Making America
A History of the United States

Making America
A History of the United States

Brief Second Edition

Volume B: Since 1865

Carol Berkin
Baruch College, City University of New York

Christopher L. Miller
The University of Texas, Pan American

Robert W. Cherny
San Francisco State University

James L. Gormly
Washington and Jefferson College

and

W. Thomas Mainwaring
Washington and Jefferson College

HOUGHTON MIFFLIN COMPANY
Boston   New York

Editor-in-chief for history and political science: Jean L. Woy
Sponsoring editor: Colleen Kyle Shanley
Senior project editor: Carol Newman
Senior production/design coordinator: Jill Haber
Senior manufacturing coordinator: Priscilla Bailey
Senior marketing manager: Sandra McGuire

Cover design: Design Associates Inc., Chicago, IL
Cover image: *Dixie Cups.* Harry Gottlieb (1895–1992). Oil on canvas. Gift of Friends of the Wichita Art Museum, Inc., 1982.42.

Text credits
Page 504: "First Fig" by Edna St. Vincent Millay. From *Collected Poems,* HarperCollins. Copyright © 1922, 1950 by Edna St. Vincent Millay. Reprinted by permission of Elizabeth Barnett, literary executor.
Page 506–507: "Song for a Dark Girl," from *Selected Poems* by Langston Hughes. Copyright © 1927 by Alfred A. Knopf Inc. and renewed 1955 by Langston Hughes. Reprinted by permission of the publisher. "I, Too" from *Selected Poems* by Langston Hughes. Copyright © 1926 by Alfred A. Knopf Inc. and renewed 1954 by Langston Hughes. Reprinted by permission of the publisher.
Page 624: Six lines from "Howl" from *Collected Poems 1947–1980* by Allen Ginsberg. Copyright © 1955 by Allen Ginsberg. Reprinted by permission of HarperCollins Publishers, Inc.

Library of Congress Catalog Card Number: 00-103016

ISBN: 0-618-04429-9

1 2 3 4 5 6 7 8 9—VH—04 03 02 01 00

BRIEF CONTENTS

C O N T E N T S

M A P S

Note: Maps listed in boldface type indicate chapter opener maps.

F E A T U R E S

P R E F A C E

Our aim in producing this second brief edition has again been to be as faithful as possible to the narrative of American history contained in the full version of *Making America*. Although the brief edition has reduced the length of *Making America* by one third, we have sacrificed very few sections and none of the features of the long edition. The clear chronology, straightforward narrative, and strong thematic structure remain. In addition, all the learning features, including chapter-opening maps and timelines, chapter outlines with focus questions, and in-text glossaries, have been retained.

Wherever possible, we have cut words and avoided excising larger sections to retain the book's narrative flow. Of necessity, the brief edition provides fewer examples and details. Where there were four examples, this edition may contain only two. We have also followed Mark Twain's advice about the adjective: "When in doubt, strike it out." We trust that in pruning the text with a discerning eye that we have allowed the major themes of *Making America* to stand out clearly.

The biggest change in this second brief edition of *Making America* is that, in response to reviewer requests, we have published it in full color. Maps, illustrations, and photographs are now more illustrative and contribute to a much livelier, visually appealing second edition.

The brief edition of *Making America* carries the story of American history through the impeachment trial of President Clinton. It also includes NATO's intervention in Kosovo.

This edition is well suited for use in courses in which additional reading is assigned or where the course is shorter than usual. It is available in a one-volume and two-volume format: Volume A covers American history from prediscovery through Reconstruction, and Volume B covers Reconstruction to Clinton's impeachment. The chapter on Reconstruction is contained in both volumes.

The Approach

Professors and students who have used the first brief edition of *Making America* will recognize that we have preserved many of its central features. We have again set the nation's remarkable and complex story within a political chronology, relying on a basic and familiar structure that is broad enough to accommodate generous attention to the social, economic, and diplomatic aspects of our national history. We remain confident that this political framework allows us to integrate the experiences of all Americans into a meaningful and effective narrative of our nation's development.

Making America continues to be built on the premise that all Americans are historically active figures, playing significant roles in creating the history that we and other authors narrate. Once again, we have written the text on the basis of our understanding that history is a dynamic process resulting from the decisions and actions of all women and men in our American past. Thus, our second brief edition continues the tradition of ECCO, our acronym for four fundamental aspects of the historical process: expectations, constraints, choices, and outcomes. In each chapter, *Making America* examines the variety of *expectations* people held about their futures; the *constraints* of time, place, and multiple social and economic factors that these historical figures faced; the *choices* they made, given the circumstances of their lives; and the expected and unexpected *outcomes* flowing from their decisions.

In this revised edition, we have chosen to retain ECCO as an explicit device in each chapter introduction and summary but have made it implicit within the chapter narrative. This strategy allows students to recognize the dynamic ECCO elements as providing an underlying structure and organizing principle rather than as a surface device.

Themes

This edition continues to thread five central themes through *Making America*. The first of these themes, the political development of the nation, is evident in the text's coverage of the creation and revision of the federal and local governments, the contests waged over domestic and diplomatic policies, the internal and external crises faced by the United States and its political institutions, and the history of political parties. The second theme is the diversity of a national citizenry created by immigrants. To do justice to this theme, *Making America* explores not only English and European immigration but immigrant communities from Paleolithic times to the present. The text attends to the tensions and conflicts that arise in a diverse population, but it also examines the shared values and aspirations that define the majority of ordinary, middle-class American lives.

Making America's third theme is the significance of regional economies and cultures. This regional theme is developed for society before European colonization and for the colonial settlements of the seventeenth and eighteenth centuries. It is evident in our attention to the striking social and cultural divergences that existed between the American Southwest and the Atlantic coastal regions as well as between the antebellum South and North. A fourth theme is the rise and impact of the large social movements, from the Great Awakening in the 1740s to the rise of youth cultures in the post–World War II generations, prompted by changing material conditions or by new ideas challenging the status quo.

The fifth theme is the relationship of the United States to other nations. In *Making America* we explore in depth the causes and consequences of this nation's role in world conflict and diplomacy. This examination includes the era of colonization of the Americas, the eighteenth-century independence movement, the removal of Indian nations from their traditional lands, the impact of the rhetoric of manifest destiny, American policies of isolationism and interventionism, and the modern role of the United States as a dominant player in world affairs.

Learning Features

The chapters in *Making America* follow a format that provides students essential study aids for mastering the historical material. Each chapter begins with a map that sets the scene for the most significant events and developments in the narrative that follows. Accompanying the map is a chronological chart of these significant events and a time line that illustrates where these events fit in a broader time frame. On the chapter-opening page, there is a topical outline of the new material students will encounter in the chapter, along with several new and, we think, thought-provoking critical thinking questions to help students focus on the broad, overarching themes of the chapter.

Each chapter offers an introduction in which we apply the ECCO model to the subject matter the students are about to explore. Each chapter ends with a summary, also structured in accordance with the ECCO model. At the end of the chapter students will also find suggestions for further reading on the events, movements, or people covered in that chapter. There is as well a selected bibliography at the end of the text citing the best scholarship in the field, old and new.

To ensure that students have full access to the material in each chapter, we provide a page-by-page glossary, defining terms and explaining their historically specific usage the first time they appear in the narrative. This running glossary will help students build their vocabularies and review for tests.

The illustrations in each chapter provide a visual connection to the past, and their captions analyze the subject of the painting, photograph, or artifact and comment on its significance. For this edition we have selected many new illustrations to reinforce or illustrate the themes of the narrative.

More than half the chapters contain an "Individual Choices" feature, which helps students understand an important point raised in the chapter. The "Individual Choices" provide intimate portraits of famous people such as President Grover Cleveland and ordinary people such as the twentieth-century farmers' advocate Milo Reno. By exploring how individuals arrived at decisions that shaped their lives, "Individual Choices" dramatize the fact that history is not inevitable but is the result of real people making real choices.

New to This Edition

In this new edition we have preserved what our colleagues and their students considered the best and most useful aspects of the first brief edition of *Making America*. We also have replaced what was less successful, revised what could be improved, and added new elements to strengthen the book.

A new chapter places the English colonial world and the empire of which it was a part in their broad historical context. Chapter 2, "A Continent on the Move, 1400–1725," prepares students to see the origins of the Anglo-American world in the expansionist ideology of western Europe, to recognize that the colonies were part of a transatlantic community of ideas and policies, and to understand that Indians, Europeans, and the English were all critical players in the development of the seventeenth- and eighteenth-century society that became the United States.

Changes that improve the coverage of content in *Making America* are evident in every chapter. The newest contributions to scholarship in American history have been integrated throughout the text. There is, for example, more coverage of the West throughout the text, and the coverage of the Kennedy and Johnson presidencies has been revised to reflect the insights of the best new work in this field. Chapters 7 through 9 have been recast into two chapters to make for more continuity in the story of the Federalists' decline and the Jeffersonian Republicans' ascendancy.

This new edition also offers a new feature: "Making History: Using Sources from the Past." This feature encourages students to work with primary documents in order to answer important historical questions. In each, "Making History" feature, the student is presented with a brief background statement entitled "The Context." This is followed by the statement of a problem, "The Historical Question." Then students are given "The Challenge" to write an essay or hold a discussion on the challenge question, drawing on

knowledge and information that they have gained from reading the text and the primary sources that accompany the feature. There is no single, correct answer, of course; students will come to different conclusions just as historians do. This feature is flexible enough to provide teachers the opportunity to hone students' essay-writing skills, critical thinking abilities, and understanding of historical methods of inquiry and standards of proof.

We the authors of *Making America* believe that this new edition will be effective in the history classroom. Please let us know what you think by sending us your views through Houghton Mifflin's American history web site, located at college.hmco.com.

Study and Teaching Aids

A number of useful learning and teaching aids accompany the second brief edition of *Making America*. They are designed to help students get the most from the course and to provide instructors with some useful teaching tools.

@history: an interactive American history source is a multimedia teaching/learning package that combines a variety of material on a cross-platformed CD-ROM—primary sources (text and graphic), video, and audio—with activities that can be used to analyze, interpret, and discuss primary sources; to enhance collaborative learning; and to create multimedia lecture presentations. @history also has an accompanying web site, located at college.hmco.com, where additional primary sources, online resources for *Making America*, and links to relevant sites can be found.

An *On-line Study Guide* is available at no charge for students. Accessible through Houghton Mifflin's @history web site (college.hmco.com), it functions as a tutorial, providing rejoinders to all multiple-choice questions that explain why the student's response is or is not correct. The online Study Guide also offers chapter outlines and other learning resources for students.

The *Instructor's Resource Manual with Test Items,* prepared by Kelly Woestman of Pittsburgh State University, includes for every chapter instructional objectives that are drawn from the textbook's critical thinking questions, a chapter summary and annotated outline, and three lecture topics that include resource material and references to the text. Each chapter also includes discussion questions, answers to the critical thinking questions that follow each major heading in the text, cooperative and individual learning activities, map activities, ideas for paper topics, and a list of audiovisual resources. The test items provide twenty key terms and definitions, forty to fifty multiple-choice questions, five to ten essay questions with answer guidelines, and an analytical exercise to test critical thinking skills.

A *Computerized Test Items File* is available for IBM PC or compatible and Macintosh computers. This computerized version of the printed Test Items file allows professors to create customized tests by editing and adding questions.

A set of over 150 full-color *American History Map Transparencies* is available in two-volume sets upon adoption.

Please contact your local Houghton Mifflin representative for more information about the ancillary items or to obtain desk copies.

Acknowledgments

The authors have benefited from the critical reading of the manuscript by our generous colleagues.

We thank the following instructors for the advice they provided on the second brief edition:

Shirley Eoff, Angelo State University

Larry Hartzell, Brookdale Community College

Daniel Lewis, California State Polytechnic University, Pomona

Pamela Riney-Kehrberg, Illinois State University

Theresa Kaminski, University of Wisconsin—Stevens Point

Pamela Robbins, Florida State University

Cornelia L. Dopkins, Fredonia State College

Ted M. Kluz, Auburn University—Montgomery

Gary L. Huey, Ferris State University

W. Thomas Mainwaring, the abridging editor of *Making America*, would like to thank Colleen Kyle at Houghton Mifflin for her faith in this project. He would like to reiterate his gratitude to James Gormly at Washington and Jefferson College for suggesting that he take on this task. He would also like to voice appreciation to his colleague Robert H. Dodge for tolerating countless interruptions to discuss many fine points of history, grammar, and style. They usually agreed. Carol Newman at Houghton Mifflin did her usual fine job of turning the manuscript into a polished book. He thanks Deborah, Amy, and Philip for everything else.

To most students, the authors of a textbook are little more than names on the spine of a heavy book. We the authors of *Making America,* however, hope you'll give us a chance to be more than "Berkin et al." If you'll give us a moment, we'll introduce ourselves—and our book—to you. We also want to give you some solid suggestions about how to get the most out of this text and out of the study of American history it is designed to assist.

We—Carol Berkin, Robert Cherny, James Gormly, Christopher Miller, and Thomas Mainwaring—have been historians, teachers, and colleagues for many years. Carol and Bob went to graduate school together; Jim and Chris taught at University of Texas—Pan American together; Jim and Tom teach at Washington and Jefferson College. As scholars, we spend much of our time in libraries or historical archives, leafing through centuries-old letters from a wife to a husband, looking at letters to an abolitionist, reading government reports on Indian policy, analyzing election returns from the 1890s, or examining newspaper editorials on the Cold War. At those moments, immersed in the past, we feel as if we have conquered time and space, traveling to eras and to places that no longer exist. This experience is part of the reason why we are historians. But we also are historians because we believe that knowing about the past is critical for anyone who hopes to understand the present and chart the future.

Our goal for this textbook is deceptively simple: we want to tell the story of America from its earliest settlement to the present, to make that story complex and interesting, and to tell it in a language and format that will help students enjoy learning that history. Achieving those goals has been hard work, and with each edition of *Making America,* we hope we move closer to success.

This textbook is organized and designed to help you master American history. Our narrative is chronological, telling the story as it happened, decade by decade or era by era. If you look at the table of contents, you can see that the chapters cover specific time periods rather than large themes. This does not mean that themes are absent; it means that we present them to you in the context of specific moments in time.

Each chapter follows the same pattern. It begins with a map of the United States on which vital information is provided. For instance, the chapter on English settlement in the colonial era shows you the boundaries of each colony, gives you the date it was founded, and tells you what type of colony it was. The map locates for you in space what the chronological narrative locates in time. Below the map you will see a time line, which gives you the dates of important events and a sense of where in the larger history of the nation these events fit. On the opposite page, you will see a chapter outline with focus questions, and when you turn the page, you will see a chart that lists in chronological order the significant events that we describe in the chapter. Together, the map, time line, outline, and chronology provide an overview of what you will be reading in the pages that follow.

The introduction to each chapter sets the scene and tells you what major themes and issues you will find as you read on. You will notice that the introductions present the story in a very particular way: as a series of *expectations,* or hopes and desires held by the people of the era; of *constraints,* or limitations that they confronted as they tried to fulfill their expectations; of *choices,* or decisions that they finally made; and of *outcomes,* or consequences of the actions prompted by those choices. Our shorthand name for this approach is ECCO, an acronym formed from the first letter of each of the four elements. Expectations, constraints, choices, outcomes—ECCO—are the dynamic elements of history. ECCO is a way to remind you that what we call "the past" was "the present" to the people who lived it. They could not know what would happen as a result of their actions—and this is the excitement of the story we have to tell.

Then the chapter itself begins. It consists of sections that you can read as mini-narratives. A summary at the end of each chapter recaps the material in the text. If you want to make sure you have focused on the important points in the chapter, you can review by reading the summary and then trying to answer the focus questions at the beginning of the chapter.

Because a serious examination of a history as rich and complex as our nation's requires us to introduce you to many new people, places, events, and ideas, it is easy to get lost in details or panic over what is most important to remember. You may also encounter words that are unfamiliar or words that seem to be used in a different way from the way you use them in everyday speech. Both problems can distract you from learning what happened—and why—and enjoying the story. To prevent this distraction, we have provided a glossary on each page to define key terms and possibly unfamiliar words. Each chapter also has suggestions for further reading on the subjects covered in the text, so that you can explore other viewpoints or look in depth at subjects that interest you.

Because students learn from visual as well as written sources, each chapter provides reproductions of paintings, photographs, artifacts, cartoons, and maps. These are not intended just to be decorative. They are there to give faces to the people you are reading about, to show you what the environment, both natural and constructed, was like in the era under discussion, and to provide images of objects from the era that make clear their similarity to or difference from material objects in the world around you today. In the captions we identify each visual aid and suggest ways to interpret it.

More than half the chapters have a feature called "Individual Choices." In this feature we present a man or woman from the past who needed to make a choice. After all, individuals, including you, shape their history at the same time that history is shaping their lives. We believe that by reading about real people—some famous, some not—as they face an important choice and an uncertain outcome, you will better understand the era in which they lived.

A feature called "Making History" also appears throughout the text. It gives you the opportunity to work with the raw materials of history: the primary sources that help historians reconstruct the past. This feature is designed to answer, the most common question students ask a history professor: "How do you know what happened or how it happened or why?" In "Making History," we pose a question to you, provide a variety of primary sources on the topic, then challenge you to offer your interpretation of the issue. "Making History" gives you a chance to be a historian, not just to read history. You will quickly see that your conclusions are not the same as those of your classmates, and these discrepancies will demonstrate why historians often disagree about issues in the past.

At the back of the textbook, you will find some additional resources. In the Appendix you will find a bibliography listing the books on which we relied in writing the chapters. You will also find reprinted two of the most important documents in American history: the Declaration of Independence and the Constitution. Here, too, are tables that give you quick access to important data on the presidents and the states. Finally, you will see the index, which will help you locate a subject quickly if you want to read about it.

We the authors of *Making America* hope that our textbook conveys to you our own fascination with the American past and sparks your curiosity about the nation's history. We invite you to share your feedback on the book: you can reach us through Houghton Mifflin's American history web site, which is located at college.hmco.com.

Carol Berkin

Born in Mobile, Alabama, Carol Berkin received her undergraduate degree from Barnard College and her Ph.D. from Columbia University. Her dissertation won the Bancroft Award. She is now professor of history at Baruch College and the Graduate Center of City University of New York, where she serves as deputy chair of the Ph.D. program in history. She has written *Jonathan Sewall: Odyssey of an American Loyalist* (1974) and *First Generations: Women in Colonial America* (1996). She has edited *Women in America: A History* (with Mary Beth Norton, 1979), *Women, War and Revolution* (with Clara M. Lovett, 1980), and *Women's Voices, Women's Lives: Documents In Early American History* (with Leslie Horowitz, 1998). She was contributing editor on southern women for *The Encyclopedia of Southern Culture* and has appeared in the PBS series *Liberty! The American Revolution* and The Learning Channel series *The American Revolution*. Professor Berkin chaired the Dunning Beveridge Prize Committee for the American Historical Association, the Columbia University Seminar in Early American History, and the Taylor Prize Committee of the Southern Association of Women Historians, and she served on the program committees for both the Society for the History of the Early American Republic and the Organization of American Historians. In addition, she has been a historical consultant for the National Parks Commission and served on the Planning Committee for the U.S. Department of Education's National Assessment of Educational Progress.

Christopher L. Miller

Born and raised in Portland, Oregon, Christopher L. Miller received his undergraduate degree from Lewis and Clark College and his Ph.D. from the University of California, Santa Barbara. He is currently associate professor of history at the University of Texas—Pan American. He is the author of *Prophetic Worlds: Indians and Whites on the Columbia Plateau* (1985), and his articles and reviews have appeared in numerous scholarly journals. In addition to his scholarship in the areas of American West and American Indian history, Professor Miller has been active in projects designed to improve history teaching, including programs funded by the Meadows Foundation, the U.S. Department of Education, and other agencies.

Robert W. Cherny

Born in Marysville, Kansas, and raised in Beatrice, Nebraska, Robert W. Cherny received his B.A. from the University of Nebraska and his M.A. and Ph.D. from Columbia University. He is now professor of history at San Francisco State University. His books include *American Politics in the Gilded Age, 1868–1900* (1997), *San Francisco, 1865–1932: Politics, Power, and Urban Development* (with William Issel, 1986), *A Righteous Cause: The Life of William Jennings Bryan* (1985, 1994), and *Populism, Progressivism, and the Transformation of Nebraska Politics, 1885–1915* (1981). His articles on politics and labor in the late nineteenth and early twentieth centuries have appeared in scholarly journals, anthologies, and historical dictionaries and encyclopedias. He has been an NEH fellow, Distinguished Fulbright Lecturer at Moscow State University (Russia), and Visiting Research Scholar at the University of Melbourne (Australia). He has also served as president of the Society for Historians of the Gilded Age and Progressive Era and of the Southwest Labor Studies Association.

James L. Gormly

Born in Riverside, California, James L. Gormly received a B.A. from the University of Arizona and his M.A. and Ph.D. from the University of Connecticut. He is now professor of history and chair of the history department at Washington and Jefferson College. He has written *The Collapse of the Grand Alliance*

(1970) and *From Potsdam to the Cold War* (1979). His articles and reviews have appeared in *Diplomatic History, The Journal of American History, The American Historical Review, The Historian, The History Teacher,* and *The Journal of Interdisciplinary History.*

W. Thomas Mainwaring

Born in Pittsburgh, Pennsylvania, W. Thomas Mainwaring received his B.A. from Yale University and his M.A. and Ph.D. from the University of North Carolina at Chapel Hill. Currently an associate professor of history at Washington and Jefferson College, he is interested in local and community history. He has edited a collection of essays on the Whiskey Rebellion and has written about a variety of topics on local and community history. He is currently engaged in a study of the Underground Railroad.

Making America
A History of the United States

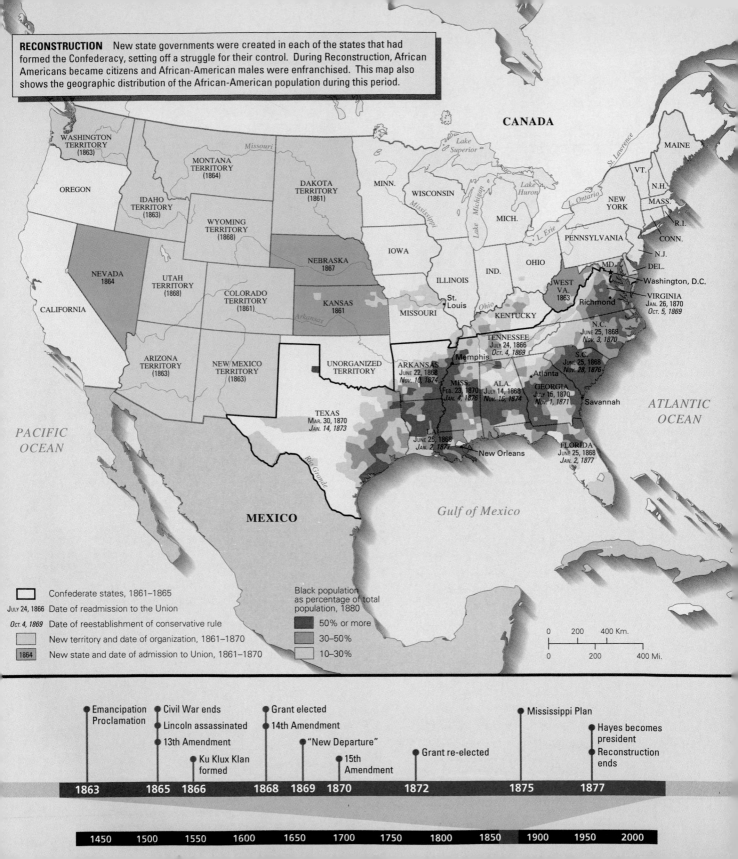

RECONSTRUCTION New state governments were created in each of the states that had formed the Confederacy, setting off a struggle for their control. During Reconstruction, African Americans became citizens and African-American males were enfranchised. This map also shows the geographic distribution of the African-American population during this period.

CANADA

WASHINGTON TERRITORY (1863)

OREGON

MONTANA TERRITORY (1864)

IDAHO TERRITORY (1863)

DAKOTA TERRITORY (1861)

MINN.

WISCONSIN

MAINE

VT.

N.H.

MASS.

NEW YORK

R.I.

CONN.

WYOMING TERRITORY (1868)

NEVADA 1864

UTAH TERRITORY (1868)

NEBRASKA 1867

IOWA

MICH.

PENNSYLVANIA

N.J.

DEL.

MD.

Washington, D.C.

COLORADO TERRITORY (1861)

CALIFORNIA

KANSAS 1861

ILLINOIS

IND.

OHIO

WEST VA. 1863

St. Louis

MISSOURI

KENTUCKY

Richmond

VIRGINIA
JAN. 26, 1870
OCT. 5, 1869

ARIZONA TERRITORY (1863)

NEW MEXICO TERRITORY (1863)

UNORGANIZED TERRITORY

TENNESSEE
JULY 24, 1866
OCT. 4, 1869

N.C.
JUNE 25, 1868
NOV. 3, 1870

ARKANSAS
JUNE 22, 1868
NOV. 10, 1874

Memphis

S.C.
JUNE 25, 1868
NOV. 28, 1876

PACIFIC OCEAN

TEXAS
MAR. 30, 1870
JAN. 14, 1873

MISS.
FEB. 23, 1870
JAN. 4, 1876

ALA.
JULY 14, 1868
NOV. 16, 1874

Atlanta

GEORGIA
JULY 15, 1870
NOV. 1, 1871

Savannah

ATLANTIC OCEAN

LA.
JUNE 25, 1868
JAN. 2, 1877

New Orleans

FLORIDA
JUNE 25, 1868
JAN. 2, 1877

MEXICO

Rio Grande

Gulf of Mexico

Confederate states, 1861–1865
JULY 24, 1866 Date of readmission to the Union
OCT. 4, 1869 Date of reestablishment of conservative rule
New territory and date of organization, 1861–1870
1864 New state and date of admission to Union, 1861–1870

Black population as percentage of total population, 1880
50% or more
30–50%
10–30%

0   200   400 Km.
0   200   400 Mi.

Emancipation Proclamation · Civil War ends · Grant elected · Mississippi Plan

Lincoln assassinated · 14th Amendment · Hayes becomes president

13th Amendment · "New Departure" · Reconstruction ends

Ku Klux Klan formed · 15th Amendment · Grant re-elected

1863   1865   1866   1868   1869   1870   1872   1875   1877

1450   1500   1550   1600   1650   1700   1750   1800   1850   1900   1950   2000

Reconstruction: High Hopes and Broken Dreams, 1865–1877

Presidential Reconstruction

- What did President Lincoln and President Johnson expect to accomplish through their reconstruction plans?
- At first, how did white southerners choose to respond to Lincoln's and Johnson's efforts at reconstruction? What were the initial outcomes of the presidents' choices?

Freedom and the Legacy of Slavery

- What expectations did freed people hold for freedom? What choices did they make based on those expectations?
- What expectations did southern whites hold at the end of the Civil War? What initial choices did they make to define the legal status of the freed people?

Congressional Reconstruction

- What did Republicans in Congress expect to accomplish by taking control of Reconstruction? What choices did they make to accomplish those goals?
- How did the Fourteenth and Fifteenth Amendments transform the nature of the federal Union?

Black Reconstruction

- Who made up the Republican party in the South during Reconstruction? Why did each major group choose to be Republican?
- What important choices did Republican state administrations make during Reconstruction? How effective were their actions?

The End of Reconstruction

- What was the Mississippi Plan, and how was it related to the end of Reconstruction?
- What were the final outcomes of Reconstruction?

INTRODUCTION

E xpectations
C onstraints
C hoices
O utcomes

By 1865, the war had touched the life of nearly every American. When the last Confederate military resistance collapsed, some 2.6 million men had served in the Union or Confederate army since 1861—about 40 percent of the male population ages 15 to 40 in 1860. More than six hundred thousand had died. Women made important contributions to the war effort as civilians and even as soldiers.

Except for Gettysburg, the major battles in the Civil War had occurred in the South or the border states. Toward the end of the war, Union armies swept across the South, leaving devastation behind them: burned and shelled buildings, ravaged fields, twisted railroad tracks. This destruction, and the collapse of the region's financial system, posed significant *constraints* on economic revival in the South.

More devastating for many white southerners than the property damage and destruction was the emancipation of four million slaves. In 1861, fearful *expectations* about the future of slavery had caused the South to *choose* secession. The *outcome* of the war made those fears a reality. The end of slavery forced southerners of both races to reconsider their *expectations* and to make a series of *choices* about social, economic, and political relations between the races.

Reconstruction, the period between 1865 and 1877, was a time of physical rebuilding throughout the South. The term "Reconstruction," however, refers primarily to the rebuilding of the federal Union and to the political, economic, and social changes that came to the South after the war. Reconstruction involved *choices* about some of the most momentous questions in American history. How was the defeated South to be treated? What was to be the future of the former slaves? Were key decisions to be made in Washington or in the state capitals? Was Congress or the president to establish policies?

As the Republicans reconstructed the Union, they redefined the very nature of the Union. They made *choices* about the terms on which the South might rejoin the Union and about the rights of the former slaves. They also permanently changed the definition of American citizenship.

These changes conflicted with the *expectations* of most white southerners. *Choices* over the future of the South and of the freedmen also produced conflict between the president and Congress. A lasting *outcome* of these *choices* was a significant increase in the power of the federal government and new *constraints* on state governments. In the end, however, the *outcome* of Reconstruction failed to fulfill African Americans' *expectations* for freedom and equality.

Presidential Reconstruction

On New Year's Day, 1863, President Abraham Lincoln began the process by which all people in the nation became free by signing the Emancipation Proclamation. Although the proclamation abolished slavery only in territory under Confederate control, where it could not be enforced, every subsequent advance of a Union army brought the reality of **emancipation** to the Confederacy.

Republican War Aims

The Emancipation Proclamation established the destruction of slavery as a war aim second in importance only to preserving the Union. Freedom for the slaves became a central concern in part be-

emancipation Release from bondage; freedom.

CHRONOLOGY

Reconstruction

1863 Emancipation Proclamation
Ten-Percent Plan

1864 Abraham Lincoln reelected

1865 Freedmen's Bureau created
Civil War ends
Lincoln assassinated
Johnson becomes president
Thirteenth Amendment (abolishing slavery)
ratified

1866 Ku Klux Klan formed
Congress begins to assert control over
Reconstruction
Civil Rights Act of 1866
Riots by whites in Memphis and New
Orleans

1867 Military Reconstruction Act
Tenure of Office Act

1868 Impeachment of President Johnson
Fourteenth Amendment (defining citizen-
ship) ratified
Ulysses S. Grant elected president

1869–1870 Victories of "New Departure"
Democrats in some southern
states

1870 Fifteenth Amendment (guaranteeing voting
rights) ratified

1870–1871 Ku Klux Klan Acts

1872 Grant re-elected

1875 Civil Rights Act of 1875
Mississippi Plan ends Reconstruction in
Mississippi

1876 Disputed presidential election: Hayes
vs. Tilden

1877 Compromise of 1877
Hayes becomes president
End of Reconstruction

cause **abolitionists** were an influential element within the Republican party. This powerful Republican **faction** developed a third objective: citizenship for the former slaves and the equality of all citizens before the law. The people who held what were then considered extreme views on black rights were called Radical Republicans or simply **Radicals.**

Thaddeus Stevens, the Radical leader in the House of Representatives, had argued as early as 1838 that voting rights should be extended to Pennsylvania's free African Americans. He became an uncompromising advocate of equal rights for African Americans. So did Charles Sumner of Massachusetts, the leading Radical in the Senate. He had argued for **racial integration** of Massachusetts schools in 1849 and won election to the U.S. Senate in 1851. A defender of slavery

abolitionist Someone who condemned slavery as morally wrong and believed that it should be abolished.

faction A group of people with shared opinions and goals who split off from a larger group.

Radicals A faction of the Republican party that advocated citizenship for former slaves; Radical Republicans believed the South should be forced to meet congressional goals for reform.

racial integration The bringing together of people of different racial groups into unrestricted and equal association in a society or organization.

◆ This engraving celebrating the Emancipation Proclamation first appeared in 1863. Although it places a white Union soldier in the center, it also portrays the important role of African-American troops and emphasizes the significance of education and literacy. *The Library Company of Philadelphia.*

had caned Sumner severely on the Senate floor in 1856 because of his outspoken views against slavery.

Most Radicals demanded a drastic restructuring not only of the South's political system but also of its economy. They had opposed slavery on moral grounds, but they also believed that free labor was crucial to democracy itself. "The middling classes who own the soil, and work it with their own hands," Stevens once proclaimed, "are the main support of every free government." The Radicals concluded that free labor would have to be elevated to a position of honor for the South to be fully democratic.

Not all Republicans accepted the proposals of the Radicals. All Republicans had objected to the expansion of slavery, but not all Republicans had been abolitionists, and not all Republicans wanted to extend citizenship rights to the former slaves. Some moderate Republicans were undecided about the proper course to take. Other **moderates** favored rapid restoration of the South so that the federal government could concentrate on stimulating economic growth and developing the West.

Lincoln's Approach to Reconstruction: "With Malice Toward None"

President Lincoln and congressional Radicals agreed that emancipation had to be a condition for the return of the South to the Union. However, major differences appeared over other terms for reunion when Lincoln issued a Proclamation of **Amnesty** and Reconstruction (the "Ten-Percent Plan") in December 1863.

The proclamation offered a full pardon to those who swore their loyalty to the Union and accepted the abolition of slavery. Only high-ranking Confederate leaders were not eligible. When those who took the oath amounted to 10 percent of a state's voters in the 1860 presidential election, the pardoned voters were to write a new state constitution that abolished slavery. They were then to elect state officials. Lincoln hoped such leniency would encourage prominent southerners to abandon the Confederacy and to accept emancipation.

Many Republicans thought that Congress should be more involved in restoring the southern states to the Union. Two leading Radicals, Benjamin F. Wade and Henry W. Davis, proposed that 50 percent of a state's white males be required to swear loyalty to the Union before a new civil government could be formed. Congress passed the Wade-Davis bill in

moderates Those whose views are midway between two more extreme positions; in this case, Republicans who favored some reforms but not all the Radicals' proposals.

amnesty A general pardon granted by a government, especially for political offenses.

July 1864. Lincoln, however, killed it with a **pocket veto.**

Lincoln continued to hope that his Ten-Percent Plan might hasten the end of the war. New state governments were established in Arkansas, Louisiana, and Tennessee during 1864 and early 1865. In Louisiana, the new government denied voting rights to black males, and it maintained restrictions on plantation laborers. Radicals complained loudly, but Lincoln urged patience. The Radicals became convinced that freed people were unlikely to receive equitable treatment from state governments formed under the Ten-Percent Plan. Moderate Republicans moved toward the Radicals' position that only **suffrage** could protect the freedmen's rights and that only federal action could secure suffrage for blacks.

All Republicans could agree by 1865 that slavery had to be destroyed permanently. The Emancipation Proclamation had not affected slavery in states such as Delaware and Kentucky, where it remained legal. To destroy slavery forever throughout the Union, Congress in early 1865 approved the **Thirteenth Amendment.**

By December 1865, only nineteen of the twenty-five Union states had ratified the amendment; however, eight of the reconstructed southern states had ratified it, bringing the total to twenty-seven, the number needed for ratification. Thus the abolition of slavery was accomplished by reconstructed state governments in the South.

◆ Radical Republicans initially hoped that Andrew Johnson would be their ally. Instead he proved to be unsympathetic to most Radical goals. His self-righteous and uncompromising personality led to conflict that eventually produced an unsuccessful effort to remove him from office in 1868. *Library of Congress.*

Andrew Johnson and Reconstruction

After the assassination of Lincoln in mid-April 1865, Vice President Andrew Johnson became president. A Tennessee Democrat who had been born into poverty, Johnson was the only southerner who did not resign from his U.S. Senate seat after **secession.** Lincoln had appointed him military governor of Tennessee early in the war. Johnson had harsh words for Tennessee secessionists, especially the wealthy planters whom he blamed for secession. Radical Republicans applauded Johnson's verbal assaults on these Confederates. He received the Republican nomination for vice president in 1864 because Lincoln wanted to appeal to Democrats and to Unionists in border states.

pocket veto The veto that occurs when Congress adjourns before the end of the ten-day period that the Constitution gives the president for considering whether to sign a bill and the president's decision is to "pocket" the bill—that is, not to sign it and let it expire.

suffrage The right to vote.

Thirteenth Amendment Constitutional amendment ratified in 1865 that abolished slavery in the United States and its territories.

secession The withdrawal of eleven southern states from the United States in 1860–1861, giving rise to the Civil War.

The Radicals hoped that Johnson as president would join in their plans for transforming the South. Johnson, however, soon made it clear that he opposed the Radicals. "White men alone must manage the South," Johnson told one visitor. He did recommend that a few freedmen be given limited political roles. But Johnson saw the major task of Reconstruction as empowering the region's white middle class and keeping the planters from regaining power.

In practice, Johnson's approach to Reconstruction differed little from Lincoln's. Like Lincoln, he relied on his power to grant pardons. Despite his bitterness toward the southern elite, he granted amnesty to most former Confederates who pledged loyalty to the Union and support for emancipation.

Johnson appointed provisional governors for the southern states that had not already been reconstructed and instructed them to call constitutional conventions. Some provisional governors, however, appointed former Confederates to state and local offices, outraging those who expected that Unionists would be appointed to these offices.

Johnson expected the state constitutional conventions to abolish slavery within each state, to ratify the Thirteenth Amendment, and to renounce secession and the state's war debts. The states were then to hold elections and resume their place in the Union. State conventions during the summer of 1865 usually complied with these provisions. Nearly all ratified the Thirteenth Amendment. They renounced secession. However, they all rejected black suffrage.

Freedom and the Legacy of Slavery

After the war, African Americans throughout the South set about creating new, free lives for themselves. Slaves and most free blacks in the South had previously led lives tightly constrained by law and custom. They had been permitted few social organizations of their own. Now freed, they faced enormous changes in almost every aspect of

their lives. They quickly developed hopes for a future free from the old constraints.

The central theme of the black response to emancipation was "a desire for independence from white control," historian Eric Foner observes. This desire for **autonomy** affected every aspect of life: family, churches, schools, newspapers, and a host of other social institutions.

Defining the Meaning of Freedom

Freedom was not something that Lincoln or the Union armies gave to enslaved blacks. It came, instead, when individual slaves stopped working for a master and claimed the right to be free. Nor did freedom come to all slaves at the same time. For some, freedom had come before the Emancipation Proclamation, when they had walked away from their owners, crossed into Union-held territory, and asserted their freedom. Toward the end of the war, many slaves simply declared their freedom and left their former masters. Owners were surprised when even their most favored slaves left them. For Kentucky slaves, freedom did not come until ratification of the Thirteenth Amendment.

Across the South, the approach of Yankee troops set off a joyous celebration that the slaves called a Jubilee. One Virginia woman remembered that "when they knew that they were free they, oh! baby! began to sing. . . . Such rejoicing and shouting you never heard in your life." A man recalled that with the appearance of the Union soldiers, "We was all walking on golden clouds. Hallelujah!" Black historian **W. E. B. Du Bois** described it this way: "A great human sob shrieked in the wind, and tossed its tears on the sea,—free, free, free."

---

autonomy   Self-government or the right of self-determination.

W. E. B. Du Bois   American historian and civil rights activist who helped found the National Association for the Advancement of Colored People and wrote several influential studies of black life in America.

◆ Before emancipation, slaves typically made their own simple and rough clothing, or they received the cast-off clothing, of their owners and overseers. With emancipation, those freed people who had an income could afford to dress more fashionably. The Harry Stephens family probably put on their best clothes for a visit to the photographer G. Gable in 1866. *Gilman Paper Company, New York.*

The freed people expressed their new freedom in many ways. Some chose new names. Many changed their style of dress. Some acquired guns. A significant benefit of freedom was the ability to travel without a pass. Many freed people took advantage of this new opportunity. Most, however, traveled only short distances to find work, to seek family members separated from them by slavery, or to return to homes that war had forced them to leave.

Many African Americans felt they had to leave the site of their enslavement to experience full freedom. One woman explained that she left the plantation where she had been a slave because "if I stay here I'll never know I'm free." Many freed people did not return to their former homes because of the poor treatment they had suffered there.

The towns and cities of the South attracted many freed people. The presence of Union troops seemed to offer protection from the random violence that occurred in many rural areas. The cities and towns also offered black churches, schools, and other social institutions begun by free blacks before the war. Urban wages were usually better than those on the plantations. Cities and towns, however, had little housing for the influx of former slaves. Most crowded into black neighborhoods of

hastily built shanties where sanitation was poor and disease common.

Creating Communities

During Reconstruction, African Americans created their own communities with their own social institutions. Freed people hoped to strengthen family ties. Some families were reunited after years of separation caused by the sale of children or spouses. Some spent years searching for lost family members.

The new freedom to conduct religious services without white supervision was centrally important. Churches became the most prominent social organization in African-American communities. Black ministers advised and helped to educate congregation members as they adjusted to the changes brought by freedom. Ministers emerged as important leaders within developing African-American communities.

Freed people understood the importance of education. Setting up a school, said one, was "the first proof" of independence. Many of the new schools were not just for children but also for adults who

◆ During Reconstruction, freed people gave a high priority to the establishment of schools, often with the assistance of the Freedmen's Bureau and northern missionary societies. This photograph of a newly established school, showing both the barefoot students and the teacher, was taken around 1870. *Library of Congress.*

had previously been barred from learning by state laws. The desire to learn was widespread and intense. One freedman in Georgia wrote: "The Lord has sent books and teachers. We must not hesitate a moment, but go on and learn all we can."

Public school systems had not existed in much of the South before the war. In many places, freed people created the first public schools. The region faced a severe shortage of teachers, books, and schoolrooms. Northern reformers assisted the transition to freedom by focusing on education.

In March 1865, Congress created the **Freedmen's Bureau,** an agency run by the War Department to assist the freed people. The nation's first welfare agency, it helped them find employment or become farmers. Its most lasting contribution, however, was helping to establish a black educational system. Northern aid and missionary societies, together with the Freedmen's Bureau, also established schools to train black teachers. By 1870, the Bureau supervised more than 4,000 schools, with more than 9,000 teachers and 247,000 students. Still, in 1870, the schools had room for only one black child in ten.

African Americans also developed political organizations. In politics, their first objective was recognition of their equal rights as citizens. Freder-

ick Douglass insisted that "slavery is not abolished until the black man has the ballot." Political conventions of African Americans in 1865 attracted hundreds of delegates. In calling for equality and voting rights, these conventions pointed to black contributions in the Civil War as evidence of patriotism and devotion. They also appealed to the Declaration of Independence's assertion that "all men are created equal."

Land and Labor

Former slaveowners reacted to emancipation in a variety of ways. Some tried to keep their slaves from learning of their freedom. A very few, like Mary Chesnut of South Carolina, actually welcomed an end to slavery. Few provided any compensation to assist their former slaves. One freedman stated, "I do know some of dem old slave owners to be nice enough to start der slaves off in

Freedmen's Bureau Agency established in 1865 to aid former slaves in their transition to freedom, especially by administering relief and sponsoring education.

freedom wid somethin' to live on ... but dey wasn't in droves, I tell you."

Many freed people looked to Union troops for assistance. When General Sherman led his army through Georgia in 1864, thousands of African Americans followed. They told Sherman that what they wanted most was to "reap the fruit of our own labor." In January 1865, Sherman responded by issuing Special Field Order No. 15. It set aside forty acres of land in the Sea Islands and coastal South Carolina and provided for the loan of an army mule for each family who settled there. By June, some forty thousand freed people had settled on 400,000 acres of "Sherman land."

Sherman's action encouraged many African Americans to expect that the federal government would order a similar redistribution of land throughout the South. "Forty acres and a mule" became a rallying cry. Land, Thaddeus Stevens proclaimed, would give the freed people control of their own labor. "If we do not furnish them with homesteads," he once said, "we had better left them in bondage."

The Freedmen's Bureau took the lead in the efforts to assist the freed people toward landownership and free labor. At the end of the war, the Bureau controlled more than 850,000 acres of land abandoned by former owners or confiscated from leading Confederates. In July 1865, General Oliver O. Howard, head of the Bureau, directed agents to divide this land into 40-acre plots.

The widespread expectation of "forty acres and a mule" came to an end when President Johnson issued pardons to the former owners of the confiscated land and ordered Howard to return the land to them. Johnson's order displaced thousands of African Americans who had already taken their 40 acres. They and others who had hoped for land now felt disappointed and betrayed. One recalled years later that they had expected "a heap from freedom dey didn't git."

Sharecropping slowly emerged across the South once expectations of **land redistribution** evaporated. Sharecropping grew out of the realities of the southern agricultural economy. Landowners owned large tracts but had no one to work them. Both black and white families wanted to raise their own crops but had no land, supplies, or money. The entire region was short of **capital**. Un-

♦ Sharecropping gave African Americans more control over their labor than did labor contracts. But sharecropping also contributed to the South's dependence on one-crop agriculture and helped perpetuate widespread rural poverty. Notice that the child standing on the right is holding her kitten, probably to be certain it is included in this family photograph. *Library of Congress.*

der sharecropping, an individual signed a contract with a landowner to rent land. The rent was typically a share of the annual harvest, ranging from a quarter to a third. If the landlord also provided mules, tools, seed, and fertilizer, however, the rent might be half or even two-thirds of the crop. Landowners preferred sharecropping because it encouraged tenants to be productive. Tenants preferred sharecropping to wage labor because they had more control over their work.

sharecropping Agricultural system in which tenant farmers give landlords a share of the crops as rent rather than cash.

land redistribution The division of land held by large landowners into small plots that are turned over to people without property.

capital Money needed to start a commercial enterprise.

Sharecroppers nevertheless often found themselves in debt to a local merchant who had advanced supplies on credit until the harvest came. Many landlords required tenants to patronize the stores they ran. All too often, the debt owed the store exceeded the value of the tenant's share of the harvest. Many southerners, black and white alike, became trapped by sharecropping and debt.

Until the 1890s, the act of casting a ballot on election day was an open process, and any observer could see how an individual was voting. Thus the power of the landlord and the merchant often extended to politics. When a landlord or merchant advocated a particular candidate, the unspoken message was often an implicit threat to cut off credit at the store or to evict a farmer from his plot if he did not vote as directed. Such forms of economic coercion had the potential to undercut voting rights.

The White South: Confronting Change

The slow spread of sharecropping was just one of many ways that the end of slavery transformed the lives of white southerners. For some, the changes were nearly as profound as for the freed people. With Confederate money worthless, savings vanished. Some found their homes and other buildings destroyed. Thousands sold their landholdings and left the South.

Southern whites were unprepared for the extent of change facing them. Their early response to emancipation suggests that, apart from the abolition of slavery, they expected conditions to return to what they had been before the war. The newly reconstructed state legislatures passed **black codes** in 1865 to define the new legal status of African Americans. Black codes placed significant restraints on the freedom of black people. They required all African Americans to have an annual employment contract, restricted them from moving about the countryside without permission, forbade them from owning guns or carrying weapons, restricted ownership of land, and required those without a job to perform forced labor. The black codes clearly represented an effort by white southerners to define a legally subordinate place for African Americans.

Other white southerners used violence to coerce the freedmen into accepting a subordinate status. Violence and terror became closely associated with the **Ku Klux Klan,** a secret organization formed in 1866. Most Klan members were small-scale farmers and workers, but the leaders were often prominent citizens. Former Confederate general Nathan Bedford Forrest became a leader of the Klan. Klan groups throughout the South aimed to restore **white supremacy** and to end Republican rule.

Klan members covered their faces with hoods, wore white robes, and rode horses draped in white. So attired, they set out to intimidate leading black Republicans and their white Radical allies. Klan members also attacked African Americans accused of not showing deference to whites. Nightriders burned black churches and schools. The Klan devastated Republican organizations in many communities.

In 1866, two events dramatized for the nation the violence routinely inflicted on African Americans. In May, a three-day riot by whites in Memphis, Tennessee, left forty-five blacks and three whites dead. In New Orleans, some forty people died in July, most of them African Americans attending a black suffrage convention, in an altercation with police. "It was not a riot," insisted General Philip Sheridan, the military commander of the district. "It was an absolute massacre by the police."

Congressional Reconstruction

By early 1866, most congressional Republicans had concluded that Johnson's Reconstruction policies

> **black codes** Laws passed by the southern states after the Civil War to limit the freedoms of African Americans and force them to return to agricultural labor.
>
> **Ku Klux Klan** A secret society organized in the South after the Civil War to resurrect white supremacy by means of violence and intimidation.
>
> **white supremacy** The racist belief that whites are inherently superior to all other races and are therefore entitled to rule over them.

had encouraged the white South to expect that it would be able to govern the region as it saw fit. The black codes, violence against freed people, and the failure of southern authorities to stem the violence turned opinion in Washington against the president's approach to Reconstruction. Increasing numbers of moderate Republicans now joined the Radicals in concluding that southern whites must be constrained.

Challenging Presidential Reconstruction

In December 1865, the Thirty-ninth Congress (elected in 1864) met for the first time. In both houses of Congress, Republicans outnumbered Democrats by more than three to one. The president's annual message proclaimed Reconstruction complete and the Union restored, but few Republicans agreed. Radical Republicans especially had been angered by Johnson's lack of support for black suffrage. To accomplish black suffrage, they needed to assert congressional power over Reconstruction. Most Republicans agreed with the Radicals' commitment to defining and protecting basic rights for the freed people. Most also agreed that Congress had the right to withhold representation from the South until state governments there met these conditions.

When the Thirty-ninth Congress first met, the newly elected congressmen from the South were excluded. Republicans were outraged that such high-ranking former Confederates as Alexander Stephens, the vice president of the Confederacy, stood ready to take his place in Congress. Republicans set up the Joint Committee on Reconstruction to determine whether the southern states were entitled to representation. Thaddeus Stevens, head of the committee, announced that he intended to investigate the whole question of Reconstruction. While the committee worked, the former Confederate states were to have no representation in Congress.

At the same time, Republicans extended the life of the Freedmen's Bureau. Congress also passed a civil rights bill that gave citizenship to African Americans and defined the rights of all citizens. Johnson vetoed both measures, but Congress passed them over his veto. Congress had asserted its control over Reconstruction.

The Civil Rights Act of 1866

The Civil Rights Act of 1866 defined all persons born in the United States (with the exception of certain Indians) as citizens. It also listed certain rights of all citizens, including the right to testify in court, own property, make contracts, bring lawsuits, and enjoy "full and equal benefit of all laws and proceedings for the security of person and property." It authorized federal officials to bring suit against violations of civil rights.

The Civil Rights Act of 1866 was the first effort to define some of the rights of American citizenship. It stipulated that the rights of national citizenship were to take precedence over the powers of the states. By expanding the power of the federal government in unprecedented ways, the law not only challenged traditional concepts of states' rights but did so on behalf of African Americans.

When President Johnson vetoed the civil rights bill, he argued that it violated states' rights. Johnson may have hoped to generate enough political support to elect a more cooperative Congress in 1866. Instead, the veto led most moderate Republicans to give up all hope of cooperation with him. Congress's passage of the Civil Rights Act over Johnson's veto in April 1866 marked the first time that Congress had overridden a veto of major legislation.

Defining Citizenship: The Fourteenth Amendment

Leading Republicans worried that the Civil Rights Act could be repealed by a later Congress or declared unconstitutional by the Supreme Court. Only a constitutional amendment could permanently safeguard the freed people's rights as citizens.

The Fourteenth Amendment, approved by Congress in June 1866, defined American citizenship in much the same way as the Civil Rights Act of 1866. It then specified:

No State shall make or enforce any law which shall abridge the privileges or immunities of citizens of the United States; nor shall any State deprive any person of life, liberty, or property, without due process of law; nor deny to any person within its jurisdiction the equal protection of the laws.

The Constitution and Bill of Rights prohibited federal interference with basic civil rights. The Fourteenth Amendment extended this protection against action by state governments. The amendment penalized states that did not **enfranchise** African Americans by reducing their congressional and electoral representation.

Some provisions of the amendment stemmed from Republicans' fears that a restored South might try to undo the outcome of the war. One section barred from public office anyone who had sworn to uphold the federal Constitution but then "engaged in insurrection or rebellion against the same." Only a two-thirds vote of both houses of Congress could counteract this provision. (In 1872, Congress pardoned nearly all former Confederates.) The amendment also prohibited either federal or state governments from assuming any of the Confederate debt or compensating slaveowners.

Although Congress adjourned in the summer of 1866, the nation's attention remained fixed on Reconstruction. The bloody riots in Memphis and New Orleans kept northern attention focused on the South. Johnson, who opposed the Fourteenth Amendment, also undertook a speaking tour in which he urged voters to turn the fall election into a **referendum** on Reconstruction policies. His reckless tirades alienated many who heard him. Republicans swept the 1866 elections, outnumbering Democrats 143 to 49 in the new House of Representatives, and 42 to 11 in the Senate.

Radicals in Control: Impeachment of the President

By March 1867, it was clear that the Fourteenth Amendment had fallen short of ratification. The amendment had been rejected by twelve states: Delaware, Kentucky, and all the Confederate states except Tennessee. Moderates became more receptive to other proposals put forth by the Radicals.

The Military Reconstruction Act of 1867, passed on March 2 over Johnson's veto, divided the Confederate states (except Tennessee) into five military districts, each governed by a military commander. The act established a military occupation of the South—the only such episode in American history. The ten states were to hold constitutional conventions, and all adult male citizens were to vote, except former Confederates barred from office under the proposed Fourteenth Amendment. The constitutional conventions were to create new state governments that permitted black suffrage and that ratified the Fourteenth Amendment. Then, perhaps, Congress might recognize those state governments as valid.

On March 2, Congress also limited some of Johnson's constitutional powers. The Tenure of Office Act specified that officials appointed with the Senate's consent were to remain in office until the Senate approved a successor. This measure was intended to prevent Johnson from replacing federal officials who opposed his policies.

Some Radicals soon began to consider **impeaching** Johnson for his obstruction of their policies. The House Judiciary Committee initially found no convincing evidence of misconduct. Johnson, however, confronted Congress over the Tenure of Office Act by removing Edwin Stanton, a Lincoln appointee, from his cabinet post as secretary of war. This action provided the Radicals with grounds for impeachment. On February 24, 1868, the House approved a recommendation for impeachment based on charges stemming from the Stanton affair. The actual motivation was that the Radicals disagreed with Johnson's actions and disliked him.

Johnson remained president after the Senate voted on his impeachment in May 1868 by the narrowest of margins. Thirty-five senators voted in favor of conviction, one vote short of the required two-thirds majority. Moderate Republicans who

---

enfranchise To grant the right to vote to a person or group of people.

referendum The submission to the public for its approval or disapproval of a law passed or proposed by the legislature.

impeach To formally charge a public official with improper conduct in office and to bring the official to trial for that offense.

regarded the charges against Johnson as dubious thus saved his presidency.

Political Terrorism and the Election of 1868

Shortly after the impeachment vote, the Republicans nominated Ulysses S. Grant for president. Grant seemed the right person to end the conflict between the White House and Congress. During the war, he had fully supported Lincoln and Congress in implementing emancipation. By 1868, he had committed himself to the congressional view of Reconstruction. The Democrats nominated Horatio Seymour, a former governor of New York, and focused most of their campaign against Reconstruction.

In the South, the campaign stirred up fierce activity by the Ku Klux Klan and similar groups. **Terrorists** assassinated an Arkansas congressman, three members of the South Carolina legislature, and several delegates to state constitutional conventions. Mobs attacked Republican newspaper offices and campaign meetings. Such coercion had its intended effect. In St. Landry Parish, Louisiana, where two hundred blacks were killed, not a single Republican vote was cast on election day.

Despite such violence, many Americans probably expected a calmer political future. In June 1868, Congress had readmitted seven southern states that met its requirements, which included ratifying the Fourteenth Amendment. In July, the Fourteenth Amendment was declared ratified. In August, Thaddeus Stevens died. In November, Grant won the presidency, taking twenty-six of the thirty-four states and 53 percent of the vote.

Voting Rights and Civil Rights

Grant's election confirmed that Reconstruction was not likely to be overturned. Radical Republicans now addressed voting rights for all African Americans. As of 1869, voting rights were still defined by the states, and only seven northern states allowed blacks to vote. To guarantee the voting rights of blacks everywhere, Congress approved the **Fifteenth Amendment** in February 1869.

Widely considered to be the final step in Reconstruction, the amendment prohibited states from denying the right to vote because of a person's "race, color, or previous condition of servitude." Democrats condemned the amendment as a "revolutionary" change in the rights of states.

Susan B. Anthony and other advocates of woman suffrage opposed the amendment for a different reason: it ignored restrictions based on sex. Before emancipation, supporters of woman suffrage had been among the staunchest opponents of slavery. Now many woman-suffrage advocates urged that the vote be extended to women and black men at the same time. The break between the women's movement and the black movement was patched over somewhat once black suffrage was accomplished, but the wounds never completely healed.

Despite such opposition, within thirteen months the proposed amendment had been ratified by the states. Success came in part because Republicans who had been reluctant to impose black suffrage in the North recognized that the party's future success required black suffrage in the South.

The Fifteenth Amendment did nothing to reduce the violence that had become almost routine in the South. When Klan activity escalated in 1870, southern Republicans turned to Washington for support. In 1870 and 1871, Congress enacted the so-called Ku Klux Klan Acts to enforce the rights specified in the Fourteenth and Fifteenth Amendments.

The prosecution of Klansmen began in 1871. Hundreds were indicted in North Carolina, and many were convicted. In Mississippi, federal officials indicted nearly seven hundred. In South Carolina, President Grant declared martial law and sent federal troops to occupy the region. Hundreds

---

terrorists Those who use threats and violence, often against innocent parties, to achieve ideological or political goals.

Fifteenth Amendment Constitutional amendment ratified in 1870 that prohibits states from denying the right to vote because of a person's race or because a person used to be a slave.

of arrests followed. By 1872, federal intervention had broken the strength of the Klan.

Congress passed one final Reconstruction measure, largely because of the persistence of Charles Sumner. Passed after Sumner's death, the Civil Rights Act of 1875 prohibited racial **discrimination** in the selection of juries, in public transportation, and in **public accommodations.**

Black Reconstruction

Congressional Reconstruction set the stage for new developments throughout the South, as newly enfranchised black men organized for political action. **Black Reconstruction** began with the efforts of African Americans to take part in politics as early as 1865 and lasted until 1877.

The Republican Party in the South

Nearly all blacks who took an active part in politics did so as Republicans. Throughout Reconstruction, they formed a large majority of the Republican party's supporters in the South. The southern wing of the party also included transplanted northerners and some native white southerners.

Suffrage made politics important in African-American communities. In Louisiana and South Carolina, more than half of the delegates to state constitutional conventions were black. With suffrage established, African Americans began to be elected to public office. Between 1869 and 1877, fourteen black men served in the national House of Representatives and two in the U.S. Senate.

At the state level, blacks were most likely to be elected to the relatively unimportant offices of lieutenant governor and secretary of state. More than six hundred black men served in southern state legislatures during Reconstruction, three-quarters of them in just four states: South Carolina, Mississippi, Louisiana, and Alabama. Only in South Carolina did African Americans ever have a majority in the state legislature.

Most African-American officeholders had some education and had been born free. Of the eighteen who served in statewide offices, only three had been slaves. Blanche K. Bruce was one of these. He had been educated, however, and after the war he attended Oberlin College in Ohio. He then moved to Mississippi, where he was elected U.S. senator in 1875.

Black Republicans achieved power only by securing at least some support from whites. Opponents referred to white Republicans as either **carpetbaggers** or **scalawags.** Both groups included idealists but also included some opportunists who hoped only to fatten their own purses.

Southern Democrats used the term "carpetbagger" to suggest that northerners who came to the South after the war were second-rate opportunists, with their belongings packed in a cheap bag made of carpet. In fact, most northerners who came south were well-educated people from middle-class backgrounds. Most men had served in the Union army and moved South soon after the war to pursue financial opportunities, not politics. Some had left behind prominent roles in northern communities. Others hoped to transform the South by creating new institutions based on free labor and free schools. Carpetbaggers made up a sixth of the delegates to the state constitutional conventions but often took key roles in the conventions and the state legislatures.

---

discrimination Treatment based on class or racial category rather than on merit; prejudice.

public accommodations Places such as hotels, bars and restaurants, and theaters set up to do business with anyone who can pay the price of admission.

Black Reconstruction The period of Reconstruction when African Americans took an active role in state and local government.

carpetbagger Derogatory southern term for the northerners who came to the South after the Civil War to take part in Reconstruction.

scalawag Derogatory southern term for white southerners who aligned themselves with the Republican party.

♦ This lithograph from 1883 depicts prominent African-American men, several of whom had leading roles in Black Reconstruction. *Library of Congress.*

Southern Democrats reserved their greatest contempt for scalawags—a term used to describe completely unscrupulous and worthless people. Scalawags were white southerners who became Republicans. Many had been political foes of the Democrats before the war. They made up the largest single category of delegates to the state constitutional conventions. Scalawags included many southern Unionists and others who thought the Republicans offered the best hope for economic recovery. Scalawags included small-town merchants, artisans, and professionals. Others were small-scale farmers from the backcountry, who had traditionally opposed plantation owners. For them, Reconstruction promised an end to political domi-

nation by the plantation counties. Still others had been Whigs before the Civil War.

Despite differences, freedmen, carpetbaggers, and scalawags used the Republican party to inject new ideas into the South. Throughout the South, Republican governments extended the role of state and local government and expanded public institutions. They established or expanded schools, hospitals, orphanages, and penitentiaries.

Creating an Educational System and Fighting Discrimination

Free public education was perhaps the most permanent legacy of Black Reconstruction. Reconstruction constitutions required tax-supported public schools. Implementation, however, was expensive and proceeded slowly. By 1875, only half of southern children attended public schools.

The Reconstruction state governments debated whether white and black children should attend the same schools. Most blacks probably favored **integrated** schools. Southern whites, however, warned that integration would drive whites away. Only Louisiana and South Carolina did not mandate that schools be segregated. Most blacks probably agreed with Frederick Douglass that separate schools were "infinitely superior" to no public education.

Funding for the new schools was rarely adequate. They had to be funded largely through **property taxes,** and property tax revenues declined during the 1870s as property values fell. Creating and operating two educational systems, one white and one black, was expensive. Black schools almost always received less support than white schools.

Reconstruction state governments moved toward equal rights in other areas. The new state constitutions prohibited discrimination and protected

integrated Open to people of all races and ethnic groups without restriction.

property taxes Taxes paid by property owners according to the value of their property; often used in the United States to provide funding for local schools.

civil rights. Some states guaranteed **equal access** to public transportation and public accommodations. White Republicans, however, often opposed such laws. Such conflicts pointed up the internal divisions within the southern Republican party. Even when equal access laws were passed, they were often not enforced.

Railroad Development and Corruption

Republicans nationally sought to use the power of government to stimulate economic growth. They typically encouraged railroad construction. In the South, Reconstruction governments granted state land to railroads, loaned them money, or helped to **underwrite** bonds. Sometimes they promoted railroads without finding out whether companies were financially sound. Such efforts often failed. During the 1870s, only 7,000 miles of new track were laid in the South, compared to 45,000 miles in the North.

Railroads sometimes tried to secure favorable treatment by bribing public officials, and all too many accepted their offers. The post–Civil War period saw the ethics of public officials reach a low point. From New York City to Mississippi, revelations and allegations of corruption became staples in political campaigning.

Conditions in the South were especially ripe for political corruption. Opportunities abounded for the ambitious and unscrupulous. Reconstruction governments included many whites and blacks who had only modest holdings but aspired to better things. One South Carolina legislator bluntly said: "I was pretty hard up, and I did not care who the candidate was if I got two hundred dollars." Corruption seemed especially prominent among Republicans only because they held the most important offices. Still, some Reconstruction Republicans remained scrupulously honest. In fact, Mississippi's government under Republican rule was far more honest than it had been under prewar Democratic rule.

The End of Reconstruction

Most white southerners resisted the new social order imposed on them. They created the black codes to maintain white supremacy and to restore elements of a bound labor system. They used terrorism against the advocates of black rights. Such resistance, however, had caused Congress to pass more severe terms for Reconstruction. This backlash drove some southern opponents of Reconstruction to rethink their strategy.

The "New Departure"

By 1869, some leading southern Democrats had abandoned their resistance to change and had chosen instead to accept key Reconstruction measures. At the same time, they also tried to restore the political rights for former Confederates. The **New Departure** Democrats believed that continued resistance would only prolong federal intervention in state politics.

Sometimes southern Democrats supported conservative Republicans. The outcome of this strategy was to dilute Radical influence in state government. Democrats first tried this strategy in Virginia. There William Mahone, a leading Democrat, forged a political **coalition** that accepted black suffrage. Mahone's organization then elected a northern-born, moderate Republican banker as governor. In this way, Virginia became the only Confederate state to avoid Radical Republican rule.

Similar coalitions won in Tennessee in 1869 and in Missouri in 1870. Leading Democrats elsewhere also endorsed the New Departure. They attacked Republicans more for raising taxes and increasing state spending than for their racial policies. Whenever possible, they added charges of corruption.

---

equal access The right of any group to use a public facility such as streetcars as freely as all other groups.

underwrite To assume financial responsibility for; in this case, to guarantee the purchase of bonds so that a project can go forward.

New Departure A policy of cooperation with key Reconstruction measures that leading southern Democrats adopted in the hope of winning compromises favorable to their party.

coalition An alliance, especially a temporary one of different people or groups.

Such campaigns brought a positive response from many taxpayers because southern tax rates had risen dramatically to support the new schools, subsidies for railroads, and other new programs.

The victories of New Departure Democrats coincided with terrorist activity aimed at Republicans. In Colfax, Louisiana, whites killed 280 African Americans in 1872 in the bloodiest racial incident of the Reconstruction era. A few southern Republicans responded by proposing to create black militias. Most Republicans, however, feared that this might provoke a race war. In most of the South, the suppression of Klan terrorism came only with federal action.

The 1872 Election

The New Departure movement coincided with a division within the Republican party. The Liberal Republican movement began in 1870 as a revolt against corruption in the Grant administration. Liberal Republicans found allies among Democrats when they came out against the Radicals.

Horace Greeley, editor of the *New York Tribune,* won the Liberal nomination for president. Although Greeley had long opposed the Democrats, the Democrats also nominated him. The Liberal Republicans and Democrats were united almost solely by their opposition to Grant and the Radicals. Few Republicans found Greeley an attractive alternative to Grant, and Greeley alienated many northern Democrats by calling for the prohibition of alcohol. Grant won convincingly in 1872 (see Map 15.1). He carried 56 percent of the vote and captured every northern state.

Redemption by Terror:
The "Mississippi Plan"

After 1872, southern whites began to abandon the Republicans. The region became polarized largely along racial lines, and the elections of 1874 proved disastrous for Republicans. Democrats won over two-thirds of the South's seats in the House of Representatives and "redeemed" Alabama, Arkansas, and Texas—meaning they regained political control of these states.

Republican candidates in 1874 lost in many parts of the North because of the economic **depression** that began in 1873. After the 1874 elections, Democrats outnumbered Republicans in the House by 169 to 109. Southern Republicans could no longer look to Congress for assistance.

Terrorism against black Republicans and their remaining white allies played a role in the victory of the **Redeemers** in 1874. The Klan had worn disguises and ridden at night, but Democrats now openly formed rifle companies and marched and drilled in public. In some areas, armed whites prevented African Americans from voting.

Political violence reached such an extreme in Mississippi in 1875 that the use of terror to overthrow Reconstruction became known as the Mississippi Plan. Democratic rifle clubs operated freely, attacking Republican leaders in broad daylight. When Mississippi's carpetbagger governor, Adelbert Ames, requested federal help, President Grant declined to give it. The president had grown weary of the continuing costs of Reconstruction and the seemingly endless bloodshed that it occasioned. The Democrats swept the Mississippi elections. When the legislature convened, it removed the black Republican lieutenant governor from office. The legislature then brought similar impeachment charges against Governor Ames. Ames resigned and left the state.

The Compromise of 1877

In 1876, the nation stumbled through a potentially dangerous presidential election. As revelations of corruption grew nationally, the issue of reform took center stage. The Democratic party nominated Samuel J. Tilden, governor of New York, as

---

depression A period of drastic decline in a national or international economy, characterized by decreasing business activity, falling prices, and unemployment.

Redeemers Southern Democrats who hoped to bring the Democratic party back into power and to suppress Black Reconstruction.

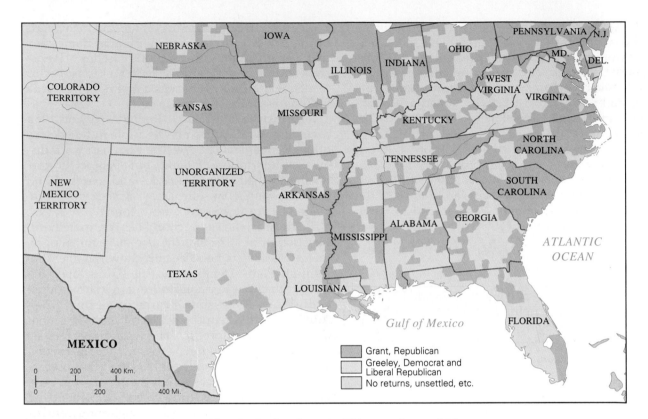

◆ **MAP 15.1.   Popular Vote for President in the South, 1872**   This map shows which candidate carried each county in the southern United States in 1872. Looking at both this map and the chapter opener map, you can see the relationship between Republican voting and African-American population, as well as where the southern Republican party drew strong support from white voters.

its presidential candidate. Tilden had earned a reputation for reform by opposing the Tweed Ring, the corrupt Democratic political machine that ran New York City government. The Republicans also selected a reform candidate, Rutherford B. Hayes, a Civil War general and governor of Ohio. Hayes's unblemished reputation proved to be his greatest asset.

First election reports indicated a close victory for Tilden, who carried most of the South and crucial northern states such as New York and Indiana. But in South Carolina, Florida, and Louisiana, Republicans still controlled the counting of ballots. Republican election boards in those states rejected enough ballots to give Hayes those three states and

thus a one-vote margin of victory in the Electoral College.

The Democrats cried fraud. Some vowed to see Tilden inaugurated by force if necessary. For the first time, Congress had to face the problem of disputed electoral votes that could decide an election. To resolve the problem, Congress created a commission consisting of five senators, five representatives, and five Supreme Court justices. Eight Republicans and seven Democrats sat on the commission.

The nation braced itself for a potentially violent confrontation. However, as commission hearings droned on into February 1877, informal discussions took place among leading Republicans and Democrats. The result was a series of informal agreements usually called the **Compromise of 1877.** Southern Democrats demanded **home rule,** by which they meant an end to federal intervention in southern politics. They also called for federal subsidies for railroad construction and waterways in the South. In return, southern Democrats were willing to abandon Tilden's claim to the White House if the commission ruled for Hayes.

Most of the agreements that were part of the Compromise of 1877 were kept. By a straight party vote, the commission confirmed the election of Hayes. Soon after his peaceful inauguration, he ordered the last of the federal troops withdrawn from the South. The Radical era of a powerful federal government pledged to protect "equality before the law" for all citizens was over. Without federal protection, the last three Republican state governments fell in 1877. The party of white supremacy held sway in every southern state.

The Compromise of 1877 marked the end of Reconstruction. The war was more than ten years in the past, and the passions it had stirred had slowly cooled. Many who had yearned to punish the South for its treason turned to other matters. Some reformers concentrated on civil service or currency issues. A major depression in the mid-1870s, unemployment and labor disputes, the growth of industry, the emergence of big business, and the economic development of the West focused public attention on economic issues.

After Reconstruction

Southern Democrats read the events of 1877 as their permit to establish new systems of politics and race relations. Most Redeemers set out to reduce taxes, to dismantle Reconstruction legislation and agencies, to take political influence away from black citizens, and eventually to reshape the South's legal system to establish African Americans as subordinate. They also began the process of turning the South into a one-party region.

Although voting and officeholding by African Americans did not cease in 1877, the political context changed profoundly once they lost federal enforcement of their rights. The threat of violence from nightriders and the potential for economic re-

taliation sharply reduced independent action by African Americans. Black political leaders increasingly recognized that efforts to mobilize black voters posed dangers to both candidates and voters. The public schools remained, segregated and underfunded, but important as both a symbol and a real opportunity to learn. Many Reconstruction era laws remained on the books.

Not until the 1890s did black disfranchisement and thoroughgoing racial segregation become widely embedded in southern law (see page 396). From the mid-1870s to the late 1890s, the South lived an uneasy compromise: African Americans had certain constitutional rights, but they exercised their rights at the sufferance of the dominant whites. Such a compromise bore the seeds of future conflict.

For generations after 1877, Reconstruction was held up as a failure. The southern version of Reconstruction—that conniving carpetbaggers and scalawags had manipulated ignorant freedmen—appealed to the racial bias of many white Americans in the North and South alike, and it gained widespread acceptance among novelists, journalists, and historians. Thomas Dixon's popular novel *The Clansman* (1905) inspired the highly influential film *The Birth of a Nation* (1915). Historically inaccurate and luridly racist, the book and the movie portrayed Ku Klux Klan members as heroes who rescued the white South, and especially white southern women, from domination and debauchery at the hands of depraved freedmen and carpetbaggers. Although black historians such as W. E. B. Du Bois challenged this picture of Reconstruction, it was not until the civil rights movement of the 1950s and 1960s that large numbers of American historians began to reconsider Reconstruction.

Compromise of 1877 Compromise in which southern Democrats agreed to allow the Republican candidate the victory in the disputed presidential election in return for the removal of federal troops from the South.

home rule Self-government; in this case, an end to federal intervention in the South.

Historians today recognize that Reconstruction was not the failure that had earlier been claimed. The creation of public schools was but one of the important changes in southern life. At a federal level, the Fourteenth and Fifteenth Amendments eventually were used to restore the principle of equality before the law. Historians also recognize that Reconstruction collapsed not so much because of internal flaws as because of the political terrorism that was unleashed in the South against blacks and Republicans.

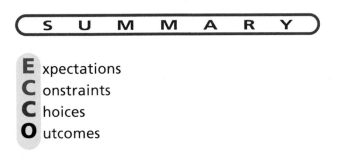

E xpectations
C onstraints
C hoices
O utcomes

At the end of the Civil War, the nation faced difficult *choices* regarding the future of the defeated South and the future of the freed people. Committed to an end to slavery, President Lincoln *chose* a lenient approach to restoring states to the Union. When Johnson became president, he continued Lincoln's approach.

The end of slavery brought new *expectations* for all African Americans. Taking advantage of the *choices* that freedom opened, they tried to create independent lives for themselves and developed social institutions that helped to define black communities. Few were able to acquire land of their own. Most became either wage laborers or sharecroppers. White southerners *expected* to keep African Americans subordinate through black codes and violence.

In reaction against the black codes and violence, Congress *chose* to wrest control of Reconstruction from President Johnson. An attempt to remove Johnson from the presidency was unsuc-

cessful. Reconstruction measures included the Fourteenth and Fifteenth Amendments, the Civil Rights Act of 1866, and the Civil Rights Act of 1875. One *outcome* of these measures was to strengthen the federal government at the expense of the states.

Enfranchised freedmen, transplanted northerners, and some southern whites created a southern Republican party that governed most southern states for a time. The most lasting contribution of these state governments was the creation of public school systems. Like government officials elsewhere, however, some southerners fell prey to corruption.

In the late 1860s, many southern Democrats *chose* a "New Departure": they grudgingly accepted some features of Reconstruction and sought to recapture control of state governments. The 1876 presidential election was hotly disputed, but key Republicans and Democrats *chose* to compromise. The Compromise of 1877 permitted Hayes to take office and brought Reconstruction to an end. Without further federal protection for their civil rights, African Americans faced severe *constraints* in exercising their rights. Sharecropping consigned most to a subordinate economic status. Terrorism, violence, and even death confronted those who *chose* to challenge their subordinate social role. The *outcome* of Reconstruction was white supremacy in politics, the economy, and social relations.

SUGGESTED READINGS

Donald, David. *Charles Sumner and the Rights of Man* (1970).

A good account not just of this important Radical leader but of important Reconstruction issues.

Du Bois, W. E. B. *Black Reconstruction in America: An Essay Toward a History of the Part Which Black Folk Played in the Attempt to Reconstruct Democracy in America, 1860–1880* (1935; reprint, 1969).

Written more than a half-century ago, Du Bois's book is still useful for both information and insights.

Foner, Eric. *Reconstruction: America's Unfinished Revolution, 1863–1877* (1988).

The most thorough recent treatment, incorporating insights from many historians who have written on the subject during the past forty years. Also available in a condensed version.

Litwack, Leon F. *Been in the Storm So Long: The Aftermath of Slavery* (1979).

Focuses on the experience of the freed people.

Woodward, C. Vann. *Reunion and Reaction: The Compromise of 1877 and the End of Reconstruction*, rev. ed. (1956).

The classic account of the Compromise of 1877.

INDUSTRIALIZATION, 1865–1900 After the Civil War, manufacturing expanded significantly, especially in the Northeast. This map indicates major types of manufacturing as of 1900 and the location of natural resources that contributed to industrialization. Some of these natural resources were not exploited until after 1900.

CANADA

WASHINGTON 1889

Ag
Pb
Cu
Ag Cu

OREGON

Timber

Timber

IDAHO 1890

MONTANA 1889

Au

WYOMING 1890

Missouri

NORTH DAKOTA 1889

SOUTH DAKOTA 1889

MINN.

Fe

Timber   Timber

Lake Superior

Minneapolis

WISCONSIN

Cu
Fe

MICH.

Lake Michigan

Lake Huron

Lake Ontario

Rochester

Buffalo

NEW YORK

Detroit

L. Erie

Cleveland

PENNSYLVANIA

Pittsburgh

New York

Jersey City

MAINE

VT.

N.H.

MASS.

Boston

CONN.

Providence R.I.

Brooklyn

Newark

Philadelphia

N.J.

DEL.

Baltimore

MD.

Milwaukee

Chicago

IOWA

C

NEBRASKA

C

ILLINOIS

IND.

C

OHIO

Cincinnati

C
C

WEST VA.

C

VIRGINIA

NEVADA

Au   Ag

San Francisco

Au
Ag

CALIFORNIA

O

O

UTAH 1896

Cu

Au
Ag

Cu

COLORADO

Au
Ag

Cu

C

KANSAS

O   C

St. Louis

MISSOURI

C

Louisville

Ohio

KENTUCKY

C

TENNESSEE

C

C

NORTH CAROLINA

SOUTH CAROLINA

ARIZONA TERRITORY

Cu

Cu   Cu

Au
Ag

NEW MEXICO TERRITORY

Cu

OK. TERR. 1890

O

O

UNORG. TERR.

ARKANSAS

O

O

MISS.

ALABAMA

Fe

C

GEORGIA

TEXAS

O

O

O

O

O

LOUISIANA

FLORIDA

PACIFIC OCEAN

MEXICO

Gulf of Mexico

ATLANTIC OCEAN

Products manufactured in 20 largest cities

- Clothing
- Flour milling
- Food, beverage, and tobacco processing
- Foundry and machine shop products
- Iron and steel
- Printing and publishing
- Slaughtering and meatpacking
- Textiles
- Mixed or other

Natural resources

Ag	Silver
Au	Gold
C	Coal
Cu	Copper
Fe	Iron ore
O	Oil (petroleum)
Pb	Lead
Timber	Timber

States with 25% or more of employees in manufacturing

0   200   400 Km.
0   200   400 Mi.

Civil War ends

Transcontinental railroad completed

Great Strike

Standard Oil Trust organized

AFL organized

Homestead Strike

Pullman Strike

Mergers peak

U.S. Steel organized

1865   1869   1877   1881   1886   1892   1894   1899 1901

1850   1900   1950   2000

Survival of the Fittest: Entrepreneurs and Workers in Industrial America, 1865–1900

INTRODUCTION

E xpectations
C onstraints
C hoices
O utcomes

In January 1901, 65-year-old Andrew Carnegie used a blunt pencil to write several lines on a sheet of paper. After receiving this paper, J. P. Morgan glanced at it and murmured, "I accept this price." Thereby did Carnegie sell the nation's largest steel company for $480 million. Thereby did Morgan, the nation's most prominent banker, acquire the central element for his plan to create the United States Steel Corporation, the first corporation in the world to be capitalized at more than a billion dollars.

By the time Morgan accepted Carnegie's offer, the U.S. economy had been dramatically transformed from what it had been during the Civil War. Back then, more than half of all American workers had toiled in agriculture. And anyone contemplating the prospects for manufacturing would have noted many potential *constraints:* a partially developed transportation system, limited amounts of capital, an unsophisticated system for mobilizing capital, and a potential shortage of workers. Some, however, would have pointed to the great potential evident in America's vast natural resources and skilled workers.

A generation later, much of that potential had been realized, and the United States stood as a major industrial power. The changes in the nation's economy far exceeded the wildest *expectations* of Americans living in 1865. Few could have imagined that steel production would increase a thousand times by 1900, or that railroads would operate nearly six times as many miles of tracks, or that farms would triple their harvests. Few could have *expected* the torrent of inventions that transformed many people's lives: adding machines, telephones, electric lights, electric streetcars, electric sewing machines, automobiles, motion pictures. By the 1890s, rapid and far-reaching change had become an ingrained part of Americans' expectations.

These economic changes were the result of *choices* made by many individuals: where to seek work, where to invest, whether to expand production, how to react to a business competitor, whom to trust. Among the many economic *choices* Ameri-

cans made, however, two general areas stand out: competition and cooperation.

As the industrial economy took off, many entrepreneurs found themselves in a love-hate relationship with competition. Carnegie loved it, expressing the *expectation* that it "insures the survival of the fittest." Morgan, by contrast, saw competition as the single most unpredictable factor in the economy and as a serious *constraint* on economic progress. Carnegie's zeal for competition was, in fact, unusual. Although many entrepreneurs paid lip service to competition, most thought more like Morgan than Carnegie.

Other Americans found themselves making *choices* regarding cooperation. Individualism was deeply entrenched in the American psyche, yet the increasing complexity of the economy presented repeated opportunities for cooperation. Entrepreneurs sometimes *chose* to cooperate by dividing a market rather than competing in it. Wage earners sometimes *chose* to join with other workers in demanding better wages or working conditions. In the process, some workers not only cooperated in a union but questioned capitalism, the economic system that paid their wages. The *outcome* of these *choices* was the industrialization of the nation and the transformation of the economy.

CHRONOLOGY

The Growth of Industry

1850s   Development of Bessemer and Kelly
             steel-making processes

1861   Protective tariff

1862   Homestead Act
           Land-Grant College Act
           Pacific Railroad Act

1865   Civil War ends

1869   First transcontinental railroad completed
           Knights of Labor founded

1870   Standard Oil incorporated
           Patent Office registers the first trademark

1872   Montgomery Ward opens its mail-order
           business

1873–1878   Depression

1875   Andrew Carnegie opens J. Edgar
           Thomson Works

1876   Invention of the telephone

1877   Great Strike
           Reconstruction ends

1879   Invention of the electric light bulb
           Henry George's *Progress and Poverty*

1880s   Railroad expansion and consolidation

1881   Standard Oil Trust organized

1882–1885   Recession

1886   Last major railroad converts to the
           standard gauge
           First Sears and Roebuck catalogue
           Peak membership in Knights of Labor
           Haymarket Square bombing
           American Federation of Labor founded

1892   Homestead strike

1893–1897   Depression

1894   Pullman strike

1901   United States Steel organized

1902   International Harvester organized

Foundation for Industrialization

By 1865, conditions in the United States were ripe for rapid industrialization. A wealth of natural resources, a capable work force, an agricultural base that produced enough food for a large urban population, and favorable government policies laid the foundation.

Resources, Skills, and Capital

At the end of the Civil War, entrepreneurs could draw on vast and virtually untapped natural resources. Americans had long plowed the fertile farmlands of the Midwest and the South. They had just begun to farm the rich black soil of Minnesota, Nebraska, Kansas, Iowa, and the Dakotas, as well as the productive valleys of California. The Pacific Northwest, the western Great Lakes region, and the South all held extensive forests untouched by the lumberman's saw.

The nation was also rich in mineral resources. Pennsylvania had vast iron ore and coal deposits. It was also the site of early efforts to tap underground pools of crude oil. California had gold. Vast reserves of other minerals lay undiscovered in

♦ In the popular imagination of most Americans in the late nineteenth century, the West was a vast and unpopulated storehouse of riches—fertile agricultural land, timber waiting to be cut, minerals there for the taking. Popular prints such as this lithograph by Currier & Ives, titled *Westward the Course of Empires Takes Its Way* (1868), which depicts ambitious pioneers moving west, encouraged such attitudes. In such imaginative depictions, there was rarely any indication that the West was already home to many American Indians and Mexican Americans. *Museum of the City of New York.*

1865: iron ore in Michigan, Minnesota, and Alabama; coal throughout the Ohio Valley and in Wyoming and Colorado; oil in the Midwest, Oklahoma, Texas, Louisiana, and California; gold or silver in Nevada and Colorado; and copper in Michigan, Montana, Utah, and Arizona.

Like natural resources, the work force and the skills and experience of workers were important for economic growth. In the early nineteenth century, New Englanders had developed manufacturing systems based on **interchangeable parts** and factories for producing cotton cloth. Their talents and inventiveness gave them a reputation for "Yankee ingenuity." Such skills, however, were not limited to New England.

Another crucial element for industrialization was capital. During the years before the war, capital became centered in the northeastern seaport cities of Boston, New York, and Philadelphia. Banks and **stock exchanges** capable of mobilizing capital had also appeared before the Civil War.

The Transformation of Agriculture

The expanding economy of the nineteenth century rested on a productive agricultural base. Improved transportation helped expand agriculture by mak-

> **interchangeable parts**   Parts that are identical and can be substituted for each other.
>
> **stock exchange**   A place where people meet to buy and sell stocks and bonds.

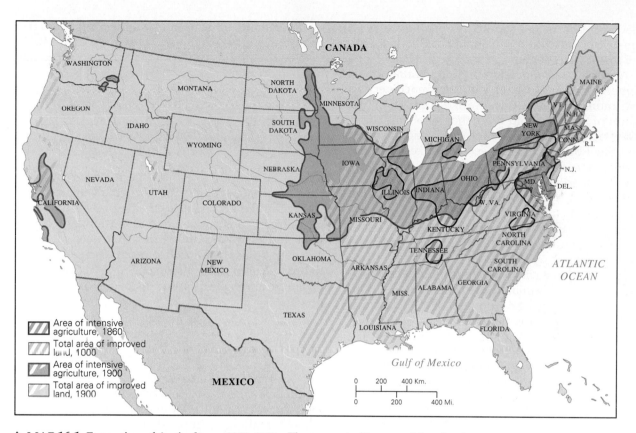

♦ **MAP 16.1 Expansion of Agriculture, 1860–1900** The amount of improved farmland
more than doubled during these forty years. This map shows two ways in which agricultural expansion came about: first, western lands were brought under cultivation; second, in other areas, especially the Midwest, land was cultivated much more intensively
than before.

ing it possible to move agricultural produce long
distances. Up to 1865, farmers had developed 407
million acres. During the next thirty-five years,
this acreage more than doubled (see Map 16.1).

The federal government contributed to the
rapid settlement of Kansas, Nebraska, the Dakotas,
and Minnesota through the **Homestead Act of
1862.** Under this act, any person could receive 160
acres of free land from the government by building
a house, living on the land for five years, and farming it. Between 1862 and 1890, 48 million acres
passed into private hands in this way. Even more
land was purchased from the government for as
little as $1.25 per acre.

As production of major crops rose, prices for
them fell. Corn sold for 66 cents per bushel in 1866
but fell steadily thereafter, hitting a low of 21 cents
in 1896. Wheat dropped from $2.06 per bushel in
1866 to a low of 49 cents in 1894. Cotton followed
the same trend. It sold for 9.7 cents per pound in
1876 but only 4.6 cents in 1894.

> **Homestead Act of 1862** Law passed by Congress
> in 1862 promising ownership of 160 acres of public
> land to any citizen who lived on and cultivated the
> land for five years.

Several factors contributed to the decline in farm prices, but the most obvious is that supply grew faster than demand. As prices for their crops fell, American farmers attempted to maintain their income by using fertilizer and new machinery to grow more crops. Between 1870 and 1890, the amount of fertilizer sold more than quadrupled.

New machinery spurred the production of grain crops. Steel-bladed plows, seed **drills,** reapers, and threshing machines all greatly increased the amount of land one person could farm. For example, a farmer with a hand-held scythe and cradle could harvest only two acres of wheat in a day. Using the McCormick reaper, first produced in 1849, a farmer and a team of horses could harvest two acres in an hour.

The growth of agriculture affected other parts of the economy. It stimulated the farm equipment industry and, in turn, the iron and steel industry. It motivated the development of railroads and sustained them. Throughout the nineteenth century, agricultural products (cotton, tobacco, wheat, and meat) constituted more than two-thirds of American exports. Thus hefty exports spurred oceanic shipping and shipbuilding.

The Impact of War and New Government Policies

In the short run, the Civil War, by diverting labor and capital into war production, probably slowed an expansion of manufacturing already under way. But the war did bring about important changes in the experience and expectations of some entrepreneurs, who began to think in terms of national markets. New government policies also quickened the rate of growth after the war.

Even in the midst of the Civil War, Republicans attempted to stimulate economic growth. They first passed a new **protective tariff** in 1861 to protect American products from foreign competition and to stimulate investment in manufacturing. Next, they used the billion acres of government-owned land to encourage economic development. The Homestead Act stimulated western settlement. The **Land-Grant College Act** (1862) gave land to states to fund public universities that would provide education in engineering and agriculture. Congress also approved the Pacific Railroad Act, a land grant for the first transcontinental railroad, in 1862.

Railroads and Economic Growth

Railroads set much of the pace for economic expansion after the Civil War. Growth of the rail network stimulated industries that supplied materials for railroad construction and operation, especially steel and coal, and industries that needed long-distance transportation to reach their markets. Railroad companies also came to symbolize big business, and some Americans began to fear their power.

Railroad Expansion

In 1865, the lack of a national rail network posed a significant constraint on economic development. Railroad companies operated on tracks of varying **gauges,** making it impossible to transfer railcars between lines. Few bridges crossed major rivers. Until 1869, no railroad connected the eastern half of the country to the Pacific coast.

By the 1880s, the final elements had fallen into place to create a national rail network. The first transcontinental rail line was completed in 1869,

---

drill A machine for planting seeds in holes or furrows.

protective tariff Tax on imported goods intended to make them more expensive than similar domestic goods, thus protecting the market for items produced at home.

Land-Grant College Act Law passed by Congress in 1862 that gave public land to each state; income from the land was to provide funding for engineering and agricultural colleges.

gauge The distance between the rails in a railroad track.

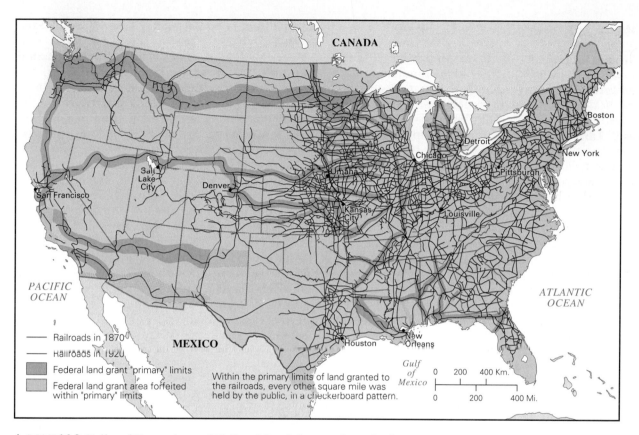

CANADA

Boston

Detroit

Chicago

New York

Salt
Lake
City

Umaha

Pittsburgh

Denver

San Francisco

Kansas
City

Louisville

PACIFIC
OCEAN

ATLANTIC
OCEAN

——— Railroads in 1870

——— Railroads in 1920

Federal land grant "primary" limits

Federal land grant area forfeited
within "primary" limits

MEXICO

Houston

New
Orleans

Within the primary limits of land granted to
the railroads, every other square mile was
held by the public, in a checkerboard pattern.

Gulf
of
Mexico

0   200   400 Km.

0   200   400 Mi.

♦ **MAP 16.2 Railroad Expansion and Railroad Land Grants**   Post–Civil War railroad expansion produced the transportation base for an industrial economy. In the West, federal land grants encouraged railroad construction. Within a grant, railroads received every other square mile. Land could be forfeited if construction did not meet the terms of the grant legislation.

connecting Sacramento, California, to Omaha, Nebraska. By 1893, four more transcontinental lines had been built. Between 1865 and 1890, railroads grew from 35,000 miles of track to 167,000 miles (see Map 16.2). By the mid-1880s, most major rivers had been bridged. Companies had replaced many iron rails with steel ones, making it possible to haul heavier loads. New inventions increased the speed, carrying capacity, and efficiency of trains. In 1886, the last major lines converted to a standard gauge, making it possible to transfer railcars from one line to another simply by throwing a switch. This rail network enabled entrepreneurs to ship raw materials and goods easily from one region to another.

Western railroads expanded with generous assistance from the federal government. Congress provided the Union Pacific and Central Pacific railroads, the first companies to build a transcontinental line, not only with sizable loans but also with 10 square miles of the public domain for every mile of track laid. Congress doubled this amount in 1864. By 1871, Congress had authorized some seventy railroad land grants, involving 128 million acres, an area the size of Colorado and Wyoming together. Most railroads sold their land to farmers and companies to raise capital for railroad operations. This practice guaranteed that the railroads would have customers and business along their tracks.

Railroads: Models for Big Business

Railroad companies differed in kind from earlier businesses. Because of their size, they encountered problems that no other businesses had faced. Railroads required much more coordination and long-range planning than previous businesses. Earlier companies typically operated at a single location, but railroads had to provide freight stations, passenger stations, and repair facilities along the entire length of their lines. Financial transactions carried on over hundreds of miles by scores of employees required a centralized accounting office. One result was the development of a bureaucracy of clerks, accountants, managers, and agents. Railroads became training grounds for the first administrators in American business and the models for many subsequent large businesses.

Railroads required far more capital than most manufacturing concerns. The largest steel furnaces in the world cost $741,000 in 1875, but in the same year the Pennsylvania Railroad was capitalized at $400 million. The railroads' huge appetite for capital made them the first American businesses to seek investors on a nationwide and international scale. By the Civil War, the New York Stock Exchange had emerged as the leading place where brokers sold railroad stocks.

Railroads faced higher **fixed costs** than most previous companies. These costs included equipment, property, and commitments to investors. To pay their fixed costs, railroad companies operated at full capacity whenever possible. Doing so sometimes proved difficult. Where two or more lines competed for the same traffic, rate wars often resulted. Competition between railroad companies sometimes became so intense that no line could show a profit. A railroad that could not cover its fixed costs faced bankruptcy.

Some railroad operators attempted to eliminate competition by forming **pools**. The most famous was the Iowa Pool, made up of the railroads operating between Chicago and Omaha. Formed in 1870, the Iowa Pool operated until 1874. Few pools lasted very long. Typically a railroad broke the pool arrangement in an effort to expand, thereby starting a new price war. Customers complained loudly when a pooling arrangement became known; they

believed that they paid higher rates because of the pool.

To compete more effectively, railroads adjusted their rates to attract high-volume shippers. Favored customers sometimes received a **rebate.** Large shipments sent over long distances cost the railroad companies less per mile than small shipments sent over short distances, so companies developed different rate structures for long and short hauls. Thus the largest shippers could secure rebates and low rates, and small businesses and farmers operated at a comparative disadvantage. Although railroads explained the rates in terms of differences in costs, small shippers still saw themselves as victims of rate discrimination.

Railroads viewed government as a source of valuable subsidies, but they constantly guarded against efforts to have government regulate their enterprises. Companies campaigned openly to secure the election of friendly politicians and **lobbied** public officials in Washington, D.C., and in state capitals. Most railroad companies issued free passes to public officials, a practice reformers attacked as a form of bribery. Railroads such as the Southern Pacific in California became the most influential political power in the state. Stories of railroad officials bribing politicians became commonplace after the Civil War.

Investment Bankers and "Morganization"

The rapid railroad expansion of the 1880s led to excessive competition, which caused some lines to earn little or no profit. Railway executives at-

---

fixed costs   Costs that a company must pay even if it closes down all its operations—for example, interest on loans, dividends on bonds, and property taxes.

pool   An agreement among businesses in the same industry to divide up the market and charge equal prices instead of competing.

rebate   The refund of part of the amount given in payment for something.

lobby   To try to influence the thinking of public officials for or against a specific cause.

tempted to solve the problem by consolidating small carriers into a large regional railway. The Santa Fe and the Southern Pacific, for example, emerged in the Southwest, and the Great Northern and the Northern Pacific held sway in the Northwest. The Pennsylvania and the New York Central controlled much of the Northeast. Railway executives expected consolidation to lead to fewer price wars and higher profits.

To raise the enormous amounts of capital necessary for construction and consolidation, railroads turned increasingly to investment bankers. **John Pierpont Morgan** had emerged as the most prominent investment banker by the late 1880s. Morgan was the son of a successful Connecticut merchant who turned to investment banking and relocated the family to London when Morgan was 17. After working in his father's London bank, Morgan moved in 1857 to New York, where his father's connections and his own abilities enabled him to become a major banking figure.

Morgan's access to capital in the United States, London, and Paris soon led to his involvement in efforts to stabilize the railroad industry. His price for investing in financially ailing railroads was the consolidation of small lines into larger systems. He often insisted that he or one of his partners be seated on the board of directors to guard against risky decisions in the future. This process became known as "Morganization." "Morganized" lines by 1900 included some of the largest in the country: the Reading, the Baltimore & Ohio, the Chesapeake & Ohio, the Santa Fe, the Erie, the Northern Pacific, and the Southern. A few other investment bankers followed similar patterns.

By 1900, railroad entrepreneurs and investment bankers had twelve large railroad systems that controlled more than half of the nation's track mileage. Twenty other railroads operated most of the rest.

Entrepreneurs and Industrial Transformation

Despite the emergence of large railroad corporations, most American businesses were relatively small. Even as late as 1899, nearly 60 percent of all manufacturing establishments were so small that they averaged only two production workers. Such businesses typically operated in a single shop, were run by the owner, and produced one item for local sale. For example, a wheelwright turned out wheels one at a time. Although a few textile factories employed a hundred workers as early as the 1820s, these companies made only one product in one location. Entrepreneurs in the late nineteenth century challenged all these patterns.

Andrew Carnegie and the Age of Steel

Steel defined the new industrial economy that emerged after the Civil War. This superior metal was difficult and expensive to make until the 1850s, when Henry Bessemer in England and William Kelly in Kentucky independently discovered ways of making it inexpensively and quickly.

In 1875, just south of Pittsburgh, Pennsylvania, **Andrew Carnegie** opened the nation's largest steel plant, the J. Edgar Thomson Works. From then until 1901, Carnegie held central place in the steel industry. Born in Scotland in 1835, Carnegie came to the United States with his penniless parents in 1848. He soon became a messenger in a telegraph office and then a telegraph operator. Because of his great skill at the telegraph key, Carnegie became the personal telegrapher for a high official of the Pennsylvania Railroad. Carnegie rose rapidly and became a superintendent at the age of 25. At the end of the Civil War, he left railroading to devote full attention to his investments in the iron and steel industry. He quickly began to apply to his iron companies the management lessons he had learned with the railroad.

> **John Pierpont Morgan**   American banker and industrialist who used investments in railroads and steel to turn his family fortune into a colossal financial empire.
>
> **Andrew Carnegie**   Scottish-born industrialist who made a fortune in steel and believed the rich had a duty to act for the public benefit.

Carnegie followed this basic rule: "Cut the prices; scoop the market; run the mills full." An aggressive competitor, he took every opportunity to cut costs so that he could charge less than his rivals. In 1864, steel rails sold for $126 per ton; by 1875, Carnegie was selling them for $69 per ton. Driven by improved technology and Carnegie's competitiveness, steel prices continued to fall, reaching less than $20 per ton in the late 1890s. By then, the nation produced nearly 10 million tons of steel each year.

Carnegie's success in reducing costs also stemmed from **vertical integration.** Like other entrepreneurs, Carnegie chose to control everything from the supply of raw materials to the distribution of finished products. Vertical integration guaranteed a reliable flow of supplies at predictable prices.

Steel plants stood at one end of the long chain of vertically integrated operations that Carnegie owned or controlled: iron ore mines in Michigan and Wisconsin, a fleet of ships that transported iron ore across the Great Lakes, hundreds of miles of railway lines, tens of thousands of acres of coal lands, ovens to produce **coke,** and plants for turning iron ore into bars of crude iron. Carnegie Steel was vertically integrated from the point where the raw materials came out of the ground through the production of steel rails and beams.

Standard Oil: Model for Monopoly

As Carnegie provided a model for other steel companies and for heavy industry, **John D. Rockefeller** revolutionized the petroleum industry. Born in 1839, Rockefeller became a partner in a grain and livestock business in Cleveland that earned large profits during the Civil War. In 1863, Rockefeller invested these profits in a refinery that had been built to process oil from northwestern Pennsylvania, where oil had been discovered in 1859. After the war, he bought more refineries and incorporated them as Standard Oil in 1870.

The refining business was highly competitive. Recognizing that improved technology could offer a decisive advantage, Rockefeller recruited engineers to make Standard the most efficient re-

finer. He secured reduced rates or obtained rebates from the railroads. He usually sought to persuade his competitors to join the **cartel** he was creating. Failing in that, he would drive them out of business.

Between 1879 and 1881, Rockefeller centralized decision making among the forty companies that he and his associates controlled by creating the Standard Oil Trust. The **trust** was a new organizational form designed to get around state laws that prohibited one company from owning stock in another. To create the trust, Rockefeller and other shareholders in the individual companies exchanged their stock for trust certificates issued by Standard Oil. Standard Oil thus was able to control all the individual companies, though technically it did not own them. The creation of Standard Oil meant that one company controlled about 90 percent of the nation's refining capacity.

Standard Oil consolidated its operations by closing more than half of its refineries and building several larger plants that incorporated the newest technology. One outcome was greater efficiency. The price of fuel and lighting products fell by more than half from 1866 to 1890. In the 1880s, Standard moved to vertical integration by gaining

> **vertical integration** The bringing together of a wide range of business activities—such as acquiring raw materials, manufacturing, and marketing and selling finished products—into a single organization.
>
> **coke** Coal from which most of the gases have been removed by heating; it burns with intense heat and is used in making steel.
>
> **John D. Rockefeller** American industrialist who amassed great wealth through the Standard Oil Company and donated much of his fortune to promote learning and research.
>
> **cartel** A group of independent business organizations that cooperate to control the production, pricing, and marketing of goods by group members; another term for *pool.*
>
> **trust** A combination of firms or corporations for the purpose of reducing competition and controlling prices throughout an industry.

control of existing oil fields, building its own pipelines and oceangoing tankers, and creating its own marketing operations. By the early 1890s, Standard Oil had achieved a near **monopoly** over an entire industry. The monopoly proved to be short-lived, however, because of the discovery of new oil fields in Texas and elsewhere. New companies emerged and quickly followed the path of vertical integration.

Technology and Economic Change

By the late nineteenth century, most American entrepreneurs had joined Rockefeller in viewing technology as an important competitive device. Railroads wanted more powerful locomotives, larger freight cars, and stronger rails. Steel companies demanded larger and more efficient furnaces. Ordinary citizens as well as entrepreneurs were infatuated with technology. One invention followed another: an ice making machine in 1865, the air brake for trains in 1868, the vacuum cleaner in 1869, the telephone in 1876, the phonograph in 1878, the electric light bulb in 1879, and the first American-made gasoline-engine automobile in 1895. By 1900, many Americans had come to expect a steady flow of new and astounding creations.

Thomas A. Edison, born in 1847, stood out in the field of electrical inventions. In 1869, Edison secured the first of the thousand-plus **patents** that he would obtain over his lifetime. In 1876, in Menlo Park, New Jersey, Edison set up the first modern research laboratory. There he and his staff worked at improving electrical technology. Sometimes building on the work of others, Edison's laboratories invented or significantly improved electric lighting, electric motors, the storage battery, the electric locomotive, the phonograph, the mimeograph, and many other products.

Investment bankers played an important role in the development of the new companies that generated and distributed electricity, manufactured electrical equipment, and sold light bulbs and other electrical devices to consumers. General Electric, for example, came about through a series of **mergers** arranged by J. P. Morgan.

Selling to the Nation

Large, vertically integrated manufacturers of consumer goods often produced goods that differed little from each other and cost virtually the same. Such companies sometimes chose not to compete on the basis of price but instead to use advertising to differentiate their products.

Most advertising in the mid-nineteenth century promoted **patent medicines** and books. By 1890, however, large-scale advertising also featured packaged foods, clothing, soap, and petroleum products. After the federal Patent Office registered the first **trademark** in 1870, companies rushed to develop logos that would distinguish their products from nearly identical rivals.

Advertising popularized new ways of selling goods. Previously, most people had purchased goods from small specialty stores, **general stores,** artisans, or door-to-door peddlers. After the Civil War, the appearance of department stores made available a wide range of choices in ready-made products such as clothing and shoes. Such stores relied heavily on newspaper advertising to attract customers. The variety presented by department stores paled, however, when compared to the goods available through the mail-order catalogues

monopoly Exclusive control by one group of the means of producing or selling a product.

Thomas A. Edison American inventor, especially of electrical devices, among them the microphone (1877), the phonograph (1878), and the light bulb (1879).

patent A government grant that gives the creator of an invention the sole right to produce, use, or sell that invention for a set period of time.

merger The union of two or more organizations.

patent medicine A medical preparation that is advertised by a brand name and can be bought without a physician's prescription.

trademark A name or symbol that identifies a product and is officially registered and legally restricted for use by the owner or manufacturer.

general store A store, common in rural areas, that sells a lot of different goods but is not divided into departments.

first offered by Montgomery Ward in 1872 and Sears and Roebuck in 1886. Aimed at rural America, these catalogues offered a wider range of choices than most country-dwellers had ever before seen. Department stores and mail-order houses were possible because manufacturers now produced all sorts of ready-made goods.

Economic Concentration and the Merger Movement

Carnegie and Rockefeller redefined the expectations of other entrepreneurs and provided models for the organization of business. One outcome was that large, complex companies appeared relatively suddenly in the 1880s. At first, they were concentrated in consumer-goods industries.

James B. Duke, for example, used efficient machinery, extensive advertising, and vertical integration to become the largest manufacturer of cigarettes. In 1890, he merged with his four largest competitors to create the American Tobacco Company, which dominated the cigarette industry. Gustavus Swift in the early 1880s began to ship fresh meat from his slaughterhouse in Chicago to the East using his own refrigerated railcars. He eventually added refrigerated storage plants in each city. Other meatpacking companies followed Swift's lead. By 1890, a half dozen firms, all vertically integrated, dominated meatpacking. Monopolies like Standard Oil were fairly rare. More typical was the situation in meatpacking, in which an **oligopoly**—a small number of firms—dominated an industry.

Many new manufacturing companies in the 1870s and early 1880s did not sell stock or use investment bankers to raise capital. Standard Oil and Carnegie Steel expanded by merging with other companies, adding partners, or purchasing companies from retained profits. Rockefeller and Carnegie, for example, concentrated ownership and control in their own hands. The same held true for many other industrial companies until late in the nineteenth century. In 1896, the New York Stock Exchange sold stock in only twenty manufacturing concerns.

At the turn of the century, however, a second phase of vertical and horizontal integration cre-

ated the need for more capital, and investment bankers began to turn their attention from railroads to heavy industry. In the late 1890s, J. P. Morgan started combining companies in the steel business to create a vertically integrated operation that might challenge Carnegie's dominance. Carnegie had never carried vertical integration to the point of making final products such as wire, barrels, or tubes. He seemed at first to relish the prospect of no-holds-barred competition with what he called "the Trust." When Morgan offered to buy him out, however, he agreed, allowing Morgan in 1901 to create United States Steel, the nation's first billion-dollar corporation.

Other large mergers followed. In 1902, competition between the two largest companies making harvesting machines became so intense that each considered creating its own steel plant. Realizing that this strategy would hurt United States Steel's business, Morgan intervened. Morgan merged the two largest and three smaller harvester firms into International Harvester in 1902, creating a company that dominated 85 percent of the market.

United States Steel and International Harvester were just two of the many new combinations in manufacturing created in a relatively short time at the turn of the century. Between 1898 and 1902, the nation witnessed an astonishing number of mergers. The high point came in 1899, when 1,208 mergers involving $2.3 billion in capital occurred.

Investment bankers sought two primary objectives in reorganizing an industry: to make the industry stable, so that investments would yield predictable **dividends;** and to make the industry efficient, so that dividends would be high. Toward that end, investment bankers placed their representatives on the boards of directors of the new companies. By 1912, the three leading New York banks held 341 directorships in 112 major companies.

Thus, by 1900, many of the characteristics of modern business had emerged. Many industries were

---

oligopoly   A market or industry dominated by a few firms.

dividend   A share of profits received by a stockholder.

oligopolistic, dominated by a few vertically integrated companies. **Product differentiation** through advertising had begun. The stock market had moved beyond the sale of railroad securities to play an important role in raising capital for industry.

With the passing of the first generation of industrial empire builders, ownership grew apart from management. Many new business executives were simply hired managers. Ownership rested with hundreds or thousands of stockholders, all of whom wanted a reliable return on their investment. The huge size of the new companies also meant that most managers rarely saw or talked with employees not involved in management or accounting. Many companies treated their employees as expenses to be increased or cut as necessary, with little regard to the impact of their decisions on people.

Workers in Industrial America

The rapid expansion of railroads, mining, and manufacturing created a demand for labor to lay the rails, dig out the ore, tend the furnaces, operate the refineries, and carry out a thousand other tasks. The new workers required to perform these tasks came from across the nation and around the world. Despite the lure of a rags-to-riches triumph like that of Andrew Carnegie, very few became wealthy.

Labor and Mobility

Horatio Alger emerged as one of America's most popular novelists after the success of *Ragged Dick* (1868), the story of an orphaned shoeshine boy who achieves financial success. Alger's books, which sold nearly a hundred million copies, had but one refrain: a poor but hardworking youth, through some unusual opportunity to do good, attracts the attention of a wealthy, powerful person and thereby achieves success, wealth, and happiness. Alger's name became a symbol of the expectation that in America anyone who worked hard and saved could succeed.

The reality of life in industrial America bore little resemblance to Alger's tales. Nearly all successful business leaders came from middle-class or upper-class families. Few workers could expect to move more than a step up the economic scale. An unskilled laborer might become a semiskilled worker, or a skilled worker might become a foreman, but few wage earners moved into the middle class. If they did, it was usually as the owner of a small business.

In industrial America, the treatment of labor differed little from that of the raw materials that went into a finished product. During boom periods, companies advertised for labor and ran their operations at full capacity. When the demand for manufactured goods fell, companies reduced production and laid off workers, cut wages, or reduced hours. Unemployed workers had little to fall back on but their savings or the earnings of other family members. Some churches and private charities gave out food, but state and federal government provided no unemployment benefits. Families that failed to find work might become homeless and go hungry. In a depression, jobs of any sort were scarce, and competition for them was intense.

Workers for Industry

Between the Civil War and 1900, the labor force more than doubled. The largest increases occurred in industries undergoing the greatest changes (see Figure 16.1). Agriculture continued to employ the largest share of the labor force (40 percent in 1900), but the growth of agricultural workers was the smallest of all major categories of workers.

Workers for the rapidly expanding economy came from within the nation and from abroad. Throughout rural New England and the Middle Atlantic states, large numbers of people moved to

> **product differentiation** The use of advertising to distinguish one product from similar products.
>
> **Horatio Alger** American writer of rags-to-riches stories about impoverished boys who become wealthy through hard work, virtue, and luck.

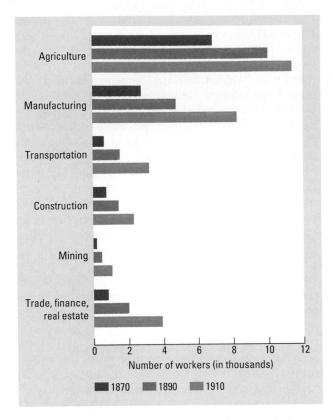

♦ **FIGURE 16.1** Distribution of the Work Force, 1870, 1890, 1910

they worked seventy-hour weeks for between 10 and 20 cents per day. Children also worked in tobacco and cotton fields in the South, operated sewing machines in New York, assisted glass blowers in West Virginia factories, and sorted vegetables in Delaware canneries. Most working children turned over all their wages to their parents.

Women as well as children found employment outside the home. Between 1890 and 1910, nearly half of all single women worked for wages, along with a third of widowed or divorced women. Among married women, only 5 to 10 percent did so. Black women were employed at much higher rates in all categories.

Children and mothers worked for wages primarily because the head of the family earned a meager income. One 1875 study showed that the average male factory worker in Lawrence, Massachusetts, earned $500 per year. The average family in Lawrence, however, required at least $600 annually to provide sufficient food, clothing, and shelter. In such circumstances, a family needed two or more incomes.

By 1900, women held a majority of jobs in some occupations. They made up more than 70 percent of the workers in textile factories, more than 70 percent of the nation's secretaries, and 80 percent of telephone operators. Office work usually paid less than factory work but was considered safer and of higher status. Women almost always earned less than their male counterparts. In most industries, the jobs commanding the best pay were reserved for adult males. Even when men and women did the same work, there was usually a pay differential. Not all women worked as wage earners. Some took in laundry, did sewing for neighbors, or rented a room to a boarder. In one eastern factory town in 1912, 90 percent of the families where the husband was the only wage earner took in boarders.

The Transformation of Work

Whether native- or foreign-born, most industrial workers had been born into a rural society. They found industrial work quite different from the work they had done previously. Farm families

urban or industrial areas. Owners abandoned small and unproductive farms to take jobs in nearby factory towns or to move west. Many country towns also lost population.

The expanding economy, however, needed more workers than the nation could supply. As a result, the period between 1865 and 1914 witnessed the largest influx of immigrants in American history: more than 26 million people. By 1910, immigrants and their children made up more than 35 percent of the population.

The expanding economy pulled children as well as adults into the ranks of industrial wage earners. In 1910, nearly two million children worked for wages, some as young as 10 years old. More children were employed in the textile industry than in any other kind of manufacturing. Mostly girls,

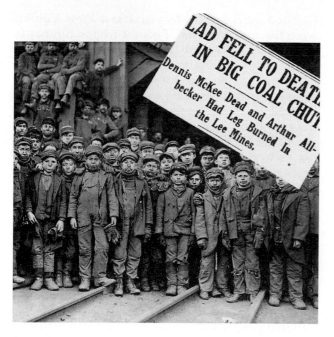

♦ The coal mines of Pennsylvania employed more than ten thousand boys under the age of 16. Known as "breaker boys," they sorted coal. Such work was dangerous and sometimes fatal, as this 1911 headline attests. *Library of Congress.*

might work from sunrise to sunset, but they worked at their own speed. Self-employed blacksmiths, carpenters, dressmakers, and other skilled workers also controlled the speed and intensity of their work. Like farmers, they could pace themselves to avoid exhaustion.

People from rural settings expected to work long hours, but they found that industrial work controlled them. The speed of the machines set the pace of the work. If managers ordered a speedup, operators worked faster. Ten- or twelve-hour days at a constant, rapid pace drained the workers. A woman textile worker in 1882 said, "I get so exhausted that I can scarcely drag myself home when night comes." During times of high demand, most steel companies required a seven-day workweek and twelve hours a day. A 27-year-old steelworker in 1910 was blunt: "It's simply a killing pace in the steel works." This was often the literal truth, as ex-

hausted workers were much more likely to be killed in accidents.

Some factory managers saw their dependence on skilled workers as a constraint on their control of production. Such workers set the pace of work, earned more than other workers, and were difficult to replace. Industrial engineer Frederick W. Taylor built a national reputation by redesigning work so that unskilled workers could replace skilled workers. Taylor broke complex tasks down into simpler ones that required few skills to perform. The replacement of skilled workers was intended to increase managers' control over the work process.

The Varieties of Labor Organization and Action

Some workers reacted to the far-reaching changes in the nature of work by choosing to join other workers in efforts to maintain or regain control over their working conditions. They experimented with a variety of organizations. **Craft unions** drew their strength from skilled workers. Some organizations sought reform, hoping to use the power of government to assist workers. Others proposed alternatives to capitalism itself. European immigrants sometimes brought union experience or a commitment to socialism with them. Strikes erupted on an unprecedented scale. Entrepreneurs responded by calling on government to protect property, to maintain order, and to suppress strikes.

Craft Unionism and Its Limits

Skilled workers in many fields outside manufacturing often remained indispensable. In construction, only an experienced carpenter could build

> **craft union** Labor union that organizes skilled workers engaged in a specific craft or trade; also called a trade union.

stairs or hang doors properly. In railroading, only a highly trained engineer could operate a locomotive. In publishing, only a skilled typesetter could transform handwritten copy into lines of lead type. Such workers took pride in the quality of their work and knew that their skill was crucial to their employer's success.

Skilled workers formed the first unions, which were called craft or trade unions because membership was limited to skilled workers in a particular craft or trade. Before the Civil War, workers in most American cities had created local trade unions in attempts to regulate the quality of work, wages, hours, and working conditions for their craft. Local unions eventually formed national trade organizations after 1865.

If most craftworkers within a city belonged to the local union, a strike could be a powerful weapon in the effort to define working conditions. Strikes most often succeeded in prosperous times, when the employer wanted to continue operating and was able to make financial concessions to workers. When the economy experienced a serious downturn, craft unions usually disintegrated because they could not strike effectively. Only after the 1880s did local and national unions develop strategies that permitted them to survive depressions.

Because craft unions limited membership to skilled workers, they were of little help to most industrial workers. Craft unions also frequently restricted their membership to white males. Membership restrictions based on gender or ethnicity were major obstacles to the economic advancement of women and ethnic minorities.

The Great Strike of 1877

In 1877, the nation witnessed widespread labor strife for the first time. When a depression began in 1873, railroad companies reduced operating costs by repeatedly cutting wages. Railroad workers' pay fell by more than a third between 1873 and early 1877. Union leaders talked of organizing a strike but failed to bring one off.

Railway workers took matters into their own hands in 1877 when companies announced additional pay cuts of 10 percent. Baltimore & Ohio

Railroad workers in Maryland and West Virginia were the first to strike. Federal troops ultimately restored service on the B & O, but the strike spread to other lines. Strikers shut down the trains in Pittsburgh. When the local militia refused to act against the strikers, the governor of Pennsylvania ordered in militia units from Philadelphia. The troops killed twenty-six people. Strikers and their sympathizers then attacked the militia, forced the troops to retreat, and burned and looted railroad property throughout Pittsburgh.

Strikes and demonstrations of support for strikers erupted across Pennsylvania, New York, and the Midwest. Everywhere, the strikers drew support from their local communities. Coal miners, factory workers, owners of small businesses, farmers, black workers, and women demonstrated their support. State militia, federal troops, and local police eventually broke up the strikes, but not before hundreds had lost their lives and the railroads had suffered property damage of $10 million, half of it in Pittsburgh.

The **Great Strike of 1877** revealed widespread dislike for the new railroad companies and significant community support for strikers. The strike also deeply worried some Americans. They saw in it a forecast of future labor unrest and even revolution. They called for better training for state militia units to suppress such domestic disorders.

The Knights of Labor

The Great Strike suggested that working people could unite across lines of occupation, race, and gender. No organization drew on that potential, however, until the early 1880s, when the **Knights of Labor** emerged as an alternative to craft unions.

Great Strike of 1877 A series of strikes in American cities triggered by railroad wage cuts; the strikes showed widespread support for the demands of workers but were put down by government troops.

Knights of Labor Labor organization founded in 1869; membership, open to all workers, peaked in 1886.

Founded in 1869, the Knights directed their appeals to members of what they called "the producing class." The "producers" included all those who produced value by their labor—the blacksmith whose labor produced tools, the farmer whose labor produced crops, the garment-factory worker whose labor produced clothing. Thus self-employed artisans and farmers were welcome along with wage-earning factory workers. The organization excluded professional gamblers, stockbrokers, lawyers, bankers, and liquor dealers. The Knights accepted African Americans and women as members and helped to provide members of both groups, including the legendary **Mary Harris ("Mother") Jones** (see Individual Choices: "Mother" Jones), with experience in labor organizing.

Terence V. Powderly, a machinist, led the Knights from 1879 to 1893. Under his leadership, they promoted organization, education, and cooperation as their chief objectives. Powderly generally opposed strikes. A lost strike, he argued, often destroyed the local union organization and thereby delayed the more important tasks of education and cooperation. The Knights' endorsement of cooperation was related to the labor theory of value. A major objective of the Knights was "to secure to the workers the full enjoyment of the wealth they create." Toward that end, they promoted a system of producers' and consumers' **cooperatives,** which they hoped would supersede the wage system. The Knights saw cooperatives as an alternative to a capitalistic system based on the payment of wages. They established some 135 cooperatives by the mid-1880s, but few lasted very long. Some folded because of lack of capital, some because of opposition from businesses with which they competed, some because of poor organization.

By the mid-1880s, the Knights of Labor was the most prominent labor organization in the country. Membership jumped from 9,000 in 1879 to 703,000 in 1886. This startling increase in membership came about primarily because local Knights' organizers won strikes against prominent railroads in 1884 and 1885. The Knights' meteoric growth suggested that many working people would band together against the emerging corporate behemoths.

1886: Turning Point for Labor?

The Great Strike of 1877 and the rise of the Knights of Labor were signs of a sense of common purpose among many working people. After 1886, however, labor organizations often found themselves on the defensive and were divided between those trying to make the best of the new realities of industrial capitalism and those seeking to change it.

On May 1, 1886, some eighty thousand Chicagoans marched through the streets in support of an eight-hour workday. Three days later, Chicago police killed several strikers at the McCormick Harvester Works. Hoping to build on the unity demonstrated by the May Day parade, a group of Chicago **anarchists** called a protest meeting for the next day at Haymarket Square. When police tried to break up the rally, someone threw a bomb into the police ranks. The police opened fire on the crowd, and some of the protesters fired back. Eight policemen died, along with an unknown number of demonstrators. About a hundred people, including sixty policemen, suffered injuries.

The Haymarket bombing sparked antiunion feelings. Employers who had opposed unions before now tried to discredit them by playing on

Mary Harris ("Mother") Jones A labor organizer who, beginning in the 1890s, traveled from region to region organizing strikes and protests among coal miners.

Terence V. Powderly Leader of the Knights of Labor who called for cooperative production instead of a wage system.

cooperative A business enterprise in which workers and consumers share ownership and take part in management.

anarchist A person who believes that all forms of government are oppressive and should be abolished.

Choosing to Serve Labor

Mother Jones

Mary Harris Jones, known as Mother Jones, faced many difficult choices in her long career as a union organizer, sometimes involving threats to her personal safety. This picture is from a protest march in 1910, when she was nearly 80 years old. Archives of Labor & Union Affairs, Wayne State University.

In 1891, a white-haired woman more than 60 years old stepped down from a train in an Appalachian mining town. A man anxiously asked her name, and she told him. Thirty years later, she still recalled his response: "The superintendent [manager for the coal-mining company] told me that if you came down here he would blow out your brains. He said he didn't want to see you 'round these parts." The threat had no effect, for she had long since chosen her life's direction. "You tell the superintendent that I am not coming to see him anyway. I am coming to see the miners." For almost fifty years, Mary Harris Jones chose "to see the miners" and to bring them the message of unionism in the face of hostility and threats from mining companies and the local officials who did the companies' bidding.

According to her own account, Mary Harris was born in Ireland in 1830 and came to the United States as a child, with her father. As a young woman, she taught school and worked as a dressmaker or seamstress, then married George Jones, an iron molder and union activist. Her expectations as a wife and mother were shattered, however, when she lost her entire family—her husband and their four children—in a yellow-fever epidemic in 1867.

fears of radical-inspired terrorism. Some people who supported what they saw as legitimate union goals shrank back in horror. In Chicago, eight leading anarchists stood trial for inciting the bombing and, on flimsy evidence, were convicted. Four were hanged, one committed suicide, and three remained in jail until they were released in 1893 by a sympathetic governor, John Peter Altgeld.

Uniting the Craft Unions: The American Federation of Labor

Two weeks after the Haymarket bombing, trade union leaders met in Philadelphia to propose an agreement between the trade unions and the Knights: trade unions would recruit skilled workers, and the Knights would limit themselves to unskilled workers. When the Knights refused to go

On her own, she opened a dressmaking shop in Chicago. Her clients included those she called "the aristocrats of Chicago," and she witnessed "the luxury and extravagance of their lives." The contrast between the opulent expectations of her wealthy clients and tightly constrained lives of the poor left her deeply disturbed.

"Often while sewing for the lords and barons who lived in magnificent houses on the Lake Shore Drive," she recalled in her autobiography, "I would look out of the plate glass windows and see the poor, shivering wretches, jobless and hungry, walking along the frozen lake front. The contrast of their condition with that of the tropical comfort of the people for whom I sewed was painful to me."

In 1871, her shop burned in the great fire that swept much of the city. Thereafter, she chose to give much of her time to helping workers, first through the Knights of Labor. In 1882, she first took part in a strike by coal miners.

As the Knights of Labor began to disintegrate after 1886, some of its trade assemblies (organizations limited to workers in one trade) chose to affiliate with the American Federation of Labor (AFL). In 1890, one received an AFL charter as the United Mine Workers of America (UMW), but it remained an industrial union that admitted both white and black members. Until her death in 1930, Jones fought for the UMW. She became a familiar figure throughout the sooty valleys of Appalachia, where miners' families lived in wretched, company-owned shacks, their lives closely constrained by the power of the mining companies, the often brutal company guards, and compliant local officials.

Jones's white hair, grandmotherly appearance, and deep loyalty to those she called "her boys" earned her the nickname "Mother." Others called her the "miners' angel." One county attorney, however, labeled her "the most dangerous woman in the country" in recognition of her ability to inspire men and women to oppose the mining companies. Her admirers recounted stories of her bravery in the face of danger. One insisted that "she wasn't afraid of the devil."

Mother Jones's talents lay in public speaking and in organizing demonstrations to capture public attention and sympathy. In one strike in 1900, she organized miners' wives to protest against strikebreakers by pounding on pots and pans and frightening the mules that pulled the mine carts. In 1903, she took up the cause of the children who worked in textile mills. By organizing a march of mill children to the home of President Theodore Roosevelt, she captured headlines with her living, walking display of the children's deformities and injuries caused by mill work.

Mother Jones made an unusual choice in her decision to spend the last half of her life as a labor organizer and agitator. But she apparently held traditional expectations about the role of women in society, arguing that their place was in the home. She seems to have seen her own work as an extension of her role as mother. Deprived of her own family, she sought to nurture and protect a much larger family of workers.

along with this plan, the trade unions formed the **American Federation of Labor (AFL).** The combined membership of the thirteen founding unions amounted to only 140,000.

Samuel Gompers became the first president of the new organization. Born in London in 1850, he learned the cigarmaker's trade before coming to the United States in 1863. He became president of the Cigarmakers' Union in 1877. Gompers contin-

---

American Federation of Labor (AFL)   National organization of trade unions founded in 1886; it used strikes and boycotts to improve the lot of workers.

Samuel Gompers   First president of the American Federation of Labor; he eventually argued to divorce labor organizing from political theory and stressed practical demands involving wages and hours.

ued as president of the AFL from 1886 until his death in 1924. Gompers opposed labor involvement with radicalism or politics. Instead, he focused on higher wages, shorter hours, and improved working conditions.

Most AFL leaders defined their task as the limited one of winning immediate struggles over wages and hours rather than the radical one of changing capitalism. Unlike the Knights of Labor, they did not try to transform the lives of all workers as a class. Instead, trade union leaders argued that unions should focus solely on their own members.

After the 1880s, the AFL suffered little competition from the Knights of Labor. By 1890, the Knights could claim only 100,000 members. This collapse stemmed only in part from the opposition of the trade unions. The failure of several strikes in the late 1880s cost the Knights many supporters.

Labor on the Defensive: Homestead and Pullman

In the late 1880s and 1890s, even highly skilled workers often found that craft unions could not withstand the power of the new industrial companies. A major demonstration of this reality came in 1892 in Pennsylvania, at Carnegie's **Homestead steel plant,** a stronghold of the Amalgamated Association of Iron, Steel, and Tin Workers. One of Carnegie's partners, Henry Clay Frick, managed the Homestead plant. When the union refused major wage cuts, Frick locked union members out of the plant and prepared to hire replacements.

Frick's first step was to bring in three hundred agents of the Pinkerton detective agency. They came by riverboat, but ten thousand strikers and community supporters resisted when they tried to land. Shots rang out. In the ensuing gun battle, seven Pinkertons and nine strikers were killed. The Pinkertons surrendered, leaving the strikers in control of the town and the plant. Soon after, the governor of Pennsylvania sent in the state militia to take control from the strikers. The militia did its job. The Amalgamated Association never recovered. This crushing defeat of the nation's largest

craft union indicated that no union could stand up to the new industrial companies.

A similar fate befell the most ambitious organizing drive of the 1890s. In 1893, under the leadership of **Eugene V. Debs,** railway workers launched the American Railway Union (ARU). Within a year, the ARU claimed 150,000 members and was the largest single union in the nation. The ARU did not affiliate with the AFL.

The twenty-four railway companies that entered Chicago had formed the General Managers Association (GMA) to combat unions. The GMA decided to challenge Debs's union when the ARU supported a strike of Pullman car workers in 1894. When the ARU disconnected **Pullman cars** from every train, the GMA insisted that only railway managers had the authority to determine which cars would make up a train. The managers promised to fire any worker who observed the boycott of Pullman cars.

Within a short time, all 150,000 ARU members were on strike. Rail traffic in Chicago came to a halt, affecting railways across the country. The GMA found an ally in U.S. Attorney General Richard Olney, a former railroad lawyer. Olney convinced President **Grover Cleveland** to use thousands of federal troops to protect trains operated by strikebreakers. Mobs lashed out at railroad property, especially in Chicago, burning trains and buildings. ARU leaders condemned the violence, but a dozen people died before it ended. Union leaders, including Debs, were jailed, and the union was destroyed.

Homestead steel plant Carnegie steel plant in Pennsylvania where state troops in 1892 put down a strike after a violent clash between striking workers and Pinkerton detectives.

Eugene V. Debs American Railway Union leader who was jailed after the Pullman strike; he converted to socialism and later ran for president.

Pullman car A railroad car with private compartments or seats that can be made up into berths for sleeping.

Grover Cleveland New York politician and advocate of clean government who was president of the United States from 1885 through 1889 and again from 1893 through 1897.

♦ This drawing of the administration building for Chicago's Columbian Exposition in 1893 emphasizes the planners' dramatic use of classical architecture and modern electric lighting. Because its buildings were all white, the exposition was called the "White City." *Culver Pictures.*

The depression that began in 1893 further weakened the unions. Many union members were unemployed. Nevertheless, the AFL hung on. By 1897, the organization claimed a membership of nearly 270,000. By then, working people had repeatedly demonstrated their discontent with the constraints they faced in the new economic order.

The Nation Transformed

By 1900, Americans could be excused if they seemed anxious about the economic changes of the previous thirty years. While some celebrated the outcomes of the economic transformation, others argued whether competition or cooperation was the best choice for achieving and maintaining progress.

Survival of the Fittest?

The concentration of power and wealth during the late nineteenth century generated comment and concern at the time. The most prominent statement on the subject was known as **Social Darwinism.** Charles Darwin's work on evolution had concluded that only the toughest, strongest, or cleverest creatures survived in competition against other creatures.

Herbert Spencer in England and William Graham Sumner, a professor of political economy at Yale, adapted Darwin's reasoning to the human situation, producing Social Darwinism. Social Darwinists contended that competition among people produced "progress" through "survival of the fittest." Further, they argued, efforts to ease the harsh impact of competition only protected the unfit. Conversely, powerful entrepreneurs constituted "the fittest" and benefited all humankind by their accomplishments.

Andrew Carnegie enthusiastically embraced Spencer's arguments. "Civilization took its start from that day that the capable, industrious workman said to his incompetent and lazy fellow, 'If thou dost not sow, thou shalt not reap,'" Carnegie wrote.

Although many Americans subscribed to the Social Darwinism propounded by Spencer, Sumner, and Carnegie, many others did not. One humorist poked fun at the three thousand libraries that Carnegie donated to the public by suggesting that they would serve the community better if they contained a kitchen and beds. Henry George,

> **Social Darwinism** The application of Darwinism to the study of human society; a theory that people who succeed in competition do so because of genetic and biological superiority.

a San Francisco journalist, concluded in *Progress and Poverty* (1879) that "material progress does not merely fail to relieve poverty—it actually produces it." The sociologist Lester Frank Ward refuted Social Darwinism by suggesting that biological competition produced bare survival, not civilization. Civilization, he concluded, represented "a triumph of mind" over "ceaseless and aimless competition."

S U M M A R Y

E xpectations
C onstraints
C hoices
O utcomes

After 1865, large-scale manufacturing developed quickly in the United States on a foundation of abundant natural resources, a pool of skilled workers, expanding harvests, and favorable government policies. The *outcome* was the transformation of the U.S. economy.

Entrepreneurs made *choices* that improved and extended railway lines, creating a national transportation network. Manufacturers and merchants developed new *expectations* based on a national market for raw materials and finished goods. Railroads were the first businesses to grapple with many problems related to size, and they made *choices* that other businesses imitated. Investment bankers combined separate rail companies into larger and more profitable systems.

Andrew Carnegie and John D. Rockefeller were the best known of many entrepreneurs whose *choices* produced manufacturing operations of unprecedented size and complexity. By 1900, oligopoly and vertical integration characterized many industries. Technology and advertising emerged as important competitive devices.

Workers *chose* to migrate to expanding industrial centers from rural areas in the United States and other countries. The new work force included not only adult males but also women and children. Industrial workers had little control over their work and often faced unpleasant or dangerous working conditions.

Some workers *chose* to form labor organizations to fight the *constraints* of low wages, long hours, and poor conditions. Espousing cooperatives and reform, the Knights of Labor *chose* to open their membership to the unskilled, to African Americans, and to women. The Knights died out after 1890. The American Federation of Labor was formed by craft unions. The AFL *chose* to reject radicalism and to work instead within capitalism to improve wages, hours, and conditions for its members. Major strikes between 1877 and 1894 revealed both the depth of workers' discontent and the strength of their organizations. By the mid-1890s, however, labor organizations were on the defensive.

Social Darwinists acclaimed unrestricted competition for producing progress and survival of the fittest. Critics countered that civilization represented a triumph of rationality and cooperation over competition.

SUGGESTED READINGS

Brody, David. *Steelworkers in America: The Nonunion Era* (1960).

    A classic study of the lives of steelworkers and the nature of their work.

Dubofsky, Melvyn. *Industrialism and the American Worker, 1865–1920*, 3rd ed. (1996).

    A brief introduction to the topic, organized chronologically.

Jones, Mary Harris "Mother." *The Autobiography of Mother Jones*, ed. Mary Field Parton (1925; reprint, 1980).

    A self-portrait of the feisty union organizer; not always precise regarding facts and dates, but fascinating for its account of one woman's activism.

Lamoreaux, Naomi. *The Great Merger Movement in American Business, 1895–1904* (1985).

An impressive study of the merger movement using detailed case histories of particular industries.

Montgomery, David. *The Fall of the House of Labor: The Workplace, the State, and American Labor Activism, 1865–1925* (1987).

Looks at the workplace and develops workers' responses to their situation from that perspective.

Porter, Glenn. *The Rise of Big Business, 1860–1910*, 2nd ed. (1992).

A brief introduction to the topic, including the role of the railroads, vertical and horizontal integration, and the merger movement.

THE WEST, 1865–1902 This map identifies various parts of the West. As you can see, the West had very few cities, and those tended to be located on the edges of the region.

CANADA

Seattle 42,837
Portland 46,385
WASH.
OR.
PACIFIC NORTHWEST
MONTANA
IDAHO
WYOMING
N.D.
S.D.
Duluth
GREAT NORTHERN R.R.
NORTHERN PACIFIC R.R.
Coastal Range
ROCKY
Great Salt Lake
Sierra
Nevada
Oakland 48,682
San Francisco 298,997
CAL.
Coastal Range
Hetch Hetchy Valley
Salt Lake City 44,843
NEV.
UTAH TERR.
Wasatch Range
CENTRAL PACIFIC R.R.
DENVER AND Rio Grande R.R.
UNION PACIFIC R.R.
Columbia
MOUNTAINS
GREAT BASIN
Owens
Los Angeles 50,395
ARIZONA TERR.
SOUTHWEST
SANTA FE R.R.
NEW MEXICO TERRITORY
CO.
Denver 106,713
Platte
NEB.
KANSAS
Lincoln 55,154
Omaha 140,452
Missouri
Chicago
St. Louis
Mississippi
OKLAHOMA TERR.
UNORGANIZED TERR.
Red
TEXAS
SOUTHERN PACIFIC R.R.
New Orleans
Nueces
Rio Grande
GREAT PLAINS
ATLANTIC OCEAN
PACIFIC OCEAN
MEXICO
Gulf of Mexico

■ Major western city
46,682 Population, 1890
┿ Western railroad

0   200   400 Km.
0   200   400 Mi.

● Civil War ends
● Cattle drives begin
● Transcontinental railroad
● Battle of the Little Bighorn
● Chinese Exclusion Act
● Dawes Severalty Act
● Reclamation Act

1865 1866 1869   1876   1882   1887   1902

1850   1900   1950   2000

Conflict and Change in the West, 1865–1902

War for the West

- What did federal policymakers hope to accomplish in their choices regarding American Indians after the Civil War?

- How did western Indians choose to respond?

- What expectations probably lay behind their responses? How were the expectations of western Indians different from those of federal policymakers?

Mormons, Cowboys, and Sodbusters: The Transformation of the West, Part I

- How did Mormons, the range cattle industry, and farmers respond to the constraints they faced in the West?

- What were the outcomes of their choices for western development?

Railroads, Mining, Agribusiness, Logging, and Finance: The Transformation of the West, Part II

- What constraints confronted western entrepreneurs engaged in mining, logging, and agriculture?

- How did choices regarding railroads, mining, agribusiness, finance capitalism, and water promote the development of the West?

Ethnicity and Race in the West

- Compare the constraints faced by Indians, Latinos, and Chinese immigrants between 1850 and 1900 and analyze the choices that each group made.

The West in American Thought

- How does the myth of the West compare with the reality?

INTRODUCTION

E xpectations
C onstraints
C hoices
O utcomes

Americans have shown a long-lasting interest in the West of the late nineteenth century. Popular fiction and drama have glorified the West as a land where pioneers overcame great odds. The reality of western life, however, was somewhat different.

At the close of the Civil War, many Americans looked to the West with high *expectations*. Previously, the issue of slavery had *constrained* federal action to develop the West. The secession of the southern states removed that *constraint*, and the Republicans who took charge in Washington in 1861 moved quickly to use federal power to open the West to economic development and white settlement.

As Americans faced west, they held some contradictory *expectations*. On the one hand, prior experience suggested the steady westward extension of family farms. On the other hand, travelers to the West had described it as an area of vast deserts, forbidding mountains, and well-armed, mounted Indian warriors. Potential *constraints* such as these suggested that parts of the West might never be developed like the eastern half of the nation.

In most of the West, rainfall was markedly lower than in the East. This scarcity of water *constrained* development and presented a new set of *choices*. What sort of development was appropriate in a region with little rain? How could western water be harnessed to support development? Who would control the water, and who would benefit from it?

Similarly, the ethnic and racial composition of the West differed significantly from that of the East and South. In 1865, the population of the northeastern and north-central United States was almost entirely of European descent. The South was a biracial society: white and black. But the West was home both to eastern Indians who had been pushed beyond the Mississippi River and to tribal groups who claimed it as their ancestral homeland. It was also home to significant numbers of people who spoke Spanish, who were often of mixed white and Indian ancestry, and whose families had lived in the region long before the arrival of the first Yankees. Finally, the West Coast had attracted

immigrants from Asia, especially China, who had *chosen* to cross the Pacific in the *expectation* of making their fortunes in America. In the late nineteenth century, these concentrations of ethnic groups marked the West as a distinctive place.

As individual Americans made *choices* that shaped the development of the West, federal officials also faced important *choices*. The basic *choice* to use the public domain to speed economic development had already been made by 1862. But a related *choice* remained: what to do about the Indians who occupied much of the land. Given the *choices* and *constraints* facing Americans in the West, the *outcome* of efforts to develop the land was sometimes quite different from previous experience and from the *expectations* of those involved. Overall, though, the *outcome* was that the western half of the United States underwent immense change during this period.

CHRONOLOGY

Conflict and Change in the West

1700s Horse culture spreads throughout the Great Plains

1847 First Mormon settlements near Great Salt Lake

1848 Treaty of Guadalupe Hidalgo

1849 California gold rush begins

1851 New federal Indian policy

1862 Homestead Act

1865 Civil War ends

1866–1880 Cattle drives north from Texas

1867–1868 Treaties establish major western reservations

1868–1869 Army's winter campaign against southern Plains Indians

1869 First transcontinental railroad completed

Early 1870s Cattle raising begins on northern Plains

1870s Destruction of buffalo herds
Silver mining boom in Nevada

1870s–1880s Extension of farming to the Great Plains

1871–1885 Anti-Chinese riots across the West

1874 Patent issued for barbed wire

1874–1875 Indian resistance ends on southern Plains

1876 Spring and summer campaign on northern Plains
Indian victory in Battle of the Little Bighorn

1877 Army subdues last major Indian resistance on northern Plains
Surrender and death of Crazy Horse
Chief Joseph and the Nez Perces flee
Workingmen's party of California attacks Chinese

1881 Surrender of Sitting Bull

1882 Chinese Exclusion Act

1884 Federal court prohibits hydraulic mining

1886 Surrender of Geronimo

1886–1887 Severe winter damages northern cattle business

1887 Dawes Severalty Act

Late 1880s Reduced rainfall

1890 Conflict at Wounded Knee Creek

1892 Sierra Club formed

1893 Frederick Jackson Turner presents his frontier thesis

1899 National Irrigation Association formed

1902 Reclamation Act

1907 Japanese immigration ends

1920s Western movies help make cowboy a mythical figure

War for the West

When Congress chose to use the public domain—western land—to encourage economic development, most white Americans considered the West to be largely vacant. In fact, American Indians lived throughout the West. The most tragic outcome of the development of the West was certainly the experience of the Indians.

The Plains Indians

By the time white Americans began to move west, the acquisition of horses and guns had already transformed the lives of many American Indians. This transformation occurred most dramatically among the tribes living on the **Great Plains,** the vast, relatively flat, treeless region that stretches across the center of the nation. The introduction of the horse to the Great Plains took place slowly, spreading in the late seventeenth century from the Spanish settlements in New Mexico. By the mid-eighteenth century, French and English traders had begun to provide guns to the Indians in return for furs. Thus guns entered the Plains from the east and northeast, and horses entered from the southwest. Together they transformed the culture of many of the Plains tribes.

The Plains Indians were divided into sedentary farmers and nomadic buffalo hunters. The Pawnees, Arikaras, Wichitas, Hidatsas, Mandans, Omahas, Otos, Osages, and similar groups lived a settled life in large, permanent villages located in river valleys. These Indians grew corn, squash, pumpkins, beans, sunflowers, and tobacco. They gathered wild fruits and vegetables and hunted and fished near their villages. Before the arrival of horses, entire villages went on extended hunting trips for buffalo twice a year, once in the early summer after the crops were planted, then again in the fall after the harvest. Horses changed the culture of these Indians only slightly.

By contrast, the horse revolutionized the way of life of some groups who became nomadic hunters. Indians on horseback could kill twice as many buffalo as Indians on foot. Thus the horse substantially increased the number of people the Plains could support. The buffalo provided food (meat), cloth-

♦ In the 1830s, George Catlin painted this buffalo hunt in what is now Montana. The acquisition of horses greatly increased the Indians' ability to kill buffalo. The Cheyennes, an extreme example, abandoned farming and staked their livelihood entirely on hunting. *"Buffalo Chase, Mouth of the Yellowstone" by George Catlin. National Museum of American Art, Washington, DC/Art Resource, NY.*

ing and shelter (made from hides), implements (made from bones and horns), and even fuel (dried dung). Some groups completely abandoned farming and followed the buffalo herds year round. By the early nineteenth century, the horse culture included the Blackfeet, Crows, **Lakotas, Cheyennes,** Arapahos, Kiowas, and Comanches. The Lakotas, the largest of these groups, were often called the Sioux, meaning "enemy," by other Indians.

Whether nomadic buffalo hunters or sedentary farmers, the Plains Indians viewed the land very differently than white settlers did. Europeans be-

Great Plains   High grassland of western North America, stretching from the Mississippi valley to the Rocky Mountains; it is generally level, treeless, and semiarid.

Lakotas   Indian people who lived on the northern Great Plains; hostile tribes called them *Sioux,* which means "enemy."

Cheyennes   Indian people who became nomadic buffalo hunters after migrating to the Great Plains in the eighteenth century.

lieved in individual ownership of land. According to Indian tradition, land was to be used but not owned. Horses, weapons, **tipis,** and clothing were all individually owned, but land was not. Among farming peoples, a tribal leader divided farmland among the female heads of each family on the basis of family size.

For the most part, the individual ownership of property was not a pressing goal for Indians. A person achieved high social standing not by accumulating possessions but by sharing. Francis La Flesche, the son of an Omaha leader, received the following advice from his mother: "When you see a boy barefooted and lame, take off your moccasins and give them to him. When you see a boy hungry, bring him to your home and give him food."

The Plains Indians did on occasion seek to gain additional hunting territory, particularly when tribes came under pressure from European westward expansion. But many conflicts stemmed from the desire to seek revenge or to display bravery, not for individual gain.

The Plains Wars

During the 1830s and after, federal Indian policy had focused on removing eastern Indians to land west of the Mississippi River. Federal Indian policy over the next fifty years reduced Indian landholdings west of the Mississippi as farmers, adventurers, and gold seekers made their way west.

In 1851, Congress approved a new Indian policy intended to provide each tribe with a definite territory on which it was to live. Federal officials initially planned large reservations taking up much of the Great Plains. After the Civil War, however, to clear the way for the construction of a transcontinental railroad across the central Plains, they hoped to restrict the Indians to three great reservations in the West—one in the northern Plains, one in the southern Plains, and one in the Southwest. The remainder of the West was to be opened up for development by white settlers. Indians on the reservations were to receive food and shelter from the government and were to be taught how to farm and raise cattle.

At the same time, federal officials encouraged growing numbers of white buffalo hunters to kill the buffalo for meat, hides, and sport. The buffalo's demise came quickly once tanneries in the East began to buy hides. In the mid-1870s, more than 10 million buffalo were killed and stripped of their hides, which sold for a dollar or more each. By 1883, a few hundred animals were left. The Plains Indians' way of life was doomed.

By mid-1868, federal officials thought their new reservation policy had made a promising start. Under treaties signed in 1867, the major southern tribes accepted reservations in Indian Territory (see Map 17.1) after the army presented a show of force. In 1868, the Lakotas agreed to a Great Sioux Reservation in what is now the western half of South Dakota. In the same year, the Crows and Navajos agreed to reservations in Montana and the Southwest, respectively.

Some southern Plains tribes, however, refused to live on reservations. Moreover, they occasionally attacked stagecoach stations, ranches, travelers crossing the Plains, and even military units. After one such attack, General William Tecumseh Sherman, the Civil War general who had become commander of the army on the Plains, declared that all Indians not on reservations "are hostile and will remain so till killed off."

In 1868–1869, Sherman launched a winter campaign on the southern Plains to deal with such "hostile" Indians. The leader of this expedition, General Philip Sheridan, another Union army veteran, directed his men to "destroy their villages and ponies, to kill and hang all warriors, and bring back all women and children." This brutal campaign convinced most southern Plains tribes that further resistance was pointless. Another campaign over the winter of 1874–1875 made all the remaining southern Plains tribes surrender.

Hunting grounds outside the Great Sioux Reservation in the Powder River region of Montana and Wyoming caused conflict on the northern Plains. As the Northern Pacific Railroad prepared to lay track in southern Montana, the government took steps to force all Indians out of the region and onto the reservation.

> **tipi** Tent made from buffalo hide and used as a portable dwelling by Indians on the Great Plains.

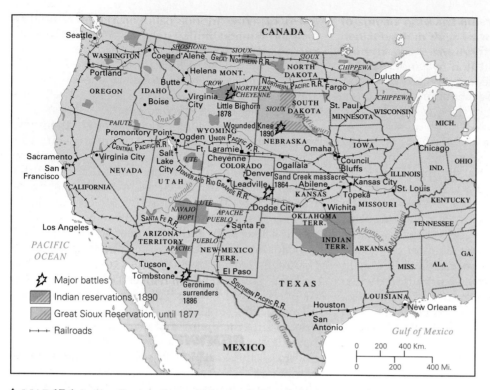

♦ **MAP 17.1 Indian Reservations** This map indicates the location of most western Indian reservations in 1890, as well as the Great Sioux Reservation before it was broken up and severely reduced in size. Note how the development of a few large reservations on the northern Plains and others on the southern Plains opened the central Plains for railroad construction and agricultural development.

The **Great Sioux War** began in 1876 when Sheridan directed troops to converge on Indians in the Powder River area from three different directions. One part of the operation went dreadfully wrong when Lieutenant Colonel George A. Custer, without waiting for the other units, sent his 7th Cavalry against an Indian camp. The encampment on the **Little Bighorn River** proved to be one of the largest ever on the northern Plains, combining several bands of Lakotas and Cheyennes led by **Crazy Horse** and **Sitting Bull.** Custer and nearly three hundred of his men lost their lives in the battle. The Indians then scattered, knowing that their victory would bring massive retaliation.

In the winter of 1876–1877, Sheridan launched another campaign of **attrition.** Troops defeated some Indian bands. Hunger and cold drove most others to surrender. Crazy Horse surrendered only

Great Sioux War War between the tribes that took part in the Battle of the Little Bighorn and the U.S. Army; it ended in 1881 with the surrender of Sitting Bull.

Little Bighorn River River in Montana where in 1876 Lieutenant Colonel George Custer discovered a large Indian encampment and ordered an attack in which he and his men were killed.

Crazy Horse Lakota leader who resisted white encroachment in the Black Hills and fought at the Little Bighorn River in 1876; he was killed by U.S. soldiers in 1877.

Sitting Bull Lakota leader who fought at the Little Bighorn River in 1876 and fled with his people to Canada before surrendering in 1881.

attrition A gradual decrease in number or strength caused by constant stress.

when the government promised that he could live in the Powder River region. Several months later, he was killed when he resisted being put into jail. Sitting Bull and his band escaped to Canada and remained there until 1881, when they finally surrendered. The Great Sioux War had ended. The government then cut up the Great Sioux Reservation to allow for white settlement, taking away the Powder River region and the Black Hills.

The Last Indian Wars

After the Great Sioux War, no Indian group had the capacity for sustained resistance. The last sizable group to refuse to live on a reservation was Geronimo's band of Chiricahua Apaches, who finally gave up in 1886. Small groups occasionally left their reservations but were tracked down by federal troops. One notable instance was the attempted flight to Canada in 1877 of the Nez Perces, led by **Chief Joseph.** They eluded the army for three months as they traveled through Montana toward Canada. More than two hundred died along the way. Joseph surrendered on the specific condition that the Nez Perces be permitted to return to their previous home. Nevertheless, federal officials sent the Nez Perces to Indian Territory.

The last major armed confrontation between the army and the Indians came in 1890, on the Pine Ridge Reservation in South Dakota. There some Lakotas had taken up a new religion, the **Ghost Dance,** that promised to return the land to the Indians, restore the buffalo, and sweep away the whites. Fearing an uprising, federal authorities ordered the Lakotas to stop their dance ritual and called for the arrest of their leader, Sitting Bull (see Individual Choices: Sitting Bull). Sitting Bull was killed when some Ghost Dancers tried to prevent his arrest. A small band of Lakotas then tried to flee, but they were captured and taken to a site near **Wounded Knee Creek.** When an Indian refused to surrender his gun, a brief battle took place that left some 250 Indians and 25 soldiers dead.

The events at Wounded Knee marked the end of armed conflict on the Plains. But the end of the horse culture had been written long before. Once the federal government chose to encourage rapid economic development in the West rather than reserving it for Indians, the outcome was inevitable.

Mormons, Cowboys, and Sodbusters: The Transformation of the West, Part I

Long before the last battles between the army and the Indians, the economic development of the West was well under way. Environmental and other constraints, as well as the cultural expectations of men and women seeking to live in that region, determined the nature of western development. The Mormons' choices in the Great Basin differed significantly from those made by the ranchers and farmers of the Great Plains.

Zion in the Great Basin

By 1865, development of the Great Basin region between the Rocky Mountains and the Sierra Nevada was already well advanced as a result of the **Mormons'** efforts. Led by Brigham Young, the Mormons in 1847 had chosen to settle near the Great Salt Lake. They expected to establish a settlement outside the United States so remote that no one would interfere with them. The Great Basin region, however, was incorporated into the United States after the Mexican War.

Chief Joseph   Nez Perces chief who led his people in an attempt to escape to Canada in 1877; after a grueling journey, they were forced to surrender and were exiled to Indian Territory.

Ghost Dance   Indian religion centered on a ritual dance; it promised the coming of an Indian messiah who would banish the whites and restore the land to the Indians.

Wounded Knee Creek   Site of a conflict in 1890 between Lakota Indians and U.S. troops attempting to suppress the Ghost Dance religion; it was the last major encounter between Indians and the army.

Mormons   Members of the Church of Jesus Christ of Latter Day Saints, founded in New York in 1830.

Choosing to Defend His Homeland

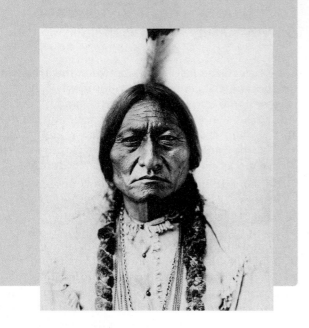

Sitting Bull

After Sitting Bull returned to the United States from Canada in 1881, he became a favorite subject for many photographers. This photo dates to the mid-1880s, when he was about 50 years old. Denver Public Library.

The U.S. Army had high expectations for the great conference of tribes from throughout the northern plains at Fort Laramie in 1868. Federal officials had two major purposes: to end attacks along the Bozeman Trail, which ran through eastern Wyoming, and to secure agreements from the northern Plains Indians to live on a reservation well to the north of the major transportation routes that ran through the new state of Nebraska. At the conference, the army agreed to close the Bozeman Trail and to abandon the forts along it if the Lakotas and their allies agreed to live on the Great Sioux Reservation—the entire western half of what is now South Dakota.

Many of the Lakota leaders were willing to consider the army's proposal. Their battles against the forts along the Bozeman Trail had included both great victories and serious losses. Red Cloud, leader of many of those struggles, was the most prominent of those who agreed to live on the reservation. Most of those who signed the treaty, however, probably had little idea of what they approved.

Sitting Bull chose not to accept any of the treaty's provisions. Instead, he continued to follow the buffalo herd and to defend the territories that his people, the Hunkpapa Lakotas, had wrested from their enemies, the Crows. Anyone—Indian or white—who invaded those regions was in peril. At the same time, he necessarily chose to fight against efforts by the U.S. Army to force the Hunkpapas to live on a reservation and to abandon their traditional way of life. Sitting Bull soon emerged as one of the most significant leaders of opposition to the treaty and to reservation life.

In 1868, Sitting Bull was in his mid-30s and had earned a reputation for fearlessness in battles with the enemies of the Hunkpapas, especially the Crows. He had counted his first coup at the age of 14, when he killed a Crow in a raid and earned the name Tatanka-Iotanka, Sitting Bull, a tribute to his fighting endurance. By 1857, when Sitting Bull was probably 26 years old, the Hunkpapas named him one of the tribal war chiefs in recognition of his many victories in battles with the Crows and other Indian enemies of the Lakotas. He also came to be considered a holy man, whose visions were messages from Wakantanka, the Great Mystery. To his people, Sitting Bull embodied the Lakota virtues of bravery, fortitude, generosity, and wisdom.

Sitting Bull was joined in his rejection of the Fort Laramie Treaty by perhaps a third of all the Lakotas, especially members of the Hunkpapas. The Oglala Lakotas divided, many following Red Cloud to the reservation and some following Crazy Horse to the west of the reservation to live on the "unceded lands" of northwestern Wyoming. In 1869, a group of Sitting Bull's supporters arranged a gathering of Lakotas and Cheyennes at which Sitting Bull was named to an unprecedented position: war chief of the entire Lakota Nation. Given the fluidity of leadership among the Lakotas, the reservation Lakotas did not accept this action, nor did all those who refused to observe the treaty. But it was a signal honor.

Over the next decade, Sitting Bull exercised greater leadership among the various Lakota tribes than any previous leader had. On June 6, 1876, many of the nonreservation Lakotas and Cheyennes had gathered into a very large village, where the Hunkpapas held a sun dance, the most important religious observance among the Plains Indians. Sitting Bull sacrificed a hundred small bits of flesh from his arms to Wakantanka and then danced and sought a vision. His vision was of soldiers falling upside down into the Lakota and Cheyenne village. It was fulfilled when, on June 25, Lieutenant Colonel George A. Custer divided his troops and personally led just over two hundred of them in an attack on a village of Lakotas and Cheyennes that included somewhere between eight hundred and eighteen hundred warriors.

The defeat of Custer was certainly the greatest victory by the Plains Indians in all their battles with the U.S. Army, but it provoked a strong counterattack. As the army attacked and attacked again, Sitting Bull and his followers lost their tipis and their provisions. Finally, they fled to Canada and remained there for several years. Soon, however, the last buffalo disappeared from the Plains, ending the Hunkpapas' traditional way of life more effectively than the army had been able to accomplish. Eventually, they were persuaded to return and to live on a reservation. After his return, Sitting Bull spent a few years touring with William F. ("Buffalo Bill") Cody's Wild West Show, then retired to live in a log cabin on the reservation. There he died at the hands of Indian policemen, some from his own Hunkpapa tribe, in 1890.

Nevertheless, isolated by mountains and deserts, the Mormons created their Zion. The Mormon community was a **theocracy** in which church officials governed every aspect of life. A church-sponsored political party dominated elections for local and territorial officials. Although streams flowed from the nearby Wasatch mountain range, meager rainfall and poor soil constrained farming. Young decreed communal ownership of both land and streams, and church officials made choices about the use of water. Young devised a system for creating farms and irrigation projects based on the right to divert water for irrigation. This system influenced laws on water rights in all the western states. The communal ownership of land ended after 1869.

The Mormon settlement thrived and established satellite communities. By the Civil War, more than twenty thousand Mormons lived in the Utah Territory. After the war, the Mormons came under great pressure to renounce their practice of **polygamy.** Efforts to make Utah a state were blocked repeatedly because of that issue. The Republican party was also concerned about the potential political power of the Mormon church. In 1890, to clear the way for statehood, the Mormon leadership dissolved the church-sponsored political party and disavowed polygamy. Utah became a state in 1896.

Cattle Kingdom on the Plains

As the Mormons were building their centralized and cooperative society in the Great Basin, the more individualistic enterprise of raising cattle was emerging on the western Great Plains. Cattle had first been brought into south Texas in the eighteenth century. Climate encouraged the growth of the herds, and Mexican ranchers developed an open-range system of cattle raising. Vaqueros (cowboys) herded the half-wild longhorns grazing on the unfenced plains. Practices developed in south Texas were subsequently transferred to the range-cattle industry, including **branding** and **roundups.**

At the end of the Civil War, five million cattle ranged across Texas, many unbranded and thus free for the taking. Others could be purchased for a few dollars each. At the slaughterhouses of Chicago, cattle brought ten times or more their price in Texas. To get cattle from south Texas to the Midwest, Texans used the cattle drive. They herded cattle north through Texas and Indian Territory to the railroads then being built westward. A half dozen cowboys, a cook, and a trail boss could drive one thousand to two thousand cattle. Enough animals survived the drive to yield a good profit. Between 1866 and 1880, some four million cattle walked north from Texas.

The first cattle drives went to Sedalia, Missouri. As railroad construction pushed west, it created a series of Kansas cattle towns such as Abilene and Dodge City. Later drives followed more westerly routes. In cattle towns, the trail boss sold his herd and paid off his cowboys, who often spent their earnings at saloons, brothels, and gambling houses. In such towns, eastern journalists and authors discovered and embroidered the exploits of town marshals such as **James B. ("Wild Bill") Hickok** and **Wyatt Earp.** The popular press credited such "town-tamers" with heroic exploits. Usually, though, the most important changes came when a town's middle class, especially the women, organized churches and schools and determined to create a law-abiding community.

Although most Texas cattle were loaded on eastbound trains for slaughtering, some were driven north to vast tracts of land still in the public domain. Thus open-range cattle raising was extended into the northern Great Plains by the early 1870s. Investors could make 50 percent annual profits from cattle raising.

---

theocracy   A state governed by religious authority.

polygamy   The practice of having more than one wife at a time.

branding   Using a hot iron to burn a unique design on the hide of cattle and other animals; the design, or brand, is used to establish ownership.

roundup   A spring event in which cowboys gathered together the cattle, branded newborn calves, and castrated most male calves.

James B. ("Wild Bill") Hickok   Western gambler and gunman; in 1876, he was shot in the back and killed while playing poker in Deadwood, Dakota Territory.

Wyatt Earp   American frontier law officer and gunfighter involved in 1881 in a controversial shootout at the O.K. Corral in Tombstone, Arizona, in which several men were killed.

By the early 1880s, so many cattle ranches were in operation that beef prices began to fall. The severe winter of 1886–1887 broke the boom. Uncounted thousands of cattle froze or starved to death on the northern Plains. Many investors went bankrupt. Surviving ranchers fenced their ranges and made certain that they could feed their cattle during the winter.

As the cattle industry expanded, so did the romanticizing of the cowboy. Popular fiction created the image of the cowboy as a brave, clean-cut hero, white and often blond, who spent his time defeating villains and rescuing fair-haired white women from danger. In reality, most real cowboys were young and unschooled. Many were African Americans or of Mexican descent. Others were former Confederate soldiers. On a cattle drive, they worked as many as twenty hours a day, faced serious danger if a herd stampeded, slept on the ground, and lived on biscuits, beans, and meager wages. Some tried to form local branches of unions, notably the Knights of Labor.

Plowing the Plains

Farmers entering the Great Plains encountered unfamiliar environmental constraints. Unlike the Indians, whose way of life was in harmony with the Plains environment, the new residents chose to alter the environment. Some succeeded, but others failed and left.

After the Civil War, the land available for new farms stretched from northern North Dakota and Minnesota southward through Oklahoma. Mapmakers in the early nineteenth century had labeled this region the Great American Desert. It was not a desert, however, and some parts of it were very fertile. But west of the line of **aridity,** around the 98th or 100th **meridian,** sparse rainfall was a serious constraint on farming (see Map 17.2). Farmers who expected to follow their usual farming practices ran the risk not only of failing but also of severely damaging the fragile **ecosystem** there.

When the **Kansas-Nebraska Act** (1854) opened up this vast region for development, the first settlers stuck to eastern areas, where the terrain and climate were similar to those they knew. After the Civil War, farmers pressed steadily westward, spurred

by the promise of free land under the Homestead Act (1862) or lured by railroad advertising that promised fertile and productive land at little cost.

Those who took advantage of the opportunities for land were quite diverse. Thousands of African Americans left the South, seeking farms of their own. Immigrants from Scandinavia, Germany, **Bohemia,** and Russia flooded in. Most homesteaders, however, moved from areas a short distance to the east, where farmland had become too expensive.

Many single women claimed 160 acres of their own land. Sometimes the wife of a male homesteader did the same. By 1886, women held one-third of all homestead claims in the Dakota Territory. Many single women seem to have viewed homesteading as a speculative venture. They intended to gain title to the land and then sell it to acquire money for other purposes, such as starting a business or creating a nest egg for marriage.

The 160 acres that the Homestead Act provided were sufficient only for farms lying east of the line of aridity. West of that line, most of the land required irrigation or was suitable only for cattle raising, which required much more than 160 acres if a ranch was to be successful. Federal officials were often lax in enforcing the Homestead Act's requirements for establishing ownership. The law required a homesteader to build a house on the land. A husband and wife could each claim 160 acres and then build a house on the boundary between their claims, thereby doubling their land. Cattle ranchers sometimes had all their cowboys file claims and then transfer the land to the rancher

---

aridity   Dryness; the lack of sufficient rainfall to support trees or woody plants.

meridian   Any of the imaginary lines representing degrees of longitude that pass through the North and South Poles and encircle the earth.

ecosystem   A community of animals, plants, and bacteria, considered together with the environment in which they are found.

Kansas-Nebraska Act   Law passed by Congress in 1854 that created the Kansas and Nebraska territories.

Bohemia   A region of central Europe now part of the Czech Republic.

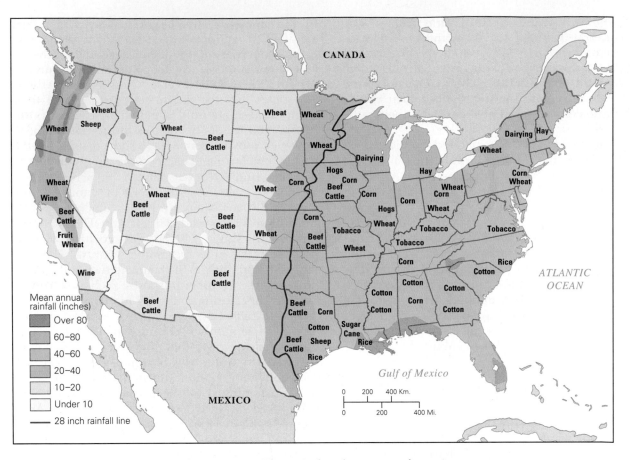

♦ **MAP 17.2 Rainfall and Agriculture, c. 1890** The agricultural prospects of any given area depended on the type of soil, the terrain, and the rainfall. Most of the western half of the nation received relatively little rainfall compared to the eastern half. Crops such as corn and cotton could not be raised in the West without irrigation.

after they received title to it. Thus individuals sometimes acquired a great deal of land by devious means.

People who wished to live on the Plains had to adapt to an environment where water and wood were scarce. The lack of wood led many families to carve homes out of the land itself by tunneling into the sides of low hills. Others cut the tough prairie **sod** into blocks, from which they fashioned one- or two-room houses. Many combined dugout and sod construction. "Soddies" seldom made satisfactory dwellings. The roof usually leaked. Snakes could drop from the ceiling or slither out of the walls. Sod houses were usually so dark inside that sewing, washing clothes, and many other house-

hold tasks were done outside whenever possible. Families nevertheless made these sod houses home by placing curtains and potted flowers at the windows.

Plains families looked to technology to meet many of their needs. Barbed wire, first patented in 1874, provided a cheap alternative to wooden fences. The barbs effectively kept ranchers' cattle off farmland. Ranchers eventually used it too.

---

sod A section of grass-covered surface soil held together by the matted roots of grass.

Much of the Plains had abundant **ground water,** but at depths greater than in the East. Windmills were used to pump water from great depths. Because the sod was so tough, special plows were developed to make the initial cut through it. These plows were so expensive that most farmers hired a specialist (a "sodbuster") to break their sod.

The most serious problem for pioneers on the Plains was lack of rainfall. During the late 1880s, rainfall fell below normal, and crop failures drove many homesteaders off the Plains. Half of the population of western Kansas left between 1888 and 1892. One covered wagon heading east bore the legend, "In God we trusted, in Kansas we busted." Only after farmers learned better techniques of **dry farming,** secured improved strains of wheat (some brought by **Russian-German** immigrants), and began to practice irrigation did agriculture become viable. Even so, farming practices often left exposed soil subject to severe wind erosion.

Railroads, Mining, Agribusiness, Logging, and Finance: The Transformation of the West, Part II

In a region of great distances, relatively few people, and widely scattered population centers, effective transportation was a necessity for economic development. Just as western cattle raisers required rail connections to send their cattle to market, so too did western miners and farmers need railroads to carry the products of their labor to markets. Given the scarcity of water in much of the West, many westerners had concluded by 1900 that water was as important as railroads in the development of the region.

Western Railroads

Railroad promoters understood that building a transcontinental line in the sparsely populated West would be very expensive and that it would not carry sufficient freight to justify the cost of construction. Thus they turned to the federal government for assistance. The Union Pacific and Central Pacific railroads were the first recipients of federal support for transcontinental railroads. The Union

Pacific began laying track west from Omaha, Nebraska Territory, and the Central Pacific began building east from Sacramento, California. Construction began slowly, partly because crucial supplies such as rails and locomotives had to be transported long distances. Both lines experienced labor shortages. The Union Pacific solved its labor shortages only after the Civil War, when former soldiers and construction workers flooded west. Many were Irish immigrants. The Central Pacific recruited Chinese immigrant laborers.

Construction proceeded slowly until the end of the Civil War in 1865. The Central Pacific laid only 18 miles of track during 1863, and the Union Pacific laid no track at all until mid-1864. It was not until May 10, 1869, that the tracks of the two companies finally met near **Promontory Point,** north of the Great Salt Lake. Other lines followed during the next twenty years, bringing most of the West into the national market system and speeding the development of western mining, lumbering, and agriculture.

Westerners greeted the arrival of the railroads with joyful celebrations, but some soon wondered whether they had traded isolation for dependence on a greedy monopoly. The Southern Pacific, successor to the Central Pacific, became known as the "Octopus" because its grasping tentacles seemed to reach everywhere. Not all western railroads acquired such bad reputations. James J. Hill of the Great Northern, for example, was called the "Empire Builder" for his efforts to build up the economy and prosperity of the region alongside his rails. Regardless of their reputation, railroads were crucial to the

> **ground water**   Water beneath the earth's surface, often between soil and rock, that supplies wells and springs.
>
> **dry farming**   Farming that makes maximum use of available moisture by using techniques such as planting drought-resistant crops and harrowing after a rainfall.
>
> **Russian-German**   Immigrants of German descent who came from Russia, often from farming colonies established in the eighteenth century.
>
> **Promontory Point**   Site in northern Utah where in 1869 the Central Pacific and Union Pacific railroads were linked, thus completing the first transcontinental railroad in the United States.

◆ Only a few of the photographs of the construction of the first transcontinental railroad show the Chinese laborers who were responsible for some of the most dangerous construction on the Central Pacific route through the Sierra Nevada. This photograph was taken, apparently by a photographer from the Union Pacific, when the two lines joined near Promontory Point, Utah Territory. *Denver Public Library.*

economic development of the West. The outcome was the rapid expansion of agriculture and mining.

Western Mining

Between 1848 and 1885, the discovery of gold and silver at many sites scattered throughout the West brought a rush of fortune seekers. **Boom towns** sprang up overnight to meet miners' needs, ranging from picks to groceries. The construction of rail lines to mining towns permitted rapid exploitation of the mineral resources by bringing in supplies and heavy equipment. Once the valuable ore gave out, however, such settlements were likely to become ghost towns.

Many of the first miners collected gold by **placer mining.** The only equipment they needed was a pan. Miners panning for gold simply washed gravel that they hoped contained gold. If present, the gold sank to the bottom of the pan as the gravel was washed away by the water. After the early gold seekers had taken the easily accessible ore, elaborate mining equipment became necessary. Gold-mining companies developed **hydraulic** systems that used great amounts of water under high pressure to demolish entire mountainsides. In the process, they wreaked havoc on the environment downstream. This practice ended only when a federal court outlawed it in 1884.

In most of the West, the exhaustion of surface deposits led to the construction of shafts and tunnels deep underground. Mine shafts in Butte, Montana, eventually reached depths of a mile. Such operations required machinery to move men and equipment and to keep the tunnels cool and dry. By the mid-1870s, the Comstock silver mines in Nevada boasted the most advanced mining equipment in the world. There temperatures soared to 120 degrees in shafts more than 2,200 feet deep. Mighty air pumps circulated air from the surface to the depths, and ice was used to reduce the temperature. Massive water pumps kept the shafts dry. Everywhere, powerful drills speeded the job of removing the ore, and enormous ore-crushing machines operated day and night on the surface.

The mining industry changed rapidly as solitary prospectors panning for gold gave way to large mining companies whose operations were financed by banks in San Francisco and the East.

---

boom town A town experiencing a sudden increase in prosperity and population.

placer mining Washing minerals from placers—deposits of sand or gravel that contain eroded particles of gold and other valuable minerals.

hydraulic Making use of water under pressure.

Mining companies became vertically integrated, operating not only mines but also ore-crushing mills and railroads. Western miners organized too, forming strong unions. Miners' unions helped secure wages five to ten times higher than those paid to miners in Britain or Germany.

The Birth of Western Agribusiness

Throughout the eastern half of the nation, the family farm was the typical agricultural unit. In California and other parts of the West, however, agriculture sometimes developed into an **agribusiness** involving huge areas, the intensive use of heavy equipment, and wage labor.

Wheat lent itself to large-scale farming because it was the first major crop to be entirely mechanized. By 1880, large wheat farms in the Red River valley of what is now North Dakota and in the San Joaquin Valley of central California measured 100 square miles. Such farming businesses involved major capital investments in land, equipment, live stock, and labor. One Dakota farm required 250 workers at harvest time. California wheat growers were using steam-powered tractors and **combines** in the late 1880s, well before such machinery was used elsewhere.

The huge wheat farms of Dakota proved to be temporary. Most of them were broken into smaller units by the 1890s. In California, however, agriculture continued to flourish on a scale largely unknown in other parts of the country. One California company, Miller and Lux, held more than a million acres. Although wheat raising had declined in significance by 1900, large-scale agriculture became established for a variety of crops. At first, the growers relied on Chinese immigrants for their field labor. When Congress prohibited most Chinese immigration in 1882, growers turned to Japanese and eventually Mexican immigrants.

Logging in the Pacific Northwest

The coastal Pacific Northwest is very different from the remainder of the West. Rainfall is so heavy that the region supports one of the few rain forests outside the tropics. Heavy winter rains and cool, damp summers nurture thick stands of tall Douglas firs and giant redwoods.

At first, in the 1850s and 1860s, the coastal redwoods of California were cut for use in San Francisco and nearby cities. Attention then shifted north to Oregon and Washington, leading to Seattle's development as a lumber town. Some companies quickly became vertically integrated, owning lumber mills in the Northwest, a fleet of schooners to haul logs, and lumberyards in the San Francisco Bay area. The railroads actively promoted the lumber industry by offering cheap rates for log shipments. Lumber production in Oregon and Washington boomed, leaving behind treeless hillsides subject to severe soil erosion.

Water Wars

From the first efforts at western economic development, water was a central concern. Prospectors needed water to separate worthless gravel from gold. Californians worked out a system of **water rights** that closely paralleled the Mormons' system. On the Great Plains, a cattle rancher staked out grazing land by establishing control over a stream. Throughout much of the West, would-be farmers learned that irrigation was vital to their success. Western cities saw lack of water as a major constraint on their ability to grow. Competition for scarce water sometimes led to conflict. Henry Miller, of Miller and Lux, once grumbled that he had spent $25 million in legal fees, mostly to protect his water rights.

Cities also battled for access to water. Beginning in 1901, San Francisco sought federal permission to put a dam on federal land near Yosemite National Park in the Sierra Nevada. Opposition came primarily from the **Sierra Club,** formed in 1892 to

---

agribusiness   Farming that is a large-scale business operation using heavy farm machinery and involving processing and distribution as well as the growing of crops.

combine   A power-operated harvesting machine that combines the cutting and threshing of grain.

water rights   The right to draw water from a particular source, such as a lake, an irrigation canal, or a river.

Sierra Club   Environmental organization dedicated to preserving and expanding the world's parks, wildlife, and wilderness areas.

preserve the Sierra Nevada wilderness. Congressional approval did not come until 1913. Los Angeles resolved its water problems by diverting the water of the Owens River to its use.

The magnitude of the efforts needed to provide enough water led many westerners to look increasingly for federal assistance. The National Irrigation Association, created in 1899, lobbied Congress successfully to secure passage of the **Reclamation Act** of 1902, which promised federal construction of irrigation facilities. To promote family farms rather than agribusiness interests, the law specified that only farms smaller than 160 acres could use this water. However, agribusiness often managed to avoid this limitation.

Ethnicity and Race in the West

In ethnic and racial composition, the West differed significantly from the rest of the nation. In 1900, the western half of the nation included 15 percent of all white Americans and 10 percent of all African Americans, but 81 percent of Americans of Chinese or Japanese ancestry, 82 percent of all American Indians, and 98 percent of immigrants born in Mexico. The West became a racially diverse society long before the rest of the country.

Immigrants to the Golden Mountain

Between 1854 and 1882, drawn initially by the California gold rush, some three hundred thousand Chinese immigrants entered the United States. Most came from southern China, which suffered from periodic famines. The Chinese accounted in 1860 for a third of all miners in California, which they called "the Golden Mountain," and more than half in 1870. They formed a major part of construction labor in the West, especially for railroad building. Chinese immigrants also worked as agricultural laborers and farmers, especially in California.

In San Francisco and in smaller western cities, they established **Chinatowns**—relatively autonomous and largely self-contained Chinese communities. In San Francisco's Chinatown, immigrants formed kinship organizations and district associa-

tions to assist and protect each other. A confederation of such associations, the Chinese Consolidated Benevolent Association, eventually exercised great power over the social and economic life in Chinese communities in the West. Such communities were largely male, for immigration officials prevented most Chinese women from entering the country. Gambling and prostitution flourished in these largely male communities, giving Chinatowns reputations as centers for vice.

From the beginning, Chinese immigrants encountered discrimination and violence. In 1854, the California Supreme Court prohibited Chinese from testifying in court against a white person. When the depression of the 1870s set in, white workers blamed the Chinese for causing unemployment. Anti-Chinese riots occurred in Los Angeles in 1871, in San Francisco in 1877 and after, and in many western towns in 1885. White miners in 1885 burned the Chinatown in Rock Springs, Wyoming, killing twenty-eight Chinese.

In these riots, the message was usually the same: "The Chinese Must Go." This slogan first gained popularity in San Francisco in 1877 as part of the appeal of the Workingmen's party of California, which blamed the Chinese for the economic woes of white members. In 1882, Congress responded to repeated pressure from West Coast labor unions by passing the **Chinese Exclusion Act,** prohibiting entry to all Chinese people except teachers, students, merchants, tourists, and officials.

In parts of the West, the Chinese were subjected to segregation similar to that imposed on blacks in the South. Chinese students were barred from the San Francisco public schools from 1871 to 1885, when the city opened a segregated Chinese school.

Reclamation Act   Law passed by Congress in 1902 that provided for publicly funded irrigation of western land and created the Reclamation Service to oversee the process.

Chinatown   A section of a city that is inhabited chiefly by Chinese people.

Chinese Exclusion Act   Law passed by Congress in 1882 that prohibited Chinese laborers from entering the United States; it was extended in 1892 and again in 1902.

Sacramento and a few other towns also established segregated schools. Local custom, enforced occasionally by mob violence, promoted residential segregation. Chinese lived outside Chinatown only as servants or in laundries. Occupational segregation was similarly enforced. Anti-Chinese violence in western small towns in the mid-1880s prompted many Chinese to retreat to the large cities.

In the larger western cities, Chinese merchants took the lead in establishing a strong economic base. Organizations based on kinship, region, or occupation sometimes opposed discrimination and segregation through the courts. When San Francisco passed a city law requiring laundry licenses, the organization of Chinese laundry owners filed suit. In 1886, the U.S. Supreme Court declared the law unconstitutional because local authorities had used it to discriminate on the basis of race. School segregation began to break down shortly before World War I.

When other immigrants began to arrive from Asia, they too concentrated in the West. Significant numbers of Japanese began coming to the United States after 1890. By 1907, nearly 150,000 had arrived. After 1907, immigration of Japanese laborers stopped because of an agreement between the United States and Japan. Whites in the West, especially organized labor, regarded Japanese immigrants in much the same way that they viewed Chinese immigrants.

Forced Assimilation

Federal policy toward American Indians aimed at their rapid assimilation into white society. The final outcome, however, was that federal policies tried to eradicate Indian culture but failed to integrate Indians into the mainstream economy and society.

After 1871, federal policy shifted from treating Indian tribes as sovereign but dependent nations with which the federal government negotiated to viewing them as wards of the federal government. This new policy meant that Indians were to be "civilized." Education was an important element in the "civilizing" process. Federal officials worked with churches and philanthropic organizations to establish schools for Indian children away from the reservations. Teachers at these schools prohibited Indian boys and girls from speaking their own language, practicing their religion, or otherwise displaying their own culture. The teachers' goal was to enable the children to live in white society and to separate them from Indian culture.

Other educational programs aimed to train adult Indian men to be farmers or mechanics. The effort to teach Indian men farming, however, was at odds with traditional gender roles in Indian society: typically women raised crops, and men hunted and fought. Many Indian men viewed farming in the same way as their white male contemporaries viewed housework: as women's work.

The **Dawes Severalty Act** (1887) was intended to make the Indians into self-sufficient, individual farmers. The law committed the government to a policy of **severalty**—that is, individual ownership of land. It divided the reservations into individual family farms of 160 acres each. Once each family had received its allotment, any surplus was to be sold by the government. This policy found support among those who coveted Indian land.

Individual landownership and acquisitiveness, however, were at odds with traditional Indian beliefs and practices. Indians maintained that the land was for the use of all and that sharing was a major obligation. Delegates from the Cherokee, Creek, and Choctaw nations petitioned Congress not to pass the Dawes Act, arguing that "our people have not asked for or authorized this," but to no avail.

The Dawes Act stripped Indians of much of their land. Once all the allotments to Indian families had been made, about 70 percent of the land area of the reservations remained, and much of it was sold outright to settlers. In the end, the Dawes Act did not end the reservation system, nor did it reduce the Indians' dependence on the federal government. Instead it separated the Indians from some of their most valuable land.

Response to the assimilation programs varied widely. Some Indians tried to become part of white

---

Dawes Severalty Act Law passed by Congress in 1887 that broke up reservations into 160-acre family plots and sought to assimilate Indians into white culture by making them farmers.
severalty The holding of property by individuals.

society; others took a middle way. Susan La Flesche, for example, daughter of an Omaha leader, graduated from medical college in 1889 at the head of her class. She disappointed some of her teachers when she set up her medical practice near the Omaha reservation, treated both white and Indian patients, and took part in tribal affairs. However, Dr. La Flesche also participated in the local white community by taking an active part in the **temperance movement** and sometimes preaching in the Presbyterian church.

Other Indians tried to cling to the old ways, hiding their children to keep them out of school and secretly practicing traditional religious ceremonies. In the late nineteenth century, the peyote cult, based on the hallucinogenic properties of the **peyote cactus,** emerged as an alternative religion. It evolved into the Native American Church by combining elements of traditional Indian culture and Christianity with peyote use. Some Indians also took solace in alcohol.

Mexican Americans in the Southwest

Throughout the Southwest during the late nineteenth century, many Mexican Americans lost their land as large numbers of **Anglos**—English-speaking whites—arrived there. Mexican Americans' landholdings were guaranteed by the Treaty of Guadalupe Hidalgo (1848), which ended the Mexican War, but the vagueness of Spanish and Mexican land grants opened the door to legal challenges. In some instances, Mexican Americans were the victims of outright fraud. In California and Texas, some Mexican-American families with large landholdings kept their land by having a daughter marry a prominent Anglo. Except in New Mexico, however, most found themselves landless laborers.

Although the California gold rush of 1849 attracted fortune seekers from around the world, including Mexico and other parts of Latin America, the vast majority came from the eastern United States and Europe. By the 1880s, the English-speaking majority had pushed aside the Spanish-speaking people of California. By the 1870s, many of the pueblos (towns) created during Mexican or Spanish rule in California had become **barrios** centered around a Catholic church. In some ways, the

barrios resembled the neighborhoods of European immigrants in the East. Both had mutual aid societies, political associations, and newspapers published in the language of the community, and both often centered on a church. There was an important difference, however. Neighborhoods of European immigrants consisted of people who had come to a new land seeking opportunity or change. By contrast, the residents of the barrios lived in regions that had been home to Mexicans for generations, but they now found themselves surrounded and dominated by English-speaking Americans who hired them for cheap wages.

Like their counterparts in California, Anglos in Texas used fraud and coercion to obtain land from the Spanish-speaking people born in Texas, the Tejanos. By 1900, much of the land in south Texas had passed out of Tejano hands. But unlike California, Anglo ranch owners usually maintained the social patterns characteristic of Tejano ranchers. A large section of Texas between the Nueces River and the Rio Grande extending west to El Paso remained Mexican culturally. This region was home both to Tejanos and to two-thirds of all Mexican immigrants in the United States before 1900. Most people living there spoke Spanish.

New Mexico presented a third pattern in the late nineteenth century. Hispanos (Spanish-speaking New Mexicans) were clearly the majority of the population in the territory. Although Hispanos were the unquestioned majority and could dominate elections, many who had small landholdings lost their land. Unlike California and Texas, many of those who enriched themselves in New Mexico were wealthy Hispanos.

From 1856 to 1910, the Latino population throughout the Southwest grew more slowly than

---

temperance movement   A movement advocating the avoidance of alcoholic drinks.

peyote cactus   A cactus native to Mexico and the southwestern United States that is able to produce a hallucinogenic effect.

Anglo   A term applied in the Southwest to English-speaking whites.

barrio   A Spanish-speaking community, especially of poor laborers.

♦ In the late nineteenth and early twentieth centuries, Mexican Americans became a major part of the work force for constructing and maintaining railroads in the Southwest. This crew of Mexican-American linemen was working in south Texas when this photograph was taken in 1910. They may have been employed by a railroad to put up and maintain its communication lines or by a telegraph or telephone company. *Texas State Library and Archives Commission.*

The West in American Thought

The West has long fascinated Americans, and the "winning of the West" has become a national myth that has obscured or distorted the facts. Since at least the 1890s, many Americans have thought of the West in terms of the frontier. According to this way of thinking, to the east of the frontier line lay established society, and to the west of it lay the wild, untamed West. The frontier thus represented the dividing point between savagery and civilization.

The West as Utopia and Myth

During the nineteenth and much of the twentieth century, the West seemed a potential **utopia.** Many Americans could dream of a better life there, even if they never ventured forth. What was the origin of this utopian view of the West? In the popular mind, the West was vacant, waiting to be formed. Nothing was predetermined there. A person or a group such as the Mormons could make a fresh start.

The West appealed as well to Americans who sought to fulfill the American dream of improving their social and economic standing. The presence of free or cheap land, the ability to start over, the idea of creating a place of one's own, all were part of the West's attraction—even for those who never acted on their dreams. Some of those who tried to fulfill their dreams did not succeed, but enough did to provide some justification for the utopian image of the West as a land of promise.

The West achieved mythical status as popular novels, and eventually movies and television, used it as the setting for stories that spoke to Americans' anxieties as well as their hopes. The development of the West gave rise to the myth of the "winning" of the West. The myth begins with the grandeur of wide grassy plains, towering craggy mountains, and vast silent deserts. In most versions, the western Indians face a tragic destiny. They are usually portrayed as a proud, noble people whose demise

the Anglo population. After 1910, however, that situation reversed itself, as political and social upheavals in Mexico prompted massive migration to the United States. Probably a million people—equivalent to one-tenth of the entire population of Mexico as of 1910—arrived over the next twenty years. More than half stayed in Texas, but significant numbers settled in southern California. Inevitably, this new stream of immigrants changed some of the patterns of ethnic relations that had characterized the region since the mid-nineteenth century.

---

utopia An ideal place.

clears the way for the transformation of the land. The starring roles in this drama are played by white pioneers who struggle to overcome natural and human obstacles. These pioneers personify rugged individualism—the virtues of self-reliance and independence—as they triumph through hard work and personal integrity. Many of the human obstacles are villainous characters: greedy speculators, vicious cattle rustlers, unscrupulous moneylenders, selfish railroad barons. Some are only doubters, too skeptical of the promise of the West to take the risks to succeed.

The Frontier and the West

Starting in the 1870s, accounts of the winning of the West suggested to many Americans the existence of an America more attractive than the steel mills and urban slums of their own day. The West was a place where people were more virtuous than the barons of industry and corrupt city politicians. Individual success was possible in the West without labor strife or racial and ethnic discord. This myth has evolved and continues to exert a hold on Americans' imaginations. The cowboy has been the most prominent embodiment of the myth. He is a brave and resourceful loner, riding across the West and dispelling trouble from his path and from the lives of others. A modern version of the medieval knight in shining armor, he rarely does the actual work of a cowboy.

In the 1920s, Hollywood discovered that this image seemed to have special appeal to Americans dissatisfied with the routine of their lives and work. In the 1950s, some found the cowboy symbolic of the American role in the Cold War, as the nation strode across the globe, rescuing grateful nations from the threat of Communist domination.

Like all other myths, the myth of the winning of the West contains elements of truth but also ignores some truths. For example, it usually treats Indians as victims of progress. It rarely considers their fate after they met defeat at the hands of the cavalry. Instead, they obligingly disappeared from the scene. The myth rarely tempers its celebration of rugged individualism by acknowledging the fundamental role government played in the transformation of the West by dispossessing the Indians, subsidizing railroad construction, using the public domain to underwrite economic development, and rerouting rivers. The myth often overlooks the role of ethnic and racial minorities from African American and Tejano cowboys to Chinese railroad construction crews. It overlooks the extent to which these people were exploited as sources of cheap labor. Women typically appear only as helpless victims or noble helpmates. Finally, the myth generally ignores the extent to which the economic development of the West replicated that of the East. If such influences appear in the myth, they are usually as constraints that the hardy pioneers overcame.

Historians have played an important role in shaping this myth of the West. In 1893, **Frederick Jackson Turner,** a young historian, wrote an essay, "The Significance of the Frontier in American History." In that essay, he challenged the prevailing idea among American historians that they should study European societies to discover the origins of American character and institutions. Rather, Turner argued, they should study the American frontier. The western frontier, he claimed, was where America had formed, because it was where individualism and democracy flourished.

Turner's theory about the frontier dominated the thinking of historians for many years. Today, however, historians focus on many elements missing from Turner's analysis. They acknowledge the importance of cultural conflicts among different groups of people; the experiences of American Indians, of the Spanish-speaking **mestizo** peoples of the Southwest, and of Asian Americans; the experiences of women; ecological issues, especially those involving water; and the ways that the western economy resembles and differs from that of the East. If frontier individualism and mobility have been important elements in American history, as Turner suggested, these other elements have been equally important in western history.

Frederick Jackson Turner American historian who argued that the receding frontier and cheap land were dominant factors in creating American democracy and shaping the national character.

mestizo A person of mixed Spanish and Indian ancestry.

SUMMARY

E xpectations
C onstraints
C hoices
O utcomes

The West changed greatly during the forty years following the Civil War. Federal policy toward that region derived from the *expectation* of rapid development, and policymakers often *chose* to use the public domain to accomplish that purpose. The Plains Indians posed *constraints* on development, but most were defeated by the army by 1877.

Patterns of development varied in different parts of the West. In the Great Basin, Mormons created a theocracy and *chose* new approaches to irrigation to meet *constraints* posed by scarce water. A cattle kingdom emerged on the western Great Plains, as railroad construction made it possible to carry cattle east for slaughter. As farming moved west, lack of rainfall *constrained* farmers' expectations. The forests of the Pacific Northwest attracted lumbering companies.

Throughout the West, change was driven by *choices* made in the face of *constraints*. Railroad construction overcame *constraints* posed by vast distances. As western mining became highly mechanized, control shifted to large mining companies able to secure the necessary capital. In California especially, landowners made *choices* that led to the development of large-scale commercial agriculture. Water posed a significant *constraint* on economic development in much of the West.

Asian immigrants, American Indians, and Latino peoples all formed substantial parts of the western population but had significantly different *expectations* and experiences. White westerners *chose* to use politics and, sometimes, terrorism to exclude and segregate Asian immigrants. Federal policies toward American Indians proceeded from the *expectation* that they should be rapidly assimilated and lose their separate cultural identity. Such policies largely failed. American citizens of Mexican descent and subsequent immigrants from Latin America had their lives and cultures *constrained* by Anglo newcomers.

The *outcomes* of the many *choices* made in the late nineteenth century were explosive economic development and population change. Americans have viewed the West as both a utopia and the source of a national myth. Those views overlook important realities in the nature of western development and in the people who accomplished it.

SUGGESTED READINGS

Billington, Ray Allen, and Martin Ridge. *Westward Expansion: A History of the American Frontier*, 5th ed. (1982).

> Presents the most detailed treatment of the West and the frontier, largely from a Turnerian perspective.

Brown, Dee. *Bury My Heart at Wounded Knee: An Indian History of the American West* (1971).

> One of the first efforts to write western history from the Indians' perspective, drawing on oral histories.

Chan, Sucheng. *Asian Americans: An Interpretive History* (1990).

> A good introduction to the history of Asian Americans.

Gomez-Quinones, Juan. *Roots of Chicano Politics, 1600–1940* (1994).

> An overview of the political history of Mexican Americans until World War II.

Hundley, Norris, Jr. *The Great Thirst: Californians and Water, 1770s–1990s* (1992).

> One of the most recent of a number of studies surveying the role of water in the West.

Limerick, Patricia Nelson. *The Legacy of Conquest: The Unbroken Past of the American West* (1987).

> The major recent criticism of the Turner thesis, posing an alternative framework for viewing western history.

Montejano, David. *Anglos and Mexicans in the Making of Texas, 1836–1986* (1987).

> An award-winning study of south Texas.

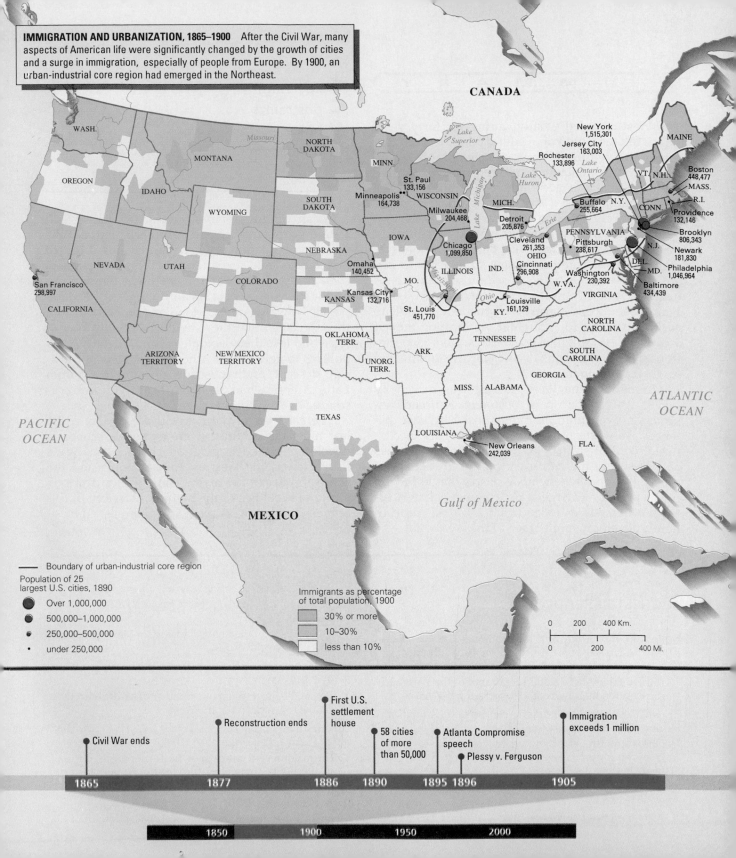

IMMIGRATION AND URBANIZATION, 1865–1900 After the Civil War, many aspects of American life were significantly changed by the growth of cities and a surge in immigration, especially of people from Europe. By 1900, an urban-industrial core region had emerged in the Northeast.

CANADA

WASH.

OREGON

IDAHO

MONTANA

WYOMING

NEVADA

UTAH

CALIFORNIA

San Francisco
298,997

ARIZONA
TERRITORY

NEW MEXICO
TERRITORY

COLORADO

NORTH DAKOTA

SOUTH DAKOTA

NEBRASKA

KANSAS

MINN.

WISCONSIN

IOWA

MO.

Omaha
140,452

Kansas City
132,716

St. Paul
133,156

Minneapolis
164,738

Milwaukee
204,468

Chicago
1,099,850

ILLINOIS

St. Louis
451,770

MICH.

Detroit
205,876

IND.

Cleveland
261,353

OHIO

Cincinnati
296,908

Louisville
161,129

KY.

Lake Superior

Lake Michigan

Lake Huron

L. Erie

Lake Ontario

New York
1,515,301

Jersey City
163,003

Rochester
133,896

Buffalo
255,664

N.Y.

PENNSYLVANIA

Pittsburgh
238,617

W.VA.

VIRGINIA

Washington
230,392

MAINE

VT. N.H.

MASS.

Boston
448,477

R.I.

CONN.

Providence
132,146

Brooklyn
806,343

N.J.

Newark
181,830

DEL.

Philadelphia
1,046,964

MD.

Baltimore
434,439

OKLAHOMA TERR.

UNORG. TERR.

ARK.

TENNESSEE

NORTH CAROLINA

SOUTH CAROLINA

TEXAS

MISS.

ALABAMA

GEORGIA

LOUISIANA

New Orleans
242,039

FLA.

PACIFIC OCEAN

ATLANTIC OCEAN

Gulf of Mexico

MEXICO

Missouri

Mississippi

Ohio

— Boundary of urban-industrial core region

Population of 25 largest U.S. cities, 1890

● Over 1,000,000
● 500,000–1,000,000
● 250,000–500,000
· under 250,000

Immigrants as percentage of total population, 1900

30% or more
10–30%
less than 10%

0   200   400 Km.
0   200   400 Mi.

Civil War ends

Reconstruction ends

First U.S. settlement house

58 cities of more than 50,000

Atlanta Compromise speech

Plessy v. Ferguson

Immigration exceeds 1 million

1865   1877   1886   1890   1895 1896   1905

1850   1900   1950   2000

The New Social Patterns of Urban and Industrial America, 1865–1917

INTRODUCTION

E xpectations
C onstraints
C hoices
O utcomes

In 1872, two neighbors in Hartford, Connecticut, concluded they could write a better novel than the ones then in vogue. The first-time novelists, Charles Dudley Warner and Samuel L. Clemens, titled their satire on business and politics *The Gilded Age: A Tale of Today*. The popular novel gave its name to the years from the 1860s through the 1890s: the Gilded Age. The label suggests both the golden gleam of a gilded surface and the cheap nature of the base metal underneath.

Many aspects of late nineteenth-century life justify terming it gilded. The dramatic expansion of business, the technology that typified "progress" for many people, the glittering wealth of the new industrial entrepreneurs, and the rapid economic development of the West all provided the gleaming surface. The grim realities of life for most industrial workers and the plight of racial and ethnic minorities, however, lay uncomfortably just below that golden surface. This chapter examines the *expectations, constraints, choices,* and *outcomes* of the period by looking at social and cultural changes in the late nineteenth and early twentieth centuries. New patterns of life rocked the burgeoning cities. Ethnic and racial groups related to each other in new ways, and new developments revolutionized education, gender roles, creative expression, and cultural participation.

Most of these *choices* and *outcomes* were related to the great transforming experiences of the late 1800s: industrialization, urbanization, immigration, and the development of the West. Together they broke down old *constraints* and created new ones. They fostered new *expectations* among Americans about how people should live and how social groups should relate to one another. Americans' *expectations* sometimes expanded individual *choices* and opportunities. However, some groups tried to impose their values and behaviors on others.

As Americans revised old *expectations* for social relations and forged new ones, the pace of growth created *constraints* that sometimes forced troubling choices. Cities expanded so rapidly that municipal governments faced difficult *choices*. For example,

should they use their limited resources to pave streets or build sewers? At the same time, however, the expansion of the educational system removed *constraints* on Americans' opportunities to learn and presented many Americans with new *choices*, such as whether to go to college. Educational opportunities for women helped to expand career *choices*, including such previously all-male professions as medicine and law, or the new profession of social work. In the South, where industrialization lagged, some people made *choices* intended to develop new social and economic patterns.

The expanding industrial economy and rapidly growing cities convinced people throughout Europe to come to America. Such *choices* were often made with the *expectation* of acquiring free land or earning high wages. Some succeeded and turned their dreams into reality. But the hopes of others were dashed by the *constraints* posed by the difficulty of finding available land or steady jobs. The *outcome* of these many *choices* about where to live, how to live, and how to relate to other groups was the transformation of American society and culture during the Gilded Age.

CHRONOLOGY   ● ● ● ● ●

Social and Cultural Change

1865	Civil War ends 248,120 immigrants enter U.S.
1868	First medical school for women
1870	25 cities exceed 50,000 people
1871	Great Chicago fire Boss Tweed indicted
1872	Clemens and Warner name the Gilded Age
1874	Women's Christian Temperance Union founded
1876	National League (professional baseball) formed
1877	Reconstruction ends
1879	Henry George's *Progress and Poverty*
1882	788,992 immigrants enter U.S.
1883	Civil Rights cases
1885	Mark Twain's *Huckleberry Finn*
1886	First U.S. settlement house
1887	American Protective Association founded Florida segregates railroads
1888	First electric streetcar system
1889	Hull House opens
1890	58 cities exceed 50,000 people Jacob Riis's *How the Other Half Lives* Second Mississippi Plan
1893	Stephen Crane's *Maggie: A Girl of the* *Streets*

1895	Booker T. Washington delivers Atlanta Compromise
1896	South Carolina adopts white primary *Plessy v. Ferguson*
1897	President Cleveland vetoes immigration restriction First southern steel mill
1899	Scott Joplin's "Maple Leaf Rag"
1901	Frank Norris's *The Octopus* Anarchists barred from U.S. Oil discovered in Texas, Oklahoma, and Louisiana
1903	First World Series
1903–1906	Pogroms against Russian Jews
1907	1,285,349 immigrants enter U.S.
1913	President Taft vetoes immigration restriction Armory Show
1916	Madison Grant's *Passing of the* *Great Race*
1917	Congress requires literacy test to limit immigration, overriding President Wilson's veto

The New Urban Environment

"The city is the nerve center of our civilization. It is also the storm center." So said Josiah Strong, a leading Protestant minister, pointing up the ambivalence with which many Americans viewed their rapidly growing cities. For recent immigrants and long-time residents, for men and women, for industrial workers and farmers, the ever-expanding cities posed the greatest challenge to their expectations and gave them the widest range of choices.

Surging Urban Growth

What Americans saw in their cities often fascinated them. Cities boasted the technological innovations that many equated with progress. When the journalist William Allen White moved to Kansas City in 1891, the city's streetcars were "marvels" to him and its telephones "a miracle." But the lure of the city stemmed from far more than telephones, streetcars, and technological gadgetry. It also offered theaters, concerts, lectures, fairs, exhibitions, and galleries.

Other visitors were repulsed by what they saw in American cities. A British traveler in 1898 described Pittsburgh as "a most chaotic city. A cloud of smoke hangs over it by day. The glow of scores of furnaces light the river banks by night. . . . All nations are jumbled up here, the poor living in tenement dens or wooden shanties thrown up or dumped down with very little reference to roads." Guillermo Prieto, visiting San Francisco in 1877, was struck by the contrast of luxurious wealth and desperate poverty: "Behind the palaces run filthy alleys, or rather nasty dungheaps without sidewalks or illumination, whose loiterers smell of the gallows."

The odd mixture of fascination and repulsion Americans felt toward cities stemmed in part from the rapidity of urban growth. Cities with more than fifty thousand people grew almost twice as fast as rural areas. The nation had twenty-five cities of that size in 1870 and fifty-eight in 1890, most of them in the Northeast and Midwest. Urban growth came largely through migration from rural areas in Europe and, to a lesser extent, in the United States. The mechanization of farm work meant that fewer workers were required than before. High rural birth rates also contributed to urban growth.

Growth of manufacturing went hand in hand with urban expansion. By the late nineteenth century, the nation had developed a **manufacturing belt** that included nearly all the largest cities as well as the bulk of the nation's manufacturing and finance (see chapter opener map). Some cities began as ports; others developed as industrial centers. Cities often became known for a particular product: iron and steel in Pittsburgh; clothing in New York; textiles in Lowell, Massachusetts; meatpacking in Chicago; flour milling in Minneapolis.

New Cities of Skyscrapers and Streetcars

As the urban population swelled, technological advances permitted cities to expand upward and outward. In the early 1800s, residents got around by foot in cities that measured only a few miles across. Buildings were seldom more than three stories high. In the late nineteenth century, however, new building and transportation technologies removed previous constraints and spelled the end of the "walking city."

Until the 1880s, construction techniques had limited building heights. The higher a building was, the thicker its lower walls had to be. Chicago architects, most notably Louis Sullivan, took the lead in designing taller buildings by using a steel frame to carry the weight of the walls. Economical and efficient, tall buildings created unique city skylines.

Just as steel-frame buildings allowed cities to grow upward, so new forms of transportation allowed cities to expand outward. Electricity transformed urban transit. Frank Sprague, a protégé of Thomas Edison, designed a streetcar driven by an electric motor. Sprague's electric streetcars first appeared in Richmond, Virginia, in 1888, and quickly replaced horse cars and cars pulled by underground cables.

> **manufacturing belt**   A region of the country in which an urban population, transportation systems, and other infrastructure support heavy industry.

By the early 1900s, networks of streetcar lines crisscrossed most large cities, connecting neighborhoods to downtown. Some carried middle-class women wearing white gloves and stylish hats to shop at downtown department stores. Skilled workers rode others to their factory jobs. Still other lines carried typists and businessmen to banks and offices. Cities expanded by annexing suburban areas that grew up along the spreading transportation lines. Chicago grew from 17 to 178 square miles between 1860 and 1890.

New railroad lines also brought outlying villages within commuting distance of cities. Wealthier urban residents could now escape the city at the end of the workday. By 1890, commuter lines brought more than 100,000 workers daily into New York City just from its northern suburbs.

The New Urban Geography

Areas within the largest cities became increasingly specialized by economic function. Iron and steel making, meatpacking, shipbuilding, and oil refining had to be established on the outskirts of cities. Land was plentiful and relatively cheap there, and the city center suffered less from the noise, smoke, and odor of heavy industry.

As heavy manufacturing moved to the outskirts of the cities, city centers tended to become more specialized as well. By 1900, a large city usually had a district of light manufacturing that might include clothing and printing. Nearby was usually a **wholesale** trade district with warehouses and offices of wholesalers. **Retail** shopping districts, anchored by department stores, emerged in a central location accessible by streetcar. In the largest cities, banks, insurance companies, and corporation headquarters clustered near one another to form a financial district. A hotel and entertainment district often lay close to both the financial and retail blocks. These areas together made up a central business district.

Residential areas as well as downtowns developed according to economic status. New suburbs ranged outward from the city center in order of wealth. Those who could afford to travel the farthest could also afford the most expensive homes. Those too poor to ride the new transportation lines lived in crowded apartments or small houses within walking distance of work.

Building an Urban Infrastructure

During the rapid urban growth after the Civil War, local governments did little to regulate urban expansion or construction practices. Cities grew with only the most basic planning. Most choices about land use and construction were made by individual landowners, developers, and builders. Everywhere, builders and owners hoped to achieve a high return on their investment by producing the most living space for the least cost. Such profit calculations rarely left room for varied designs or open space.

Private companies sometimes provided gas, electricity, telephone, and public transit under **franchises** from the city. Companies eagerly competed for such franchises, sometimes bribing city officials to secure one. As a result, cities usually found themselves well supplied with franchised utilities. New residential areas sometimes had gas and electric lines before any houses were framed.

The unplanned nature of most urban growth meant that cities could rarely keep up with the demands for fire and police protection, schools, sewage disposal, street maintenance, parks, and water. As a result, city residents sometimes faced contaminated drinking water, inadequate disposal of sewage and garbage, and epidemic disease. By 1900, however, most cities had improved their infrastructure substantially. The quality and quantity of the water supply varied greatly from city to city. To enlarge its water supply, New York City spent seven years and $24 million constructing what was then the largest aqueduct in the world. Baltimore and Boston also undertook huge water projects. Water quality, though, remained a problem. As city officials began to understand that germs caused

---

wholesale Engaged in the sale of goods in large quantities, usually for resale by a retailer.

retail Engaged in the sale of goods in small quantities directly to consumers.

franchise Government authorization allowing a private company to provide a public service in a certain area.

♦ Monday was laundry day throughout much of America in the late nineteenth and early twentieth centuries. New York tenements were no exception, as is clear from this photograph taken around 1900. Because buildings were so close together, hanging the laundry became a social event, as neighbors leaned out their windows, pinned their clothes to the line, and exchanged greetings. Note the high population density in such areas. *Library of Congress.*

many diseases, cities introduced filtration and **chlorination** of their water to eliminate disease-carrying organisms. Even so, only 6 percent of urban residents received filtered water by 1900.

Cities faced similar constraints in disposing of sewage, cleaning streets, and removing garbage. Even when cities built sewer lines, they usually emptied the untreated sewage into some nearby body of water. One sanitary expert in 1877 called Boston Harbor "one vast cesspool." In most cities, few streets were paved. The rest became mudholes in the rain, threw up clouds of dust in dry weather, and froze into deep ruts in the winter. Chicago counted 2,048 miles of streets in 1890, but only 629 miles were paved. In the late nineteenth century, however, most eastern cities began using asphalt paving, following the lead of Washington, D.C.

Everywhere, urban growth outstripped cities' ability to provide for it. Despite the introduction of uniformed police during the Civil War era, urban crime mushroomed. The **great Chicago fire** of 1871, which devastated three square miles, killed more than 250 people, and left 18,000 homeless, demonstrated the inadequacy of existing fire protection. The Chicago fire spurred efforts to improve fire protection by creating a well-trained and well-equipped staff of firefighters and by regulating construction practices.

Although change came slowly, city utilities and services improved significantly between 1870 and

chlorination   The treatment of water with the chemical chlorine to purify and disinfect it.

great Chicago fire   The 1871 disaster that destroyed much of the city and spurred national efforts to improve fire protection.

1900. By the early twentieth century, large American cities had more extensive sewer systems and provided more water to each resident than similar cities in Germany. But as late as 1900, no city larger than 150,000 people had a sewage treatment plant.

Poverty and the City

In 1879, in *Progress and Poverty*, Henry George pointed out that the "enormous increase in productive power" had failed to eliminate poverty or to improve the lives of working people. He concluded that progress and poverty went hand in hand: "The 'tramp' comes with the locomotive, and almshouses and prisons are as surely the marks of 'material progress' as are costly dwellings, rich warehouses, and magnificent churches." George was one of many who focused attention on the growing numbers and problems of the urban poor.

"How the Other Half Lives"

In 1890, **Jacob Riis** shocked many Americans with his book *How the Other Half Lives: Studies Among the Tenements of New York.* In a city of a million and a half inhabitants, Riis claimed, half a million had begged for food at some time over the preceding eight years. Of them, only 6 percent were physically unable to work. Most of Riis's book describes the appalling conditions of the **tenements** that housed three-quarters of the city's population. The living space for an entire family often consisted only of a 10-by-12-foot living room and one or two dark, tiny bedrooms. A tenement might house a dozen or more families. Such accommodations, Riis insisted, "make for evil; because they are the hotbeds of the epidemics that carry death to rich and poor alike; the nurseries of pauperism and crime that fill our jails and police courts; . . . above all, they touch the family life with deadly moral contagion."

Crowded conditions in working-class areas developed in part because so many people were constrained by the need to live within walking distance of their work. By dividing buildings into small rental units, landlords packed in more tenants and collected more rent. Rents were high com-

pared to wages, so tenants often took in boarders. Such practices produced alarmingly high population densities. No other American city was as densely populated as New York, but nearly all urban, working-class neighborhoods throughout the United States were crowded.

Few agreed on the causes or cures for the widespread urban poverty. Riis divided the blame among greedy landlords, corrupt officials, and the poor themselves. Henry George pointed to private ownership of property as the culprit. The influential Charity Organization Society (COS), by contrast, argued that individual character defects such as immorality and laziness produced poverty. COS officials expected the recipients of aid to be moral, thrifty, and hardworking.

The Mixed Blessings of Machine Politics

Not everyone blamed the urban poor for their own distress. In most cities, political organizations built loyal followings in poor neighborhoods by addressing desperate needs in a direct and personal way. Instead of repentance, they wanted the votes of the poor.

George W. Plunkitt illustrates the kind of politics such organizations practiced. Born in a poor Irish neighborhood of New York City, Plunkitt became a district leader of **Tammany Hall,** which dominated the city's Democratic party. Plunkitt described how he kept the loyalty of the voters in his neighborhood in a 1905 newspaper interview:

Go right down among the poor families and help them in the different ways they need help. . . . It's philanthropy, but it's politics, too—mighty good politics. . . . The poor are the most grateful people

---

Jacob Riis New York journalist whose exposure of slum conditions in American cities appalled middle-class Americans and led to calls for slum clearance and new building codes.

tenement An unsafe and often unsanitary apartment building usually occupied by poor families.

Tammany Hall A New York political organization whose "machines" dominated city and sometimes state politics.

in the world, and, let me tell you, they have more friends in their neighborhoods than the rich have in theirs. If there's a family in my district in want I know it before the charitable societies, and me and my men are first on the ground. . . . The consequence is that the poor look up to George W. Plunkitt as a father, come to him in trouble—and don't forget him on election day.

Plunkitt typified many big-city politicians across the country. Neighborhood **saloons** often served as social gathering places, especially for working-class men. Not surprisingly, would-be politicians frequented these saloons and often owned them. They responded to the needs of the urban poor by providing a bucket of coal on a cold winter day, a basket of food at Thanksgiving, or a job on a city crew. In return, they expected recipients to follow their lead in politics. Political organizations based among working-class and poor voters, usually led by men of poor, immigrant parentage, emerged in nearly all large cities. Opponents denounced the leader of the organization as a **boss** and the organization itself as a machine.

One of the earliest city bosses was **William Marcy Tweed,** who became head of the Tammany Hall organization in 1863. Tweed and his associates built public support by spending tax funds on various charities, and they gave to the poor from their own pockets—pockets often lined with public funds or bribes. Under Tweed's direction, city government launched such major construction projects as public buildings and improvements in streets, parks, sewers, and docks. Much of the construction was riddled with corruption. Between 1868 and 1871, the Tweed Ring may have plundered as much as $200 million from the city, mostly in **kickbacks** from contractors. In 1871, evidence of corruption led to Tweed's conviction and imprisonment. Reformers in practically every city subsequently charged officeholders with corruption, but most bosses were more cautious than Tweed.

Perhaps the most important single function the bosses served was to centralize political decision making. As one Boston boss said, "There's got to be in every ward somebody that any bloke can come to—no matter what he's done—to get help." If a pushcart vender needed a permit to sell tinware or a railroad president needed permission to

build a bridge, the machine could help him—if he showed the proper gratitude.

Combating Urban Poverty: The Settlement Houses

By the 1890s, young college-educated men and women began to confront urban poverty in an altogether different way. These humanitarians took an environmental approach in assisting the poor. The **settlement house** idea, which originated in London in 1884, involved opening a house in the slums where idealistic university graduates lived among the poor and tried to help them. The first settlement house in the United States opened in New York in 1886.

Jane Addams and Ellen Gates Starr opened **Hull House** in Chicago in 1889. For many Americans, Jane Addams became synonymous with the settlement house movement. Settlement house workers provided a wide range of assistance to slum families: cooking and sewing classes, public baths, childcare facilities, instruction in English, and housing for unmarried working women. Ad-

---

saloon A place common to middle-class and working-class neighborhoods where patrons could buy and drink alcoholic beverages.

boss Name applied to the head of an urban political organization that based its success on lower-income voters.

William Marcy Tweed New York City political boss who used the Tammany machine to maintain control over city and state government from the 1860s until his downfall in 1871.

kickback A sum of money that a contractor illegally gives "under the table" to the official who awarded the contract.

settlement house Community center operated by resident social reformers in a slum area to help poor people in their own neighborhood.

Jane Addams Illinois social worker who sponsored child labor laws and was a leader in the settlement house movement. She won the Nobel Peace Prize in 1931.

Hull House Settlement house founded by Jane Addams and Ellen Gates Starr in Chicago in 1889 to improve community and civic life in the slums.

dams and other settlement house workers became forces for urban reform, promoting better education, improved public health, and honest government. Settlement houses spread rapidly, with some four hundred operating by 1910. The settlement houses became the first institutions to be created and staffed primarily by college-educated women.

Church-affiliated settlement houses often reflected the **Social Gospel,** a movement initiated by Protestant ministers who were concerned about the social and economic problems of the cities. One of the best known, Washington Gladden of Columbus, Ohio, called for an "Applied Christianity"—the adoption of Christian principles by businesses. By this he meant that businesses should follow Christ's injunctions to love one another and to treat others as you would have them treat you.

New Americans from Europe

The flood of immigrants that fed the burgeoning cities and industrial labor force from the Civil War to World War I represents the highest level of immigration in American history. In 1865, when the Civil War ended, 248,120 immigrants entered the United States. The number rose to 788,992 in 1882 and peaked at 1,285,349 in 1907.

Most immigrants came from Europe and settled in cities. By 1910, in eighteen of the twenty-five largest cities, immigrants and their children made up more than half the population. Three-fourths of New Yorkers and Chicagoans were first- or second-generation immigrants.

A Flood of Immigrants

Before 1890, most immigrants came from Great Britain, Ireland, Germany, and **Scandinavia.** After 1890, most came from southern and eastern Europe, especially Austria-Hungary, Italy, and Russia.

Most immigrants came because of the United States' reputation as the "land of opportunity," where farms were cheap or free, labor was in demand, and wages were high. Some were attracted by America's reputation for religious toleration and commitment to democracy. Others were re-

♦ The photographer Lewis Hine took this picture of a family from eastern Europe who arrived in the United States in 1905. After 1890, immigrants came ashore at Ellis Island and were processed by the Immigration Service. For millions of immigrants, Ellis Island was their portal to America. *Courtesy George Eastman House.*

cruited by agents sent to Europe by sparsely populated western states or by railroad companies seeking buyers for their land. The reasons for coming varied from country to country, year to year, and person to person.

Groups exhibited distinctive patterns of settlement in the United States. The greatest number of

> **Social Gospel** A moral reform movement of the late nineteenth century led by Protestant clergymen who drew attention to urban problems and advocated social justice for the poor.
>
> **Scandinavia** The region of northern Europe consisting of Norway, Sweden, and Denmark.

Irish immigrants, many desperately poor, arrived between 1847 and 1854, after the potato blight hit, but Irish immigration continued at high levels until the 1890s. Ninety percent were Catholic. They settled initially in the cities of the Northeast, composing a quarter of the population of New York City and Boston as early as 1860. Although many Irish immigrants worked in the West, the Irish as a group remained urban.

Germans outnumbered all other immigrant groups in the United States before 1900. Rural **overpopulation,** changes in agriculture, and crop failures in the 1840s and 1850s all contributed to the desire to move from Germany. Religious and political persecutions affected some as well. German peasants sold their holdings at home and thus arrived in the United States with the expectation of buying farms. Many did so, especially in the north-central states. Even more German immigrants, however, settled in midwestern towns and cities.

Scandinavian immigration followed the German patterns. The high point of Scandinavian immigration came in the 1880s and 1890s, when Scandinavians accounted for 12 percent of American immigrants. Scandinavian farmers left because of overpopulation and changes in agriculture. Many settled on farms in Minnesota, the Dakotas, Montana, and Nebraska; others landed in Washington State.

Italian immigrants illustrate a different situation. Landless farm laborers from southern Italy and Sicily began to leave in significant numbers in the 1880s. Their numbers increased slowly until, between 1900 and 1915, Italians outnumbered any other single group of immigrants arriving in the United States. At first, many young men worked in construction or agriculture during the summer and returned to Italy during the winter. Eventually, some chose to stay and sent for their families. Large numbers of Italians made the cities of the Northeast their home. In California, Italians became prominent in growing grapes and making wine.

The immigration of Eastern European Jews reveals still a different pattern. In the late nineteenth and early twentieth centuries, one-third of the Jews living in eastern Europe left there, and 90 percent of those came to the United States. The largest number came from Russia, accounting for nearly one-eighth of all immigrants after 1900. Extended

pogroms occurred in Russia in the early 1880s and from 1903 to 1906. This religious persecution was the most important reason for Jewish migration. Jewish immigration was also different in that entire communities chose to emigrate as a group. They became the most urban of immigrant groups. Half of all the eastern European Jews in America resided in New York in 1914.

Large numbers of Slavic-speaking immigrant groups came only in the 1890s and after, accounting for more than a third of all European immigrants between 1900 and 1914. They immigrated primarily for economic opportunity. The largest single group, Poles, were nearly all Catholic and settled in New York and in the cities of the Midwest. By 1910, Chicago, Milwaukee, Detroit, and Buffalo had large Polish populations. Most Slavic-speaking groups tended to locate in urban and industrial areas.

An Ethnic Patchwork

Immigrant groups tended to congregate in ethnic neighborhoods in American cities. For example, in Manhattan in 1890, the Irish predominated on the West Side and the Germans on the East Side. Neighborhoods of Italians, African Americans, Jews, Chinese, Czechs, Arabs, Finns, Greeks, and Swiss completed the ethnic patchwork. Ethnic patchworks composed of distinctive immigrant communities were not limited to cities. Scandinavians, Dutch, Swiss, Czechs, and Germans were most likely to be farmers, but there were rural farming settlements of many groups. The map at the beginning of the chapter reveals concentrations of immigrants both in the manufacturing belt and in western areas with cheap farmland or mines.

These patterns of settlement reflect the expectations immigrants held about America as well as the opportunities they found when they arrived. The British, Germans, Scandinavians, and Czechs came with capital in the 1870s and 1880s, when good

---

overpopulation　The growth of a population beyond the point where it can be supported by its environment.

pogrom　Violent mob attacks on Jewish communities, often resulting in massacres.

farmland could still be acquired relatively cheaply in the north-central states. By contrast, fewer Irish had the necessary capital, and so fewer came with the expectation of becoming farmers. Some post-1900 immigrants, especially Italians and Poles, came without any expectations of staying in America permanently. They planned to work for a time and then return home with full pockets. After 1890, farmland was more difficult to obtain. Newcomers at that point were more likely to find work in the rapidly expanding industrial sectors of the economy.

Hyphenated America

In the nineteenth century, many **old-stock Americans** (sometimes only a generation removed from immigrant forebears themselves) assumed that immigrants should learn English quickly and become citizens resembling themselves. Immigrants from Britain often did assimilate rapidly. They already spoke English and had similar religious values. Most other immigrants, however, resisted rapid assimilation. They held fast to elements in their own culture at the same time that they took up a new life in America. Conscious of being a German or an Italian in America, they often came to think of themselves as **hyphenated Americans:** German-American or Italian-American.

On arriving in America, with its strange language and unfamiliar customs, many immigrants reacted by seeking people who shared their cultural values, practiced their religion, and spoke their language. Ethnic communities thus played significant roles in newcomers' transition from the old country to America. They gave immigrants a chance to learn about their new home with the assistance of those who had come before. At the same time, the newcomers could retain the values and behaviors from their old country that they found most important.

Hyphenated America developed a unique blend of ethnic institutions. Ethnic fraternal lodges sprang up to provide not only social ties but also benefits in case of illness or death. Among them were the Ancient Order of Hibernians (Irish), the Sons of Hermann (German), and the Sons of Italy. Singing societies devoted themselves to the music of the old country. Foreign-language newspapers were vital in connecting the old country to the new, for they provided news from the old country as well as from other similar communities in the United States.

For nearly every group, the church provided the single most important element in ethnic group identity. Immigrant churches shared religion, language, and culture. By 1900, for example, there were separate Lutheran churches speaking German, Norwegian, Swedish, Danish, Finnish, and Icelandic. Catholic services were sometimes conducted in the language of the parish's largest ethnic group and sometimes featured special observances transplanted from the old country.

Nativism

Many old-stock Americans expected that immigrants would embrace the behaviors and beliefs of old-stock Americans and blend neatly into their culture. These expectations came to be identified with the image of the **melting pot.** But the melting-pot metaphor rarely described the reality of immigrants' lives. Most immigrants changed their ways slowly, over their lifetimes.

Few old-stock Americans understood the immigrants' adjustment to their new home. Instead of seeing the ways immigrants changed, many old-stock Americans saw only immigrants' efforts to retain their own culture. They fretted over the multiplication of foreign-language newspapers and feared to go into communities where they rarely heard English. Such fears and misgivings fostered the growth of nativism: the view that old-stock values and social patterns were preferable to those of

---

old-stock Americans   Term used by the Census Bureau to describe people who were born in the United States.

hyphenated Americans   Americans with a strong ethnic identity based on their ancestry who felt that they had been shaped by two cultures—Irish-American, for example.

melting pot   A phrase describing the vision of American society as a place where immigrants set aside their distinctive cultural identities and were absorbed into a homogeneous culture.

immigrants. Nativists argued that only their values and institutions were genuinely American.

American nativism was often linked to anti-Catholicism because so many immigrant groups were Catholic. The American Protective Association (APA), founded in 1887, noisily proclaimed itself the voice of anti-Catholicism. Its members pledged not to hire Catholics, not to vote for them, and not to strike with them. The APA claimed a half million members by 1894. It dominated the Republican party in parts of the Midwest and occasionally fomented mob violence against Catholics.

Jews, too, faced religious antagonism. Beginning in the 1870s, organizations and businesses began to discriminate against Jews. By the early twentieth century, such discrimination intensified. Some employers refused to hire Jews, many college fraternities and sororities refused to admit them, and **restrictive covenants** constrained them from buying homes in certain areas.

Labor organizations sometimes looked at unlimited immigration as a threat to jobs and wage levels. Anti-Chinese sentiment among Pacific Coast unions contributed to the passage of the Chinese Exclusion Act in 1882 (see page 378). The depression of the 1890s convinced the American Federation of Labor in 1897 to call for a literacy test as a way to reduce the influx of immigrants.

The rise of labor and radical political organizations also contributed to anti-immigrant sentiment. By 1900, a few employers had begun to argue that unions represented foreign, un-American interests. Far more serious was the association of immigrants with radicalism, especially anarchism. Congress banned anarchists from immigrating after Leon Czolgosz, an American-born anarchist with a foreign-sounding name, assassinated President William McKinley in 1901. The link between immigrants and radicalism seemed to be confirmed later when Socialist party candidates received strong support from immigrant voters.

The shift in the sources of immigration from northwestern Europe to southern and eastern Europe also contributed to the rise of nativism in the 1890s. Nativists viewed these **new immigrants** as less desirable than **old immigrants** from northwestern Europe.

The arrival of significant numbers of new immigrants coincided with the glorification of Anglo-

Saxons (Germanic ancestors of the English). Relying on Social Darwinism and its argument for survival of the fittest (see page 359), proponents of Anglo-Saxonism were alarmed by statistics that showed old-stock Americans having fewer children than the new immigrants. Some voiced fears of a "race suicide" in which Anglo-Saxons were bred out of existence. Madison Grant, a wealthy New Yorker, epitomized this thinking. Grant claimed in *The Passing of the Great Race* (1916) that all civilization had been created by Nordics—tall, blond, blue-eyed northern Europeans—and that other Europeans had proven themselves unable to sustain civilization.

By the 1890s, these religious, economic, political, and racist strains resulted in demands that the government restrict immigration from Europe. Advocates of restriction initially called for immigrants to pass a literacy test. Opposition came from immigrant organizations and from employers seeking a larger supply of labor. Congress passed literacy measures in 1897, 1913, and 1917, but presidential vetoes prevented the first two from passing. The 1917 law, which did not specify literacy in English, had little impact because most immigrants by then were literate in their own language.

New South, Old Issues

The term **New South** refers to efforts by some southerners to diversify the region's economy and

---

restrictive covenant Provision in a property title designed to restrict subsequent sale or use of the property, often specifying sale only to a white Christian.

new immigrants Newcomers to America from southern and eastern Europe who began to arrive in large numbers in the 1880s.

old immigrants Newcomers to America from Britain, Germany, Ireland, and Scandinavia who came in waves that peaked during the years 1840–1880.

New South Term first used by southern journalist Henry Grady to promote the image of an industrialized South as the region recovered from the devastation of the Civil War.

to industrialize after Reconstruction. These efforts took place as the South grappled with the legacy of slavery, the Civil War, and Reconstruction. One outcome of these efforts was a modest diversification of the southern economy. Another was that white southerners created a society based on racial segregation that lasted for more than a half-century.

The New South

Following the Civil War, the state of southern railroads was a critical constraint on the region's economic growth. During the 1880s, however, southern railroads more than doubled their miles of track. In the 1890s, J. P. Morgan reorganized southern railroads into three large systems.

The emergence of better transportation led some entrepreneurs to think in terms of new industries, particularly textiles. The 1880s marked a boom era for that industry. New southern mills had more modern equipment and were more productive than the mills of New England. By the 1890s, many New England firms had moved their operations south rather than compete with southern mills. Southern textile mills had cheaper labor costs than those in New England, partly because they relied on child labor. An estimated 70 percent of southern cotton-mill workers were under 21 years of age. A few other industries also developed in the South, including tobacco and cottonseed oil processing, but they did little to transform the regional economy. Nearly all these industries took advantage of the South's cheap, unskilled, and nonunionized labor.

Of greater potential was the iron and steel industry that emerged in northern Alabama. Dominated by the Tennessee Coal, Iron, and Railroad Company, the industry drew on coal from Tennessee and Alabama mines and iron ore from northern Alabama. By the late 1890s, Birmingham, Alabama, had become one of the world's largest producers of pig iron. In 1897, the first southern steel mill opened in Ensley, Alabama, and soon became a serious rival of Pittsburgh's mills. In 1907, J. P. Morgan arranged the merger of the Tennessee Company into his United States Steel Corporation.

The turn of the century also saw the beginning of a southern oil industry near Beaumont, Texas, with the tapping of the Spindletop Pool. The center of petroleum production now shifted from the Midwest to Texas, Oklahoma, and Louisiana, where important discoveries were made in 1901. These discoveries prompted the growth of new companies, notably Gulf and Texaco.

Some southerners tried to diversify the region's agriculture. In doing so, however, they ran up against the cotton textile and cigarette industries. In the end, southern agriculture changed little: owners and sharecroppers farmed small plots, obligated by their rental contracts or **crop liens** to raise cotton or tobacco.

The late nineteenth century also saw the myth of the **Old South** and of the so-called **Lost Cause** blossom. Popular fiction and song, North and South, romanticized the pre–Civil War South as a place of gentility and gallantry, where "kindly" plantation owners cared for "loyal" slaves. The Lost Cause myth portrayed the Confederacy as a heroic effort to retain the life and values of the Old South. Leading southerners, especially Democrats, promoted the Lost Cause myth. Hundreds of statues of Confederate soldiers appeared on courthouse lawns.

The Second Mississippi Plan and the Atlanta Compromise

Dreams of the Old South and the Lost Cause helped fuel the politics of white supremacy that dominated the South after Reconstruction. As long as the Civil Rights Act of 1875 remained in place,

crop lien A claim against a crop, typically held by a storekeeper as the price for extending credit.

Old South Term used to describe the antebellum, or pre–Civil War, South, especially by those who characterized the period as a time of gentility and gallantry.

Lost Cause Term used to describe the Confederate struggle in the Civil War, especially by white southerners who characterized it as a noble but doomed effort to preserve a way of life.

African Americans were theoretically protected against discrimination in public places. Segregation existed, to be sure, but largely without force of law. Restrictions on black political voting and officeholding were also extralegal.

Then, in the **Civil Rights cases** (1883), the U.S. Supreme Court ruled the Civil Rights Act of 1875 unconstitutional. The Court's decision specified that the "equal protection" of the Fourteenth Amendment applied only to state governments, not to individuals and companies. This meant that private businesses need not offer equal access to their facilities. In response, southern lawmakers slowly began to require businesses to practice segregation. In 1887, the Florida legislature required separate accommodations on railroad trains. By 1891, six other states had passed similar laws. Both social custom and local laws began to specify greater racial separation as well.

Mississippi whites took a bolder step in 1890, holding a state constitutional convention to eliminate political participation by African Americans. Shrewdly, the new provisions did not mention the word race. Instead they specified payment of a poll tax, passing a literacy test, and other requirements for voting. Everyone understood that these measures were intended to disfranchise black voters. Those who failed the literacy test could still vote if they could understand a section of the state constitution or law after it was read it to them. This "understanding" clause gave white officials discretion in deciding who passed the test, and they usually permitted white illiterates to vote. The South followed this so-called Second Mississippi Plan with great interest. Except for the **poll tax,** however, no other state imitated its provisions immediately.

Then, in 1895, a black educator signaled his apparent willingness to accept disfranchisement and segregation in a speech at the opening of the Cotton States and International Exposition in Atlanta. Founder of the Tuskegee Institute in Alabama, **Booker T. Washington** seemed to accept an inferior status for blacks, at least for the present: "No race can prosper till it learns that there is as much dignity in tilling a field as in writing a poem. It is at the bottom of life we must begin, and not at the top." He also seemed to condone segregation: "In all things that are purely social, we can be as sepa-

rate as the fingers, yet one as the hand in all things essential to mutual progress. . . . The wisest among my race understand that the agitation of questions of social equality is the extremest folly." He agreed that equal rights had to be earned rather than belonging to all citizens.

The speech, soon dubbed the **Atlanta Compromise,** earned great acclaim for Washington among whites. His message that blacks were willing to accept segregation and disfranchisement in return for interracial peace and economic opportunity was one that southern whites wanted to hear. Northern whites, too, were receptive to the notion that the South would work out its race relations by itself. Until his death in 1915, Washington held sway as the most prominent black leader in the nation. His message found a mixed reception among African Americans. Some accepted his approach as the best that might be secured at the time. Others criticized his willingness to sacrifice black rights. Henry M. Turner, a bishop of the African Methodist Episcopal church in Atlanta, declared that Washington "will have to live a long time to undo the harm he has done our race."

Separate but Not Equal

Southern lawmakers continued to redefine the legal status of African Americans after Washington's

---

Civil Rights cases   A series of cases that came before the Supreme Court in 1883, in which the Court ruled that private companies could legally discriminate against blacks.

poll tax   A tax that many southern states used as a prerequisite to voting to discourage blacks from taking part in the electoral process.

Booker T. Washington   A former slave, this educator founded and built the Tuskegee Institute into a leading black educational institution and urged blacks to accept segregation for the time being.

Atlanta Compromise   Landmark speech given by Booker T. Washington in 1895, in which he encouraged blacks to accommodate to segregation and work for economic advancement in the available paths.

and then carved holes through which only whites could squeeze. South Carolina and other southern states added the white primary as an additional barrier. Southern Democrats, the "white man's party," restricted their primaries and conventions to whites only.

Southern lawmakers also extended segregation by law. The U.S. Supreme Court's decision in *Plessy v. Ferguson* (1896), a case involving segregated railroad cars, aided the advocates of such segregation. The Court ruled that "separate but equal" facilities did not violate the equal protection clause of the Fourteenth Amendment. Southern legislators soon applied that reasoning to everything from prisons to restaurants.

Violence against blacks accompanied the new laws. From 1885 to 1900, when the South was redefining race relations, the region witnessed more than twenty-five hundred lynching deaths, almost all of them African Americans. Once the new order was in place, lynchings declined to about eleven hundred between 1900 to 1915.

African Americans fought against lynching in various ways, primarily by publicizing the record of brutality. One of the most prominent opponents was **Ida B. Wells.** In *Free Speech*, the black newspaper that she helped found in Memphis, Tennessee, in 1891, she attacked lynching, arguing that several local victims had been targeted as a means of eliminating successful black businessmen. In response, a mob destroyed her newspaper office. She moved north and spent most of the 1890s crusading against lynching.

◆ During the 1890s, Ida B. Wells emerged as the leading opponent of lynching, refusing to be silenced even when threatened herself. She appealed to women especially, through the various women's organizations that developed in the late nineteenth century. *Schomburg Center for Research in Black Culture/New York Public Library/photo by Oscar B. Willis.*

Atlanta speech. State after state followed the lead of Mississippi and disfranchised black voters. In 1898, Louisiana added the infamous **grandfather clause.** Under it, men who would otherwise be prohibited from voting were allowed to vote if their fathers or grandfathers had been eligible to vote in 1867, when the Fourteenth Amendment was enacted. The ruling reinstated whites into the electorate but kept blacks out. Throughout the South, states set up substantial barriers to voting

grandfather clause Provision in various southern state constitutions restricting suffrage to those whose fathers or grandfathers could vote in 1867, thus depriving blacks of the vote.

Plessy v. Ferguson Case in 1896 in which the Supreme Court upheld a Louisiana law requiring segregated railroad facilities on the grounds that "separate but equal" accommodations were constitutional.

Ida B. Wells Reformer and journalist who crusaded against lynching and advocated racial justice and woman's suffrage. Upon marrying in 1895, she changed her name to Wells-Barnett.

African Americans also sought ways to resist disfranchisement and segregation. Some promoted an exodus from the South to **Liberia,** the nation created in western Africa before the Civil War as a home for free blacks. But few could afford to go to Liberia. Other blacks proposed leaving the South for homestead and railroad land in Kansas. "Kansas Fever" swept through the South in the late 1870s and early 1880s. Perhaps as many as twenty thousand blacks from Louisiana, Mississippi, and Texas moved to Kansas in just a few months in 1879. The 1890s saw another swell in migration. In the 1880s, interest grew in creating all-black communities. A number of such communities were organized, most of them in the South, but others were scattered from New Jersey to California. Between 1892 and 1910, some twenty-five all-black towns were founded in Oklahoma.

New Patterns of American Social and Cultural Life

The decades following the Civil War brought far-reaching social change to Americans in nearly every part of the nation. The educational system, gender roles, sexual relationships, artistic expression, and cultural and leisure activities also changed significantly during this period.

The New Middle Class

The Gilded Age brought substantial changes to the lives of middle-class Americans. In the cities, an army of accountants, lawyers, secretaries, insurance agents, and middle-level managers developed to staff the emerging giant corporations and professional offices. The streetcar made it possible for the middle class to live beyond walking distance of their work. Thus industrialization and urban expansion produced not only sprawling working-class neighborhoods and wealthy enclaves but also distinctively middle-class neighborhoods and suburbs.

Single-family homes set amid wide and carefully tended lawns were common in the new middle-class neighborhoods. Such neighborhoods accelerated the tendency of American urban areas to spread outward and to have lower population densities than their European counterparts. To acquire a single-family house in the leafy suburbs away from urban noise and filth became a part of the American middle-class dream.

Suburban households often followed different patterns than those of working-class or farm families. Middle-class families often hired a servant to assist with household chores, and middle-class women were much more likely to take part in social organizations outside the home. Such families rarely expected their children to contribute to the family's finances but emphasized education instead. Middle-class households were likely to subscribe to daily newspapers and to family magazines such as the *Ladies' Home Journal* and the *Saturday Evening Post*. The new advertising (see page 349) featured in these newspapers and magazines helped create a "consumer culture," particularly among middle-class women, who by 1900 were responsible for nearly all of their families' shopping.

Ferment in Education

The Gilded Age witnessed important changes in education, from kindergarten through the university. Kindergartens, created to provide childcare for working mothers, grew from two hundred in 1880 to three thousand in 1900. Between 1870 and 1900, most northern and western states established school attendance laws, typically requiring children between the ages of 8 and 14 to attend school for a minimum number of weeks annually. School enrollment among those ages 5 to 19 increased significantly, particularly at the secondary level. By 1890, high schools had added a fourth year everywhere but in the South. The high school curriculum changed significantly, including courses such as science, civics, business, home economics, and drafting. The number of high school graduates tripled between 1878 and 1898.

> **Liberia**   A nation on the west coast of Africa founded through the efforts of the American Colonization Society and settled mainly by freed slaves between 1822 and the Civil War.

College enrollments also grew, especially in the new state universities created under the Land-Grant College Act of 1862. Still, college students came disproportionately from middle-class and upper-class urban families. The college curriculum changed greatly, from a set of courses required of all students (mostly Latin, Greek, mathematics, rhetoric, and religion) to a system in which students chose a major and electives. New subjects included economics, political science, modern languages, and laboratory sciences. Many universities also began to offer engineering, business administration, and education classes.

Far fewer women than men marched in college graduation processions. **Vassar College** became the first college exclusively for women in 1861. Only one college graduate in seven was a woman in 1870, and this improved only to one in four by 1900. In 1879, fewer than half the nation's colleges even admitted women. Twenty years later, four-fifths did so. Some prestigious private institutions such as Harvard, Princeton, and Yale, however, remained all-male enclaves.

Redefining Women's Gender Roles

Greater educational opportunities for women marked part of a change in social definitions of gender roles. Throughout the nineteenth century, most Americans defined women's social role in terms of the **cult of domesticity.** This held that the proper place for a woman was in the home as wife and mother. Advocates of domesticity conceded that women might also have important roles in the church and the classroom. They contended that women should avoid business and politics, where lax moral standards might corrupt them. Women should occupy a **separate sphere,** immune from such dangers. Widely advocated in the pulpits and journals of the day, the concept of domesticity proved most typical of white middle-class and upper-class women in towns and cities. Farm women and working-class women worked too hard and witnessed too much of the world to fit the model of innocence and daintiness prescribed by advocates of domesticity.

The late nineteenth century saw increasing challenges to domesticity. One challenge came as more

women finished college and chose to enter the professions. Important early successes came in medicine. In 1849, Elizabeth Blackwell became the first woman to complete medical school and helped establish the first medical school for women in 1868. By the 1880s, some twenty-five hundred women held medical degrees. About 3 percent of all physicians were women, more proportionately than in most of the twentieth century. After 1900, however, medical schools began to impose enrollment restrictions on women. Access to the legal profession proved surprisingly difficult. Arabella Mansfield was the first woman to be admitted to the bar in 1869, but the entire nation counted only sixty practicing women attorneys ten years later. Most law schools refused to admit women until the 1890s. Women predominated in the new field of social work.

Professional careers attracted relatively few women, but many more became involved outside their homes through women's clubs or in reform activities. Women's clubs became popular among middle- and upper-class women in the late nineteenth century, claiming 800,000 members by 1910. Crusader Ida B. Wells actively promoted the development of black women's clubs. Such clubs often began as forums to discuss literature or art, but they sometimes led women into reform movements. In 1904, Sarah Platt Decker, president of the General Federation of Women's Clubs, bluntly proclaimed, "**Dante** is dead. He has been dead for several centuries, and I think it is time that we dropped the study of his Inferno and turned our attention to

---

Vassar College   The first collegiate institution for women, founded in Poughkeepsie, New York, in 1861.

cult of domesticity   The nineteenth-century notion that women's activities were ideally rooted in domestic labor and the nurture of children.

separate sphere   The notion that women were meant to pursue occupations having to do with family, church, or school and not those in such traditionally male fields as business and politics, which were considered too competitive and corrupt for women.

Dante   Italian poet (1265–1321) best known for his *Inferno,* about a descent into hell.

our own." Female reform organizations often had some link to domesticity: temperance, opposition to prostitution, and abolition of child labor. The **Women's Christian Temperance Union,** one of the most prominent, was formed in 1874.

Women's church organizations, clubs, and reform societies all provided experience in working together under the leadership of women. Through them, women developed networks of working relationships. These experiences and contacts contributed to the effectiveness of women's efforts to establish their right to vote (see page 414).

Emergence of a Gay and Lesbian Subculture

Challenges to domesticity involved women seeking to redefine society's gender roles. A quite different redefinition occurred as gay and lesbian **subcultures** developed in America's burgeoning cities. Homosexuals and lesbians recognized that large cities offered an anonymity not possible in rural areas. Rural communities where practically everyone knew everyone else either prompted people physically attracted to members of their own sex to suppress such tendencies or to exercise them very discreetly. After the Civil War, however, homosexuals and lesbians gravitated toward the largest cities and began to create distinctive subcultures. By the 1890s, one researcher reported that "perverts of both sexes maintained a sort of social set-up in New York City, had their places of meeting, and [the] advantage of police protection." Boston, Chicago, New Orleans, St. Louis, and San Francisco also had clubs, restaurants, and steambaths that catered to homosexuals. Although most homosexuals were secretive about their sexual identity, some flouted their sexuality at "drag balls."

In the 1880s, physicians created medical names for these emerging subcultures, including "homosexual," "lesbian," "invert," and "pervert." Earlier, law and religion had defined particular actions as illegal or immoral. The new medical definitions emphasized not the actions but instead the persons taking the actions. Some theorists proposed that such behavior resulted from a mental disease, but others concluded that homosexuals and lesbians were born that way. The medical definition of *homo-*

sexual stigmatized expressions of deep affection between heterosexuals of the same sex, which became less common as individuals tried to avoid any suggestion that they were anything but heterosexual.

New Patterns in Cultural Expression: From Realism to Ragtime

Shortly after 1900, the director of the prestigious Metropolitan Museum of New York observed "a state of unrest all over the world" in art, literature, music, painting, and sculpture. Unrest meant dramatic changes in American art, literature, and music—many directly influenced by the new urban, industrial, multiethnic society.

Walt Whitman's *Leaves of Grass*, first published in 1855 and reissued in revised editions until his death in 1892, stands as a major work in world literature. Whitman gloried in democracy and in ordinary people. He dealt, too, with topics considered inappropriate for public print, including intimate relationships and the human body:

> *Have you ever loved the body of a woman?*
> *Have you ever loved the body of a man?*
>
> *Do you not see that they are exactly the same to all*
>   *In all nations and times all over the earth?*

Emily Dickinson, whose poetry first appeared after her death in 1890, rejected the formal strictures of most previous verse to probe the depths of anxiety and emotion:

> *I can wade Grief—*
> *Whole Pools of it—*
> *I'm used to that—*
> *But the least push of Joy*
> *Breaks up my feet*
> *And I tip—drunken—*

Women's Christian Temperance Union Women's organization founded in 1874 that opposed the evils of drink and supported reforms such as woman's suffrage.

subculture A cultural subgroup, unified by status, interests, or practices, which differentiates its members from the dominant culture on the basis of shared values or loyalties.

American novelists increasingly turned to realistic, critical portrayals of life, rejecting the romantic idealism characteristic of the pre–Civil War period. The towering figure of the era was **Mark Twain** (Samuel Langhorne Clemens). His *Huckleberry Finn* (1885) pokes fun at the social pretensions of the day, scorns the Old South myth, and challenges racial biases against blacks. The novels of William Dean Howells and Henry James, by contrast, present restrained, realistic portrayals of upper-class men and women. After 1890, Stephen Crane, Theodore Dreiser, and Frank Norris sharpened the critical edge of fiction. Crane's *Maggie: A Girl of the Streets* (1893) depicts how urban squalor turned a young woman to prostitution. Norris's *The Octopus* (1901) portrays the abusive power of a railroad. Kate Chopin's *The Awakening* (1899) deals with the repression of a woman's sexual desires.

As American literature moved toward realism, most American painting was moving in the opposite direction. An important exception was Thomas Eakins. Although he received little recognition in the 1870s and 1880s, his work is now considered a major contribution to realism. American painting changed late in the century largely in response to French **impressionism,** which emphasized less an exact reproduction of the world and more the artist's impression of it. James Whistler's work showed impressionist influences. Mary Cassatt was the only American (and the only woman) to rank among the leaders of impressionism, but she lived and painted mostly in France. A prominent American impressionist was Childe Hassam, who often presented urban landscapes.

Robert Henri and his associates in the **Ash Can school** also were preoccupied with urban poverty and ordinary people. The Ash Can adherents faced a challenge from artists influenced by the abstract approach then becoming prominent in France by 1910 or so. In 1913, the so-called Armory Show in New York City presented the art of radical European innovators such as Pablo Picasso, Henri Matisse, and Wassily Kandinsky. Critics dismissed the modernists, but the abstract style caught on.

The most innovative musician at the turn of the century was African-American composer Scott Joplin. Joplin studied piano with a German-born music teacher and then traveled through African-American communities from New Orleans to Chicago. As he traveled, he encountered **ragtime** music and soon began to write his own. In 1899, he published "The Maple Leaf Rag" and soared to fame as the best-known ragtime composer in the country.

The Origins of Mass Entertainment

Better transportation and communication and increased leisure time fostered new forms of entertainment in the late nineteenth century. Companies now organized entertainers into traveling groups and sent them from city to city to perform. Circuses also took advantage of improved transportation to establish regular circuits. Thus mass entertainment had its birth.

Gilded Age booking agencies scheduled traveling dramatic and musical troupes into every corner of the country. Traveling groups of actors, singers, and other performers provided the entertainment mainstay, performing everything from Shakespeare to **slapstick.** In the late nineteenth century, these agencies developed the star system, in which each traveling company had one or two accomplished performers who attracted audiences.

One of the most unusual traveling shows was the **Chautauqua,** a blend of inspirational oratory,

---

Mark Twain   Pen name of Samuel Clemens, an American author who drew on his childhood along the Mississippi River to create novels such as *The Adventures of Huckleberry Finn.*

impressionism   A style of painting that developed in France in the 1870s. It emphasized the play of light on surfaces and attempted to convey the impression of observing nature directly.

Ash Can school   New York artists of varying styles who shared a dislike of academicism.

ragtime   Music blending African rhythms and European form to create a unique style; popularized by Scott Joplin and others in the late nineteenth century.

slapstick   A boisterous form of comedy marked by chases, collisions, and crude practical jokes.

Chautauqua   Traveling shows offering educational, religious, and recreational activities; part of a nationwide movement of adult education that began in the town of Chautauqua, New York.

education, and entertainment. Thousands of towns held annual Chautauqua assemblies that featured comedians, inspirational orators, opera, glee clubs, lectures, string quartets, or magic-lantern shows on foreign countries.

Professional baseball emerged as a quite different form of mass entertainment after the Civil War. Teams traveled by train from city to city, and urban rivalries built loyalty among hometown fans. The formation of the National League in 1876 established an owners' cartel that monopolized the industry by excluding rival clubs and by controlling the movement of players from team to team. Because African Americans were barred from the National League, separate Negro Leagues emerged. In the 1880s and 1890s, the National League successfully warded off challenges from rival leagues and a players' union. Not until 1901 did another league—the American League—successfully organize. In 1903, the two leagues merged into a new, stronger cartel and staged the first World Series. Other professional sports often adopted baseball's patterns of organization, labor relations, and racial discrimination.

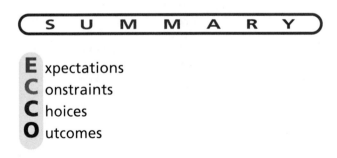

S U M M A R Y

E xpectations
C onstraints
C hoices
O utcomes

In the Gilded Age, industrialization transformed the economy, while urbanization and immigration challenged many established social patterns. In the midst of economic and social change, Americans developed new *expectations* and faced new *choices* about their relations with each other. The *outcomes* of their many individual *choices* marked a major redefinition of American social and cultural life.

As rural Americans and European immigrants sought better lives in the cities, urban America changed dramatically. New technologies in transportation and communication broke down old *constraints* on individual *choices* about where to live and work. The *outcome* was a new urban geography with separate retail, wholesale, finance, and manufacturing areas and residential neighborhoods defined by economic status.

Many urban Americans struggled under the *constraints* of poverty. To gain support from the poor, political machines like Tammany Hall in New York City helped them in various ways. Social reformers established settlement houses to address the problems of the urban poor in a different way.

Many Europeans immigrated because of their *expectations* of better opportunities in America. Immigrants often formed separate communities, usually centered on a church. The flood of immigrants from southern and eastern Europe spawned nativist reactions among some old-stock Americans.

Some southerners proclaimed the creation of a New South and promoted industrialization. The *outcome* was mixed. The South did acquire some industry, but regional poverty remained. After 1890, white southerners disfranchised African Americans and extended segregation. Booker T. Washington emerged as the best-known African-American leader.

Education underwent far-reaching changes from kindergartens through universities. Challenged in part by the *expectations* of college-educated women, socially defined gender roles began to change as some women *chose* professional careers. Some also *chose* active roles in reform. Urbanization offered new *choices* to gay men and lesbians by permitting the development of urban subcultures. The new *expectations* and *choices* generated by an urban, industrial, multiethnic society contributed to critical realism in literature, new patterns in painting, and ragtime music. Urbanization and changes in transportation and communication also fostered the emergence of an entertainment industry.

SUGGESTED READINGS

Addams, Jane. *Twenty Years at Hull House* (1910; reprint, 1960).

Nothing can convey the complex world of Hull House and the striking personality of Addams as well as her own account.

Ayers, Edward L. *The Promise of the New South: Life After Reconstruction* (1992).

A comprehensive survey of developments in the South during this period.

Clinton, Catherine. *The Other Civil War: American Women in the Nineteenth Century* (1984).

The section on the post–Civil War period surveys the subject, although so many recent works have appeared that no synthesis could cover them all.

Higham, John. *Strangers in the Land: Patterns of American Nativism, 1860–1925* (1965).

This classic of American history played a major role in defining the contours of American nativism and still provides an excellent introduction to the subject.

Kraut, Alan M. *The Huddled Masses: The Immigrant in American Society, 1880–1921* (1982).

A helpful introduction to immigration, especially the so-called new immigration.

McDonald, Terrence J., ed. *Plunkitt of Tammany Hall*, by William L. Riordon (1993).

McDonald provides excellent context for and editing of this classic account of Tammany's relationship with voters.

Mohl, Raymond A. *The New City: Urban America in the Industrial Age, 1860–1920* (1985).

An informative but concise introduction to nearly all aspects of the growth of American cities.

• • • New Choices for Women

The Context

The late nineteenth and early twentieth centuries saw a good deal of public attention given to the emergence of the "New Woman," a consequence of the emergence of a mature industrial economy and a complex, urban society. The era of "separate spheres" was rapidly passing, as women moved out of the home and into the larger society. Young women of upper- and middle-income families attended college, and some of them entered careers. Some women, mostly of middle- and upper-income levels, joined women's associations and sought political changes. Young women of working-class families entered the wage-earning work force as factory or office workers, and some of them became involved in unions. (For further information on the context, see pages 400–402.)

The Historical Question

At the time and since then, some people asked whether the breakdown of separate spheres called into question the concept of domesticity—the expectation that a woman has a special responsibility for the nurturing and protection of the family. Did the emergence of the "New Woman" significantly change expectations about women's roles in American society? Or were the older expectations of domesticity still prominent?

The Challenge

Using the sources provided, along with other information you have read, write an essay or hold a discussion on the following question. Cite evidence in the sources to support your conclusions. **Did the emergence of the "New Woman" significantly change expectations about women's roles in American society?**

The Sources

1 Mrs. Burton Harrison, writing in *Harper's Bazaar* in 1900 on "Home Life as a Profession," had this to say:

Today, when hundreds of young women of our best blood and culture in America are standing within the open doors of schools and colleges, eagerly straining their gaze out into the future, hoping to catch a glimpse of the opportunity for a "career," it seems to behoove the conservative thinkers among us to suggest to some of them the profession of home life. . . . Now, as a matter of historic fact, the cornerstone of the highest civilization has always been the home, and wifehood and motherhood the happiest estate of woman. To my mind, it is a cruel wrong to a young girl to launch her in life unadvised on these points,

and imbued with the determination to independence of the other sex. . . .

Far be it from me to suggest a relapse to those dark ages of home life when a girl strummed on the piano or worked in cross-stitch tapestry. . . . On the contrary, I would have her carry back into her home her sheaves of knowledge and accomplishment, and there try to enrich and broaden the domestic sphere. . . . I do not think our homes as they are now a sufficiently satisfying exchange for the broader, more interesting channels for women's work everywhere available. But I earnestly wish they might be made so; and the question of how to accomplish this enormously important result lies largely in the palm of the girl graduate of today.

2 Rena Rietveld Verduin, an Illinois farm wife and mother with only a fifth-grade education, presented these views in 1907 in a community debate sponsored by a local club that organized cultural activities. She spoke in opposition to the proposition "Resolved that women should not enter higher education."

Through an education girls are enabled to become self-supporting and acquainted with the ways of the world. Through an education girls learn to earn a livelihood and are not so liable to throw themselves away in marriage on some worthless man. . . . When [men] discover that the girls don't have to marry— by getting an education and going into some profession—they will be more likely to behave themselves and be at some pains to make themselves worthy of the girl's acceptance. . . . Men seem to think that the women have no business on the face of the earth except to work and slave for them. . . . Girls, get an education and escape slavery.

3 Susan W. Fitzgerald prepared this argument for woman's suffrage in the early twentieth century.

We are forever being told that the place of woman is in the HOME. . . .

SHE is responsible for the cleanliness of her house.

SHE is responsible for the wholesomeness of the food.

SHE is responsible for the children's health.

SHE, above all, is responsible for their morals, for their sense of truth, of honesty and decency, for what they turn out to be.

How Far Can the Mother Control These Things? . . . [The pamphlet then surveys problems of urban life—filthy streets, lack of adequate sanitation, fire hazards, and more.]

It is the MEN and NOT THE WOMEN that are really responsible for the unclean houses, unwhole-

some food, bad plumbing, danger of fire, risk of tuberculosis and other diseases, immoral influences of the street. In fact, MEN are responsible for the conditions under which the children live, but we hold WOMEN responsible for the results of those conditions. If we hold women responsible for the results, must we not, in simple justice, let them have something to say as to what those conditions shall be? . . . LET THEM VOTE.

Women are by nature and training, housekeepers. Let them have a hand in the city's housekeeping, even if they introduce an occasional house cleaning.

4 Charlotte Perkins Gilman, who made her living as a writer and lecturer, was largely self-educated. This excerpt is from her article "Are Women Human Beings?" which appeared in *Harper's Weekly* in 1912.

[The] things the women want to do and be and have are not in any sense masculine. They do not belong to men. They never did. They are departments of our social life, hitherto monopolized by men. . . . We find everywhere this same pervasive error, this naïve assumption, which would be so insolent if it were not so absurd, that only men are human creatures, able and entitled to perform the work of the world; while women are only female creatures, able to do nothing whatever but continue in the same round of duties to which they have been so long restricted. . . .

Women will never cease to be females, but they will cease to be weak and ignorant and defenseless. They are becoming wiser, stronger, better able to protect themselves, one another, and their children. Courage, power, achievement are always respected. . . . [As they take] their full place in the world as members of society, as well as their partial places as mothers of it, they will gradually rear a new race of men, men with minds large enough to see in human beings something besides males and females.

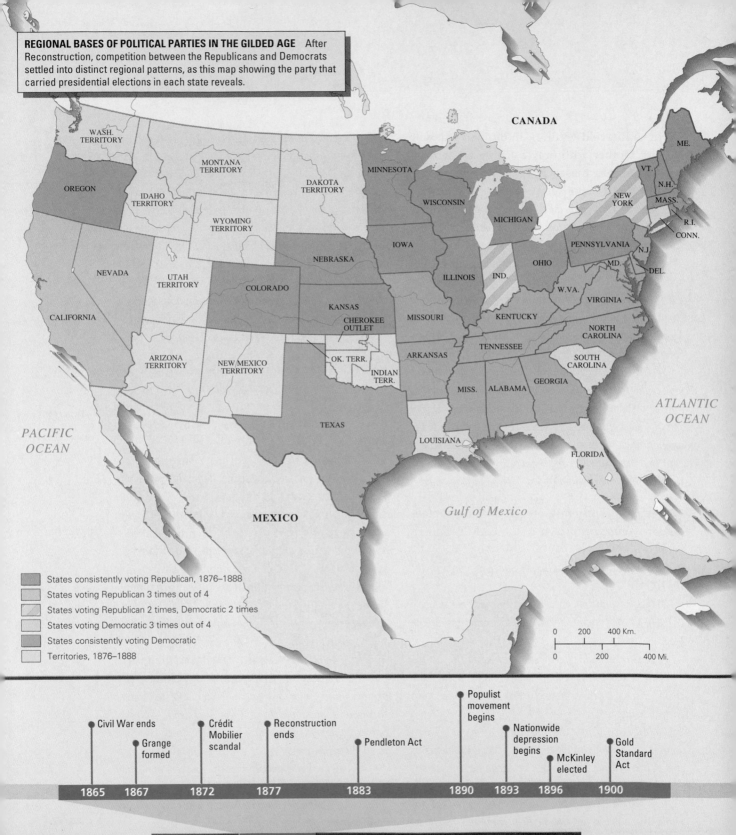

REGIONAL BASES OF POLITICAL PARTIES IN THE GILDED AGE After Reconstruction, competition between the Republicans and Democrats settled into distinct regional patterns, as this map showing the party that carried presidential elections in each state reveals.

CANADA

WASH. TERRITORY

OREGON

IDAHO TERRITORY

MONTANA TERRITORY

WYOMING TERRITORY

DAKOTA TERRITORY

MINNESOTA

WISCONSIN

MICHIGAN

ME.

VT.

N.H.

NEW YORK

MASS.

R.I.

CONN.

NEVADA

UTAH TERRITORY

COLORADO

NEBRASKA

IOWA

ILLINOIS

IND.

OHIO

PENNSYLVANIA

N.J.

MD.

DEL.

CALIFORNIA

KANSAS

CHEROKEE OUTLET

MISSOURI

KENTUCKY

W.VA.

VIRGINIA

NORTH CAROLINA

ARIZONA TERRITORY

NEW MEXICO TERRITORY

OK. TERR.

INDIAN TERR.

ARKANSAS

TENNESSEE

SOUTH CAROLINA

TEXAS

MISS.

ALABAMA

GEORGIA

LOUISIANA

FLORIDA

PACIFIC OCEAN

ATLANTIC OCEAN

MEXICO

Gulf of Mexico

States consistently voting Republican, 1876–1888
States voting Republican 3 times out of 4
States voting Republican 2 times, Democratic 2 times
States voting Democratic 3 times out of 4
States consistently voting Democratic
Territories, 1876–1888

0   200   400 Km.
0   200   400 Mi.

Civil War ends

Grange formed

Crédit Mobilier scandal

Reconstruction ends

Pendleton Act

Populist movement begins

Nationwide depression begins

McKinley elected

Gold Standard Act

1865   1867   1872   1877   1883   1890   1893   1896   1900

1850   1900   1950   2000

Political Stalemate and Political Upheaval, 1868–1900

Parties, Voters, and Reformers

- What were people's expectations about the role of parties in the politics of the Gilded Age?
- What choices did the political parties offer voters?

Political Stalemate

- How did the stalemate that deadlocked politics from 1874 into the 1890s constrain both parties?

Agricultural Distress and Political Upheaval

- Why did farmers choose to take political action outside the major parties?

- What did they expect to accomplish?
- What was the immediate outcome of their choices?

Economic Collapse and Political Upheaval

- What choices did voters face in the 1896 presidential election?
- What were the long-term outcomes of that election?

INTRODUCTION

E xpectations
C onstraints
C hoices
O utcomes

In July 1892, a new political party, the People's party, met in Omaha to *choose* its candidates for president and vice president. The new party, also called the Populists, contended that the *outcome* of industrialization had been material and moral ruin, political corruption, and exploited labor. The Populists also proclaimed their *choices* for dealing with the *outcome* of industrialization. They urged immediate federal action to rescue debtors, break up monopolies, and bring railroads under government ownership. They proposed reforms to increase the power of voters to control the government. And they made clear the *expected outcome* of these changes: that "oppression, injustice, and poverty shall eventually cease in the land."

Most Americans, however, held different *expectations* from the Populists. Most were unwilling to create a vastly more powerful federal government, to place severe *constraints* on the rights of property owners, or to entrust the federal government to self-proclaimed representatives of impoverished farmers and angry workers. In the end, the Populists failed to establish their new party as a major factor in American politics. The *outcome* of their efforts, however, was significant change in the nature of politics in the 1890s—and in the twentieth century as well.

Although most Americans rejected the Populists' remedies, few doubted that there had been a profound transformation of the nation's social and economic life following the Civil War. Congress and the president had grappled with complex *choices* affecting the South and Reconstruction, the future of American Indians, and the role of the federal government in developing the West. But a protracted stalemate gripped national politics from 1875 to 1896, *constraining* those who advocated political changes that would address the issues created by rapid social and economic change.

Throughout those years, men were *expected* to hold intense party loyalties. (Nearly all women were *constrained* from voting throughout this period.) Despite such *expectations*, a few people *chose* to break with the major parties to call for changes in policies or in the nature of politics. Prominent among those demanding change were advocates of woman suffrage. A succession of organizations and parties also spoke out for impoverished farmers and tried, largely unsuccessfully, to forge an alliance among all the disadvantaged—rural and urban, black and white.

The Populist party was the *outcome* of a quarter-century of agrarian radicalism that was fueled by the economic misfortunes of farmers. Eventually, the Populists *chose* to merge with the Democrats in support of the presidential candidacy of William Jennings Bryan in 1896. In the process, the Democratic party shed its deep commitment to minimal government and embraced a more activist role for the government in the economy. In 1896, however, voters *chose* William McKinley, the Republican candidate for president, thereby endorsing a more conservative approach to government. The long-term *outcome*, however, was the transformation of the very nature of American politics.

CHRONOLOGY

Politics

1865	End of the Civil War
1867	First Grange
1868	Grant elected president
1869	National Woman Suffrage Association formed Wyoming Territory adopts woman suffrage
1870	Utah Territory adopts woman suffrage
1872	Crédit Mobilier scandal Grant reelected
1872–1874	Granger laws
1875	Whiskey Ring scandal
mid-1870s	Grange membership peaks
1877	Reconstruction ends *Munn v. Illinois*
1878	Greenback party peaks Bland-Allison Act
1880	Garfield elected president
1881	Garfield assassinated; Arthur becomes president
1883	Pendleton Act
1884	Cleveland elected president
1886	*Wabash Railway v. Illinois*
1887	Congress disfranchises women in Utah Territory Interstate Commerce Act
1880s	Farmers' Alliances spread
1888	Harrison elected president

1888–1892	Australian ballot adopted
1890	Wyoming becomes a state, with woman suffrage Idaho becomes a state McKinley Tariff, Sherman Anti-Trust Act, and Sherman Silver Purchase Act "Force Bill" defeated Populist movement begins
1892	Homestead strike Cleveland elected president
1893	Colorado adopts woman suffrage Nationwide depression Sherman Silver Purchase Act repealed
1894	Coxey's Army Wilson-Gorman Tariff
1895	Morgan stabilizes gold reserve
1896	Utah becomes a state, with woman suffrage Bryan's "Cross of Gold" speech McKinley elected president Idaho adopts woman suffrage
1897	Dingley Tariff
1900	Gold Standard Act

Parties, Voters, and Reformers

Political parties dominated nearly every aspect of the political process from the 1830s until the early 1900s. During those years, Americans expected all meaningful political choices to come through parties. An understanding of politics therefore must begin with an analysis of political parties: what they were, what they did, what they stood for, and what choices they offered to voters.

Republicans and Democrats

Important differences characterized the two parties in their campaign arguments, their actions at state and local levels, and the voters who supported them. Some of those differences appear in the ways the two parties described themselves in their platforms, newspapers, speeches, and other campaign appeals.

Republicans asserted a virtual monopoly on patriotism by pointing to their defense of the Union during the Civil War. They claimed that Democrats had proved themselves disloyal during the conflict. "Every man that shot a Union soldier," one Republican orator proclaimed, "was a Democrat." Republicans exploited the Civil War legacy in other ways too. Republicans in Congress voted generous federal pensions to disabled Union army veterans and to the widows and orphans of those who died. Republican party leaders urged the **Grand Army of the Republic (GAR),** the organization of Union veterans, to "vote as you shot." Republican candidates were frequently Union veterans.

Prosperity formed another persistent Republican campaign theme. Republicans boasted that the economic growth of the postwar era stemmed from their wise policies. They accused the Democrats of endangering prosperity by pledging to reduce the protective tariff. Republicans also claimed to be the party of decency and respectability. Republican campaigners delighted in portraying Democrats as "the old slave-owner and slave-driver, the saloon-keeper, the ballot-box-stuffer, the Kuklux [Klan], the criminal class of the great cities, the men who cannot read or write."

Whereas Republicans defined themselves in terms of what their party did and who they were, Democrats typically explained what they opposed. Most leading Democrats stood firm against "governmental interference" in the economy, especially tariffs and land grants. The Republicans' protective tariff, Democrats claimed, protected manufacturers from international competition at the expense of consumers. Land grants should provide farms for citizens, not subsidies for railroads. Democrats favored a strictly limited role for the government in the economy. This commitment to minimal government went back to the days of Andrew Jackson, who equated governmental activism with privileges for a favored few.

Democrats also opposed governmental interference in social relations and behavior. In the North, especially in Irish and German communities, they condemned **prohibition,** which they called a violation of personal liberty. They defended Catholics against the political attacks of groups like the **American Protective Association (APA).** In the South, Democrats rejected federal enforcement of equal rights for African Americans.

Efforts to mobilize supporters on election day produced all-time records for voter participation. In 1876, more than 80 percent of the eligible voters cast their ballots. At the polling places, party workers distributed lists, or "tickets," of their party's candidates, which voters then used as ballots. Voting was not secret until the 1890s. Before then, everyone could see which party's ticket a voter deposited in the ballot box.

Most voters developed strong party loyalties on the basis of **ethnicity,** race, or religion. Nearly all

---

Grand Army of the Republic Organization of Union army veterans.

prohibition A legal ban on the manufacture, sale, and use of alcoholic beverages.

American Protective Association An anti-Catholic organization founded in Iowa in 1887 and active during the next decade.

ethnicity Ethnicity, or ethnic background, can include a shared racial, religious, linguistic, cultural, or national heritage.

Catholics and many Irish, German, and other immigrants supported the Democrats as the party that defended them against the APA, nativism, and prohibition. Poor voters in the disproportionately Catholic big cities usually supported the local Democratic machine. Most southern whites supported the Democrats as the party that opposed federal enforcement of black rights. After 1876, the Democrats dominated the South and found pockets of ethnic supporters throughout the North. They comprised a very diverse coalition.

Outside the South, most old-stock Protestants voted Republican, as did most Scandinavian and English immigrants. Most African Americans and former abolitionists supported the Republicans as the party of emancipation. Union veterans supported the Republicans overwhelmingly. Republicans did well in New England, Pennsylvania, much of the Midwest, and among Hispanic voters in the Southwest. The Republicans comprised a more coherent political organization than the Democrats. They agreed that the federal government should encourage economic growth and protect black rights. The Democrats opposed such measures. Neither party advocated government action to regulate, restrict, or tax the developing industrial corporations.

Parties and Patronage

The spoils system, or patronage system, played an important role in Gilded Age politics. Under this system, the winner of an election, whether a mayor or a president, rewarded his loyal followers with appointments to the many government jobs at his disposal. These patronage jobs were considered an appropriate reward for working hard for the candidate during the campaign. Everyone understood that those appointed to such jobs were expected to contribute part of their salaries to the party and to work for that party's candidates. Thus the existence of patronage jobs helped ensure a high voter turnout.

Competition for patronage jobs was always fierce. In 1869, Congressman James A. Garfield grumbled that all "the adult population of the United States" seemed involved in "the rush for office." When

Garfield himself became president in 1881, he was so overwhelmed with demands for jobs that he exclaimed in disgust, "My God! What is there in this place that a man should ever want to get into it?"

The government jobs most in demand involved purchasing supplies or handling government contracts. Purchasing and contracts themselves became another form of spoils, awarded to entrepreneurs who supported the party. This system invited corruption. In the 1890s, for example, a Post Office Department official pressured **postmasters** across the country to buy clocks from a political associate. Business owners competing for government contracts sometimes paid bribes to the officials who made the decisions.

Some critics charged that the fundamental defect of the politics of patronage was that it ignored principles and issues. George F. Hoar, a Republican congressman from Massachusetts, complained in 1876 that some of his colleagues believed that the only way to win power was "to bribe the people with the offices" and that these politicians used power primarily for "promotion of selfish ambition." The spoils system did have its defenders. Tammany Hall politician George Plunkitt explained, "You can't keep an organization together without patronage. Men ain't in politics for nothin'. They want to get somethin' out of it."

The most persistent critics of the spoils systems were known as the **Mugwumps.** Centered in Boston and New York, these reformers were largely Republicans who enjoyed high social status. Mugwumps argued that eliminating patronage would drive out the machines and opportunists and restore political decency. Instead of basing appointments on political loyalty, the Mugwumps advocated a **merit system**

---

postmaster An official appointed to oversee the operations of a local post office.

Mugwumps A group of Republicans who opposed political corruption and campaigned for reform in the 1880s and 1890s, sometimes crossing party boundaries to achieve their goals.

merit system Practice of hiring government workers based on their abilities and their scores on competency tests instead of through patronage.

◆ This sketch of women voting in Cheyenne, Wyoming Territory, appeared in 1888. In 1869, Wyoming became the first state or territory to extend suffrage to women. This drawing apppeared shortly before Wyoming requested statehood, a request made controversial by the issue of woman suffrage. *Library of Congress.*

based on a job seeker's ability to pass a comprehensive examination. Educated, dedicated civil servants, they believed, would stand above party politics and provide capable, honest administration. Because the Mugwumps sometimes broke with their party, they drew the contempt of most party politicians.

Challenging the Male Bastion: Woman Suffrage

In the late nineteenth century, some bold women accelerated the efforts to secure the right to vote

for women. The struggle for woman suffrage was of long standing. In 1848, Elizabeth Cady Stanton and four other women had organized the world's first Women's Rights Convention, held at Seneca Falls, New York. Stanton was the most prominent leader in the struggle for women's rights, especially voting rights, until her death in 1902. After 1851, Susan B. Anthony became her constant partner in these efforts. They achieved important successes in convincing lawmakers to modify laws that discriminated against women, but all their labor could not change the laws that limited voting to men.

In 1869, Stanton and Anthony formed the **National Woman Suffrage Association (NWSA).** The NWSA sought a constitutional amendment to secure woman suffrage. They built alliances with other reform organizations and worked to improve women's status. For example, members pressed for easier divorce laws and birth control (which Stanton called "self-sovereignty") and promoted women's unions. The major support for the NWSA came from middle-class women—and some men— who were of old-stock American Protestant descent.

The first victories for woman suffrage came in the West. In 1869, the Wyoming territorial legislature extended the **franchise** to women. This action may have been intended to attract women to Wyoming, which had many more males than females. In 1889, when Wyoming asked for statehood, many congressmen balked at admitting a state that permitted women to vote. Congress ultimately relented and approved Wyoming statehood in 1890. In 1893, Colorado became the first state to adopt woman suffrage through a popular vote.

National Woman Suffrage Association   New York–based woman-suffrage organization led by Elizabeth Cady Stanton and Susan B. Anthony; it accepted only women as members and worked for related issues such as unionizing female workers.

franchise   The right to vote; another word for *suffrage.*

The Utah Territory adopted woman suffrage in 1870. This action strengthened the Mormons' political power, because Mormon women greatly outnumbered non-Mormon women. The Mormons also may have hoped to silence critics who claimed that polygamy degraded women. In an act aimed primarily at the Mormons, Congress outlawed polygamy in 1887 and disfranchised the women in the Utah Territory at the same time. Not until Utah became a state in 1896 did Utah women regain the vote. Neighboring Idaho also adopted woman suffrage in 1896.

Several states began to permit women limited voting rights, especially on matters usually outside party politics, such as school board elections and school bond issues. These concessions reflected the widespread assumption that women's gender roles included child rearing. By 1890, women could vote in school elections in nineteen states and on bond and tax issues in three. But no state passed a suffrage proposal between 1896 and 1910.

Structural Change and Policy Change

The Mugwumps and advocates of woman suffrage were only two of the many groups that identified issues seldom addressed by the two major parties: prohibition, the secret ballot, an end to child labor, and the regulation of business, among others. Most of the reforms these groups called for fall into two categories. *Structural reform* refers to efforts to change the manner in which political decisions are made. Structural issues include the way in which public officials are chosen and eligibility to vote. Thus the Mugwumps and woman suffragettes both advocated structural change. *Policy reform,* by contrast, refers to changes in the way government uses its power. The debate over federal economic policy in the Gilded Age provides an array of contrasting positions. Democrats typically favored laissez faire, believing that federal interference in the economy created a privileged class. Republicans believed in distributing economic benefits to companies and individuals (land, tariff protection) to encourage economic growth. The Grangers (discussed on page 420) wanted federal regulation of corporations.

Although many reform groups had little in common with each other, some formed alliances. The tiny Prohibition party, for example, wanted government to eliminate alcohol, but it also favored woman suffrage because it assumed most women voters would oppose alcohol.

Many political groups supported one important structural change: the **Australian ballot,** which was printed and distributed by the government, not political parties, and marked by voters in the privacy of an enclosed booth. Use of the secret ballot spread rapidly after its introduction in the late 1880s. By 1892, most states had adopted it. This reform had important implications for political parties. It enabled voters to cross party lines and vote a **split ticket.** It also prevented party officials from seeing how a voter cast his ballot. The adoption of the secret ballot and the merit system marked the first significant efforts to limit parties' power and influence.

Political Stalemate

A political stalemate made it difficult for either party to put through major changes in federal policy between 1875 and 1896. Instead, politics often revolved around scandal and spoils rather than issues of policy. When the Republicans briefly broke the stalemate in 1889 and 1890, they found themselves rejected by the voters.

Formula for Stalemate

Competition between Republicans and Democrats at a national level was very close from 1874 to 1896. In the elections of 1880, 1884, and 1888, New York State cast its electoral votes for the winning

---

Australian ballot   A method of voting adopted from Australia, in which the voter's choices of candidates are secret.

split ticket   A ballot cast by an individual who has voted for candidates of more than one political party.

candidate. Had it voted for the other candidate, he would have won. Thus a different choice by one or two voters out of every hundred in New York would have changed the result of the national election.

Although most presidential elections during these decades were very close, the Republicans usually won. The Democrats carried only two of the eleven presidential elections between 1860 and 1900. However, from 1877 until 1895, the two parties had nearly equal numbers in the Senate and House of Representatives. The Democrats usually held a slim majority in the House, and the Republicans usually held a similar margin in the Senate. Thus the Republican Senate could block any proposal by a Democratic president, and the Democratic House could block any proposal by a Republican president.

Other factors also made significant changes in policy unlikely. The struggle between Andrew Johnson and the congressional radicals had tipped the balance of power from the presidency to the Congress. Johnson's successors did little to challenge that dominance. Also, both parties held attitudes toward the presidency that made it improbable that a president would seek a leadership role in policy. In the words of John Sherman, a highly influential Republican, the executive "should be subordinate to the legislative department." Virtually no one expected the president to be a major policy initiator, and no president was.

The Grant Administration: Spoils and Scandals

The dogged determination that made Ulysses S. Grant a winning general failed to make him even a satisfactory president. Grant never grasped the potential for presidential leadership. Congress had taken control of domestic policymaking during Andrew Johnson's troubled presidency, and Grant accepted that situation.

Although Grant himself was not involved, his two terms in office (1869–1877) were mired in scandal. Grant all too often named friends or acquaintances to federal posts for which they were unqualified. Many of them saw their positions as little

more than a way to enrich themselves. The **Whiskey Ring** provides a prime example. This "ring" of federal officials and distillers, centered in St. Louis, had conspired to evade paying whiskey taxes. In 1875, Treasury Secretary Benjamin Bristow had 230 men indicted for this offense. The indictment included several of Grant's appointees and even his private secretary. Despite the evidence, Grant could not believe his close associates were guilty. He helped his secretary avoid conviction and forced Bristow to resign.

Congress also supplied its share of scandal. In 1868, several prominent congressional leaders had become stockholders in the **Crédit Mobilier,** a construction company created by the chief shareholders in the Union Pacific Railroad. The Union Pacific officers awarded Crédit Mobilier a very generous contract to build the railroad. Thus the company's chief shareholders paid themselves handsomely for constructing their own railroad. To protect this arrangement from congressional scrutiny, the company sold shares cheaply to key members of Congress. Purchasers included many leading Republicans, two of whom later became vice president. Revelation of these arrangements in 1872 and 1873 scandalized the nation.

Hayes, Garfield, and Arthur: The Politics of Faction

Repeated exposures of corruption led Republicans in 1876 to nominate **Rutherford B. Hayes,** whose

---

Whiskey Ring   Distillers and revenue officials in St. Louis who were revealed in 1875 to have defrauded the government of millions of dollars in whiskey taxes, with the collusion of federal officials.

Crédit Mobilier   Company created to build the Union Pacific Railroad. It sold shares cheaply to congressmen who approved federal subsidies for railroad construction. The scandalous deal was uncovered in 1872–1873.

Rutherford B. Hayes   Reform governor of Ohio who was elected president in 1876 on the Republican ticket.

reputation was unblemished. Hayes helped restore the reputation of the Republican party after the scandals of the Grant administration. In Congress, however, Hayes found few allies when he tried to modify the patronage system. He did not seek re-election in 1880.

The Republicans were badly divided that year. James G. Blaine of Maine, a powerful leader of one Republican faction, sought the presidential nomination. Roscoe Conkling of New York, the leader of the other faction, the **Stalwarts,** promoted the candidacy of former president Grant. The convention ultimately compromised on **James A. Garfield,** a Civil War general and an able congressman from Ohio. The Democrats nominated Winfield Scott Hancock, a distinguished Civil War general. The campaign dealt less with policy issues than with Garfield's minor role in the Crédit Mobilier scandal and with Hancock's Catholic wife. Garfield won by a tiny margin, 48.5 percent to 48.0 percent.

On July 2, 1881, four months after taking office, Garfield was shot by Charles Guiteau, who was mentally unstable. Garfield died in September. Vice President Chester A. Arthur then assumed the presidency. Defying his previous reputation as a loyal Stalwart, Arthur proved that the presidential office can improve the stature of its occupant. He prosecuted Stalwarts involved in post office corruption and even suggested that Congress should reform the spoils system. This suggestion bore fruit in 1883, when Congress passed the **Pendleton Act,** as civil service reformers took advantage of the widespread but false belief that Guiteau was a disappointed office seeker. The act established the merit system for government employment. Competitive examinations became the basis for appointment to **classified positions,** which were removed from the patronage system.

Initially, only 15 percent of federal positions were classified, but the law authorized the president to add positions to the list. The person who held an office when it was first classified was protected from removal on political grounds, so presidents used the law to protect their own patronage appointees. Once those people retired, however, their replacements came through the merit system. In this way, positions were gradually withdrawn from the patronage system. By 1901, the law ap-plied to 44 percent of federal employees. The Pendleton Act laid the basis for the current civil service system.

Cleveland and the Democrats

Because of his failing health, Arthur exerted little effort to win his party's nomination in 1884, allowing Blaine to capture it. The Democrats nominated Grover Cleveland, the governor of New York State, who had earned a reputation for integrity and political courage by attacking Tammany Hall. Tammany voters—many of them Irish—therefore disliked Cleveland.

The campaign quickly turned nasty. Many Mugwumps disliked Blaine and embarrassed him by revealing that he had profited from prorailroad legislation. Blaine supporters gleefully trumpeted the fact that Cleveland had avoided military service during the Civil War and had once fathered a child outside marriage. The election hinged on New York State, where Blaine expected to cut deeply into the usually Democratic Irish vote. A few days before the election, however, a Republican preacher in New York City called the Democrats the party of "rum, Romanism [Catholicism], and rebellion." Blaine ignored this insult to his Irish Catholic supporters until newspapers blasted it the next day. By then the damage was done. Cleveland won New York State by a tiny margin, and New York's electoral votes gave him the victory.

Cleveland was deeply committed to minimal government and to restraining spending. Between

---

Stalwart Faction of the Republican party led by Roscoe Conkling that was committed wholeheartedly to the spoils system.

James A. Garfield Ohio congressman who was chosen as a compromise candidate at the 1880 Republican convention, elected twentieth president of the United States, and shot to death only four months after taking office.

Pendleton Act Law passed in 1883 that created the Civil Service Commission and the merit system for government hiring and jobs.

classified position Government job filled through the merit system instead of by patronage.

1885 and 1889, he vetoed 414 bills, most of them granting pensions to individual Union veterans. This was twice as many vetoes as for all previous presidents combined. Cleveland provided little leadership but did approve the Dawes Severalty Act (see page 379) and the Interstate Commerce Act.

The Interstate Commerce Act grew out of political pressure from farmers and small businesses that led several states to regulate railroads. In 1871, Illinois had created a railroad and warehouse commission to set maximum rates. Iowa and Wisconsin passed laws regulating railroad freight rates in 1874. In 1877, in *Munn v. Illinois*, the Supreme Court held that businesses with "a public interest," including warehouses and railroads, "must submit to be controlled by the public for the common good." In *Wabash Railway v. Illinois* (1886), however, the Supreme Court put severe limits on the states' power to regulate railroad rates.

The *Wabash* decision prompted Congress in 1887 to pass the Interstate Commerce Act, which created the **Interstate Commerce Commission (ICC)**, the first federal regulatory commission. The law prohibited pools, rebates, and different rates for short and long hauls. The prohibitions proved to be largely unenforceable, however, because the law was vague and the ICC had little real power.

Cleveland considered the nation's greatest problem to be the persistent federal budget surplus. Throughout the 1880s, the surplus was often more than $100 million per year. Worried that the surplus encouraged wasteful spending, Cleveland demanded in 1887 that Congress cut tariff rates on raw materials and necessities. Cleveland's action provoked a serious division within his own party. The Democrats could not agree on a bill, and Congress adjourned without voting on the tariff.

In the 1888 presidential election, the Democrats renominated Cleveland. The Republicans nominated **Benjamin Harrison,** senator from Indiana and grandson of former president William Henry Harrison. The Republicans' campaign focused on the virtues of the protective tariff. They raised unprecedented amounts of campaign money by systematically approaching business leaders on the tariff issue. The Republicans also attacked Cleveland's vetoes of pensions for Union veterans.

Harrison won in the electoral voting but received fewer popular votes than Cleveland: 47.9 percent to Cleveland's 48.7 percent. The Republicans also secured majorities in both the House and Senate. In 1889, the Republicans stood poised to create new public policies.

Harrison: Ending the Stalemate?

The new Republican majority's first major task when Congress opened in 1889 was tariff reform. The Republicans wanted to cut the federal surplus without reducing protection. The **McKinley Tariff** of 1890 (named for the congressman chiefly responsible for it, William McKinley) moved some items to the free list (notably sugar, a major source of tariff revenue) but raised tariff rates prohibitively on other items. The House passed the McKinley Tariff in late May 1890 and sent it on to the Senate.

In July, the House approved the Federal Elections Bill, nicknamed the "Force Bill" by its Democratic opponents. The bill proposed federal supervision over congressional elections to prevent disfranchisement, fraud, and violence. The bill did not single out the South, but everyone knew that the South was its target. The measure passed the House and went to the Senate, where approval seemed likely.

Harrison wanted the tariff and election bills passed as a party package. Senate Republicans, however, feared that a Democratic filibuster against the election bill would prevent passage of either measure. Finally, the Republicans agreed to postpone the elections bill if the Democrats would not delay the tariff bill. Over the strong protests of a few New England Republicans, the rest of the

Interstate Commerce Commission Federal commission established in 1887 to oversee railroads.

Benjamin Harrison Indiana Republican senator elected president in 1888 on a platform of high protective tariffs.

McKinley Tariff Tariff law passed in 1890 that sought not only to protect established industries but also, by prohibitory duties, to create new industries; it soon became extremely unpopular.

party sacrificed African Americans' voting rights to gain the revised tariff. (Some seventy years would pass before Congress finally acted to protect black voting rights in the South.) By raising import duties, the McKinley Tariff soon reduced imports, tariff income, and the budgetary surplus.

Another significant law to emerge from the Republican Congress in 1890 was the **Sherman Anti-Trust Act.** Created in response to growing public concern about trusts and monopolies, the law declared that "every contract, combination in the form of trust or otherwise, or conspiracy, in restraint of trade or commerce among the several states, or with foreign nations, is hereby declared to be illegal." The United States thereby became the first industrial nation to regulate business combinations. But the law proved difficult to enforce. Since it did not define "trust," "conspiracy," or "restraint of trade," it was left to courts that were generally sympathetic to business to supply these definitions.

Republicans seemed to have broken the political logjam in 1889–1890. The McKinley Tariff and the Sherman Anti-Trust Act were among a record number of new laws. Other legislation included a major increase in pension eligibility for disabled Union army veterans, admission to statehood for Idaho and Wyoming, and appropriations that laid the basis for a modern navy.

Agricultural Distress and Political Upheaval

Curiously enough, the first strong winds of political change blew not in the industrial cities but in the farm communities of the Great Plains and the South and in the mining camps of the Rocky Mountain region. In the early 1890s, those regions witnessed the birth of a new political party, the People's party or **Populists.**

The Farmers' Complaints

During the Gilded Age, farmers became increasingly dependent on the national railroad network, on fertilizer and laborsaving equipment, on grain and cotton brokers, and on sources of credit in distant cities. At the same time, some began to feel increasingly helpless in the face of the great concentrations of economic power that seemed to be taking over their lives.

Farmers were most distressed by steadily declining crop prices after the Civil War. Many farmers argued that this decline in prices was not attributable to the fluctuations of supply and demand, but rather to the monopolistic practices of grain and cotton buyers. Most agricultural regions were served by only one buyer, who paid the prices set by **commodity markets** in Chicago and New York. Farmers had no choice but to accept the price that was offered. They needed cash to pay their debts. Farmers blamed commodity brokers for the fact that the bushel of corn they sold in Kansas for 10 cents in October brought three or four times that amount in New York in December.

The debts that farmers had contracted to expand production magnified the impact of falling prices. Suppose a farmer borrowed $1,000 for five years in 1881, when corn sold for 63 cents per bushel. The borrowed $1,000 would have been equivalent to 1,587 bushels of corn. In 1886, when the loan came due, corn sold for 36 cents per bushel, requiring 2,777 bushels to repay the $1,000. And this example does not take into account the interest on the loan. Further, the prices of most farm supplies did not fall as rapidly as crop prices. As a result, farmers raised more and more each

---

Sherman Anti-Trust Act   Law passed in 1890 authorizing the federal government to prosecute any "combination" "in restraint of trade"; because of adverse court rulings, it initially proved ineffective as a weapon against monopolies.

Populists   Members of the People's party, who held their first presidential nominating convention in 1892 and called for reforms such as the eight-hour workday, direct election of senators, and the secret ballot.

commodity market   Financial market in which brokers buy and sell agricultural products in large quantities, thus determining the prices paid to farmers for their harvests.

year just to pay their debts and buy necessities. The more they raised, the lower prices fell.

The railroads also angered farmers. The railroads, farmers claimed, were greedy monopolies that charged them as much as possible. It sometimes cost four times as much to ship freight in the West as in the East. Farmers also protested the railroads' dominance of state politics and distribution of free passes to all manner of politicians.

Crop prices and railroad practices were only two of the farmers' complaints. They protested that bankers charged much higher interest rates in the South and West than in the Northeast. They argued that federal monetary policies contributed to falling prices and thereby compounded their debts. Southern farmers, especially, condemned the tariff for creating artificially high prices on manufactured goods that farmers had to buy. Farmers complained as well that the corporations that made farm equipment and fertilizer overcharged them.

Grangers, Greenbackers, and Silverites

Following the Civil War, farmers joined organizations that they hoped would provide them some relief. Oliver H. Kelley formed the first, the Patrons of Husbandry, in 1867. Usually known as the **Grange,** the new organization included women as well as men. Kelley hoped that the Grange would provide a social outlet for farm families and also educate them about new agricultural methods. It far exceeded his expectations.

The Grange grew rapidly, especially in the Midwest and the central South. In the 1870s, it became a leading proponent of cooperative buying and selling. Many local Granges set up cooperative stores, and some even tried to sell their crops cooperatively. Grangers laid ambitious plans for cooperative factories producing everything from wagons to sewing machines. Some Grangers formed mutual insurance companies, and a few experimented with cooperative banks.

Although the Grange was initially nonpartisan, its membership began talking about political action in the 1870s. "Granger parties" emerged in

eleven states. Their most prominent demand was state legislation to prohibit railroad rate discrimination. The resulting state laws were called **Granger laws.**

The Grange reached its zenith in the mid-1870s. Hastily organized cooperatives then began to suffer financial problems because of the nationwide depression. The collapse of cooperatives often pulled down Grange organizations. Political activity brought some successes but also generated bitter disputes within the Granges. The surviving Granges usually avoided cooperatives and politics.

With the decline of the Grange in the late 1870s, some farmers looked to monetary policy for relief. Following the Civil War, the money supply did not grow as rapidly as the economy. The Greenback party argued that the supply of money should be increased through printing more **greenbacks,** the paper money issued during the Civil War. More money in circulation, they believed, would raise prices.

Greenbackers found their most receptive audience among farmers who were in debt. In the congressional elections of 1878, the Greenback party received nearly a million votes and elected fourteen congressmen. However, it proved unsuccessful in attracting votes nationwide. In the 1880 presidential election, the Greenback party endorsed not only inflation but also the eight-hour workday, legislation to protect workers, the abolition of child labor, regulation of transportation, a **graduated income tax,** and woman suffrage. For president, they nominated James B. Weaver of Iowa, a former

---

Grange Farmers' organization that combined social activities with education on new methods of farming and cooperative economic efforts; officially, known as the Patrons of Husbandry.

Granger laws State laws establishing standard freight and passenger rates on railroads passed because of the lobbying of the Grange.

greenbacks Paper money, not backed by gold, that the federal government issued during the Civil War.

graduated income tax Percentage tax levied on income that varies with income. People who earn more money pay a higher tax rate.

Union general. Weaver got only 3.3 percent of the vote. In 1884, the Greenbackers fared even worse.

A similar monetary analysis motivated those who wanted the government to resume issuing silver dollars. Until 1873, federal mints had accepted gold and silver in unlimited quantities and made them into coins at virtually no charge. Throughout most of the nineteenth century, however, owners of silver made more money selling it commercially than taking it to the mint. Hence, no silver dollars existed for many years. In 1873, Congress dropped the silver dollar from the list of approved coins. Thus the United States joined Britain and Germany on the **gold standard.**

Soon after 1873, silver discoveries in Nevada and elsewhere drove down the price of silver. The rallying cry of farmers and silver miners became "**Free silver** at 16 to 1." This meant that both silver and gold would be coined into dollars in unlimited quantities and that a silver dollar would weigh sixteen times as much as a gold dollar. In 1878, Congress passed the **Bland-Allison Act,** authorizing a limited amount of silver dollars. However, it was not enough to counteract **deflation.** The Sherman Silver Purchase Act of 1890 increased the amount of silver to be purchased and appeased western Republicans, but it did not require free coinage of silver. It satisfied neither silverites nor advocates of the gold standard.

Birth of the People's Party

In the 1880s, three organizations emerged to fill the vacuum left by the Grange's decline. All were called **Farmers' Alliances.** One was centered in the north-central states. Another, the Southern Alliance, began in Texas and spread eastward across the South. Because its membership was limited to white farmers, a third Alliance, the Colored Farmers' Alliance, was formed for black farmers in the South. Like the Grange, the Alliances looked to cooperatives as a partial solution to their problems. The Texas Alliance experimented with cooperative cotton selling, and some midwestern local Alliances built cooperative **grain elevators.**

The alliances worked initially within the framework of the major parties. This was especially im-

portant in the South, where any white person who challenged the Democratic party ran the risk of being viewed as a traitor to both race and region. Not until 1890 did widespread farmer support materialize for independent political action in the Midwest. Corn prices had fallen so low by then that some farmers found it cheaper to burn their corn than to buy fuel.

During the summer of 1890, members of the Farmers' Alliance in Kansas, Nebraska, the Dakotas, Minnesota, and surrounding states formed new political parties to contest state and local elections. One leader explained that the political battle they waged was "between the insatiable greed of organized wealth and the rights of the great plain people." Organization of the new party launched a decade of dramatic political change.

The Populist party was launched by parades of farm wagons passing down the hot, dusty main streets of scores of country towns. The festivities ended with a picnic and rally, where speakers decried the plight of the farmer and proclaimed the sacred cause of the new party. Women played a prominent part in Populist campaigning. Mary Elizabeth Lease of Kansas was widely quoted in newspapers as urging farmers to "raise less corn and more hell!"

When the Populists organized a national party in 1892, they emphasized three themes: antimonopolism, government action on behalf of farmers and

---

gold standard A monetary system based on gold.

free silver The proposal to allow the coinage of all available silver to supplement gold as currency; repeatedly suggested as a solution to the nation's economic troubles.

Bland-Allison Act Law passed in 1878 providing for federal purchase of silver to be coined into silver dollars.

deflation Falling prices, a situation in which the purchasing power of the dollar increases.

Farmers' Alliances Agricultural organizations of the 1880s and 1890s that carried forward the agrarian cause after the decline of the Grange.

grain elevator Storehouse usually located near railroad tracks where farmers stored grain prior to shipping.

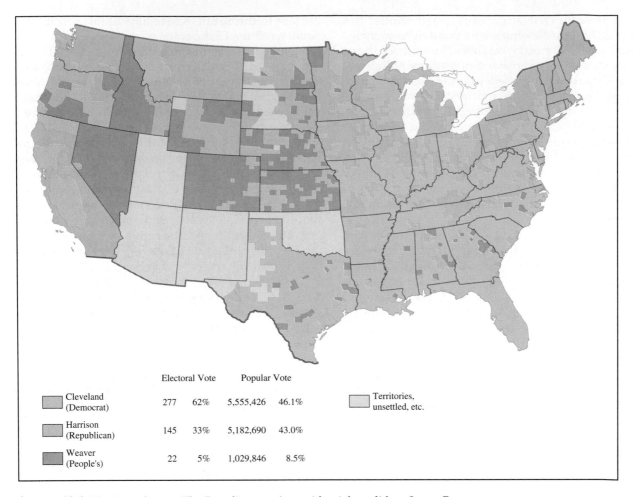

	Electoral Vote		Popular Vote	
Cleveland (Democrat)	277	62%	5,555,426	46.1%
Harrison (Republican)	145	33%	5,182,690	43.0%
Weaver (People's)	22	5%	1,029,846	8.5%

Territories, unsettled, etc.

◆ **MAP 19.1 Election of 1892**   The Populist party's presidential candidate, James B. Weaver, made a strong showing in 1892. This map indicates that his support was concentrated regionally in the West and South and that he had relatively little support in the northeastern states.

workers, and increased popular control of government. Their antimonopolism drew on their own unhappy experiences with railroads, grain buyers, and farm equipment companies. But it derived as well from a long American tradition of opposition to concentrated economic power. Populists often compared themselves to Andrew Jackson in his fight against the Bank of the United States.

The Populists' solution to the dangers of monopoly was government action on behalf of farmers and workers. They proposed federal ownership of the railroads and the telegraph and telephone systems, and government alternatives to private banks. "We believe the time has come," Populists proclaimed in 1892, "when the railroad companies will either own the people or the people must own the railroads." They also demanded inflation (through greenbacks or silver) and a graduated income tax to replace the tariff. They hoped to gain broad support among urban and industrial workers. Their platform called for the eight-hour day for workers and the prohibition of private armies like the one used against the Homestead strikers (see page 358). Some Populists also advocated a proposal called the Sub-Treasury Plan, under which crops stored in government warehouses might be collateral for low-interest loans to farmers.

Finally, the People's party favored a series of changes to make government more responsive to the people: expansion of the merit system for government employees, election of U.S. senators by direct ballot instead of by state legislatures, a one-term limit for the president, the **secret ballot,** and the **initiative** and **referendum.** Many Populists also favored woman suffrage. In the South, they posed a serious challenge to the prevailing politics by seeking to forge a political alliance of the disadvantaged of both races. Thus the Populists wanted to use government to control, even to own, the corporate behemoths that had evolved in their lifetimes, and they wanted to increase the influence of the individual voter in political decision making.

The Elections of 1890 and 1892

The issues in the 1890 elections varied by region. In the West, the Populists lambasted both major parties for ignoring the needs of the people. In the South, Democrats held up the Force Bill as a symbol of the dangers posed by abandoning the party of white supremacy. There the Farmers' Alliance worked within the Democratic party to secure favorable candidates. In the Northeast, Democrats attacked the McKinley Tariff for producing higher consumer prices. In the Rocky Mountain region, nearly all candidates pledged their support for unlimited silver coinage.

The Populists became the most successful new party since the appearance of the Republicans in the 1850s. Populists elected state legislators, representatives in the House of Representatives, and two U.S. senators. Across the South, the Alliance claimed that Democratic candidates owed their victories to its voters. Democrats captured congressional seats across the Midwest and made some gains elsewhere as well. Everywhere, Republicans suffered defeat. In the House of Representatives, the Republicans went from 166 seats in 1889 to only 88 in 1891.

The Republicans renominated Harrison in 1892, but without enthusiasm. The Democrats chose Grover Cleveland as their candidate. The southern Farmers' Alliance joined western Populists to form a national People's party and to nominate James Weaver, the former Greenbacker, for president. Democrats and Populists again earned impressive victories. Cleveland secured 46.1 percent of the popular vote, Harrison 43.0 percent, and Weaver 8.5 percent (see Map 19.1). The Democrats kept control of the House of Representatives and, for the first time in twelve years, also won the Senate. Despite their weak showing nationally, Populist candidates displayed strength in the West and South. The Democrats now found themselves fully able to translate their campaign promises into law.

Economic Collapse and Political Upheaval

After the Democrats swept to power in the 1892 elections, they suddenly faced difficult choices. Could they fulfill their campaign promises for tariff reform? Could they also halt the collapse of the national economy?

Economic Collapse and Depression

Ten days before Cleveland took office, the Reading Railroad declared bankruptcy. A financial panic soon set in as other companies followed it

> **secret ballot** Voting methods in which individual votes are marked in private, so no one knows how an individual is voting.
>
> **initiative** Procedure allowing any group of people to propose a law by gathering signatures on a petition; the proposed law is then voted on by the electorate.
>
> **referendum** Procedure whereby a bill or constitutional amendment is submitted to the voters for their approval after having been passed by a legislative body.

Choosing Principle over Party

Grover Cleveland

President Grover Cleveland, confronted with a shattered economy, had to choose between his conservative principles and maintaining the unity of his party. Portrait Grover Cleveland by Anders Zorn. National Portrait Gallery, Smithsonian Institution / Art Resource, N.Y.

Grover Cleveland took the presidential oath of office for the second time on March 4, 1893. Soon after, he faced a series of choices so difficult that he had every reason to expect intense criticism no matter what choice he made or what outcome resulted. He could not escape from making the choices, either, for he was afraid that the economic collapse that had begun shortly before he took office might threaten even the federal government itself.

Like many in his day, Cleveland held a traditional expectation about money. Because money must have intrinsic value, he contended, only precious metals could serve as money. In 1885, during his first term as president, he urged Congress to repeal the silver coinage act passed in 1878, on the grounds that the United States could not, by itself, maintain both gold and silver as money. To attempt to do so, Cleveland feared, would inevitably mean that gold would leave the country. Congress, however, refused to follow his advice in 1885.

When Cleveland's first presidency ended in 1889, the government's gold reserves stood at $197 million. When he took office again in 1893, it seemed that his earlier fears were coming

into bankruptcy. More than fifteen thousand businesses failed in 1893, more than in any previous year.

At the time, no one really understood why the economy collapsed so suddenly. The collapse began when the failure of a major English bank led some British investors to recall their investments in the United States. This recall, combined with the

reduction in revenues caused by the McKinley Tariff, resulted in a sharp decline in federal **gold reserves.** Fears about low gold reserves and bank-

gold reserves   The stockpile of gold with which the federal government backs up the currency.

true, for the gold reserves had fallen to $103.5 million. This was dangerously close to the $100 million mark that Congress had earlier fixed as the point below which the nation might not be able to maintain the gold standard. The decline in gold reserves was in part the result of cuts in tariff revenues and greatly increased federal expenditures approved by the Republican Congress of 1889–1890. Another factor was widespread anxiety about the economy. Uncertain about the future, many investors chose to liquidate their holdings in return for gold. The shrinking gold reserves alarmed Cleveland.

Because so many business and financial leaders shared the expectation that money must have intrinsic value, they argued that silver coinage (authorized under the Sherman Silver Purchase Act) was dishonest, because it required that silver worth only 53 cents on the open market be made into a dollar coin. The president was pressured from one side by bankers and manufacturers eager to end silver coinage and to restore the gold reserve, and from the other side by members of his own party hostile to banking interests and favorable to silver coinage. Cleveland thus faced a difficult choice. Should he do what he believed to be necessary to maintain the nation's financial integrity? Or should he compromise and thereby preserve the unity of the Democratic party and his own political popularity?

In the midst of these pressures and counterpressures, Cleveland demonstrated his courage when he underwent surgery to remove a cancer from the roof of his mouth and kept his illness secret. Seriously weakened by the surgery and uncertain that he was out of danger, Cleveland labored over a message to a special session of Congress. In his message, he made his choice clear: he asked Congress to repeal the Sherman Silver Purchase Act, knowing his action would divide his own party and bring upon him an avalanche of criticism.

The battle in Congress over repeal of the Sherman Silver Purchase Act was hard fought. Cleveland at times felt depressed about the prospects for success, once writing that "if I did not believe in God I should be sick at heart." But he stubbornly refused all efforts at compromise, and took comfort in the knowledge that he was following his sense of integrity and duty. "I think so often of Martin Luther's 'Here I stand—God help me,'" he told a friend.

The immediate outcome was that Cleveland won in Congress, with the assistance of most Republicans and some Democrats, including some who had previously opposed him. Another outcome was that Cleveland confirmed his personal reputation for integrity, courage, and stubbornness. But the most far-reaching outcome was that the president had splintered the Democratic party and doomed any hopes he may have had for leading it.

ruptcies precipitated a stock market crash in May 1893, which brought on the depression.

Major underlying factors included the end of agricultural expansion and railroad construction. A slow agricultural economy before 1893 produced a decline in sales of farm machinery and, hence, steel. More important were the railroads. Railroad building drove the industrial economy in the 1880s. In the 1890s, however, a number of large lines declared bankruptcy, including the Erie, Northern Pacific, Santa Fe, and Union Pacific. Railroad construction fell by half between 1893 and 1895. The sharp decline in railroad construction produced a domino effect. Production of steel rails fell by more than a third between 1892 and 1894. Thirty-two steel companies closed down as a result. Banks that had invested in railroads and steel companies then collapsed. Nearly five hundred banks failed just in 1893.

These business failures threw at least a third of the wage earners in manufacturing out of work. During the winter of 1893–1894, Chicago counted 100,000 unemployed—roughly two workers out of five. Crowds swarmed at factory gates in response to a rumor that the plant was hiring. Many who kept their jobs received smaller paychecks, as employers cut wages and hours. In 1892, the average nonfarm wage earner received $482 per year. By 1894, this fell to $420.

The depression produced widespread suffering. Many who lost their jobs had little to fall back on except the soup dispensed by charities. Newspapers told of people who committed suicide when faced with starving to death or stealing food. Many men and some women left home desperate to find work. Some walked the roads, but most hopped freight trains. A few found work, but most failed. Some families were never reunited. Those who kept their jobs and homes could not escape the pitiful sight of jobless, homeless men and women walking the streets.

A dramatic demonstration against unemployment began in late January 1894, when Ohio Populist Jacob S. Coxey proposed that the government hire the unemployed to build roads and repair public works. The response to Coxey's call for the unemployed to join him in a march on Washington was electric. All across the country, hundreds of men and a few women tried to join the march. Western groups hijacked some fifty trains and headed east pulling boxcars loaded with unemployed men. (None of the pirated trains traveled far before authorities stopped them and arrested the leaders.) Several thousand people took part in Coxey's march in some way, but most never reached Washington.

When Coxey and his group of several hundred arrived in Washington, he was not permitted to speak at the Capitol. When he tried to do so on May 1, police arrested him for trespassing and dispersed the crowd. The trek of **Coxey's Army** marked the first time that so many protesters had gone to Washington to urge the government to create jobs for the unemployed.

The Divided Democrats

When Congress met in 1893, the majority Democrats faced several divisive issues. Their platform called for cutting the tariff, but the party disagreed over how to do that. The party was also divided over the **Sherman Silver Purchase Act.** Many business leaders believed that the act had caused the depression, but western and southern Democrats disagreed. In addition, the depression and unemployment demanded attention. President Cleveland held to his staunch beliefs in minimal government and **laissez faire.**

Convinced that silver coinage had contributed to the economic collapse, Cleveland asked Congress to repeal the Sherman Act (see Individual Choices: Grover Cleveland). Cleveland won, but at the cost of pitting the northeastern branch of his party against the West and much of the South. This division persisted for the remainder of his term. It plagued discussions of the tariff. The Wilson-Gorman Tariff of 1894 was riddled with so many provisions for special interests that Cleveland refused to sign it. The bill became law without his signature.

In the 1894 elections, voters turned decisively to the Republicans, as the disorganized Democrats lost everywhere but in the Deep South. The Republicans scored their biggest gain in Congress ever, adding 117 seats. The Populists lost support even in their previous strongholds.

To Cleveland's regret, the end of silver purchases did not stop the flow of gold from the treasury. Investors responded to continuing economic uncertainties by converting their securities to gold. Government gold reserves fell dangerously low. In desperation, Cleveland turned for assistance to

Coxey's Army   Unemployed workers led by Jacob S. Coxey who marched to Washington to demand relief measures from Congress following the Panic of 1893.

Sherman Silver Purchase Act   Law passed in 1890 requiring the federal government to increase its purchases of silver.

laissez faire   An economic doctrine under which the free-enterprise system operates with little government interference.

♦ In 1896, William Jennings Bryan (left), candidate of the Democratic, Populist, and Silver Republican parties, traveled some eighteen thousand miles in three months, speaking to about five million people. William McKinley (right), the Republican, stayed home in Canton, Ohio, greeting thousands of well-wishers. *Bryan: Nebraska State Historical Society; McKinley: Ohio Historical Society.*

J. P. Morgan, the symbol of Wall Street and the trusts. Morgan agreed in 1895 to take charge of a bond issue that stabilized the gold reserve, but Cleveland came under heavy criticism for consulting Morgan and for the price that Morgan charged.

The 1896 Election: Bryan Versus McKinley, Silver Versus Protection

In 1896, **William McKinley** garnered the Republican nomination for president. A former Ohio congressman and governor, McKinley billed himself as the "Advance Agent of Prosperity." Although the Republican platform touted the advantages of

the gold standard, McKinley focused on the benefits of the protective tariff.

William Jennings Bryan of Nebraska emerged as the Democrats' candidate after delivering a

William McKinley Republican who defeated Bryan in presidential elections in 1896 and 1900; he led the country into the Spanish-American War and was shot by an anarchist in 1901.

William Jennings Bryan Nebraska congressman who advocated free coinage of silver, opposed imperialism, and ran for president unsuccessfully three times on the Democratic ticket.

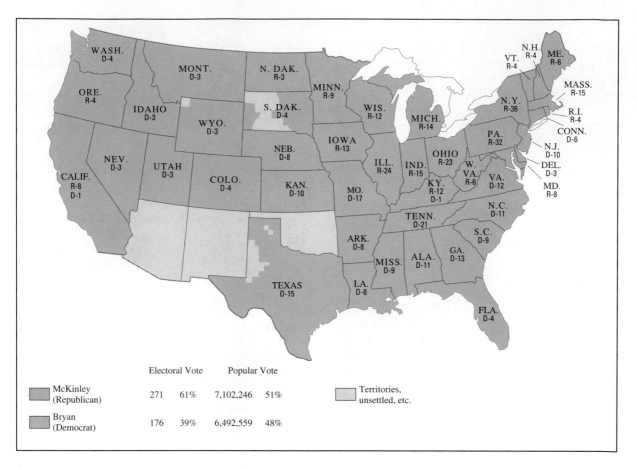

♦ **MAP 19.2 Election of 1896** Bryan could not win with just the votes of the South and West, which had few electoral votes. Even if he had won all the West, South, and border states, he would have needed one or more northeastern states. McKinley won in the urban, industrial core region and the more prosperous farming areas of the Midwest.

masterful speech defending silver at the party's convention. He argued that the conflict between silver and gold was one between "the producing masses" and "the idle holders of idle capital." His closing statement rang defiant: "We will answer their demand for a gold standard by saying to them: You shall not press down upon the brow of labor this crown of thorns. You shall not crucify mankind upon a cross of gold." This "Cross of Gold" speech stunned the convention and se-cured the Democratic nomination for Bryan. Given his commitment to silver, to the income

tax, and to a broad range of other reforms, the Populists felt compelled to give Bryan their nomi-nation too.

Bryan and McKinley both fought an all-out campaign but used sharply contrasting tactics. Bryan, vigorous and young, knew that his speak-ing voice was his greatest campaign tool. He took his case directly to the voters in four grueling train journeys through 26 states and more than 250 cities. Delivering up to 30 speeches a day and ad-dressing a total of perhaps 5 million people, he stressed that the most important issue was silver.

He found large crowds of enthusiastic supporters nearly everywhere he went.

McKinley campaigned from his front porch in Canton, Ohio. The Republican party carried the campaign to the voters for him. They also chartered trains that brought thousands to hear McKinley. Campaign manager Marcus A. Hanna played on the fears of business leaders that Bryan and silver coinage would bring complete financial collapse to raise an enormous campaign fund of $4 million—more than ten times as much as the Democrats raised.

McKinley scored the largest margin of victory since 1872, taking 51.1 percent of the popular vote and 23 states with 271 electoral votes. Bryan won 22 states and 176 electoral votes. As Map 19.2 indicates, Bryan carried the South and nearly all of the West. McKinley's victory came in the urban, industrial Northeast. Of the twenty largest cities in the nation, only New Orleans went for Bryan.

Bryan's defeat spelled the end of the Populist party. Some Populists moved into the Democratic party; others returned to the Republicans; a few joined the Socialist party; and a few simply ignored politics. The Populists' influence lived on, however, in Bryan's wing of the Democratic party.

After 1896: The New Republican Majority

The presidential election of 1896 stands as one of the most important in American history. The campaigns of 1896 focused on economic issues. Bryan's silver crusade appealed most to debt-ridden farmers and western miners. McKinley forged a broader appeal by emphasizing the gold standard and protective tariff as keys to economic recovery. Many urban residents—workers and the middle class alike—believed that the protective tariff meant manufacturing jobs.

McKinley's victory ushered in a generation of Republican dominance of national politics. The depression and the political campaigns of the 1890s caused a significant number of voters to re-evaluate their partisan commitments and to change parties. After 1896, no one could doubt that the Re-

publicans were the national majority. Republicans ruled in the House of Representatives for twenty-eight of the thirty-six years after 1894 and in the Senate for thirty of those thirty-six years. Republicans won seven of the nine presidential elections between 1896 and 1932. Similar patterns of Republican dominance appeared in state and local government outside the South.

The events of the 1890s also worked significant changes in the party. As Bryan solidified his hold on the party, he moved it away from its commitment to minimal government and laissez faire. While retaining the Jacksonians' distrust of monopoly and their opposition to governmental favoritism toward business, Bryan and other new Democratic leaders now agreed with the Populists that the solution to the problems of economic concentration lay in an active government that could limit monopoly power. "A private monopoly," Bryan never tired of repeating, "is indefensible and intolerable." In other ways, the Democrats changed little. Southern Democrats remained committed to states' rights. Northern Democrats continued to oppose nativism and moral reform.

McKinley provided strong executive leadership and worked closely with leaders of his party in Congress to fulfill Republican campaign promises. In 1897, the **Dingley Tariff** drove tariff rates even higher than the 1890 McKinley Tariff. In 1900, the **Gold Standard Act** wrote that Republican commitment into law. Fabulous gold discoveries in the **Klondike** and Alaska increased the nation's currency supply and stopped the clamor for silver coinage.

Although the majority of American voters considered themselves Republican, many held their

---

Dingley Tariff   Bill passed in 1897 enacting a high protective tariff, averaging 57 percent.

Gold Standard Act   Law passed in 1900 that declared gold the nation's monetary standard for all currency issued.

Klondike   A region of Canada's Yukon Territory where gold was discovered in 1896, triggering a gold rush that attracted more than 25,000 people to the frozen north.

new party commitments less intensely than before. Before 1890, ethnicity and choice of party went hand in hand. Now voters sometimes felt pulled toward one party by their economic situation and toward the other party by their ethnicity. Such voters sometimes voted a split ticket, supporting Republicans for some offices and Democrats for others. This was much easier than before because most states had adopted the secret ballot by 1892. As more government positions became subject to the merit system, there were fewer rewards for party workers. Voter participation dropped from 79 percent in 1896 to 59 percent in 1912.

American politics in 1888 looked much like American politics in 1876 or even 1844. But in 1896, American politics changed decisively. Political parties would never be as important thereafter.

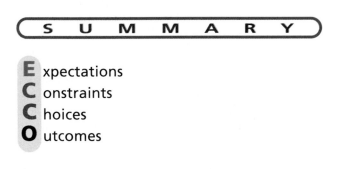

E xpectations
C onstraints
C hoices
O utcomes

Americans in the late nineteenth century expected political parties to dominate politics. All elected public officials were nominated by party conventions and elected through efforts of party campaigners. Most civil service employees were appointed in return for party loyalty. Republicans *chose* to use government to promote rapid economic development, but Democrats argued that government is best when it governs least. Voters *chose* between the major parties along the lines of ethnicity, race, and religion.

Some people rejected the *constraints* of party government and sought reform. Mugwumps argued for the merit system in the civil service, ac-

complished through the Pendleton Act of 1883. By the late nineteenth century, a well-organized woman-suffrage movement had also emerged.

The closely balanced strengths of the two parties contributed to a long-term political stalemate. Republicans broke the *constraints* of stalemate in 1890, passing the McKinley Tariff, Sherman Anti-Trust Act, Sherman Silver Purchase Act, and other measures. But voters subsequently turned against the Republicans.

The 1890s saw important and long-lasting changes in political patterns and people's *expectations* for politics. The political upheaval began when long-suffering western and southern farmers turned to political action. In 1890, members of the Farmers' Alliances *chose* to launch a new political party, usually called the Populists. In 1892, voters rejected the Republicans in many areas, *choosing* either the new Populist party or the Democrats.

President Grover Cleveland proved unable to meet the political challenges of a major depression that began in 1893. In 1896, the Democrats nominated for president William Jennings Bryan, a supporter of silver coinage. The Republicans *chose* William McKinley, who favored the protective tariff as most likely to end the depression. McKinley won, and important long-term *outcomes* were felt well into the twentieth century. First was the beginning of Republican dominance in national politics that lasted until 1930. And second, under Bryan's leadership, the Democratic party discarded its commitment to minimal government and instead adopted a willingness to use government against monopolies and other powerful economic interests.

SUGGESTED READINGS

Bryce, James. *The American Commonwealth,* 2 vols. (1889).
    Fascinating firsthand account of the politics of this period.

Cherny, Robert W. *American Politics in the Gilded Age, 1868–1900* (1997).
    The most recent survey of the politics of this period.

Lebsock, Suzanne. "Women and American Politics, 1880–1920." In *Women, Politics, and Change.* Ed. Louise A. Tilly and Patricia Gurin (1990).

An overview of women and politics, incorporating summaries of much of the most interesting recent research.

McMath, Robert C., Jr. *American Populism: A Social History, 1877–1898* (1993).

A recent, concise introduction to the populist movement.

Williams, R. Hal. *Years of Decision: American Politics in the 1890s* (1978).

A concise survey of national politics; strongest on congressional decision making.

EXPANSION OF THE UNITED STATES, 1865–1917 As a result of the Spanish-American War, the United States acquired island possessions stretching halfway around the world, from Puerto Rico to the Philippines. These and other acquisitions established the United States as one of the major powers in the Pacific and East Asia, and as the dominant power in the Caribbean.

ARCTIC OCEAN

RUSSIA

CANADA

CHINA

KOREA

JAPAN

PACIFIC OCEAN

Alaska
(Purchased from
Russia, 1867)

UNITED STATES

ATLANTIC OCEAN

Midway
(Annexed, 1867)

Tropic of Cancer

Cuba
(Protectorate
1902–34)

Dominican Republic
(Santo Domingo)
(Protectorate, 1905–24)

Puerto Rico
(Acquired from
Spain, 1898)

Philippines
(Acquired from
Spain, 1898)

Guam
(Acquired from
Spain, 1898)

Wake Island
(Annexed, 1899)

Hawai'i
(Annexed, 1898)

Haiti
(Protectorate
1915–33)

Nicaragua
(Protectorate
1912–25,
1927–33)

Virgin Islands
(Purchased from
Denmark, 1917)

Equator

Panama
(Protectorate
1904–36)

Canal Zone
(Acquired by treaty,
1904)

AUSTRALIA

Samoa
(Acquired by treaty
with Britain and
Germany, 1899)

Tropic of Capricorn

PACIFIC OCEAN

| 0 | 750 | 1500 Km. |
| 0 | 750 | 1500 Mi. |

120°E 135°E 150°E 165°E 180° 165°W 150°W 135°W 120°W 105°W 90°W 75°W 60°W

Spanish-American War

Hawai'i annexed

Civil War ends

Philippine insurrection begins

Open Door notes

Alaska purchased

Queen
Liliuokalani
overthrown

Roosevelt becomes president

Roosevelt Corollary

1865 1867 1893 1898 1899 1901 1904

1850 1900 1950 2000

Becoming a World Power: America and World Affairs, 1865–1913

The United States and World Affairs, 1865–1889

- How did American choices with regard to Alaska, Mexico, and eastern Asia reflect traditional American expectations regarding world affairs?

- How did American choices with regard to eastern Asia and the Pacific reflect new conditions in world affairs?

Stepping Cautiously in World Affairs, 1889–1897

- How and why did some Americans' expectations about the U.S. role in world affairs begin to change between 1889 and 1897?

Striding Boldly: War and Imperialism, 1897–1901

- What were the outcomes of the war with Spain?

- What new expectations about America's role in world affairs were expressed in the debate over the acquisition of new possessions?

"Carry a Big Stick": The United States and World Affairs, 1901–1913

- What were Theodore Roosevelt's expectations about the role of the United States in world affairs?

- What choices did he make to bring about the outcomes he desired?

(I N T R O D U C T I O N)

E xpectations
C onstraints
C hoices
O utcomes

In 1898, the United States went to war with Spain and quickly inflicted a stinging defeat. The *choice* to go to war climaxed a turnabout in American *expectations* regarding foreign affairs. During much of the nineteenth century, the nation's role in world affairs was slight at best, and most Americans *expected* that their nation would stay out of foreign conflicts.

Similarly, Americans had few worries about being pulled into European wars, for Europe remained relatively peaceful. The insulation afforded by the Atlantic and Pacific oceans reinforced Americans' feeling of security, and the powerful British navy provided a protective umbrella for American commercial shipping. Thus George Washington's advice that the nation "steer clear of permanent alliances with any portion of the foreign world" became the cornerstone of American foreign relations for most of the nineteenth century.

In the late nineteenth century, however, the United States took a place among the leading industrial nations of the world. The simultaneous emergence of Germany and Japan as industrial and naval giants contributed to a growing instability in world affairs. Japan joined the European powers in a race for empire in which much of the world seemed fair game for colonial capture. In Africa, major European nations scrambled to claim territory. In eastern Asia, they were joined by Russia and Japan. Britain and Germany sometimes looked toward Latin America as another field for expansion. In eastern Asia, the Pacific, and Latin America, the United States also had long-standing interests, often derived from commerce.

Toward the end of the nineteenth century, some Americans began urging that the nation boldly *choose* to seek a prominent role in world affairs. Most presidents after the Civil War were highly cautious about such a commitment. But a revolution in transportation and communication erased many former *constraints* on foreign relations. American diplomatic representatives abroad had once been connected to Washington only by an occasional memorandum carried by an American ship. Now they could communicate daily by telegraph. Sailing ships had once taken weeks to traverse the Atlantic and Pacific. Now steam-powered, steel-hulled vessels crossed in days and carried many times as much cargo.

Challenges to traditional *expectations* of U.S. isolationism and the dissolving of long-standing *constraints* on action presented American policymakers of the late nineteenth century with more *choices* in foreign relations than their predecessors had faced. One *outcome* of their *choices* was a foreign policy usually described as imperialism. Its foundation was the acquisition of possessions scattered halfway around the world (see chapter opener map). But the emerging U.S. foreign policy resulted in more than just colonies and the navy necessary to maintain and protect them. The larger *outcome* was a redefinition of nearly every aspect of American relations with the rest of the world.

CHRONOLOGY

The United States and World Affairs

1823	Monroe Doctrine
1865	Civil War ends
1867	French troops leave Mexico Alaska purchased from Russia
1872	Arbitration of *Alabama* claims
1887	Constitution forced on Hawaiian monarchy Pearl Harbor granted to U.S. Navy
1889	First Samoa treaty
1890	Mahan's *The Influence of Sea Power upon History* McKinley Tariff
1891	Liliuokalani becomes Hawaiian queen Harrison threatens war with Chile
1893	Queen Liliuokalani overthrown
1894	Wilson-Gorman Tariff
1895–1896	Venezuelan boundary crisis
1896	Reconcentration policy in Cuba McKinley elected
1898	De Lôme letter U.S. warship *Maine* explodes Spanish-American War Hawai'i annexed by joint resolution Treaty of Paris signed
1899	Treaty of Paris ratified Open Door notes Permanent Court of Arbitration created
1899–1902	Philippine insurrection suppressed
1900	Foraker Act McKinley reelected Boxer Rebellion

1900–1901	Hay-Pauncefote Treaties
1901	McKinley assassinated; Roosevelt becomes president
1902	Civil government in the Philippines Cuba becomes a protectorate
1903	Arbitration of Alaska-Canada boundary dispute
1904	Hay–Bunau-Varilla Treaty makes Panama a protectorate, provides for construction of a canal there Roosevelt Corollary
1904–1914	Panama Canal constructed
1905	Dominican Republic becomes a protec- torate Roosevelt mediates Russo-Japanese War
1907	Roosevelt's "Great White Fleet"
1912	Nicaragua becomes a protectorate

The United States and World Affairs, 1865–1889

Americans took their first steps toward a new foreign policy following the Civil War, but those steps occurred largely in isolation from each other. Until the 1890s, American foreign policy proceeded largely on a case-by-case basis.

Alaska, Canada, and the *Alabama* Claims

In 1866, the Russian minister to the United States hinted to Secretary of State **William H. Seward** that Russia might sell its holdings in North America if the price were right. Seward made an offer, and in 1867 the two diplomats agreed on a price slightly over $7 million for Alaska. Some journalists derided the new purchase as a frozen, worthless wasteland and labeled it "Seward's Folly." The Senate, however, greeted it with considerable enthusiasm. Charles Sumner, chairman of the **Senate Foreign Relations Committee,** spoke for many in regarding the purchase of Alaska as the first step to the ultimate possession of Canada.

The acquisition of Canada figured prominently in American claims against Great Britain arising out of the Civil War. Several Confederate naval vessels built in British shipyards, notably the *Alabama,* had badly disrupted northern shipping. British ports had also offered refuge, repairs, and supplies to Confederate ships. Although Sumner suggested that Britain should compensate the United States by ceding Canada, Britain proved unresponsive to American demands for any damages. In 1869, however, as relations between Britain and Russia grew tense, the British began to fret that American shipyards might provide similar services for the Russians. In the Treaty of Washington (1871), the two countries agreed to **arbitration.** The 1872 arbitration decision held Britain responsible for the direct claims amounting to $15.5 million in damages.

Testing the Monroe Doctrine: The United States and Latin America

Ever since the formulation of the Monroe Doctrine in 1823, the United States had declared its intentions of preventing further European colonization and meddling in the Western Hemisphere. The first real test of that doctrine came after the Civil War in 1865.

In late 1861, as the United States lurched into civil war, France, Spain, and Britain sent a joint force to Mexico to collect debts that Mexico could not pay. Spain and Britain soon withdrew their contingents, but France remained. Despite resistance led by Benito Juarez, president of Mexico, French troops occupied key areas. Some of Juarez's conservative political opponents cooperated with the French emperor, Napoleon III, to name **Archduke Maximilian** of Austria emperor of Mexico. But Maximilian antagonized many and held power only because of the French army.

During the Civil War, the United States continued to recognize Juarez as president of Mexico but could do little else. As soon as the war ended, however, Secretary of State Seward demanded that Napoleon withdraw his troops. Seward underscored his demand by moving fifty thousand battle-hardened troops to the Mexican border. Thus confronted, Napoleon III withdrew his army

---

William H. Seward U.S. secretary of state under Lincoln and Johnson; a former abolitionist who had expansionist views and who arranged the purchase of Alaska from Russia.

Senate Foreign Relations Committee One of the standing, or permanent, committees of the Senate; it deals with foreign affairs, and its chairman wields considerable power.

arbitration Process by which parties to a dispute submit their case to the judgment of an impartial person or group and agree to abide by the decision of the arbiter.

Archduke Maximilian Austrian archduke appointed by France to be emperor of Mexico in 1864; he lacked popular support and was executed by Mexican republicans when the French withdrew from the country.

♦ Located on the Hawaiian island of Oahu, Pearl Harbor is one of the finest harbors in the Pacific. This painting was done in 1889, two years after the Hawaiian king granted use of the harbor to the United States. In return, the United States granted preferred status to Hawaiian sugar in the American market. *"Pearl Harbor from the Ocean" by Joseph Strong, 1889. Bishop Museum, Honolulu, Hawai'i.*

in early 1867. Juarez defeated Maximilian in battle and then executed him. The French withdrawal helped create new respect in Europe for the role of the United States in Latin America.

Eastern Asia and the Pacific

Americans had taken a strong commercial interest in eastern Asia since the opening of the China trade in 1784. Following the Civil War, however, American exports to that area made up less than 2 percent of all exports. Some Americans began dreaming of profits from selling to China's hundreds of millions of potential consumers.

Growing trade prospects between eastern Asia and the United States thus fueled American interest in ports in the Pacific that could provide supplies and repairs. Interest focused on two groups of islands with excellent harbors, Hawai'i and **Samoa,** both independent nations. The Hawaiian Islands' location near the center of the Pacific made them an ideal supply depot for ships crossing the ocean. New England missionaries had gone to the islands as early as 1819. By 1842, President John Tyler stated that the United States would not allow the islands to pass under the control of another power.

Hawai'i's relationship to the United States changed significantly after 1875, when the Senate yielded to pressure from *haole* sugar growers and exempted Hawaiian imports from the tariff. The outcome was a rapid expansion of the Hawaiian sugar industry, as children of New England missionaries joined American sugar refiners in developing huge sugar plantations. Sugar soon tied the Hawaiian economy closely to the United States. In 1887, a group of *haole* business leaders and plantation owners pressured King Kalakaua into accepting a constitution that limited the monarch's powers and permitted *haoles* to dominate the government. Although the royal family resented *haole* control of the government, they reluctantly granted Pearl Harbor to the American navy in 1887 to secure the renewal of tariff exemptions for Hawaiian sugar.

Samoa   A group of volcanic and mountainous islands in the South Pacific.

haole   Hawaiian word used to describe persons not of indigenous Hawaiian ancestry, especially whites.

Samoa, in the South Pacific, drew attention not just from the United States but also from Britain and Germany. When German actions in the islands suggested an attempt at annexation, President Cleveland vowed to maintain Samoan independence. All three nations dispatched warships to the vicinity in 1889, and conflict seemed likely until a typhoon scattered and damaged the ships. A subsequent treaty provided for Samoan independence under the protection of the three Western nations.

Stepping Cautiously in World Affairs, 1889–1897

During Benjamin Harrison's administration (1889–1893), the United States began to take its first, cautious steps toward redefining its role in world affairs. One step involved a new role for the U.S. Navy and the commissioning of modern ships able to carry it out. Another involved the emergence of a more coherent set of foreign policy objectives and commitments.

Building a Navy

At the end of the Civil War, the navy, like the army, was rapidly **demobilized.** Unlike the army, which was needed to fight Indians in the West, the navy was largely ignored. Few Americans appreciated the significance of the Civil War experiments with armor-plated, steam-powered ships. Even the navy's wooden sailing vessels deteriorated to the point that some people ridiculed them as fit only for firewood.

Alfred Thayer Mahan played a key role in the emergence of the modern navy. As president of the Naval War College, Captain Mahan exerted a powerful influence, especially during the Harrison administration. In his book *The Influence of Sea Power upon History* (1890), Mahan argued that sea power had been the determining factor in the great European power struggles from the mid-seventeenth to the early nineteenth centuries.

Mahan drew a number of lessons for government policy from his study of history. First, Mahan urged support for a strong **merchant marine.** Sec-

ond, he advocated a large, modern navy centered on huge, powerful battleships. Third, he stressed a vision for empire. Extend American power beyond the national boundaries, he exhorted, to establish and control a canal through Central America, command the Caribbean, dominate Hawai'i and other strategic locations in the Pacific, and create naval bases at key points in the Atlantic and Pacific.

In 1889, during the Harrison administration, Secretary of the Navy Benjamin F. Tracy urged Congress to modernize and expand the navy significantly. He requested eighteen more battleships, nearly fifty more cruisers, and more smaller vessels. Congress did not give him all that he asked but did begin to create a modern, two-ocean navy centered on battleships that were equal to the world's best.

Revolution in Hawai'i

In 1890, the McKinley Tariff allowed imported sugar to enter the United States without being subject to a tariff. To protect domestic sugar producers, sugar grown within the United States received a subsidy of 2 cents per pound. Hawaiian sugar now encountered stiff competition in the American market, notably from Cuban sugar. Facing economic disaster, many Hawaiian planters craved the 2-cent subsidy and began to talk of annexation to the United States. In 1891, King Kalakaua died and was succeeded by his more assertive sister, **Liliuokalani.** She hoped to restore Hawai'i to the **indigenous** Hawaiians. Fearing that they might

---

demobilize   To discharge from military service.

Alfred Thayer Mahan   Lecturer and writer on naval history who stressed the importance of sea power in determining political history and who justified imperialism on the basis of national self-interest.

merchant marine   Ships engaged in commerce.

Liliuokalani   Last reigning queen of Hawai'i, whose desire to restore land to the Hawaiian people and perpetuate the monarchy prompted *haole* planters to depose her in 1893.

indigenous   Original to or belonging in an area or environment.

lose not only their political clout but also their economic holdings, *haole* entrepreneurs set out to overthrow the monarchy. On January 17, 1893, the plotters announced a provisional republican government that would seek annexation by the United States. John L. Stevens, the U.S. minister to Hawai'i, provided crucial assistance for the rebellion by ordering the landing of 150 marines. Liliuokalani surrendered, as she put it, "to the superior force of the United States."

The Harrison administration was unable to annex Hawai'i before Harrison's term of office expired. The succeeding president, Grover Cleveland, withdrew the annexation treaty when he learned how Liliuokalani had been deposed. He asked the new government of Hawai'i to restore the queen. It refused, and Hawai'i became a republic, dominated by its *haole* business and planter community.

Crises in Latin America

Although Harrison and Cleveland acted at cross-purposes regarding Hawai'i, they moved in similar directions with regard to Latin America. Both presidents extended American involvement, and both threatened the use of force.

A rebellion in Chile in 1891 ended with victory for the rebels. Because the American minister to Chile had seemed to side against the rebels, anti-American feelings ran high. In October 1891, a mob in Valparaiso killed two American sailors on shore leave. When the Chilean government failed to apologize, Harrison responded with threats of war. Chile gave in, apologized, and promised to pay damages.

In 1895 and 1896, Grover Cleveland also took the nation to the edge of war over a long-standing boundary dispute between Venezuela and **British Guiana.** Venezuela repeatedly proposed arbitration, but Britain refused. In July 1895, Secretary of State Richard Olney demanded that Britain submit the boundary issue to arbitration. Resting his argument on the Monroe Doctrine, he bombastically proclaimed the United States to be pre-eminent throughout the Western Hemisphere. The British still refused arbitration. Cleveland then asked Congress for authority to determine the boundary

and enforce it. Britain faced the possibility of conflict with the United States at a time when it was becoming increasingly concerned about Germany and when tensions were mounting between the British colony in South Africa and the neighboring **Boer republics.** Britain agreed to arbitration.

Cleveland took a more restrained position on Cuba, one of the few vestiges of Spain's New World empire. Cuba had rebelled against the mother country repeatedly. A new rebellion broke out after 1894, when the Wilson-Gorman Tariff placed a high duty on Cuban sugar and sent the Cuban economy into a depression. In 1896, General Valeriano Weyler, the Spanish commander in Cuba, established a **reconcentration** policy to combat guerrilla warfare waged by **insurgents** seeking independence. Weyler ordered the civilian population into fortified towns or camps. Everyone outside these fortified areas was subject to attack. The insurgents responded by ravaging sugar and tobacco plantations, including those owned by Americans.

The U.S. government vehemently protested reconcentration, particularly after disease and starvation swept through the camps, killing an estimated one of every eight Cubans in two years. American newspapers vied with each other in portraying Spanish atrocities and in exaggerating them to attract readers. Such **yellow journalism** swayed many Americans to clamor for action that would rescue the Cubans from Spanish oppression.

British Guiana   British colony in northeast South America on the Atlantic coast; its boundary with Venezuela was the source of a long-standing dispute.

Boer republics   Self-governing nations established by white South Africans of Dutch descent; they were formed in an effort to escape British rule but were eventually annexed by Britain into its South African colony.

reconcentration   Spanish policy in Cuba in 1896 under which the civilian population was ordered into fortified camps as part of a plan to isolate and annihilate Cuban revolutionaries.

insurgents   Rebels or revolutionaries.

yellow journalism   Journalism that exploits or exaggerates the news to attract readers.

Cleveland reacted cautiously. He proclaimed American neutrality and warned Americans not to support the insurrection. When members of Congress began to push for action to secure Cuban independence, Cleveland ignored the pressure. He did urge Spain to grant concessions to the insurgents, but he considered the insurgents incapable of replacing Spanish rule. Just as he had opposed the annexation of Hawai'i, Cleveland feared that American intervention might lead to annexation regardless of the will of the Cuban people. Nonetheless, by early 1897 he had begun to warn Spain of possible American intervention.

Striding Boldly: War and Imperialism, 1897–1901

In 1898, the United States went to war with Spain over Cuba. Some who promoted American intervention on behalf of the suffering Cubans envisioned a quick war to establish a Cuban republic. Others saw war with Spain as an opportunity to acquire a colonial empire for the United States.

McKinley and War

William McKinley assumed the presidency in 1897 amid increasing demands for action regarding Cuba. McKinley gradually stepped up diplomatic efforts to resolve the crisis. Late that year, Spain responded by recalling General Weyler, softening the reconcentration policy, and offering the Cubans limited self-government but not independence.

In February 1898, however, two events scuttled progress toward a negotiated solution. First, Cuban insurgents stole a letter written by **Enrique Dupuy de Lôme,** the Spanish minister to the United States, and released it to the *New York Journal.* In it, de Lôme criticized President McKinley as "weak and a bidder for the admiration of the crowd." The letter implied that Spain was not seriously committed to reform in Cuba. De Lôme's immediate resignation could not undo the damage. The letter aroused intense anti-Spanish feeling among Americans.

Second, on February 15, a few days after publication of the de Lôme letter, an explosion ripped open the American warship *Maine,* anchored in Havana harbor. The *Maine* sank, with the loss of more than 260 American officers and sailors. The yellow press accused Spain of sabotage, claiming that a submarine mine had sunk the ship. Regardless of how the explosion occurred, those advocating intervention now had a rallying cry: "Remember the *Maine!*"

McKinley demanded that Spain put an immediate end to the fighting and submit to his **mediation.** One possible outcome of this mediation was Cuban independence. In reply, the Spanish government consented to end the fighting if the insurgents asked for an **armistice.** Spain was silent, though, on mediation by McKinley and independence for Cuba. On April 11, McKinley asked Congress for authority to stop the war in Cuba. On April 19, Congress passed four resolutions that (1) declared that Cuba was and should be independent, (2) demanded that Spain withdraw "at once," (3) authorized the president to force Spanish withdrawal, and (4) disavowed any intention to annex the island. The first three resolutions amounted to a declaration of war. The fourth has usually been called the **Teller Amendment** for its sponsor, Senator Henry M. Teller of Colorado. In response, Spain declared war.

Nearly all Americans reacted enthusiastically to what they understood to be a war whose purpose was to bring independence to the long-suffering

---

Enrique Dupuy de Lôme Spanish minister to the United States whose private letter criticizing President McKinley was stolen and made public, increasing anti-Spanish sentiment.

Maine American warship that exploded in Havana harbor in 1898; later investigation suggested an internal explosion.

mediation An attempt to bring about the peaceful settlement of a dispute through the intervention of a neutral party.

armistice An agreement to halt fighting at least temporarily.

Teller Amendment Resolution approved by U.S. Senate in 1898, by which the United States promised not to annex Cuba.

Cubans. From the beginning, however, some voiced distrust of the McKinley administration's motives. This distrust intensified when the McKinley administration defeated efforts to have the Cuban insurgents recognized as the legitimate government of Cuba.

The "Splendid Little War"

Many Americans were taken by surprise when the first engagement in the war occurred not in Cuba but in the **Philippine Islands,** on the other side of the world. A Spanish colony for more than three hundred years, the Philippines, like Cuba, were engaged in a rebellion against Spanish rule.

Assistant Secretary of the Navy **Theodore Roosevelt,** however, was not surprised. In late February 1898, more than six weeks before McKinley's war message to Congress, Roosevelt cabled the American naval commander in the Pacific, George Dewey, and instructed him to crush the Spanish fleet at Manila Bay in the event of war. On May 1, Dewey carried out those orders. His squadron of four cruisers and three smaller vessels steamed into Manila Bay and quickly destroyed or captured ten Spanish cruisers and gunboats. The Spanish lost 381 men; the Americans lost 1, a victim of heat prostration. Dewey became an instant national hero.

Dewey's victory at Manila immediately raised the prospect of establishing a permanent American presence there. This, in turn, revived interest in annexing Hawai'i as a base for supplying and protecting future American involvement in eastern Asia. The annexation of Hawai'i was accomplished on July 7, some five years after the planters had **deposed** Queen Liliuokalani.

Dewey's victory demonstrated that the American navy was clearly superior to that of Spain. By contrast, the Spanish army in Cuba outnumbered the entire American army by more than five to one. The Spanish troops also had years of experience fighting in Cuba. When war was declared, the American army numbered only twenty-eight thousand soldiers. A call for volunteers brought nearly a million—five times as many as the army could take.

The sudden declaration of war caught the army unprepared. Sent to training camps in the South, the new soldiers found chaos and confusion. Food, uniforms, and equipment arrived at one location while the men for whom they were intended stood hungry and idle at another. The heavy wool uniforms were totally unsuited for the climate. Disease raged through some camps, killing many men. Others died from tainted food.

Once in Cuba, American forces concentrated on the port city of Santiago, where the Spanish Atlantic fleet had taken refuge. Inexperienced, poorly equipped, and unfamiliar with the terrain, the Americans doggedly assaulted the fortified hills surrounding the city. At Kettle Hill, Theodore Roosevelt, who had resigned as assistant secretary of the navy to organize a volunteer cavalry regiment, led a successful but costly charge of his **"Rough Riders"** and regular army units. Driving the Spanish from the crest of Kettle Hill cleared a serious impediment to the assault on nearby San Juan Heights and San Juan Hill. Roosevelt's units took a minor part in the attack on those heights. With little regard for accuracy, newspapers declared Roosevelt the hero of the Battle of San Juan Hill.

Once the Americans secured control of the high ground around Santiago Harbor, the Spanish fleet of four cruisers and two destroyers tried to escape from the harbor. A larger American fleet under Admiral William Sampson and Commodore Winfield Schley sank or disabled every Spanish ship. The Spanish suffered 323 deaths, the Americans 1.

Their fleet destroyed and the surrounding hills in American hands, the Spanish in Santiago still waited two weeks before surrendering. A week later, American forces took Puerto Rico. Early in the war, on June 21, an American cruiser had

---

Philippine Islands   A group of islands in the Pacific Ocean southeast of China that came under U.S. control in 1898 after the Spanish-American War.

Theodore Roosevelt   American politician and writer who advocated war against Spain in 1898; McKinley's vice president in 1900, he became president in 1901 upon McKinley's assassination.

depose   To dethrone or remove from power.

Rough Riders   Cavalry volunteers in the Spanish-American War recruited by their lieutenant colonel, Theodore Roosevelt.

♦ Theodore Roosevelt's Rough Riders, on foot because there was not room aboard ship for their horses, are shown in the background of this artist's depiction of the battle for Kettle Hill, a part of the larger battle for San Juan Hill, overlooking the city of Santiago. The artist has put into the foreground members of the 9th and 10th Cavalry, both African-American units that also played a key role in that engagement, but one often overlooked because of the attention usually given Roosevelt and the Rough Riders. *Chicago Historical Society.*

forced Spanish forces on Guam to surrender without a contest. Spanish land forces in the Philippines surrendered when the first American troops arrived in mid-August (see Map 20.1). The "splendid little war," as John Hay, the American ambassador to Great Britain described it, lasted only sixteen weeks. The war cost the United States 385 battlefield deaths and more than 5,000 deaths because of disease and other causes.

The Treaty of Paris

On August 12, the United States and Spain agreed to stop fighting. The truce specified that Spain was to give up Cuba and transfer Puerto Rico and one of the **Ladrone Islands** to the United States. Until a peace conference determined the Philippines' fate, the United States was to occupy Manila.

The only real question remaining was the disposition of the Philippines. McKinley at first seemed inclined to request only a naval base and to leave Spain the remainder of the islands. Spanish authority collapsed everywhere on the islands by mid-August, however, as Filipino insurgents took charge. Britain, Japan, and Germany seemed likely to step in if the United States withdrew.

McKinley then apparently decided that defending a naval base on Manila Bay would require control of the entire island group. No one seems to have seriously considered the Filipinos' desire for independence.

McKinley was well aware of the political and strategic importance of the Philippines for establishing an American presence in eastern Asia. He invoked other reasons, however, when he explained his decision to a group of visiting Methodists. He repeatedly prayed for guidance on the Philippine question, he told them. Late one night, he realized that "there was nothing left for us to do but to take them all, and to educate the Filipinos, and uplift and civilize and Christianize them and by God's grace do the very best we could by them, as our fellow men, for whom Christ also died." In fact, most Filipinos had been Catholics for centuries.

Ladrone Islands Islands in the western Pacific now known as the Marianas; they include the island of Guam, which the United States acquired from Spain under the 1898 Treaty of Paris.

◆ **MAP 20.1 The United States and the Pacific, 1866–1900** In the 1890s, the United States became a major power in the Pacific and in eastern Asia. This map indicates major acquisitions and activities up to 1900.

Map labels

NORTH AMERICA

ALASKA (Purchased from Russia 1867)

Aleutian Islands

U.S.

PACIFIC OCEAN

ASIA

RUSSIA

Sakhalin

U.S. troops involved in Boxer Rebellion, 1900

Peking

CHINA

Shanghai

KOREA

JAPAN — Tokyo

Formosa (Japanese)

Hong Kong (Br.)

FRENCH INDOCHINA

PHILIPPINE ISLANDS 1898

GUAM 1898

MIDWAY Annexed 1867

WAKE ISLAND Annexed 1899

Overthrow of Hawaiian monarchy by white business and planter leaders, 1893 Establishment of a republic, 1894

HAWAIIAN ISLANDS Annexed 1898

Threat of naval conflict over Samoa, 1889

Samoa Islands

AMERICAN SAMOA 1899

NETHERLANDS EAST INDIES

New Guinea

Timor

Celebes

Borneo

Java

AUSTRALIA

Scale at Equator
0   750   1500 Mi.
0   750   1500 Km.

✦ Major battle

■ U.S. acquisitions

⊥ U.S. naval bases

Inset 1

CHINA

South China Sea

PACIFIC OCEAN

Formosa (Japanese)

PHILIPPINE ISLANDS (Acquired from Spain, 1898)

Luzon I.

Manila
Manila Bay May 1, 1898

Mindoro I.

Samar I.

Leyte I.

Panay I.

Negros I.

Cebu I.

Bohol I.

Mindanao I.

Palawan I.

Sulu Sea

BRITISH NORTH BORNEO

0   200   400 Km.
0   200   400 Mi.

Inset 2

PACIFIC OCEAN

Kauai

Niihau

Oahu — Pearl Harbor

Molokai

Lanai

Maui

Kahoolawe

Hawai'i

HAWAIIAN ISLANDS (Annexed 1898)

0   50   100 Km.
0   50   100 Mi.

Inset 3

PACIFIC OCEAN

WESTERN SAMOA (German)

Savai'i

Upolu

AMERICAN SAMOA (Acquired by treaty with Britain and Germany, 1899)

Tutuila — Pagopago

Manua Is.

0   50   100 Km.
0   50   100 Mi.

The **Treaty of Paris,** signed in December 1898, required Spain to surrender all claim to Cuba, cede Puerto Rico and the island of Guam to the United States, and sell the Philippines for $20 million. For the first time in American history, a treaty acquiring new territory failed to confer U.S. citizenship on the residents. Thus these acquisitions represented a new kind of expansion. The United States now owned territories with no prospect for statehood and whose residents lacked the rights of American citizens. America had become a colonial power.

The terms of the Treaty of Paris dismayed Democrats, Populists, and some conservative Republicans. An active anti-imperialist movement quickly formed, including William Jennings Bryan, Grover Cleveland, Andrew Carnegie, Mark Twain, Jane Addams, and others. The treaty, they argued, amounted to a denial of self-government for the newly acquired territories and therefore violated the Declaration of Independence. For the United States to hold colonies, they claimed, threatened the very concept of democracy. "The Declaration of Independence will make every Filipino a thoroughly dissatisfied subject," Andrew Carnegie warned. Others worried about the perversion of American values. "God Almighty help the party that seeks to give civilization and Christianity hypodermically with 13-inch guns," prayed Senator William Morris of Illinois.

Those who defended the acquisition of the Philippines echoed McKinley's lofty pronouncements about America's solemn duty, along with more mundane claims about economic benefits. Albert Beveridge, senator from Indiana after 1899, stated the need for expansion: "Today, we are raising more than we can consume, making more than we can use. Therefore we must find new markets for our produce." Expansionists also argued that possession of the Philippines would make the United States a leading power in eastern Asia. American business would then have access to the China market. In contrast to the heated debates over the Philippines, virtually no one challenged the acquisition of Puerto Rico.

Bryan, the Democratic presidential candidate in 1896, urged his followers in the Senate to approve the treaty. That way, he reasoned, the United States alone could determine the future of the Philippines. Once the treaty was approved, he argued, the United States should immediately grant them independence. By a narrow margin, the Senate approved the treaty on February 6, 1899, but senators rejected a proposal for Philippine independence.

Republic or Empire: The Election of 1900

Bryan, who easily won the Democratic nomination for a second time, hoped to make independence for the Philippines the central issue in the 1900 presidential election. Bryan found, however, that many conservative anti-imperialists would not support his candidacy because he insisted on silver coinage and attacked big business.

The Republicans renominated McKinley. For vice president, they chose Theodore Roosevelt, the "hero of San Juan Hill." The McKinley re-election campaign seemed unstoppable. Republican campaigners pointed proudly to a short and highly successful war, legislation that had fulfilled party campaign promises on the tariff and the gold standard, and the return of prosperity. Whereas Bryan repeatedly attacked imperialism, McKinley and Roosevelt took pride in expansion. McKinley easily won a second term with 51.7 percent of the vote. He even carried most of the western states where populism had once flourished.

Organizing an Insular Empire

The Teller Amendment specified that the United States would not annex Cuba (see Map 20.2). The McKinley administration, though, consistently refused to recognize the insurgents as a legitimate government, so the U.S. Army took over the job of running the island when the Spanish left. Among other tasks, the army undertook public improvements, including sanitation projects intended to reduce disease, especially yellow fever. After two years of army rule, the McKinley administration permitted Cuban voters to hold a constitutional convention.

> **Treaty of Paris** Treaty ending the Spanish-American War, under which Spain granted independence to Cuba, ceded Puerto Rico and Guam, and sold the Philippines to the United States for $20 million.

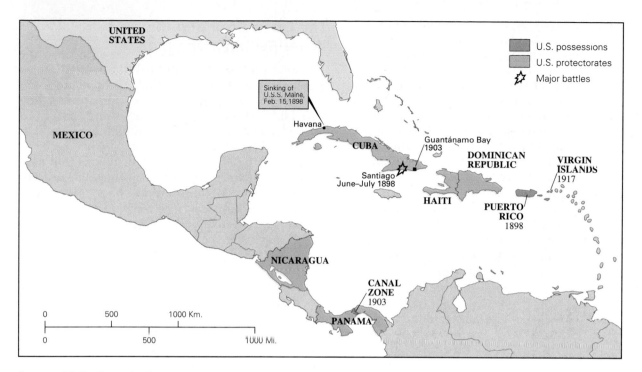

♦ **MAP 20.2 The United States and the Caribbean, 1898–1917** Between 1898 and 1917, the United States expanded into the Caribbean by acquiring possessions and establishing protectorates. As a result, the United States became the dominant power in the region during this time period.

The convention drafted a constitution in 1900 modeled on that of the United States. It did not define relations between Cuba and the United States, however. In March 1901, the McKinley administration specified, and Congress adopted, detailed provisions for Cuba to adopt before the army would withdraw, including these stipulations: (1) Cuba was not to make any agreement with a foreign power that impaired the island's independence, (2) the United States could intervene in Cuba to preserve Cuban independence and maintain law and order, and (3) Cuba was to lease facilities to the United States for naval bases and coaling stations. The Cubans reluctantly accepted the conditions, added them to their constitution, and agreed to a treaty with the United States stating the same conditions. In 1902, Cuba thereby became a protectorate of the United States.

The Teller Amendment did not apply to Puerto Rico. On that island, too, the army provided a military government until 1900, when Congress approved the **Foraker Act.** That act made Puerto Ricans citizens of Puerto Rico but not citizens of the United States. It specified that Puerto Rican voters were to elect a legislature but final authority was to rest with a governor and council appointed by the president of the United States. In 1901, in the **Insular cases,** the U.S. Supreme Court issued a complex decision that, in effect, confirmed the colonial status of Puerto Rico and, by implication,

---

Foraker Act Law passed by Congress in 1900 that established civilian government in Puerto Rico; it provided for an elected legislature and a governor appointed by the U.S. president.

Insular cases Cases concerning Puerto Rico in which the U.S. Supreme Court ruled in 1901 that people in new island territories did not automatically receive the constitutional rights of U.S. citizens.

the other new possessions. The Court ruled that they were not equivalent to earlier territorial acquisitions and that their people did not possess the constitutional rights of citizens.

Establishment of a civil government in the Philippines took longer. Between Dewey's victory and the arrival of the first American soldiers three months later, a Philippine independence movement, led by **Emilio Aguinaldo,** had established a provisional government. Its forces controlled all the islands except Manila, which remained in Spanish hands until American troops arrived. Aguinaldo and his government wanted independence, not a new colonial master. When the United States decided to keep the islands, many Filipinos resisted and eventually turned to guerrilla warfare. In an ironic turn of events, the United States now found itself in the role that Spain had previously played.

Quelling what American authorities called the "Philippine insurrection" required three years, took the lives of more than forty-two hundred American soldiers (more losses than in the Spanish-American War) and perhaps twenty thousand guerrillas, and cost $400 million (twenty times the price of the islands). In crushing the resistance, U.S. troops resorted to the practice of reconcentration that the American public had so widely condemned when Spain used it in Cuba. Both sides committed atrocities during the conflict. Anti-imperialists saw their fears confirmed that a colonial policy would corrupt American values.

Aguinaldo's eventual defeat and McKinley's re-election ended any prospect for immediate Philippine independence. In 1902, Congress set up a government for the Philippines similar to that of Puerto Rico. Filipinos became citizens of the Philippine Islands, not of the United States. The president of the United States appointed the governor. Filipino voters elected one house in the two-house legislature, and the governor appointed the other. Both the governor and the United States Congress could veto laws passed by the legislature. **William Howard Taft,** governor of the islands from 1901 to 1904, tried to build local support for American control but met with little success. When the first Philippine legislature met in 1907, over half of its members favored independence from the United States.

The Open Door and the Boxer Rebellion in China

The new Pacific acquisitions of the United States greatly strengthened its ability to gain access to markets in eastern Asia, especially China. They also laid a broad basis for asserting American power in eastern Asia. The United States now began to act like a major East Asian power.

The McKinley administration flexed this new American power first in China. By 1899, Britain, Germany, Russia, and France had carved out spheres of influence in China where they claimed special rights—usually a monopoly over trade. The United States claimed no such privileges in China. Fearing the breakup of China into separate European colonies, Secretary of State John Hay in 1899 circulated a letter to Germany, Russia, Britain, France, Italy, and Japan. The Open Door notes asked these countries to permit Chinese authorities to continue to collect tariff duties within their **spheres of influence.** Hay hoped that this measure would preserve some semblance of Chinese sovereignty. He also urged them not to discriminate against citizens of other nations engaged in commerce within their spheres. Thus Hay sought to prevent other nations from carving up China and, at the same time, to make American trade possible throughout China. Although some replies proved less than fully supportive, he announced that the **Open Door policy** was in effect.

The next year, in 1900, a Chinese secret society took up arms to expel foreigners from China. Be-

Emilio Aguinaldo Leader of struggles for Philippine independence, first against Spain and then against the United States.

William Howard Taft Appointed governor of the Philippines from 1901 to 1904; he was elected president of the United States in 1908 and became chief justice of the Supreme Court in 1921.

spheres of influence Areas of a country where foreign nations exercise considerable authority.

Open Door policy Policy advocated by the United States in 1899 under which all nations would have equal access to trading and development rights in China.

A FAIR FIELD AND NO FAVOR!
UNCLE SAM: "I'M OUT FOR COMMERCE, NOT CONQUEST."

♦ In this 1899 cartoon celebrating the Open Door policy, Uncle Sam insists that the nations of Europe must compete fairly for China's commerce and must not seize Chinese territory. In the background, John Bull (Britain) lifts his hat in approval. *Library of Congress.*

cause the rebels used a clenched fist as their symbol, Westerners called them Boxers. After attacking missionaries, the Boxers laid siege to the foreign **legations** in Peking, the Chinese capital. Hay foresaw that the major powers might use the **Boxer Rebellion** as a pretext to take full control of China. To block such a move, the United States took part in a joint international military expedition to crush the rebellion. Hay insisted that American action was not against the Chinese government but against the rebels.

Although China did not lose territory after the Boxer Rebellion, the intervening nations required it to pay an **indemnity**. After compensating American citizens for losses suffered during the rebellion, the U.S. government returned the remainder of its indemnity to China. As a show of gratitude, the Chinese government used the money to send Chinese students to the United States to develop good will between the two countries.

"Carry a Big Stick": The United States and World Affairs, 1901–1913

In 1901, an assassin's bullet cut down President McKinley and put Theodore Roosevelt in the White House. Roosevelt remolded the presidency, established new federal powers in the economy, and expanded America's role in world affairs. Few other presidents have had so great an impact. He once expressed his fondness for what he described as a West African proverb: "Speak softly and carry a big stick; you will go far." As president, however, Roosevelt seldom spoke softly. Everything he did, it seemed, he did strenuously. Well-read in history and current events, Roosevelt entered the presidency with definite ideas on the proper role for the United States in the world. He envisioned a future in which major powers, particularly the United States, would exercise international police powers.

Taking Panama

Following the American victory over Spain, American diplomats pursued efforts to build a canal through Central America to create a passage between the Atlantic and the Pacific. The considerable time that it took an American battleship stationed on the West Coast to reach Cuba during the Spanish-American War led McKinley to pronounce that an American-controlled canal was "indispensable." The **Hay-Pauncefote Treaties** of 1900 and 1901, in which Britain renounced its interests in an

> **legation** A diplomatic mission in a foreign country.
> **Boxer Rebellion** Uprising in China in 1900 directed against foreign powers; it was suppressed by an international army that included American participation.
> **indemnity** Payment for damage, loss, or injury.
> **Hay-Pauncefote Treaties** Two separate treaties (1900 and 1901) signed by the United States and Britain giving the United States the exclusive right to build, control, and fortify a canal through Central America.

isthmian canal, cleared the way. Experts identified two possible locations for a canal, Nicaragua and Panama (then part of Colombia). In its favor, the Panama route was shorter, and a French canal company had completed some work in the 1870s. **Philippe Bunau-Varilla,** a major stockholder in the French company, did his utmost to sell that company's interests to the United States. Building through Panama, however, meant overcoming both formidable mountains and fever-ridden swamps. Previous studies had shown Nicaragua to be preferable because of fewer natural obstacles. Bunau-Varilla's lobbying led the Senate to approve the Panama route, provided that Colombia agreed to give up land for a canal.

Negotiations with Colombia bogged down over treaty language that significantly limited its sovereignty. Pressure from the United States did lead the Colombian government to accept such limitations— but only in return for more money. Roosevelt, outraged, called it "pure bandit morality." To break the impasse, Bunau-Varilla financed a revolution in Panama. Anticipating such a possibility, Roosevelt had ordered U.S. warships to prevent Colombian troops from crushing the uprising. The revolution succeeded, and Panama declared its independence. The United States immediately extended diplomatic recognition. Bunau-Varilla, named Panama's minister to the United States, promptly signed a treaty that gave the United States much the same arrangement earlier rejected by Colombia.

The **Hay–Bunau-Varilla Treaty** (1904) granted the United States perpetual control over a strip of Panamanian territory 10 miles wide, for a price of $10 million and annual rent of $250,000. The United States also purchased the assets of the French company and in 1904 began construction of the canal. Building the canal proved difficult. Just over 40 miles long, the canal took ten years to build and cost nearly $400 million. Completed in 1914, just as World War I began, the canal was considered one of the world's great engineering feats.

Making the Caribbean an American Lake

Well before the canal was finished, Roosevelt determined to establish American dominance in the Caribbean and Central America to protect the canal. The threat of European intervention in the Caribbean led Roosevelt in 1904 to present what became known as the **Roosevelt Corollary** to the Monroe Doctrine. The corollary stated that the United States would act as the police power in the Western Hemisphere in cases where governments defaulted on their debts or otherwise misbehaved. Roosevelt thus warned European nations against any intervention whatsoever in the Western Hemisphere. If outside authority became necessary in the Caribbean and Central America, Roosevelt insisted that the United States would handle it. He exempted Argentina, Brazil, and Chile from the Roosevelt Corollary as "civilized" powers in their own right.

Roosevelt acted forcefully to establish his new policy. In 1905, the Dominican Republic agreed to permit the United States to supervise government expenditures and thereby became an American protectorate. Roosevelt's successors, William Howard Taft and Woodrow Wilson, expanded his policy of American domination in the Caribbean region. Under Taft, the United States encouraged Americans to invest in the region. Taft hoped that American investment would stabilize and develop the Caribbean economies. Taft supported such **dollar diplomacy** throughout the region, especially in Nicaragua. In 1912, Taft sent marines there to suppress a rebellion against President Adolfo Díaz. Nicaragua, too, became an American protectorate.

Philippe Bunau-Varilla Chief engineer of the French company contracted to build the Panama Canal and later minister to the United States from the new Republic of Panama.

Hay–Bunau-Varilla Treaty Treaty with Panama that granted the United States sovereignty over the Canal Zone in return for a $10 million payment plus an annual rent.

Roosevelt Corollary Extension of the Monroe Doctrine voiced by Theodore Roosevelt in 1904, in which he proclaimed the right of the United States to police Caribbean areas.

dollar diplomacy Policy during the Taft administration of supporting U.S. commercial interests abroad for strategic purposes, especially in Latin America.

The marines remained after the turmoil settled to prop up the Díaz government.

Roosevelt and Eastern Asia

Roosevelt's East Asian policy built on the Open Door notes and American participation in the suppression of the Boxer Rebellion. He found cause for both concern and optimism in Japan's rise as a major industrial and imperial power. His friend Alfred Thayer Mahan, the naval strategist, had warned of the potential danger to the United States posed by Japan. But Roosevelt was also hopeful. He admired Japanese accomplishments and looked forward to Japan's exercising the same degree of international police power in its vicinity that the United States did under the Roosevelt Corollary.

In 1904, Russia and Japan went to war over **Manchuria,** the northern part of China. After the Boxer Rebellion, Russia had pressured China to grant concessions that slowly turned Manchuria into a Russian colony. Russia seemed also to have designs on Korea. Japan responded with force to Russian encroachment on its interests. The Japanese scored smashing naval and military victories over the Russians but lacked the resources to sustain a long war.

Early in the war, Roosevelt indicated some support for Japan. When Japan's resources ran low, Japan asked Roosevelt to act as mediator. The president agreed in hopes of preserving a regional balance of power. The **Treaty of Portsmouth** (1905) recognized Japan's dominance in Korea and gave Japan both the southern half of Sakhalin Island and Russian concessions in southern Manchuria. Russia kept its railroad in northern Manchuria. China was to have responsibility for civil authority in Manchuria. For his mediation, Roosevelt received the 1906 Nobel Peace Prize.

That same year, Roosevelt mediated another significant dispute. The San Francisco school board had ordered children of Japanese parentage to attend the city's segregated Chinese school. The Japanese government regarded this as a serious insult. Roosevelt convinced the board to withdraw the segregation order in return for his efforts to cut off Japanese immigration. Japan agreed informally to limit the departure of laborers to the United States.

In 1908, the American and Japanese governments further agreed to respect each other's territorial possessions and to maintain "the independence and integrity of China" and the Open Door. During the Taft administration, the United States extended the concept of dollar diplomacy to China. Proponents sought Chinese permission for American citizens not just to trade with China but also to invest there, especially in railroad construction. Taft hoped that such investments could head off further Japanese expansion. The effort received Chinese governmental sanction, but little came of it.

The United States and the World: 1901–1913

Before the 1890s, the United States had no clear or consistent set of foreign policy commitments or objectives. After that, its commitments were obvious to all. Acquisition of the Philippines, Guam, Hawai'i, Puerto Rico, eastern Samoa, and the **Canal Zone** represented highly visible components in a new American role in world affairs.

Central to that role was a large, modern, two-ocean navy. Roosevelt was so proud of the navy that, in 1907, he dispatched sixteen battleships—painted white to indicate their peaceful intent—on a fourteen-month world tour. Roosevelt later claimed that his purpose in sending the Great White Fleet "was to impress the American people." But he was clearly interested in impressing other nations too.

Another aspect of America's new role in the world revolved around the principle that the

---

Manchuria   A region of northeast China that the Russians and Japanese fought to control in the late nineteenth and early twentieth centuries.

Treaty of Portsmouth   Treaty in 1905 ending the Russo-Japanese War, which was negotiated at a conference in Portsmouth, New Hampshire, through Theodore Roosevelt's mediation.

Canal Zone   Territory under U.S. control including the Panama Canal and land extending 5 miles on either side of it.

United States should control an **isthmian** canal. Protecting that canal led the United States to establish **hegemony** in the Caribbean and Central America as a means of preventing any other major power from threatening the canal. The new American role also focused on the Pacific. Captain Mahan had pointed out that the Atlantic Ocean had been the theater of conflict among European nations in the eighteenth century. He looked to the Pacific Ocean as the likely theater of twentieth-century conflict. Again, considerations of commercial enterprise and naval strategy coincided in leading the United States to acquire naval bases at strategic points in the central Pacific (Hawai'i), south Pacific (eastern Samoa), and off eastern Asia (the Philippines).

America's new vision of the world divided nations into two broad categories. On the one hand were all the "civilized" nations. On the other were those nations that Theodore Roosevelt described as "barbarous." American policy toward "civilized" countries—the European powers, Japan, and the large, stable nations of Latin America—focused on finding peaceful ways to realize mutual objectives, especially through arbitration. In eastern Asia, McKinley, Roosevelt, and Taft looked to a balance of power among the contending "civilized" powers as most likely to realize the American objective of maintaining access to the China market.

The conviction that arbitration was the appropriate means to settle disputes among "civilized" countries was widespread. An international conference in 1899 created a Permanent Court of Arbitration in the Netherlands. Housed in a marble "peace palace" built through a donation from Andrew Carnegie, the **Hague Court** functioned as a source of neutral arbitrators for international disputes. Both Roosevelt and Taft tried to negotiate arbitration treaties with major powers, only to find that the Senate was not willing to ratify them. Senators feared that such treaties might diminish their future role in approving agreements with other countries.

The United States and Britain repeatedly used arbitration to settle disputes between themselves. In addition to the *Alabama* claims, they used arbitration in 1903 to settle questions over the boundary between Alaska and Canada and in 1909 to end a dispute over the rights of American fishermen operating off the coast of Canada.

Throughout the late nineteenth and early twentieth centuries, American relations with Great Britain improved steadily. As Germany expanded its army and navy and increasingly challenged Britain, British policymakers sought to improve ties with the United States, the only nation besides Great Britain with a navy comparable to Germany's. During the Spanish-American War, Britain alone among the major European powers sided with the United States and encouraged its acquisition of the Philippines. In signing the Hay-Pauncefote Treaties and reducing its naval forces in the Caribbean, Britain delivered a clear signal: it not only accepted American dominance there but even depended on the United States to protect its own holdings in the region.

> **isthmian** Pertaining to a narrow strip of land connecting two larger landmasses; in this case, the isthmus was Panama.
> **hegemony** The dominance of one over another.
> **Hague Court** Body of delegates from about fifty member nations created in the Netherlands in 1899 for the purpose of peacefully resolving international conflicts; also known as the Permanent Court of Arbitration.

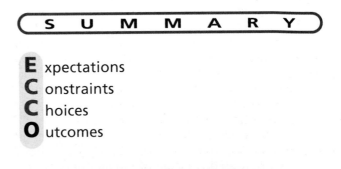

S U M M A R Y

E xpectations
C onstraints
C hoices
O utcomes

From 1865 to 1889, few Americans *expected* their nation to take a major part in world affairs. The United States did make *choices* to acquire Alaska and to expel the French from Mexico. Other American *choices* brought some involvement in the Caribbean and Central America and in eastern Asia and the Pacific.

The 1890s witnessed the development of enlarged *expectations* and daring *choices* in foreign affairs. During the administration of Benjamin Harrison, Congress approved the creation of a modern navy. Although a revolution presented the United States with an opportunity to annex Hawai'i, President Grover Cleveland *chose* to reject that course. However, Cleveland boldly threatened war with Great Britain over a disputed boundary between Venezuela and British Guiana, and Britain *chose* to back down.

A revolution in Cuba led the United States into a one-sided war with Spain in 1898. The immediate *outcome* of the war was acquisition of an American colonial empire that included Cuba, the Philippines, Guam, and Puerto Rico. Congress annexed Hawai'i in the midst of the war, and the United States acquired Samoa by treaty in 1899. The Filipinos *chose* to resist the imposition of American authority, leading to a three-year war that cost more lives than the Spanish-American War. With the Philippines in hand and an improved navy on the seas, the United States was free of old *constraints* on

its influence in East Asia. It now *chose* to assert the principle of the Open Door in China, where American troops helped suppress the Boxer Rebellion.

President Theodore Roosevelt's *choices* played an important role in defining America's status as a world power. He secured rights to build a U.S.-controlled canal through Panama and established Panama as an American protectorate. The Roosevelt Corollary declared that the United States was the dominant power in the Caribbean and Central America. In eastern Asia, by contrast, Roosevelt *chose* to bolster the Open Door policy by maintaining a balance of power.

Roosevelt and many others *expected* that "civilized" nations had no need to go to war. Thus he *chose* to seek arbitration treaties with leading nations, efforts that failed because of Senate opposition. Faced with the rise of German military and naval power, Great Britain *chose* to improve its relations with the United States.

One *outcome* of America's *choices* in foreign affairs was the acquisition of colonies in a foreign policy usually described as imperialism. A larger *outcome* was that the United States took on the role of a world power, thereby redefining its relations with the rest of the world.

SUGGESTED READINGS

Beisner, Robert L. *From the Old Diplomacy to the New, 1865–1900,* 2nd ed. (1986).

A concise introduction to American foreign relations for this period.

Gould, Lewis L. *The Spanish-American War and President McKinley* (1980).

The political decisions involved in war, peacemaking, and the acquisition of Spanish possessions.

LaFeber, Walter. *The New Empire: An Interpretation of American Expansion, 1860–1898* (1963).

A leading treatment, the first to emphasize the notion of a commercial empire.

Langley, Lester D. *The Banana Wars: United States' Intervention in the Caribbean, 1898–1934* (1983; reprint, 1988).

Sprightly and succinct account of the role of the United States in the Caribbean and Central America.

McCullough, David G. *The Path Between the Seas: The Creation of the Panama Canal, 1870–1914* (1977).

Perhaps the most lively, engrossing coverage of its subject.

Miller, Stuart Creighton. *"Benevolent Assimilation": The American Conquest of the Philippines, 1899–1903* (1982).

A thorough account of its subject.

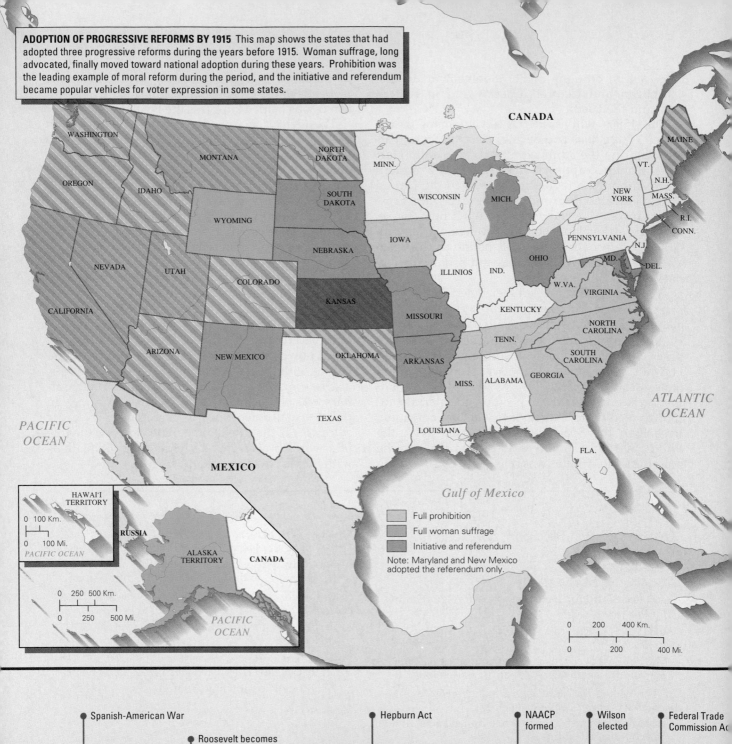

ADOPTION OF PROGRESSIVE REFORMS BY 1915 This map shows the states that had adopted three progressive reforms during the years before 1915. Woman suffrage, long advocated, finally moved toward national adoption during these years. Prohibition was the leading example of moral reform during the period, and the initiative and referendum became popular vehicles for voter expression in some states.

CANADA

WASHINGTON

MONTANA

NORTH DAKOTA

MINN.

WISCONSIN

MICH.

MAINE

VT.

N.H.

NEW YORK

MASS.

OREGON

IDAHO

WYOMING

SOUTH DAKOTA

IOWA

OHIO

PENNSYLVANIA

R.I.

CONN.

N.J.

MD.

DEL.

NEBRASKA

ILLINOIS

IND.

NEVADA

UTAH

COLORADO

KANSAS

MISSOURI

W.VA.

VIRGINIA

KENTUCKY

CALIFORNIA

ARIZONA

NEW MEXICO

OKLAHOMA

ARKANSAS

TENN.

NORTH CAROLINA

SOUTH CAROLINA

GEORGIA

TEXAS

MISS.

ALABAMA

LOUISIANA

FLA.

PACIFIC OCEAN

MEXICO

ATLANTIC OCEAN

Gulf of Mexico

Full prohibition

Full woman suffrage

Initiative and referendum

Note: Maryland and New Mexico adopted the referendum only.

HAWAI'I TERRITORY

0   100 Km.

0   100 Mi.

PACIFIC OCEAN

RUSSIA

ALASKA TERRITORY

CANADA

0   250   500 Km.

0   250   500 Mi.

PACIFIC OCEAN

0   200   400 Km.

0   200   400 Mi.

● Spanish-American War

● Hepburn Act

● NAACP formed

● Wilson elected

● Federal Trade Commission Ac

● Roosevelt becomes president

1898   **1901**   **1906**   **1910**   **1912**   **1914**

1850   1900   1950   2000

The Progressive Era, 1900–1917

Organizing for Change

- How did progressivism and organized interest groups reflect the changing political expectations of many Americans and their new political choices?
- What choices by women and African Americans produced new organizations devoted to political change?

The Reform of Politics, the Politics of Reform

- How did city and state reforms reflect new expectations for political parties and government?
- How did the rise of interest groups reflect new expectations about politics and government?

Roosevelt, Taft, and Republican Progressivism

- What constraints did Roosevelt face, and how did he choose to deal with them?

- What were the outcomes for the role of the federal government in the economy and for the power of the presidency?

Wilson and Democratic Progressivism

- What choices confronted American voters in the presidential election of 1912?
- How did choices by Wilson and the Democrats influence the role of the federal government in the economy and the power of the presidency?

Progressivism in Perspective

- Were the progressives successful in light of their expectations?
- What lasting outcomes of progressivism affect modern American politics?

INTRODUCTION

E xpectations
C onstraints
C hoices
O utcomes

"Nothing is done in this country as it was done twenty years ago," wrote President Woodrow Wilson in 1913. He exaggerated only slightly. The late 1890s and first twenty years of the twentieth century—the Progressive Era—were a time when "reform was in the air," as one journalist later recalled. In 1912, Walter Weyl, a former settlement house worker, described the state of American politics this way:

We are in a period of clamor, of bewilderment, of an almost tremulous unrest. We are hastily revising all our social conceptions. We are hastily testing all our political ideals.

Weyl's description reflected the widespread popular *expectation* for change. Many different individuals and groups joined the crusade for reform, often with quite different *expectations.* The variety of competing organizations seeking to reform politics produced nearly as much clamor and bewilderment as Weyl described.

At the dawn of the new century, however, few Americans could have anticipated the extent of change that lay ahead. Most probably *expected* a continuation of nineteenth-century political patterns, in which parties dominated politics and government's role in the economy was very limited. Yet many Americans also believed that something should be done to curb the power of the new industrial corporations and to correct the problems of the cities.

Progressivism took shape through many *choices* by voters and political leaders. The basic question in most of these *choices* was this: Should government play a larger role in the lives of Americans? This question lay behind debates over regulation of railroads in 1906 and regulation of banking in 1913, as well as behind proposals to prohibit alcoholic beverages and to limit working hours of women factory workers. Time after time, Americans *chose* a greater role for government. Many times, in fact, all agreed on the need for greater government intervention, and the only *choices* were about the form intervention would take. As

they gave government more power, Americans also sought to make it more responsive to ordinary citizens. Americans sometimes impatiently cast former *constraints* aside by putting stricter limits on political parties and by introducing ways for people to participate more directly in politics.

The *constraints* imposed by traditional values of private property and individualism proved more hardy. Although progressives imposed restrictions on the rights of private property, few Americans responded to calls by socialists to eliminate it. Although some reformers proposed to limit individual liberties in the name of morality, a more lasting *outcome* proved to be the breakdown of separate spheres for men and women in politics.

The *outcome* of the political changes of the Progressive Era was a revamped pattern of politics, significantly different from that of the nineteenth century. The long-term changes in the structure and function of government wrought during these decades fundamentally altered American politics and government in the twentieth century. The Progressive Era gave birth to many aspects of modern American politics.

CHRONOLOGY ● ● ● ● ● ●

Reform in the Progressive Era

1889	Pingree elected Detroit mayor
1893	Anti-Saloon League formed
1895	*U.S. v. E. C. Knight*
1896	McKinley elected
1897	Jones elected Toledo mayor
1898	Spanish-American War
1900	First city commission, Galveston, Texas La Follette elected Wisconsin governor McKinley re-elected
1901	Socialist Party of America formed McKinley assassinated; Roosevelt becomes president
1902	Muckraking journalism begins Oregon adopts initiative and referendum Antitrust action against Northern Securities Company Roosevelt intervenes in coal strike Newlands Act
1903	Women's Trade Union League formed Du Bois's *Souls of Black Folk*
1904	Steffens's *The Shame of the Cities* Tarbell's *History of Standard Oil* Roosevelt elected
1905	Niagara Movement Industrial Workers of the World organized
1906	Sinclair's *The Jungle* Hepburn Act Pure Food and Drug Act Meat Inspection Act
1907	Financial panic
1908	*Muller v. Oregon* Race riot in Springfield, Illinois Taft elected

1909	First "red-light abatement" law Payne-Aldrich Tariff
1910	Mann Act National Association for the Advancement of Colored People formed Johnson elected California governor Wilson elected New Jersey governor Taft fires Pinchot
1911	Triangle factory fire
1912	Progressive ("Bull Moose") party formed Wilson elected president
1913	Sixteenth and Seventeenth Amendments Underwood Tariff Federal Reserve Act
1914	Clayton Antitrust Act Federal Trade Commission Act
1916	Montana elects Rankin first woman in Congress Wilson reelected Brandeis appointed to Supreme Court
1917	U.S. enters World War I

Organizing for Change

During the **Progressive Era,** politics dramatically expanded to embrace a much wider range of concerns. And, more than ever before, politics came to reflect the interaction of organized **interest groups.**

The Changing Face of Politics

As the United States entered the twentieth century, the lives of Americans had changed in important ways. The railroad, telegraph, and telephone had transformed concepts of time and space and had fostered the formation of many new organizations. Executives of the new industrial corporations now thought in terms of a national market for their products. Union members allied with others of their trade in distant cities. Farmers studied grain prices in Chicago and Liverpool, England. Physicians organized to establish national standards for medical schools.

Manufacturers, farmers, merchants, carpenters, teachers, lawyers, physicians, and many other occupational groups established national organizations or associations to advance their economic or professional interests. But it was not just occupational groups that formed national associations. So did college graduates, churches, ethnic and racial groups, reformers, humanitarians, and middle-class women. Sooner or later, many of these new organizations sought changes in laws to help them reach their objectives.

The rise of these new organizations transformed American politics. Increasingly, citizens related to politics through organized **interest groups.** At the same time, the typical voter became less and less likely to give his total loyalty to one political party.

Many of these new groups optimistically believed that responsible citizens could achieve social progress and improve the human condition if they acted together and made use of technical know-how. As early as the 1890s, some had begun to call themselves "progressive citizens." By 1910, they were calling themselves simply "progressives."

The term *progressivism* signifies three related developments: (1) the emergence of new concepts of the purpose of government, (2) changes in government policies and institutions, and (3) the political agitation that produced those changes. A progressive can be defined as a person involved in one or more of these activities. The many individuals and groups promoting their own visions of change made progressivism a complex political phenomenon. There was no one progressive movement. Progressivism did, however, reflect the concerns of the urban middle class, especially of urban middle-class women.

Progressivism appeared at the local, state, and federal levels. And progressives promoted a wide range of new government activities: regulation of business, moral reform, consumer protection, conservation of natural resources, educational improvement, tax reform, and more. In all these ways, they brought government more directly into the lives of most Americans.

Women and Reform

Organizations formed or dominated by women burst upon politics during the Progressive era. By 1900, a new ideal for women had emerged from women's colleges and clubs. The "New Woman" stood for self-determination rather than unthinking acceptance of prescribed social roles. By 1910, this fresh attitude, sometimes called **feminism,** was accelerating the transition from the nineteenth-century women's movement for suffrage to the twentieth-century struggle for equality and individualism.

Women's increasing control over one aspect of their lives is evidenced in the birth rate, which fell steadily throughout the nineteenth and early twentieth centuries. They began to challenge laws that banned information about contraception.

> **Progressive Era** A period of reform in the late nineteenth and early twentieth centuries.
>
> **interest group** A coalition of people working on behalf of a particular cause, such as a change in policy, a particular industry, or a special segment of society.
>
> **feminism** The conviction that women are and should be the social, political, and economic equals of men.

♦ Margaret Sanger is seen here in 1916 leaving court after being charged with distributing birth-control information illegally. During the Progressive Era, women worked to remove legal barriers to obtaining information on preventing conception. *Smith College Collection, Smith College.*

Union League (1903) tried to improve the lives of workingwomen. Such efforts received a tragic boost in 1911 when a fire in the Triangle Shirtwaist Company's clothing factory in New York City killed 146 workers—most of them women—who were trapped in a building with no outside fire escapes and with the exit doors locked. The public outcry produced a new state factory safety law.

Some states passed laws specifically to protect workingwomen. In *Muller v. Oregon* (1908), the Supreme Court approved the constitutionality of a law limiting women's hours of work. The decision was widely hailed as a vital and necessary protection for women wage earners. By 1917, all but nine states had laws restricting women's working hours.

Support for suffrage grew as more women recognized the need for political action to bring social reforms. Between 1910 and 1915, eight additional western states approved female suffrage. In 1916, **Jeannette Rankin** of Montana became the first woman elected to the House of Representatives. Suffrage, however, scored few victories outside the West.

Convinced that only a federal constitutional amendment would gain the vote for all women, the **National American Woman Suffrage Association (NAWSA)** developed a national organization geared to lobbying in Washington. Despite the predominantly white and middle-class cast of its leaders, the cause of woman suffrage mobilized young, old, rich, poor, black, and white women during the 1910s. Opponents of woman suffrage had long argued that voting would bring women into the

Margaret Sanger, a nurse practicing among the poor of New York City, became convinced that large families contributed to poverty and damaged the health of women. She saw women die after botched abortions. By 1914, Sanger had concluded, "Women cannot be on an equal footing with men until they have full and complete control over their reproductive function." In 1916, she went to jail for informing women about birth control, a term she originated.

Other women also formed organizations to advance specific causes. The National Consumers' League (formed in 1890) and the Women's Trade

Margaret Sanger   Birth-control advocate who believed that birth-control information was essential to help women escape poverty and who disobeyed government laws against its distribution.

Muller v. Oregon   Supreme Court case in 1908 in which the Court upheld an Oregon law that limited the hours of employment for women.

Jeannette Rankin   Montana social worker who in 1916 became the first woman elected to Congress.

National American Woman Suffrage Association   Organization formed in 1890 that united the two major woman suffrage groups at the time.

male sphere and thereby corrupt them. But some suffrage advocates now turned the domesticity argument to their favor, claiming that instead of politics corrupting women, women would purify politics. Feminists took a different approach, arguing that women should vote because they deserved full equality with men.

Moral Reform

Women were prominent as well in organizations intended to bring moral reform, especially those targeting alcohol. By the late nineteenth century, the temperance movement looked increasingly to government to prohibit the sale and consumption of alcohol. Many saw prohibition as a Progressive reform, enlisting government to safeguard the public interest. Few Progressive reforms claimed as many women activists as prohibition.

The drive against alcohol developed a broad base during the Progressive era. Some **old-stock** Protestant churches, notably the Methodists, termed alcohol one of the most significant obstacles to a better society. Many prohibitionists emphasized the need to protect families from the destructive influence of alcohol on husbands and fathers. At the same time, scientists tied alcohol to certain diseases. Sociologists added studies demonstrating unmistakable links between liquor and prostitution, venereal disease, poverty, crime, and broken families.

The **Anti-Saloon League,** formed in 1893, became the model for successful interest group politics. Proudly describing itself as "the Church in action against the saloon," it usually operated through the large old-stock Protestant denominations. The League attacked the saloon for corrupting not only individual patrons but politics as well. Saloons had long been identified with the party machines that dominated many large cities. The League endorsed only politicians who opposed Demon Rum, regardless of their party. As prohibition demonstrated its growing political clout, politicians increasingly lined up against the saloon. At the same time, the League also promoted statewide referendums to ban alcohol. Between 1900 and 1917, voters in nearly half of the states, including most of the West and South, adopted prohibition.

Although prohibitionists had many worthy aims, they also had a hidden agenda. For many, prohibition offered a way to control and "Americanize" immigrants. Factory owners favored the campaign against alcohol because they wanted sober workers. Protestant politicians crusaded against saloons and political machines on moral grounds, but the real stakes were often political control.

Opposition to prohibition came from Irish, German, and southern and eastern European immigrants, who regarded beer or wine as an accepted part of social life. Their churches did not regard the use of alcohol as inherently sinful. These groups regarded prohibition as an infringement on their "personal liberty." Distillers and beer brewers also organized in opposition to the prohibitionists.

The drive against alcohol was by no means the only target for moral reformers. During the Progressive era, they tried to eliminate prostitution completely through legislation. Beginning in Iowa in 1909, states passed "red-light abatement" laws designed to close down brothels. In 1910, Congress passed the **Mann Act,** making it illegal to take a woman across a state line for "immoral purposes."

Racial Issues

Racial issues received little attention during the Progressive era. Only a few white progressives actively opposed disfranchisement and segregation in the South (see page 398). Indeed, southern white progressives often took the lead in enacting discriminatory laws. Journalist Ray Stannard Baker, one of the few white progressives to address the plight of African Americans, asked in his book *Following the Color Line* (1908), "Does democracy really

---

old-stock People whose families had been in the United States for several generations.

Anti-Saloon League Political lobby for temperance founded in 1893, which organized through churches and offered its endorsement to politicians who favored prohibition.

Mann Act Law passed by Congress in 1910 designed to suppress prostitution. It became illegal to transport a woman across state lines for immoral purposes.

include Negroes as well as white men?" For most white Americans, the answer appeared to be no.

Lynchings and violence continued as facts of life for African Americans. Between 1900 and World War I, lynchings claimed more than eleven hundred victims, mostly in the South, but many in the Midwest. The same years also saw race riots in Atlanta and Springfield, Illinois, that left half a dozen blacks dead and many injured. Little effort was made anywhere to prosecute the leaders of such mobs.

During the Progressive Era, some African Americans challenged the accommodationist leadership of Booker T. Washington. W. E. B. Du Bois, the first African American to receive a Ph.D. from Harvard, argued that blacks should struggle for their rights "unceasingly," and, "if they fail, die trying" (see Individual Choices: W. E. B. Du Bois). In 1905, Du Bois and other black leaders met secretly in Canada, near Niagara Falls, to organize a movement for racial equality. In the wake of the Springfield riot in 1908, some white progressives in 1909 called a biracial conference to seek ways to improve race relations. In 1910, these progressives and the **Niagara Movement** formed the **National Association for the Advancement of Colored People (NAACP)**. Du Bois served as the NAACP's director of publicity and research.

Challenging Capitalism: Socialists and Wobblies

Many progressive organizations reflected middle-class and upper-class concerns. Not so the Socialist Party of America (SPA), formed in 1901. Proclaiming themselves the political arm of workers and farmers, the Socialists argued that industrial capitalism had produced "an economic slavery which renders intellectual and political tyranny inevitable." They called for a cooperative commonwealth in which workers would share in the ownership and control of the means of production.

The Socialists' best-known national leader was Eugene V. Debs, leader of the Pullman strike (see page 358). Strong among immigrants, some of whom had become socialists in their native lands, the SPA also took in Christian Socialists (who drew their inspiration from religion rather than from Marx), farmers, and trade union activists. In addition, the party attracted support from some intellectuals such as W. E. B. Du Bois and Margaret Sanger.

In 1905, a variety of radicals, including socialists, organized the Industrial Workers of the World (IWW). The IWW set out to organize the unskilled and semiskilled workers at the bottom of the socioeconomic structure. They aimed at the **sweatshop** workers of eastern cities, **migrant workers,** southern sharecroppers, women workers, African Americans, and the "new" immigrants from southern and eastern Europe. The American Federation of Labor (AFL), which emphasized skilled white males, usually ignored these workers.

IWW members, called Wobblies, had a simple objective: after most workers joined the IWW, they would call a general strike, labor would refuse to work, and capitalism would collapse. The IWW did organize a few dramatic strikes and even scored a few significant victories. A textile strike in Lawrence, Massachusetts, in 1912 gained national attention. But more often, the Wobblies met with brutal suppression by local authorities and rarely made lasting gains.

The SPA counted considerably more victories. Hundreds of cities and towns—including Milwaukee, Wisconsin; Reading, Pennsylvania; and Berkeley, California—elected Socialist mayors or council members. Socialists also won election to state legislatures. Districts in New York City and Milwaukee sent Socialists to Congress. Most Americans, however, had no interest in eliminating private property.

Niagara Movement Civil rights movement that began in 1905 with the meeting at Niagara Falls of W. E. B. Du Bois and others interested in ending segregation and racial inequality in the United States.

National Association for the Advancement of Colored People Biracial civil rights organization founded in New York City in 1910, which worked to end segregation and discrimination in the United States.

sweatshop A shop or factory in which employees work long hours at low wages under poor conditions.

migrant workers Laborers who travel from one area to another in search of work.

Fighting for Equality

W. E. B. Du Bois

A brilliant young intellectual, W. E. B. Du Bois had to choose between leading the quiet life of a college professor and challenging Booker T. Washington's claim to speak on behalf of all African Americans. Schomburg Center for Research in Black Culture; New York Public Library, Astor, Lenox and Tilden Foundations.

In 1904 and 1905, William Edward Burghardt Du Bois moved toward a difficult choice. Should he challenge the leadership of Booker T. Washington, the "Wizard of Tuskegee," the most powerful African American in the nation? In the decade after his Atlanta Compromise address (see pages 397–398), Washington emerged as head of the "Tuskegee Machine." His access to northern white philanthropists made him the chief channel for donations to African-American institutions. And his access to leaders of the Republican party gave him a hand in influencing many, if not most, African-American political patronage appointments, North and South alike. Du Bois, by contrast, was a college professor with few connections to funds or politics, but he was well-known and highly respected among black intellectuals.

Born in Great Barrington, Massachusetts, an area with a very small black population, Du Bois experienced little racial hostility before leaving home. At Fisk University in Nashville, Tennessee, however, he encountered both the constraints of racism and the African-American culture of the South. He completed his undergraduate studies at Harvard, graduated with honors, studied in Germany, and wrote a doctoral dissertation on the suppression of the African slave trade to the United States. In 1895,

The Reform of Politics, the Politics of Reform

In their quest to make politics more honest and to change the structure of government, progressive reformers sometimes found themselves in conflict with the entrenched leaders of political parties. In response, some reformers dedicated themselves to limiting the power of political parties.

Exposing Corruption: The Muckrakers

Journalists played an important role in preparing the ground for reform. In the early 1900s, magazines discovered that their sales boomed when they he became the first African American to receive a Ph.D. from Harvard.

Du Bois then taught at the college level and undertook research and scholarly writing. By the early twentieth century, however, he had chosen to do more than research and teach. In his third book, *Souls of Black Folk* (1903), he challenged Washington's accommodationist approach and insisted that African Americans should never acquiesce in the surrender of their rights. He also presented the concept of *double consciousness,* by which he meant that African Americans had both an African identity and an American identity and needed to be aware of both parts of their cultural heritage. He argued that the "talented tenth"—the African-American intellectual elite—had special leadership obligations. Refuting Washington's claim that African Americans should start at the bottom, Du Bois insisted instead that denial of educational opportunities for the talented tenth constrained all African Americans.

Although the book created a sensation among African-American intellectuals and some white philanthropists, Washington's first response was to invite Du Bois to Tuskegee, apparently to co-opt him into the Tuskegee Machine. Du Bois, however, held back, weighing his choices against the potential for retribution that Washington could bring to bear against his opponents. By late 1904, Du Bois decided to challenge Washington directly, and early in 1905, he charged that Washington had bought and paid for much of the support he had received from the black press.

The next important step, in July 1905, was the formation of the Niagara Movement. This body was to be the organizational vehicle for mobilizing African Americans for an assault both on white supremacy and on Washington's accommodationism. Proclaiming that "persistent manly agitation is the way to liberty," the new organization chose Du Bois as its general secretary. Despite a promising beginning, the movement failed to thrive. In 1910, what was left of the Niagara Movement was transformed into the NAACP, and Du Bois became editor of its journal, *The Crisis.* About the same time, Du Bois briefly joined the Socialist Party of America. He continued to espouse socialist ideas, and the experience of World War I moved him closer to anti-imperialism and pacifism.

Du Bois's uncompromising leadership in the struggle for civil rights and his voluminous writings on both current events and black history made him probably the single most influential African-American intellectual of the twentieth century. By the end of his long life, he concluded that America would never accomplish racial equality. In 1961, he joined the Communist party and accepted citizenship in Ghana, then a socialist nation. There he died during the night of August 27, 1963, the day before one of the greatest civil rights gatherings in American history (see page 647). In announcing Du Bois's death to the huge crowd in Washington, D.C., Roy Wilkins, executive secretary of the NAACP, noted that "at the dawn of the twentieth century his was the voice calling you to gather here today in this cause."

published dramatic exposés of political corruption and corporate wrongdoing. Those who practiced this provocative journalism acquired the name **muckrakers.** *McClure's Magazine* led the surge in muckraking journalism beginning in 1902. *McClure's* readers were treated to **Lincoln Steffens**'s revelations of municipal corruption (published separately in 1904 as *The Shame of the Cities*),

muckrakers Journalists in the Progressive era who wrote investigative articles exposing corruption in city government, business, and industry.

Lincoln Steffens Muckraking journalist and managing editor of *McClure's Magazine* best known for revealing political corruption in city governments.

Ida Tarbell's exposures of Standard Oil's sordid past (published in 1904 as *History of Standard Oil*), and Ray Stannard Baker's discoveries of corruption in labor unions. Sales of *McClure's* soared, and other monthlies soon were detailing the defects of patent medicines, fraud in the insurance industry, the horrors of child labor, and more.

The most famous muckraking exposé, however, was **Upton Sinclair**'s novel *The Jungle* (1906). *The Jungle* exposed in disgusting detail the shortcomings of the meatpacking industry. Sinclair, a socialist, hoped his readers would recognize that the offenses portrayed in his book were the results of industrial capitalism. He described in chilling detail the afflictions of packinghouse workers, from severed fingers to tuberculosis and blood poisoning.

Finley Peter Dunne, a political humorist, claimed that he hadn't "been able to eat anything more nourishing than a cucumber" since reading Sinclair's book. President Roosevelt appointed a commission that confirmed Sinclair's charges. Pressured by Roosevelt and the public, Congress in 1906 passed the **Pure Food and Drug Act,** which banned impure or mislabeled food and drugs, and the **Meat Inspection Act,** which required federal inspection of meatpacking. Sinclair, however, was disappointed that his revelations had not converted readers to socialism. "I aimed at the public's heart," Sinclair later complained, "and by accident I hit it in the stomach."

Reforming City Government

Many municipal reformers argued that corruption and inefficiency were inevitable without major changes in the structure of city government. Usually **city councils** consisted of members elected from neighborhood **wards.** Reformers condemned the ward system for producing city council members unable to see beyond the needs of their own blocks. They concluded that the ward leaders' small favors for neighborhood voters kept the machine in power despite its corruption. Reformers argued that citywide elections, with all city voters choosing from one list of candidates, would result in council members with broader perspectives and would undercut the machines.

James Phelan of San Francisco is one example of an early municipal reformer. Phelan attacked corruption in city government and won election as mayor in 1896. He then led the fight in adopting a new charter that strengthened the office of mayor and required citywide election of supervisors, San Francisco's term for councilmen.

Some municipal reformers proposed new forms of city government, notably the **commission system** and the **city-manager plan.** Both reveal prominent traits of progressivism: a distrust of political parties and a desire for expertise and efficiency.

The commission system first developed in Galveston, Texas, after a hurricane and tidal wave nearly destroyed that city in 1900. The governor appointed five businessmen to run the city. They attracted widespread attention for their efficiency in administering city government. Within two years, more than two hundred communities had adopted a commission system. Typically, all the city's voters elected the commissioners, and each commissioner then took charge of a specific city function.

Ida Tarbell Journalist in the Progressive era whose exposé on the Standard Oil Company revealed its ruthless business ethics.

Upton Sinclair Socialist writer and reformer whose novel *The Jungle* helped bring about government regulation of meatpacking and other industries.

Pure Food and Drug Act Law passed in 1906 that discouraged the use of dyes and preservatives in foods; it forbade the sale of impure or improperly labeled food and drugs.

Meat Inspection Act Law passed in 1906 requiring federal inspection of meatpacking; it was the result of Upton Sinclair's exposé of unsanitary conditions in the industry.

city council A body of representatives elected to govern a city.

ward A division of a city or town, especially an electoral district, for administrative or representative purposes.

commission system System of city government in which all executive and legislative power is vested in a small elective board, usually composed of five members.

city-manager plan System of city government under which a small council, chosen on a nonpartisan ballot, hires a professional to manage the affairs of city government.

The city-manager plan adapted the administrative structure of the corporation to city government. It featured a professional city manager (similar to a corporate executive) who was appointed by an elected city council (similar to a corporate board of directors) to handle much of municipal administration. In 1913, a serious flood led Dayton, Ohio, to adopt a city-manager plan, and other cities then followed.

A few progressives went beyond changing the structure of city government to advocate social reform. Hazen Pingree attracted national attention as mayor of Detroit. Elected in 1889 as an advocate of honest, efficient government, he soon began to criticize the city's gas, electric, and streetcar companies for overcharging customers and providing poor service. His solution was municipal ownership of such utilities. The depression of 1893 led him to address the needs of the unemployed with measures such as work projects and community gardens. Samuel "Golden Rule" Jones, elected mayor of Toledo, Ohio, in 1897, brought the Golden Rule—do unto others as you would have them do unto you—to city government. Under his leadership, Toledo acquired free concerts, free public baths, kindergartens, and the eight-hour workday for city employees.

The Progressive era also saw city governments take up **city planning.** Throughout most of the nineteenth century, urban growth had been driven by a market economy. Cities, however, came to recognize the need to establish separate zones for residential, commercial, and industrial use and to develop efficient transportation systems to reduce traffic congestion. In 1907, Hartford, Connecticut, set up one of the first city-planning commissions. The emergence of city planning represents an important transition in thinking about government and the economy, for it presumed greater government control over use of private property.

Saving the Future

The Progressive Era also saw the development of other professions that were to have an impact on the whole social fabric. In public health, mental health, social work, and education, professionals worked to reshape government to solve the problems of an urban, industrial, multiethnic society. Their objective was to use knowledge to control social forces, to mold society in their own image, and thereby to define the future.

The public schools presented an important arena in which professionals sought change. In the cities especially, graduates of recently established university programs for the preparation of teachers and school administrators began to seek greater control over education. Professional educators pushed for greater centralization in school administration. They particularly pushed to reduce the role of elected **school boards** and school superintendents who had no professional qualifications for their positions.

Advances in medical knowledge and the American Medical Association's efforts to raise the standards of medical colleges and to restrict access to the profession improved the status of physicians. Scientific discoveries helped transform hospitals from charities that provided minimal help for the poor into centers for dispensing the most up-to-date care to all who could afford it. Physicians helped launch public health programs for the eradication of hookworm in the South, **tuberculosis** in the slums, and venereal disease. In the process, public health emerged as a new medical field.

Other emerging professional fields that carried important implications for public policy included mental health and social work. Psychiatrists and psychologists tried to transform the nineteenth-century asylums from places for confining the mentally ill into places where they could be treated and perhaps cured. Social workers often found themselves allied with public health and mental health professionals in their efforts to bring greater governmental control over urban health and safety codes.

---

city planning The practice of planning urban development by regulating the location of transportation, public buildings, recreational facilities, and zoning.

school board A local board of policymakers that oversees a city or town's public schools.

tuberculosis An infectious disease that attacks the lungs, causing coughing, fever, and weight loss; it was common and often fatal in the nineteenth and early twentieth centuries.

Reforming State Government

As reformers launched changes in various cities, **Robert M. La Follette** pushed Wisconsin state government to the forefront of reform. Elected governor of Wisconsin in 1900, La Follette saw conservative members of his own Republican party defeat his proposals to regulate railroad rates and to replace party nominating conventions with the **direct primary.** He then threw himself into an energetic campaign to elect a state legislature that would support reform. He traveled the state, speaking wherever a crowd gathered. La Follette built a strong political following among Wisconsin's farmers and urban wage earners. The political organization he built not only elected reformers to the state legislature but also re-elected La Follette as governor in 1902 and 1904.

La Follette then led the way to a wide range of reform legislation designed to limit both corporations and political parties. Wisconsin adopted a direct primary, set up a commission to regulate railroad rates, increased taxes on railroads and other corporations, enacted a merit system for hiring and promoting state employees, and limited the activities of lobbyists. La Follette also drew on the expertise of faculty members at the University of Wisconsin. These reforms and reliance on experts came to be called the **Wisconsin Idea.** La Follette won election to the U.S. Senate in 1905 and was re-elected until his death in 1925.

La Follette's success prompted imitators elsewhere. But only in California did progressives produce a volume of reform that rivaled Wisconsin's. Hiram W. Johnson, elected governor in 1910 after revealing widespread bribery in San Francisco government, proved to be an uncompromising foe of corporate influence in politics. At his urging, the legislature regulated railroads and public utilities, placed restrictions on political parties, provided protections for labor and conservation, and adopted woman suffrage. Johnson showed more sympathy for labor than did most other reformers. He appointed union leaders to state positions and supported a variety of measures to benefit working people, including an eight-hour-day law for women, **workers' compensation,** and restrictions on child labor. The sympathies of California progressives, however, did not extend to Asians or

Asian Americans. In 1913, California prohibited Asian immigrants from owning land in the state.

California progressives worked to limit the influence of political parties. By 1913, California exceeded all other states in the range of offices that were nonpartisan, including all judges, school administrators, and local and county officials. Only members of the federal Congress, a few statewide officers, and members of the state legislature ran for office as party candidates.

The Decline of Parties and the Rise of Interest Groups

Although California represents the extreme in weakening political parties, nearly all states took steps in that direction. City and state reformers charged that party bosses manipulated nominating conventions, managed public officials, and controlled law enforcement. They claimed too that bosses, in return for payoffs, used their influence on behalf of companies that did business with city or state government. Muckrakers convinced many voters that the reformers were correct. The party organizations that had dominated politics so completely during the nineteenth century now found themselves under attack on every side.

Reformers increased the power of the individual voter and reduced the power of political parties nearly everywhere. State after state adopted the direct primary. Most reformers also sought to introduce or strengthen the merit system to reduce

---

Robert M. La Follette Governor of Wisconsin at the turn of the century, who instituted a series of reforms including direct primaries, tax reform, and anticorruption measures.

direct primary A primary in which the voters who identify with a party choose that party's candidates directly through an election.

Wisconsin Idea The program of political reforms sponsored by Robert La Follette in Wisconsin, which were designed to decrease political corruption and foster direct democracy.

workers' compensation Payments that employers are required by law to award to workers injured on the job.

the number of patronage positions. Most states made judgeships, school-board seats, and educational offices nonpartisan. A number of states also adopted the initiative and referendum, first approved by Oregon in 1902. Some states adopted the **recall,** under which voters could remove a public official from office. The direct primary, initiative and referendum, and recall are sometimes called "direct democracy" because they remove intermediate steps between the voter and final political decisions.

One outcome of the switch to direct primaries and direct election of U.S. senators was a new style of campaign. Candidates now appealed directly to voters rather than to party leaders and convention delegates. Individual candidates thus ran for office on their records and personal attributes, not their party identification. As campaigns focused more on individual candidates than on party positions, advertising supplanted the armies of party retainers who had mobilized voters previously. Without party efforts to get out the vote, voter turnout began to fall.

Political participation changed not only through the instruments of direct democracy but also through organized interest groups. As the power of political parties faded, organized interest groups became more involved in politics to advance their special concerns. The many groups that advocated change sometimes fought among themselves over which reform goals were most important. Groups increasingly pressured candidates for office to commit themselves to the group's stand on issues. In 1904, for example, the National Association of Manufacturers (NAM) targeted and defeated two key prolabor members of Congress. The American Federation of Labor (AFL) responded in 1906 with a similar strategy and managed to elect six union members to the House of Representatives.

Interest groups also focused greater attention on the legislative process. They began retaining the services of full-time **lobbyists** in Washington. Lobbyists urged congressmen to support their group's position on issues, reminded congressmen of the electoral power of the group, and arranged campaign support for those who favored the group. Lobbyists also appeared at the state level.

Thus, as political parties receded from the dominant position they had once occupied, organized interest groups moved in. Some elected officials came to see themselves less as loyal members of a political party and more as mediators among competing interest groups. Pushed one way by the AFL and the other by the NAM, some politicians responded by counting the number of voters each group could influence in their districts and voted accordingly.

Roosevelt, Taft, and Republican Progressivism

The American public came to identify Theodore Roosevelt with progressivism more than any other single person. Elected vice president in 1900, he became the youngest president in American history in 1901 after the assassination of President William McKinley. In seven years, he changed the nation's domestic policies more than any other president since Lincoln and made himself a legend in the process.

Roosevelt: Asserting the Power of the Presidency

Roosevelt was unlike most other politicians of his day. Independently wealthy, he saw politics as a duty rather than as an opportunity for personal advancement. He defined his political views in terms of character, morality, hard work, and patriotism rather than in terms of party rhetoric. He considered political power a tool to achieve an ethical and socially stable society. Confident in his own personal principles, he did not hesitate to wield the full powers of the presidency. Roosevelt often used the office of the presidency as a "bully pulpit"—a forum for preaching—to gain attention for his message of character and responsibility.

> **recall** Procedure by which voters can seek to remove an elected official from office, submitting a petition to bring the matter to a public vote.
>
> **lobbyist** A person who tries to influence the opinions of legislators or other public officials for or against a specific cause.

In his first message to Congress, in December 1901, Roosevelt sounded a theme that he was to repeat throughout his political career: the growth of powerful corporations was "natural," but some of them exhibited "grave evils." He set out to remedy those evils. Roosevelt's chief obstacle was the Supreme Court's decision in *U.S. v. E. C. Knight* (1895). This decision held that the Sherman Anti-Trust Act did not apply to manufacturing companies because they were not involved in interstate commerce. Roosevelt soon found an opportunity to challenge the *Knight* decision. The creation of the Northern Securities Company set up a railroad monopoly in the Northwest. If any industry qualified as interstate commerce, the railroads did. In February 1902, Roosevelt advised Attorney General Philander C. Knox to seek dissolution of the Northern Securities Company for violating the Sherman Act. For the first time, Americans witnessed a serious federal challenge to the ever-increasing might of powerful corporations. In 1904, the Supreme Court agreed that the Sherman Act applied to the Northern Securities Company and ordered it dissolved.

Bolstered by this confirmation of federal power, Roosevelt launched additional antitrust suits and gloried in his reputation as a **trustbuster.** But he never regarded the trustbusting route as the best way to regulate the economy. He regarded large corporations as natural, inevitable, and potentially beneficial. He thought it made more sense to regulate them than to break them up, so he used trustbusting selectively. Companies that met Roosevelt's standards of public service had no reason to fear antitrust action.

Roosevelt's willingness to take bold action did not stop at reining in the trusts. He interjected himself into a labor dispute in 1902 when **anthracite** coal miners went on strike in Pennsylvania, seeking higher wages and an eight-hour workday. Mine owners refused even to meet with representatives of the **United Mine Workers.** As cold weather approached and coal prices edged upward, public concern grew. In early October, Roosevelt called both sides to Washington to urge them to submit their differences to arbitration. The owners haughtily refused. Roosevelt, now angry, considered their attitude "well-nigh criminal."

Roosevelt began preparations to use the army to dispossess the mine owners and reopen the mines.

He also sent Secretary of War Elihu Root to talk with J. P. Morgan, who held a significant stake in the railroads that owned the mines. The threat of military intervention led Morgan to convince the companies to accept arbitration. The arbitration board granted the miners higher wages and a nine-hour workday. No president before had ever intervened in a strike by treating a union as equal to the owners. The coal strike settlement represented what Roosevelt liked to call a **Square Deal,** in which each side received fair treatment.

The Square Deal in Action: Creating Federal Economic Regulation

Roosevelt's trustbusting and settlement of the coal strike brought him great popularity. When he sought election in 1904, he defeated Democratic candidate Alton B. Parker by one of the largest margins up to that time, securing more than 56 percent of the popular vote.

Elected in his own right, Roosevelt now set out to implement meaningful regulation of the railroads, the largest of the nation's big businesses. In 1905, he asked Congress to pass laws regulating railroad rates, opening financial records of railroads to government inspection, and increasing governmental power in strikes involving interstate commerce. Although he had to compromise occasionally with conservative Republicans, Roosevelt accomplished most of his agenda. On June 29,

U.S. v. E. C. Knight Supreme Court ruling in 1895 that the Sherman Anti-Trust Act did not prohibit manufacturing monopolies; it seriously impaired the application of antitrust laws.

trustbuster Label applied to Theodore Roosevelt and others who sought to prosecute or dissolve business trusts.

anthracite Type of coal that contains high levels of carbon and burns with a clean flame; widely used for heating homes and businesses in the early twentieth century.

United Mine Workers Union of coal miners organized in 1890.

Square Deal Phrase used by Theodore Roosevelt to describe the effort to deal fairly with all.

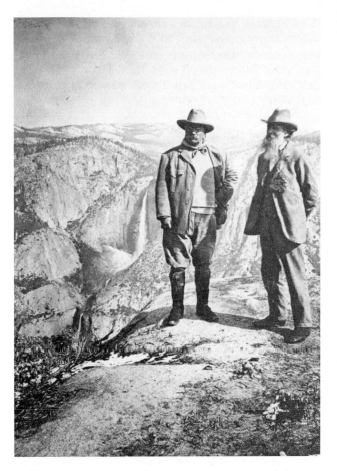

◆ Theodore Roosevelt (left) met with John Muir, a leading advocate for the preservation of wilderness, in 1903 at Yosemite National Park. Although Roosevelt made important contributions to the preservation of parks and wildlife refuges, he was more interested in the careful management of national resources, including federal lands. *Culver Pictures, Inc.*

preserves to save what he called "beautiful and wonderful wild creatures whose existence was threatened by greed and wantonness." Roosevelt, however, deserves to be called a conservationist, not a preservationist. He did not believe that nature should be kept in a pristine condition.

For Roosevelt and Chief Forester **Gifford Pinchot,** conservation involved carefully planning the use of federally owned resources. Pinchot, trained in scientific forestry in Europe, worked to conserve timber and grazing resources by withdrawing large tracts of federal land from public sale or use. They hoped that federal management of these lands would provide for the needs of the present and for the future. While president, Roosevelt more than quadrupled the land under federal protection.

Roosevelt's attitude toward western water clearly reveals his definition of conservation. He strongly supported the National Reclamation Act of 1902, also known as the Newlands Act, which set aside proceeds from the sale of federal lands in sixteen western states to finance irrigation projects. The act established the federal government's responsibility for constructing the dams and canals that made agriculture possible in the arid West. Thus water was to be managed. Far from preserving the western landscape, federal water projects profoundly transformed it.

Taft's Troubles

Soon after Roosevelt won the election of 1904, he announced that he would not seek another term in 1908. He virtually named his successor, William Howard Taft, who had served as governor of the Philippines before joining Roosevelt's cabinet as secretary of war in 1904. William Jennings Bryan faced no serious opposition in winning the Democratic

1906, Congress passed the **Hepburn Act,** which allowed the Interstate Commerce Commission (ICC) to establish maximum railroad rates. The act also limited railroads' ability to issue free passes, a practice reformers had long considered bribery.

Regulating Natural Resources

An outspoken proponent of strenuous outdoor activities, Roosevelt took great pride in establishing five national parks and more than fifty wildlife

> **Hepburn Act** Law passed in 1906 that authorized the Interstate Commerce Commission to fix maximum railroad rates and extended ICC authority to other forms of transportation.
>
> **Gifford Pinchot** Head of the Bureau of Forestry from 1898 to 1910; helped begin the conservation movement.

party's nomination for the third time. Roosevelt's popularity and his endorsement of Taft overcame a lackluster Republican campaign. Taft won just under 52 percent of the vote, and Republicans kept control of the Senate and the House. Soon after turning the reins over to Taft, Roosevelt set off to hunt big game in Africa.

Although Taft's political approach was far more restrained than his predecessor's, he supported Roosevelt's Square Deal. His attorney general initiated some ninety antitrust suits in four years, twice as many as during Roosevelt's seven years. Taft also approved efforts to extend the power of the Interstate Commerce Commission to cover most communication companies.

Taft's administration oversaw the passage of two constitutional amendments. Reformers had long considered the income tax as the fairest means of raising federal revenues. With support from Taft, the **Sixteenth Amendment,** permitting a federal income tax, was ratified in 1913. The **Seventeenth Amendment,** proposed in 1912 and adopted in 1913, changed the method of electing U.S. senators from election by state legislatures to direct election by the voters of the state.

Despite these accomplishments, Taft presided over an increasingly divided Republican party. He alienated the progressive wing of the party in 1909 when he signed the **Payne-Aldrich Tariff,** which retained high rates on most imports. Taft further angered progressives by siding with Joseph Cannon, the highhanded Speaker of the House of Representatives, who used his power to support conservatives. Taft's firing of Roosevelt's friend Gifford Pinchot also greatly annoyed the progressive branch of the party, particularly Roosevelt. By 1912, when Taft faced re-election, he also faced opposition from most progressive Republicans.

Wilson and Democratic Progressivism

In 1912, Theodore Roosevelt bolted the Republican party to run for president as the candidate of the newly formed **Progressive party.** The Democratic presidential candidate that year was Woodrow Wilson, who, like Roosevelt, claimed to be the true voice of progressivism. Roosevelt and Wilson attacked each other's right to claim the title "progressive." They agreed only that William Howard Taft, the Republican candidate, was not a progressive at all.

Debating the Future: The Election of 1912

When Theodore Roosevelt returned from Africa and Europe in 1910, he had already met with the indignant Pinchot, who complained that Taft had betrayed the cause of conservation. He then undertook a speaking tour to propose a broad program of reform that he labeled the **New Nationalism.** Roosevelt did not openly question Taft's re-election, but other Republican progressives began to do so. In the 1910 congressional elections, Republican candidates lost control of the House of Representatives for the first time since 1892.

In February 1912, Roosevelt announced that he would oppose Taft for the Republican presidential nomination. Roosevelt enjoyed great popularity in the thirteen states that had established primaries, winning 278 delegates to 48 for Taft and 36 for La Follette. Taft, however, controlled the party machinery. At the Republican nominating convention, many states sent contesting delegations, one pledged to Taft and the other to Roosevelt. Taft's

---

Sixteenth Amendment   Constitutional amendment ratified in 1913 that gave the federal government the right to establish an income tax.

Seventeenth Amendment   Constitutional amendment ratified in 1913 that authorized the direct popular election of U.S. senators.

Payne-Aldrich Tariff   Tariff bill in 1909 that began as a Republican attempt to reduce tariffs but that ultimately retained high tariffs on most imports.

Progressive party   Party formed in 1912 with Theodore Roosevelt as its candidate for president; it disintegrated when Roosevelt lost the election.

New Nationalism   Program of labor and social reform that Theodore Roosevelt advocated in 1910; he made an unsuccessful bid to regain the presidency using this platform in 1912.

supporters controlled the **credentials committee** and gave most of the contested seats to Taft delegates. Roosevelt's delegates walked out, claiming that Taft had stolen the nomination.

Roosevelt's angry supporters regrouped to form the Progressive or "Bull Moose" party. The new party's platform, which was based on the New Nationalism, called for tariff reduction, regulation of corporations, a minimum wage, an end to child labor, and woman suffrage. Women were more prominent at the Progressive convention than at any other presidential nominating session since the Populists'. Jane Addams seconded Roosevelt's nomination.

The hotly contested Democratic nomination went to Woodrow Wilson, the progressive governor of New Jersey. The Democrats' platform attacked monopolies and called for limits on corporate campaign contributions, a single term for the president, and major tariff reductions. Wilson labeled his program the **New Freedom.**

Much of the campaign focused on big business. Roosevelt continued to maintain that the behavior of corporations was the problem, not their size. Wilson depicted monopoly itself as the problem, not the misbehavior of individual corporations. Breaking up monopolies and restoring competition, he argued, would benefit consumers through better products and lower prices. He also pointed out that as long as monopolies faced regulation, they would naturally seek to control the regulator: the federal government. Only antitrust actions, Wilson argued, could protect democracy from this threat.

Taft was clearly the most conservative of the candidates; Eugene V. Debs, the Socialist candidate, was clearly the most radical. The real contest, however, was between Roosevelt and Wilson. In the end, Wilson received most of the usual Democratic vote and won with 42 percent of the total. The Democrats also won sizable majorities in both houses of Congress. Roosevelt and Taft split the traditional Republican vote. Debs, with but 6 percent, did come in first in some counties and in some city precincts (see Map 21.1).

Wilson and Reform, 1913–1914

Born in Virginia in 1856, Woodrow Wilson first gained national attention when he became president of Princeton University in 1902 and initiated educational reforms. In 1910, New Jersey Democrats turned to him when they needed a respectable candidate for governor. Wilson won the election and suddenly embraced reform, shocking the conservatives who had nominated him. In two years, he led the legislature to adopt a direct primary, a corrupt practices act, workers' compensation, and regulation of railroads and public utilities. Many Democratic progressives supported Wilson when he sought the 1912 presidential nomination.

As president, Wilson focused first on tariff reform. Despite the opposition of many manufacturers, Congress passed the Underwood Tariff in 1913, establishing the most significant reductions since the Civil War. To offset the subsequent federal revenue losses, the **Underwood Act** initiated an income tax, recently authorized by the Sixteenth Amendment.

Wilson tackled banking reform next. Although a national banking system had existed since 1863, periodic financial panics such as the one in 1907 had made the system's shortcomings evident. Chief among these was that it had no way to adjust the **money supply** to the needs of the economy. In 1913, a congressional investigation also revealed highly concentrated power in the hands of the few investment bankers. For Wilson and the Democrats in Congress, the crucial question of banking reform was that of control. Conservatives and bankers favored minimal governmental regulation. Progressive Democrats favored strong federal control.

credentials committee Party convention committee that settles disputes arising when rival delegations from the same state demand to be seated.

New Freedom Program of reforms advocated by Woodrow Wilson during his 1912 presidential campaign, including reducing tariffs, revising the monetary system, and breaking up monopolies.

Underwood Act Law passed in 1913 that substantially reduced tariffs and made up for the lost revenue by providing for a small graduated income tax.

money supply The amount of money in the economy, such as cash and the contents of checking accounts.

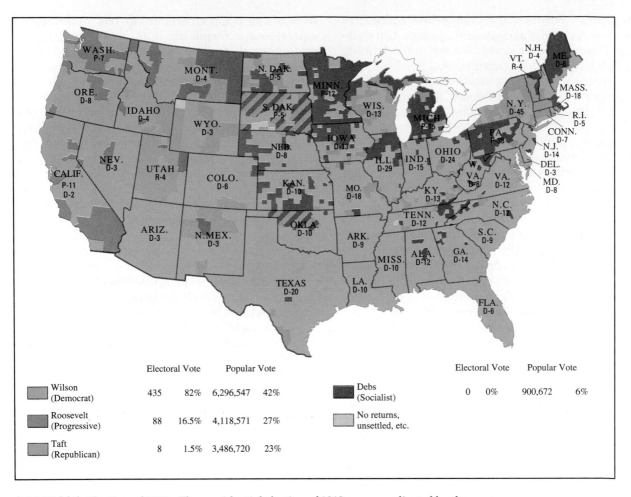

	Electoral Vote		Popular Vote	
Wilson (Democrat)	435	82%	6,296,547	42%
Roosevelt (Progressive)	88	16.5%	4,118,571	27%
Taft (Republican)	8	1.5%	3,486,720	23%

	Electoral Vote		Popular Vote	
Debs (Socialist)	0	0%	900,672	6%
No returns, unsettled, etc.				

◆ **MAP 21.1 Election of 1912**   The presidential election of 1912 was complicated by the campaign of former President Theodore Roosevelt, running as a Progressive. Roosevelt's campaign split the usual Republican vote without taking away much of the usual Democratic vote. Woodrow Wilson, the Democratic candidate, carried many parts of the West and Northeast that Democratic candidates rarely won.

The debate over control ended in compromise. In 1913, the **Federal Reserve Act** established twelve regional Federal Reserve Banks. These were "banker's banks," places where banks kept their reserves. All national banks were required to belong to this Federal Reserve System. The participating banks exercised significant control over the twelve district banks, but the district banks were regulated and supervised by the Federal Reserve Board, a new federal agency with members chosen by the president. In his appointments, Wilson named men sympathetic to banking and thereby reassured the banking community that the "Fed" posed no threat. The Federal Reserve Act created a flexible currency that was no longer solely depen-

> **Federal Reserve Act**   Law passed in 1913 establishing twelve Federal Reserve Banks to hold the cash reserves of commercial banks.

dent on the price of gold. It still provides the framework for regulating the nation's banking system.

In 1914, Congress passed the **Clayton Antitrust Act,** which prohibited specified business practices, including **interlocking directorates** among large companies. It also exempted farmers' organizations and unions from the Sherman Act. The antitrust sections of the Clayton Act, however, provided little basis for breaking up big corporations. One senator claimed that the bill started out as "a raging lion with a mouth full of teeth" but ended up as "a tabby cat with soft gums." The weakening of the Clayton Act partly reflected a change of course by Wilson. Instead of breaking up big business, Wilson now moved closer to Roosevelt's position that regulation had more potential for protecting small businesses. Wilson did energetically support passage of the **Federal Trade Commission Act** (1914), a regulatory measure designed to prevent unfair business competition.

Wilson and Social Reform

Apart from establishing a separate department of labor, Wilson did little to appeal to progressives who favored social reform. He considered efforts to outlaw child labor unconstitutional and was not convinced of the need to amend the Constitution for woman suffrage.

Wilson did draw sharp criticism from some northern social reformers in 1913 when his appointees began to institute racial segregation in several federal agencies. A southerner by birth, Wilson believed in segregation. Even though he resisted the most extreme racists in his party, he appointed adamant segregationists to many federal positions. In the South, some Wilson appointees even began to fire African Americans from federal jobs.

Late in 1914, Wilson announced that he was satisfied with the legislation that had been passed and would seek no further reforms. Early in 1916, however, he reversed direction in anticipation of the coming election. Wilson had won the White House in 1912 only because of the split among Republicans. He joined Democratic progressives in Congress, therefore, in pushing measures intended to capture the loyalty of all progressive voters.

As a first step, Wilson nominated **Louis Brandeis** for the Supreme Court. Brandeis's reputation as a staunch progressive and critic of business aroused intense opposition from conservatives. He was confirmed with support from a few progressive Republicans and became the first Jewish member of the Court. Wilson followed up the Brandeis nomination with support for improved credit facilities for farmers, workers' compensation for federal employees, and a law to eliminate child labor.

Wilson's shift toward the social reformers may have been a significant factor in the election. His support for organized labor gave him strong backing among unionists. In states where women could vote, they supported Wilson in disproportionate numbers, probably because he backed issues such as outlawing child labor. Wilson furthermore vowed to keep the United States out of World War I, which had broken out in 1914. In a very close election, Wilson won with 49 percent of the popular vote against Charles Evans Hughes, a moderately progressive Republican.

Progressivism in Perspective

The Progressive Era began with efforts at municipal reform in the 1890s and sputtered to a close

> **Clayton Antitrust Act** Law passed in 1914 banning such monopolistic business practices as price fixing and interlocking directorates; it also exempted farmers' organizations and unions from prosecution under antitrust laws.
> **interlocking directorate** Situation in which the same individuals sit on the boards of directors of various "competing" companies in one industry.
> **Federal Trade Commission Act** Law passed in 1914 that outlawed unfair methods of competition in interstate commerce and created a commission appointed by the president to investigate illegal business practices.
> **Louis Brandeis** Lawyer and reformer who opposed monopolies and defended individual rights; in 1916 he became the first Jewish justice on the Supreme Court.

during World War I. The war diverted public attention from reform, and by the end of the war, political concerns had changed. By the mid-1920s many of the major leaders of progressivism had passed from the political stage.

The Progressive Era transformed American politics and government. Before the Hepburn Act and the Federal Reserve Act, the federal government's role in the national economy consisted largely of instituting land-grant subsidies and protective tariffs. After the Progressive Era, the federal government became a significant player in the economy, regulating a wide range of economic activity. The income tax quickly became the most significant source of federal funds.

The decline of political parties and the emergence of political campaigns based largely on personality and advertising stemmed from progressive reforms. So did the proliferation of organized pressure groups. Women's participation in politics also increased greatly during the era.

The assertion of presidential authority by Roosevelt and Wilson transformed Americans' expectations regarding the presidency. Throughout the nineteenth century, Congress dominated the making of domestic policy. During the twentieth century, however, Americans came to expect forceful executive leadership in the White House.

Perhaps the most instructive legacy from progressivism is the understanding that reforms rarely fulfill all the expectations of their **proponents.** Some advocates of prohibition, for example, predicted that crime and poverty would diminish once alcohol was banned. Prohibition, however, helped give birth to organized crime, as the makers of illegal liquor began to cooperate among themselves rather than engage in cutthroat competition. Those who reduced the power of political parties hoped to destroy political machines and bosses, but instead fostered the growth of interest-group politics. Some machines also proved highly resilient, adapting themselves to new conditions. The Progressive Era taught America that even the most well-intended reforms are not cure-alls.

proponent   One who argues in support of something.

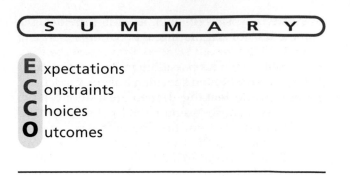

S U M M A R Y

E xpectations
C onstraints
C hoices
O utcomes

Progressivism, a phenomenon of the late nineteenth and early twentieth centuries, refers to new concepts of government, changes in government that made those concepts a reality, and the political process by which change occurred. Those years marked a time of far-reaching political transformation, brought about through many *choices* by groups and individuals, who approached politics with fresh but often quite different *expectations*. Organized interest groups became an important part of this process. Women broke through previous *constraints* to take a more prominent role in politics. The Anti-Saloon League was the most successful of a number of organizations that *chose* to reshape government to enforce their moral standards. Some African Americans *chose* to fight the *constraints* of segregation and disfranchisement, looking to W. E. B. Du Bois for leadership. Socialists and the Industrial Workers of the World saw capitalism as the source of many problems, but few Americans *chose* their radical solutions.

Political reform took place at every level, from cities to the federal government. Muckraking journalists exposed corruption, wrongdoing, and suffering. Municipal reformers introduced modern methods of city government in a quest for efficiency and expertise. Some *chose* to use government to remedy social problems by employing the expertise of new professions such as public health and social work. Reformers also *chose* to attack the power of party bosses and machines by reducing the role of political parties.

At the federal level, Theodore Roosevelt set the pace for progressive reform. He challenged judicial *constraints* on federal authority over big business and advocated other forms of economic regulation. The *outcome* was an increase in the federal government's role in the economy. He also *chose* to regulate the use of natural resources.

In 1912, Roosevelt *chose* to form a new political party, the Progressives, calling for the regulation of business. Wilson, the Democrat, favored antitrust action. Wilson won the election but soon *chose* regulation over antitrust action. He presided over the creation of the Federal Reserve System of regulating banking nationwide. Before the 1916 election, Wilson also pushed for social reforms to unify all progressives behind his leadership.

Progressive reforms have had a profound impact on American politics throughout the twentieth century. In many ways, the *outcome* of the Progressive Era was modern American politics.

SUGGESTED READINGS

Chambers, John Whiteclay, II. *The Tyranny of Change: Americans in the Progressive Era, 1890–1920,* 2nd ed. (1992).

A concise overview of American life during the Progressive Era.

Kerr, K. Austin. *Organized for Prohibition: A New History of the Anti-Saloon League* (1985).

A recent treatment of the organization that formed the prototype for many organized interest groups.

Lewis, David Levering. *W. E. B. Du Bois: Biography of a Race, 1868–1919* (1993).

A powerful biography of Du Bois that delivers on its promise to present the "biography of a race" during the Progressive Era.

Link, Arthur S., and Richard L. McCormick. *Progressivism* (1983).

A thorough survey of progressivism, including the views of historians.

Roosevelt, Theodore. *An Autobiography* (1913; abr. ed. reprint, 1958).

Roosevelt's account of his actions sometimes needs to be taken with a grain of salt but nevertheless provides insight into Roosevelt, the person.

Sinclair, Upton. *The Jungle.* With an introduction by James R. Barrett (1988).

This socialist novel about workers in Chicago's packinghouses is a classic example of muckraking.

THE DOMESTIC IMPACT OF WAR World War I had a major impact on the lives of Americans. This map shows two different examples: (1) labor shortages in industry encouraged African Americans to leave the South and move north or, in some cases, west, and (2) increased food demand encouraged more farming, especially of wheat.

CANADA

WASHINGTON
OREGON
IDAHO
MONTANA
NORTH DAKOTA
SOUTH DAKOTA
WYOMING
NEVADA
UTAH
COLORADO
CALIFORNIA
ARIZONA
NEW MEXICO
Los Angeles

MINN.
WISCONSIN
IOWA
NEBRASKA
KANSAS
OKLAHOMA
TEXAS

MICH.
Detroit
Gary
Toledo
Akron
ILLINOIS
IND.
OHIO
Cleveland
MISSOURI
KENTUCKY
TENNESSEE
ARKANSAS
MISS.
LOUISIANA
ALABAMA
GEORGIA
W. VA.
VIRGINIA
NORTH CAROLINA
SOUTH CAROLINA
FLA.

MAINE
VT
N.H.
NEW YORK
MASS.
New York
RHODE ISLAND
CONNECTICUT
PENNSYLVANIA
NEW JERSEY
Philadelphia
DELAWARE
MARYLAND

PACIFIC OCEAN

ATLANTIC OCEAN

Gulf of Mexico

MEXICO

HAWAI'I TERRITORY
0   100 Km.
0   100 Mi.
PACIFIC OCEAN

RUSSIA
ALASKA TERRITORY (1912)
CANADA
0   250 500 Km.
0   250   500 Mi.
PACIFIC OCEAN

Proportion of increase of African-American population in selected cities, 1910–1920

Arrived 1910–1920
Present in 1910

Areas of increases in wheat acreage, 1909–1919
Some increase
Heaviest increase

0   200   400 Km.
0   200   400 Mi.

Fourteen Points
World War I ends
Treaty of Versailles defeated
Harding elected

Wilson elected
War in Europe begins
Sinking of Lusitania
U.S. enters World War I
Red Scare
Labor unrest

1912   1914   1915   1917   1918   1919   1920

1850   1900   1950   2000

America and the World, 1913–1920

Inherited Commitments and New Directions

- In what ways did existing foreign policy commitments constrain Wilson's choices?
- What major foreign policy choices did Wilson make before the United States entered World War I?

From Neutrality to War: 1914–1917

- What were Wilson's expectations regarding American neutrality?
- What constraints did he face in seeking to maintain neutrality?
- What choices did he make in an effort to do so?
- What was the final outcome?

The Home Front

- What constraints hindered the United States' contribution to the Allied war effort?
- What choices did the federal government make in mobilizing the economy and society?

Americans "Over There"

- What constraints prevented the bulk of the AEF from being sent to Europe until 1918?
- Why did Wilson choose to keep the AEF as separate as possible from the troops of the other Allies?

Wilson and the Peace Conference

- What were Wilson's expectations regarding peace?
- What constraints did he face in realizing those objectives?
- What choices did he make, and what was the outcome?

Trauma in the Wake of War

- How did Americans' expectations change as a result of the outcome of the war and the events of 1919?
- How did these new expectations affect their choice in the 1920 presidential election?

┤ I N T R O D U C T I O N ├

E xpectations
C onstraints
C hoices
O utcomes

On June 28, 1914, a Bosnian Serb killed Archduke Franz Ferdinand, heir to the throne of Austria-Hungary, in Sarajevo, Bosnia-Herzegovina. To punish the assassination, Austria first consulted with its ally, Germany, then made stringent demands on Serbia. Serbia sought help from Russia, which was allied with France. Tense diplomats invoked elaborate, interlocking alliance systems. Huge armies began to move. By August 4, most of Europe was at war.

Earlier, Theodore Roosevelt had probably voiced the *expectations* of many Americans when he claimed in 1899 that war had become practically obsolete among the world's "civilized" nations. As president, Roosevelt helped shape Americans' *expectations* of security when he argued that the best way to preserve peace was by *choosing* to develop naval strength. Given such *expectations,* many Americans were shocked, saddened, and repelled in August 1914 when the leading "civilized" nations of the world lurched into war.

When Europeans *chose* war in August 1914, the United States had already assumed a major role in world affairs. Since 1898, it had acquired the Philippines and the Panama Canal, come to dominate the Caribbean and Central America, and pursued an active involvement in the balance of power in eastern Asia. All three presidents of the Progressive era—Theodore Roosevelt, William Howard Taft, and Woodrow Wilson—agreed wholeheartedly that the United States should exercise a major role in world affairs. But in 1914, the United States was the only large, industrial nation that had *chosen* not to become part of the elaborate network of treaties and understandings among the powers of Europe and Asia. Woodrow Wilson *chose* to maintain U.S. neutrality.

When Wilson entered the White House in 1913, he *expected* to spend most of his time dealing with domestic issues. As a political scientist, he had mostly studied domestic politics, and his winning presidential campaign in 1912 had focused primarily on domestic issues. Although well-read on international affairs, he brought to the White House neither significant international experience nor carefully considered foreign policies. For secretary of state, he *chose* William Jennings Bryan, who had also devoted most of his political career to domestic matters. Both devout Presbyterians, Wilson and Bryan shared a confidence that God had a plan for humankind and that all people shared a basic bond. Both hoped that their foreign policy *choices* might make the United States a model among nations for the peaceful settlement of international disputes. Neither man *expected* that he and the nation were soon to face difficult *choices* over a war so immense and so horrible that its *outcome* would be a profoundly altered world.

Inherited Commitments and New Directions

When Woodrow Wilson entered the White House in 1913, he first fixed his foreign policy attention on Latin America, the Pacific, and eastern Asia. There he tried to balance the anti-imperialist principles of his Democratic party against the **inter**-**ventionist** commitments of his Republican predecessors. In the end, he not only accepted but actually extended most of these previous Republican commitments.

> **interventionist** Tending to interfere in the affairs of another sovereign state.

CHRONOLOGY

The United States and World Affairs

1912	Wilson elected
1913	Huerta takes power in Mexico
	Wilson denies recognition of Huerta
1914	U.S. Navy occupies Veracruz
	War breaks out in Europe
	U.S. neutrality declared
	Stalemate on the western front
1915	German U-boat sinks the *Lusitania*
	United States occupies Haiti
1915–1920	Great Migration
1916	U.S. troops pursue Villa into Mexico
	National Defense Act
	Congress promises Philippine independence
	Sussex pledge
	United States occupies Dominican Republic
	Wilson re-elected
1917	Wilson calls for "peace without victory"
	American troops leave Mexico
	Germany resumes submarine warfare
	Czar overthrown in Russia
	United States declares war on Germany
	Committee on Public Information
	War Industries Board
	Selective Service Act
	Espionage Act
	Race riot in East St. Louis

	Government crackdown on IWW
	Bolsheviks seize power in Russia
	Russia withdraws from war
	Secret treaties published
	Railroads placed under federal control
1917–1918	Union membership rises sharply
1918	Wilson presents Fourteen Points
	Germans launch major offensive
	National War Labor Board
	Sedition Act
	Successful Allied counteroffensive
	Armistice in Europe
1918–1919	Rampant U.S. inflation
1919	Versailles peace conference
	Seattle general strike
	Urban race riots
	Lynchings increase
	Wilson suffers stroke
	Boston police strike
	Senate defeats Versailles treaty
1919–1920	Steel strike
	Red Scare
	Palmer raids
1920	Senate defeats Versailles treaty again
	Harding elected president
1921	Sacco and Vanzetti convictions

Anti-Imperialism and Intervention

Wilson's party had criticized the imperialist foreign policies of McKinley, Roosevelt, and Taft. Secretary of State Bryan was a leading anti-imperialist who had faulted Roosevelt's "Big Stick" approach to foreign affairs. "The man who speaks softly does not need a big stick," Bryan claimed. Wilson shared Taft's commitment to American commercial expansion, but he criticized dollar diplomacy for using the State Department to benefit particular companies.

During the Wilson administration, the Democrats' long adherence to anti-imperialism produced two measures. In 1916, Congress established a bill of rights for residents of the Philippine

Islands and promised them independence at an unspecified date. The next year, Puerto Rico became a U.S. territory, and its residents became U.S. citizens. Thus the Democrats wrote into law a limited version of the anti-imperialism they had proclaimed for more than twenty years.

Yet Wilson was to intervene more in Central America and the Caribbean than any previous president. He sent American marines into Haiti in 1915 after a mob killed the dictatorial president. A subsequent treaty made Haiti a protectorate in which American forces controlled the government until 1933. In 1916, Wilson sent marines into the Dominican Republic, where they remained until 1924.

Wilson and the Mexican Revolution

In Mexico, Wilson similarly engaged in brazen power politics. A rebellion forced dictator **Porfirio Díaz,** who had ruled Mexico for a third of a century, to resign in 1911. Francisco Madero, a wealthy landowner but also a leading reformer, assumed the presidency to great acclaim but proved incapable of uniting the country. Discontent rolled across Mexico, as peasant armies calling for *tierra y libertad* ("land and liberty") attacked the mansions of great landowners. Conservatives feared Madero as a reformer at the same time radicals dismissed him as too timid. Conservative forces led by **General Victoriano Huerta** launched a successful uprising in Mexico City in February 1913 and executed Madero.

Most European governments quickly recognized the Huerta government, but Wilson refused to do so because he considered Huerta a murderer and because Huerta's regime did not rest on the consent of the governed. Telling one visitor, "I am going to teach the South American republics to elect good men," Wilson waited for an opportunity to act against Huerta. In the meantime, anti-Huerta forces in northern Mexico, led by Venustiano Carranza, began to make significant gains.

In April 1914, Wilson found an excuse to intervene when Mexican officials arrested a few American sailors in Tampico. The city's army commander immediately released them and apologized. Wilson, however, used the incident to justify the occupation of **Veracruz,** Mexico's leading port. Veracruz's customs revenue was also the major

source of government income. Huerta, facing Carranza's armies and deprived of munitions and customs revenues, fled the country in mid-July. Wilson withdrew the last American forces from Veracruz in November.

Carranza succeeded Huerta as president, and Wilson officially recognized his government. Carranza faced armed opposition, however, from **Pancho Villa** in northern Mexico. When Villa suffered serious defeats, he apparently decided his best hope for defeating Carranza was to incite a war with the United States. Villa's men murdered several Americans in Mexico and then, in March 1916, killed several Americans in New Mexico. After securing reluctant approval from Carranza, Wilson sent an expedition of nearly seven thousand men, commanded by General John Pershing, into Mexico to punish Villa.

Villa deftly evaded the American troops, drawing them ever deeper into Mexico. Carranza then became alarmed about the American expedition. When a clash between Mexican and American forces resulted in casualties, Carranza asked Wilson to withdraw the American troops. Wilson refused. Villa subsequently doubled behind the American army and raided into Texas, killing more Americans. Wilson sent more men into Mexico despite Carranza's insistence that all the American forces be withdrawn. Only in early 1917, when the prospect of war with Germany began to loom large, did Wilson order the troops to withdraw. The episode left a deep reservoir of Mexican resentment toward the United States.

Porfirio Díaz Mexican soldier and politician who became president after a coup in 1876 and governed the country until 1911.

General Victoriano Huerta Mexican general who overthrew the president, Francisco Madero, in 1913, and established a military dictatorship until forced to resign in 1914.

Veracruz The major port city of Mexico, located on the Gulf of Mexico; in 1914, Wilson ordered the U.S. Navy to occupy the port.

Pancho Villa Mexican bandit and revolutionary who led a raid into New Mexico in 1916, which prompted the U.S. government to send troops into Mexico in unsuccessful pursuit.

From Neutrality to War: 1914–1917

At first, Americans paid only passing attention to the assassination of Franz Ferdinand in Sarajevo in 1914. But when Europe plunged into war, Wilson and all Americans faced difficult choices.

The Great War in Europe

Europe's great powers had avoided armed conflict with each other since the Franco-Prussian War ended in 1871. Since then, however, competition for world markets and colonies had encouraged nations to accumulate arms and seek allies. European diplomats had constructed two major alliance systems by 1907. The **Triple Entente** linked Britain, France, and Russia. The **Triple Alliance** of Germany, Austria-Hungary, and Italy stood in opposition. As European nations formed their alliance networks, nationalism fueled aspirations for independence among the various cultural or linguistic groups of central and eastern Europe. These aspirations were especially powerful in the **Balkan Peninsula** (see Map 22.1), where Austro-Hungarian and Serbian interests clashed.

The primary point of conflict involved Bosnia, a territory annexed by Austria-Hungary in 1908. The Slavs in Serbia had previously eyed Bosnia, which contained a substantial Slavic population, as a candidate for Serbian annexation. Ironically, the Serbian nationalists who plotted the Austrian archduke's assassination did so because they feared that his liberal policies toward Bosnian Slavs would dampen their desire to break way from Austria.

After the assassination, Austria first assured itself of Germany's backing, then declared war on Serbia. In turn, Russia confirmed France's support and began slowly mobilizing in support of Serbia. Rather than wait for Russia to marshal its army, Germany declared war on Russia on August 1 and on France two days later. German strategists planned to bypass French defenses along the Franco-German border by moving through neutral Belgium (see Map 22.1). The Germans expected to knock France out of the war quickly and then turn their full power against Russia. Britain entered the conflict in defense of Belgium on August 4. Eventually, Germany and Austria-Hungary combined with Bulgaria and Turkey to form the Central Powers. Italy abandoned its Triple Alliance partners and joined Britain, France, Russia, Romania, and Japan to make up the Allies.

Instead of the quick knockout blow the Germans had anticipated, the armies settled into defensive lines over the **western front:** 475 miles of French countryside extending from the English Channel to the Alps (see Map 22.1). By the end of 1914, the troops had dug elaborate networks of trenches, separated from each other by a desolate **no man's land** filled with coils of barbed wire, where any movement brought a burst of machine-gun fire. As the war progressed, terrible new weapons—poison gas, aerial bombings, tanks—took many thousands of lives but failed to break the deadlock.

American Neutrality

Wilson's initial reaction to the European conflagration was to announce American neutrality. On August 19, he urged Americans to be "neutral in fact as well as in name . . . impartial in thought as well as in action." He hoped not only that America would remain outside the conflict but that he might serve as the peacemaker.

Wilson's hopes for peace proved unrealistic. Most of the warring nations wanted to gain territory, and only a decisive victory could deliver such a prize. The longer they fought, the more territory they coveted to satisfy their losses. As long as they

Triple Entente   Informal alliance that linked France, Great Britain, and Russia in the years before World War I.

Triple Alliance   Alliance that linked Germany, Italy, and Austria-Hungary in the years before World War I.

Balkan Peninsula   Region of southeast Europe bounded by the Adriatic, Aegean, and Black seas; once ruled by Turkey, it included a number of relatively new and sometimes unstable states.

western front   The line of battle between the Allies and Germany in World War I, which was located in French territory.

no man's land   The field of battle between the lines of two opposing, entrenched armies.

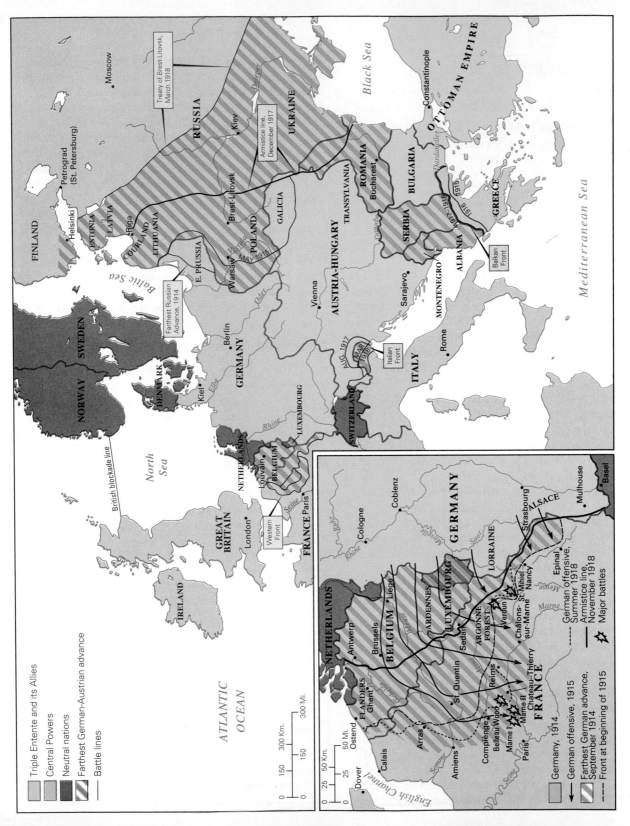

◆ **MAP 22.1 The War in Europe, 1914–1918** This map identifies the members of the two great military coalitions: the Central Powers and the Allies. Notice how much territory Russia lost by the Treaty of Brest-Litovsk as compared to the armistice line (the line between the two armies when Russia sought peace with Germany).

**Legend (main map):**

Triple Entente and its Allies

Central Powers

Neutral nations

Farthest German-Austrian advance

Battle lines

**Main map labels:**

ATLANTIC OCEAN

North Sea

Baltic Sea

Black Sea

Mediterranean Sea

British blockade line

NORWAY

SWEDEN

FINLAND

Helsinki

Moscow

Petrograd (St. Petersburg)

RUSSIA

Kiev

UKRAINE

ESTONIA

LATVIA

Riga

COURLAND

LITHUANIA

Treaty of Brest-Litovsk, March 1918

Armistice line, December 1917

Brest-Litovsk

E. PRUSSIA

Warsaw

POLAND

MAY 1915

GALICIA

Vistula

Oder

Elbe

Rhine

Dnieper

Danube

Farthest Russian Advance, 1914

DENMARK

Kiel

Berlin

GERMANY

NETHERLANDS

Louvain

BELGIUM

LUXEMBOURG

Western Front

Paris

FRANCE

Seine

GREAT BRITAIN

London

IRELAND

SWITZERLAND

Vienna

AUSTRIA-HUNGARY

TRANSYLVANIA

ROMANIA

Bucharest

Sarajevo

MONTENEGRO

SERBIA

BULGARIA

ALBANIA

GREECE

1917–1918

1915

1916

Balkan Front

Dardanelles

Constantinople

OTTOMAN EMPIRE

Rome

ITALY

Italian Front

AUG. 1917

MAR. 1918

Scale: 0   150   300 Km.
0   150   300 Mi.

Inset map legend:

Germany, 1914

German offensive, 1915

Farthest German advance, September 1914

Front at beginning of 1915

German offensive, Summer 1918

Armistice line, November 1918

Major battles

**Inset map labels:**

English Channel

Dover

Calais

Ostend

FLANDERS

Ghent

Antwerp

Brussels

NETHERLANDS

BELGIUM

Liege

ARDENNES

LUXEMBOURG

Sedan

St. Quentin

Arras

Amiens

Compiègne

Belleau Wood

Marne

Marne II

Chateau-Thierry

Paris

Reims

Châlons-sur-Marne

ARGONNE FOREST

Verdun

St. Mihiel

Nancy

LORRAINE

ALSACE

Strasbourg

Epinal

Mulhouse

Basel

GERMANY

Coblenz

Cologne

Ruhr

Rhine

Moselle

Saar

Meuse

Marne

Seine

Somme

Scheldt

FRANCE

Inset scale: 0   25   50 Mi.
0   25   50 Km.

saw a chance of winning, they had no interest in Wilson's appeals.

Wilson's hope that Americans could remain impartial was also unrealistic. Most Americans sided with the Allies. Britain had cultivated American friendship since the mid-1890s. A shared language and culture joined the upper classes in both countries, and trade and finance united many members of their business communities. Memories of French assistance during the American Revolution fueled enthusiasm for France. The German invasion of neutral Belgium aroused American sympathy as well. Allied propagandists worked hard to generate anti-German sentiment in America, portraying the war as a conflict between civilized peoples and brutal **Huns.**

Not all Americans sympathized with the Allies. Nearly 8 million of the 97 million people in the United States had one or both parents from Germany or Austria. Not surprisingly, many of them disputed the depictions of their cousins as bloodthirsty barbarians. Ethnic loyalties also influenced some 5 million Irish Americans, who disliked the English and held no sympathy for them.

Neutral Rights and German U-Boats

Wilson and Bryan agreed on the need to keep American interests separate from those of the parties to the European conflict. However, they developed different approaches for carrying out that policy. Bryan proved willing to sacrifice neutral rights if insistence on those rights posed the prospect of war. Wilson stood firm on maintaining all traditional rights of neutral nations. Bryan initially opposed loans to **belligerent** nations as incompatible with neutrality. Wilson first agreed, but once it became clear that the ban hurt the Allies more than the **Central Powers,** Wilson modified it to permit buying goods on credit. Finally, he dropped the ban on loans altogether.

Traditional neutral rights also included the freedom of neutrals to trade with all belligerents. However, European powers saw the war as a struggle for survival. Wilson soon found himself in conflict with both sides as they turned to naval warfare to break the deadlock on the western front.

Britain began to redefine neutral rights by announcing a blockade not only of German ports but also of neutral ports. Britain also expanded traditional definitions of **contraband** to include anything that might give even indirect aid to an enemy, including food. Germany responded by declaring a blockade of the British Isles, to be enforced by its submarines, called **U-boats.** U-boats were relatively fragile, and even a lightly armed merchant ship stood a reasonable chance of sinking one that surfaced and ordered a ship to stop. Consequently, submarines struck from below the surface, without warning. When Britain began disguising its ships with neutral flags, Germany countered that neutral flags no longer guaranteed protection from U-boat attacks. Whereas Wilson issued token reprimands over Britain's practices, he strongly denounced those of Germany.

On February 10, 1915, Wilson warned that the United States would hold Germany to "strict accountability" for its actions. On May 7, 1915, a German U-boat torpedoed the British passenger liner *Lusitania,* which sank with the loss of 1,198 passengers, including 128 Americans. Americans reacted with horror. When Bryan learned that the *Lusitania* carried rifle cartridges and other contraband, he urged restraint. Wilson, however, prepared a protest message that stopped just short of demanding an end to submarine warfare against unarmed merchant ships. When the German response was noncommittal, Wilson composed an even stronger ultimatum. Bryan feared the words would lead to war, and he resigned as secretary of state.

Huns   Disparaging term used to describe Germans during World War I; the name came from a warlike tribe that invaded Europe in the fourth and fifth centuries.

belligerent   A nation formally at war.

Central Powers   In World War I, the coalition of Germany, Austria-Hungary, Bulgaria, and the Ottoman Empire.

contraband   Goods prohibited by law or treaty from being imported or exported.

U-boat   A German submarine (in German, *Untersee-boot*).

Lusitania   British passenger liner torpedoed by a German submarine in 1915; more than 1,000 drowned, including 128 Americans, bringing the United States closer to war with Germany.

As other U-boat attacks followed, Wilson continued to protest. But after the sinking of the unarmed French ship *Sussex* in March 1916, which injured several Americans, Wilson warned Germany that if unrestricted submarine warfare did not stop, "the United States can have no choice" but to sever diplomatic relations. Germany responded with the **Sussex pledge,** promising that U-boats would no longer strike merchant vessels without warning.

America's economic ties to the Allies grew as the war progressed. The British blockade stifled Americans' trade with the Central Powers, which fell from around $170 million in 1914 to almost nothing two years later. Meanwhile, trade with Britain and France more than offset this decline. American companies sent $756 million in exports to those two nations in 1914 and $2.7 billion in 1916. And by April 1917, American bankers had loaned more than $2 billion to the Allied governments.

Deeply convinced that the best way to keep the United States neutral was to end the war, Wilson sent his close adviser Edward M. House to London and Berlin early in 1916 to sound out the British and Germans on the possibility for peace. House concluded that neither side wanted a negotiated end to the war. Discouraged, Wilson yielded to the increasing numbers of Americans who sought "preparedness"—a military buildup. In the summer of 1916, Congress passed the **National Defense Act,** more than doubling the size of the army, and appropriated the largest naval expenditures in the country's peacetime history.

The Decision for War

After the 1916 election, Wilson tried again to end the war by asking the belligerents to state their terms for ending the fighting. Hoping to cultivate Wilson, Germany announced its support for a peace conference but refused to specify terms. The Allies likewise refused to state their terms.

Still hoping to secure a peace conference, Wilson presented his views on the best way to achieve peace to the Senate in late January 1917. He urged that the only lasting peace would be a "peace without victory" and a "peace among equals" in which neither side exacted gains from the other. The speech received an enthusiastic welcome from most Democrats and progressives. But the British, French, and Germans had no interest in "peace without victory."

In Germany, the initiative passed to those who wanted to resume unrestricted submarine warfare. By denying the Allies American food and supplies, they hoped to achieve a decisive advantage and a quick victory. Germany announced it would resume submarine attacks effective February 1, 1917. Germany knew this move was likely to bring the United States into the war but gambled on being able to win the war before American troops could arrive in large numbers. Wilson accordingly broke off diplomatic relations with Germany on February 3, 1917.

Revelation of the Zimmermann Telegram on March 1 caused a further deterioration in U.S. relations with Germany. In January 1917, **Arthur Zimmermann,** the German foreign secretary, proposed to the German minister in Mexico that Mexico ally itself with Germany. If war broke out between Germany and the United States, Mexico should attack the United States. The incentive for Mexico would be the recovery of its "lost provinces" in the American Southwest. The British intercepted Zimmermann's message and passed it to American representatives on February 24. A public outcry followed the release of the telegram, but Wilson still hesitated to ask for war.

The Germans' sinking of five American ships between March 12 and March 21 removed all doubts from Wilson's mind. On April 2, 1917, Wilson asked Congress for a declaration of war. In asking for war, Wilson tried to unite Americans in a righteous, progressive crusade. He condemned German U-boat attacks as "warfare against mankind" and defined

---

Sussex pledge   German promise in 1916 to stop sinking merchant ships without warning if the United States would compel the Allies to obey "international law."

National Defense Act   Law passed in 1916 enlarging the army, strengthening the National Guard, and providing for an officers' reserve corps.

Arthur Zimmermann   German foreign minister who proposed in 1917 that if the United States declared war on Germany, Mexico should become a German ally and win back Texas, Arizona, and New Mexico.

American war aims idealistically. "The world must be made safe for democracy," he pleaded. He promised that the United States would fight for democracy, self-government, "the rights and liberties of small nations," and a league of nations.

Not all members of Congress agreed that war was necessary. Senator George W. Norris, a progressive Republican from Nebraska, claimed that the nation was going to war to "preserve the commercial right of American citizens to deliver munitions of war to belligerent nations." Only five other senators, however, joined Norris in opposing the declaration of war on Germany. The House voted 373 to 50 for war.

The Home Front

The war altered nearly every aspect of the American economy, as the progressive emphasis on expertise and efficiency produced unprecedented centralization of economic decision making. Mobilization extended beyond war production to the people themselves, their attitudes toward the war, and their response to the need for labor.

Mobilizing the Economy

In the United States, shortages of military supplies, railway transportation snarls, and serious delays in military equipment deliveries proved to be major constraints for the war effort. As a result, federal direction over manufacturing, food and fuel production, and transportation increased dramatically. The extent to which the federal government exercised control over the economy during World War I has never since been matched.

Much of the nation welcomed government intervention. Business enlisted as a partner with government and supplied its cooperation and expertise. Prominent entrepreneurs volunteered their full-time services for a dollar a year. The wartime centralization of economic decision making came about through new agencies composed of government officials, business leaders, and prominent citizens.

The **War Industries Board (WIB),** established in 1917, oversaw the production of war materials. It did little to improve industrial productivity until Wilson appointed Bernard Baruch, a successful Wall Street investor, to head the board in early 1918. By pleading, bargaining, and sometimes threatening, Baruch usually persuaded companies to set and meet production quotas, to allocate raw materials, and to make the entire economy more efficient. Baruch accomplished most WIB goals without coercing corporate America, and industrial production increased by 20 percent.

Efforts to conserve fuel included the first use of **daylight-saving time.** To make rail transportation more efficient, the federal government ran the railroads as a single system, although it left them under private ownership. The government similarly took over the telegraph and telephone systems and launched a huge shipbuilding program.

The National War Labor Board, created in 1918 to mediate labor disputes, endorsed **collective bargaining** and gave some support for an eight-hour workday in return for a no-strike pledge from labor. Many unions secured contracts that brought significant wage increases. Union membership boomed from 2.7 million in 1916 to more than 4 million by 1919. Most established labor leaders, such as Samuel Gompers, president of the American Federation of Labor (AFL), fully supported the war.

One crucial American contribution to the Allies was food, for the war severely disrupted European agriculture. Food Administrator **Herbert Hoover** promoted increased production and conservation of food. He urged American families to observe

---

War Industries Board Board headed by Bernard Baruch that coordinated American production during World War I, setting production quotas, fixing prices, and allocating raw materials.

daylight-saving time Setting clocks one hour or more ahead of standard time to provide more daylight at the end of the workday during late spring, summer, and early fall.

collective bargaining Negotiation between the representatives of organized workers and their employers to determine wages, hours, and working conditions.

Herbert Hoover U.S. food administrator during World War I known for his proficient handling of relief efforts; he was elected president in 1928, only to see the country enter a major depression.

Meatless Mondays and Wheatless Wednesdays and to plant "war gardens." Farmers also brought large areas under cultivation for the first time (see chapter opener map). As a result, food shipments to the Allies tripled.

Mobilizing Public Opinion

Not all Americans fully supported the war. Some German Americans were reluctant to see their sons sent to war against their cousins. Some Irish Americans took little interest in saving Britain, especially after the brutal suppression of an attempt at Irish independence in 1916. The Socialist party voted to oppose American participation in the war. This stance greatly increased the Socialists' share of the vote in several cities in 1917.

To mobilize public opinion in support of the war, Wilson in 1917 created the Committee on Public Information, headed by George Creel. Once a muckraker, Creel set out to sell the war to the American people. The **Creel Committee** eventually counted 150,000 lecturers, writers, artists, actors, and scholars championing the cause and whipping up hatred of the "Huns." Most of those serving with the Creel Committee did so as "Four-Minute Men"—ready to make a four-minute speech anywhere a crowd gathered.

The fierce patriotism fanned by the Creel Committee sometimes sparked harsh measures against those considered "slackers" and "Kaiserites." "Woe to the man or group of men that seeks to stand in our way in this day of high resolution," warned Wilson. Zealots across the country took up the cry. Some states prohibited the use of foreign languages in public. Some communities removed German books from libraries and publicly burned them; others banned the music of Bach and Beethoven. Even words with German connections became objectionable: sauerkraut became "liberty cabbage," German measles were renamed "liberty measles," and dachshunds trotted as "liberty pups." Mobs even lynched people suspected of antiwar sentiments.

Civil Liberties in Time of War

German Americans suffered the most from the wartime hysteria, but pacifists, socialists, and other radicals also became targets for government and vigilantes. Congress passed the **Espionage Act** in 1917 and the **Sedition Act** in 1918, prohibiting interference with the draft and outlawing criticism of the government. Some fifteen hundred people were arrested for violating the Espionage and Sedition acts, including Eugene V. Debs, leader of the Socialist party.

Those who voiced dissenting opinions found they could not rely on the courts for protection. When opponents of the war challenged the Espionage Act, the Supreme Court ruled that freedom of speech was never absolute. Just as no one has the right to shout "Fire" in a crowded theater, said Justice Oliver Wendell Holmes, Jr., so in wartime no one has a constitutional right to say anything that might endanger the nation. The Court also upheld the Sedition Act in 1919.

The IWW came under relentless attack. In July 1917, in Bisbee, Arizona, managers of local copper mines, law enforcement officials, and deputized citizens rounded up more than eleven hundred IWW members, marched them at gunpoint into railroad boxcars, transported them over one hundred miles into the desert, and abandoned them. In September 1917, Justice Department agents arrested IWW leaders throughout the West, who were then sentenced to jail terms of up to twenty-five years. Deprived of its leaders and virtually bankrupt, the IWW never recovered.

A few Americans protested the abridgment of civil liberties. One group formed the Civil Liberties Bureau, forerunner of the American Civil Liberties Union. Most Americans, however, did not object to

---

Creel Committee The U.S. Committee on Public Information (1917–1919), headed by journalist and editor George Creel, which used films, posters, pamphlets, and news releases to mobilize American public opinion in favor of World War I.

Espionage Act Law passed in 1917 that mandated severe penalties for anyone found guilty of interfering with the draft or encouraging disloyalty to the United States.

Sedition Act Law passed in 1918 that supplemented the Espionage Act by extending the penalty to anyone deemed to have abused the government in writing.

the repression. Others who were sympathetic to the victims kept silent. Jane Addams, who had been maligned for expressing her pacifist views before the war, would not sign the Civil Liberties Bureau's appeal for funds, explaining, "I am obliged to walk very softly in all things suspect."

Changes in the Workplace

Intense activism and remarkable productivity characterized American labor's wartime experience. Union membership almost doubled, and a significant number of women became new cardholders. In addition, unions benefited from the encouragement that the **National War Labor Board** gave to collective bargaining between unions and companies. The board also helped settle labor disputes through mediation. Never before had a federal agency interceded this way.

Demands for increased production at a time when millions of men were marching off to war opened opportunities for women. Employment of women in factory, office, and retail jobs had increased before the war, but the war accelerated those trends. Most women who worked outside the home were young and single. Some middle-class women who now entered the paid labor force not only gave up their homebound roles but also rejected their parents' standards of morality and behavior. They adopted instead the less restricted lifestyles that had long been experienced by many wage-earning, working-class women. One commentator observed, "For the first time in the memory of man, girls from well-bred, respectable middle-class families broke through these invisible chains of custom and asserted their right to a nonchalant, self-sustaining life of their own."

The Great Migration and White Reactions

The war also had a great impact on African-American communities. Until the war, about 90 percent of all African Americans lived in the South. By 1920, perhaps as many as 500,000 had moved north in what has been called the **Great Migration.** The largest proportional increases in the African-American population came in the industrial cities of the Midwest. Gary, Indiana, showed one of the greatest gains: 1,284 percent between 1910 and 1920. New York City, Philadelphia, and Los Angeles also attracted many blacks (see chapter opener map). Several factors combined to stimulate this migration. "Every time a lynching takes place in a community down South," T. Arnold Hill of Chicago's Urban League pointed out, "colored people will arrive in Chicago within two weeks." Economic disaster in the South in the form of drought, floods, and the **boll weevil** in 1915 and 1916 was another impetus.

The sharp decline in European immigration caused by the war also spurred the Great Migration. The wartime labor needs of northern cities attracted hundreds of thousands of African Americans seeking better jobs and higher pay. Many industrial jobs paid $3 a day, compared to 50 cents for picking cotton. The impact on some southern cities was striking. Jackson, Mississippi, for example, lost half of all working-class African Americans and a quarter to a third of black business owners and professionals.

The war heightened racial tensions in the South because some whites resented the new options available to blacks. For example, black women who received money from their men in uniform or in wartime jobs sometimes found that they no longer needed farm work. Pine Bluff, Arkansas, officials tried to extend the nation's "work or fight" rule, under which anyone not aiding the war effort by either working or fighting could be arrested, to black women who refused to work in the cotton fields.

Severe wartime racial conflicts erupted in several cities on the northern end of the Great Migration trail. The worst race riot in American history swept through East St. Louis, Illinois, on July 2, 1917. Thousands of African Americans had settled in the city during the previous two years. At least

---

National War Labor Board   Board appointed by President Wilson in 1918 to act as the court of last resort for labor disputes.

Great Migration   Mass movement of black people from the rural South to the urban North during World War I; about a half million people relocated.

boll weevil   Small beetle of the southern United States that infests cotton plants and whose larvae hatch in and damage cotton bolls.

thirty-nine perished in the riot, and six thousand found themselves homeless. Incensed that such brutality could occur so soon after the nation's moralistic entrance into the war, W. E. B. Du Bois charged, "No land that loves to lynch 'niggers' can lead the hosts of Almighty God."

Americans "Over There"

With the declaration of war, the United States needed to mobilize quickly for combat. The navy was already large and powerful after nearly three decades of shipbuilding. The army, however, was tiny. Millions of men had to be enlisted or drafted, trained, supplied, and transported to Europe.

Mobilizing for Battle

The navy was able to strike back quickly at the German fleet. The convoy technique, in which several ships traveled together under the protection of destroyers, helped cut shipping losses in half by late 1917. By the following spring, the U-boat ceased to pose a significant danger.

The army, however, with only 372,000 men, was not ready for action in April 1917. Many men volunteered but not enough. Congress therefore passed the **Selective Service Act** in May, requiring men ages 21 to 30 to register with local boards to determine who was to be called to duty. For the most part, Americans accepted the draft. Eventually, 24 million men registered, and 2.8 million were drafted. By the end of the war, the combined army, navy, and marine corps counted 4.8 million members.

No women were drafted, but some women chose to serve in the military. Almost thirteen thousand women joined the navy and marines, mostly in clerical capacities. They were permitted to hold full military rank and status for the first time. The army, however, considered enlisting women a "most radical departure" and refused to do it. Women could serve in the Army Corps of Nurses, which enrolled nearly eighteen thousand women but denied them army rank, pay, or benefits. At least five thousand civilian women served in various capacities in France, sometimes near the frontlines, most through the Red Cross, which helped staff hospitals and rest facilities.

Nearly 400,000 African Americans served during World War I. Almost 200,000 served overseas, nearly 30,000 on the frontlines. Most black soldiers were treated as second-class citizens. They marched in segregated **Jim Crow** units in the army, were limited to food service duties in the navy, and were excluded from the marines altogether. Only about 600 African Americans earned commissions as officers. White officers commanded most black troops.

"Over There"

As the first troops of the **American Expeditionary Force (AEF)** trickled into France in June 1917, the Central Powers seemed close to victory. French offensives in April 1917 had failed, and a British summer effort in Flanders had resulted in enormous casualties but little gain. A Russian drive in midsummer proved disastrous, and in November, following the triumph of the **Bolsheviks,** Russia withdrew from the war. Hoping to win the war before many American troops arrived, the Germans planned a massive spring offensive for 1918.

The German offensive came in Picardy at the point where the French and British lines joined. AEF units were hurried to the front to block the German advance. By late May, the Germans had moved to within 50 miles of Paris, which French officials considered evacuating. AEF units fought bravely and effectively. At Château-Thierry and Belleau Wood, they took eight thousand casualties during a monthlong battle over a single square mile of wheat fields and woods.

> **Selective Service Act** Law passed in 1917 establishing compulsory military service for men ages 21 to 30.
>
> **Jim Crow** Name for any laws or forms of organization that discriminate against blacks; probably derived from a minstrel-show stock character named Jim Crow.
>
> **American Expeditionary Force** American army commanded by General John J. Pershing that served in Europe during World War I.
>
> **Bolsheviks** Communists who seized power in Russia in November 1917.

◆ This painting depicts British troops being sent into the no man's land between their trenches and those of the Germans. The development of the machine gun made such efforts highly dangerous and contributed to the staggering losses of World War I. The artist, one of only twelve survivors of a company of eighty sent against the enemy's trenches, recalled that "it was bitterly cold and we were easy targets in snow and daylight." *"Over the Top" by Paul Nash. Imperial War Museum.*

The Allies launched a counteroffensive in July 1918, as American troops finally began to pour into France. The American command insisted on being assigned its own sector of the front to make the American contribution to victory clear. In September, General John J. Pershing launched a stunning one-day offensive against the St. Mihiel **salient** (see Map 22.1). AEF forces then joined a larger Allied offensive in the Meuse-Argonne region, the last major assault of the war. In the Argonne Forest on October 8, Corporal Alvin York, armed with only a rifle and a pistol, killed 25 German soldiers, eliminated 35 enemy machine guns, and took 132 prisoners, thus becoming the most heroic figure of the war. By the time of his exploits, the German general staff was pleading with its government to seek an armistice. Fighting ended on the eleventh hour of the eleventh day of the eleventh month of 1918. By then, more than 2 million American soldiers were in France.

When the clamor of celebration replaced the din of battle, thirty-two nations had entered the war against the Central Powers. Nearly 9 million men in uniform died: Germany lost 1.8 million, Russia 1.7 million, Austria-Hungary 1.2 million, the British Empire 908,400. France lost 1.4 million, including half of its men between the ages of 20 and 32. American losses of 115,000 men were small in comparison.

Wilson and the Peace Conference

When the war ended, Wilson hoped that the peace treaty would not contain the seeds of future wars. He also hoped to create an international organization to keep the peace. Most of the Allies, however, had more interest in grabbing territory and punishing Germany.

Bolshevism, the Secret Treaties, and the Fourteen Points

In December 1917, the Bolsheviks, who had seized power in Russia only a month earlier, tried to demonstrate that the war was nothing more than a capitalist scramble for imperial spoils. They published secret treaties by which the Allies had agreed to take colonies and territories from the Central Powers. These exposés strengthened Wilson's efforts to impose his war objectives on the Allies.

salient　Battle line that projects closest to the enemy.

On January 8, 1918, Wilson directly challenged the secret treaties and tried to seize the initiative in defining a basis for peace in a speech to Congress. Wilson presented fourteen specific objectives, soon called the **Fourteen Points.** Points 1 through 5 provided a general context for lasting peace: no secret treaties, freedom of the seas, reduction of barriers to trade, reduction of armaments, and adjustment of colonial claims based partly on the interests of colonial peoples. Points 6 through 13 addressed particular situations: return of territories France had lost to Germany in 1871 and self-determination in Central Europe and the Middle East. The fourteenth point called for "a general association of nations" that could afford "mutual guarantees of political independence and territorial integrity to great and small states alike."

The major Allies reluctantly accepted Wilson's Fourteen Points as a basis for discussion but expressed little enthusiasm for them. When the Germans asked for an end to the fighting, however, they based their request on the Fourteen Points.

Wilson at Versailles

When Woodrow Wilson toured France, Italy, and Britain in December 1918, huge welcoming crowds paid homage to the great "peacemaker from America." Delegates to the peace conference at **Versailles,** which opened on January 18, 1919, assembled amid far-reaching change. The Austro-Hungarian Empire had crumbled, producing the new nations of Poland, Czechoslovakia, and Yugoslavia and the republics of Austria and Hungary. In Germany, **Kaiser Wilhelm II** had **abdicated,** and a republic was being formed. In Russia, a civil war was raging between the Bolsheviks and their anti-Communist opponents. Amid the ruins of the Russian Empire, Finland, Estonia, Latvia, and Lithuania were asserting their independence. The Ottoman Empire was collapsing too, as Arabs revolted with aid from Britain and France. Throughout Europe and the Middle East, national self-determination and government by the consent of the governed seemed to be becoming a reality.

Although representatives were on hand from all the nations that had declared war against the Central Powers, the Big Four made the major decisions at the conference: Woodrow Wilson of the United States, David Lloyd George of Britain, Georges Clemenceau of France, and Vittorio Orlando of Italy. Germany was excluded. Terms of peace were to be imposed, not negotiated. Russia was also excluded on the grounds that it had made a separate peace with Germany in the Treaty of Brest-Litovsk, signed in March 1918. But the specter of Bolshevism hung over the conference.

Wilson learned at the outset that the European leaders were far more interested in pursuing their own national interests than in implementing his Fourteen Points. Clemenceau carried painful memories of Germany's humiliating defeat of France in 1871 and wanted to disable Germany so that it could never again invade his nation. Lloyd George came to Paris with a mandate from British voters for exacting heavy **reparations** from Germany. Orlando insisted on reaping all the territories promised when Italy joined the Allies in 1915.

Facing the insistent and acquisitive Allies, Wilson had no choice but to compromise. He did secure the creation of the **League of Nations,** but only after threatening to make a separate peace with Germany. Rather than achieving a "peace without victory," however, the treaty imposed harsh terms. A "war guilt" clause forced Germany to accept the blame for starting the war. Other provisions required Germany to pay the Allies $33 billion in

---

Fourteen Points   President Wilson's program for maintaining peace after World War I, which called for arms reduction, national self-determination, and a league of nations.

Versailles   Magnificent estate near Paris built by Louis XIV in the seventeenth century; the treaty ending World War I was signed there in 1919.

Kaiser Wilhelm II   German emperor who had worked to create the great military machine and system of alliances that precipitated the outbreak of World War I.

abdicate   To formally relinquish a high office.

reparations   Payments required from a defeated nation as compensation to the victors for damage or injury during a war.

League of Nations   A world organization proposed by President Wilson and founded in 1920; it worked to promote peace and international cooperation.

reparations and to surrender Alsace-Lorraine, all its colonies, and other European territories (see Map 22.2). To prevent further aggression, the treaty deprived Germany of its navy and limited its army to 100,000 men. German representatives signed on June 28, 1919.

In the end, Wilson compromised on nearly all of his Fourteen Points. He hoped the League of Nations would resolve future controversies without war and would also solve the problems created by the compromises he had reluctantly accepted. He was especially pleased with Article 10 of the **League Covenant,** which specified that League members would take joint economic and military action against aggressors.

The Senate and the Treaty

While Wilson was in Paris, opposition to his plans was taking shape in the Republican-controlled Senate, which had to approve any treaty. The Senate split into three groups over the treaty. **Henry Cabot Lodge,** chairman of the Senate Foreign Relations Committee, led the largest opposition group, called the *reservationists* after the reservations, or amendments, to the treaty that Lodge had proposed. At least part of Lodge's opposition was personal. He disliked Wilson intensely and had been angered by the president's failure to include any Republicans in the Versailles treaty delegation. Lodge's chief public misgiving was that Article 10 might be used to commit American troops to war without congressional approval. A smaller group, the *irreconcilables*, consisted primarily of Republicans who opposed any American involvement in European affairs. A third Senate group, mostly Democrats, favored the treaty.

Wilson decided to appeal directly to the people to win support for the treaty. In September 1919, he undertook an arduous speaking tour of twenty-nine cities. The effort proved too demanding for his fragile health. He collapsed in Pueblo, Colorado, on September 25, and returned to Washington. Soon after, he suffered a serious stroke. Half-paralyzed, Wilson remained in seclusion and carried on few of his duties.

Lodge proposed that the Senate accept the treaty with his reservations. Wilson, however, refused to compromise. On November 19, 1919, the Senate defeated the treaty with the Lodge reservations and then defeated the original version of the treaty. The treaty with reservations came to a vote again in March 1920 but failed to gain a two-thirds majority. The United States would not join the League of Nations.

Legacies of the Great War

Roosevelt, Wilson, and most other prewar leaders had projected the progressive mood of optimism and confidence. Wilson invoked this tradition in claiming that the United States was going to war to make the world "safe for democracy." In doing so, however, he fostered unrealistic expectations that world politics might be transformed overnight.

Americans who believed that rational, civilized people had outgrown war found the conflict a disillusioning experience. For some, wartime suppression of civil liberties called into question their belief in the inevitability of progress. Many Americans became disenchanted by the contrast between Wilson's lofty idealism and the Allies' cynical opportunism. The war to make the world safe for democracy turned out to be a chance for Italy to grab Austrian territory and for Japan to seize German concessions in China.

In the end, the peace conference left unresolved many problems. Wilson's elevation of self-government and **self-determination** encouraged aspirations for independence throughout the colonial empires retained by the Allies. Above all, the war and the treaty helped produce economic and political instability in much of Europe, making it a breeding ground for totalitarian and nationalistic movements that were eventually to bring on another world war.

League Covenant The constitution of the League of Nations, which was incorporated in the Versailles treaty in 1919.

Henry Cabot Lodge Massachusetts Republican senator who led congressional opposition to the Versailles treaty and the League of Nations.

self-determination The freedom of a given people to determine their own political status.

MAP 22.2 Postwar Boundary Changes in Central Europe and the Middle East This map shows the boundary changes in Europe and the Middle East that resulted from the defeat of the four large multiethnic empires—Austria-Hungary, Russia, Germany, and the Ottoman Empire.

Trauma in the Wake of War

The United States began to demobilize almost as soon as French church bells pealed for the **Armistice.** By November 1919, nearly the entire force of 4 million men and women was out of uniform. Industrial demobilization occurred even more quickly, as officials canceled war contracts with no more than a month's notice. The year 1919 saw not only the return of the troops from Europe but also raging inflation, massive strikes, bloody race riots, widespread fear of radical **subversion,** violations of civil liberties, and passage of Prohibition.

Inflation and Strikes

Inflation was the most pressing single problem Americans faced after the war. Between 1913 and 1919, the average American family saw its cost of living double. Such inflation contributed to labor unrest. When the Armistice ended the no-strike pledge taken by unions, they made wage demands to keep up with the soaring cost of living. In 1919, however, management was ready for a fight.

After the war, some companies determined to return labor relations to prewar patterns. They blamed organized labor for the rise in prices and connected strikes and unions to "dangerous foreign ideas" from Bolshevik Russia. Seattle's mayor claimed that a five-day general strike called by all the city's unions in February 1919 was a Bolshevik plot. Boston's police struck in September 1919 after the city's police commissioner fired nineteen policemen for joining an AFL union. Massachusetts governor **Calvin Coolidge** activated the state guard to maintain order and break the union. "There is no right to strike against the public safety by anybody, anywhere, anytime," he proclaimed. By mid-1919, it was clear that conservative political and business leaders had joined forces to roll back the union gains of the war years.

The largest and most dramatic labor conflict in 1919 came against United States Steel. Most steelworkers had not had a recognized union since the 1892 Homestead strike. Many steelworkers put in twelve-hour days and, when they changed shifts, sometimes slogged through twenty-four hours in the mills without rest. Wages had not increased as fast as inflation. When the AFL launched an ambitious unionization drive in the steel industry in 1919, many steelworkers responded eagerly.

The steel industry firmly refused to deal with the new organization, provoking a strike in late September. United States Steel, however, blamed the strike on radicals. Company guards protected strikebreakers, and military forces commanded by General Leonard Wood moved into Gary, Indiana, to help round up what they called "the Red element." By January 1920, after eighteen workers had been killed and hundreds beaten, the strike was over and the unions ousted.

The Red Scare

The steel industry's charges of Bolshevism to discredit strikers came at a time when many government and corporate leaders decried the dangers of Bolshevism at home and abroad. In late April 1919, the discovery in various post offices of thirty-four bombs addressed to prominent Americans such as John D. Rockefeller lent credibility to these fears. In June, bombs in several cities damaged buildings and killed two people. Although the work of a few anarchists, the explosions set off a panic over a radical conspiracy to overthrow the government.

With President Wilson still bedridden, Attorney General A. Mitchell Palmer organized an anti-Red campaign, hoping to enhance his presidential prospects in 1920. "Like a prairie fire," Palmer claimed, "the blaze of revolution was sweeping over every American institution." In November 1919, Palmer launched the first of what came to be called the **Palmer raids** to arrest suspected radicals.

Armistice   An agreement to stop fighting.

subversion   Efforts to undermine or overthrow an established government.

Calvin Coolidge   Massachusetts governor and conservative Republican who became Harding's vice president in 1921; he served as president from 1923 to 1929.

Palmer raids   A series of government attacks on individuals and organizations in 1919 and 1920, carried out in a climate of anti-Communist hysteria to search for political radicals.

Authorities rounded up some five thousand people between November and January 1920, and although they found only a few firearms, they **deported** several hundred aliens.

State legislatures joined in with antiradical measures of their own. In January 1920, the New York state legislature expelled five members solely because they were Socialists. When a wide range of respected public figures denounced the assembly action as undemocratic, public opinion regarding the **Red Scare** began to shift. The Red Scare finally spent itself after Palmer's dire predictions of radical activities on May 1, 1920, the major day of celebration for Socialists and Communists alike, came to nothing.

As the Red Scare sputtered to an end, police in Massachusetts arrested two Italian-born anarchists, **Nicola Sacco and Bartolomeo Vanzetti,** and charged them with robbery and murder. Despite inconclusive evidence and the accused men's protestations of innocence, a jury in 1921 found them guilty, and they were sentenced to death. While appeals delayed their execution, many Americans became convinced that the two had been convicted because of their political beliefs and Italian origins. Further, many doubted that they had received a fair trial. Over loud protests at home and abroad, both men were executed in 1927.

Race Riots and Lynchings

The racial tensions of the war years continued into the postwar period. Black soldiers encountered more acceptance and less discrimination in Europe than they had ever known at home. Some whites, however, were determined to restore the state of race relations that had prevailed before 1917. Southern mobs lynched ten returning black soldiers, some still in uniform. Mobs lynched more than seventy blacks in 1919 and burned eleven victims alive.

Rioting also struck outside the South. In July, violence reached the nation's capital, where white mobs attacked blacks throughout the city for three days, killing several. A few days later, in Chicago, whites apparently caused the death of a young African American swimming in Lake Michigan by throwing rocks at him. The incident sparked two weeks of rioting by racial mobs that left fifteen whites and twenty-three blacks dead. By the end of 1919, race riots had flared in more than two dozen places.

The Election of 1920

Republicans confidently expected to regain the White House in the 1920 election. The Democrats had lost their congressional majorities in the 1918 elections, and the postwar confusion and disillusionment often focused on Wilson. One reporter described the stricken president as the "sacrificial whipping boy for the present bitterness."

The reaction against Wilson almost guaranteed the election of any Republican nominee. Several candidates attracted significant support, but no candidate could muster a majority of the convention delegates. Senator **Warren G. Harding** of Ohio emerged as a compromise candidate. Even some of his supporters characterized him as "the best of the second-raters." The Democrats chose James Cox, the governor of Ohio, as their presidential candidate.

The election was a Republican landslide. Harding won 60 percent of the popular vote, the largest popular majority up to that time. Wilson had hoped the election might be a "solemn referendum" on the League of Nations, but it proved to be more of a response to the disappointments of the Wilson years. Americans, it seemed, had had enough idealism and sacrifice.

---

deport To expel an undesirable alien from a country.

Red Scare Wave of anticommunism in the United States in 1919 and 1920, which included a government crackdown that focused on foreigners and labor unions.

Nicola Sacco and Bartolomeo Vanzetti Italian anarchists convicted in 1921 of the murder of a Braintree, Massachusetts, factory paymaster and the theft of a $16,000 payroll; in spite of public protests on their behalf, they were electrocuted in 1927.

Warren G. Harding Ohio politician and Republican who was elected president in 1920; his administration was marred by corruption and scandal.

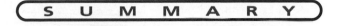

S U M M A R Y

Expectations
Constraints
Choices
Outcomes

Woodrow Wilson took office *expecting* to focus on domestic policy, not foreign affairs. He fulfilled some Democratic party commitments to anti-imperialism but *chose* to intervene extensively in the Caribbean and in Mexico.

When war broke out in Europe in 1914, Wilson proclaimed the United States to be neutral. German submarine warfare and British restrictions on commerce, however, *constrained* traditional *expectations* for neutrality. Wilson secured a German pledge to refrain from unrestricted submarine warfare. He was re-elected in 1916 on the platform that "he kept us out of war." Shortly after his re-election, however, the Germans violated their pledge, and Wilson *chose* to ask for war against Germany.

The war brought new *expectations* in nearly every aspect of the nation's economic and social life. To overcome *constraints* of inefficiency, the federal government *chose* to develop a high degree of centralized economic planning. Fearing that opposition to the war might pose a *constraint* on full mobilization, the Wilson administration *chose* to secure new laws that *constrained* some civil liberties. When the federal government *chose* to back collective bargaining, unions registered important gains. And when labor shortages threatened to *constrain* the war effort, more women and African Americans *chose* to enter the industrial work force. One *outcome* was that many African Americans *chose* to move to northern and midwestern industrial cities.

Germany *chose* to launch a major offensive in early 1918, *expecting* to achieve victory before American troops could make a difference. However, the AEF was able to play a significant part in breaking the German advance. The *outcome* was the Germans' request for an armistice.

In his Fourteen Points, Wilson expressed his *expectations* for peace. *Constrained* by opposition from the Allies, Wilson *chose* to compromise at the peace conference, but he still *expected* that the League of Nations would be able to maintain the peace. Fearing the *constraints* that League membership might place on the United States, enough senators opposed the treaty to defeat it. The *outcome* was that the United States did not become a member of the League.

In the United States, the immediate *outcome* of the war was disillusionment and a year of high prices, costly strikes, the Red Scare, and race riots and lynchings. In 1920, the nation returned to its usual Republican preference when it sent Warren G. Harding to the White House.

SUGGESTED READINGS

Clements, Kendrick A. *The Presidency of Woodrow Wilson* (1992).

More than half of this recent account of Wilson's presidency is devoted to foreign policy matters and the war.

Friedel, Frank. *Over There: The Story of America's First Great Overseas Crusade*, rev. ed. (1990).

A vivid survey of American participation in the fighting in Europe, with many firsthand accounts.

Lewis, Sinclair. *Main Street* (1920; reprint, 1961).

An absorbing novel about a woman's dissatisfaction with her life and her decision to work in Washington during the war.

Link, Arthur S. *Woodrow Wilson: Revolution, War, and Peace* (1979).

A concise introduction to Wilson's role in and thinking about foreign affairs.

Remarque, Erich Maria. *All Quiet on the Western Front.* Trans. A. W. Wheen (1930; reprint, 1982).

The classic and moving novel about World War I, seen through German eyes.

Tuchman, Barbara W. *The Guns of August* (1962; reprint, 1976).

A popular and engaging account of the outbreak of the war, focusing on events in Europe.

The Choice to Declare War

The Context

On April 2, 1917, President Woodrow Wilson spoke to a joint session of Congress and requested that it declare war on Germany in response to the German government's decision to resume unrestricted submarine warfare. Congress did declare war on April 6, and for the first time, the United States found itself involved in a military conflict in Europe. U.S. involvement in World War I lasted for a year and seven months, during which more than 115,000 Americans died on the battlefields of Europe. Once Wilson decided for war, he had to choose the way he would present his decision to Congress and to the American people.

The Historical Question

In asking Congress to declare war on Germany, President Wilson had to choose between a narrow justification, based on American self-interest, and a broader vision of transforming international politics. Wilson chose the broad approach, but members of Congress did not necessarily agree. In calling for war, to what values did Wilson appeal? On what values did Senator Borah base his decision to vote for war? On what values did Senators La Follette and Norris base their opposition to war?

The Challenge

Using the sources provided, along with other information you have read, write an essay or hold a discussion on the following question. Cite evidence in the sources to support your conclusions. **On what values did Wilson, Borah, La Follette, and Norris base their decisions about going to war? What evidence is there that they all drew on the same values as they came to different conclusions about war?**

The Sources

1 President Woodrow Wilson, in a speech to a joint session of Congress on April 2, 1917, asked for a declaration of war against Germany. *I am not now thinking of the loss of property involved, immense and serious as that is, but only of the wanton and wholesale destruction of the lives of non-combatants, men, women, and children, engaged in pursuits which have always, even in the darkest periods of modern history, been deemed innocent and legitimate. Property can be paid for; the lives of peaceful and innocent people cannot be. The present German submarine warfare against commerce is a warfare against mankind. . . .*

We are accepting this challenge of hostile purpose because we know that in such a Government [Germany], following such methods, we can never have a friend; and that in the presence of its organized power, always lying in wait to accomplish we know not what purpose, there can be no assured security for the democratic Governments of the world. . . . We are glad, now that we see the facts with no veil of false pretense about them, to fight thus for the ultimate peace of the world and for the liberation of its peoples, the German people included: for the rights of nations great and small and the privilege of men everywhere to choose their way of life and of obedience. The world must be made safe for democracy. Its peace must be planted upon the tested foundations of political liberty. We have no selfish ends to serve. We desire no conquest, no domination.

2 Senator William E. Borah, progressive Republican from Idaho, spoke in the Senate on April 4, 1917.

There can, to my mind, be only one sufficient reason for committing this country to war, and that is the honor and security of our own people and our own Nation. . . . I join no crusade; I seek or accept no alliances; I obligate this Government to no other power. I make war alone for my countrymen and their rights, for my country and its honor.

3 Senator Robert M. La Follette, progressive Republican from Wisconsin, spoke in the Senate on April 4, 1917.

I had supposed until recently that it was the duty of Senators and Representatives in Congress to vote and act according to their convictions on all public matters that came before them. . . . Another doctrine has recently been promulgated by certain newspapers . . . and that is the doctrine of "standing behind the President," without inquiring whether the President is right or wrong. . . . [President Wilson] says that this is a war "for the things which we have always carried nearest to our hearts—for democracy, for the right of those who submit to authority to have a voice in their own government.". . . [But] the President has not suggested that we make our support of Great Britain conditional to her granting home rule to Ireland, or Egypt, or India. . . .

Will the President and the supporters of this war bill submit it to a vote of the people before the declaration of war goes into effect? Until we are willing to do that, it illy becomes us to offer as an excuse for our entry into the war the unsupported claim that this war was forced upon the German people by their Government. . . . Who has registered the knowledge or approval of the American people of the course this Congress is called upon to take in declaring war upon Germany? Submit the question to the people, you who support it. You who support it dare not do it, for you know that by a vote of more than ten to one the American people as a body would register their declaration against it.

4 Senator George W. Norris, progressive Republican from Nebraska, spoke in the Senate on April 4, 1917.

There are a great many American citizens who feel that we owe it as a duty to humanity to take part in this war. . . . I think such people err in judgment and to a great extent have been misled as to the real history and the true facts by the almost unanimous demand of the great combination of wealth that has a direct financial interest in our participation in the war.

We are taking a step to-day that is fraught with untold danger. We are going into war upon the command of gold. . . . By our act we will make millions of our countrymen suffer, and the consequences of it may well be that millions of our brethren must shed their lifeblood, millions of broken-hearted women must weep, millions of children must suffer with cold, and millions of babes must die from hunger, and all because we want to preserve the commercial right of American citizens to deliver munitions of war to belligerent nations. . . . I feel as though we are about to put the dollar sign upon the American flag. . . .

The troubles of Europe ought to be settled by Europe. . . . [Declaring war will take] America into entanglements that will not end with this war but will live and bring their evil influence upon many generations yet unborn.

IMPROVED HIGHWAYS AND MAJOR CITIES, 1920–1930 During the 1920s, as many Americans became automobile owners, they quickly called for more and better highways. This map shows highway expansion during that decade. The nation also became increasingly urban during the 1920s. This map locates the largest cities.

CANADA

WASHINGTON
OREGON
MONTANA
NORTH DAKOTA
MINN.
WISCONSIN
MICH.
NEW HAMPSHIRE
VERMONT
MAINE
MASSACHUSETTS
NEW YORK
Boston 748,060

IDAHO
SOUTH DAKOTA
Buffalo 506,775
RHODE ISLAND
Milwaukee 457,147
Detroit 993,678
New York 5,620,048
CONNECTICUT
Newark 414,524

WYOMING
Chicago 2,701,705
Cleveland 796,841
Pittsburgh 588,343
PENNSYLVANIA
NEW JERSEY
Philadelphia 1,823,779

NEVADA
IOWA
ILLINOIS
IND.
OHIO
DELAWARE
Baltimore 733,826
MARYLAND

San Francisco 506,676
NEBRASKA
W. VA.
Washington, D.C. 437,571

UTAH
COLORADO
KANSAS
MISSOURI
St. Louis 772,897
KENTUCKY
VIRGINIA
NORTH CAROLINA

CALIFORNIA

Los Angeles 576,673
ARIZONA
NEW MEXICO
OKLAHOMA
ARKANSAS
TENNESSEE
SOUTH CAROLINA
GEORGIA

PACIFIC OCEAN

TEXAS
MISS.
ALABAMA
ATLANTIC OCEAN

FLA.

MEXICO

LOUISIANA

Gulf of Mexico

HAWAI'I TERRITORY
0   100 Km.
0   100 Mi.
PACIFIC OCEAN

U.S.S.R.

ALASKA TERRITORY
CANADA
PACIFIC OCEAN

0   250   500 Km.
0   250   500 Mi.

Improved highways as of 1920

Improved highways as of 1930

Population of 15 largest U.S. cities, 1920

- Over 5,000,000
- 1,000,000–5,000,000
- 500,000–1,000,000
- Under 500,000

0   200   400 Km.
0   200   400 Mi.

Harding elected

World War I ends

Agricultural depression begins

Coolidge reelected

15 millionth Model T

First radio broadcast

Coolidge elected

Klan peaks

First talking movie

| 1918 | 1920 | 1921 | 1923 | 1924 | 1925 | 1927 | 1928 |

| 1850 | 1900 | 1950 | 2000 |

The 1920s, 1920–1928

The Prosperity Decade
- What new economic choices opened for consumers during the 1920s? What new choices opened for business?
- What constraints did farmers face?

The "Roaring Twenties"
- What new expectations and choices shaped American society in the 1920s?
- How did they reflect or contribute to the important social changes of the period?

Traditional America Roars Back
- How did some Americans try to restore traditional social expectations and values during the 1920s?
- What were the outcomes of their choices?

Race, Class, and Gender in the 1920s
- During the 1920s, what expectations and constraints influenced choices faced by American Indians, Mexicans, working people, women, and homosexuals?
- What were the outcomes of their choices?

The Politics of Prosperity
- What were the expectations of the Republican administrations of the 1920s?
- What were their resulting policy choices?

INTRODUCTION

E xpectations
C onstraints
C hoices
O utcomes

Called the "Jazz Age" and the "Roaring Twenties," the decade of the 1920s sometimes seems to be a swirl of conflicting images. Prohibition attempted to control Americans' drinking habits at the same time the flapper was flaunting the liberation of women from previous *constraints.* The booming stock market promised prosperity to all with money to invest at the same time that thousands of farmers were abandoning the land because they could not survive financially. Business leaders celebrated the expansion of the economy at the same time many wage earners in manufacturing endured the destruction of their unions and their legal protections. White-sheeted armies of the Ku Klux Klan marched as self-proclaimed defenders of Protestant American values and white supremacy at the same time African Americans were creating impressive art, literature, and music. The values of big business reigned supreme in politics at the same time the economy was lurching toward a collapse that few anticipated.

In the 1920s, business turned as never before to focus on the consumer. Americans suddenly found themselves facing a range of consumer *choices* beyond all previous *expectations,* as they were deluged with new products such as automobiles, radios, and electric household appliances of every description. Americans began to purchase on credit as installment-plan buying swept the nation, shattering old *constraints* about paying cash and avoiding debt. By the mid-1920s, it seemed as though much of the nation had *chosen* to borrow money and go on an extended buying binge.

Not everyone shared in the *expectations* bred by the consumer culture of postwar America. The poorest farmers and wage earners were *constrained* from doing so by their economic situations. Some others *chose* not to. Disillusioned with the "war to end war" and scornful of the widespread infatuation with consumer buying, many intellectuals became alienated from American culture. Some *chose* to move to Europe to escape what they saw as the emptiness of American life. For them, modern America had become a spiritual and cultural wasteland.

Few other Americans shared the gloom of such intellectuals. For most, the 1920s were a time of glittering *expectations.* Many revealed an unfettered optimism as they picked out their new radio or signed papers to buy a new automobile on the installment plan. For them, the immediate *outcome*—new car, new radio, new styles—seemed to fulfill the rosy *expectations* bred by advertising.

This optimism fed into an expansive popular culture that seemed to reflect a nationwide "age of excess." Radio and movies popularized nationwide tastes, trends, and "heroes" as never before. Led primarily by youths of white, middle-class background, many young people *chose* to flaunt behavior that defied the values of their parents' generation.

Like the shiny new roadsters that filled the advertising in popular magazines, the economy roared along at high speed, fueled by easy credit and consumer spending, virtually unregulated. It carried most Americans with it—until the economic engine sputtered and seemed to die in 1929.

C H R O N O L O G Y

America in the 1920s

1908	Ford introduces Model T General Motors formed
1914	Universal Negro Improvement Association founded War breaks out in Europe
1915	Ku Klux Klan revived
1917	United States enters World War I
1918	World War I ends
1920	Eighteenth Amendment (Prohibition) takes effect Nineteenth Amendment grants women the vote Sinclair Lewis's *Main Street* Harding elected president
1920–1921	Nationwide recession Agricultural depression begins
1921	Temporary immigration quotas First commercial radio broadcasts Bad breath sells Listerine Farm Bloc formed
1922	Sinclair Lewis's *Babbitt* T. S. Eliot's *The Waste Land*
1923	Harding dies; Coolidge becomes president Marcus Garvey convicted of mail fraud Jean Toomer's *Cane* American Indian Defense Association formed
1923–1925	Harding administration scandals revealed
1924	National Origins Act Coolidge elected president Wheaties marketed as "Breakfast of Champions"

	Crossword puzzle fad Full citizenship for American Indians
1925	Scopes trial F. Scott Fitzgerald's *The Great Gatsby* Ku Klux Klan claims 5 million members Klan leader convicted of murder One automobile for every three residents in Los Angeles Chrysler Corporation formed
1926	Railway Labor Act Florida real-estate boom collapses Ernest Hemingway's *The Sun Also Rises*
1927	Coolidge vetoes McNary-Haugen bill Charles Lindbergh's transatlantic flight 15 millionth Model T sold Duke Ellington conducts jazz at Cotton Club
1928	Coolidge vetoes McNary-Haugen again Confederacion de Uniones Obreras Mexicanas formed Ford introduces Model A
1931	Frederick Lewis Allen's *Only Yesterday* Al Capone convicted and imprisoned

The Prosperity Decade

After World War I ended in 1918, the economy completed an important shift toward consumer goods. Previously, U.S. manufacturing efforts had been dominated by railroads, steel, and heavy-equipment manufacturing, few of which made products for sale to the average consumer. During the 1920s, though, the rise of the automobile industry dramatized the new prominence of **consumer-goods** industries.

The Economics of Prosperity

The 1920s was a prosperous decade for most Americans. Although the economy experienced a sharp recession in 1920–1921, it quickly rebounded. By 1923, unemployment had fallen to 2 percent and remained under 5 percent for the rest of the decade. Manufacturing workers saw their average weekly paycheck grow from $21 in 1922 to $25 in 1929 (see Figure 23.1). Increased productivity meant that prices for most manufactured goods remained stable or even went down. Declining prices for agricultural products brought lower food and clothing prices. Thus many Americans seemed better off by 1929 than in 1920: they earned about the same, and they paid somewhat less for necessities.

Advertisers encouraged Americans to spend their money on more than just necessities. In 1931, journalist Frederick Lewis Allen noted in *Only Yesterday*, a perceptive history of the 1920s, that "business had learned as never before the immense importance to it of the ultimate consumer." Persuading Americans to consume an array of products became crucial to keeping the economy healthy.

The marketing of Listerine demonstrates the rising importance of advertising. Listerine had been devised as a general antiseptic, but in 1921 Gerard Lambert devised a more persuasive approach. Through aggressive advertising, he fostered anxieties about the impact of bad breath on popularity and made millions by selling Listerine to combat the offensive condition. In 1924, General Mills first advertised Wheaties as the "Breakfast of Champions," thereby tying the consumption of cold cereal to success in sports. Americans responded by buy-ing those products and others with similarly creative pitches. "We grew up founding our dreams on the infinite promises of American advertising," wrote Zelda Fitzgerald, wife of F. Scott Fitzgerald.

Changes in fashion also encouraged increased consumption. The popularity of short hairstyles for women, for example, led to the development of hair salons. Cigarette advertisers began to target women. The American Tobacco Company advised women to "Reach for a Lucky instead of a sweet" to attain a slim figure. Technological advances also contributed to the growth of consumer-oriented manufacturing. In 1920, about one-third of all residences had electricity. By 1929, electrical power had reached most urban homes. Advertisers began to stress the time and labor that housewives could save by using vacuum cleaners, washing machines, irons, and toasters. Between 1919 and 1929, consumer expenditures for household appliances grew by more than 120 percent.

This increased consumption contributed to a change in people's spending habits. Before the war, most urban families paid cash for what they bought. But many consumers in the 1920s listened to the advice of retailers: "Buy now, pay later." By the late 1920s, about 15 percent of all retail purchases came through the installment plan. Charge accounts in department stores also became popular.

The Automobile: Driving the Economy

The automobile more than any other single product epitomized the consumer-oriented economy of the 1920s. Automobiles remained a luxury item until **Henry Ford** developed a mass-production system that drove down costs. Other companies jostled with Ford for the patronage of American car buyers. By the late 1920s, America's roadways sported nearly one automobile for every five people.

---

consumer goods Products such as food and clothing that directly satisfy human wants.

Henry Ford Inventor and manufacturer who founded the Ford Motor Company in 1903 and pioneered mass production in the auto industry.

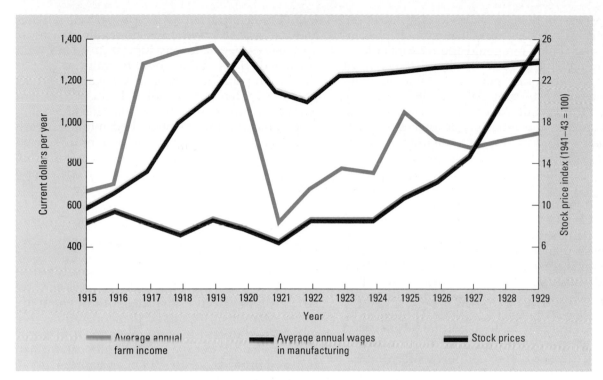

◆ **FIGURE 23.1 Economic Indicators, 1915–1929** This figure presents three measures of economic activity for the period covering World War I and the 1920s. Farm income and wages should be read on the left-hand scale; stock prices should be read on the right-hand scale. *Note:* Incomes are in current dollars, not adjusted for changes in purchasing power. *Source:* U.S. Department of Commerce, Bureau of the Census, *Historical Statistics of the United States, Colonial Times to 1970,* Bicentennial Edition, 2 vols. (Washington, D.C.: U.S. Government Printing Office, 1975), I: 483, 170; II: 1004.

Ford built his success on the **Model T,** introduced in 1908. By 1927, Ford had produced more than 15 million of them, dominating the market by selling at the lowest possible prices. "Get the prices down to the buying power," Ford ordered. His dictatorial management, technological advances, and high worker productivity brought the price of a new Model T as low as $290 by 1927. Cheap to buy and maintain, the Model T made Henry Ford into a wealthy folk hero.

Competition helped keep prices low for middle-class automobile purchasers. General Motors (GM), established in 1908, and Chrysler Corporation, founded in 1925, adopted some of Ford's techniques but also emphasized comfort and style, both missing in the purely functional Model T. Ford finally ended production of the Model T in 1927 and introduced the more stylish Model A the next year.

Ford's company also illustrates how efforts to reduce labor costs by improving labor efficiency caused work on Ford's assembly line to become a thoroughly **dehumanizing** experience. He prohibited his workers from talking, sitting, smoking,

Model T Lightweight automobile produced by Ford from 1908 to 1927 and sold at the lowest possible price, on the theory that an affordable car would be more profitable than an expensive one.

dehumanizing That which deprives of human qualities, such as individuality, by rendering a task mechanical and routine.

singing, or even whistling while working. However, Ford paid his workers more than any of his competitors so that they, too, could afford a Model T.

The automobile industry in the 1920s often led the way in promoting new sales techniques. Installment buying became so widespread that, by 1927, two-thirds of all American automobiles were sold on credit. The introduction of new models every year enticed owners to trade in their cars to keep up with the latest fashions in design, color, and options. Dozens of small automakers closed down when they could not compete with the low prices and yearly models offered by the Big Three. By 1929, Chrysler, Ford, and GM manufactured 83 percent of all the cars in the country.

Business giants like Henry Ford emerged as popular and respected figures in the 1920s. In 1925, in a book titled *The Man Nobody Knows*, Bruce Barton suggested that Jesus Christ could best be understood as a chief executive who "had picked up twelve men from the bottom ranks of business and forged them into an organization that conquered the world." Barton's book led the nonfiction bestseller lists for two years.

"Get Rich Quick": The Speculative Mania

The stock market captured people's fancy in the 1920s as a certain route to riches. Speculation—buying a stock and expecting to make money by selling it at a higher price—ran rampant. Magazine articles proclaimed that everyone could get rich in no time. By 1929, some 4 million Americans, or about 10 percent of American households, owned stock.

Driven partly by real economic growth and partly by speculation, stock prices rose higher and higher. Standard and Poor's index of common stock prices tripled between 1920 and 1929. As long as prices kept going up, it seemed that prosperity would never end.

Although the stock market held the nation's attention as the most popular path to instant riches, other speculative opportunities abounded. One of the most prominent was the Florida land boom. The mania was fed by rapid growth in the population of Florida, especially Miami. People poured into Florida, attracted by the climate, the beaches, and the ease of travel from the chilly Northeast. Speculators began to buy almost any land amid slick predictions that it would boom in value. Stories of land that had increased in value by 1,500 percent over ten years circulated. Like stocks, land was bought on credit with the intention of reselling it at a quick profit. The boom began to falter early in 1926, however, as the population influx slowed, and collapsed later that year when a hurricane slammed into Miami. By 1927, many speculators faced bankruptcy.

Agriculture: Depression in the Midst of Prosperity

Prosperity never extended to agriculture. Farmers never recovered from the postwar recession and struggled to survive financially throughout the 1920s. Many had expanded their operations during the war in response to government demands for more food. After the war, as European farmers resumed production, the glut of agricultural goods on world markets caused prices to fall. Exports of farm products tumbled by half within a few years of the end of the war.

Prices fell as a consequence of this **overproduction.** When adjusted for inflation, corn and wheat prices never rebounded to their prewar levels. The average farm's net income for the years 1917 to 1920 had ranged between $1,196 and $1,395 per year. This fell to a dreadful $517 in 1921, then slowly began to rise. But farm prices did not reach 1917 levels until World War II.

Throughout the 1920s, farmers pressed the government for help. In 1921, the bipartisan congressional **Farm Bloc** formed to promote legislation to assist farmers. Congress passed a few assistance measures in the early 1920s, but none addressed the central problems of overproduction and low prices. In the mid-1920s, proposals to tackle these

> **overproduction**   Production that exceeds consumer need or demand.
>
> **Farm Bloc**   Bipartisan group of senators and representatives formed in 1921 to promote legislation to assist farmers.

two key issues invariably met with presidential vetoes. The average farmer saw the value of his land fall by more than half between 1920 and 1928. Hundreds of thousands of people left farms each year in the 1920s. The prosperity decade did not include rural America.

The "Roaring Twenties"

"The world broke in two in 1922 or thereabouts," wrote novelist Willa Cather. She disliked much that came after. F. Scott Fitzgerald, another novelist, agreed with the date but embraced the change. He thought 1922 initiated an "age of miracles" and an "age of art." For most Americans, evidence of sudden and dramatic social change was on all sides, from automobiles, radios, and movies to a new youth culture and an impressive cultural outpouring by African Americans.

The Automobile and American Life

During the 1920s, the automobile profoundly changed American patterns of living. Highways significantly shortened the travel time from cities to rural areas, thereby reducing the isolation of farm life. One farm woman, when asked why her family had an automobile but not indoor plumbing, responded, "Why, you can't go to town in a bathtub." Trucks allowed farmers to take more products to market more quickly and conveniently than ever before. The spread of gasoline-powered farm vehicles also reduced the need for human farm labor and so stimulated migration to urban areas.

If the automobile changed rural life, it had an even more profound impact on life in the cities. Cities continued to grow. The 1920 census recorded more Americans living in urban areas than in rural ones for the first time. The automobile freed suburban developments from their dependence on commuter rail lines. Suburbs mushroomed, sprouting single-family houses. From 1922 through 1928, construction began on an average of 883,000 new homes each year. New home construction rivaled the auto as a driving force behind economic growth.

A look at Los Angeles shows the automobile's pervasive impact on urban life. From 1920 to 1930 the population of Los Angeles County more than doubled, from fewer than 1 million to 2.2 million. Los Angeles became the first large city organized around the auto. By 1925, Los Angeles counted one automobile for every three residents, twice the national average. The auto made it possible for residents to live farther from work than ever before. In the 1920s, Los Angeles developed the lowest urban population density in the United States. By 1930, about 94 percent of all residences in Los Angeles were single-family homes, an unprecedented figure. The first modern supermarket appeared in Los Angeles. So did the first large shopping district designed for the automobile. Los Angeles set the precedent for organizing life around the automobile.

By the late 1920s, the automobile had also begun to demonstrate its ability to strangle urban traffic. Detroit introduced the first traffic lights in 1920. Although they spread rapidly to other large cities, traffic congestion worsened. By 1926, cars in Manhattan's rush hour crawled along at less than three miles an hour—slower than a person could walk.

A Homogenized Culture Searches for Heroes

As the automobile cut travel times, restrictive immigration laws were closing the door to immigrants. These factors, together with the new technologies of radio and film, began to **homogenize** the culture by breaking down cultural differences based on region or ethnicity.

In 1921, the first commercial radio broadcasting station opened. Within six years, 681 were operating. By 1930, 40 percent of all households had radio sets. Movie attendance increased rapidly as well, from a weekly average of 40 million people in 1922 to 80 million in 1929. The equivalent of two-thirds of the nation went to the cinema every week. As Americans across the country tuned into the

homogenize To make something uniform throughout.

same radio broadcast and families laughed or wept at the same movie, radio and film did their part in homogenizing American life, particularly in urban areas.

Radio and film joined newspapers and magazines in prompting national trends, fashions, and fads. In 1923, the opening of the fabulous tomb of the Egyptian pharaoh Tutankhamen led to a passion for things Egyptian. Crossword puzzles captured the attention of many Americans in 1924. Such fads, in turn, created markets for new consumer goods, from Egyptian-style furniture to crossword dictionaries.

The media also contributed to the development of national sports heroes. By the 1920s, as Frederick Lewis Allen observed, sports "had become an American obsession." Radio now began to broadcast baseball games nationwide. Boxing and college football vied with baseball for spectators' dollars. Most Americans were familiar with the exploits of such baseball greats as Lou Gehrig, Ty Cobb, and Babe Ruth, as well as boxers like Jack Dempsey and Gene Tunney and golfers like Bobby Jones.

The rapid spread of movie theaters created a new category of fame: the movie star. Charlie Chaplin, Buster Keaton, Harold Lloyd, and others brought laughter to the screen. Tom Mix was the best-known cowboy of the silver screen. Sex made stars of Theda Bara, the **vamp,** and Clara Bow, the "It Girl," whose publicists not only said she had "it" but also insisted that no one had to ask what "it" was. Rudolph Valentino soared to fame as a male sex symbol in *The Sheik.* Several women committed suicide after Valentino's death in 1926. "Valentino had silently acted out the fantasies of women all over the world," claimed screen star Bette Davis.

The greatest popular hero of the 1920s, however, was neither an athlete nor an actor but a small-town airmail pilot named **Charles Lindbergh.** In 1927, Lindbergh decided to collect the prize of $25,000 offered to the pilot of the first successful nonstop flight between New York and Paris. Flying *The Spirit of St. Louis* for 33½ sleepless hours, Lindbergh earned the $25,000 and the adoration of crowds on both sides of the Atlantic. His accomplishment seemed to proclaim that old-fashioned individualism, courage, and self-reliance could still triumph over adversity.

Alienated Intellectuals

Other Americans went to Paris in the 1920s, but for a different reason. They left to escape what they considered America's dull conventionalism and dangerous materialism. Whether they left for Paris or not, many American writers bemoaned what they saw as the shallowness, greed, and homogenization of American life. **Sinclair Lewis** in *Main Street* (1920) and *Babbitt* (1922) presented small-town, middle-class existence as not just boring but stifling. The title character, George F. Babbitt, is Lewis's version of a typical, narrow-minded suburban businessman who speaks in clichés and buys every gadget on the market. **H. L. Mencken,** the influential editor of the *American Mercury,* relentlessly pilloried the "booboisie," jeered at all politicians, and celebrated only those writers who shared his distaste for most of American life.

Other writers also rejected traditional values in their disillusionment with postwar society and search for self. Edna St. Vincent Millay captured the spirit of rebellion and pleasure seeking in 1920:

> *My candle burns at both ends;*
> *It will not last the night;*
> *But ah, my foes, and oh, my friends—*
> *It gives a lovely light!*

F. Scott Fitzgerald, in *The Great Gatsby* (1925), revealed the dark side of the hedonism of the 1920s, as he portrayed the pointless lives of wealthy pleasure seekers. Ernest Hemingway, in *The Sun Also Rises* (1926), depicted jaded and disillusioned

---

vamp   A woman who uses her sexuality to entrap and exploit men.

Charles Lindbergh   American aviator who made the first solo transatlantic flight in 1927 and became an international hero.

Sinclair Lewis   Novelist who satirized middle-class America in works such as *Babbitt* (1922) and who became the first American to win a Nobel Prize for literature.

H. L. Mencken   Editor and critic who founded the *American Mercury* and who wrote essays of scathing social criticism.

F. Scott Fitzgerald   Fiction writer who captured the Jazz Age in novels such as *The Great Gatsby* (1925).

expatriates who go to Spain to see the bullfights in an effort to introduce some excitement into their lives. The novel's dominant tone is one of frustration, futility, and suffering.

Others took the theme of hopelessness even further. **T. S. Eliot,** a poet who had fled America for England in 1915, published *The Waste Land* in 1922, in which he presented a grim view of the barrenness of modern life, where a search for meaning yielded "the empty chapel, only the wind's home." Some writers predicted the end of Western civilization. Joseph Wood Krutch in 1929 concluded that modern civilization was so decadent that it could not rejuvenate itself and would be overthrown by barbarians.

Renaissance Among African Americans

Krutch's fear of the imminent end of Western civilization was limited largely to white intellectuals. Such views were little reflected in the striking outpouring of literature, music, and art by African Americans in the 1920s.

Harlem, a predominantly black neighborhood in New York City, quickly became a symbol of the new, urban life of African Americans. The term **Harlem Renaissance** describes a literary and artistic movement in which black artists and writers insisted on the value of black culture and used African and African-American traditions in literature, painting, and sculpture. Pointing to this renaissance in 1925, the black writer Alain Locke argued that African Americans were "achieving something like a spiritual emancipation" and that henceforth the nation "must reckon with a fundamentally changed Negro." Black actors, notably Paul Robeson (see page 612), began to appear in serious theaters and earn acclaim for their abilities.

Among the movement's poets, **Langston Hughes** became the best known. His poetry rang with the voice of the people, as he sometimes used folk language to convey powerful images (see Individual Choices: Langston Hughes). Zora Neale Hurston began her long writing career with several short stories in the 1920s. Jean Toomer's novel *Cane* (1923) has been praised as "the most impressive product of the Negro Renaissance." In it, Toomer combined poetry and prose to produce sketches and short stories dealing with African Americans in rural Georgia and Washington, D.C.

The Renaissance included **jazz,** which was becoming a central element in distinctly American music. Created and nurtured by African-American musicians in southern cities, especially New Orleans, jazz had been introduced to northern and white audiences by World War I. It became so popular that the 1920s have been called the Jazz Age. Jazz also began to influence leading white composers, notably George Gershwin, whose *Rhapsody in Blue* (1924) brought jazz into the symphony halls. Some attacked the new sound, claiming it encouraged people to abandon their self-restraint, especially with regard to sex. Despite such condemnation, the wail of the saxophone became an integral part of the 1920s.

Louis "Satchmo" Armstrong emerged as the leading jazz trumpeter. Bessie Smith, the "Empress of the Blues," was the outstanding vocalist of the decade. The great black jazz musicians drew white audiences into black neighborhoods to hear them. As increasing numbers of whites went "slumming" to Harlem, the area came to be associated with exotic nightlife and glittering jazz clubs such as the Cotton Club. Edward Kennedy "Duke" Ellington went there in 1927 and began to develop the works that made him a respected composer.

---

expatriate A person who has taken up residence in a foreign country or renounced his or her native land.

T. S. Eliot American poet who settled in England and whose long poem *The Waste Land* (1922) chronicles the barrenness of modern life.

Harlem Renaissance Literary and artistic movement in the 1920s centered in Harlem, in which black writers and artists described and celebrated African-American life.

Langston Hughes Poet of the Harlem Renaissance whose work, inspired by the rhythms of jazz and the blues, dealt with the joys and sorrows of African Americans.

jazz Style of music developed in America in the early twentieth century, characterized by strong, flexible rhythms and improvisation on basic melodies.

Choosing to Live in Harlem

Langston Hughes

Langston Hughes, an acclaimed author, chose to celebrate black people in his writing and to develop opportunities for other black artists to cultivate their creativity. This portrait by Winold Reiss was made in 1925, when Hughes, in his early twenties, was already a significant figure in the Harlem Renaissance. National Portrait Gallery, Smithsonian Institution/Art Resource, NY.

In the late 1940s, Langston Hughes bought a house on East 127th Street in central Harlem. He could have afforded a house in a wealthy suburb if he had wished, but he chose Harlem. It symbolized other choices he had made throughout his writing career, for he chose to write for and about African Americans.

Born in Joplin, Missouri, in 1902, he lived for a time with his grandmother Mary Langston, from whom he learned lessons in social justice. He began to write poetry in high school, briefly attended college, then chose to work and travel in Africa and Europe. He continued writing poetry, some of which won prizes from African-American journals.

Hughes had become a significant figure in the Harlem Renaissance by 1925, sometimes reading his poetry to the musical accompaniment of jazz or the blues. Some of his work then presented images from black history, like "The Negro Speaks of Rivers" (1921). Other works, like "Song for a Dark Girl" (1927), vividly depicted the constraints of racism.

*Way Down South in Dixie
(Break the heart of me)
They hung my black young lover
To a cross roads tree.*

The sparkle of the Cotton Club was remote from the experience of most African Americans. But one Harlem leader affected black people throughout the country and beyond. **Marcus Garvey,** born in Jamaica, advocated a form of **black separatism.** His organization, the Universal Negro Improvement Association (UNIA), founded in 1914,

Marcus Garvey Jamaican black nationalist active in America in the 1920s.

black separatism Doctrine of cultural separation of blacks from white society.

Way Down South in Dixie
(Bruised body high in air)
I asked the white Lord Jesus
What was the use of prayer.

Way Down South in Dixie
(Break the heart of me)
Love is a naked shadow
On a gnarled and naked tree.

Other poems looked to the future with an expectation for change and for new choices, as in "I, Too" (1925).

I, too, sing America.

I am the darker brother.
They send me
To eat in the kitchen
When company comes,
But I laugh,
And eat well,
And grow strong.

Tomorrow
I'll sit at the table
When company comes.
Nobody'll dare
Say to me,
"Eat in the kitchen,"
Then.
Besides
They'll see
How beautiful I am
And be ashamed.

I, too, am America.

In the early 1930s, as the Harlem Renaissance waned and the Depression deepened,

Hughes, like other American intellectuals, turned to socialism. He traveled again and began writing short stories and plays. Few theaters at that time would stage works by or about African Americans, and few hired African-American actors. Hughes, therefore, chose to use his prestige and his time to create black theater companies in Harlem, Los Angeles, and Chicago.

Hughes's writings poured forth in a near-torrential stream. By the end of his life, in 1967, he had produced ten volumes of poetry; sixty-six short stories; some twenty plays, musicals, and operas; two autobiographical volumes; more than a hundred published essays, both serious and humorous; and several novels, histories, and children's books. The outcome of Hughes's devotion to writing and his choice to focus on the African-American experience was that he established a prominent place for himself among American authors of his time. Also, and perhaps more significant, he helped define the Harlem Renaissance, and he greatly encouraged the development of African-American poetry, fiction, drama, and other writing.

stressed racial pride and solidarity across national boundaries. Garvey argued that whites would always be racist. Therefore blacks from around the world needed to assist Africans in overthrowing colonial rule and building a strong African state. Garvey established a steamship company, the **Black Star Line,** which he hoped would carry

Black Star Line   Steamship company founded by Marcus Garvey to carry blacks to Africa; Garvey was convicted of mail fraud in connection with its finances and imprisoned in 1923.

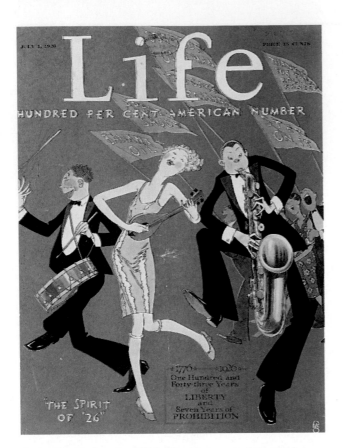

♦ On the one hundred fiftieth anniversary of the Declaration of Independence, *Life* presented this cover parodying the famous painting *The Spirit of '76* by depicting *"The Spirit of '26"*—an uninhibited flapper, a jazz saxophonist and drummer, and banners with the snappy sayings of the day. The caption reads, "One Hundred and Forty-three Years of LIBERTY and Seven Years of PROHIBITION." *Harvard College Library.*

American blacks to Africa. UNIA attracted wide support among urban blacks in the United States.

Black integrationist leaders, however, condemned UNIA for its separatism. The NAACP, especially W. E. B. Du Bois, took the lead in opposing Garvey, arguing that the first task facing blacks was integration and equality in the United States. Garvey and Du Bois called each other traitors.

Federal officials eventually charged Garvey with irregularities in his fundraising for the Black Star Line, and he was convicted of mail fraud in

1923. He spent two years in jail and then was deported to his native Jamaica. Garvey continued to lead UNIA in exile, but most of the local organizations lost members and influence.

"Flaming Youth"

Although African Americans created jazz, those who danced to it, in the popular imagination of the 1920s, were white: a male college student, clad in a swank raccoon-skin coat with a hip flask of illegal liquor in his pocket, and his female counterpart, the uninhibited **flapper** with bobbed hair and a daringly short skirt. This stereotype of "flaming youth" reflected startling changes among many white, college-age youths of middle- or upper-class background.

The prosperity of the 1920s allowed many middle-class families to send their children to college. The proportion of the population ages 18 to 24 enrolled in college more than doubled between World War I and 1930. On campus, students reshaped colleges into youth centers, where football games and dances assumed as much significance as examinations and term papers.

For some college women, the changes of the 1920s seemed particularly dramatic. Young women scandalized their elders by wearing skirts that stopped at the knee, stockings rolled below the knee, short hair often dyed black, and generous amounts of rouge and lipstick. Many observers assumed that the outrageous look reflected outrageous behavior. In fact, women's sexual activity outside marriage had begun to increase before the war, especially among working-class women and radicals. In the 1920s, such changes began to affect middle-class college and high school students. About half of the women who came of age during the 1920s had intercourse before marriage, a marked increase from prewar patterns.

---

flapper Name given in the 1920s to a young woman with short hair and short skirts, who discarded old-fashioned standards of dress and behavior.

Such changes in behavior were often linked to the automobile. It brought greater freedom to young people, for they could go where they wanted. Sometimes they went to a **speakeasy.** Before Prohibition, few women who valued their reputations entered saloons. Prohibition, however, seemed to glamorize drinking. Now men and women went to speakeasies to drink and smoke together, and to dance to popular music derived from jazz. While some adults criticized the frivolities of the young, others emulated them.

Traditional America Roars Back

Many Americans felt threatened by the upheaval in social values that originated in the cities. Although their efforts to stop the tide of changes that threatened their way of life dated to the prewar era, several movements to preserve traditional values came to fruition in the 1920s.

Prohibition

Prohibition epitomized the cultural struggle to preserve white, old-stock Protestant values and to make immigrants whose values were judged to be quite different conform to "American" standards. Spearheaded by the Anti-Saloon League, prohibition advocates gained strength throughout the Progressive era. They convinced Congress to pass a temporary prohibition measure in 1917 to conserve grain during the war. A more important victory for the "drys" came later that year, when Congress adopted the **Eighteenth Amendment,** prohibiting the manufacture, sale, and transportation of alcoholic beverages. The amendment took effect in January 1920 after three-fourths of the state legislatures ratified it.

Many Americans simply ignored the Eighteenth Amendment from the beginning, and it grew less popular the longer it lasted. By 1926, a poll indicated that only 19 percent of Americans supported Prohibition. Nonetheless, Prohibition remained the law until 1933. Prohibition did reduce drinking and apparently drunkenness. It was most effective among those groups and in those areas that had provided its greatest support. It was never well enforced anywhere, however, and was ignored in most cities. Congress never provided enough money for more than token federal enforcement, and most city police didn't even try because of the immensity of the task. New York State admitted the impossibility of enforcing Prohibition by repealing its enforcement act in 1923.

Prohibition produced unintended consequences. It glamorized drinking. **Bootlegging** flourished. The thirst for alcohol provided criminals with a fresh and lucrative source of income. **Al Capone** and his gang took in more than $60 million from bootlegging in 1927 alone. The scar-faced Capone realized such huge gains in part by systematically eliminating the competition. Gang warfare raged in Chicago throughout the 1920s, producing some five hundred slayings. Despite Capone's undoubted role in murders, bootlegging, and other illegal activities, his extensive political influence kept him immune from local prosecution. Only in 1931 did federal officials finally convict him of income-tax evasion and send him to prison.

The gangs of Chicago had their counterparts elsewhere. Profits from bootlegging not only provided bribes to police and political officials but also led gangsters into gambling, prostitution, and **racketeering.** Through racketeering, they gained power in some labor unions. Some Americans blamed these developments on Prohibition. For other Americans, however, the gangs, killings, and corruption confirmed their long-standing distrust

speakeasy A place for the illegal sale and consumption of liquor during Prohibition.

Eighteenth Amendment Amendment to the Constitution ratified in 1919 forbidding the manufacture, sale, and transportation of alcoholic beverages.

bootlegging Illegal production, distribution, or sale of liquor.

Al Capone Italian-born American gangster who ruthlessly ruled the Chicago underworld until he was imprisoned for tax evasion in 1931.

racketeering Commission of crimes such as extortion, loansharking, bribery, and obstruction of justice in the course of illegal business activities.

of cities and immigrants, and they clung to the vision of a dry America as the best hope for renewing traditional values.

Fundamentalism and the Crusade Against Evolution

Fundamentalist Protestantism also sought to maintain traditional values. **Fundamentalism** emerged from a conflict between Christian modernism and **orthodoxy.** Where modernists tried to reconcile their religious beliefs with modern science, fundamentalists rejected anything incompatible with a literal reading of the Scriptures.

In the early 1920s, some fundamentalists focused on **evolution** as contrary to the Bible. Fundamentalists saw in evolution not just a challenge to the Bible's account of creation, but also a challenge to religion itself. William Jennings Bryan, the former Democratic presidential candidate, provided fundamentalists with their greatest champion. His energy, eloquence, and enormous following guaranteed that the issue received wide attention.

Bryan played a central role in the **Scopes trial,** the most famous dispute over evolution. In March 1925, the Tennessee legislature made it illegal for any public school teacher to teach evolution. Promised the assistance of the American Civil Liberties Union (ACLU), John T. Scopes, a young biology teacher in Dayton, Tennessee, challenged the law. Bryan volunteered to assist the local prosecutors. He claimed that the only issue was the right of the people to regulate public education in the interest of morality. But defense attorney **Clarence Darrow** insisted that he was there to prevent "bigots and ignoramuses from controlling the education of the United States."

Toward the end of the trial, Darrow called Bryan to the witness stand as an authority on the Bible. Under Darrow's withering questioning, Bryan revealed that he knew little about findings in archaeology, geology, and linguistics that cast doubt on biblical accounts. He also admitted that he did not always interpret the Bible literally. "Bryan was broken," one reporter wrote. "Darrow never spared him. It was masterful, but it was pitiful." Bryan died a few days later. Scopes was found guilty, but the Tennessee Supreme Court threw out his sentence on a technicality, preventing appeal. The Tennessee law remained on the books until 1968, although it was not enforced.

Nativism and Immigration Restriction

Since the 1890s, nativists had urged Congress to cut off immigration, but earlier efforts met with either congressional indifference or presidential vetoes. However, the disquieting presence of so many German Americans during World War I, the Red Scare, and the continued influx of poor immigrants from southern and eastern Europe after the war combined in 1921 to convince Congress to approve a temporary act limiting immigration.

The **National Origins Act** of 1924 established permanent restrictions. It limited total immigration to 150,000 people each year and established quotas for each country based on how many Americans came from that country as of 1890. The law thus attempted to freeze the nation's ethnic composition by stopping immigration from southern and eastern Europe. The law completely excluded

fundamentalism An organized, evangelical movement originating in the United States in the early twentieth century in opposition to liberalism and secularism.

orthodoxy Traditional or established doctrine of faith.

evolution The central organizing theorem of the biological sciences, which holds that organisms change over generations, mainly as a result of natural selection; it includes the concept that humans evolved from nonhuman ancestors.

Scopes trial Trial in 1925 in which a high school biology teacher was prosecuted for teaching evolution in violation of Tennessee law; it raised issues concerning the place of religion in American education.

Clarence Darrow Lawyer known for his defense of unpopular causes; his merciless cross-examination of Bryan in the Scopes trial made the argument against evolution look weak.

National Origins Act Law passed in 1924 establishing quotas that discouraged immigration from southern and eastern Europe and encouraged immigration from Scandinavia and western Europe; it also prohibited Asian immigration.

Asians but permitted unrestricted immigration from Canada and Latin America.

Nativism and discrimination flourished throughout the 1920s. In West Frankfort, Illinois, for example, rioting townspeople beat and stoned Italians in 1920 before setting their houses on fire. Nativist-inspired discrimination was more subtle. Exclusive eastern colleges placed quotas on the number of Jews admitted each year. In 1920, Henry Ford, writing in the *Dearborn Independent,* began to accuse international Jewish bankers of controlling the American economy. In 1927, Ford was forced to retract his charges and to apologize when he was sued for libel and challenged to prove his charges.

The Ku Klux Klan

Nativism, anti-Catholicism, anti-Semitism, and fear of radicalism all contributed to the spectacular growth of the Ku Klux Klan in the early 1920s. The original Klan, created during Reconstruction to intimidate former slaves, had long since died out. Formed by William Simmons, the new Klan portrayed itself as a patriotic order devoted to America, Protestant Christianity, and white supremacy.

The new Klan grew spectacularly after 1920, when local organizers were offered $4 of every $10 initiation fee. Membership grew from 5,000 in 1920 to as many as 5 million by 1925. The Klan attacked Catholics, Jews, immigrants, and blacks, along with bootleggers, corrupt politicians, and gamblers in the name of old-fashioned Protestant morality. In rural areas, the Klan's terror was sometimes carried out by **nightriders,** who roved country roads to carry out beatings, kidnappings, torture, brandings, floggings, and even murder.

The Klan was strong not only in the South but also in the Midwest, West, and Southwest. It sometimes exerted a powerful political influence, most notably in Texas, Oklahoma, Oregon, and Indiana. In Oklahoma, the Klan led a successful impeachment campaign against a governor who tried to restrict their nightriding.

Extensive corruption underlay the Klan's self-righteous rhetoric. Some Klan leaders joined primarily for the profits, both legal (from recruiting) and illegal (from political payoffs). And some lived personal lives in stark contrast to the morality they preached. In 1925, D. C. Stephenson, a prominent Klan leader, was convicted of the second-degree murder of a woman who had accused him of raping her. When the governor of Indiana refused to pardon him, Stephenson produced records that proved the corruption of the governor, a member of Congress, the mayor of Indianapolis, and other officials endorsed by the Klan. Thereafter, Klan membership fell sharply.

Race, Class, and Gender in the 1920s

For most people of color, the reality of daily life fell somewhere between the liberation experienced by those in the Harlem Renaissance and the terror felt by those who confronted Klan nightriders. For working people, the 1920s represented a time when many gains from the Progressive Era and World War I were lost. For women, the 1920s opened with a political victory in the form of suffrage, but the unity developed in support of that measure soon broke down.

Race Relations: North, South, and West

Race relations changed little during the 1920s. Terror against African Americans continued after the rioting and bloodshed of 1919. Southern legislators defeated every effort by the NAACP to secure a federal antilynching law. Discrimination and violence were not directed only at blacks. In the West and Southwest, American Indians and those of Asian and Latino descent were frequently the victims of racism.

Californians led the way in passing laws discriminating against Asian immigrants and Asian Americans. In 1920, California voters by a margin of 3 to 1 approved an initiative forbidding Asian

> **nightriders** Bands of masked white men associated with the Ku Klux Klan who roamed rural areas at night, terrorizing and murdering blacks.

immigrants to own or lease land in the state. Some Californians even sought a constitutional amendment to remove citizenship from Asian Americans.

Beginnings of Change in Federal Indian Policy

In the early 1920s, American Indians experienced an intensification of previous assimilationist policies (see page 379). Interior Secretary Albert Fall's attempts to wrest lands along the Rio Grande from the Pueblo Indians, however, did not succeed. In fact, his schemes prompted the formation of the **American Indian Defense Association (AIDA)** in 1923. The AIDA soon emerged as the leading voice for change in federal Indian policy. Its goals were to end land allotments, to improve health and educational services on the reservations, to create tribal governments, and to gain tolerance for Indian religious ceremonies. The AIDA encouraged recognition of Indian cultures and values.

The political pressure applied by the AIDA and by Indians themselves secured several new laws favorable to American Indians. One measure, in 1924, extended full citizenship to all Indians who were still not citizens—about one-third of the total. Some had been reluctant to accept citizenship for fear of losing their tribal rights, so the law included provisions specifically protecting those rights.

Mexicans in California and the Southwest

California and the Southwest attracted growing numbers of Mexican immigrants in the 1920s. Many Mexicans went north to escape the revolution and civil war that devastated their nation from 1910 into the 1920s. Nearly one Mexican in ten may have fled to the United States between 1910 and 1930. More than half went to Texas, but by the mid-1920s, increasing numbers were arriving in California.

Population changes in southern California and south Texas followed change in the agricultural economies of those regions. In south Texas, some cattle ranches were converted to farms, especially for cotton. The 1920s also saw dramatic increases in the commercial production of fruits and vegetables. By 1925, the Southwest produced 40 percent

of the nation's fruits and vegetables, crops that were highly labor-intensive. In the late 1920s, Mexicans made up 80 to 85 percent of farm laborers in southern California and south Texas. These changes in population and economy reshaped relations between Anglos and Mexicans.

In south Texas, many Anglo newcomers looked on Mexicans as a "partly colored race" and tried to import sharecropping, disfranchisement, and segregation. Disfranchisement was relatively unsuccessful, but some schools and other social institutions were segregated despite Mexican opposition.

In California, Mexican workers' efforts to organize and strike for better pay and working conditions often sparked violent opposition. In the early 1920s, strikes involving thousands of workers were broken brutally. Workers began organizing on a larger scale in 1928, with the formation of the Confederacion de Uniones Obreras Mexicanas, an umbrella group for various unions in southern California. Local authorities arrested and often beat strikers. Leaders found themselves subject to deportation. But growers adamantly opposed any proposals to restrict immigration from Mexico.

Labor on the Defensive

Difficulties in establishing unions among Mexican workers mirrored a larger failure of unions in the 1920s. When unions tried to recover lost purchasing power by striking in 1919 and 1920, they nearly all failed. After 1921, business took advantage of the conservative political climate to challenge Progressive-era legislation benefiting workers. The Supreme Court responded by limiting workers' rights, voiding laws that eliminated child labor, and striking down minimum wages for women and children.

Many companies undertook anti-union drives. Arguing that unions had become either corrupt or radical, some employers refused to recognize them. At the same time, many companies initiated an approach known as "welfare capitalism." The strat-

---

American Indian Defense Association Organization founded in 1923 to defend the rights of American Indians; it pushed for an end to allotment and a return to tribal government.

egy was to provide workers with benefits such as insurance, retirement pensions, cafeterias, paid vacations, and stock purchase plans. Such innovations stemmed both from genuine concern about workers' well-being and from the expectation that such improvements would increase productivity and discourage unionization.

Only the railroad unions made significant gains in the 1920s. The **Railway Labor Act** of 1926 established collective bargaining for railroads. But the gains of the railroad unions were unique. The 1920s marked the first period of prosperity since the 1830s when union membership declined. Hostile government policies, welfare capitalism, and lost strikes all contributed to this decline.

Changes in Women's Lives

The attention given to the flapper in the 1920s should not obscure other significant changes in women's gender roles during the decade. Marriage among middle-class couples came to be increasingly valued as a companionship between two partners. Although the ideal of marriage was often expressed in terms of equality, the actual responsibility for the smooth functioning of the family typically fell on the woman.

The 1920s also saw a significant decline in the birth rate. This decline reflected changing social values and the wider availability of birth-control information and devices. More women used diaphragms rather than relying on males to use condoms. Margaret Sanger, the pioneer in the birth-control movement, was able to persuade more doctors to spread birth-control information. As birth control gained the backing of male physicians, it became more respectable. Nonetheless, until 1936, federal law restricted public distribution of information about contraception.

Although the lives of many middle-class women lightened with the introduction of labor-saving devices such as vacuum cleaners, working-class women still spent long days struggling to maintain families. As before, these women often worked outside the home because the family needed the income. The proportion of women working for wages remained quite stable during the 1920s, at about one in four.

Perhaps the most publicized event in women's lives was national woman suffrage. In June 1919, Congress approved the **Nineteenth Amendment** and sent it to the states for ratification. After a grueling state-by-state battle, ratification came in August 1920.

The unity of the suffrage movement quickly disintegrated thereafter. Some suffrage activists joined the League of Women Voters, a nonpartisan group committed to social and political reform. The Congressional Union converted itself into the National Woman's party and, after 1923, focused its efforts on securing an **Equal Rights Amendment** to the Constitution. The League of Women Voters argued that such an amendment would endanger laws that provided special rights and protections for women. In the end, woman suffrage did not dramatically change either women or politics.

Development of Gay and Lesbian Subcultures

In the 1920s, gay and lesbian subcultures became more established and, in places such as New York, Chicago, New Orleans, and Baltimore, relatively open. *The Captive,* a play about lesbians, opened in New York in 1926, and some movies included unmistakable references to gays or lesbians. Novels with gay and lesbian characters circulated in the late 1920s and early 1930s. By the late 1920s, some nightclub acts included material about gays and lesbians in performances intended for largely heterosexual audiences. A relatively open black gay and lesbian community emerged in Harlem.

Railway Labor Act   Law passed in 1926 that replaced the Railway Labor Board with a board of mediation only loosely connected with the federal government.

Nineteenth Amendment   Amendment to the Constitution in 1920 that prohibited federal or state governments from restricting the right to vote on account of sex.

Equal Rights Amendment   Constitutional amendment first proposed by the National Woman's party in 1923, giving women in the United States equal rights under the law.

As many as seven thousand revelers of all races attended the annual Hamilton Lodge drag ball in Harlem, the nation's largest gay and lesbian event.

At the same time, however, more psychiatrists and psychologists were labeling homosexuality a **perversion.** As the work of Sigmund Freud became well known, psychiatrists and psychologists came to regard homosexuality as a sexual disorder that required a cure. Thus Freud may have been a liberating influence with regard to heterosexual relations, but he proved harmful for same-sex relations.

The late 1920s and early 1930s brought increased suppression of gays and lesbians. New state laws gave police greater authority to crack down on them. In 1927, New York police raided *The Captive*, and the New York legislature banned all such plays. In 1929, Adam Clayton Powell, a leading Harlem minister, launched a highly publicized campaign against gays. Motion-picture studios instituted a morality code that prohibited any depiction of homosexuality. The end of Prohibition after 1933 allowed local authorities to use their regulatory power to close businesses with liquor licenses that tolerated gay or lesbian customers. Thus, by the late 1930s, many gays and lesbians were forced to become more secretive about their sexual identities.

The Politics of Prosperity

After 1918, the Republicans returned to the majority role they had played from the mid-1890s to 1912, and they were the unquestioned majority party throughout the 1920s. Progressivism largely disappeared, although Robert La Follette and George Norris persisted in their vigil to limit corporate power. The Republican administrations of the 1920s, however, thought that government should be the partner of business, not its regulator.

Harding's Failed Presidency

Warren G. Harding, elected in 1920, looked like a president—handsome, gray-haired, dignified—but he displayed little intellectual depth below the

charming surface. For some cabinet positions, he named the most respected leaders of his party. He chose Charles Evans Hughes for secretary of state, Andrew Mellon for secretary of the treasury, and Herbert Hoover for secretary of commerce. Harding, however, was most at home in a smoke-filled room, drinking whiskey and playing poker with friends. He gave hundreds of government jobs to his cronies. They betrayed his trust and turned his administration into one of the most corrupt in American history. Harding tried to ignore their misdeeds.

The full extent of corruption became clear after Harding died in August 1923. Interior Secretary Albert Fall had accepted huge bribes from oil companies for leases on government oil reserves at Elk Hills, California, and **Teapot Dome,** Wyoming. Attorney General Harry Daugherty had accepted bribes to approve the sale of government property for less than its value. The head of the Veterans Bureau had swindled the government out of more than $200 million. In all, three cabinet members resigned, four officials went to jail, and five men committed suicide.

The Three-Way Election of 1924

Fortunately for the Republican party, the new president, Calvin Coolidge of Vermont, exemplified the honesty, virtue, and sobriety associated with New England. In 1924, Republicans quickly chose him as their candidate for president. The Democratic convention, however, sank into a long and bitter deadlock between its northern and southern wings before turning to John W. Davis, a leading corporate lawyer. The remaining progressives welcomed the independent candidacy of Senator Robert M. La Follette of Wisconsin. La Follette at-

> **perversion** A sexual practice considered abnormal or deviant.
>
> **Teapot Dome** Government-owned Wyoming oil field that Interior Secretary Albert B. Fall leased to private developers in return for a bribe, causing one of the scandals that disgraced the Harding administration.

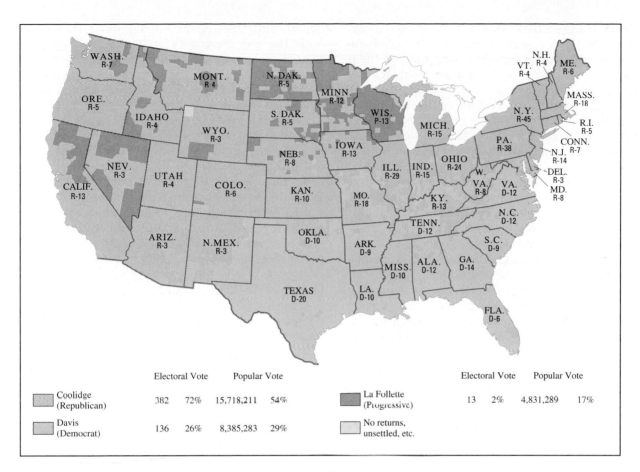

	Electoral Vote		Popular Vote				Electoral Vote		Popular Vote	
Coolidge (Republican)	382	72%	15,718,211	54%	La Follette (Progressive)		13	2%	4,831,289	17%
Davis (Democrat)	136	26%	8,385,283	29%	No returns, unsettled, etc.					

♦ **MAP 23.1 Election of 1924**   The presidential election of 1924 was complicated by the campaign of Senator Robert La Follette of Wisconsin, who ran as a Progressive. Much of his support came from Republicans living in the north-central and northwestern regions, where the agricultural economy was most hard hit.

tacked big business, embraced collective bargaining, and advocated public ownership of railroads.

Republican campaigners largely ignored Davis and focused on portraying La Follette as a dangerous radical. Coolidge claimed the key issue was "whether America will allow itself to be degraded into a communistic or socialistic state or whether it will remain American." Coolidge won with nearly 16 million votes and 54 percent of the total. Davis held onto most traditional Democratic voters, especially in the South, receiving 8 million votes. La Follette carried only his home state of Wisconsin but garnered almost 5 million votes nationwide (see Map 23.1).

The Politics of Business

Resolved to limit government, Coolidge tried to reduce the significance of the presidency—and succeeded. Having once announced that "the business of America is business," he believed that the free market would provide economic prosperity for all.

The Coolidge administration's commitment to an unfettered market economy meant it had little sympathy for proposals to assist the faltering farm economy. Congress tried to address the related problems of low prices for farm products and persistent agricultural surpluses with the

McNary-Haugen bill. This bill would have created federal price supports and authorized the government to buy farm surpluses and sell them abroad at prevailing world prices. Coolidge vetoed the bill in 1927 and again in 1928.

Secretary of the Treasury Andrew Mellon did secure substantial tax cuts for the wealthy and for corporations. He argued that these tax cuts would cause the wealthy to make "productive investments" that would benefit everyone. Secretary of Commerce Herbert Hoover, however, was unsuccessful in urging Coolidge to regulate the increasingly wild use of credit, which encouraged stock market speculation.

Coolidge cut federal spending and staffed Washington's agencies with people who shared his distaste for government. Unlike Harding, Coolidge found honest and competent appointees. Like Harding, he named probusiness figures to regulatory commissions and put conservative, probusiness judges in the courts. The *Wall Street Journal* described the outcome: "Never before, here or anywhere else, has a government been so completely fused with business."

> **McNary-Haugen bill** Farm relief bill that provided for government purchase of crop surpluses during years of large output; it was vetoed by Coolidge in 1927 and again in 1928.

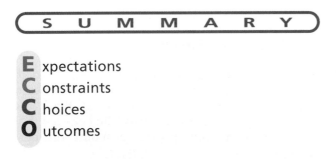

S U M M A R Y

E xpectations
C onstraints
C hoices
O utcomes

The 1920s were a decade of prosperity: unemployment was low, gross national product (GNP) grew steadily, and many Americans fared well. Sophisticated advertising campaigns created bright *expec-*tations, and installment buying freed consumers from the old *constraints* of having to pay cash. Many consumers did *choose* to buy more and to buy on credit—stimulating manufacturing and an expansion of personal debt. Easy credit and *expectations* of continuing prosperity also helped to loosen *constraints* on speculation. Fueled by many individual *choices*, the stock market climbed higher and higher. Agriculture, however, did not share in this prosperity.

As *expectations* changed during the Roaring Twenties, Americans experienced significant social change. The automobile, radio, and movies broke down old *constraints* on travel and communication and produced, as one *outcome*, a more homogeneous culture. Many American intellectuals, however, *chose* to reject the consumer-oriented culture. During the 1920s, African Americans produced an outpouring of significant art, literature, and music. Some young people *chose* to reject traditional *constraints*.

Not all Americans embraced change. Some *chose* instead to try to maintain or restore earlier cultural values. The *outcomes* were mixed. Prohibition was largely unsuccessful. Fundamentalism grew and prompted a campaign against teaching evolution. Nativism helped produce significant new restrictions on immigration. The Ku Klux Klan, committed to nativism, traditional values, and white supremacy, experienced nationwide growth until 1925, but membership declined sharply thereafter.

Discrimination and occasional violence continued to *constrain* the lives of people of color. Federal Indian policy had long stressed assimilation and allotment, but some groups *chose* to promote different policies based on respect for Indian cultural values. Immigration from Mexico greatly increased the Latino population in California and the Southwest. Nearly all unions faced strong opposition from employers, and only the railroad unions made significant gains during the twenties.

Some older *expectations* and *constraints* regarding women's roles broke down as women gained the right to vote and exercised more control over the *choice* to have children. An identifiable gay and lesbian subculture emerged in cities.

Politics became less prominent. Warren G. Harding and his successor, Calvin Coolidge, both *expected* that government should act as a partner with business, and they made *choices* that minimized regulation and encouraged speculation. Progressive reform largely disappeared from politics, and efforts to secure federal assistance for farmers fizzled. One *outcome* was a federal government that was strongly conservative and probusiness.

SUGGESTED READINGS

Allen, Frederick Lewis. *Only Yesterday: An Informal History of the Nineteen-Twenties* (1931; reprint, 1964).
   Filled with anecdotes that bring the decade to life.

Fitzgerald, F. Scott. *The Great Gatsby* (1925).
   A fictional portrayal of high living and pleasure seeking among the wealthy of New York.

Huggins, Nathan Irvin. *Harlem Renaissance* (1971).
   Thorough and thoughtful, this work places the Harlem Renaissance in the larger context of race relations in the 1920s.

Leuchtenburg, William E. *The Perils of Prosperity, 1914–1932*, rev. ed. (1993).
   A comprehensive account of the 1920s by a leading historian.

The Smithsonian Collection of Classic Jazz (1987).
   An outstanding collection of compact discs that reflects the development of American jazz, with annotations and biographies of performers.

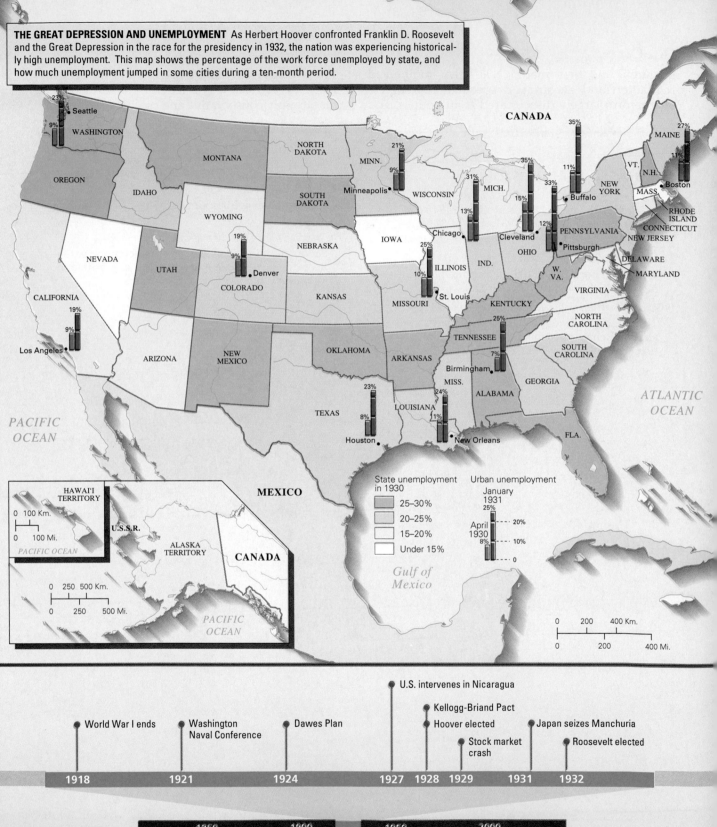

THE GREAT DEPRESSION AND UNEMPLOYMENT As Herbert Hoover confronted Franklin D. Roosevelt and the Great Depression in the race for the presidency in 1932, the nation was experiencing historically high unemployment. This map shows the percentage of the work force unemployed by state, and how much unemployment jumped in some cities during a ten-month period.

CANADA

23% Seattle
9% WASHINGTON
OREGON
MONTANA
NORTH DAKOTA
MINN.
21% 9% Minneapolis
IDAHO
SOUTH DAKOTA
WISCONSIN
35% 11% Buffalo
MAINE 27%
11% N.H.
VT.
NEW YORK
MASS.
Boston
RHODE ISLAND
CONNECTICUT
NEW JERSEY

WYOMING
19% 9% Denver
NEBRASKA
IOWA
31% 13% Chicago
MICH. 35%
15% Cleveland
33%
12% Pittsburgh
OHIO
PENNSYLVANIA
W. VA.
DELAWARE
MARYLAND

NEVADA
UTAH
COLORADO
KANSAS
25% 10% St. Louis
ILLINOIS
IND.
KENTUCKY
VIRGINIA
NORTH CAROLINA

CALIFORNIA
19% 9% Los Angeles
ARIZONA
NEW MEXICO
OKLAHOMA
ARKANSAS
MISSOURI
TENNESSEE 25%
7% Birmingham
SOUTH CAROLINA
GEORGIA

PACIFIC OCEAN
TEXAS
23% 8% Houston
LOUISIANA
24% 11% New Orleans
MISS.
ALABAMA
FLA.
ATLANTIC OCEAN

Gulf of Mexico

HAWAI'I TERRITORY
0 100 Km.
0 100 Mi.
PACIFIC OCEAN
U.S.S.R.
ALASKA TERRITORY
CANADA
MEXICO
0 250 500 Km.
0 250 500 Mi.
PACIFIC OCEAN

State unemployment in 1930
■ 25–30%
■ 20–25%
□ 15–20%
□ Under 15%

Urban unemployment
January 1931
25%
20%
April 1930
8%
10%
0

0 200 400 Km.
0 200 400 Mi.

U.S. intervenes in Nicaragua
Kellogg-Briand Pact
Hoover elected
World War I ends
Washington Naval Conference
Dawes Plan
Stock market crash
Japan seizes Manchuria
Roosevelt elected

1918 1921 1924 1927 1928 1929 1931 1932

1850 1900 1950 2000

From Good Times to Hard Times, 1920–1932

The Diplomacy of Prosperity

- How did the strength of the American economy, along with America's desire to remain unconstrained in foreign affairs, shape the choices in U.S. foreign policy during the 1920s?

The Failure of Prosperity

- What expectations did Americans have when they chose Herbert Hoover instead of Al Smith to be president?

- What weaknesses constrained the American economy? What expectations caused these constraints not to be clearly seen?

Government and Economic Crisis

- What choices did Hoover make to deal with the Great Depression? How did his expectations about government limit his choices?

- Why were the outcomes of Hoover's efforts to fight the Depression unsuccessful?

Depression America

- What economic and social constraints and choices did the Depression generate for industrial workers, minorities, and women?

- What choices did Americans make during the Depression that reflected the continuity of social and cultural values?

INTRODUCTION

Expectations
Constraints
Choices
Outcomes

As the Roaring Twenties drew to a close, the United States seemed to have reached new levels of success. American prosperity bloomed, fueling much of the world's economic growth. American business interests swept into Europe, Asia, the Middle East, and Latin America. At the same time, the United States government *chose* to avoid a direct role in world politics. Instead, American policymakers from Harding to Hoover *expected* indirect and private means to promote American interests and a stable and peaceful world.

Domestically, the Republican presidents of the twenties *chose* to rely less on governmental supervision and more on unfettered American business to build a prosperous and stable America. For Herbert Hoover, the outlook in 1928 seemed bright. He *expected* to be elected president and to guide the continued growth of American and world prosperity. He was confident that domestic poverty would nearly disappear and international peace would prevail.

This chapter examines the failure of Hoover's *expectations* in the face of the Great Depression. Hoover *chose* to face the decline of the economy with policies that he *expected* would produce continued growth. He found, however, that they only heightened disillusionment and individual hard-ship. Confronted with dismal realities, Hoover altered policy, but his new *choices* failed to change the course of the Depression. As individuals and society responded to the Depression, many, like Hoover, questioned their long-held values and revised their *expectations*, especially about the role of government. By 1932, it was obvious that the Depression had thwarted Hoover's hopes and ruined his political career. The American people *chose* a president pledged to activism: Franklin D. Roosevelt.

The Depression also revealed the weaknesses of the *expectations* and *choices* that had governed American foreign policy throughout the 1920s. The *constraints* of economic failure dashed hopes of basing peace and international stability on economic growth and voluntary agreements. The *outcome* was an increasingly dangerous world, as nations moved to protect and promote their own economic goals at the expense of others' and, in the case of Japan, of world peace.

The Diplomacy of Prosperity

Two realities shaped American foreign policy in the 1920s: the rejection of Woodrow Wilson's internationalism following World War I and the continuing quest for economic expansion by American business. President Warren Harding, elected in 1920, dismissed any American role in the League of Nations and refused to accept the **Treaty of Versailles.** The administration and Congress simply declared the war to be over. Harding's secretary of state, Charles Evans Hughes, then quickly concluded separate peace treaties with the Central Powers. Hughes also supported efforts by American banks and corporations to expand their business activities around the world. The Great War had made America the world's major industrial producer and banker. Throughout the 1920s, American businesses helped shape the global economy by lending money to other nations.

Because Harding and his successor, Calvin Coolidge, had little interest in foreign affairs, they

> **Treaty of Versailles** Treaty that ended World War I, which was signed at Versailles, France, in 1919.

CHRONOLOGY

A New Era

1918	World War I ends
1920	Harding elected president
1921–1922	Washington Naval Conference
1922	Fordney-McCumber Tariff
1923	France occupies the Ruhr
	Harding dies in office; Coolidge becomes president
1924	Coolidge elected president
	Dawes Plan
	U.S. forces withdraw from Dominican Republic
1927	United States intervenes in Nicaragua
	Henry Stimson negotiates the Peace of Titiapa
	Augusto Sandino begins guerrilla war in Nicaragua
1928	Kellogg-Briand Pact
	Hoover elected president
1929	Agricultural Marketing Act (Farm Board)
	Stock market crash
1930	Rafael Trujillo seizes power in Dominican Republic
	Hawley-Smoot Tariff
1931	Japan seizes Manchuria
	Scottsboro Nine convicted
1932	32,000 U.S. businesses fail
	U.S. forces begin withdrawal from Nicaragua
	Reconstruction Finance Corporation (RCF) begins emergency relief
	Farmers' Holiday Association founded
	Bonus March
	Franklin Roosevelt elected president
1933	4,000 U.S. banks fail
	Unemployment reaches 25 percent
	Japan withdraws from League of Nations
1934	U.S. forces withdraw from Haiti
	Sandino murdered by Anastasio Somoza
1936	Somoza becomes president of Nicaragua

deferred to their secretaries of state: Hughes and Frank Kellogg, respectively. Both were capable men interested in developing American business and influence abroad through "independent internationalism." Independent internationalism had two central thrusts: avoiding international responsibilities—sometimes called **isolationism**—and expanding economic opportunities overseas. As secretary of commerce, Herbert Hoover was equally involved in promoting American business activities worldwide. In Asia, the Commerce and State departments encouraged private American investments in Japan and China. In the Middle East, the United States worked hard to overcome British opposition and provide openings for American oil companies seeking drilling rights. Successes in Asia and the Middle East were limited, but efforts to expand the American economic position in Latin America and Europe were quite successful.

isolationism A national policy of avoiding political or economic entanglements with other countries.

CANADA

UNITED
STATES

San Francisco

Ottawa★

Washington, D.C.★

Roosevelt's Good Neighbor Policy, 1933

U.S. upholds right of intervention at
Pan American Conference, 1928

U.S. troops, 1917–1922
U.S. investors dominate sugar industry
Revolution of 1933
U.S. abrogates Platt Amendment, 1934
Batista era, 1934–1959

U.S. troops, 1915–1934
Financial supervision, 1916–1941

MEXICO

Constitution of 1917 challenges U.S. interests
Nationalization of foreign oil companies, 1938
U.S.-Mexico agreement settles oil dispute, 1942

Gulf
of
Mexico

Miami

THE BAHAMAS
Nassau

Guantánamo

Havana CUBA

JAMAICA

HAITI
Port-au-
Prince

DOMINICAN
REP.

Santo
Domingo

San
Juan

U.S. financial supervision, 1905–1941
U.S. troops withdrawn, 1924
Trujillo era, 1930–1961

VIRGIN IS. (US,UK)

PUERTO
RICO (US)

U.S. colony since 1917

Mexico
City

Belmopan
BELIZE
GUATEMALA
Guatemala
EL SALVADOR San
Salvador

Kingston

HONDURAS
Tegucigalpa

NICARAGUA
Managua

Caribbean Sea

U.S. colony
Jones Act grants U.S. citizenship, 1917

U.S. invasion, 1924
United Fruit Company active

COSTA
RICA

San José
Panama

PANAMA

Caracas

VENEZUELA

Georgetown
Paramaribo
Cayenne

GUYANA
SURINAM

FRENCH
GUIANA
(FR.)

U.S. financial supervision, 1911–1924
U.S. military occupation, 1912–1925
U.S. war against Sandino, 1927–1933
Somoza era, 1936–1979

Bogotá

COLOMBIA

U.S. control of Canal Zone
Declaration of Panama, 1939

ECUADOR
Quito

U.S. oil investments

PERU
Lima

BRAZIL

La Paz

Brasília

BOLIVIA

U.S. copper interests

CHILE

PARAGUAY

Asunción

PACIFIC

OCEAN

ATLANTIC

OCEAN

Santiago

Buenos Aires

URUGUAY
Montevideo

ARGENTINA

U.S. votes for nonintervention pledge
at Pan American Conference, 1936

0   500   1000 Km.

0   500   1000 Mi.

♦ **MAP 24.1 The United States and Latin America, 1919–1939** As this map shows, the United States continued to play an active role in promoting its interests throughout Central and South America and the Caribbean between the two world wars. In some cases, as in Nicaragua in the 1920s, this included military intervention, but during the 1920s and the terms of Hoover and Roosevelt, political and economic pressure replaced military force as the primary means to protect U.S. interests.

The United States and Latin America

The 1920s marked a gradual American retreat from direct intervention in Latin America (see Map 24.1). President Harding intended to end the American occupation of Haiti and the Dominican Republic. The withdrawal of American troops proceeded slowly, however, because Harding, Coolidge, and Hoover did not want anti-American governments to seize power. To ensure friendly and stable governments, Americans maintained control over these countries' national finances and trained national guards to act as police forces. With such precautions in place, U.S. troops left the Dominican Republic in 1924, Nicaragua in 1925, and Haiti in 1934.

When American troops withdrew from the Dominican Republic and Haiti, they left better roads and improved sanitary systems. But years of occupation had not advanced educational systems, national economies, or the standard of living. In Haiti, American-imposed segregation and favoritism toward the minority, lighter-colored **mulattos** made social divisions worse. Nor did the United States promote the cause of democracy, favoring stability over freedom, even if that meant dictatorship. In 1930, Rafael Trujillo, an American-trained national guard officer, declared himself dictator of the Dominican Republic. He ruled the country brutally until his death in 1961.

In Nicaragua, civil war broke out when American forces left in 1925. President Coolidge reintroduced American forces in 1927 to protect the pro-American, conservative government and sent special envoy Henry L. Stimson to negotiate a truce. Stimson arranged the **Peace of Titiapa,** which ended most of the fighting. However, **Augusto Sandino,** whose primary goal was to see Nicaragua free of American influence, rejected the truce. Between 1927 and 1932, he carried on a guerrilla war against the government and American forces. Throughout Latin America, his resistance earned him many admirers who saw the United States as an imperial power wielding its might over Latin Americans. The United States withdrew its forces from Nicaragua in 1933. After the U.S. Marines left, the commander of the Guardia Nacional, **Anastasio Somoza,** arranged a peace conference with the rebel. After a farewell dinner, Somoza executed Sandino and his aides. Using the national guard as a political weapon, Somoza was elected president in 1936. He ruled either directly or through puppet presidents until his assassination in 1956. His family would remain in power until 1979, when rebels calling themselves the Sandinistas—after their hero, Sandino—drove the Somozas out of Nicaragua.

Elsewhere in Latin America, the 1920s saw American business interests expand. Throughout Central America, American firms such as the United Fruit Company purchased or pressured governments to give them thousands of acres for plantations on which to grow tropical fruits, especially bananas. In Venezuela and Colombia, American oil companies, with State Department help, successfully negotiated profitable contracts for drilling rights, pushing aside European oil companies. American investment in Latin America rose from $2 billion in 1919 to nearly $3.5 billion by 1929.

Oil also played a key role in American relations with Mexico. American businessmen objected strongly when Mexico began to **nationalize** its oil (see Map 24.1). By 1925, American oilmen were calling for military action to protect their interests in northern Mexico. Coolidge, however, instructed ambassador Dwight W. Morrow "to keep us out of war with Mexico." Morrow understood Mexican nationalism and pride and clearly appreciated

---

mulatto   A person of mixed black and white ancestry.

Peace of Titiapa   Agreement negotiated by U.S. Secretary of State Henry L. Stimson in 1927 that sought to end factional fighting in Nicaragua.

Augusto Sandino   Rebel who sought to rid Nicaragua of American influence; he was murdered by his rival, Anastasio Somoza.

Anastasio Somoza   General who established a military dictatorship in Nicaragua in 1934, deposed his uncle to become president in 1936, and ruled the country for two decades, amassing a personal fortune and suppressing all opposition.

nationalize   To convert an industry or enterprise from private to governmental ownership and control.

Mexico and its people. He cultivated a personal relationship with Mexican president Plutarco Calles. Together they reached a compromise that recognized Mexican sovereignty over its oil but delayed nationalization of existing oil properties until 1938.

America and the European Economy

World War I had shattered most of Europe physically and economically, while the United States had climbed during wartime to unprecedented economic heights. After the war, the United States sought to expand exports and restrict imports. High tariffs inched higher throughout the 1920s. In 1922, the **Fordney-McCumber Tariff** set records in protective rates for most imported industrial goods. The effect was not only to limit European imports but also to weaken Europe's ability to acquire the dollars needed to repay its war debts to the United States.

While the tariff was shutting off the entry of European goods into the American market, Secretary of State Hughes and Secretary of Commerce Hoover worked to expand American economic interests in Europe, especially Germany. They believed that if Germany recovered economically and was able to pay its $33 billion war reparations to the victors of World War I, those nations would be able to repay their war debts to the United States. Over $4 billion in American investments flowed into Europe during the decade, doubling American investment there. General Motors purchased Opel, a German automobile firm. Ford built the largest automobile factory outside the United States in England.

Even with the infusion of American capital, Germany could not keep up with its reparations burden by 1923. France responded by sending troops to occupy the industrial **Ruhr Valley** of Germany, igniting an international emergency. Hughes sent Chicago banker Charles G. Dawes to Europe to negotiate a plan to resolve the crisis. Under the **Dawes Plan,** passed in 1924, American bankers loaned $2.5 billion to Germany for economic development, while the Germans promised to pay $2 billion in reparations to the Europeans. The Euro-

peans, in turn, paid $2.5 billion in war debts to the United States. The remedy worked fairly well until 1929, when the Depression ended nearly all loans and payments.

In Europe and the United States, the destruction caused by World War I spurred postwar pacifism and calls for disarmament. In the United States, support for arms cuts was widespread and vocal. In November 1921, Harding invited the major naval powers to Washington for discussions on reducing "the crushing burdens of military and naval establishments."

Pacifism was not the only American motive for hosting the **Washington Naval Conference.** Harding and Hughes were worried about continued Japanese naval expansion and growing Japanese pressures on China. Disarmament suggested a way of dealing with this Japanese threat without expanding the American navy. Hughes shocked conference delegates with a radical proposal that called for scrapping more than 200 tons of warships, primarily battleships. He also called for a ten-year ban on naval construction and for limits to the size of navies, based on a ratio of existing tonnage, that would keep the Japanese behind the British and American navies. Hughes put forth a ratio of 5 to 5 to 3 for the United States, Britain, and Japan. Lesser naval powers like Italy and France would receive even smaller ratios. Most of the nations attending applauded Hughes's

---

Fordney-McCumber Tariff Law passed in 1922 that raised tariff rates to record levels, fostering the growth of monopolies and provoking foreign tariff reprisals.

Ruhr Valley Region surrounding the Ruhr River in northwestern Germany, which contained many major industrial cities and valuable mines.

Dawes Plan Plan for collecting World War I reparations from Germany, which scheduled annual payments and stabilized German currency by reorganizing the Reichsbank under Allied supervision.

Washington Naval Conference International conference held in Washington, D.C., in November 1921 through February 1922; it produced a series of agreements to limit naval armaments and prevent conflict in the Far East.

proposal, but not Japan, which called the ratio a national insult. The conference dragged on for more than two months, but finally the Japanese agreed—as Hughes had known they would. Prior to the conference, the United States had broken the Japanese **diplomatic code** and had intercepted secret messages instructing the Japanese delegates to concede if Hughes held firm on his ratio.

Many Americans and Europeans applauded the achievements of the Washington conference but wanted to go even further. They sought total disarmament and a repudiation of war. In 1923, Senator William E. Borah of Idaho introduced a resolution in the Senate to outlaw war. It failed, but the idea remained active. In 1927, French foreign minister Aristide Briand suggested a French-American pact to outlaw war between them, privately hoping that such an agreement would commit the United States to aid France if attacked. Secretary of State Kellogg wanted to avoid any such American commitment and deflected the proposal by suggesting a multinational statement opposing war. Kellogg thereby removed any hint of an American commitment to aid any nation under attack. On August 27, 1928, the United States and fourteen other nations, including Britain, France, Germany, Italy, and Japan, signed the **Kellogg-Briand Pact.** Each country renounced war "as an instrument of national policy" and promised to settle disputes by peaceful means. The pact included no enforcement provisions.

By the end of 1928, American independent internationalism seemed to be a flourishing success. American business investments and loans were fueling an expansive world economy and adding to American prosperity. Avoiding entangling alliances, the United States had acted to protect its Asian and Pacific interests against Japan while promoting world disarmament and peace. In Latin America, it had moderated its interventionist image by withdrawing American troops in the Caribbean and trying to mediate a peace among warring factions in Nicaragua (see Map 24.1). It appeared that foreign policies based on economic expansion and noncoercive diplomacy were establishing a promising era of cooperation and peace in world affairs.

The Failure of Prosperity

In August 1927, Calvin Coolidge called reporters from his vacation spot in South Dakota and told them, "I do not choose to run in 1928." Coolidge's announcement stunned the country and his party. Secretary of Commerce Herbert Hoover immediately declared his candidacy.

He seemed the ideal person for the job. A Quaker farm boy from Iowa, Hoover had grown up among thrifty, self-sufficient farmers who believed that hard work was the only way forward. He worked his way through Stanford University. He formed his own mining engineering company in 1908, and by 1914 he had offices in London, Petrograd, Paris, New York, and San Francisco. *Fortune* estimated that he and his wife were worth more than $4 million. Having reached the top in business, Hoover wanted to apply his belief in hard work and sound planning to public service. When the Great War broke out, he offered to help provide relief to Belgium. Hoover traveled across war-torn Europe, seeking funds and materials for Belgium, and earned a reputation as "the Great Humanitarian." When the United States entered the war, President Wilson named him to head the U.S. Food Administration. By war's end, Hoover was an international hero.

The 1928 Election

The theme of Hoover's candidacy in 1928 was American prosperity. "We in America today are nearer to the final triumph over poverty than ever before," he boldly announced. The Democrats nominated Al Smith, four-time governor of New York. Like Hoover, Smith was a self-made man. Smith had entered politics as part of Tammany

---

diplomatic code Secret code in which diplomatic messages are transmitted.

Kellogg-Briand Pact Treaty signed in 1928 by fifteen nations, including Britain, France, Germany, the United States, and Japan, renouncing war as a means of solving international disputes.

Hall, the Democratic machine that ran New York City, and quickly proved to be an able politician. As a reform-minded, progressive governor, Smith had streamlined government, improved governmental efficiency, and supported legislation to set a minimum wage and maximum hours of work.

Despite his progressive record, Smith had a number of liabilities. Opponents attacked his Catholicism, his big-city background, his opposition to Prohibition, and his Tammany connections. Anti-Catholic sentiment burned hotly in many parts of the country, often fanned by the remnants of the Klan. Evangelist Billy Sunday called Smith supporters "damnable whiskey politicians, bootleggers, crooks, pimps and businessmen who deal with them." For many voters, the choice seemed to be between a candidate who represented hard work and the pious values of small-town, old-stock, Protestant America and one who represented urban upheaval, machine politics, foreigners, and Catholics.

Hoover won easily, with 58 percent of the popular vote. He owed his victory in large part to the prosperity that Republicans claimed as their accomplishment. Also, Smith's religion and position against Prohibition cost him substantial support in the South.

Unlike his predecessors, Hoover came to the White House with the intention of being an active president. He wanted to create a "New Day" for America. Hoover's goal was to encourage economic and social growth by using government to promote cooperation among business and other parts of society. Hoover did not want the federal government to step in to solve society's problems directly. He feared that such governmental involvement would cause the people to give up their freedom. The government should help people solve their problems, not solve their problems for them.

Origins of the Depression

When Herbert Hoover took office, ever-rising stock prices, shiny new cars, and rapidly expanding suburbs seemed to verify Hoover's observation about "the final triumph over poverty." But behind the rush for radios, homes, and vacuum cleaners lay several economic weaknesses. The prosperity of the 1920s depended in large part on a few major industries such as construction, automobiles, and household appliances. Other important sectors of the economy—textiles, railroads, steel, and iron—barely made a profit, while farming and mining suffered steady losses. Farmers saw their income and property values decline to about half their wartime highs. Hundreds of thousands of people left farms throughout the twenties.

Agriculture's troubles were only part of a growing economic distress. By 1929, even the boom industries were showing signs of weakness. New construction starts fell from 11 million to 9 million units between 1926 and 1929. Furniture companies cut their labor force in 1928 after huge inventories piled up. A similar story held for many makers of household appliances. Only the automobile industry was strong in 1928 and 1929.

The economic slowdown in 1929 stemmed from overproduction, poor distribution of income, and too much credit buying. Although the 1920s was a prosperous decade for the upper and middle classes, minorities and those living in rural areas enjoyed no increase in wages or savings. As Hoover assumed the presidency, over 70 percent of all American families lived on less than the $2,500 a year that the Brookings Institute considered an adequate standard of living. Few people, however, took notice of this vast majority of Americans who spent all they earned and for whom missing a single paycheck meant economic hard times.

The Stock Market Plunge

When Americans awoke on Thursday, October 24, 1929, no one realized they would experience one of those days that would change their lives. It was business as usual as men and women prepared to go to work. In the Midwest, people braced themselves against a frigid, unseasonable ice and snow storm. Across the country, Americans followed the lurid story of millionaire theater owner Alexander Pantangas, on trial for assaulting a 17-year-old dancer. Most Americans hardly noticed the rise and fall of stock prices on Wall Street.

Despite the lack of public concern, the activity on the New York Stock Exchange that day would have profound consequences for all Americans. On **Black Thursday,** the bottom suddenly fell out of the stock market. By noon, millions of stocks had been sold as the stock exchange became a frenzied sea of waving arms, raised fists, and screaming voices. In brokerage offices across the country, brokers rushed to place sell orders.

As the exchange closed for lunch, New York's financial leaders hurriedly met to deal with the panic. They concluded that they needed to support stock prices. Twenty-two years earlier, in 1907, New York bankers had stopped a panic and thwarted a possible depression by pooling funds to buy stocks. Now they hoped to repeat history. Led by the bank of J. P. Morgan, financial leaders put together a fund of nearly $50 million. The bankers then told Richard Whitney, vice chairman of the exchange, to use the fund to buy stocks as soon as the market reopened.

At 1:30, Whitney jauntily announced that he was buying ten thousand shares of steel at 205—ten points higher than the existing market price. Amid cheers, others quickly joined the buying drive. By the end of the day, nearly half of the $6 billion lost in the morning had been recovered. Confidence seemed to have been restored.

On Monday, October 28, prices dropped again. But this time no rescuer appeared. Bankers and Wall Street leaders, having already committed $50 million, were hesitant to add to their bailout. On Black Tuesday, October 29, prices plunged drastically and continued to fall throughout November. Between early September and mid-November, the New York Times **industrials** fell from 469 to 221. RCA plummeted from 101 to 28, Montgomery Ward from 138 to 49, Union Carbide from 138 to 59. Hundreds of brokers and speculators were ruined.

The stock market crash that began in October 1929 was not solely responsible for the **Great Depression.** Rather, it pushed an already weakened economy into a steep decline. Since 1927, the overall economy had been slowing down and consumption had been declining. Like much of the public, many corporations were in debt. When the market crashed, brokers and banks found their resources dwindling and began demanding repayment of loans. Many borrowers could not meet this demand, and as a result, lenders found themselves unable to meet the demands of depositors. Banks failed, and a substantial portion of the savings of the upper and middle classes vanished.

The crash undermined economic confidence throughout the country. Americans had viewed the soaring stock market as a symbol of the vigor of the economy and of the nation. Now investors were wary. Corporations cut production and laid off workers. Consumers hesitated to spend money. Coupled with the weaknesses of the economy, the stock market crash resulted in the worst and longest depression in American history.

The plummeting domestic economy had international repercussions as well. American banks cut their European loans, and American corporations reduced their purchases. To protect American business from foreign competition, Congress in 1930 passed the **Hawley-Smoot Tariff,** which drastically raised tariffs. It proved to be a catastrophe for world trade. Angered by American actions, twenty-three foreign governments raised their tariffs on American goods, further stifling trade. By 1932, American exports had fallen to their lowest level since 1905. Rather than protect national economies, the high tariffs only spread the global depression. With fewer goods being sold, businesses faced declining profits and slashed production and payrolls.

Stock prices continued downward until 1932. The New York Times industrials sank to 58 by

---

Black Thursday October 24, 1929, when the stock market fell dramatically in what proved to be the beginning of the crash.

industrials Industrial stocks chosen as indicators of trends in the economy.

Great Depression The years 1929 to 1941 in the United States, during which the economy was in a severe decline and millions of people were out of work.

Hawley-Smoot Tariff Law passed in 1930 in response to the Depression, setting the highest tariff rates in U.S. history and thus undermining world trade.

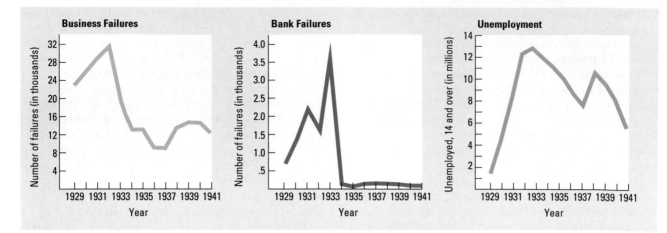

♦ **FIGURE 24.1 Charting the Economics of the Depression**   Between 1929 and 1933, there was an expanding number of unemployed people seeking work, and more and more banks and businesses were closing their doors. By 1933, over 4,000 banks had failed, unemployment had reached 24.9 percent, and over 100,000 firms had closed. As the New Deal began, not only did the statistics improve, but for most Americans there was also a feeling of hope.

mid-1932. United States Steel fell from a precrash high of 262 to a low of 22. Many companies did not survive. Between 1929 and 1933, ninety thousand businesses failed, and nine thousand banks closed (see Figure 24.1). As banks collapsed, depositors lost $2.5 billion. The money supply shrank by a third between 1930 and 1933, and expenditures for goods plummeted 45 percent. Purchases of automobiles dropped 75 percent. Unemployment rose from 3 percent in 1929 to 25 percent in 1933 (see chapter opener map). As the downward economic spiral continued, nearly everyone in the nation felt the effects of what was becoming the Great Depression.

Government and Economic Crisis

Shortly after the stock market crash, Hoover called together leaders of banking, industry, and labor. He pleaded with employers not to cut wages or production or to lay off workers. He exhorted

unions not to demand higher wages. At the same time, he assured the public that the economy was sound and would soon improve. These efforts worked for only a short time.

When cheerleading failed, public pressure grew for the federal government to take more direct action. Hoover also began to lean toward more direct government involvement. In December 1929, he asked Congress to increase spending for the construction of **public works** projects, including highways, government facilities, and **Boulder Dam.** Federal, state, and local governments doubled their spending on public works, but the economy continued to worsen. Increasingly, Americans blamed Hoover and his admin-

public works   Construction projects such as highways and dams, financed by public funds and carried out by the government.

Boulder Dam   Dam on the Colorado River between Nevada and Arizona, which was renamed in honor of Hoover.

istration for the hardships they faced. A popular jingle went:

Mellon pulled the whistle
Hoover rang the bell
Wall Street gave the signal
And the country went to hell.

By the end of 1932, workers' income had dropped 40 percent and unemployment had risen to an alarming 25 percent. Small industrial towns were especially hard hit. Donora, Pennsylvania, had only 277 jobs for its population of over 14,000. Many, like Donora's future baseball great Stan Musial, left home seeking greener pastures. Most were unsuccessful. Even rumors of jobs drew thousands to factory gates. Ed Paulson, who roamed the country looking for work, recalled that he developed a "coyote mentality." "You were a predator," he said. "You had to be. The coyote is crafty. . . . We were coyotes in the Thirties, the jobless." Private, state, and local charities and relief agencies vainly tried to meet the needs of the millions out of work. Bread lines and soup kitchens did their best to feed the growing army of hungry and displaced Americans, but the numbers were overwhelming. Across the country, shantytowns bitterly named **Hoovervilles** housed the homeless.

When the stock market crashed, agriculture was already in a depression. Drought in the Mississippi valley soon spread throughout the South and Midwest. It would last a decade. Adding to the misery of farmers, swarms of grasshoppers ate their way across the nation's midsection. The region became known as the **Dust Bowl** (see Map 24.2) in the 1930s, when winds whipped up clouds of dust, sometimes stretching more than 200 miles across and 7,000 to 8,000 feet high. In 1938, the worst year for dust storms, erosion claimed over 850 million tons of **topsoil.** Dust hung in the air and filtered into homes, covering clothing, furniture, food, everything.

Even before the Crash, Hoover had responded to the crisis on American farms by proposing the creation of a national farm board. The board would help stabilize prices by buying agricultural products on the open market. Congress passed the **Agricultural Marketing Act** in May 1929. The Farm Board was initially successful in supporting

♦ The Great Depression produced large-scale unemployment, which reached 25 percent in 1933. This picture by Reginald Marsh, titled *Unemployed,* effectively captures the despair of men and women seeking jobs. *"Unemployed" by Reginald Marsh, 1932. Library of Congress.*

Hooverville   Crudely built camp set up by the homeless on the fringes of a town or city during the Depression.

Dust Bowl   Name given to the Great Plains region devastated by drought and dust storms during the 1930s.

topsoil   Surface layer of the soil, in which crops grow.

Agricultural Marketing Act   Law passed in 1929 that created the Farm Board to stabilize farm prices by buying crop surpluses; the price support program ended in 1931.

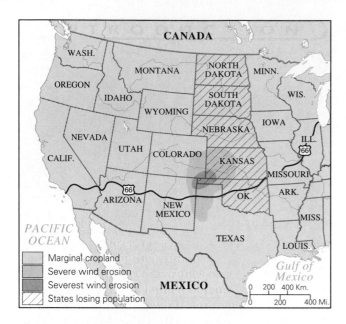

CANADA

WASH.
OREGON
IDAHO
MONTANA
NORTH DAKOTA
MINN.
SOUTH DAKOTA
WIS.
WYOMING
NEBRASKA
IOWA
ILL.
66
NEVADA
UTAH
COLORADO
KANSAS
MISSOURI
CALIF.
66
ARIZONA
NEW MEXICO
OK.
ARK.
MISS.
TEXAS
LOUIS.

PACIFIC OCEAN

Gulf of Mexico

MEXICO

Marginal cropland
Severe wind erosion
Severest wind erosion
States losing population

0   200   400 Km.
0   200   400 Mi.

♦ **MAP 24.2 The Dust Bowl** Throughout the 1930s, wind eroded millions of acres of cropland, sending tons of topsoil into the air and generating tidal waves of dust. This map shows the regions most affected by the Dust Bowl and the loss of population. Many chose to travel Route 66, hoping that it would lead to a better life in California.

farm prices. The world price of wheat sank to $.55 a bushel in February 1931, but Farm Board purchases held the American price steady at $.80 a bushel. By the end of 1931, however, the Farm Board had run out of funds. Agricultural prices then tumbled downward, forcing more farmers into bankruptcy.

As declining farm prices, drought, and dust destroyed farmers' hopes, many turned to direct action. The **Farmers' Holiday Association,** founded in 1932 by Milo Reno, called on midwestern farmers to destroy their products and to resist **foreclosures** (see Individual Choices: Milo Reno). Angry and frequently armed, farmers used their numbers and threats of violence to ensure that foreclosed properties were sold at auction to their previous owners for a fraction of their value. One such "penny auction" returned Walter Crozier's farm in Haskins, Ohio, for a high bid of $1.90. Critics linked the protests with "international Jews, the

IWW, Socialists, and Communists." In fact, the protesters were homegrown and simply wanted government support for the farmer.

Hoover's Final Efforts

By December 1931, confronted with a still-worsening economy, Hoover moved in a new direction. He asked Congress for banking reforms, financial support for home mortgages, and the creation of the **Reconstruction Finance Corporation (RFC).** Congress approved all three proposals.

Hoover's primary weapon in fighting the Depression was the RFC, through which he intended to pump money into the economy. Using federal funds, the RFC was to provide loans to banks, savings and loans, railroads, insurance companies, and large corporations to keep them operating. Hoover believed that the money would "trickle down" to workers and the unemployed through higher wages and new jobs. It was an unprecedented effort by the federal government to intervene in the private sector and stimulate the economy. Conservatives called it "an experiment in socialism." Within five months, the RFC had loaned over $805 million to large businesses, but little money trickled down to workers. Liberal critics labeled the program "welfare for the rich" and insisted that Hoover do more for the poor and unemployed through **direct relief** payments and more public works projects.

Farmers' Holiday Association Farmers' organization led by Milo Reno of Iowa that led a strike in the summer of 1932 to protest the drastic decline in farm income.

foreclosure Confiscation of a property by the bank when mortgage payments are delinquent.

Reconstruction Finance Corporation Organization to promote economic recovery established at Hoover's request in 1932; it provided emergency financing for banks, life insurance companies, railroads, and farm mortgage associations.

direct relief Payments directly to the poor and unemployed.

Hoover opposed direct federal relief, or the "dole," for several reasons. He believed that it would be too burdensome for the federal budget and that relief should instead be distributed by private organizations and local government. "Where people divest themselves of local government responsibilities," he explained, "they at once lay the foundation for the destruction of their liberties." He was also convinced that the dole would erode the work ethic and bring about a class of idle Americans.

In 1932, Hoover finally relented and agreed to create the Emergency Relief Division within the RFC and lend $300 million to states for relief. Like other RFC efforts, actual relief spending did not match the potential. Headed by a conservative board of directors, the RFC loaned money cautiously. Further, states whose budgets were already overstrained hesitated to borrow more money. By the end of 1932, the RFC had spent only 10 percent of its relief fund.

The patience of many Americans seemed at an end by the summer of 1932. The Farmers' Holiday movement was spreading across the Midwest, and thousands of veterans, the Bonus Expeditionary Force, were making their way toward Washington. The **Bonus Army,** twenty thousand unemployed veterans of the Great War, headed to the capital to lobby for the Wright-Patman bill, which stipulated early payment of their veterans' bonus, originally scheduled to be paid in 1945. Against his advisers' warnings, Hoover allowed the Bonus Marchers to set up their Hooverville across from Congress in Anacostia Flats.

Hoover respected the veterans' right to assemble, but when the Senate rejected the Patman bill, the president thought the marchers should go home. Nearly half of them, however, stayed in Washington. When the police attempted to clear condemned buildings of marchers, nearly five thousand veterans and eight hundred police clashed, resulting in the deaths of two Bonus Marchers. Hoover then turned to the army to evict the squatters. Using sabers, rifles, tear gas, and fixed bayonets, the army, led by Army Chief of Staff General Douglas MacArthur, drove the veterans from the abandoned buildings. Hoover had given orders to leave the Bonus Marchers at Ana-

costia Flats alone, but MacArthur ignored these orders. To the horror of most Americans, the army drove off the veterans and their families and set their huts and tents afire. Over one hundred veterans were injured in the melee. What slim chance Hoover had for re-election died at the "Battle of Anacostia Flats."

The Diplomacy of Depression

When Hoover entered the presidency, the world appeared stable and peaceful. Like his predecessors, Hoover intended to use economic and noncoercive means to protect American interests and promote world prosperity. Hoover promised not to intervene in Latin American affairs and continued the process of removing troops. During Hoover's administration, relations between Latin America and the United States improved greatly.

Elsewhere, however, Hoover's efforts to promote prosperity and peace abroad came to little. As the Depression became entrenched, so did Isolationism. Most Americans were far more concerned about keeping their jobs and homes than about international affairs. Republican senator George W. Norris of Nebraska urged the United States to look out for its own interests and let Europe be damned. Unfortunately, like the Depression, world problems would not go away.

If most Americans reacted to the Depression by spurning foreign involvements, the opposite was true in Japan. Japan relied heavily on international trade for its economic growth and its food supply. As declining world trade weakened their economy, the Japanese called for their government to protect their national interests. Japanese nationalists began to look hungrily toward Manchuria, a Chinese province. Rich in iron and coal, Manchuria accounted for 95 percent of Japanese

---

Bonus Army   Unemployed World War I veterans who marched to Washington in 1932 to demand early payment of a promised bonus; Congress refused, and protesters who remained were evicted by the army.

Choosing Confrontation

Milo Reno

In 1918 Milo Reno chose to become a spokesman for the farmer and organized the Farmers' Holiday Association. In 1933, he chose to reject Roosevelt's agricultural recovery program, and lost the support of most farmers, who backed the president. State Historical Society of America.

Born in 1866, Milo Reno was raised in the heartland of Populism and enthusiasm for William Jennings Bryan. Ordained as a Cambellite minister by Oskalossa College, Reno chose to give up the ministry to pursue his true calling—organizing farmers for political action. He joined the Farmers' Union in 1918, dominating it until his death in 1936, and was the driving force behind the Farmers' Holiday Association. Wearing a ten-gallon hat and a flaming red necktie, Reno captured farmers' hearts with evangelical-style speeches that combined simple explanations, personalized enemies, biblical quotes, and farm wisdom.

In 1932, he claimed that Hoover's farm policies were driving hardworking, decent people from the land, and in August he called for a farmers' strike. "Stay home, buy nothing, sell nothing," he commanded the farmers in an effort to force change and break "the grip of Wall Street and international bankers on government." Farmers across Iowa and neighboring states heeded his call, refusing to sell their products. Others erected barricades across highways to prevent farmers' products from reaching processors. Outside Sioux City and other midwestern towns, farmers armed with clubs and pitchforks clashed with truck drivers

overseas investment and supplied vital foodstuffs to the island nation.

In September 1931, a small group of young, anti-Western Japanese army officers in Manchuria executed a plan to establish Japanese rule over the region. They blew up a section of track of the Southern Manchurian Railroad and blamed the Chinese. Then, without informing the civilian

government of Japan, they used this as an excuse to attack Chinese forces and take control of the province.

World reaction was one of shock and eventual condemnation, but little else. The League of Nations sheepishly called for peace and appointed a committee to investigate the conflict. Neither the United States nor Great Britain, the two major Pa-

and hastily dispatched sheriff's deputies. By mid-August, over eighty picketers had been arrested, and fearful of further violence and arrests, Reno called a "temporary halt" to the strike.

With the barricades, the strike had received national news coverage focused on the distress of farmers, and politicians had responded. Midwest governors listened to Farmers' Holiday spokesmen and pushed Hoover for increased support for farmers. Presidential candidate Franklin D. Roosevelt emphasized that Democrats promised farm prices "in excess of cost." Reno, like millions of other Americans, saw in Roosevelt a chance for hope, cheered his election, and waited anxiously for the New Deal to begin.

As Roosevelt assumed office, Reno and the Farmers' Holiday movement—now claiming ninety thousand members—continued to attract national attention by stopping farm foreclosures and forcing "penny auctions." Again, direct action seemed to work, as many companies halted foreclosures and ten states even passed foreclosure "moratorium laws." But with Roosevelt in office, farmers were also receiving less and less public support for their activism. Many politicians and journalists now linked their movement with communism. Reno was faced with a hard choice. Should he continue direct action or support Roosevelt's agriculture program?

Responding to negative public opinion, Reno asked farm activists to pull back from confrontation and give Roosevelt time to implement his farm programs. Still, Reno had doubts. He considered Roosevelt an "enigma," and was angry when the New Deal's agriculture program—the Agricultural Adjustment Act—did not include cost-of-production provisions. He told a friend, "I have no faith whatever in the gestures that are being made by the administration. It is simply the same old tactic to hand the people a little measure of relief to suppress rebellion, with no intention of correcting a system that is fundamentally wrong."

In October 1933, Reno made a difficult decision, but one he believed necessary. Roosevelt, he was sure, was taking the nation down the wrong path, which would eventually "crush all . . . independence and liberty . . . setting up a bureaucratic, autocratic, dictatorial government." He renewed the call for a strike and stated that a third political party was the only possible solution "to clean up the stinking mess" in Washington. The strike call was largely ignored by farmers, who had begun to trust Roosevelt's promise of federal support. The momentum of the farmers' protest had vanished, consumed by the spread of the federal government into agricultural affairs.

Increasingly out of touch with most farmers, Reno fell into periods of depression and heavy drinking until, stricken with influenza in March 1936, he checked into a sanitarium. "Tell them I'm really sick," he said. Milo Reno died on May 5, 1936.

---

cific naval powers, wanted to become involved in an Asian war. Invoking the **Stimson Doctrine,** the United States refused to recognize Japan's newly created puppet state of **Manchukuo.** In American eyes, Manchuria remained a part of China.

The Japanese had violated the Kellogg-Briand Pact and principles of the League of Nations, but the ensuing barrage of protests did nothing to

Stimson Doctrine   Declaration by the U.S. secretary of state in 1932 that the United States would not recognize Manchukuo or any other arrangement that threatened China's independence.

Manchukuo   Puppet state established by Japan in 1932 and not recognized by the United States.

deter their aggression. In Japan, the conquest of Manchuria magnified the power of pro-imperial and anti-Western groups. In 1933, Japan withdrew from the League of Nations.

At the end of Hoover's presidency, the world was a much different place than in 1928. The cheery optimism of a prosperous world at peace had dissipated.

Depression America

Few Americans in November 1932 were concerned about Japanese militarism in distant Manchuria. Their concerns were much closer to home. The Depression had touched every American, forcing changes in lifestyle, thought, and politics. Poverty was no longer reserved for those viewed as lazy or unworthy; it was no longer relegated to remote areas and inner cities. Now poverty dragged down blue- and white-collar workers, and even a few of the once-rich.

Families in the Depression

The 35 percent drop in average annual income between 1929 and 1933 caused many people to worry about basic survival during the Depression. Some also worried that the Depression was causing a decline in family values and morality. Pointing to the drifters uprooted by hard times, to families without fathers, and to reports of increasing abortions and premarital and deviant sexual activities, they forecast the end of American civilization.

Their fears were unfounded. The vast majority of Americans clung tightly to traditional family values and emphasized family unity. Church attendance actually rose during the Depression, and the number of divorces declined. The percentage of people getting married did drop slightly, but marriages were only delayed, not put off entirely. Moralists decried an increasing abortion rate, but in fact the estimated number of abortions remained steady. Studies also indicated that sexual activity, rather than becoming more varied and promiscuous, actually decreased.

The Depression did tear many families apart, but ironically it brought many others closer together. Economic necessity kept families at home playing board games and cards, reading, and listening to the radio. The game of Monopoly allowed players to fantasize about becoming a millionaire and laugh about going broke.

The Middle and Working Classes and Hard Times

For many of the American middle class and most of the working class, the most common fear was economic insecurity. Would the next day bring a reduction in wages, the loss of a job, or the closing of a business? Some saw their businesses go bankrupt and found new careers. Harry S Truman closed his haberdashery and turned to politics. E. Y. Harburg lost his family's hardware store, borrowed $500 from a friend, and started writing songs. One of them, "Brother, Can You Spare a Dime?" became one of the most famous songs of the Depression era. Other people worked for less, lost and found other jobs, or, disheartened, accepted relief.

Observers in Muncie, Indiana, noted that middle-class neighborhoods during the Depression looked much as they had in the mid-1920s. Clean, neatly kept houses stood behind green lawns. But closer examination showed the growing impact of harder and harder times. Newspapers carried more pages of tax delinquencies, evictions, and foreclosures. Signs appeared in yards and windows announcing a variety of services—household beauty parlors, kitchen bakeries, rooms for boarders. A Milwaukee wife recalled, "I did baking at home to supplement our income. I got 9 cents for a loaf of bread and 25 cents for an apple cake. . . . I cleared about $65 a month."

In Muncie and across the country, families adopted the motto "Use it up, wear it out, make it do, or do without." To save money, many women sewed, baked bread, and canned, reaffirming traditional female roles. A Singer sewing machine salesman commented that he was selling machines to people who in the past would not have sewn. Feed sacks became a source of material.

During the 1920s, the automobile had pulled families away from their porches and backyards. They returned during the Depression. Men tended backyard grills, and entire families looked after vegetable and flower gardens. A "mania for flower gardens," and flower shows struck the middle class. Away from the house, use of the local park and library, dances, and movies provided inexpensive entertainment. Family togetherness was praised as one positive outcome of the Depression. An Indiana newspaper editorialized, "All . . . are hoping for a quick return of prosperity . . . but in the mean time millions of Americans already have a kind of prosperity that includes strengthening the family."

Working-class Americans confronted the same challenges as did Middle America but more often faced the prospect of losing a job and being evicted. In Gary, Indiana, nearly the entire working class was out of a job by 1932. Approximately one-sixth of all urban families, having lost their homes, "doubled up" with relatives. Don Blincoe remembered that most households seemed like his, "where father, mother, children, aunts, uncles and grandma lived together" and pooled their earnings.

Living with relatives, however, did not always help. Unemployed males, especially fathers, often felt shamed by their economic problems. A social worker wrote, "I used to see men cry because they didn't have a job. . . . They were belittled before the eyes of their families and they couldn't take it." John Boris, a Slavic immigrant, was devastated by being laid off by Ford after having worked loyally for the company for fourteen years. "Last July, I was a good man," he lamented. "I ain't a man now."

Many former breadwinners deserted their families and took to the road. Some, called hoboes, rode the rails, hitching rides in boxcars, living in shantytowns, and begging and scrounging for food along the road. Estimates in 1932 placed the number of homeless migrants at between 1 million and 2 million. Suicides increased, as did the number of people admitted to state mental hospitals and the number of children placed in orphanages.

Included in the so-called migration of despair were thousands from rural areas, especially parts of Texas, Arkansas, and Oklahoma. Many **"Arkies" and "Okies,"** like those characterized in John Steinbeck's novel *The Grapes of Wrath* (1939), were forced from their farms by insects, dust, debt, and landlords. They loaded their meager possessions into their jalopies and headed for California. By the end of the decade, California's population had jumped by over a million. Some migrants found jobs, but most continued to wander.

Discrimination in the Depression

The Depression intensified the economic and social difficulties of minorities. For the majority of African Americans who lived in the rural South, the Depression started in the 1920s with the decline of agricultural prices. By 1930, few were making more than $200 a year. As agricultural prices continued to shrink, black sharecroppers, farm hands, and tenant farmers either left or were forced from the farm. Nearly 400,000 left the South. Most headed north to urban centers like Harlem. Those who stayed behind were unemployed or worked for extremely meager wages. In some parishes of Louisiana, cotton pickers earned only 40 cents a day, some only $40 a year.

Racial violence and injustice increased as whites used violence and intimidation to drive blacks from jobs and maintain social dominance. Nowhere was racial bigotry more glaring than in the celebrated Scottsboro case. In 1931, nine black men were arrested in Alabama for raping two white prostitutes. Without any physical evidence, an all-white male jury quickly found the **Scottsboro Nine** guilty. Eight were sentenced to death. Years of appeals and retrials followed. The Supreme Court twice ordered a new trial. Though

"Arkies" and "Okies" Names applied to dispossessed farmers and sharecroppers from Arkansas and Oklahoma, both black and white, who migrated to California during the Depression.

Scottsboro Nine Nine African Americans convicted of raping two white women in a freight train in Alabama in 1931; their case became famous as an example of racism in the legal system.

never acquitted, all nine defendants were free by 1950.

Generally, African Americans living in the North found that white racial attitudes there were much like those in the South. As jobs grew scarce, whites demanded and got the jobs previously held by minorities. Unemployment among urban blacks ran 20 to 50 percent higher than among urban whites. Nationally, 50 percent of the black population was out of work or on relief. In Harlem, low wages, limited relief funds, and racial tensions sparked a race riot in 1935 that cost four lives and millions of dollars in damage.

African-American women, especially in northern cities, also saw significant drops in employment, even though they held low-paying jobs. In Chicago, Cleveland, and Philadelphia, the decline in employment among black women averaged 22.6 percent between 1929 and 1940, as white women and men pushed them out of the labor force.

Like African Americans, Latinos found that the Depression aggravated Anglo hostility and made a hard life harder. Between 1914 and 1929, the Mexican population in California, the Southwest, and the Midwest had grown rapidly. Most Mexican nationals and Mexican Americans squeezed out a meager living. They filled menial jobs, worked in the fields, and farmed small plots of land. The Depression forced many into deeper poverty.

Racial hostility intensified as Anglos demanded that Latino workers be fired to provide jobs for whites. In Tucson, Arizona, Anglos accused Mexicans of "taking the bread out of our white children's mouths." Across the country, by 1937 the lack of jobs, together with Anglo pressure and the Mexican government's encouragement, had convinced more than half a million Mexicans to leave the United States. Those who remained found jobs scarce and pay pitiful.

On the farms in California, the average wage was $289 a year, about a third of what the government described as a subsistence budget. As farm wages dropped and working conditions deteriorated, Mexican-American agricultural unions organized strikes. In a few cases, the unions won small pay raises, but usually the growers, sup-

ported by local authorities and public opinion, easily broke the strikes.

Asians, too, faced hardships and growing hostility. In San Francisco, nearly one-sixth of the Asian population was on relief. They received about 10 to 20 percent less than whites because relief agencies concluded that Asians could subsist on a less expensive diet. Some second-generation Japanese hoped that by assimilating, by becoming "200 percent American," they could remove economic and social barriers. The Japanese-American Citizens League was organized in 1930 and worked to overcome discrimination and to repeal anti-Asian legislation. By 1940, it had six thousand members but had made little headway. Asians remained isolated in ethnic enclaves.

Women in the Depression

While African Americans and Latinos found their already low status declining, some women discovered new opportunities. More white women entered the work force than ever before, primarily at the bottom of the occupational ladder. But in the professions, gender worked against women. The number of women in the professions declined from 14.2 to 12.3 percent during the Depression. Public opinion polls consistently found that most people, including women, believed that men, not women, should have the available jobs. Women were accused of stealing jobs from men. Opinion was especially hostile toward married women who worked. A survey of fifteen hundred school districts found that 77 percent did not hire married women as teachers and 63 percent fired women when they married. In 1932, 2 million women were out of work, and by 1933, an estimated 145,000 women were homeless.

For many rural women, the Depression took away a major avenue to new status: migration to the city. Throughout the 1920s, an increasing number of rural women, white and black, had moved to urban areas, taking domestic and other service jobs. But during the 1930s, such jobs in the cities became scarce, and many women were forced to remain on the farm. Too frequently, foreclosures and drought destroyed farm life. Rural women like

Ma Joad, heroically depicted in *The Grapes of Wrath*, had to adapt to life on the road, as over 2.5 million farm families were forced to migrate.

Among women who did enter the work force, few found that bringing home the paycheck changed either their status or their role within the family. Husbands still maintained authority and dominance in the home. Unemployed husbands rarely helped with household chores. One husband agreed to help with the laundry but refused to hang the wash outside for fear that neighbors might see him doing woman's work. Still, as wives and mothers, women were praised as pillars of stability in a changing and perilous society.

Franklin D. Roosevelt

As Americans sought to adapt to the economic crisis, many looked to the Democratic party for leadership and a change. Throughout early 1932, **Franklin D. Roosevelt** had campaigned for the Democratic presidential nomination, saying that government needed to be concerned about the "forgotten man," who, through no fault of his own, suffered from the Depression.

Born into wealth and privilege, Roosevelt had attended elite schools: Groton Academy, Harvard University, and Columbia Law School. The popular Roosevelt entered New York politics in 1910, winning a seat in the legislature. Tall, handsome, charming, glib, and willing to work with Tammany Hall, Roosevelt moved up the political ladder quickly. In 1920, he was selected as James Cox's running mate. Roosevelt came off well in a losing campaign.

The climb seemed suddenly over in 1921, however, when Roosevelt was stricken with polio and paralyzed from the waist down. But he and his wife, Eleanor, were determined to overcome his disability. For two years, Roosevelt worked hard to advance from bedridden invalid to barely mobile. He was never able to walk except with the aid of heavy steel leg braces and crutches. At the same time, Eleanor Roosevelt toiled tirelessly to keep his political career alive. Making his return to the political battlefield in 1928, Roosevelt ran for governor of New York and won.

♦ In the 1932 election, Roosevelt campaigned across the nation, always appearing confident and cheerful. Some said that his smile was the biggest political weapon he had—not only against Hoover but also against the Depression. *FPG.*

As governor, Roosevelt saw nothing wrong with governmental activism to deal with economic disaster. He was one of the few governors to mobilize his state's limited resources to help the unemployed and the poor. Although he made little

> **Franklin D. Roosevelt**   New York governor elected president in 1932 with the promise of a "new deal for the American people"; he would lead the country through the Depression and World War II.

headway against the Depression, his efforts projected an image of a caring and energetic leader. His brave struggle to overcome polio, combined with his effectiveness as governor and his cheery disposition, made him the logical candidate for the presidency.

The 1932 Election

In accepting the Democratic nomination, Roosevelt emphasized two points: he was a man of action who promoted change, and his paralysis in no way hindered his capacity for work. Roosevelt also established the theme for the coming campaign by promising a "new deal for the American people." Although Roosevelt offered no concrete solutions to the problems plaguing the country, he stirred people's hopes.

The election was a huge success for the Democratic party and Roosevelt. Across the nation, people voted for Democrats: for state and local officials, for Congress, and, most important, for president. Roosevelt won in a landslide, garnering 57.4 percent of the popular vote. Hoover carried only six states.

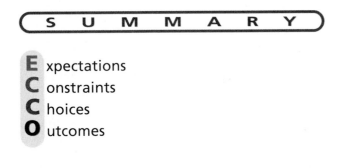

S U M M A R Y

E xpectations
C onstraints
C hoices
O utcomes

In the period from 1928 to 1932, the United States underwent major changes of lasting impact. Hoover assumed the presidency in 1929 a heroic figure. *Expectations* were high that further growth in the economy would enhance the quality of American life. The onslaught of the Depression, however, quickly changed Hoover's and the nation's fortunes. The economic flaws that had remained hidden during the apparent prosperity of the 1920s were soon exposed as banks and businesses closed. The economic collapse originated in part from internal weaknesses in the economy and the government's *choices* to promote easy money and to encourage speculation.

More than any previous president, Hoover *chose* to expand the role of the federal government to meet the economic crisis. He initiated a series of measures, including the Reconstruction Finance Corporation, by which the federal government tried to stimulate the economy. But Hoover's philosophy of limited government *constrained* the effort. The outcome was that the economy continued to worsen.

The Depression forced Americans to adjust their values and lifestyles to meet the economic and psychological crisis. Industrial workers and minorities faced extra burdens of discrimination and loss of status. Although many Americans had to make difficult *choices* that disrupted their lives, the *outcome* was that society generally remained stable as most people learned to cope with the Depression.

The Depression also made a mockery of Hoover's *expectations* about a prosperous and peaceful world. During the 1920s, the United States had *chosen* a path of independent internationalism that stressed voluntary cooperation among nations, while at the same time enhancing private American economic opportunities around the world. Although relations with Latin America improved under Hoover, elsewhere an *outcome* of the worldwide depression was international instability, as symbolized by Japan's invasion of Manchuria. *Constrained* by economic worries, however, more and more Americans withdrew into isolationism.

By 1932, most Americans had lost their faith in Hoover, the Republicans, and American business. Voters *chose* to put their faith instead in Franklin D. Roosevelt.

SUGGESTED READINGS

Bernstein, Michael A. *The Great Depression* (1987).

A detailed economic examination of the causes and effects of the Depression.

Bird, Carolyn. *The Invisible Scar* (1966).

An excellent study of how people responded to the impact of the Depression.

Macaulay, Neill. *The Sandino Affair* (1985).

An examination of Nicaraguan affairs and the American role in Central America through the eyes of Augusto Sandino.

Nash, Gerald D. *The Crucial Era: The Great Depression and World War II, 1929–1945* (1992).

A comprehensive and straightforward history of the period.

Terkel, Studs. *Hard Times: An Oral History of the Great Depression* (1970).

A classic example of how oral histories can give a human dimension to history.

Thomas, Gordon, and Max Morgan-Witts. *The Day the Bubble Burst: The Social History of the Wall Street Crash of 1929* (1979).

A view of the American economy and the stock market crash as experienced by selected individuals.

Wilson, Joan Hoff. *Herbert Hoover: Forgotten Progressive* (1970).

A positive evaluation of the life of Herbert Hoover that stresses his accomplishments as well as his limitations.

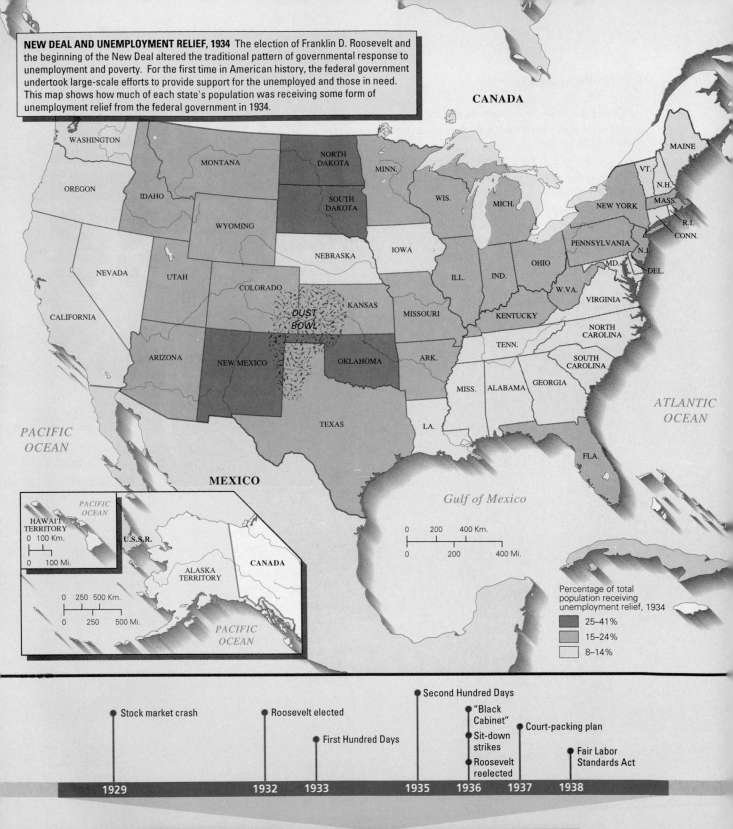

NEW DEAL AND UNEMPLOYMENT RELIEF, 1934 The election of Franklin D. Roosevelt and the beginning of the New Deal altered the traditional pattern of governmental response to unemployment and poverty. For the first time in American history, the federal government undertook large-scale efforts to provide support for the unemployed and those in need. This map shows how much of each state's population was receiving some form of unemployment relief from the federal government in 1934.

CANADA

WASHINGTON
MONTANA
NORTH DAKOTA
MINN.
OREGON
IDAHO
SOUTH DAKOTA
WIS.
MICH.
MAINE
VT.
N.H.
NEW YORK
MASS.
R.I.
CONN.
WYOMING
IOWA
PENNSYLVANIA
N.J.
NEBRASKA
OHIO
MD.
DEL.
NEVADA
UTAH
COLORADO
ILL.
IND.
W.VA.
VIRGINIA
CALIFORNIA
KANSAS
MISSOURI
KENTUCKY
NORTH CAROLINA
DUST BOWL
ARIZONA
NEW MEXICO
OKLAHOMA
ARK.
TENN.
SOUTH CAROLINA
GEORGIA
MISS.
ALABAMA
TEXAS
LA.
FLA.

PACIFIC OCEAN

MEXICO

ATLANTIC OCEAN

Gulf of Mexico

PACIFIC OCEAN
HAWAI'I TERRITORY
0 100 Km.
0 100 Mi.
U.S.S.R.
CANADA
ALASKA TERRITORY
PACIFIC OCEAN
0 250 500 Km.
0 250 500 Mi.

0   200   400 Km.
0   200   400 Mi.

Percentage of total population receiving unemployment relief, 1934

- 25–41%
- 15–24%
- 8–14%

Timeline:

- Stock market crash
- Roosevelt elected
- First Hundred Days
- Second Hundred Days
- "Black Cabinet"
- Sit-down strikes
- Roosevelt reelected
- Court-packing plan
- Fair Labor Standards Act

| 1929 | 1932 | 1933 | 1935 | 1936 | 1937 | 1938 |

| 1850 | 1900 | 1950 | 2000 |

The New Deal, 1933–1940

A New President, a New Deal

- How did public and political expectations and constraints shape Roosevelt's choices during the First Hundred Days?
- How well did the NRA and the AAA meet the expectations of Roosevelt and his advisers?
- How did political and social constraints shape the outcomes of New Deal relief efforts?

The Second Hundred Days

- What were the sources of opposition to Roosevelt's First Hundred Days?
- What was the outcome of Roosevelt's response to his critics?

The New Deal and Society

- What were the outcomes of the New Deal for cities across America?
- What were Roosevelt's expectations regarding civil rights? How did the New Deal affect the choices of women, African Americans, Latinos, and American Indians?

The New Deal Winds Down

- Why did Roosevelt choose to pack the Supreme Court? What was the outcome of this effort?
- What was the outcome of the New Deal for the structure of government and Americans' expectations about government?

INTRODUCTION

E xpectations
C onstraints
C hoices
O utcomes

The Depression brought to the presidency an individual who would dominate American history for the next thirteen years: Franklin D. Roosevelt. The dire economic situation gave Roosevelt unparalleled opportunities to reshape the federal government's relationship to the country. Roosevelt had few qualms about using the power of the government to combat the Depression.

Americans' *expectations* created opportunities for Roosevelt, but he faced serious *constraints* as well. Crisis or not, there were political and ideological limits on how much the president could change. To many on the political left, Roosevelt's election offered the perfect chance to reform society, to achieve social justice for all, and to restructure American capitalism to make it more humane. But Roosevelt had no intention of abandoning capitalism or restructuring American society. Eleanor Roosevelt, more socially liberal than her husband, reflected, "I'm the agitator; he's the politician." As a politician, Roosevelt knew that the nature of two-party politics loomed as a *constraint* to any significant shift toward the political left. Indeed, many conservatives *chose* to oppose any form of government activism and expansion of federal power. Another obstacle was the lack of precedent: no one knew what kinds of intervention would work on the reeling economy. Even among Roosevelt's advisers, there was disagreement on the nature of programs and the extent and type of governmental activism.

Roosevelt's *choices* were thus shaped by both public and political *expectations* and *constraints.* The *outcome* was the New Deal, which witnessed a barrage of legislation along three paths: economic recovery, relief for the victims of the Depression, and reforms to regulate the economy. This *outcome* was to change the responsibilities and power of the federal government. Roosevelt would be revered and hated, but no one could deny his impact.

In 1933, riding a wave of popular support, Roosevelt faced few political *constraints* as he initiated the First Hundred Days of the New Deal. A year later, that tide had changed. Many who had given Roosevelt a free hand in 1933 were now beginning to oppose him and his programs. Conservatives condemned economic and business controls and excessive federal spending. Liberals called for fewer compromises with business, increased spending, and more programs for workers, minorities, the poor, and the unemployed. With his popularity confirmed by the 1934 elections, Roosevelt *chose* to consider new approaches that placed a stronger emphasis on people than on business. The *outcome* was a Second Hundred Days of legislation passed in 1935 and 1936.

The New Deal expanded not only the functions of government but also the ranks of those voting Democrat. New Deal programs attracted women, minorities, and blue-collar workers. The president's overwhelming victory in 1936 verified the party's increased strength and raised the possibility of further expansion of government social programs. Such *expectations* quickly evaporated, however, as new *constraints* appeared after Roosevelt's unsuccessful challenge to the Supreme Court. By 1938, the New Deal had achieved its final shape. It had not promoted a full economic recovery, but it had restored Americans' faith in the economic and political system. The New Deal had rescued American capitalism. It also had profoundly changed the role and function of government. The long-term *outcome* of the New Deal was that the federal government emerged as the most powerful and important level of government in the nation. Before the 1930s, people looked to local, county, and state government for help. After the New Deal, people looked to Washington for assistance. Government and politics would never be the same.

CHRONOLOGY

Out of Depression

1929	Stock market crash
1932	Roosevelt elected president
	Milo Reno forms Farmers' Holiday Association
	32,000 U.S. businesses fail
1933	Dust bowl begins
	4,000 U.S. banks fail
	Bank Holiday
	First Fireside Chat
	12 million Americans (25 percent) unemployed
	First Hundred Days: AAA, TVA, NIRA, CCC
	Twenty-first Amendment
	Home Owner's Loan Corporation formed
1934	Huey Long's Share the Wealth plan
	Father Coughlin forms National Union for Social Justice
	Indian Reorganization Act
	Securities and Exchange Commission formed
	American Liberty League established
	Townsend movement begins
1935	Second Hundred Days: WPA, Social Security Act, Wagner Act
	Rural Electrification Administration formed
	National Youth Administration created
	Long assassinated
	Committee for Industrial Organizations established
	NRA ruled unconstitutional in *Schechter* case
1936	AAA ruled unconstitutional in *Butler* case
	Roosevelt re-elected
	"Black Cabinet" established
	Sit-down strikes begin
1937	Court-packing plan
	"Roosevelt's recession"
1938	Fair Labor Standards Act
	AAA re-established
	10.4 million Americans unemployed
	Republican victories in congressional elections
1939	Marian Anderson's concert at Lincoln Memorial
	John Steinbeck's *The Grapes of Wrath*
1940	Richard Wright's *Native Son*

A New President, a New Deal

During the long winter of despair between the November 1932 election and the March 1933 inauguration, Roosevelt and his advisers debated what course of action to take against the Depression. His advisers, often called the **Brain Trust** because of the many professors who joined the administration, were deeply divided. One group led by Columbia professors Rexford Tugwell and Raymond Moley believed that the concentration of American business in fewer and fewer hands was inevitable and favorable. Like Theodore Roosevelt, they applauded big business as efficient, economical, and, with the proper controls, beneficial. Their solution to the economic crisis was corporate regulation and public planning.

> **Brain Trust** Group of specialists in law, economics, and social welfare who, as advisers to President Roosevelt, helped develop the social and economic principles of the New Deal.

Felix Frankfurter represented another faction within the Brain Trust. He disagreed about the benefits derived from the concentration of business and the centralization of planning. Frankfurter distrusted big business and wanted more competition, along with social programs to help those most harmed by the Depression. Despite their differences, the Brain Trust agreed on the necessity of federal action to combat the Depression.

Roosevelt relished his advisers' debates, but in the end he made up his own mind about what to include in the **New Deal.** He would do what seemed expedient and would discard whatever did not work and whatever cost too much, politically or socially.

Bank Holiday

As Roosevelt's inauguration approached, the nation faced a severe banking crisis. Many banks had gone out of business since the Crash, leaving depositors penniless. In 1932, 1,456 banks had failed. The public's dwindling confidence in banks caused a growing number of **runs** on banks as depositors demanded their money. Most banks had no money and were forced to close their doors. By March 4, 1933, Inauguration Day, nearly all the country's banks were either closed or operating under severe restrictions. With the banks unable to operate, the economy of the United States was stiffening with paralysis.

On Inauguration Day, Roosevelt reassured the American public that he was going to take action. Millions listened to the radio as the president calmly stated that Americans had "nothing to fear but fear itself." The American economy was sound and would revive, but the nation would not revive by merely talking about it. "We must act quickly," he cautioned, adding that he intended to ask Congress for sweeping powers to deal with the crisis.

On March 6, Roosevelt announced a national **Bank Holiday** that closed all the country's banks. Three days later, as freshmen congressmen were still finding their seats, the president presented Congress with a request for an emergency banking bill. Without even seeing the written bill, Democrats and Republicans gave Roosevelt what he

wanted in less than four hours. The **Emergency Banking Act** allowed the Federal Reserve to examine banks and to certify those that were sound. It also allowed the Federal Reserve and the Reconstruction Finance Corporation to support the nation's banks by providing funds and buying stocks of preferred banks.

On Sunday evening, March 12, in the first of his so-called **Fireside Chats,** Roosevelt confidently told Americans that the federal government was solving the banking crisis. Federal banking officials were going to inspect banks, he announced, and those banks determined to be sound would be allowed to reopen. Banks would be safe again. "I can assure you," he joked, "it is safer to keep your money in a reopened bank than under the mattress."

Most of the 60 million Americans who listened to the speech believed the president. When banks in the twelve Federal Reserve cities reopened on Monday, customers deposited rather than withdrew money. Within a month, nearly 75 percent of the nation's banks were operating again. Roosevelt's quick and effective action established a positive national mood. The New Deal was under way. Over the next one hundred days, the new president

---

New Deal Roosevelt's program for attacking the problems of the Depression, which included relief for the poor and unemployed, efforts to bring about economic recovery, and reform of the nation's financial system.

run A panic during which depositors fearful of bank failure demand to withdraw their money, thus forcing the bank to close.

Bank Holiday Temporary shutdown of banks throughout the country by executive order of President Roosevelt in March 1933, until government authorities could examine each bank's condition to determine its soundness.

Emergency Banking Act Law passed in 1933 that permitted sound banks in the Federal Reserve System to reopen and allowed the government to supply funds to support private banks.

Fireside Chats Radio talks in which President Roosevelt promoted New Deal policies and reassured the nation.

would sign fifteen major pieces of legislation. The legislation, Roosevelt explained, had three different objectives: relief, recovery, and reform.

As the legalization of beer and wine sales in March 1933 illustrates, actual legislation often addressed several of these objectives. Legalizing their sale put people to work. It was also a reform measure aimed at curbing bootlegging. Similar motives informed Roosevelt's support for the repeal of Prohibition, accomplished by passage of the **Twenty-first Amendment** in December 1933.

Primary targets for reform included the banking and stock market industries. In June 1933, Congress passed the Glass-Steagall Banking Act, which reorganized the banking and financial system, gave new powers and responsibilities to the Federal Reserve System, and created the **Federal Deposit Insurance Corporation (FDIC).** The FDIC provided federal insurance for bank accounts of less than $5,000 and thus provided safety to millions of customers. Reforms for the stock market came in May 1933 with the Federal Security Act, which required companies to provide information about their economic condition to stock buyers. The **Securities and Exchange Commission (SEC),** created in June 1934, regulated stock market activities. Public approval for the reforms was widespread.

Seeking Agricultural Recovery

As Roosevelt assumed office, the plight of farmers appeared near disaster. The Farmers' Holiday Association threatened to call a farmers' strike across the nation unless Congress acted to restore farm profits. Roosevelt responded sympathetically because he believed that the family farm was an essential part of American life and needed to be saved. His goal was to raise farm prices through national planning to **parity**—the level of prices that farmers received in the profitable years prior to World War I. Secretary of Agriculture Henry A. Wallace was convinced that the nation's economic problems could not be solved without first resolving the problem of agricultural overproduction and farm profits. The challenge was to convince farmers to cut production. The **Agricultural Adjustment Act (AAA),** passed on May 12, proposed a way to do that.

The act encouraged farmers to reduce production by paying them not to plant. A national planning board determined the amount of land to be removed from production and then allocated specific reductions for wheat, cotton, corn, rice, tobacco, hogs, and dairy products to the states. State boards divided production cuts among participating farmers and compensated them for lost crops and livestock. The money for paying farmers not to plant was generated by a special tax on industrial food processors.

Because the AAA was not approved until May, after spring sowing, hundreds of acres of corn and tobacco crops had to be plowed under. Likewise, farmers had to destroy thousands of hogs and dairy cows and huge quantities of milk. In the Midwest, the continuing drought made it easier for ranchers and farmers to take land out of production. Many shuddered at the waste and pressed for the surplus food to be made available to the needy rather than being destroyed. Others complained that small farmers did not have enough land to remove from cultivation to gain from the program. They also pointed out that sharecroppers and tenant farmers were often evicted when landlords took land out of production to meet AAA quotas. Evictions and the Depression pushed more than 3 million people off the land.

Twenty-first Amendment Amendment to the Constitution in 1933 that repealed the Eighteenth Amendment and thus brought Prohibition to an end.

Federal Deposit Insurance Corporation Created by the Glass-Steagall Banking Act of 1933, it insured deposits up to a fixed sum in member banks of the Federal Reserve System.

Securities and Exchange Commission Bipartisan agency created by Congress to license stock exchanges and supervise their activities, including the setting of margin rates.

parity The fair value of a commodity, as opposed to its market value.

Agricultural Adjustment Act Law passed in 1933 that sought to reduce overproduction by paying farmers to keep land fallow; it was struck down by the Supreme Court in 1936.

Although large amounts of land were left fallow, production did not drop substantially. Farmers took their least productive land out of cultivation and used more scientific farming methods to grow more crops on fewer acres. To ensure crop reduction in 1934, Congress passed the Bankhead Cotton Control Act and the Kerr-Smith Tobacco Control Act. These acts levied special taxes on cotton and tobacco farmers who exceeded their production quotas.

By 1935, recovery in the agricultural sector had clearly started. Farm prices were rising, and the purchasing power of farmers was increasing. Then, in 1936, the Supreme Court declared the AAA unconstitutional in *Butler v. the United States.* The Court ruled that the special tax on food processing was illegal. The Roosevelt administration pushed the Soil Conservation and Domestic Allotment Act through Congress quickly to maintain the agricultural recovery. Under this act, the **Soil Conservation Service** paid farmers for cutting back on soil-depleting crops like cotton, tobacco, and wheat and for adopting better conservation methods. Finally, in 1938, Congress approved a second Agricultural Adjustment Act that re-established the principle of federally set commodity quotas, acreage reductions, and parity payments. The second AAA avoided the legal difficulties of the first AAA by using general revenue funds as the source of payments.

The combination of drought and governmental policies stabilized farm prices and saved farms. From 1932 to 1939, farm income more than doubled, and the government provided over $4.5 billion in aid to farmers. Initially regarded as a short-term measure to revitalize agriculture, the second AAA became an accepted solution to farm problems. The policy would contribute to stable agricultural prices for over fifty years. Equally important, Roosevelt's farm programs significantly changed the relationship between agricultural producers and the federal government.

Seeking Industrial Recovery

The **National Industrial Recovery Act (NIRA)** was Roosevelt's answer to the problem of industrial recovery. Approved by Congress in June 1933, the NIRA quickly earned widespread support from business, labor, the unemployed, and community leaders. In a two-part offensive, the **Public Works Administration (PWA)** was given $3.3 billion to put people to work immediately, while the **National Recovery Administration (NRA)** provided programs to restart the nation's industrial engine and create permanent jobs.

The NRA called for business and labor leaders, consumers, and government officials to work together on planning boards to promote industrial growth. The NRA was, Roosevelt explained in a Fireside Chat, a "partnership in planning." To achieve their goals, the boards developed "industrial codes" that set limits on prices, production, and wages. In turn, the government suspended antitrust laws for two years. Roosevelt selected General Hugh Johnson to command the NRA.

Johnson, who had headed the War Industries Board during World War I, relished the opportunity to wage war against the Depression. He immersed himself in forming the planning boards and drafting the codes for the nation's major industries.

Business supported the NRA because it allowed price fixing, which raised prices and profits. Labor

Butler v. the United States Supreme Court ruling in 1936 that declared the Agricultural Adjustment Act invalid on the grounds that it overextended the powers of the federal government.

Soil Conservation Service Agency established by Congress for the prevention of soil erosion; by paying farmers to cut back on soil-depleting crops, the government also addressed the problem of overproduction.

National Industrial Recovery Act Law passed in 1933 establishing the National Recovery Administration to supervise industry and the Public Works Administration to create jobs.

Public Works Administration New Deal agency created in 1933 to increase employment and to stimulate economic recovery.

National Recovery Administration New Deal agency created in 1933 that was responsible for implementing national industrial codes.

was attracted by Section 7a, which gave workers the right to organize and bargain collectively, outlawed child labor, and established minimum wages and maximum hours of work. Although consumers, workers, and government officials were represented on the boards, the boards were dominated by business elements.

Initially, Johnson's zealous efforts were remarkably successful. The blue eagle that was chosen as the NRA's symbol appeared everywhere as Americans promised to do their part. Within six months, the National Recovery Administration had written 557 specific codes covering industries of every size.

But the early enthusiasm for the NRA soon waned. The boards typically emphasized profits rather than market expansion or wage increases. Workers complained that too many codes instituted low wages and that employers frequently violated the wage, hour, and unionization provisions of the codes. Consumers lost faith in the blue eagle as prices rose without any corresponding growth in wages or jobs. Farmers complained that NRA-generated price increases ate up any AAA benefits they received. Businesses complained about mountains of paperwork, criticized Section 7a, and feared further restrictions on their activities.

To nearly everyone's relief, on May 27, 1935, the Supreme Court declared the NRA unconstitutional in *Schechter Poultry Corporation v. the United States.* Noting that the Schechter Corporation was not involved in interstate commerce, the high court ruled that the government could not set wages and hours in local plants. The PWA remained in place, but with the NRA gone, Roosevelt was forced to consider other means to rekindle the economy.

TVA and REA

Perhaps the most innovative and successful recovery program of the New Deal was the **Tennessee Valley Authority (TVA).** The Tennessee River and its **tributaries** ran through some of the nation's most economically disadvantaged areas. The TVA harnessed the river system of the Tennessee Valley through the construction of flood-control and hydroelectric dams (see Map 25.1). The first benefit was new jobs, but the chief outcome was long-term

economic development. The TVA's directors used the AAA to improve agriculture while the TVA provided electricity through federally owned hydroelectric systems. Only 2 percent of the homes and farms in the region had electricity in 1933. Twelve years later, the number of electrified homes had reached 75 percent. The TVA's cheap electricity attracted businesses like Monsanto Chemical and American Aluminum to the area.

Although many hailed the TVA's accomplishments, the TVA had its critics. Liberals condemned the agency's practice of segregation. Private utility companies and conservatives opposed the idea of a government-owned agency operating factories and power companies. Such conservative opposition was largely responsible for Congress's failure to approve seven more proposed TVA-like projects in 1937.

The TVA's electrification program nevertheless became a precedent for a nationwide effort. Utility companies had argued that rural America was too isolated and poor to make service profitable. Only about 30 percent of farms had electricity in the early thirties. In 1935, the Roosevelt administration created the **Rural Electrification Administration (REA)** to bring electricity to rural America. Working with rural electrical cooperatives, the REA had electrified 45 percent of rural America by 1945 and 90 percent by 1951. The electrification of rural America was one of the most important social and economic changes that took place as a result of the New Deal. It integrated rural America with the culture of modern, urban America.

Tennessee Valley Authority   Independent public corporation created by Congress in 1933 and authorized to construct dams and power plants in the Tennessee Valley region—Tennessee, North Carolina, Kentucky, Virginia, Mississippi, Georgia, and Alabama.

tributary   A river or stream that flows into a larger river.

Rural Electrification Administration   Government agency established in 1936 for the purpose of loaning money to rural cooperatives to start power plants that would bring electricity to isolated farms.

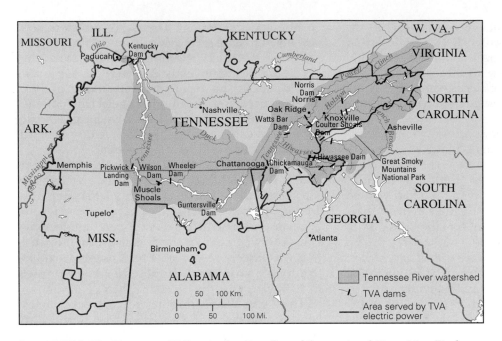

♦ **MAP 25.1 The Tennessee Valley Authority**   One of the most ambitious New Deal projects was developing the Tennessee Valley by improving waterways, building hydroelectric dams, and providing electricity to the area. This map shows the various components of the TVA and the region it changed.

Remembering the "Forgotten Man"

Roosevelt did not forget his campaign promises to help the "forgotten man," the 25 percent of the population—nearly 12 million people—who were out of work in March 1933 (see chapter opener map). Recognizing that state and private relief sources were unable to cope with the Depression, Roosevelt proposed four major relief programs during his First Hundred Days.

The **Civilian Conservation Corps (CCC)** established army-style camps to house unemployed urban males ages 18 to 25. Within months, the program had enrolled over 300,000 men, paying them $30 a month, $25 of which they had to send home. By 1941, enrollment was over 2 million men. The "Conservation Army" built national park facilities, cut out roads and **firebreaks,** erected telephone poles, dug irrigation ditches, and planted trees.

The **Federal Emergency Relief Administration (FERA)** and the PWA provided relief for the general population. **Harry Hopkins,** a former social

worker, headed the FERA and oversaw a $500 million fund to give to states for their relief efforts. Hopkins soon discovered that some states showed little compassion for the poor. Oregon's governor, for example, opposed payments to anyone able-

Civilian Conservation Corps   Organization created by Congress in 1933 to hire young, unemployed men for conservation work, such as planting trees, digging irrigation ditches, and caring for national parks.

firebreak   Strip of cleared or plowed land used to stop the spread of a fire.

Federal Emergency Relief Administration   New Deal agency created in 1933 to provide direct grants to cities and states to spend on relief.

Harry Hopkins   Head of several New Deal agencies, first organizing emergency relief and then public works; he remained a close adviser to Roosevelt during World War II.

bodied enough to work and thought that the feeble-minded and aged should be **chloroformed.** But by 1935, the FERA was spending over $300 million a year on relief measures.

The Public Works Administration, directed by **Harold Ickes,** eventually provided over $4 billion to state and local governments for more than thirty-four thousand **public works** projects, including construction of sidewalks and roads, schools, and community buildings. Ickes wanted PWA projects that were socially and economically desirable, but not all fulfilled his criteria. Urban bosses used PWA monies to make jobs for political supporters, and many communities often ignored their poorest neighborhoods when spending PWA funds.

In November 1933, as high unemployment continued despite the CCC, FERA, and PWA, Roosevelt established the **Civil Works Administration (CWA)** to provide nearly 4 million jobs during the winter of 1933–1934. CWA workers participated in a wide variety of work programs. Critics complained of "make-work" projects that wasted money, but overall CWA funds were well spent. The CWA built over half a million miles of roads and forty thousand schools. It paid the salaries of over fifty thousand rural schoolteachers. Despite its success, Roosevelt ended the CWA in February 1934 when the immediate crisis was over.

Not all relief programs were aimed at the homeless and the poor. Two aided homeowners. The Home Owner's Loan Corporation (HOLC), established in May 1933, permitted homeowners to **refinance** their mortgages at lower interest rates through the federal government. Before it stopped making loans in 1936, the HOLC had refinanced 1 million homes, including 20 percent of all mortgaged urban homes. The National Housing Act, passed in June 1934, created the **Federal Housing Administration (FHA),** which still provides federally backed loans for home mortgages and repairs.

The Second Hundred Days

The New Deal began with almost total support in Congress and among the people. That support did not last. By mid-1933, most Republicans actively opposed New Deal legislation, objecting to relief programs, federal spending, and increased governmental control over business. Conservatives fumed that Roosevelt threatened free enterprise, if not capitalism itself, and that he had betrayed his own class—the rich and privileged. They thought it bad enough when Roosevelt pulled the nation off the **gold standard** in April 1933, but in January 1934 he devalued the gold value of the dollar to $.59. To warn the country about Roosevelt and his "baloney dollars," conservatives became increasingly vocal in their attacks on the president. The Hearst newspaper chain instructed its editors to warn the public that Roosevelt planned to lead the nation into socialism. In August 1934, a coalition of anti–New Deal Democrats, Republicans, and business leaders formed the **American Liberty League (ALL).** By 1935, the ALL was the center of conservative

chloroformed To use the anesthetic chloroform to end a person's life painlessly.

Harold Ickes Secretary of the interior under Roosevelt and Truman and director of the Public Works Administration; he was an efficient administrator who opposed racial discrimination.

public works Construction projects, such as highways or dams, financed by public funds and carried out by the government.

Civil Works Administration Emergency unemployment relief program in 1933 and 1934, which hired 4 million jobless people for federal, state, and local work projects.

refinance To pay off an old mortgage with the proceeds of a new mortgage obtained at a lower interest rate.

Federal Housing Administration Agency created in 1934 to help homeowners finance repairs and to stimulate residential construction through federal mortgages.

gold standard An internationally established value for a nation's currency based on its exchange rate with gold.

American Liberty League Conservative organization that existed between 1934 and 1940 to oppose the New Deal.

opposition to Roosevelt and claimed nearly 150,000 supporters.

Populist Voices

For the majority of the American people, however, Roosevelt and the New Deal still spelled hope and faith in the future. Voters in the 1934 elections gave Democrats friendly to Roosevelt overwhelming victories. They won twenty-six of thirty-five Senate races and nine additional seats in the House. The segment of the Republican party vehemently opposed to the New Deal was virtually wiped out. Those election results made Roosevelt less willing to cooperate with conservatives and business. The president was also aware that economic recovery was not progressing as projected. Unemployment had been reduced, but government work programs still supported nearly 8 million households, or 22 percent of the population. Roosevelt was ready to switch approaches to fighting the Depression. Grassroots criticism that the New Deal was not doing enough to help the "forgotten man" also pushed the president in a new direction.

One of the leading critics was **Father Charles Coughlin,** a Roman Catholic priest who used the radio every Sunday afternoon to reach out to nearly 30 million Americans. Coughlin had lashed out at Hoover and anyone else who opposed relief. "God would have been condemned for giving manna in the desert because it was a dole," he told his audience. Throughout 1933, the "radio priest" of Royal Oak, Michigan, had strongly supported Roosevelt and the New Deal. But by mid-1934, he had turned his influential radio voice first against the National Recovery Administration and then against Roosevelt himself for being too probusiness. In November, he formed the National Union for Social Justice to promote legislation that would help the masses and to peddle his message of blatant anti-Semitism. (Coughlin thought many businessmen and bankers were Jewish.) Coughlin advocated a guaranteed annual income, the redistribution of national wealth, tougher antimonopoly laws, and the nationalization of banking. Within a year, the organization claimed more than 5 million members.

Coughlin was not alone in broadcasting that Roosevelt was not doing enough for the "forgotten man." Senator **Huey Long** of Louisiana, another onetime supporter, hotly criticized the president. Long had achieved power in Louisiana by attacking big money and promising to help poor whites. As governor, he had built roads, schools, and hospitals; provided free textbooks; and imposed new taxes on oil companies and the wealthy. In 1934, he broke with Roosevelt and advocated the **Share the Wealth** plan. The plan called for the federal government to provide every American family with an annual check for $2,000; a home, car, and radio; and a college education for each child. The plan would be funded by having incomes over $1 million taxed at 100 percent and by inheritance laws that would limit inheritances to $5 million. Crying "Soak the Rich!" Share the Wealth societies soon enrolled over 4 million followers.

By 1936, Democratic leaders feared that Long might join forces with Father Coughlin and run for president. Prospects of a third party soared when **Francis Townsend,** a popular spokesman for the elderly poor, appeared willing to join with Long and Coughlin. A doctor in Long Beach, California, Townsend, nearly 70, was well aware of the elderly's plight. Ignored by work programs and frequently denied relief because they owned property,

> **Father Charles Coughlin** Roman Catholic priest whose influential radio addresses in the 1930s at first emphasized social justice but eventually became anti-Semitic and pro-fascist.
>
> **Huey Long** Louisiana governor, then U.S. senator, who ran a powerful political machine and whose advocacy of the redistribution of income was gaining him a national political following at the time of his assassination in 1935.
>
> **Share the Wealth** Movement that sprang up around the nation in the 1930s urging the redistribution of wealth through government taxes or programs; its slogan was "Every man a king."
>
> **Francis Townsend** California physician who proposed the Townsend Plan in 1933, under which every retired person over age 60 would be paid a $200 monthly pension to be spent within the month.

♦ The Works Progress Administration not only built roads and buildings but also provided employment for teachers, writers, and artists. A common theme among WPA artists and writers was the strength and dignity of common people as they faced their difficult lives. Here a Michigan WPA artist sketches WPA workers. *National Archives.*

the elderly were among those most cruelly hit by the Depression. Dr. Townsend advocated a federal old-age pension plan. He wanted the government to provide every American age 60 and over with a monthly $200 pension check. Recipients would be required not to work and to spend the money within the month. Townsend proposed a national sales tax to finance the payments. Several million people joined Townsend Clubs.

The growing popularity of Long, Coughlin, and Townsend reflected the frustration of a large segment of the American population who believed that the New Deal was doing little to help them. Long's and Townsend's programs were attractive because they would aid people, not businesses.

A Shift in Focus

Responding to the growing pressure to modify the New Deal, Roosevelt announced in his 1935 State of the Union address that his administration would adopt a new strategy to combat the Depression. The focus would now be on helping people rather than on helping business increase profits. He asked Congress to provide more work relief, to develop an old-age and unemployment insurance program, and to regulate holding companies and utilities. During the Second Hundred Days, a solidly Democratic and largely liberal Congress responded with a series of acts. In April 1935, Congress allocated nearly $5 billion for relief to be divided among the CCC, the PWA, the FERA, and the newly created **Works Progress Administration (WPA).**

Roosevelt named Harry Hopkins to head the WPA, whose goal was to provide jobs as quickly as possible. Between 1935 and 1938, the WPA

> **Works Progress Administration** Agency established in 1935 and headed by Harry Hopkins, which hired the unemployed for construction, conservation, and arts programs.

employed over 2.1 million people a year. Most performed manual labor, but the WPA employed professional and white-collar workers as well. Teachers, writers, artists, actors, photographers, composers, and musicians were among the professionals who benefited from New Deal programs. The WPA's Writers Project provided future Pulitzer Prize–winning novelist Saul Bellow with a job writing short biographies and allowed African-American author Richard Wright to write his highly acclaimed *Native Son*. Professional theater groups toured towns and cities performing Shakespearean and other plays. By 1939, an estimated 30 million people had watched WPA productions that included known actors such as Orson Welles and John Housman.

The WPA also made special efforts to help women, minorities, and students and young adults. Prodded by Eleanor Roosevelt, the WPA employed between 300,000 and 400,000 women a year. Although some were hired as teachers and nurses, the majority worked on sewing and canning projects. WPA efforts to ensure African-American employment thrived in the northeastern states but stalled in the South. The **National Youth Administration (NYA)** provided aid for college and high school students and programs for young people not in school. In 1936, over 200,000 students were receiving aid. Mary McLeod Bethune, an African-American educator, directed the NYA's Office of Negro Affairs. Through constant pressure, she obtained support for black schools, colleges, and vocational programs.

More dramatic than the WPA was passage of the **Social Security Act** of 1935. Whereas the WPA was a temporary expedient, the establishment of a federal old-age and survivor insurance program was to be a permanent modification of the government's role in society. Previously, only 15 percent of workers had been covered by any sort of pension. The primary force behind the Social Security Act was **Frances Perkins** , the first woman cabinet member (see Individual Choices: Frances Perkins). In 1934, encouraged by the popularity of Dr. Townsend's plan, Perkins chaired the Committee on Economic Security to draft a social security bill. Passed by Congress in August 1935, the Social Security Act had three sections.

The most controversial part of the legislation created the Social Security system. Conservatives insisted that it would remove the incentive to work. Social Security provided a pension plan for retirees 65 or older. They would receive initial payments ranging from $10 to $85 a month, depending on how much they paid into the system. The more a worker paid into the system, the larger his or her pension would be. The program would begin in 1937, when a new tax (mandated by the Federal Insurance Contributions Act, or FICA) would be collected from workers and employers. Not all workers were covered. Many occupations, including domestic and agricultural laborers, were exempt. Compared to Townsend's dream and many existing European systems, U.S. Social Security was limited and conservative. Nonetheless, it represented a major leap in government's responsibility for the welfare of society.

A less controversial section of the bill established a federally supported system of unemployment compensation. Within two years, every state was part of the system, paying the jobless between $15 and $18 a week in unemployment compensation. A third section of the Social Security Act made federal funds available to states for aid to families with dependent children and the disabled. This provision aided nearly 3.8 million female-headed families that had been helplessly impoverished.

The National Labor Relations Act, generally called the **Wagner Act,** strengthened the union

National Youth Administration Program established by executive order in 1935 to provide employment for young people and to help needy high school and college students continue their education.

Social Security Act Law passed in 1935 that created systems of unemployment, old-age, and disability insurance, and provided for child welfare.

Frances Perkins Industrial reformer who, as Roosevelt's secretary of labor from 1933 to 1945, was the first woman cabinet member.

Wagner Act Law passed in 1935 that defined unfair labor practices and protected unions against such coercive measures as the blacklist and company unions.

movement by pulling the power of government behind the workers' right to organize. It created the National Labor Relations Board to ensure workers' rights, to conduct elections for union representatives, and to prevent unfair labor practices like firing workers for union activities. Roosevelt's support for the Wagner Act helped clinch labor support for himself and the Democrats.

The combination of the Wagner Act and the Social Security Act reduced the credibility of those who called Roosevelt too conservative. Similar political goals were evident in other acts of the Second Hundred Days. The Revenue Act of 1935 placed higher taxes on inheritance and gifts, raised income-tax rates for the wealthy, and instituted a graduated income tax for corporations. Conservatives, the business community, and the wealthy all blasted the tax changes, but among the not-so-wealthy, the law was clearly popular. The new tax structure actually did little to redistribute wealth. In fact, from 1933 to 1939, the wealthiest 1 percent increased their personal wealth 2.3 percent, controlling 30.6 percent of the nation's wealth. Still, Roosevelt's tax measures further angered business interests and raised conservative cries of a New Deal dictatorship.

Other acts of the Second Hundred Days reasserted Roosevelt's support for the "forgotten man." To help small farmers, sharecroppers, and tenant farmers, the **Resettlement Administration (RA)** and the Farm Mortgage Moratorium Act were passed. The latter allowed federal courts to reduce the debts of farmers to that equal to their property value. It also provided a three-year **moratorium** against farm seizures for farmers who had court permission. The RA tried to resettle marginal farmers on better land.

The New Deal and Society

Just as the Depression had an impact on every segment of society, so too did the New Deal. Newly restored confidence found expression in the popular entertainment of the time. The New Deal encouraged hope for overcoming obstacles that had long limited opportunities for some minorities.

The New Deal and Urban America

As the Depression set in, city governments found that their resources were too few to maintain the city, much less care for the needy. In 1933, 145 of the largest cities collected only 75 percent of the property-tax revenues they were owed. To "save" their budgets, cities cut wages and laid off policemen, firemen, teachers, and other municipal workers. In most cities, relief programs were among those targeted for elimination or reduction. "I am as much in favor of relief for the unemployables as anyone, but I am unwilling to continue this relief at the expense of bankrupting the City of Birmingham," stated the head of the city commission.

The New Deal provided new hope for cities by providing public works projects that eased the burdens of unemployment and relief. In many cities, especially in the West and South, public works projects also improved the existing **infrastructure** by constructing roads, bridges, hospitals, schools, and other public buildings. San Francisco saw the construction of the Golden Gate Bridge. Southern California, especially the Los Angeles basin, drew additional benefits from the water and cheap electrical power supplied with the completion of Boulder Dam in 1935. There were also political gains to be made from federal money and projects. "Roosevelt Is My Religion" was the 1936 campaign slogan of Mayor Edward J. Kelly, who kept Chicago solvent with federal funds.

Other federal programs shaped the growth of urban areas in subtler ways. Agencies like the HOLC and the FHA saved thousands of urban homes

---

Resettlement Administration Agency established in 1935 to resettle poor families on new farms or in new communities and to make loans enabling sharecroppers to buy their own land.

moratorium Suspension of an ongoing or planned activity.

infrastructure An underlying base for a system or organization; the basic facilities, services, and installations needed for the functioning of a community.

Choosing to Serve

Frances Perkins

Beginning in 1911, Francis Perkins sought to improve working conditions for the nation's men, women, and children. Perkins was the first woman cabinet member, and as secretary of labor, she tirelessly worked to create the Social Security system, establish a minimum wage for workers, and limit the number of hours people could be required to work. New York Historical Society.

On February 1, 1933, responding to a month-long flurry of rumors in the press and among "those in the know" that she was to be chosen secretary of labor, Frances Perkins wrote to President-elect Franklin D. Roosevelt saying that she "honestly" hoped the rumors were wrong. Shortly after the letter, Mary Dewson, director of the Women's Division of the Democratic National Committee, visited Perkins to convince her to take the cabinet position if offered. Dewson, who had recommended Perkins to Roosevelt, reminded Perkins of the many years she had spent fighting to establish unemployment compensation and a minimum wage and to abolish child labor. "You want these things done," Dewson argued. "You have ideas. . . . Nobody else will do it." She told Perkins, "You owe it to the women. . . . Too many people count on what you do."

On February 22, Roosevelt asked Perkins to be secretary of labor. She replied that, if she accepted, she would push for the abolition of child labor and the establishment of unemployment insurance, old-age pensions, a minimum wage, and a limit on maximum hours of work. Roosevelt responded that she would "have to invent the way to do these things" and that she should not "expect too much help from" him. She chose to accept the position. After some opposition from organized labor, she was easily confirmed by the Senate and became secretary of labor—"Madam Secretary," the first woman to serve in a president's cabinet.

She arrived at the position through hard work and a commitment to improving workers' lives. The daughter of a conservative middle-class family, she had been introduced to the lives of workers while taking an economics class at Mount Holyoke College. She quickly immersed herself in the spirit of the Progressive era, participating in the settlement house movement and helping to investigate working conditions as part of the New York Factory Commission that arose after the tragic fire at the Triangle Shirtwaist Company in 1911.

Through her work on the commission and with the Consumers' League, she became involved in New York politics as a supporter of Al Smith. She served Governor Smith as a member of the Industrial Commission, working to improve the circumstances of workers. When Franklin D. Roosevelt replaced Smith as governor in 1929, he named her industrial commissioner, a state cabinet-level position—making her the first woman to hold such a position at the state level. Beginning in 1930, she moved to support legislation that reduced the workweek for women to 48 hours, created a minimum wage, and developed unemployment insurance. Thus, when appointed secretary of labor in 1933, she already was experienced in the politics of improving the life of the worker.

During the First Hundred Days of Roosevelt's administration, Perkins and the Department of Labor helped to create the Civilian Conservation Corps and the Federal Emergency Relief Administration. In 1934, as the chair of the newly created Committee on Economic Security, she began to draft a social security bill. In encouragement, Roosevelt told her: "You care about this thing. You believe in it. Therefore I know you will put your back to it more than anyone else, and you'll drive it through."

The Social Security Act of 1935 was the outcome of many choices, most of which involved Perkins, Harry Hopkins, and Roosevelt. It was decided, for fiscal and political reasons, to have workers pay into the system as opposed to having the government pay for it out of taxes. Perkins wanted to include medical coverage, but it had to be excluded from the Social Security package, in large part because of the hostile reaction of the medical profession. To convince

Congress to pass the Social Security program, she made hundreds of public speeches and countless appearances before countless congressional committees. With its passage on August 14, 1935, the relationship between the federal government and the people permanently changed.

Frances Perkins took pride in the passage of the Social Security Act, but she was overjoyed when the Fair Labor Standards Act became law in 1938. "A self-supporting and self-respecting democracy," she testified, "can plead no justification for the existence of child labor, no economic reason for chiseling workers' wages or stretching workers' hours." The bill was attacked by conservatives and union leaders as allowing too much government intrusion. Conservatives called it a form of socialism, while union leaders argued that collective bargaining—not the government—should gain wage and hour benefits for workers. Nevertheless, when the bill became law on June 25, 1938, more than 12 million workers felt its effect. It immediately raised the pay of 300,000 people and shortened the workday for a million more. Together, the Social Security Act and the Fair Labor Standards Act changed the economic and social values of the nation and ushered in a new relationship between the government and the people.

Frances Perkins continued to serve Roosevelt and his successor, Harry S Truman, as an advocate of government support of workers and their families. Retiring in 1953, she wrote, lectured, and joined the faculty at Cornell University. She died in 1965, and her tombstone reflects the fateful choice she made in 1933:

FRANCES PERKINS WILSON
1880–1965
SECRETARY OF LABOR OF U.S.A.
1933–1945

and supported the building of single-family units, rather than high-density multifamily structures. The outcome was to encourage suburbanization rather than the development of central metropolitan areas.

Popular Culture

Movies and radio, the most popular form of entertainment throughout the thirties, provided a break from the worries of Depression life. On average, 60 percent of Americans saw a movie a week. *Gone with the Wind, The Wizard of Oz,* and dozens of musicals like *Top Hat* afforded a brief escape from the daily routine. Movies offered not only escape, though. Some also reflected the social and political changes generated by the Depression and the New Deal. In *Golddiggers of 1933,* unemployed men march across the stage while the lead singer demands,

> *Remember my forgotten man,*
> *You put a rifle in his hand,*
> *You sent him far away,*
> *You shouted, "Hip Hooray!"*
> *But look at him today.*

Cops-and-robbers films remained popular but underwent a slight change. Before the New Deal, famous stars frequently played gangsters. But as the New Deal became part of the American experience, those big names increasingly appeared as brave government officials who brought villains to justice. James Cagney became an FBI agent in *G-Men;* Humphrey Bogart was a crusading district attorney in *Crime School* and *Marked Woman;* and even Edward G. Robinson became a respectable good guy in *Bullets or Ballots.* All three actors had achieved fame playing tough guys, usually convicts or con men. Such character changes reflected a more positive vision of government than ever before.

Like movies, radio provided escape from the "De-repression," as the Depression was frequently called on the "Amos 'n' Andy Show," radio's most popular broadcast from 1928 to 1932. The Depression created a sudden demand for "gloom chasers" like the Marx Brothers, George Burns and Gracie

Allen, and Jack Benny. It also sustained crazes like the "Original Amateur Hour," which first aired in 1934. When amateur programs began to fade in 1937, radio turned to quiz shows. Keeping pace in popularity with comedians, amateur shows, and quiz programs were crime fighters like the Shadow, the Green Hornet, Dick Tracy, the Lone Ranger and Tonto, and Sergeant Preston of the Yukon Mounted Police. These heroes proved again and again that truth, justice, honor, and courage always prevailed.

Whereas movies and radio rarely criticized American politics and society, many novelists certainly did. Michael Gold, a young Communist writer, urged other writers and artists to produce works that furthered revolutionary change. Many responded by stressing the immorality of capitalism and the inequities caused by racism and class differences. But few advocated an end to capitalism. Instead they found heroes among those who refused to break under the strain of the Depression. Erskine Caldwell's *Tobacco Road,* John Steinbeck's *The Grapes of Wrath,* and Richard Wright's *Native Son* described "losers" whose misery was not of their own making but society's fault. In these and similar novels, authors assailed the rich and powerful while praising the poor's noble humanitarian spirit.

Still, popular culture typically affirmed traditional American values. Popular themes expressed faith that the long-term effects of democracy would allow the integrity of the nation's people and leaders to emerge.

A New Deal for Minorities and Women

Even more than the president, Eleanor Roosevelt was sensitive to the needs of average Americans. The first truly active First Lady, she crisscrossed the country talking with coal miners, waitresses, farmers, and housewives. Thousands wrote to her to describe their hardships and to ask for help. Although rarely able to provide any direct assistance, Eleanor Roosevelt constantly urged her husband not to neglect the poor, women, and minorities.

♦ In 1935, Mary McLeod Bethune (front center) became the first African-American woman to hold a high-ranking government position, serving as the head of the Office of Negro Affairs in the National Youth Administration. Here she is shown with the Council of Negro Women, which she helped organize in 1935 to focus on the problems faced by African Americans at the national level. *New York Public Library, Schomburg Center for Research in Black Culture.*

Eleanor Roosevelt took the lead in working to reduce discrimination in the government and throughout the country. In 1933, she helped to convene a special White House conference on the needs of women to ensure that women received more than just token consideration from New Deal agencies. Her outspoken support helped Democratic women to organize their own division within the party and to lobby for more important roles in the party and the government. Her efforts resulted in more opportunities for women in government than at any previous time in American history.

Eleanor Roosevelt was just as determined to affirm the equality of African Americans. Working with black educators and administrators like Mary Bethune, she sought to generate new opportunities for blacks. In 1939, she demonstrated her commitment to racial equality when the Daughters of the American Revolution (DAR) refused to allow renowned black opera singer Marian Anderson to sing at their concert hall in Washington, D.C. In protest, Eleanor Roosevelt resigned her membership in the DAR and helped arrange a larger, public concert on the steps of the Lincoln Memorial. Marian Anderson's performance attracted seventy-five thousand people.

Most black leaders complained, however, that the New Deal did little to challenge existing patterns of prejudice, discrimination, and segregation. A political realist, the president recognized the key role of white southern Democrats in Congress, and so he retreated from promoting civil rights legislation, even an antilynching law. When black leaders complained, he admitted, "If I come out for the antilynching bill now, they will block every bill I ask Congress to pass. . . . I just can't take that risk."

Nonetheless, the New Deal brought about some positive changes in favor of racial equality. In August 1936, Mary Bethune organized African Americans within the administration into the

"Black Cabinet," which acted as an unofficial advisory commission on racial relations. Among the most pressing needs for African Americans, the Black Cabinet concluded, was access to relief and jobs. In northern cities, it was not uncommon for state and local agencies to deny African Americans relief. Fortunately, Ickes and Hopkins were proponents of racial equality and used the PWA, CWA, and WPA to provide African Americans with relief and jobs. The WPA alone supported nearly 1 million African-American families and in northern cities, nearly eliminated discrimination from its programs.

Not every New Deal administrator or agency was as committed to equality as Hopkins and the WPA were. The Civilian Conservation Corps and the Tennessee Valley Authority openly practiced segregation and discrimination. African-American skilled workers were almost always given unskilled, lower-paying public works jobs. Even in the best of cases, federal support was not enough to help more than a segment of the black population. In Cleveland, for example, 40 percent of PWA jobs were reserved for African Americans, but black unemployment and poverty still remained high.

Still, most African Americans praised Roosevelt and promised their political support. By 1934, wherever African Americans could vote, blacks were bolting from the Republican party. In the 1936 presidential election, Roosevelt would receive nearly 90 percent of the nation's black vote.

Mexican Americans benefited from the New Deal in much the same way as African Americans. Agencies such as the PWA and WPA not only included Mexican Americans but paid wages that usually exceeded those in the **private sector.** New Deal legislation also helped union organizers trying to assist Latino workers throughout the West and Southwest. San Antonio's Mexican-American pecan shellers, mostly women, were among the lowest-paid workers in the country, earning less than $180 a year. Local union activist "Red" Emma Tenayuca and Congress of Industrial Organizations (CIO) representatives led the pecan shellers in strikes, finally gaining higher wages and union recognition in 1938. In the fields of central California, however, Mexican-American unions had little success in organizing farm workers. Where they were permitted to vote, Mexican Americans deserted the Republican party to vote Democrat.

Unlike most Mexican Americans and African Americans, American Indians benefited directly from the New Deal. Secretary of the Interior Harold Ickes and Commissioner of Indian Affairs John Collier both opposed existing Indian policies, which since 1887 had sought to destroy the reservation system and obliterate Indian cultures. At Collier's urging, Congress passed the **Indian Reorganization Act** in 1934. The act returned land and community control to tribal organizations. It provided Indian self-rule on the reservations and prevented individual ownership of tribal lands. To improve the squalid conditions of most reservations and to provide jobs, Collier organized a CCC-type agency solely for Indians. He also tried to promote American Indian culture. Working with tribal leaders, Collier took measures to protect, preserve, and encourage Indian customs, languages, religions, and folkways. Reservation school curricula incorporated Indian languages and traditions. Collier's New Deal for American Indians did little to improve their standard of living. Funds were too few, and problems created by years of poverty and government neglect were too great.

The New Deal Winds Down

By 1936, the Second Hundred Days had effectively reasserted Roosevelt's leadership and popularity. The prospect of a successful Republican or third-party challenge to Roosevelt was remote. Huey

---

"Black Cabinet" Members of the Roosevelt administration organized by Mary McLeod Bethune into a semiofficial advisory committee on racial issues.

private sector Businesses run by private citizens rather than by the government.

Indian Reorganization Act Law passed in 1934 that ended Indian allotment and returned surplus land to tribal ownership; it also sought to encourage tribal self-government and improve economic conditions on reservations.

Long had died in 1935, the victim of an assassin's bullet. Another Louisianan, Gerald L. K. Smith, took up Long's populist standard but was no match for the colorful "Kingfish." Smith joined forces with Coughlin and Townsend to form the Union party, but it never posed a threat to Roosevelt. Nor did the Socialist or Communist parties mount any noticeable opposition.

The Republican party, which nominated Kansas governor **Alfred Landon,** was hardly more of a worry. Although Landon accepted most New Deal programs in principle, most Republicans wanted him to attack Roosevelt and the New Deal. Reluctantly, Landon agreed. Roosevelt responded by reminding voters of the New Deal's achievements and stressing his support for the "forgotten man." He attacked big business, the "economic royalists" who wanted to rule like kings over the people. The tactics worked, and Roosevelt won in a landslide. Landon carried only Maine and Vermont.

The Democratic victory in 1936 demonstrated not only the personal popularity of Roosevelt but also the realignment of political forces. Prior to 1930, only two major interest groups successfully influenced government: big business and the South. With Roosevelt and the New Deal, other interest groups—some new, like the CIO, and some old, like agriculture—became integrally involved in the political process. Workers, farmers, women, minorities, and the aged now competed with the South and business for government favor and legislation. Roosevelt recognized the political importance of those who cast their vote for him, and he promised a government intent on seeking "social justice."

His second inaugural address raised expectations that there would be a third one hundred days. "I see millions of families trying to live on incomes so meager that the pall of family disaster hangs over them day by day," he announced. "I see one-third of a nation ill-housed, ill-clad, ill-nourished." The words seemed to promise new legislation aimed at helping the poor and the working class.

Roosevelt and the Supreme Court

Instead of promoting new social legislation, however, Roosevelt pitched his popularity against the Supreme Court— and lost. The president's anger at the Court had been growing since the *Schechter* case. It ruled in the *Butler* case (1936) that the AAA was unconstitutional. The Court also had declared illegal a quota plan for the oil industry, the Railroad Retirement Act, and a New York law establishing a minimum wage for women. As 1937 began, legal challenges to the Wagner Act and the Social Security Act were on the Court's docket. Roosevelt feared that the Court would undo much of the New Deal. He thus proposed to appoint new justices to give the Court a pro–New Deal majority.

Without consulting congressional leaders, Roosevelt presented a plan to reorganize the Court to Congress in early February 1937. Claiming that the Court's elderly judges could not meet the demands of the office, he asked for additional justices to help carry the judicial load. His goal was a new justice for every one over age 70 who had served more than ten years on the Court. Although Congress could change the size of the Supreme Court, many thought that Roosevelt's action threatened the checks and balances of government established by the Constitution. He made a major political miscalculation with his **Court-packing plan.** Many Democrats who had reservations about the New Deal now joined Republicans to say no to Roosevelt.

Roosevelt ignored the growing opposition and pressed on. Roosevelt's case weakened, however, when the Court in a series of 5-to-4 decisions upheld Washington State's minimum wage law, the Wagner Act, and the Social Security system. Even Roosevelt's supporters in Congress now questioned the need to enlarge the Court. The president's position collapsed completely in May when conservative justice Willis van Devanter announced his retirement. By July, Roosevelt had conceded defeat.

Alfred Landon   Kansas governor who ran unsuccessfully for president in 1936.

Court-packing plan   Roosevelt's unsuccessful proposal in 1937 to increase the number of Supreme Court justices; it was an effort to circumvent the Court's hostility to the New Deal.

He took solace in appointing Hugo Black, a southern New Dealer, to the Court.

Despite the Court's favorable decisions, Roosevelt had lost a great deal. He had lost control over conservative southern Democrats. Having safely broken with Roosevelt on the Court issue, many such Democrats now found it possible to oppose other Roosevelt initiatives. The Court fight had produced a new conservative grouping composed of Republicans, business interests, and southern Democrats. Consequently, a Third Hundred Days was now impossible.

The Resurgence of Labor

Labor strife also dampened many Americans' enthusiasm for the New Deal. During his first administration, Roosevelt had supported unions and workers through the National Recovery Administration and passage of the Wagner Act. "President Roosevelt wants you to join the union," was a common plug that labor organizers used to recruit workers. Mostly, the response was positive, and by mid-1934 unions were growing and becoming more militant.

There were over eighteen hundred strikes in 1934, involving more than 1.5 million workers. Union membership doubled that year. The rise of organized labor was especially pronounced in the mass-production industries. When the leadership of the craft-based American Federation of Labor (AFL) discouraged industry-wide unionization in 1935, a minority element formed the Committee for Industrial Organizations (CIO) to continue organizing industrial unions. Unionization drives were launched in the automobile, rubber, and electrical industries. The CIO also took an active political stance, pushing workers to support only those politicians who were friends of labor. In 1938, the CIO completed its break from the AFL and formed an independent labor organization: the **Congress of Industrial Organizations.**

In March 1936, the CIO supported workers striking against the rubber industry in Akron, Ohio, home of Firestone, Goodyear, and Goodrich. Wanting recognition of their union and higher wages, workers stopped work and refused to leave the factory, launching one of the first major **sit-down strikes** in the United States. With the strikers occupying the factory, the employer could not use **strikebreakers.** When the rubber industry quickly agreed to most of the strikers' demands, the benefits of sit-down strikes seemed clear to labor.

Encouraged by the Akron results, the **United Automobile Workers (UAW)** planned a sit-down strike against General Motors. The UAW focused on plants in Cleveland, Ohio, and Flint, Michigan. Because most General Motors plants received car bodies from Cleveland and Flint, successful strikes in those plants would eventually shut down most of GM's assembly lines. The sit-down strike began on November 30, 1936, when Flint workers took over the factory. Despite cutting off the heat, trying to block deliveries of food, and attacking the plant with company guards and city police, GM was unable to dislodge the strikers. When Michigan Governor Frank Murphy refused to send in state militia units to remove the strikers, the company settled with the UAW. Weeks later, Chrysler gave in to sit-down strikers and also recognized the UAW. In March, United States Steel accepted the steelworkers' union without a strike. Throughout 1937, labor staged more than forty-seven hundred strikes and won 80 percent of them. Union membership soared.

Congress of Industrial Organizations Labor organization established in 1938 by a group of powerful unions that left the AFL to unionize workers by industry rather than by trade.

sit-down strike Strike in which workers refuse to leave their place of employment until their demands are met.

strikebreakers Temporary workers hired by employers to substitute for striking workers.

United Automobile Workers Union of workers in the automobile industry, which used sit-down strikes in 1936 and 1937 to end work speed-ups and win recognition for the fledgling labor organization.

As strikes spread and violent incidents multiplied, unions did not fare well in public opinion. Many people equated strikes and labor militancy with radicalism and communism. Critics also blamed unions for most of the strike-related violence and considered sit-ins illegal. In 1939, the Supreme Court agreed, declaring sit-down strikes unconstitutional.

The End of New Deal Legislation

By 1937, with the economy apparently well on the road to recovery, Secretary of the Treasury Henry Morgenthau argued that the administration should cut relief programs, balance the budget, and allow business a freer hand in shaping the economy. Roosevelt agreed. He cut government spending and closed down many federal job programs. But unemployment rapidly soared to 19 percent, and the recovery collapsed. **Roosevelt's recession** had begun.

Roosevelt's liberal advisers won his ear in calling for a resurrection of the New Deal. The WPA rehired those dropped from the rolls, and Roosevelt attempted to marshal support for new legislation. But the political mood had changed since 1933, and a coalition of conservatives in Congress blocked passage of most of Roosevelt's requested programs.

Prodded by a strong agricultural lobby, Congress did enact a second Agricultural Adjustment Act that paid farmers to reduce production. In June 1938, congressional New Dealers overcame strong opposition to pass the **Fair Labor Standards Act.** The act established an initial maximum workweek of forty-four hours, set a minimum wage of $.25 an hour, and outlawed child labor (under age 16). The act proved to be the last New Deal legislation. In 1938, Roosevelt campaigned unsuccessfully for liberal candidates. The new Congress was more conservative and determined to oppose the president's "socialistic" ideas. Roosevelt recognized political reality and asked for no new domestic programs. By 1939, the economy had recovered to the point where it had been in 1929, and there seemed no reason to expand government programs. The New Deal was over.

The New Deal's Impact

New Deal programs failed to achieve a complete economic recovery largely because Roosevelt never spent enough money to generate rapid economic growth. It was spending connected with the outbreak of another world war that would propel the American economy to new levels of prosperity. Despite the New Deal's failure to promote economic prosperity, it changed the country and its people. It ended the fear generated by the Depression and encouraged a return to a stable and orderly society and economy. Equally important, it altered the basic relationships between government and society and between government and the economy.

Evaluations of the New Deal generally reflect attitudes about the proper role of government in society. Conservatives, during the New Deal and since, argue that the positive legacy of the New Deal is an illusion. Government intervention, they say, was the problem rather than the solution because it undermined individualism and created an expensive and overbearing government. Liberals praise Roosevelt and the New Deal for balancing the needs of the economy with those of society. From the liberal viewpoint, the New Deal promoted stable economic growth and contributed to the overall health of American society. More radical critics of the New Deal focus on what the New Deal failed to accomplish. They point out that the same groups who held power and wealth before the New Deal were still in control afterward and contend that Roosevelt made no effort to combat racism or economic inequalities.

What is indisputable is that the New Deal caused government to play a much larger role in the life of Americans than anyone had previously

Roosevelt's recession Economic downturn of 1937–1938 that was blamed on Franklin D. Roosevelt.

Fair Labor Standards Act Law passed in 1938 that established a minimum wage and a maximum workweek and forbade labor by children under 16.

expected. Before the New Deal, the federal government had remained remote from most Americans. By 1939, it had assumed new and expanded responsibilities. Institutions created by Roosevelt still regulate the nation's banking and financial systems. The economic health of agriculture continues to rely on a series of price-support and loan programs. The Wagner Act remains the overseer of labor-management relations. Social Security continues to provide for the economic welfare of the elderly. The belief in governmental responsibility for the needy has remained part of the American memory and experience. Since the New Deal, the American people have come to look to the federal government and the president for leadership, for legislation, and for solutions to the nation's problems.

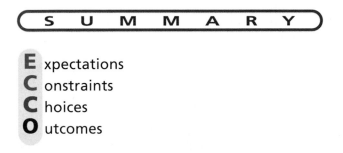

E xpectations
C onstraints
C hoices
O utcomes

The Great Depression brought Franklin D. Roosevelt to power amid widespread *expectations* that he would initiate a major shift in the nature of government. Through a variety of programs, Roosevelt *chose* to use the federal government to regenerate economic growth, to aid millions of Americans in need, and to regulate the economy. Although never a specific overarching plan, the New Deal attacked the Depression on three fronts: recovery, relief, and reform.

The First Hundred Days witnessed a barrage of legislation that dealt with immediate problems of unemployment and economic collapse. In 1935, Roosevelt *chose* to initiate a second burst of legislation that focused on social reform and putting people to work. The overwhelming Democratic victory in 1936 confirmed the popularity of Roosevelt and raised *expectations* of further social and economic regulatory legislation. A Third Hundred Days, however, never materialized. The Court-packing scheme, an economic downturn, labor unrest, and growing conservatism created formidable political constraints against further change. The *outcome* was that the New Deal wound down after 1937.

Although the New Deal failed to restore economic prosperity quickly, it left a lasting imprint on American society. Reforms of the financial and securities systems left a much more secure and stable industry. In the end, the New Deal strengthened capitalism and removed *constraints* for many who had been prevented from achieving the American dream.

The New Deal opened doors for those frequently ignored by government. Farmers, blue-collar workers, women, and minorities all had their New Deal. Each group emerged with stronger *expectations* about government's role in promoting their interests. The New Deal's *outcome* was a profound shift in society's *expectations* about the federal government.

SUGGESTED READINGS

Bergman, Andrew. *We're in the Money: Depression America and Its Films* (1971).

An interesting look at the movie industry and how it reflected the Great Depression.

Blackwelder, Julia Kirk. *Women of the Depression: Caste and Culture in San Antonio, 1929–1939* (1984).

A tightly focused study on Mexican-American, African-American, and Anglo women in the world of San Antonio during the Depression.

Fine, Sidney. *Sit-Down: The General Motors Strike of 1936–1937* (1969).

Using the United Auto Workers' strike against General Motors, Fine examines the industrial union movement and the use of the sit-down strike.

Leuchtenberg, William. *Franklin D. Roosevelt and the New Deal* (1983).

A comprehensive, classic account of how Roosevelt directed the nation from his 1932 election until 1941.

Sitkoff, Harvard. *A New Deal for Blacks* (1978).

A review of how African Americans benefited from and were otherwise affected by the New Deal and the Roosevelts.

Steinbeck, John. *The Grapes of Wrath* (1939).

A classic novel about the survival of the Joad family during the Depression that was later turned into an award-winning film.

Ware, Susan. *Holding Their Own: American Women in the 1930s* (1982).

An examination of the impact of the Depression on the lives and lifestyles of women.

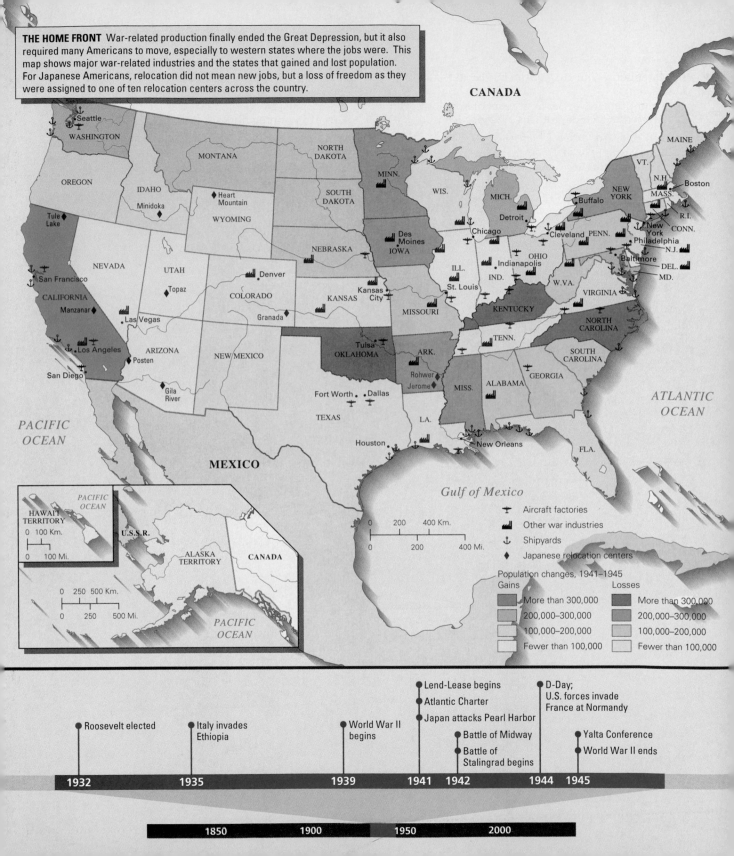

THE HOME FRONT War-related production finally ended the Great Depression, but it also required many Americans to move, especially to western states where the jobs were. This map shows major war-related industries and the states that gained and lost population. For Japanese Americans, relocation did not mean new jobs, but a loss of freedom as they were assigned to one of ten relocation centers across the country.

CANADA

Seattle
WASHINGTON
OREGON
MONTANA
NORTH DAKOTA
MINN.
WIS.
MAINE
VT.
N.H.
Boston
MASS.
NEW YORK
Buffalo
IDAHO
Minidoka
Heart Mountain
WYOMING
SOUTH DAKOTA
MICH.
Detroit
Chicago
Cleveland
PENN.
New York
Philadelphia
R.I.
CONN.
N.J.
Tule Lake
Des Moines
IOWA
OHIO
Indianapolis
Baltimore
DEL.
MD.
NEVADA
UTAH
Topaz
NEBRASKA
Denver
ILL.
St. Louis
IND.
W.VA.
VIRGINIA
San Francisco
CALIFORNIA
Manzanar
Las Vegas
COLORADO
Granada
KANSAS
Kansas City
MISSOURI
KENTUCKY
NORTH CAROLINA
Los Angeles
ARIZONA
Posten
Tulsa
OKLAHOMA
ARK.
TENN.
SOUTH CAROLINA
San Diego
Gila River
NEW MEXICO
Rohwer
Jerome
MISS.
ALABAMA
GEORGIA
ATLANTIC OCEAN
PACIFIC OCEAN
Fort Worth
Dallas
TEXAS
LA.
MEXICO
Houston
New Orleans
FLA.
Gulf of Mexico

PACIFIC OCEAN
HAWAII TERRITORY
0 100 Km.
0 100 Mi.

U.S.S.R.
ALASKA TERRITORY
CANADA
0 250 500 Km.
0 250 500 Mi.
PACIFIC OCEAN

0   200   400 Km.
0   200   400 Mi.

Aircraft factories
Other war industries
Shipyards
Japanese relocation centers

Population changes, 1941–1945

Gains	Losses
More than 300,000	More than 300,000
200,000–300,000	200,000–300,000
100,000–200,000	100,000–200,000
Fewer than 100,000	Fewer than 100,000

Lend-Lease begins
Atlantic Charter
Japan attacks Pearl Harbor
D-Day; U.S. forces invade France at Normandy

Roosevelt elected
Italy invades Ethiopia
World War II begins
Battle of Midway
Battle of Stalingrad begins
Yalta Conference
World War II ends

1932   1935   1939   1941 1942   1944 1945

1850   1900   1950   2000

America's Rise to World Leadership, 1933–1945

Roosevelt and Foreign Policy

- In what ways did Roosevelt's choices in dealings with Latin America reflect the ideals of the Good Neighbor policy?
- How did isolationism constrain American foreign-policy choices from 1932 to the outbreak of World War II?

The Road to War

- What constraints did Roosevelt face in trying to implement a more interventionist foreign policy?
- In reshaping American neutrality, what choices did Roosevelt make regarding Britain and Japan?

America Responds to War

- What actions did Roosevelt choose to mobilize the nation for war?

- What new social and economic choices did Americans confront as the nation became the "arsenal of democracy"?
- What new opportunities and old constraints did women and minorities encounter on the home front and in their military experiences?

Waging World War

- What choices and constraints did Roosevelt and Truman confront in shaping America's strategy for global conflict?
- What were the stresses within the Grand Alliance?
- What expectations prompted Truman and his advisers to choose to use the atomic bomb?

(I N T R O D U C T I O N)

E xpectations
C onstraints
C hoices
O utcomes

When Roosevelt assumed office in 1933, the cheery optimism of a prosperous world at peace that had greeted Herbert Hoover in 1929 was gone. By then, three nations seemed willing to *choose* military conquest if necessary to achieve their goals. Japan, seeking an empire in Asia, had annexed Manchuria and was threatening China. In Germany, Adolf Hitler and the National Socialist (Nazi) party had gained political dominance amid promises of restoring Germany's military and diplomatic prowess. Having seized power in 1922, Benito Mussolini had used nationalism, imperial designs, and military power to tighten his control over Italy. Roosevelt faced the events in Asia and Europe as an internationalist. He wanted the country to take a more active role in world affairs, but he was *constrained* by strong isolationist views in Congress and among the public. In addition, he understood that American economic recovery was his first priority.

The onslaught of war in 1939, however, allowed Roosevelt to chart a path away from neutrality. He *chose* to help defeat Hitler by providing economic and military assistance to Britain and to *constrain* Japanese expansion by using trade restrictions. Japan's attack on Pearl Harbor in December 1941 drew the United States into World War II.

The war managed to do what the New Deal had not—to restore American prosperity. An *out-come* of America's becoming the "arsenal of democracy" was full recovery and full employment, as 15 million Americans marched off to war. Those remaining at home faced new opportunities and *constraints*. Americans *chose* to move to take war-related jobs, especially on the West Coast. The *outcome* for women and minorities was mixed: they experienced greater opportunities, but they also were *expected* to give up their new opportunities once the war was over.

For Presidents Franklin D. Roosevelt and Harry S Truman, defeating the Axis Powers entailed making strategic decisions that shaped the course of the war. Roosevelt *chose* to allocate most of the nation's resources to defeat Hitler first. By the end of May 1945, Hitler's Third Reich was in ruins and American forces were on the verge of victory over Japan. Roosevelt had died. Truman, facing the prospect of huge casualties with an invasion of Japan, *chose* to use the atomic bomb. The *outcome* was the surrender of Japan, the beginning of a new age of atomic power, and the emergence of the United States as a super power.

Roosevelt and Foreign Policy

Until Franklin Roosevelt ran for the presidency, he was an internationalist who had supported an active American role in world affairs. But as a presidential candidate, he stated his opposition to American participation in the League of Nations and other world organizations. At heart, however, Roosevelt remained an internationalist who believed that international cooperation would create a better world.

The Good Neighbor Policy

In Latin America, Roosevelt built on the improving relations already begun by Hoover. He promised that the United States would be a "good neighbor" and would not interfere in Latin American affairs. His promise was soon tested in Cuba, where President Gerardo "the Butcher" Machado's harsh regime stirred political unrest. In the summer of 1933, Roosevelt sent special envoy Sumner Welles to Cuba to encourage Machado to

C H R O N O L O G Y

A World at War

1931   Japan occupies Manchuria

1932   Roosevelt elected president

1933   Gerardo Machado resigns as president
of Cuba
United States recognizes Soviet Union
Hitler and Nazi party take power in Germany

1934   Fulgencio Batista assumes power in Cuba

1935   Italy invades Ethiopia
Neutrality Act of 1935

1936   Spanish Civil War begins
Germany reoccupies the Rhineland
Roosevelt reelected president

1937   Japan invades China
Panay attacked by Japanese aircraft
Neutrality Act of 1937

1938   Austria annexed by Germany
Munich Conference

1939   Germany invades Czechoslovakia
Ribbentrop-Molotov Nonaggression Pact
World War II begins as Germany invades
Poland
Soviets invade Poland and Finland
Neutrality Act of 1939

1940   Germany occupies most of western Europe
Roosevelt reelected president
Burke-Wadsworth Act
Destroyers-for-bases agreement

1941   Lend-Lease begins
Fair Employment Practices Commission
created
Atlantic Charter
Germany invades Soviet Union
U.S. warships attacked by U-boats
Japan attacks Pearl Harbor
United States enters World War II

1942   War Production Board created
Japanese conquer Philippines
Japanese Americans interned
Battles of the Coral Sea and Midway
Manhattan Project begins
Congress of Racial Equality founded
U.S. troops invade North Africa

1943   U.S. forces capture Guadalcanal
Soviets defeat Germans at Stalingrad
Detroit race riot
U.S. forces invade Italy
Tehran Conference

1944   D-day: U.S. forces invade France at
Normandy and reach the Rhine
Roosevelt reelected president
U.S. forces capture Philippines
Soviet forces liberate Eastern Europe
Battle of the Bulge

1945   Yalta Conference
Roosevelt dies; Truman becomes president
Soviets capture Berlin
Germany surrenders
U.S. forces capture Iwo Jima and Okinawa
Potsdam Conference
Atomic bombs dropped on Hiroshima and
Nagasaki
Japan surrenders

resign. He succeeded, but Welles considered the new government of Ramón Grau San Martín too radical and recommended using American military force to overthrow Grau. Roosevelt refused to send in the marines. Instead, the United States refused to recognize the Cuban government. Meanwhile, Welles encouraged **General Fulgencio Batista** to overthrow Grau and install a government acceptable to the United States. Batista did so in 1934. As a result, the United States recognized the new government; rescinded the 1902 Platt Amendment, which authorized American intervention in Cuban affairs; and signed a favorable trade agreement. Batista would control the island nation until 1959.

Watching American actions in Cuba, many Latin Americans questioned the reality of Roosevelt's **Good Neighbor Policy.** Secretary of State Cordell Hull raised further doubts when he declared that the United States maintained the right to intervene in Latin America to protect American citizens. At Pan American conferences in 1936 and 1938, however, the United States rejected all reasons for armed intervention.

Roosevelt's commitment to **nonintervention** was tested when, in 1938, Mexico's president, **Lázaro Cárdenas,** nationalized foreign-owned oil properties. American oil interests quickly called on the United States to take action against Mexico. But the American ambassador to Mexico, Josephus Daniels, recommended to Roosevelt that the United States accept Mexico's actions and negotiate a fair settlement with the American companies. Roosevelt took Daniels's advice. By 1940, Roosevelt had vastly improved America's image throughout Latin America.

Roosevelt and Isolationism

While Roosevelt was improving the image of the United States in Latin America, tensions were increasing in Europe and Asia. In Germany, Adolf Hitler by 1935 had ruthlessly instituted a **dictatorship** and expanded the military. The Japanese spoke openly of establishing a larger Japanese sphere of influence and increased pressure on China. Eyeing the Japanese and the Germans un-

easily, the Soviet Union, led by Joseph Stalin, sought to improve relations with the United States. Roosevelt also sought improved relations. In November 1933, the United States recognized the Soviet Union.

Within the United States, Roosevelt's decision to establish relations with the Soviets prompted protests that he meant to abandon isolationism. Many voices urged the avoidance of foreign entanglements. A congressional investigation chaired by Senator Gerald P. Nye determined that America's entry into World War I had been the product of arms manufacturers, bankers, and war profiteers— "the merchants of death." Novelists such as Ernest Hemingway (*A Farewell to Arms*, 1929) and John Dos Passos (*Three Soldiers*, 1921) added to antiwar and isolationist sentiments with their powerful stories depicting the senseless horror of war. A Gallup poll revealed that 67 percent of Americans believed that the nation's intervention in World War I had been wrong.

By 1935, tensions in Asia and Europe combined with American isolationism to generate neutrality laws designed to prevent American involvement in future foreign wars. The **Neutrality Act of 1935**

General Fulgencio Batista Dictator who ruled Cuba from 1934 through 1958; his corrupt authoritarian regime was overthrown on New Year's Day, 1959, by Fidel Castro's revolutionary movement.

Good Neighbor Policy Phrase used to describe Roosevelt's Latin American policy, which was based on the belief that the United States had no right to intervene in Latin American affairs.

nonintervention Refusal to interfere, especially in the affairs of another nation.

Lázaro Cárdenas Mexican president from 1934 to 1940, who distributed land to peasants, instituted social reforms, and nationalized foreign-owned oil properties.

dictatorship State or government controlled by a tyrant, or absolute ruler.

Neutrality Act of 1935 Congressional resolution prohibiting arms shipments to nations at war and authorizing the president to warn U.S. citizens against traveling on belligerents' vessels.

prohibited the sale of arms and munitions to any nation at war. Anxious to see the Second Hundred Days successfully through Congress, Roosevelt signed the measure.

Many Americans felt that the Neutrality Act of 1935 came just in time. On October 3, Benito Mussolini's Italian troops invaded the African nation of Ethiopia. Roosevelt immediately announced American neutrality toward the Ethiopian conflict. The arms embargo had little effect on Italy, whose modern army overpowered Ethiopia's antiquated forces. On May 9, 1936, Italy annexed Ethiopia.

International tensions increased in Europe itself in 1936. In March, German troops violated the Treaty of Versailles by occupying the **Rhineland,** and in July, civil war broke out in Spain. Roosevelt proclaimed that the remilitarization of the Rhineland was of no concern to the United States. Most Americans agreed, but public opinion was sharply divided about the conflict in Spain. Liberals and leftists supported the Spanish government's **Republican** forces. Conservatives and most Catholics supported the rebels led by the **fascist** general **Francisco Franco.** However, most Americans agreed when Roosevelt applied the neutrality acts to both sides.

Italy and Germany actively aided Franco, taking the opportunity to test their military capability. German and Italian planes, tanks, and troops augmented Franco's soldiers in attacks on Republican forces and towns. Facing better-equipped and larger armies, the Republican forces fought bravely but were forced to surrender city after city. With the fall of Madrid in March 1939, Franco defeated the last Republican forces.

The Ethiopian War, German militarization, and the Spanish Civil War strengthened American isolationism. The **Neutrality Act of 1937** went beyond the previous act in requiring nations to pay cash for all "nonwar" goods and to carry those goods on their own ships, and in barring Americans from sailing on belligerents' ships. The new act did give the president a small victory by allowing him to determine which nations were at war and which goods were nonwar goods.

Roosevelt used that provision in late July 1937 following a Japanese invasion of northern China.

He refused to recognize that China and Japan were at war and allowed American trade to continue with both nations. That fiction did not last long. On December 12, 1937, Japanese aircraft bombed the American gunboat *Panay* and two Standard Oil tankers. Roosevelt wanted to retaliate, but public opinion and Congress insisted otherwise. Within two days of the *Panay* bombing, isolationists in the House had pushed forward a constitutional amendment that would require a public referendum before Congress could declare war. Only after Roosevelt had expended a great deal of political effort did the House return the amendment to committee, effectively killing it. Roosevelt had no choice but to accept Japan's apology and payment of damages for the *Panay*.

The Road to War

World peace was crumbling fast as 1938 began. The fighting in China and Spain raged on. From Berlin, Hitler pronounced his intentions of unifying all German-speaking lands in a new German empire, or Reich. Hitler's first step in creating this

---

Rhineland   Region of western Germany along the Rhine River, which, under the terms of the Versailles Treaty, was to remain free of troops and military fortifications.

Republican   In Spain, a left-wing political group that won national elections in 1936 but was prevented from carrying out its programs by a military rebellion and the outbreak of civil war.

fascist   Supporter of a political system and dictatorship that glorifies the state, nation, and race over individual liberties and rights.

Francisco Franco   Fascist general whose rebel forces defeated the Republicans in the Spanish Civil War (1936–1939); he ruled as dictator of Spain until his death in 1975.

Neutrality Act of 1937   Law that required warring nations to pay cash for "nonwar" goods and barred Americans from sailing on belligerents' ships.

empire was the forced **Anschluss,** or merger, of Austria with Germany.

Hearing only mild protests from other nations, Hitler confidently moved to incorporate other German-speaking areas into the Reich. He next demanded the annexation of the Sudeten region of western Czechoslovakia, which had a substantial German population. The Czechoslovakian government was prepared to resist and appealed for help as German troops massed along the Sudeten border. France, the Soviet Union, and Britain, however, did not want a confrontation with Hitler. On September 30, Britain's prime minister, **Neville Chamberlain,** met with Hitler in Munich and accepted Germany's annexation of the Sudetenland (see Map 26.1). Without British and French support, the Czechs had no option but to concede the loss of territory. Chamberlain returned to England smiling and promising "peace in our time."

Within Germany, Hitler stepped up the persecution of the country's nearly half a million Jews. In 1938, Hitler had Jewish synagogues, businesses, and homes looted and destroyed. Detention centers at Dachau and Buchenwald soon confined over fifty thousand Jews. Thousands of German and Austrian Jews fled to other countries. Many applied to enter the United States, but most were turned away. American anti-Semitism was strong, and the State Department routinely denied entry to German Jews whose property had been seized by the German government. The State Department enforced the immigration laws so strictly between 1933 and 1939 that nearly three-fourths of the 27,400-person quota for Germany and Austria went unfilled.

Convinced that Hitler was a threat to humanity, Roosevelt sounded a dire warning to Americans in his 1939 State of the Union address. "Events abroad have made it increasingly clear to the American people that the dangers within are less to be feared than dangers without," he observed. "This generation will nobly save or meanly lose the last best hope of earth." Events verified Roosevelt's prediction of danger. Hitler ominously concluded a military alliance with Italy, invaded and seized what remained of Czechoslovakia, and demanded that Poland cede the **Polish corridor,** which connected Poland to the Baltic Sea. British and French officials, unwilling to appease Hitler any longer, pledged to protect Poland. Meanwhile, the Soviet Union had reached a secret agreement with Germany—the Ribbentrop-Molotov Nonaggression Pact of August 23, 1939—which divided Poland between them. No longer worried about a Soviet attack, Hitler invaded Poland on September 1, 1939. Two days later, Britain and France declared war on Germany. Within a matter of days, German troops had overrun nearly all of Poland. On September 17, acting under the terms of a nonaggression pact signed with Germany, Soviet forces seized the eastern parts of Poland and subsequently invaded Finland (see Map 26.1). World War II had begun.

Roosevelt and American Neutrality

In the United States, there was little desire to come to the aid of Poland, Britain, or France. Isolationism remained strong. But Roosevelt was determined to do everything possible short of war to help those nations opposing Hitler.

When Germany invaded Poland, the president proclaimed American neutrality. But he also asked Congress to modify the Neutrality Act of 1937 to allow the sale of any goods, including arms, to any nation that paid cash for those goods and carried them away in its own ships. Roosevelt calculated that only Britain and France would be able to take advantage of this cash-and-carry provision, since the British navy denied German ships access to American ports. Although a congressional "peace bloc" argued that the request would drag the nation into the war, Con-

Anschluss Political union, especially the one absorbing Austria into Nazi Germany in 1938.

Neville Chamberlain British prime minister who pursued a policy of appeasement toward the fascist regimes of Europe before World War II.

Polish corridor Territory adjoining the city of Danzig, which connected Poland with the Baltic Sea and which Germany demanded from Poland in 1939.

♦ **MAP 26.1 German and Italian Expansion, 1933–1942** By the end of 1942, the Axis nations of Italy and Germany, through conquest and annexation, had occupied nearly all of Europe. This map shows the political and military alignment of Europe as Germany and Italy reached the limit of their power.

gress granted the president's request in the **Neutrality Act of 1939.**

To protect merchant ships approaching American ports, Roosevelt established a 300-mile neutrality zone around American waters. Warships of belligerent nations were forbidden in the zone. If the navy happened to sink any German submarines, Roosevelt joked to his cabinet, he would respond like "the Japs do, 'So sorry. Never do it again.' Tomorrow we sink two."

Roosevelt was even more determined to aid the British after the fall of France in the spring of 1940. Hitler's first attack that spring had been on Denmark and Norway, which fell quickly. The German

> **Neutrality Act of 1939** Law repealing the arms embargo and authorizing cash-and-carry exports of arms and munitions even to belligerent nations.

offensive against France began on May 10 with an invasion of Belgium and the Netherlands. The German **blitzkrieg** overwhelmed Belgian, French, and British forces. That 350,000 British and French forces were able to escape from the French port of Dunkirk across the channel was the only bright spot for Britain and France. On June 10, Mussolini entered the war on Germany's side. Twelve days later, France surrendered.

Germany and Italy, called the **Axis Powers,** controlled almost all of Western and Central Europe, leaving Britain to face them alone. Britain's new prime minister, the feisty **Winston Churchill,** pledged never to surrender until the Nazi scourge was destroyed. On August 8, 1940, the **Battle of Britain** began. The German air force bombed targets throughout Britain in preparation for an invasion. Outnumbered eight to one, the Royal Air Force (RAF) outfought the German Luftwaffe. British pilots shot down over seventeen hundred German planes and forced Hitler to call off his planned invasion. "Never has so much been done by so few for so many," Churchill declared.

While the outcome of the Battle of Britain was still uncertain, Roosevelt lobbied Congress to provide the British with destroyers and aircraft and to increase the military budget. He argued that with American support, Britain could defeat the Axis without America's having to enter the conflict. Isolationists bitterly denounced Roosevelt for pushing the nation toward war, but Roosevelt got his support for Britain. In September 1940, he signed the **Burke-Wadsworth Act,** creating the first peacetime military draft in American history. By executive order, he exchanged fifty old, mothballed destroyers for ninety-nine-year leases over British military bases in Newfoundland, the Caribbean, and British Guiana. By the end of the year, Congress had approved over $37 billion for military spending.

In 1940, faced with a world becoming more dangerous by the minute, Roosevelt chose to take the unprecedented step of running for a third term in office. The Republicans nominated **Wendell Willkie** of Indiana, a public utilities executive. Initially, Willkie supported aid to Britain and increased military spending. But Republican

leaders convinced Willkie to present himself as the peace candidate. Willkie's popularity surged upward, forcing Roosevelt to affirm more strongly his commitment to peace. "Your boys," the president promised American mothers, "are not going to be sent into any foreign wars." The election demonstrated solid personal support for Roosevelt, who won easily, but not for the Democratic party, which lost seats in the Senate and the House.

The Battle for the Atlantic

As Roosevelt knew, the destroyers-for-bases deal was only a temporary solution to Britain's growing shortage of cash. In December 1940, Churchill asked Roosevelt for loans to pay for supplies and for help to protect merchant ships from German submarines. Roosevelt agreed. In his December Fireside Chat, he told his audience that a strong Britain was America's best defense against Germany. If Britain fell, Hitler would attack the United States next. He urged the people to make the nation the "arsenal of democracy" and to supply

---

blitzkrieg Sudden, swift military offensive that allowed Germany to defeat Poland in a matter of days.

Axis Powers Coalition of nations that opposed the Allies in World War II, first consisting of just Germany and Italy and later joined by Japan.

Winston Churchill Prime minister who led Britain through World War II; he was known for his eloquent speeches and his refusal to give in to the Nazi threat.

Battle of Britain Series of air battles between British and German planes fought over Britain from August to October 1940, during which English cities suffered heavy bombing.

Burke-Wadsworth Act Law passed in 1940 creating the first peacetime draft in American history and providing for the training of 1.2 million troops.

Wendell Willkie Business executive and Republican presidential candidate who lost to Roosevelt in 1940.

Britain with all the material help it needed to defeat Hitler. He then presented Congress with the **Lend-Lease bill,** which would allow the president to lend or lease war materials to any country considered vital to American security. The bill passed easily on March 11, 1941.

For a while, it appeared that Lend-Lease might have been passed too late. German submarines were sinking so many ships that not even Britain's minimal needs were reaching ports. In March 1941, Churchill warned Roosevelt that Germany's foes could not afford to lose the battle for the Atlantic. In response, Roosevelt extended the neutrality zone to include Greenland. By the summer of 1941, the United States Navy's patrol of the neutrality zone overlapped Hitler's Atlantic war zone. It was only a matter of time before American and German ships confronted each other. In May, a German submarine had sunk the American merchant ship *Robin Moor*.

Hitler's attention, however, was focused eastward. During the spring of 1941, he was preparing for an invasion of the Soviet Union. The nonaggression pact of 1939 had served its purpose. Hitler assembled the largest military force ever massed on a single front: 2,700 planes, 3,350 tanks, and 3.3 million men. On June 22, German forces opened the eastern front.

As German armies raced across the vast expanse of Russia toward Moscow, Roosevelt and Churchill met secretly off the coast of Newfoundland in August 1941. They discussed strategies, supplies, and future prospects. For the first time, both leaders sensed some room for optimism. More ships were getting safely across the Atlantic. But Roosevelt's main concern at the meeting was to develop a set of political principles that would support America's entry into the war. He and Churchill produced the **Atlantic Charter.** The charter reaffirmed the Wilsonian goals of self-determination, freedom of trade and the seas, and the establishment of a "permanent system of general security."

Shortly thereafter, on September 4, 1941, the inevitable encounter between an American destroyer and a German submarine took place. Claiming that the attack on the destroyer was totally unprovoked, Roosevelt obtained congres-

♦ From the beginning of World War II, Roosevelt was determined to help defeat the forces of fascism. Meeting with Churchill on board a cruiser off the coast of Newfoundland in August 1941, the two leaders signed the Atlantic Charter as a prelude to America's waging war against Germany. *FDR Library.*

sional permission to arm American merchant ships, to use the navy to convoy ships all the way to Britain, and to allow American ships to attack Axis warships. By the fall of 1941, the U.S. Navy was unofficially at war with Germany. On October 17, the U.S.S. *Kearney* was damaged while protecting a convoy. Two weeks later, the U.S.S. *Reuben James* was sunk, with 115 deaths. On November 13, Congress rescinded all neutrality laws. War was imminent, but Roosevelt

Lend-Lease bill   Bill that became a law in 1941, providing that any country whose security was vital to U.S. interests could receive arms and equipment by sale, transfer, or lease from the United States.

Atlantic Charter   Joint statement issued by Roosevelt and Churchill in 1941 to formulate the postwar aims of the United States and Britain, including international economic and political cooperation.

♦ **MAP 26.2 Japanese Advances, December 1941–August 1942** Beginning on December 7, 1941, Japanese forces began carving out a vast empire, the East Asian Co-Prosperity Sphere, by attacking American, British, Dutch, and Australian forces from Pearl Harbor to the Dutch East Indies. This map shows the course of Japanese expansion until the critical naval battles of the Coral Sea and Midway in the spring of 1942 that halted Japanese advances in the Pacific.

envisioned it as a war involving only American naval and air forces.

Facing Japan

Since 1937, Japanese troops had seized more and more of coastal China while the United States did little but protest. In July 1940, Roosevelt responded by forbidding the sale of aviation fuel and scrap iron to Japan.

In September 1941, the situation in East Asia worsened. Japan took over French Indochina (see Map 26.2) and signed a defense treaty with Germany and Italy. Roosevelt promptly increased American forces in the Philippines and added more trade restrictions. Within the Japanese government, there were opposing views on how to react to the American economic sanctions. Those seeking to avoid war hoped that negotiations would settle Japanese-American differences. But those negotiations stalled when Secretary of State Cordell Hull demanded Japan's withdrawal from Indochina and China. Hull's demand played into the hands of Japanese military leaders, who had argued all along that war was unavoidable to break the "circle of force" being created around it.

For Minister of War Hideki Tojo, the choice had become simple: either submit to American demands, giving up the achievements of the past ten years, or safeguard the nation's honor by initiating a war. If negotiations did not produce a more favorable American policy toward Japan by December 1941, the choice was for war. Naval aircraft would target the American fleet at Hawai'i, while the army would invade the Philippines, Malaya, Singapore, and the Dutch East Indies. The negotiations remained stalled.

Pearl Harbor

At 7:49 A.M. (Hawai'i time) on December 7, 1941, Japanese planes struck the American naval base at Pearl Harbor. By 8:12, seven battleships of the American Pacific fleet were aflame, sinking, or badly damaged. Eleven other ships had been hit, nearly two hundred American aircraft had been destroyed, and twenty-five hundred Americans had lost their lives. Fortunately, U.S. aircraft carriers were on maneuvers in the Pacific. Pearl Harbor's repair shops, dry docks, and oil storage tanks also incurred only light damage.

Elsewhere that day, Japanese planes struck Singapore, Guam, the Philippines, and Hong Kong. The Japanese overwhelmed British and American positions throughout the Pacific and East Asia. Roosevelt declared December 7, 1941, "a day which will live in infamy" and asked Congress for a declaration of war against Japan. The December 8 declaration fell one vote short of being unanimous. Three days later, Germany and Italy declared war on the United States.

America Responds to War

The attack on Pearl Harbor unified the nation as no other event had done. Afterward, it was almost impossible to find an isolationist. Thousands of young men rushed to enlist, especially in the navy and marines. On December 8, the navy recruiting station in New York City was besieged by twelve hundred applicants, some of whom had waited outside all night.

The shock of Japan's attack on Pearl Harbor raised fears of further attacks, especially along the Pacific coast. Throughout the week after December 7, West Coast cities reported phantom enemy planes. Rumors circulated that Japanese Americans intended to sabotage factories and military installations. Within a week, the Federal Bureau of Investigation (FBI) had arrested 1,370 Japanese, 1,002 Germans, and 169 Italians.

Japanese-American Internment

The feelings against Japanese Americans were the product of long-standing racist attitudes. Of the nearly 125,000 Japanese Americans in the country, about three-fourths were **Nisei,** those born in the United States. The rest, the **Issei,** were officially citizens of Japan, although nearly all had lived in the United States since 1924, when American law barred them from becoming naturalized citizens.

Echoing its anti-Japanese actions in the 1880s, California moved to "protect" itself. Japanese Americans were fired from state jobs and had their law and medical licenses revoked. Banks froze Japanese-American assets, stores refused service, and loyal citizens vandalized Nisei and Issei homes and businesses. Although some doubted the reality of any threat from the Japanese-American community, no one protested the growing cry that they be relocated away from the coast. On February 19,

Nisei A person born in America of parents who emigrated from Japan.
Issei A Japanese immigrant to the United States.

1942, President Roosevelt signed **Executive Order #9066,** which allowed the military to remove anyone deemed a threat from official military areas. When the entire West Coast was declared a military area, the eviction of the Japanese Americans from the region began. By the summer of 1942, over 110,000 Nisei and Issei had been transported to ten **internment camps** (see chapter opener map). The Supreme Court upheld the internment order twice.

The orders to relocate gave Japanese Americans almost no time to prepare. Families had to pack the few personal possessions they were allowed to take and to store or **liquidate** the rest of their property. Some had two weeks to get ready; others had two days. Most families had to sell their possessions at ridiculously low prices. A twenty-six-room hotel was sold for $500; a pickup truck went for $25; farms sold for a fraction of what they were worth. Japanese-American families lost an estimated $810 million to $2 billion in property and possessions. Decades later, in 1988, the federal government paid $20,000 in compensation to each of the surviving sixty thousand internees.

Internment produced a feeling of helplessness and isolation. Tags with numbers were issued to every family to tie to luggage and coats—no names, only numbers. "From then on," wrote one woman, "we were known as family #10710." Going to the camp, she lost her identity, dignity, and privacy. The Nisei and Issei were surrounded by barbed wire and watched over by guards in towers mounted with machine guns. Photographers were not allowed to take pictures of the wire or the guard towers. In camp, families and individuals were assigned to apartments 20-by-25-foot located in long barracks. An average of eight people were assigned to each apartment. Cots, straw-filled mattresses, and three army blankets were furnished each person.

Some internees were able to leave the camps by working outside, especially on farms. Others volunteered for military service, the other escape route from the camps. Japanese-American units served in both the Pacific and European theaters. The most famous unit was the 442nd Combat Team. The men of the 442nd were among the most decorated in the war.

Aware of rabidly anti-Japanese public opinion, Roosevelt waited until after the 1943 elections to allow internees who passed a loyalty review to go home. A year later, the camps were empty. Returning home, the Japanese Americans discovered that nearly everything was gone. Stored belongings had been stolen. Land, homes, and businesses had been seized by the government for unpaid taxes. Quietly demonstrating their loyalty, Japanese Americans began to re-establish their homes and businesses.

Mobilizing the Nation for War

When President Roosevelt made his first Fireside Chat following Pearl Harbor, "Dr. New Deal" became "Dr. Win the War." He called on factories to run twenty-four hours a day, seven days a week. Gone was every trace of the antibusiness attitude that had characterized much of the New Deal rhetoric. Roosevelt welcomed big business back into the heart of government. Corporate executives left their companies and flocked to Washington to become **dollar-a-year men,** contributing their business skills to help the war effort.

By 1942, one-third of all American production was geared to the war, and the government was allocating millions of dollars to build new plants in vital industries like aluminum and synthetic rubber. By the end of the war, U.S. manufacturers had built over 300,000 aircraft, 88,140 tanks, and 86,000 warships.

As the nation's economy began to retool, Roosevelt acted to provide government direction and

---

Executive Order #9066 Order of President Roosevelt in 1942 that authorized the removal of "enemy aliens" from military areas and that was used to isolate Japanese Americans in internment camps.

internment camps Camps where over 110,000 Japanese Americans living in the West were isolated on the grounds that they were "enemy aliens" dangerous to U.S. security.

liquidate To convert assets into cash.

dollar-a-year men Corporate executives who volunteered for government jobs to help the war effort.

planning. His first step was to establish the **Office of Price Administration (OPA)** to control prices. In January 1942, Roosevelt established the War Production Board (WPB) and the War Labor Board (WLB). Working together, these boards plus the OPA were to coordinate and plan production, establish the allotment of materials, and ensure harmonious labor relations. Initially, however, they did not create a smoothly working economy. By the fall of 1942, confused priorities and soaring food prices had created a public outcry and labor unrest. To give the government still more control, in September Congress expanded the powers of the OPA and regulated agricultural prices. In turn, Roosevelt created the Office of Economic Stabilization (OES) to coordinate prices, rents, and wages. He appointed former Supreme Court Justice James F. Byrnes as its chief.

Armed with extensive powers and the president's trust, Byrnes became the second most powerful man in the country. "If you want something done, go see Jimmie Byrnes" became the watchword. Almost immediately, Byrnes and the new director of the OPA, Chester Bowles, set maximum prices and froze wages and rents at their March 1942 levels. To deal with scarce commodities, Bowles and Byrnes expanded the existing rationing system, adding gasoline, tires, butter, sugar, cheese, and meat. By the end of 1942, most Americans had a ration book. Despite all government efforts, a strong black market thrived. The right amount of money could buy nearly any item.

By mid-1943, production was booming, jobs were plentiful, wages and family incomes were rising, and inflation was under control. Even farmers were climbing out of debt, as farm income had tripled since 1939. Taxes also went up, especially for businesses and the affluent. Those making $500,000 or more a year paid 88 percent in taxes. Corporate taxes averaged 40 percent, with a 90 percent tax on excess profits. The 1942 Revenue Act also slapped everyone making more than $645 a year with a special "victory tax" of 5 percent, greatly expanding the number of people paying personal income taxes from 13 million to 50 million. The tax changes from 1940 to 1945 moderately altered the basic distribution of wealth by reducing the percentage of income held by the wealthy.

Increased tax revenues funded about half of the total cost of the war. The government borrowed the rest. The national debt jumped from $40 billion to $260 billion by 1945. The most publicized borrowing effort encouraged the purchase of **war bonds.** Movie stars and celebrities asked Americans to "do their part" and buy bonds. The public responded by purchasing over $40 billion of bonds, but the majority of bonds was sold to corporations and financial institutions.

Roosevelt sought to prevent labor disputes while protecting workers through the creation of the War Labor Board. To prevent strikes and keep down labor costs, the WLB allowed workers a maximum 15 percent increase in wages above January 1941 levels. Although most workers accepted this cap on wages as a patriotic duty, some did not. In 1943, John L. Lewis and his United Mine Workers went out on strike. An angry president threatened to seize the mines and jail Lewis. Eventually, the parties reached a compromise that established special circumstances to exceed the cap. Other strikes broke out during the war, but war production was never in jeopardy.

Wartime Politics

As Roosevelt mobilized the nation for war, Republicans and conservative Democrats moved to bury what was left of the New Deal. The congressional elections of November 1942 indicated that Roosevelt and liberal Democrats were facing hard political times. People secure in wartime jobs were no longer as concerned about the social welfare programs of the New Deal. They griped about higher taxes, rents, and prices; about the scarcity of goods, especially gasoline and meat; and about government inefficiency. And they aimed their

Office of Price Administration Agency established by executive order in 1941 to set prices for critical wartime commodities.

war bond Bond sold by the government to finance the war effort.

complaints at Roosevelt and the Democrats. Early military defeats in the Pacific added to the dissatisfaction. Consequently, many Americans who had once supported the New Deal voted Republican in 1942. Business-oriented publications like *Fortune* and the *Wall Street Journal* sounded the attack on remaining New Deal social welfare agendas. Congress axed the CCC, WPA, and NYA and slashed the budgets of several other government agencies.

The Republicans nominated Governor Thomas Dewey of New York as their 1944 presidential candidate. Responding to the conservative tone of the nation, Roosevelt dropped the liberal Henry Wallace as vice president and selected the moderately conservative Harry S Truman from Missouri in his place. Roosevelt campaigned on a strong wartime economy, his record of leadership, and, by November 1944, a successful war effort. Dewey had little with which to attack Roosevelt except suggestions that Roosevelt, at age 62, was too old for the job. Roosevelt's winning totals, though not as large as in 1940, were still greater than pollsters had predicted.

A People at Work and War

Within sixteen days of Pearl Harbor, nearly 600,000 men were in uniform. But still more were needed, and there were not enough volunteers. The United States conscripted over 10 million men during the war. Those drafted were required to serve until the war was over.

At home, the call-up and need to manufacture war-related goods changed everyday life. Cotton, silk, and gasoline became increasingly scarce. The War Production Board established fashion rules to conserve cotton and wool. Garment makers eliminated vests and shirt cuffs and narrowed the lapels on men's suits. The amount of fabric in women's skirts was also reduced. Families collected scrap metals, paper, and rubber to be recycled for the war effort and grew victory gardens. When people complained about shortages, more would challenge, "Don't you know there's a war on?"

One sure sign that there was a war on was that people were moving and taking new jobs as never before. Prior to the war, nearly 3.8 million Americans were unemployed; by the end of 1942, a severe labor shortage existed. To fill the gaps in the work force, employers increasingly turned to women and minorities. Even the Nisei were allowed to leave their relocation camps if their labor was needed. Between 1941 and 1945, 15 million Americans relocated to work in new jobs. Two hundred thousand people, many from the rural South, headed for Detroit, but more went west, where defense industries beckoned. Shipbuilding and the aircraft industry sparked boomtowns that could not keep pace with the growing need for local services and facilities. San Diego, California, mushroomed into a major military and defense industrial city almost overnight. Nearly fifty-five thousand people flocked there each year of the war. Mobile, Alabama; Norfolk, Virginia; Seattle, Washington; and Denver, Colorado, experienced similar rapid growth (see chapter opener map).

Such cities experienced massive problems providing homes, water, electricity, and sanitation for all the newcomers. Crime flourished. Marriage, divorce, family violence, and juvenile delinquency rates soared. The flood of people brought other disturbing social problems. The twelve thousand sailors and soldiers looking for a good time gave Norfolk a reputation as a major sin city. Police estimated that between two thousand and three thousand prostitutes worked in its alleys, taxis, clubs, and restaurants.

New Opportunities and Old Constraints in Wartime

As the wartime labor shortage deepened, employers turned to women and minorities to work the assembly lines. The federal government conducted an emotional campaign suggesting that women could shorten the war if they left the home and went to work. The image of Rosie the Riveter became the symbol of the patriotic woman doing her part. As more jobs opened, women did fill them—some because of patriotism, but most because they wanted the wages. Peggy Terry worked in a munitions plant and

♦ More than 350,000 women served in the military during the war, including Lieutenant Hazel Ying Lee, a Women's Airforce Service Pilot. WASPs flew "noncombat" missions, ferrying planes and supplies across the United States and Canada. Already an experienced pilot in China, Lieutenant Lee is seated here in the cockpit of a trainer. She died in 1943 when her plane crashed. *Texas Woman's University.*

considered it "an absolute miracle. . . . We made the fabulous sum of $32 a week. . . . Before, we made nothing." By 1944, 37 percent of all adult women were working.

But not all was rosy at work. Male workers resented and harassed women. Employers and most men expected that when the war was over, women would happily return to their traditional roles at home. For women, the war experience was a mixed one. They became more aware of their potential and ability. But when the war was over, many were required to sacrifice their newly discovered potential for traditional American values that kept women less than equal.

Like the war experiences of women, those of minorities were mixed. New employment and social opportunities existed, but they were accompanied by increased racial and ethnic tensions. Initially, the war provided few opportunities for African Americans. Shipyards and other defense contractors wanted white workers. The antiblack bias began to change by mid-1942 as the labor shortage worsened. West Coast shipyards were the first to integrate. Lockheed Aircraft then broke the color barrier in August. Word soon spread to the South that blacks could find work in California. Between the spring of 1942 and 1945, over 340,000 African Americans moved to Los Angeles alone.

The growing availability of jobs for African Americans was also the product of increased pressure on government from African-American leaders. In early 1941, **A. Philip Randolph,** leader of the powerful Brotherhood of Sleeping Car Porters union, proposed that African Americans march en masse on Washington to demand equality in jobs and the armed forces. In June, fearing that over 100,000 African Americans would descend on Washington, Roosevelt signed a law that created the Federal Employment Practices Commission (FEPC) and forbade racial job discrimination by the government and companies holding government contracts. Black wages during the war rose from an annual average of $457 to $1,976.

Across the nation, blacks supported the "Double V" campaign: victory over racist Germany and victory over racism at home. Membership in the NAACP and Urban League increased as these organizations took bolder steps to attack segregation, lynching, and discrimination. In 1942, the newly formed **Congress of Racial Equality (CORE)** adopted the sit-in tactic to attempt to integrate public facilities and met with some minor successes. In 1944, the Supreme Court ruled in *Smith v. Allwright* that Texas could not use the "all-white primary" to deny African Americans the right to vote. This decision changed the law, but whites soon found other ways to keep blacks from the polls in Texas.

In the North, patterns of hostility, discrimination, and violence hardened as the population of

A. Philip Randolph   African-American labor leader who organized the 1941 march on Washington that pressured Roosevelt to issue an executive order banning discrimination in defense industries.

Congress of Racial Equality   Civil rights organization founded in 1942 and committed to using nonviolent techniques such as sit-ins to end segregation.

African Americans increased. White workers went on strike when three black workers were promoted, harping, "We'd rather see Hitler and Hirohito win than work beside a nigger on the assembly line." A violent confrontation in Detroit in June 1943 left twenty-five blacks and nine whites dead.

The opportunities and realities of African Americans in uniform matched those of black civilians. Prior to 1940, blacks served at the lowest ranks and in the most menial jobs in a segregated army and navy. The Army Air Corps and the Marine Corps refused to accept blacks at all. President Roosevelt had made no effort to integrate the military. Blacks and civil rights supporters, including Eleanor Roosevelt, lobbied hard for changes. In 1940, the army began to encourage the recruitment of black officers and promoted **Benjamin O. Davis** from colonel to general. By the beginning of 1942, the Army Air Corps had an all-black unit and eventually would commission six hundred African-Americans as pilots. In April 1942, Secretary of the Navy James Forrestal permitted black **noncommissioned officers** in the U.S. Navy.

Higher ranks for a few did not disguise the fact that for most blacks, military life was often demeaning. In Indiana, over a hundred black officers were arrested for trying to integrate the officers' club. In Salina, Kansas, German prisoners could eat at any local lunch counter, but their black guards could not.

Latinos, too, found new opportunities and continued frustrations during the war. Latinos rushed to enlist as the war started. More than 300,000 Latinos served—the highest percentage of any ethnic community. Unlike African Americans and most Nisei, Latinos served in integrated units and generally faced less discrimination in the military than in society.

For those remaining at home, there were more jobs available, but still most Latinos worked as common laborers and agricultural workers. A serious shortage of farm workers developed during the war. After having deported Mexicans during the Depression, the government had to ask Mexico to supply agricultural workers. Mexico agreed but insisted that the *braceros* (Spanish for "helping arms") receive fair wages and adequate housing, transportation, food, and medical care. In practice, ranchers and farmers commonly paid low wages and provided barely livable facilities.

American Indians eagerly supported the war effort, realizing that it offered both individual and tribal opportunities. At least twenty-five thousand Indians served in the military. Among the most famous were three hundred Navajos who served as **code talkers** for the Marine Corps, using their native language as a secure means of communication. American Indians, unlike other minorities, met with little discrimination in the military. For most, military life and wages compared favorably to reservation life. During the war, jobs and higher wages lured over forty thousand American Indians away from their reservations. Mostly unskilled, these wartime workers boosted their families' average income from $400 a month in 1941 to $1,200 in 1945. Many who left the reservation assimilated into American culture and never returned to the old patterns of life.

Waging World War

The Japanese attack on Pearl Harbor convinced most Americans that defeating Japan should be the country's first priority. To Churchill's relief, Roosevelt still considered victory in Europe more important, regarding Hitler as the more dangerous enemy. In late April 1942, Soviet foreign minister V. M. Molotov arrived in Washington to confirm Roosevelt's commitment to the Europe-first strat-

Benjamin O. Davis Army officer who, in 1940, became the first black general in the U.S. Army.

noncommissioned officer Enlisted member of the armed forces, such as a corporal or sergeant, who has been promoted to a rank conferring leadership over others.

braceros Mexican nationals who worked on U.S. farms beginning in 1942 because of the labor shortage during World War II.

code talkers Navajo Indians serving in the U.S. Marines who communicated by radio in their native language so that the enemy could not interpret messages.

egy. Further, Molotov asked for a second front in Western Europe to relieve pressure on the Soviet Union. Roosevelt promised a second front sometime in 1942. His commitment to the European theater of operations cemented the Grand Alliance between the United States, Great Britain, and the Soviet Union to defeat Hitler.

The British, however, vigorously opposed an invasion across the English Channel in 1942, claiming it was too risky. Instead, the British proposed an Allied landing in western North Africa. This would be a safer venture that would also help the British army fighting in western Egypt. Roosevelt agreed to the plan. General **Dwight David Eisenhower** was selected to command American forces in North Africa and Europe.

As planning began for the invasion of North Africa in 1942, the course of the war seemed to darken for the Allies. German forces under General Erwin Rommel were advancing toward Egypt and the Suez Canal. A renewed German offensive was penetrating deeper into the Soviet Union. In the Atlantic, German U-boats were sinking ships at an appalling rate. In the Pacific, Japanese successes continued. In May, commanding general Douglas MacArthur fled by sea as the last American forces in the Philippines surrendered. Japanese forces also captured Singapore and the Dutch East Indies and were establishing bases on New Guinea and the Solomon Islands (see Map 26.2).

Halting the Japanese Advance

The first major American action in the Pacific occurred on May 7, 1942, at the **Battle of the Coral Sea** (see Map 26.3). "Magic," the code name for deciphering Japanese codes, had alerted American forces that Japan was preparing to invade Port Moresby, New Guinea, a step that would threaten Australia. The aircraft carriers *Lexington* and *Yorktown* intercepted the invasion fleet, and in the air-to-ship battle that followed, they turned back the invasion fleet despite the loss of the *Lexington*.

American aircraft carriers also foiled Admiral Yamamoto's plan to seize **Midway Island.** Again alerted by Magic, the carriers *Hornet, Enterprise,* and *Yorktown* lay in wait northeast of Midway (see

Map 26.3). The engagement on June 4, 1942, changed the course of the war in the Pacific. Thirty-seven American dive-bombers surprised the Japanese carriers in the middle of rearming and refueling their planes. Four Japanese carriers went down. Although the *Yorktown* sank as well, the air superiority of the Japanese had been destroyed. Hundreds of superb Japanese pilots had perished. The United States, with its greater industrial and population base, now held the upper hand. It was able to launch fourteen new aircraft carriers between 1942 and 1945, whereas Japan launched only six.

With the victories at the Coral Sea and Midway, the next step was to begin retaking lost territory. General MacArthur and the army were given the task of leading an offensive toward the Philippines from the south. The navy, under the direction of Admiral Chester Nimitz, would seize selected islands and atolls and approach the Philippines from the east. Eventually, both forces would join for the final attack on Japan. On August 7, 1942, soldiers of the 1st Marine Division waded ashore on **Guadalcanal Island** in the Solomons. Japan furiously defended the island. Fierce fighting dragged on for the next six months, but in early February 1943, Japan withdrew its last troops from Guadalcanal. By early 1943, American and Australian forces were also

Dwight David Eisenhower Supreme commander of Allied forces in Europe during World War II who planned the D-day invasion; he later became president of the United States.

Battle of the Coral Sea Major U.S. victory in the Pacific in May 1942, which prevented the Japanese from invading New Guinea and thus isolating Australia.

Midway Island Strategically located island in the Pacific that the Japanese navy tried to capture in June 1942; naval intelligence warned American forces of the Japanese plans, and they repulsed the attack.

Guadalcanal Island Pacific island that was the site of the first major U.S. offensive action in the Pacific. In November 1942, U.S. troops finally secured the island from the Japanese.

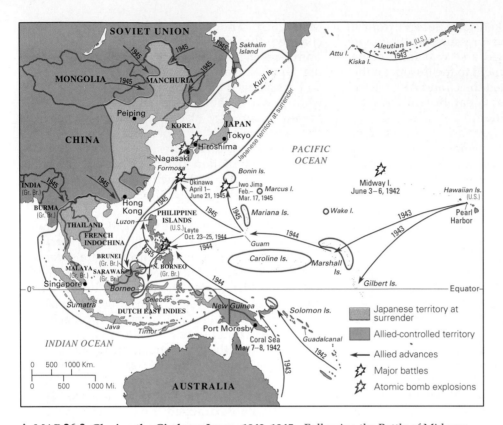

♦ **MAP 26.3 Closing the Circle on Japan, 1942–1945** Following the Battle of Midway, with the invasion of Guadalcanal (August 1942), American forces began the costly process of island hopping. This map shows the paths of the American campaign in the Pacific, closing the circle on Japan. After the Soviet Union entered the war and Hiroshima and Nagasaki were destroyed by atomic bombs, Japan surrendered on August 14, 1945.

driving Japanese forces out of southeastern New Guinea.

The Tide Turns in Europe

In Europe, too, the Allies began to meet with some success. By late 1942, British and American forces were closing in on Rommel's Afrika Corps (see Map 26.4). After halting Rommel's advance at El Alamein, a British offensive led by General Bernard Montgomery drove the German "Desert Fox" westward out of Egypt toward Tunisia. To the west, British and American forces landed in Morocco and Algeria. American forces under General

George S. Patton overcame stiff resistance to link up with Montgomery. Caught between two Allied armies, the last German forces in North Africa surrendered on May 13, 1943.

German losses in North Africa were light compared to those in Russia. Although Soviet forces had stopped the German advance short of Moscow dur-

> **George S. Patton** American general who commanded troops in North Africa, Sicily, and Europe in World War II and who was known as a brilliant tactician.

♦ **MAP 26.4 The North African and Italian Campaigns**   Having rejected a cross-channel attack on Hitler's "Atlantic Wall," British and American forces in 1942 and 1943 invaded North Africa and Italy, where victory seemed more assured. This map shows the British and American advances across North Africa and the invasions of Sicily and Italy. German forces fought stubbornly in Italy, slowing Allied advances up the peninsula.

ing the winter of 1941–1942, Germany's 1942 summer offensive had made dramatic gains, especially in southern Russia. But Stalingrad stood in the way of further advances. Bitter fighting quickly reduced the city to rubble, but the Soviets stood fast.

From August through November, the German 6th Army fought to take the city; after November, it fought to survive. On February 2, 1943, the German 6th Army surrendered, having lost over 140,000 men. The number of Soviet losses was probably just as large, but the tide of the war had turned in Europe (see Map 26.5).

In February 1943, however, Stalin knew only that the **Battle of Stalingrad** had cost the Russians dearly. To ease the pressure on his forces, the So-

viet leader again demanded that the Allies open up a second front in Europe. Again, he would be disappointed. Churchill had already met with Roosevelt at Casablanca in January 1943 and convinced him to invade **Sicily** and Italy, which

Battle of Stalingrad   Battle over the Soviet city of Stalingrad, which was besieged by the German army in 1942 and recaptured by Soviet troops in 1943.

Sicily   Large island in the Mediterranean west of Italy, which the Allies conquered in July 1943 as a first step to invading Italy.

Legend

- Hitler's Greater Germany
- Allied with Germany
- Occupied by Germany and its allies
- Grand Alliance
- Neutral nations
- Major battles
- Siege
- Advances by U.S. and British forces
- Advances by Soviet forces

Map labels (main map)

Siege of Leningrad, Sept. 1941–Jan. 1944

Russian front, Nov. 1942

Siege of Stalingrad, Aug. 21, 1942–Jan. 31, 1943

Russian front, Dec. 1941

Russian front, Spring 1944

Russian front, Feb. 1945

Rhine crossing, March 7, 1945

German surrender: Reims, May 7, 1945 Berlin, May 8, 1945

Battle of the Bulge, Dec. 1944

Western front, Feb. 1945

Invasion of Normandy, June 6, 1944

Allies land in Provence, Aug. 15, 1944

Italian front, Feb. 1945

VICHY FRANCE (occupied Nov. 1942)

Place / region names

SOVIET UNION, FINLAND, NORWAY, SWEDEN, DENMARK, GREAT BRITAIN, IRELAND, NETHERLANDS, BELGIUM, GERMANY, FRANCE, SWITZ., SPAIN, PORTUGAL, ITALY, SLOVAKIA, HUNGARY, CROATIA, YUGOSLAVIA, SERBIA, ROMANIA, BULGARIA, UKRAINE, TURKEY, SYRIA, IRAQ, SAUDI ARABIA, TRANS-JORDAN (Br. Mandate), PALESTINE (Br. Mandate), CYPRUS, EGYPT

Cities: Leningrad, Moscow, Tula, Smolensk, Kiev, Stalingrad, Yalta, Pinsk, Riga, Helsinki, Oslo, Stockholm, Copenhagen, Berlin, Posen, Warsaw, Krakow, Vienna, Budapest, Bucharest, Sofia, Bologna, Reims, Paris, Dunkirk, Vichy, London, Madrid, Ankara, Cairo

Seas: Caspian Sea, Black Sea, Baltic Sea, North Sea, ATLANTIC OCEAN

Rivers: Volga, Don, Dnieper, Dniester, Danube, Vistula, Rhine, Rhône, Po, Ebro, Nile, Suez Canal

Scale: 400 Mi., 400 Km., 200, 0

BATTLE OF THE BULGE (inset)

GERMANY, BELGIUM, LUXEMBOURG

Namur, Manhay, Celles, Rochefort, St.-Hubert, Bastogne, Clervaux, Luxembourg, Vith

Line Dec. 16, 1944
Line Dec. 25, 1944
Line Jan. 16, 1945

Rivers: Meuse, Ourthe, Cerf, Our, Moselle, Prüm

Scale: 20 Km., 20 Mi., 10, 0

Legend:
- U.S. forces
- British forces
- German forces

NORMANDY INVASION (inset)

ENGLAND, FRANCE

London, Southampton, Dover, Dunkirk, Calais, Boulogne, Abbeville, Amiens, Dieppe, Le Havre, Rouen, Paris, Cherbourg, Caen, St.-Lô, Avranches, St.-Malo, Brest

JUNO, SWORD, GOLD, UTAH, OMAHA

Beachhead, June 12, 1944
Line Aug. 15, 1944
Line Aug. 1, 1944
Paris Aug. 25, 1944

English Channel

Rivers: Seine, Orne, Vire

Legend:
- U.S. forces
- British and Canadian forces
- Fortified German stronghold
- Airborne forces

Scale: 50 Km., 50 Mi., 25, 0

◆ **MAP 26.5 The Fall of the Third Reich** In 1943 and 1944, the war turned in favor of the Allies. On the eastern front, Soviet forces drove German forces back toward Germany. On June 6, 1944, D-day, British, Canadian, and American forces landed on the coast of Normandy to begin the liberation of France. This map shows the course of the Allied armies as they fought their way toward Berlin. On May 7, 1945, Germany surrendered.

Churchill called the "soft underbelly of the Axis." To placate Stalin, Roosevelt and Churchill promised an increased flow of supplies and promised they would make no separate peace with Hitler.

The invasion of Sicily—Operation Husky—took place in early July 1943. In a month, the Allies controlled the island (see Map 26.4). In response, the Italians overthrew Mussolini, installed a new government, and changed sides in the war. Italy surrendered unconditionally on September 8, just hours before American troops landed at Salerno. Immediately, German forces assumed the defense of Italy. German troops also freed Mussolini, taking the Italian dictator to German-controlled northern Italy, where they proclaimed him ruler of Italy. The "soft underbelly" turned out to be far from soft. Strong German defenses halted the American advance just north of Salerno. Not until late May 1944 did Allied forces finally break through the German defenses. On June 4, U.S. General Mark Clark's forces entered Rome.

Two days later, the world's attention turned toward Normandy along the west coast of France. The second front demanded by Stalin had at long last begun (see Map 26.5).

Approval for the cross-channel attack had come at the **Tehran Conference** (November 27–December 1, 1943). In the Iranian capital, Roosevelt and Churchill met with Stalin to discuss strategy and to consider a postwar settlement. Roosevelt wanted to establish Soviet support for a new world organization and to obtain a Soviet commitment to declare war against Japan. The three agreed on plans to coordinate a Soviet offensive with the Allied landings at Normandy, and Stalin pledged he would declare war on Japan once the European war was over.

The invasion of Normandy, **Operation Overlord,** was the grandest amphibious assault ever assembled: 6,483 ships, 1,500 tanks, and 176,000 men. Opposing the Allies were thousands of German troops behind the Atlantic Wall they had constructed to stop such an invasion. On **D-day,** June 6, 1944, American forces landed on Utah and Omaha beaches, while British and Canadian forces hit Sword, Gold, and Juno beaches (see

Map 26.5). At the landing sites, German resistance varied. The fiercest fighting was at Omaha Beach. By nightfall, all five beaches were secure. After a week, the five beachheads were finally linked, and British and American forces coiled to break through the German positions blocking the road to the rest of France. On July 25, American forces under General Omar Bradley pierced the stubbornly held German defensive lines at St.-Lô and rumbled toward Paris and the German border. The Allies liberated Paris on August 23, and by early November they had taken Aachen on the west side of the Rhine River, the first German city to fall. From November to March, American forces consolidated and regrouped for the final assault on Germany across the Rhine (see Map 26.5).

While the British and Americans advanced across France, Allied bombers were bombing German-held Europe night and day. German cities and civilians were not spared. In one of the worst raids, during the night of February 13–14, 1945, British and American bombers set **Dresden** aflame, creating a firestorm that killed over 135,000 civilians. Nearly 600,000 German civilians would die in Allied air raids.

Stresses Within the Grand Alliance

As Allied forces moved eastward toward the Rhine, the Soviets advanced rapidly westward,

---

Tehran Conference   Meeting in Iran in 1943 at which Churchill, Roosevelt, and Stalin discussed the invasion of Western Europe and plans for a new international organization.

Operation Overload   Code name for Allied invasion of France.

D-day   Allied invasion of Europe on June 6, 1944, which was carried out by transporting tanks and soldiers from England across the channel to Normandy; *D-day* is short for "designated day."

Dresden   Industrial city in eastern Germany, which was almost totally destroyed when it was firebombed by the Allies in 1945.

pushing the last German troops from Russia by the end of June 1944. Behind Germany's retreating eastern armies, the Soviets occupied parts of Poland, Romania, Bulgaria, Hungary, and Czechoslovakia. Following the Red Army came Soviet officials and Eastern European Communists who had lived in exile in the Soviet Union during the war. The Soviet goal was to establish new Eastern European governments that would be friendly to the Soviet Union. A Communist Lublin government (named after the town where the government was installed) was established in Poland, while in Romania and Bulgaria, "popular front" governments, heavily influenced by Communists, took command. Only Czechoslovakia and Hungary managed to establish non-Communist governments as the German occupation collapsed. Britain and the United States eyed the political changes in Eastern Europe with suspicion.

On February 4, 1945, the Big Three met at the Black Sea resort of **Yalta** amid growing apprehension about Soviet territorial goals in Eastern Europe. Roosevelt hoped to secure a Soviet declaration of war on Japan and support for the new **United Nations.** He believed that both were necessary to usher in peace and international stability. He also wanted the Soviets to modify their control over Eastern Europe. Stalin's diplomatic goals were Western acceptance of a Soviet sphere of influence in Eastern Europe, the weakening of Germany, the economic restoration of the Soviet Union, and reassurances that any postwar international system would be based on Big Three cooperation.

Roosevelt and Stalin concurred on Germany. To prevent Germany from ever again posing a military threat to its neighbors, they desired to divide their enemy into smaller, weaker states. Churchill disagreed, saying that the dismemberment of Germany would be too harsh. Unable to agree on the future of Germany, the Big Three postponed further discussions until their next meeting.

The question of which Polish government represented Poland, however, could not be put off. The Soviet Union supported the Lublin government as the only legitimate one. Roosevelt and Churchill, however, hoped to establish a Polish government on the basis of free and honest elections. Their goal matched the ideals of the Atlantic Charter but not the **geopolitics** of the Soviet Union. Stalin argued that Soviet security demanded a friendly government in Poland. The powers agreed on a very ambiguous compromise that called for non-Communist participation in the Polish government but that provided no means of enforcement. On the related issue of Soviet influence throughout Eastern Europe, Roosevelt fared little better. The Yalta Conference left control over Eastern Europe firmly in Soviet hands. Roosevelt did accomplish his two major goals: Stalin promised to enter the war against Japan within three months of Germany's surrender and to support the formation of the United Nations.

Believing that there could be no postwar stability and security without Soviet cooperation, Roosevelt permitted Stalin to keep what he already had or could easily take. Short of ending friendly relations with the Soviet Union, Roosevelt had no means to reduce Soviet power in Eastern Europe. Roosevelt hoped that his good will would encourage Stalin to respond in kind. Both Stalin and Roosevelt were buoyed by the "spirit of Yalta." Only Churchill, who distrusted Stalin, left Yalta in a gloomy mood.

Hitler's Defeat

With his forces crumbling in the east, Hitler approved a last-ditch attempt to halt the American advance. Taking advantage of bad weather that

---

Yalta   Site in the Crimea of the last meeting, in February 1945, between Roosevelt, Churchill, and Stalin; they discussed the final defeat of the Axis Powers and the problems of postwar occupation.

United Nations   International organization established in 1945 to maintain peace among nations and foster cooperation in human rights, education, health, welfare, and trade.

geopolitics   Government policy based on the influence of geographic and political factors on national interests.

♦ Hitler ordered the "Final Solution"—the extermination of Europe's Jews—soon after the United States entered the war. In this picture, German troops arrest residents of the Warsaw ghetto for deportation to concentration camps. Few would survive the camps, where over 6 million Jews died. *YNO Institute for Jewish Research.*

grounded Allied aircraft, German forces launched an attack in December 1944 through the Ardennes Forest, pushing back the Americans. It was a desperate gamble that failed. The **Battle of the Bulge** delayed Eisenhower's westward assault only briefly and cost Germany valuable reserves and equipment (see Map 26.5). Ultimately, it merely hastened the end of the war. The war was also winding down in Italy. By the end of 1944, British and American forces had taken most of northern Italy. When German armies began to surrender in April 1945, Italian partisans captured Mussolini and hanged him.

On March 7, 1945, American forces crossed the Rhine at Remagen and began to battle their way into the heart of Germany. In Berlin, Hitler and the German High Command waited for the end. American and British troops were moving steadily eastward toward Berlin, while Soviet forces were dangerously close to Berlin's eastern suburbs. Unwilling to be captured, Hitler committed suicide on April 30 and had aides burn his body. Berlin fell to the Soviets two days later. On May 8, 1945, German officials surrendered. The war in Europe was over.

Although Roosevelt had worked since 1939 to ensure Hitler's defeat, he did not live to see it. On April 12, 1945, he died of a massive cerebral hemorrhage at Warm Springs, Georgia. Nor did Roosevelt live to know the full horror of what came to be called the **Holocaust.** No horror could match what advancing Allied armies found as they fought their way toward Berlin. In 1941, the Nazi political leadership had adopted the **Final Solution** to rid Europe of Jews. In concentration camps,

---

Battle of the Bulge   Battle in December 1944 that was the last major Axis counteroffensive against the Allied invasion of Europe; German troops gained territory in France but were eventually driven back.

Holocaust   Genocide of European Jews systematically carried out by the Nazis during World War II.

Final Solution   German plan to destroy the Jews by isolating them in concentration camps and committing mass executions; by the end of the war, the Nazis had killed 6 million Jews.

Jews, along with homosexuals, Gypsies, and the mentally ill, were brutalized, starved, worked as slave labor, and systematically exterminated. At Auschwitz, the Nazis used gas chambers to execute twelve thousand victims a day. When the camps and their remaining inmates were liberated in 1945, 6 million Jews had been slaughtered, nearly two-thirds of prewar Europe's Jewish population.

Closing the Circle on Japan

Victory in Europe—**V-E Day**—touched off parades and rejoicing in the United States, but Japan still had to be defeated. Japan's strategy was to force the United States to invade a seemingly endless number of Pacific islands before it could attack Japan. The Japanese hoped that pressure would build in the United States for a negotiated settlement. The strategy was based on wrong assumptions. After Pearl Harbor, few Americans would accept anything less than the total defeat of Japan. Equally important, the American military realized that it had to seize only the most strategic islands. With carriers providing air superiority, the Americans could bypass and isolate many Japanese-held islands.

Throughout 1943, General MacArthur advanced up the northern coast of New Guinea, while the navy and marines fought their way through the Solomon Islands. By mid-1944, MacArthur was ready to fulfill his promise to return to the Philippines. At the same time, far to the northeast, the U.S. Navy and the Marine Corps were establishing a foothold in the Gilbert Islands (see Map 26.3).

Next, Admiral Nimitz prepared to take Guam and Saipan in the Mariana Islands. The Japanese rushed a fleet with nine carriers to halt the American invasion of Saipan. Warned of their approach, Admiral Marc Mitscher turned his fifteen carriers to intercept. When the "Great Marianas' Turkey Shoot" ended on June 20, 243 of 373 Japanese planes had been shot down and 3 Japanese carriers had been sunk. All of Saipan's Japanese defenders, including 22,000 Japanese civilians, committed suicide rather than surrender.

By July 1944, the southern and eastern approaches to the Philippines were in American hands. From airfields on Tinian, Saipan, and Guam, long-range B-29 bombers began devastating raids against Japan. In October, American forces landed on Leyte in the center of the Philippine archipelago. Again, the Japanese navy acted to halt the invasion. In the largest naval battle in history, the **Battle of Leyte Gulf** (October 23–25, 1944), American naval forces shattered what remained of Japanese air and sea power. On October 23, General MacArthur returned to the Philippines.

After the Battle of Leyte Gulf, the full brunt of the American Pacific offensive bore down on Okinawa and Iwo Jima in the Ryukyu Islands, only 750 miles from Tokyo. To defend the islands, Japan resorted to kamikaze, or suicide, attacks in explosive-laden airplanes. The American assault on Iwo Jima began on February 19, 1945. Iwo Jima was the worst experience faced by U.S. Marines in the war. Virtually all of the 21,000 Japanese defenders died, and American losses approached one-third of the landing force: 6,821 dead and 20,000 wounded. The battle for Okinawa, begun on April 1, proved even costlier. By the end of June, Okinawa was in American hands, but at a fearful price: 12,000 Americans, 110,000 Japanese soldiers, and 160,000 Okinawan and Japanese civilians dead.

Entering the Nuclear Age

Okinawa proved a painful warning for those planning the invasion of Japan. Fighting for their homeland, the Japanese could be expected to resist until death. American casualties would be extremely high, perhaps as many as a million. But by the summer of 1945, the United States had a new and untried weapon: the atomic bomb. The

> **V-E Day**   Official end of the war in Europe on May 8, 1945, following the unconditional surrender of the German armies.
>
> **Battle of Leyte Gulf**   Largest naval battle in history, which occurred in the Philippines in October 1944 as American naval forces crushed Japanese air and sea power.

A-bomb was the product of the **Manhattan Project,** which British and American scientists had been working on since 1942. When the bomb was tested at Alamogordo, New Mexico, on July 16, 1945, the results were spectacular.

President Harry S Truman decided to use the bomb as quickly as possible against Japan. Using the atomic bomb, Truman hoped, would force Japan to surrender without an invasion and perhaps make the Soviets more amenable to American views. Soon after his arrival at Potsdam to meet with Churchill and Stalin in July, Truman informed Stalin that the United States had a new and powerful weapon to use against Japan. The **Potsdam Declaration,** called on Japan to surrender by August or face total destruction.

On July 25, Truman ordered the use of the atomic bombs as soon after August 3 as possible if the Japanese did not surrender. Moral reasons for not using the bomb were not seriously considered. Massive American bombing raids against Japanese cities already had killed tens of thousands of Japanese civilians. The losses at Iwo Jima and Okinawa, along with growing distrust of Stalin, had only strengthened Truman's desire to end the war as quickly as possible.

The first bomb, "Little Boy," was dropped from a B-29 bomber named the *Enola Gay* over **Hiroshima** at 9:15 A.M. on August 6. The atomic blast killed or terribly maimed almost a hundred thousand Japanese. Another hundred thousand would eventually die from radiation. The United States announced that unless the Japanese surrendered immediately, they could "expect a rain of ruin from the air, the like of which has never been seen on this earth."

In Tokyo, peace advocates in the Japanese government sought to use the Soviets as an intermediary. But the Soviet response was to declare war on August 8, exactly as promised, three months after V-E day. On August 9, a second atomic bomb, "Fat Man," destroyed **Nagasaki** and killed nearly sixty thousand people. Emperor Hirohito decided that Japan must "bear the unbearable" and surrender. On August 14, Japan officially surrendered.

World War II was over, but much of the world now lay in ruins. Some 50 million people, military and civilian, had been killed (see Table 26.1). The

◆ On August 6, 1945, the world entered the atomic age when the city of Hiroshima was destroyed by an atomic bomb. "We had seen the city when we went in," said the pilot of the *Enola Gay,* "and there was nothing to see when we came back." The city and most of its people died. *National Archives.*

United States was spared most of the destruction. It had suffered almost no civilian casualties, and its cities and industrial centers stood intact. In many ways, the war had been good to the United

A-bomb   The first nuclear weapon, which used a chain reaction involving uranium and plutonium to create an explosion of enormous destructive force.

Manhattan Project   Scientific research effort to develop an atomic bomb begun in 1942 and carried on in a secret community of scientists and workers near Oak Ridge, Tennessee.

Potsdam Declaration   The demand for Japan's unconditional surrender, made after the July 1945 Potsdam Conference attended by Truman, Churchill, Clement Attlee (who replaced Churchill as British Prime Minister just before the meeting) and Stalin.

Hiroshima   Japanese city that became the target on August 6, 1945, of the first atomic bomb used in World War II.

Nagasaki   City in western Japan devastated on August 9, 1945, by the second atomic bomb used in World War II.

TABLE 26.1 War Dead	
Country	**Dead**
Soviet Union	13.5 million
China	7.4 million
Poland	6.0 million
Germany	4.6 million
Japan	1.2 million
Britain and Commonwealth	430,000
United States	405,000

States. It had decisively ended the Depression. Government regulation and planning took root during the war. And as the war ended, only a few wanted a return to the laissez-faire style government that had characterized the 1920s. Big government was here to stay, and at the center of big government was a powerful presidency ready to direct and guide the nation.

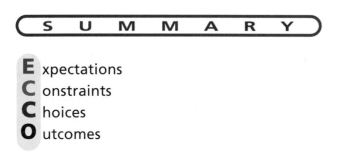

S U M M A R Y

E xpectations
C onstraints
C hoices
O utcomes

At the start of his presidency, Franklin Roosevelt *chose* to promote better relations with Latin America and succeeded. But elsewhere, the international situation grew steadily worse. Japan seized Manchuria in 1931 and invaded China in 1937, while Mussolini and Hitler were seeking to expand their nations' power and territory. In the lengthening shadow of world conflict, the majority of Americans still *chose* isolationism. Wanting to take a more active role in world affairs, Roosevelt found himself *constrained* by isolationist sentiment and by his own *choice* to fight the Depression at home first. Even as Germany invaded Poland in September 1939, the majority of Americans were still anxious to remain outside the conflict. Roosevelt, however, was determined to provide all necessary aid to those nations fighting Germany and Italy.

Roosevelt also *chose* to increase economic and diplomatic pressure on Japan to halt its conquest of China and its occupation of Indochina. But the pressure only convinced the Japanese government that the best *choice* was to attack the United States before it grew in strength. Japan's attack on Pearl Harbor on December 7, 1941, brought a fully committed American public and government into World War II.

Mobilizing the nation for war ended the Depression and increased government intervention in the economy. Another *outcome* of the war was a range of new *choices* for women and minorities in the military and the workplace. For Japanese Americans, however, the *outcome* was internment and the loss of property.

American planners *chose* to give first priority to defeating Hitler. The British and American offensive to recover Europe began in North Africa and expanded to Italy in 1943 and to France in 1944. By the beginning of 1945, Allied armies were threatening Nazi Germany from the west and the east, and on May 8, 1945, Germany surrendered. In the Pacific, the victory at Midway in 1942 gave American forces naval and air superiority over Japan and allowed them to begin tightening the noose around Japan. Worried about casualties if America had to invade Japan, Truman *chose* to use the atomic bomb. The *outcome* of the war was that the United States became economically and militarily stronger than when the war started. Confident Americans *expected* the postwar years to begin "America's Century."

SUGGESTED READINGS

Blum, John Morton. *V Was for Victory* (1976).
 A good introduction to society and politics during the war.

Dallek, Robert. *Franklin D. Roosevelt and American Foreign Policy, 1932–1945* (1979).

An excellent, balanced study of Roosevelt's foreign policy.

Daniels, Roger. *Concentration Camps, USA* (1971).

An in-depth and compassionate look at the internment of Japanese Americans.

Gluck, Sherna B. *Rosie the Riveter Revisited: Women, the War, and Social Change* (1987).

An important work examining the changes that took place among women in society during the war.

Jonas, Manfred. *Isolationism in America* (1966).

A solid examination of the varieties of isolationist attitudes in the United States, especially in the 1930s.

Keegan, John. *The Second World War* (1990).

An excellent work that summarizes the military and diplomatic aspects of World War II.

Spector, Ronald. *Eagle Against the Sun* (1988).

One of the best-written general accounts of the war in the Pacific.

Wyman, David. *The Abandonment of the Jews* (1985).

A balanced account of the Holocaust.

● ● ● The Decision to Drop the Atomic Bomb

The Context

On August 6, 1945, at 8:15 A.M., the *Enola Gay* dropped the first atomic bomb on the Japanese city of Hiroshima. More than 100,000 people died and another 100,000 were injured. Three days later, the United States exploded a second atomic bomb over Nagasaki, killing about 60,000 Japanese. On August 14, Japan surrendered. Within the United States, there was widespread rejoicing—the bomb had ended the war. Many also realized that the development of the atomic bomb and the decision to use it heralded a new age: the atomic era. The bomb was not just a powerful weapon but also a revolutionary development with far-ranging military, ethical, international, and scientific consequences. (For further information on the context, see pages 588–590.)

The Historical Question

Since the detonation of the atomic bomb, historians and others have asked if the choice to destroy the cities was necessary. Did military expediency necessitate dropping the bomb? What other expectations did those involved in building and deciding to use "the gadget" have? Did they consider moral and other aspects of their decision?

The Challenge

Using the sources provided, along with other information you have read, write an essay or hold a discussion on the following question. Cite evidence in the sources to support your conclusions. **What did those involved in planning the use of the atomic bomb consider, and what goals lay behind the final decision?**

The Sources

1 Secretary of War Henry L. Stimson was directly involved in planning the use of the atomic bomb. In an article for *Harper's* in 1947, he explained the military-based decision to use the new weapon. He wrote:

To extract a genuine surrender from the Emperor and his military advisers, they must be administered a tremendous shock which would carry convincing proof of our power to destroy the Empire. Such an effective shock would save many times the number of lives, both American and Japanese, than it would cost. . . . We estimated . . . that such an operation might cost over a million casualties to American forces . . . Enemy casualties would be much larger than our own.

2 A committee of scientists involved in building the atomic bomb met throughout May, June, and July to consider the use of the bomb. In June 1945, the Franck Committee reported:

The military advantages and the saving of American lives, achieved by the sudden use of the atomic bombs against Japan, may be outweighed by the ensuing loss of confidence and wave of horror and repulsion sweeping over the rest of the world, and perhaps dividing even public opinion at home.

. . . If we consider international agreement on total prevention of nuclear warfare as the paramount objective . . . this kind of introduction of atomic weapons to the world may easily destroy all

our chances of success. Russia, and even allied countries which bear less mistrust of our ways and intentions, as well as neutral countries, will be deeply shocked. It will be very difficult to persuade the world that a nation which was capable of secretly preparing and suddenly releasing [such] a weapon . . . is to be trusted in its proclaimed desire of having such weapons abolished by international agreement.

3 Most of the planning to use the atomic bomb was delegated to a special Interim Committee approved by President Harry Truman shortly after he assumed office. It was chaired by Secretary of War Stimson and was composed of three scientists, representatives of the State of War departments, and a special representative of the president. Except for Stimson, none of the committee members knew about the military plans for the invasion of Japan. Another group within the committee also considered which cities made suitable targets for atomic weapons. In May 1945, the committee reported:

We should not give the Japanese any warning. . . . We should seek to make a profound psychological impression on as many of the inhabitants as possible . . . The most desirable target would be a vital war plant employing a large number of workers and closely surrounded by workers' houses.

Hiroshima—This is an important army depot and port . . . in the middle of an urban industrial area. It is a good . . . target and it is such a size that a large part of the city could be extensively damaged . . . Adjacent hills . . . are likely to produce a focusing effect which would considerably increase the blast damage.

4 President Truman told Secretary of War Stimson to move ahead with the plans to drop the atomic bomb. On July 26, 1945, the United States demanded Japan's unconditional surrender and warned that Japan would face total destruction if surrender did not come. Recounting his thoughts on using the bomb, Truman wrote in his diary on July 18, 1945.

This weapon is to be used against Japan between now and August 10th. I have told the Sec. of War, Mr. Stimson, to use it so that military objectives and soldiers and sailors are the target and not women and children. Even if the Japs are savages, ruthless, merciless and fanatic, we as the leader of the world for the common welfare cannot drop that terrible bomb on the old capital or the new.

. . . We will issue a warning statement asking the Japs to surrender and save lives. I'm sure they will not do that, but we will have given them the chance. It is certainly a good thing for the world that Hitler's crowd or Stalin's did not discover this atomic bomb. It seems to be the most terrible thing ever discovered, but it can be made the most useful.

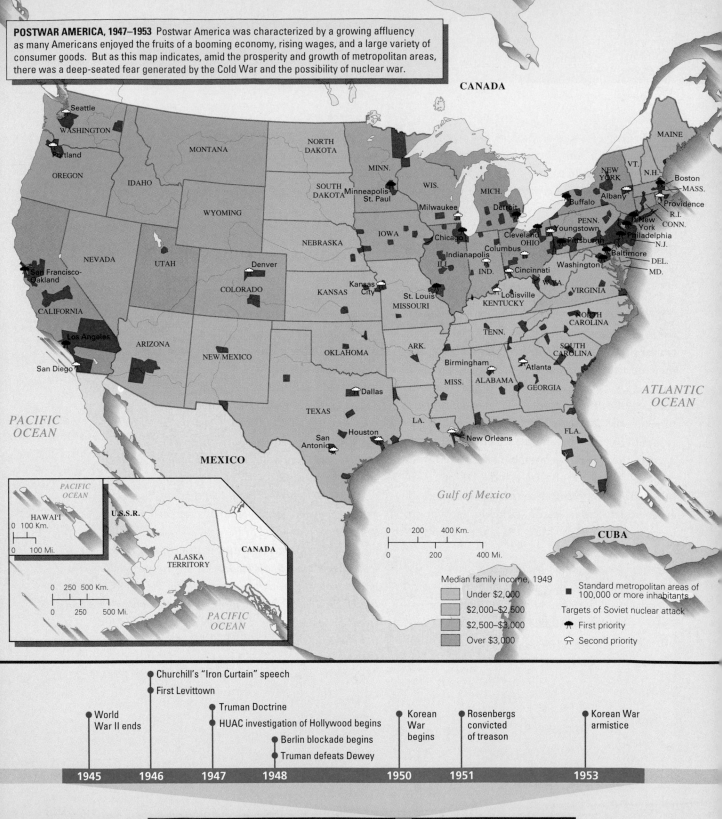

POSTWAR AMERICA, 1947–1953 Postwar America was characterized by a growing affluency as many Americans enjoyed the fruits of a booming economy, rising wages, and a large variety of consumer goods. But as this map indicates, amid the prosperity and growth of metropolitan areas, there was a deep-seated fear generated by the Cold War and the possibility of nuclear war.

CANADA

Seattle
WASHINGTON
Portland
OREGON
MONTANA
NORTH DAKOTA
MINN.
Minneapolis-St. Paul
Milwaukee
WIS.
MICH.
Detroit
MAINE
N.H.
VT.
NEW YORK
Boston
MASS.
Albany
Buffalo
Providence
R.I.
CONN.
Youngstown
New York
Philadelphia
N.J.

IDAHO
SOUTH DAKOTA
WYOMING
NEBRASKA
IOWA
Chicago
ILL.
PENN.
Cleveland
OHIO
Pittsburgh

NEVADA
UTAH
Denver
COLORADO
KANSAS
Kansas City
St. Louis
MISSOURI
Indianapolis
IND.
Columbus
Cincinnati
Louisville
KENTUCKY
Washington
W.VA.
VIRGINIA
Baltimore
DEL.
MD.

San Francisco-Oakland
CALIFORNIA
Los Angeles
ARIZONA
NEW MEXICO
OKLAHOMA
ARK.
TENN.
NORTH CAROLINA
SOUTH CAROLINA

San Diego
PACIFIC OCEAN
Dallas
TEXAS
San Antonio
Houston
LA.
Birmingham
MISS.
ALABAMA
Atlanta
GEORGIA
ATLANTIC OCEAN

MEXICO
New Orleans
Gulf of Mexico
FLA.
CUBA

Inset maps:

PACIFIC OCEAN
HAWAI'I
0   100 Km.
0   100 Mi.

U.S.S.R.
CANADA
ALASKA TERRITORY
PACIFIC OCEAN
0   250   500 Km.
0   250   500 Mi.

0   200   400 Km.
0   200   400 Mi.

Median family income, 1949
Under $2,000
$2,000–$2,500
$2,500–$3,000
Over $3,000

■ Standard metropolitan areas of 100,000 or more inhabitants

Targets of Soviet nuclear attack
First priority
Second priority

Timeline:

Churchill's "Iron Curtain" speech
First Levittown
World War II ends
Truman Doctrine
HUAC investigation of Hollywood begins
Berlin blockade begins
Truman defeats Dewey
Korean War begins
Rosenbergs convicted of treason
Korean War armistice

1945   1946   1947   1948   1950   1951   1953

1850   1900   1950   2000

Truman and Cold War America, 1945–1952

The Cold War Begins

- What expectations did Americans have about the postwar world and the Soviet Union?

- How was the containment theory applied to Western Europe between 1947 and 1951?

- Outside Western Europe, what choices did the Truman administration make to promote and protect American interests?

The Korean War

- As the North Koreans invaded South Korea, what choices and constraints did Truman confront when considering policy options?

- What expectations did Truman and General MacArthur have about defeating the North Koreans and unifying Korea? What was the outcome for both leaders?

Homecomings and Adjustments

- What were the social and economic expectations of most Americans as World War II ended? What

were the outcomes of these expectations for women and minorities?

- What constraints did proposals to expand New Deal programs encounter as the Cold War developed?

- What constraints did Truman face in implementing his domestic programs? How did they influence his choices?

- Why did Truman win the 1948 election? What choices did members of the New Deal coalition have in 1948, and why did most Democrats vote for Truman?

Cold War Politics

- What fears and events heightened society's fear of internal subversion, and what choices did politicians make in response to them?

- Why and how did Joseph McCarthy become so powerful by 1952?

INTRODUCTION

E xpectations
C onstraints
C hoices
O utcomes

When World War II ended, Americans hoped for a bright future. The Great Depression was over, the war had reignited American industry, and the United States stood as the world's biggest economic and military power. Returning veterans looked forward to living the "American dream," which included owning a home, a car, and a variety of consumer products. More than ever before, women and minorities shared in *expectations* for greater opportunity.

Although everyone hoped for postwar prosperity, political conservatives anticipated the demise of the New Deal. They argued that the New Deal was no longer necessary and that society and the economy should revert to traditional norms. They sought to place *constraints* on the economic and social gains made by minorities, women, and workers. Unions, they asserted, had become too powerful and must be restrained. Women, conservatives argued, should give up their jobs and return full-time to the roles of wife and mother. African Americans and other minorities should return to their customary place in American society.

Which direction would the nation *choose:* the path of the liberal New Deal or a more conservative one? The *outcome* pleased neither ardent liberals nor staunch conservatives. It reflected an acceptance and even some expansion of existing governmental activism but few new programs.

Truman also faced *choices* in shaping a new international order. Isolationism had virtually vanished amid the wreckage of Pearl Harbor and Hiroshima. Truman tried between 1945 and 1952 to seek a lasting peace, but the *outcome* was not what he *expected.* By the end of 1947, American and Soviet leaders had made *choices* that produced a bitter rivalry. The *outcome*, the Cold War, polarized the world, expanded America's global role, and added a new force in American society: the fear of the Soviet Union and communism. When North Korea invaded South Korea, Truman *chose* to commit American troops to halt Communist aggression. At home, the activities of anti-Communists like Senator Joseph McCarthy exposed a dark side of American politics and society.

Despite increased prosperity, American society began to seem less stable and unified, clouding *expectations* for a bright future. Labor unions clashed with employers, many women and minorities found their *expectations* thwarted, and the Korean War dragged on in a stalemate. The *outcome*, by the end of Truman's second term, was widespread political dissatisfaction and a general desire for change.

The Cold War Begins

Germany, Italy, and Japan had been defeated, and the world hoped that an enduring peace would follow. But could the cooperative relationship of the victorious Allies continue into the postwar era without a common enemy to bind them together?

Before 1941, suspicion and distrust had marked the normal relationship between the United States and the Soviet Union. In 1917, when the Soviets seized power, the Wilson administration refused to recognize the new Soviet state and intervened in the civil war between Soviet and anti-Communist forces. The last American troops left in 1920, but Washington refused to recognize the Soviet Union until 1933. Even after President Franklin D. Roosevelt established official ties with Moscow, relations remained frosty. When the Soviets signed their alliance with Nazi Germany in 1939 and claimed parts of Poland for themselves, most Americans saw little real differ-

CHRONOLOGY

From World War to Cold War

1945
Roosevelt dies; Truman becomes president
United Nations formed
Germany surrenders
Potsdam Conference
United States drops atomic bombs
Japan surrenders

1946
George Kennan's "Long Telegram"
Winston Churchill's "Iron Curtain" speech
Iran crisis
Railroad and coal miners' strikes
Construction begins on first Levittown

1947
Truman Doctrine
Truman's Federal Employee Loyalty Program
Taft-Hartley Act
House Un-American Activities Committee begins investigation of Hollywood
Jackie Robinson joins Brooklyn Dodgers
Marshall Plan announced
To Secure These Rights issued

1948
Communist coup in Czechoslovakia
State of Israel founded
Western zones of Germany unified
Berlin blockade begins
Congress approves Marshall Plan
Truman defeats Dewey

1949
North Atlantic Treaty Organization created
Berlin blockade lifted
Peekskill riot
West Germany created
Soviet Union explodes atomic bomb
Communist forces win civil war in China
Alger Hiss convicted of perjury

1950
Hydrogen bomb project announced
Joseph McCarthy's announcement of Communists in the State Department
NSC-68
Korean War begins
Rosenbergs arrested for treason
Inchon landing
North Korean forces retreat from South Korea
U.S. forces cross into North Korea; China enters Korean War

1951
General Douglas MacArthur relieved of command
Korean War armistice talks begin
Rosenbergs convicted of treason

1952
Hydrogen bomb tested

1953
Korean War armistice signed

ence between the brutal totalitarianism of nazism and communism.

American policy toward the Soviets altered in 1941, when Hitler invaded the Soviet Union. Relations with the Soviets improved quickly, as the United States supported the Communists in their war against the Germans. Ideological and other differences were de-emphasized. But even during the war, the two powers viewed each other suspiciously over issues such as the timing of the second European front and the creation of pro-Soviet governments in Eastern Europe.

When Roosevelt died on April 12, 1945, Harry S Truman was left to face the imposing job of finishing the war and creating the peace. Winning the war was mostly a matter of following existing policies, but formulating a new international order required new ideas and policies. In facing this formidable task, the new president counted on his common sense and what he believed would be best for the country. Truman was determined to be a decisive, hard-working president. He had read history; now he would shape it. A plaque on his desk proclaimed, "THE BUCK STOPS HERE."

In July 1945, Truman met with Stalin and Churchill for the first time at Potsdam on the outskirts of Berlin. He was surprised that the Soviet leader was shorter than he and thought that Churchill talked too much, giving him "a lot of hooey." Later Truman wrote, "You never saw such pig-headed people as are the Russians." Here Stalin and Truman (*left*) and advisers Byrnes and Molotov (*right*) pose for photographers. *Truman Library.*

Truman and the Soviets

Truman and other American leaders identified two overlapping paths to peace: international cooperation and **deterrence** based on military strength. They concluded that the United States must continue to field a strong military force with bases in Europe, Asia, and the Middle East. But deterrence alone could not guarantee peace and a stable world. That required the presence of a strong world organization to preserve collective security, a determination not to appease aggressors, and a prosperous world economy.

Not all nations accepted the American vision for peace and stability. Having been invaded twice in the twentieth century, the Soviets advanced different goals. They wanted to have Germany reduced in power and to see "friendly" governments in Eastern Europe. The Soviets were unwilling to allow an open political and economic system to function in neighboring countries. They put little faith in Roosevelt's call for the creation of the United Nations, although they agreed to go along with Roosevelt's idea.

The basic organization of the United Nations was mapped out at the **Dumbarton Oaks** conference in the fall of 1944. The United Nations charter, written at a meeting in San Francisco in April 1945, established a weak **General Assembly** composed of all the world's nations. The smaller **Security Council,** composed of the Big Five (now including France) and six other nations elected for two-year terms, possessed the power to make all real decisions, including taking action against aggressor nations. Each of the Big Five could veto Security Council decisions to ensure that the council could not interfere with their national interests. New York City became the permanent UN headquarters.

When Truman became president, he developed a rapid distrust of the Soviets. He regarded Soviet ac-

> **deterrence** Measures taken by a state, often including a military build-up, to discourage another state from attacking it.
>
> **Dumbarton Oaks** Conference in Washington, D.C., at which representatives of China, Britain, the USSR, and the United States drew up a blueprint for the charter of the United Nations.
>
> **General Assembly** Assembly of all members of the United Nations, which debates issues but neither creates nor executes policy.
>
> **Security Council** Executive agency of the United Nations, which includes five permanent members (China, France, Russia, Britain, and the United States) and six members chosen by the General Assembly for two-year terms.

tions in Poland and Romania as violations of proper behavior, the principles of the Atlantic Charter, and the Yalta agreements. Truman quickly confronted Soviet foreign minister V. M. Molotov over the Soviets' failure to fulfill promises made at Yalta to allow self-determination in Eastern Europe. Truman was less willing to consider Soviet "needs" than Roosevelt had been. In July 1945, Truman had his only face-to-face meeting with Stalin at the Potsdam Conference. The meeting accomplished little. Truman became more convinced than ever before that the Soviets were a major obstacle to world stability.

By early 1946, Truman believed that it was past time for the Soviets to prove their peaceful intentions. In Eastern Europe, every indication suggested that the Soviets were tightening their controls over Poland, Romania, and Hungary. On February 9, 1946, Stalin asserted that future wars were inevitable because of "present capitalist conditions," which most American observers saw as proof of Soviet hostility. Supreme Court Justice William O. Douglas called Stalin's speech "A Declaration of World War III." The Joint Chiefs of Staff agreed and recommended a foreign policy that would support nations threatened by Soviet hostility. The State Department was less alarmed, but it too concluded that the Soviets were following an "ominous course."

George F. Kennan, the **chargé d'affaires** in Moscow, plotted the American response to threatened Soviet expansionism. Asked by the State Department to evaluate Soviet policy, Kennan described Soviet totalitarianism as internally weak. Soviet leaders, he wrote in a report that became known as the "Long Telegram," held Communist ideology secondary to remaining in power. To rule, Soviet leaders relied on fear, repression, and resistance to a foreign enemy. To stay in control, Soviet leaders needed Western capitalism to serve as that enemy, Kennan wrote. Therefore, they could not afford to reach meaningful, long-lasting agreements with the West. He recommended a policy of **containment.** That meant meeting any attempted expansion of Soviet power head-on. Based on Kennan's advice, Truman adopted a policy designed to "set will against will, force against force, idea against idea . . . until Soviet expansion is finally worn down."

Fear of Soviet expansion quickly became a bipartisan issue. Both parties sought to convince the public that the United States must resist Soviet **global-ism.** The most sensational warning about the Soviet danger came from Winston Churchill on March 5, 1946, at Westminster College in Fulton, Missouri. With President Truman sitting beside him, the former British prime minister warned that an **"iron curtain"** had fallen across Europe. He called for a "fraternal association of the English-speaking peoples" to halt the Russians. Churchill, *Time* magazine pronounced, had spoken with the voice of a "lion."

As Churchill gave his address, it appeared that an "American lion" was needed in Iran. During World War II, the Big Three had stationed troops in Iran to ensure the safety of lend-lease materials going by that route to the Soviet Union. The troops were to be withdrawn by March 1946, but as that date neared, Soviet troops remained in northern Iran. Britain and the United States sent harshly worded telegrams to the Soviets and petitioned the United Nations to consider an Iranian complaint against the Soviet Union. Soviet forces soon evacuated Iran. The crisis was defused, but it convinced many Americans that the Soviets would retreat only when confronted with firmness.

Throughout the rest of 1946, the United States hardened its resolve in Europe. Postwar credits and loans were determined on the basis of ideology. Thus Britain received a $3.8 billion loan and France a $650 million loan, but the Soviet Union and Czechoslovakia received nothing. In Germany, the United States merged its occupation zone with those of the British and French and promised that American troops would remain as long as necessary to protect the German people.

---

chargé d'affaires   A high-ranking member of an embassy, frequently the highest-ranking career diplomat of the mission.

containment   Policy of checking the expansion or influence of a hostile power by means such as strategic alliances or the support of weaker states in areas of conflict.

globalism   National geopolitical policy in which the entire world is regarded as the appropriate sphere for a state's influence.

"iron curtain"   Name given to the military, political, and ideological barrier established between the Soviet bloc and Western Europe after World War II.

The Division of Europe

Throughout western and southern Europe, postwar economic and social turmoil was adding to the popularity of **leftist** and Communist groups. In the eastern Mediterranean, the Soviets were pressuring Turkey to permit some degree of Soviet control over the Dardanelles, the straits linking the Black Sea to the Mediterranean. Nearby, Greece was torn by a civil war between Communist-backed rebels and the British-supported conservative government (see Map 27.1). Communist influence seemed to be growing everywhere.

Truman responded by asserting in a speech to Congress that it was the duty of the United States "to support free people" who resisted subjugation "by armed minorities or by outside pressure." Truman asked Congress for $400 million in aid for Greece and Turkey.

Secretary of State **George Marshall** and Assistant Secretary of State **Dean Acheson** backed Truman's request for aid by warning select Democratic and Republican senators that Greece was on the brink of collapse. A Communist victory there would endanger neighboring states and eventually the entire eastern Mediterranean and Middle East. The Soviets were on the move, Acheson told the senators, and would triumph unless the United States stepped forward and stopped them. Impressed, Senator Arthur Vandenberg said that Truman needed to "scare the hell" out of the country. The president took the advice. In his **Truman Doctrine** speech of March 12, 1947, he blamed almost every threat to peace and stability on an unnamed villain, the Soviet Union. With American support, Turkey resisted Soviet pressure and retained control of the straits, and the Greek government was able to defeat the Communist rebels in 1949.

On June 5, 1947, in a commencement address at Harvard, Secretary of State Marshall uncovered a new weapon in the fight against communism: the **Marshall Plan.** The United States had already loaned nearly $9 billion to Western European nations, but more was needed to ward off a possible European economic collapse. Wartime destruction, drought, and an extremely bitter winter had, by 1947, brought Europe close to social and economic chaos. Millions of people could not heat their homes and were existing on a starvation diet. Communist

and Socialist parties were gaining in popularity and strength. Italian Communists represented a third of the electorate, whereas in France nearly a quarter voted Communist. European prosperity had to be restored to preserve democracy and freedom.

For the Truman administration, the question was not whether to aid Western Europe but whether to aid the Soviets and Eastern Europeans as well. To allow the Soviets and their satellites to participate seemed contrary to the Truman Doctrine. If the plan excluded the Soviets, however, the United States might seem to be encouraging the division of Europe. Chaired by George Kennan, the State Department planning staff recommended that the United States offer economic aid to all Europeans. Kennan believed that the Soviets' unwillingness to cooperate with capitalists would keep them from taking part.

Britain and France accepted the American offer within two weeks and called for a meeting in Paris of all interested parties on June 26, 1947. To nearly everyone's surprise, a Soviet delegation arrived. It appeared for a moment that Kennan's gamble had failed. But Soviet foreign minister Molotov rejected a British and French proposal for an economically integrated Europe, joint economic planning, and a requirement to purchase mostly American goods. The Soviets left the conference. Attracted by the

---

leftist Holding various liberal or radical political beliefs, often resting on a sympathy with the working class and a conviction that government should provide for the basic needs of the people.

George Marshall Chief of staff of the U.S. Army during World War II, who became Truman's secretary of state in 1947 and worked to rebuild the economy of Western Europe.

Dean Acheson Diplomat who took over as secretary of state in 1949; he helped formulate U.S. policy in Korea and advocated a firm stand against Soviet aggression in the Berlin crisis.

Truman Doctrine Anti-Communist foreign policy enunciated by Truman in 1947, which called for military and economic aid to countries whose political stability was threatened by communism.

Marshall Plan Program to foster economic recovery in Western Europe in the postwar period through massive amounts of U.S. financial aid, which began in 1948.

ATLANTIC OCEAN

$ Participants in the Marshall Plan

☐ Member of NATO, formed in 1949

■ Member of COMECON, formed in 1949, and the Warsaw Pact, organized in 1955

Exploded first atomic bomb, 1960 Withdrew from NATO, 1966

Zones of occupation ended, 1955

Joined NATO, 1955

Joined NATO, 1982

Berlin blockade, 1948–1949

Exploded first atomic bomb, 1949

Communist coup, 1948

Joined NATO, 1952

Joined NATO, 1952

♦ **MAP 27.1 Cold War Europe** Following World War II, Europe was separated by what Winston Churchill called the "iron curtain," which divided most of the continent politically, economically, and militarily into an eastern bloc (the Warsaw Pact) led by the Soviet Union and a western bloc (NATO) supported by the United States. This postwar division of Europe lasted until the collapse of the Soviet Union in the early 1990s.

prospect of American aid, sixteen other nations stayed in Paris and drafted a European recovery program. Completed on September 22, the plan called for four years of American assistance amounting to over $20 billion. Congress consented in 1948 to give $12.5 billion.

The Marshall Plan produced far-reaching consequences east and west of the iron curtain. One condition of the aid was that Western European countries had to purge Communist elements from their governments. The Soviet sphere responded with a hardening of Communist influence and control over Eastern Europe. In September 1947, the Soviet Union formed the Communist Information Bureau

(Cominform) to ensure Soviet direction of Europe's Communist parties. And in February 1948, the Soviets engineered a **coup** in Czechoslovakia and installed a Communist government. The death of political freedom in Czechoslovakia proved to many Americans the hostile intent of the Soviets. "We are faced with exactly the same situation with which Britain and France were faced in 1938 and

coup Sudden overthrow of a government by a small group of people in or previously in positions of authority.

♦ In many people's views, Truman's decision to support Greece and Turkey and his announcement of the Truman Doctrine (March 1947) represented the transfer of world responsibility from Great Britain to the United States. In Truman's words, "The free peoples of the world look to us for support in maintaining their freedoms."

1939 with Hitler," Truman announced. But Truman was no Neville Chamberlain.

The United States, Britain, and France responded to the "sovietization" of Eastern Europe by unifying their German occupation zones into a West German state. Faced with the prospect of a pro-Western and resurgent Germany, Stalin reacted. On June 24, 1948, the Russians blockaded all land traffic to Berlin and shut off the electricity to the city's western zones. With a population of over 2 million, West Berlin lay isolated 120 miles inside the Soviet zone of Germany. The Soviet goal was to force the West either to abandon the creation of West Germany or to face the loss of Berlin. The Americans were determined not to retreat. Churchill affirmed the American stand. We want peace, he stated, "but we should by now have learned that there is no safety in yielding to dictators, whether Nazi or Communist." The prospect of war loomed.

American strategists confronted the question of how to stand fast without starting a shooting war. Truman chose to use the three air corridors to Berlin from the West that the Soviets had earlier agreed to recognize. British and Americans flew through these corridors to three Berlin airports on an average of one flight every three minutes. To drive home to the Soviets the depth of American resolve, Truman ordered a wing of B-29 bombers, the "atomic bombers," to Berlin. In fact, these planes carried no atomic weapons.

The **Berlin airlift** was a tremendous victory for the United States. The unceasing flow of supplies testified to American resolve to contain Soviet power and to protect Europe. The Soviets ended the blockade of Berlin in May 1949. The crisis ended virtually all congressional opposition to the Marshall Plan and the creation of West Germany.

Truman followed the Berlin action with a call for an American military alliance with Western Europe. By April 1949, negotiations to create the **North Atlantic Treaty Organization (NATO)** were completed (see Map 27.1). Congress approved American entry into NATO in July. Membership in the alliance ensured that American forces would remain in the newly created West Germany and that Western Europe would be eligible for additional American economic and military aid. The Mutual Defense Assistance Act, passed in 1949, provided $1.5 billion in arms and equipment for NATO member nations. By 1952, 80 percent of American assistance to Europe was military aid.

A Global Presence

American foreign policy from 1945 to 1950 focused on rebuilding Western Europe and containing Soviet

---

Berlin airlift Response to the Soviet blockade of West Berlin in 1948, in which American and British planes made continuous flights to deliver supplies and keep the city open.

North Atlantic Treaty Organization Alliance formed in 1949 that includes most of the nations of Western Europe and North America; its mutual defense agreement was a basic element of the effort to contain communism.

power, but American policy did not ignore the rest of the world. To the south, the Truman administration rejected requests from Latin Americans for a Marshall Plan for the Western Hemisphere. Instead, it encouraged private firms to develop the region through business and trade. The United States did sponsor the creation of the **Organization of American States** to coordinate defense, economic, and social concerns. In the Middle East, fear of future oil shortages led the United States to promote American petroleum interests. In Saudi Arabia, Kuwait, and Iran, the goal was to replace Britain as the major economic and political influence.

Simultaneously, the United States became a powerful supporter of a new Jewish state that was to be created out of **Palestine,** then under British rule. Considering the Nazi terror against the Jews, Truman believed that the Jews should have their own nation. In May 1947, Britain announced that it no longer had the resources to maintain control over Palestine. The United States recognized Israel almost immediately when the United Nations voted to **partition** Palestine into Arab and Jewish states on May 14, 1948. When war broke out between the surrounding Arab states and Israel, Truman and most Americans applauded the victories of Israeli armies.

If Americans were pleased with events in Latin America and the Middle East, Asia provided one bright spot but several disappointments. Under American occupation, Japan's government had been reshaped into a democratic system and placed safely within the American orbit. Success in Japan was offset by reverses in China and Korea. During World War II, the **Nationalist Chinese** government of Jiang Jieshi (Chiang Kai-shek) and the Chinese Communists under Mao Zedong (Mao Tse-tung) had moderated their hostility toward each other to fight the Japanese. Old animosities quickly resurfaced when the war ended. By February 1946, civil war again ravaged China. American supporters of Jiang, most notably his friend, Time-Life publisher Henry R. Luce, recommended that the United States increase its economic and military support for the Nationalist government. Luce and others argued that the civil war in China was as important as the one that threatened Greece. Truman and Marshall disagreed. Although dreading a Communist success in China, they blamed the corrupt and inefficient Nationalist government for China's po-

litical and economic turmoil. Truman and Marshall were willing to continue some aid for China but did not want to commit America to an Asian war. Jiang's forces steadily lost the civil war. In 1949, Jiang's army disintegrated, and the Nationalist government fled to the island of Formosa (Taiwan).

Conservative Democrats and Republicans labeled the rout of Jiang as a humiliating American defeat. To quiet critics and to protect Jiang, Truman refused to recognize the People's Republic of China on the mainland and ordered the U.S. 7th Fleet to waters near Taiwan. Increasingly, Truman was feeling pressure to expand the containment policy beyond Europe. The pressure intensified in late August 1949, when the Soviets detonated their own atomic bomb, shattering the American nuclear monopoly. Suddenly, it seemed that the United States was losing the Cold War. From inside and outside the administration came calls for a more aggressive policy against communism. The **National Security Council,** in its Memorandum #68 (NSC-68), called in 1950 for global containment and a huge buildup of American military force.

Truman studied the report but hesitated to implement its recommendations. He worried about the impact of such large-scale military production on domestic goods manufacturing. He eventually agreed to a "moderate" $12.3 billion military budget

---

Organization of American States   An international organization composed of most of the nations of the Americas, including the Caribbean, which deals with the mutual concerns of its members. Cuba is not currently a member.

Palestine   Region on the Mediterranean that was a British mandate after World War I; the UN partitioned the area in 1948 to allow for a Jewish and a Palestinian state.

partition   To divide a country into separate, autonomous nations.

Nationalist Chinese   Supporters of Jiang Jieshi, who fought the Communists for control of China in the 1940s; in defeat they retreated to Taiwan in 1949, where they set up a separate government.

National Security Council   Executive agency established in 1947 to coordinate the strategic policies and defense of the United States; it includes the president and four cabinet members.

for 1950 that included building the **hydrogen bomb,** which was first tested in 1952. Supporters of NSC-68, however, won the final argument on June 24, 1950, when North Korean troops stormed across the **38th parallel.**

The Korean War

When World War II ended, Soviet forces occupied Korea north of the 38th parallel, and American forces remained south of it (see Map 27.2). As with Germany, the division of Korea was expected to be temporary. A reunified Korean nation was to appear after the war. But mutual Soviet and American fears soon led to the establishment of an American-supported government in the south, led by **Syngman Rhee,** and a Communist-backed government in the north, headed by **Kim Il-Sung.** By mid-1946, the division of Korea appeared more permanent than temporary.

In 1949, believing Korea to be of little political or strategic importance, the Soviet and American governments withdrew their forces, leaving behind two hostile regimes, each claiming to be Korea's rightful government. Both Koreas launched raids across the border, but neither side gained much ground. Then, on June 25, 1950, Kim Il-Sung launched a full-scale invasion of the south. Truman quickly announced that Korea was, after all, a region vital to American interests and needed American protection. In Truman's mind, Moscow had directed the invasion. The wisdom of NSC-68's recommendations for global containment was undeniably confirmed.

The UN Responds to Communist Aggression

Within days, the South Korean army (ROK) was fleeing before stronger, better-equipped North Korean forces. Immediately, the United States asked the UN Security Council to intervene. The Security Council asked member nations to provide assistance to South Korea. Truman ordered **General Douglas MacArthur** to commit American naval and air units south of the 38th parallel. Two days later, as North Koreans captured the South Korean capital of Seoul, the Security Council approved an international military force to defend South Korea and named MacArthur commander of the United Nations forces. As one of the five permanent members of the Security Council, the Soviet Union could have vetoed the mission to South Korea, but the Russians were boycotting the council for its refusal to recognize the People's Republic of China.

Fearful that a congressional declaration of war against Korea might expand the conflict to involve the Chinese and Russians, Truman never sought one. American troops served in Korea under United Nations resolutions and followed Truman's orders as commander in chief. For the record, the war was called the Korean Conflict or a "police action." Few in Congress objected to Truman's actions.

The infusion of American troops did not halt the North Korean advance. By the end of July 1950, North Korean forces occupied most of South Korea except for the southeastern corner of the peninsula, the **Pusan perimeter.** But in a bold maneuver, MacArthur on September 15 landed some seventy thousand American forces at Inchon, near **Seoul,** nearly 200 miles north of the Pusan perimeter. It

hydrogen bomb Explosive weapon of enormous destructive power fueled by the fusion of the nuclei of various hydrogen isotopes.

38th parallel Negotiated dividing line between North and South Korea, which was the focus of much of the fighting in the Korean War.

Syngman Rhee Korean politician who became president of South Korea in 1948; his dictatorial rule ended in 1960, when he was forced out of office into exile.

Kim Il-Sung Installed by the Soviets as leader of North Korea. He served as premier from 1948 to 1972, when he became president, holding that office until his death in 1994.

General Douglas MacArthur Commander of Allied forces in the South Pacific during World War II and of UN forces in Korea until a conflict over strategy led Truman to dismiss him.

Pusan perimeter Area near the city of Pusan in South Korea, which was the center of a beachhead held by UN forces in 1950.

Seoul Capital of South Korea, which suffered extensive damage during its occupation by Communist forces in 1950 and 1951.

♦ **MAP 27.2 The Korean War, 1950–1953** Seeking to unify Korea, North Korean forces invaded South Korea in 1950. To protect South Korea, the United States and the United Nations intervened. After driving North Korean forces northward, Truman sought to unify Korea under South Korea. But as UN and South Korean forces pushed toward the Chinese border, Communist China intervened, forcing UN troops to retreat. This map shows the military thrusts and counterthrusts of the Korean War as it stalemated roughly along the 38th parallel.

was a brilliant tactical move that surprised the enemy completely. The next day, the United Nations forces along the Pusan perimeter began their advance. The North Koreans fled back across the 38th parallel. Seoul was liberated on September 27. United Nations forces had achieved the purpose of the police action.

Seeking to Liberate North Korea

MacArthur, Truman, and most other Americans now wanted to unify the peninsula under South Korean rule. Bending under American pressure, the United Nations approved the new goal on October 7, 1950. MacArthur had a green light to "liberate" North Korea from Communist rule (see Map 27.2).

An invasion seemed safe. North Korean forces were in disarray, and intelligence sources discounted the possibility of either Soviet or large-scale Chinese involvement. By mid-October, United Nations forces were moving quickly northward toward the Korean-Chinese border at the Yalu River. The Chinese, however, threatened intervention if the invaders approached the border. Some UN units had already encountered Chinese "volunteers." Anxious that the Chinese might move in force, Truman flew to Wake Island to confer with MacArthur. The United Nations commander was supremely confident. If Chinese forces did cross the border, he explained, they could not number more than thirty thousand. American airpower would slaughter them. Unconvinced, Truman ordered MacArthur to use only South Korean forces in approaching the Yalu River. MacArthur violated Truman's orders. On November 24, he moved American, British, and Korean forces to within a few miles of the Yalu. Two days later, nearly 300,000 Chinese soldiers entered the conflict.

In the most brutal fighting of the war, the Chinese attacked in waves, nearly trapping several American and South Korean units. MacArthur had believed that vastly superior American airpower would deal with any Chinese invaders. But his calculations had not foreseen the bitter winter weather or night battles that severely limited the role of American aircraft.

Within three weeks, the North Koreans and Chinese had shoved the United Nations forces back to the 38th parallel. During the retreat, General MacArthur asked for permission to bomb bridges on the Yalu River and Chinese bases across the border. He also urged a naval blockade of China and the use of Nationalist Chinese forces against the mainland. Believing that such an escalation could lead to World War III, Truman allowed only the Korean half of the bridges to be bombed and flatly rejected MacArthur's other suggestions. Truman abandoned the goal of a unified pro-Western Korea and sought a negotiated settlement to end the conflict.

The decision was not popular. Americans wanted victory. MacArthur publicly took exception to the limitations his commander in chief had placed on him. He put it simply: there was "no substitute for victory." Already dissatisfied with MacArthur's arrogance, Truman used the general's direct challenge to presidential power as grounds to fire him and replaced him with General Matthew Ridgway. MacArthur returned to the United States and received a hero's welcome, including a ticker-tape parade down New York's Fifth Avenue. He continued his criticism of Truman's policies at congressional hearings in June 1951, arguing that an expanded war could achieve victory. The administration countered that an expanded war could mean nuclear world war.

In their face-off, neither MacArthur nor Truman won. Truman's public approval rating continued to plummet. At the same time, MacArthur's hopes for a presidential candidacy collapsed as most Americans feared that his aggressive policies might result in another world war. By the beginning of 1952, the vast majority of Americans were weary of the war and wanted it over. The Korean front had meanwhile stabilized along the 38th parallel. Peace talks involving the United States, South Korea, China, and North Korea had begun on July 10, 1951. The negotiations did not go smoothly. For two years, the powers bickered about prisoners, **cease-fire** lines, and a multitude of lesser issues. Over 125,000 UN casualties occurred during the two years of peace negotiations. When the cease-fire finally was concluded by the Eisenhower administration on July 26, 1953, the Korean Conflict had cost over $20 billion and 33,000 American lives.

The "hot war" in Korea had far-reaching military and diplomatic results for the United States. In Europe, Truman moved forward with plans to rearm West Germany in case of a confrontation with the Soviet Communists. Throughout Asia and the Pacific, a large American presence was made permanent. In 1951, the United States concluded a settlement with Japan that kept American forces in Japan and Okinawa. The United States increased its military aid to Nationalist China and French **Indochina.** The containment policy that George F. Kennan had envisioned to protect Western Europe had expanded to include East Asia and the Pacific. According to the philosophy of the day, a Communist victory anywhere threatened the national security of the United States.

Homecomings and Adjustments

By November 1945, 1.25 million GIs were returning home each month wanting to rediscover family, jobs, and the American dream. Armed with the 1944 **G.I. Bill,** which provided low-interest home loans, a year's unemployment compensation, and economic support to attend school or college, returning veterans were eager to begin civilian life.

Adjusting to Peace at Home

Those veterans faced a massive housing shortage in 1945 and 1946. Streetcars were converted into homes in Chicago, grain silos became apartments in North Dakota, and across the country families doubled up. By mid-1946, however, developers like William Levitt were supplying mass-produced, prefabricated houses to meet the demand. Using building techniques developed during the war, Levitt boasted that he could construct a house on

---

cease-fire A truce that brings an end to fighting.

Indochina French colony in Southeast Asia, which included the present-day states of Vietnam, Laos, and Cambodia; it began fighting for its independence in the mid-twentieth century.

G.I. Bill Law passed in 1944 that provided financial and educational benefits for American veterans after World War II; *G.I.* stands for "government issue."

an existing concrete slab in sixteen minutes. Standardized and with few frills, his homes cost slightly less than $8,000, a very attractive price to many returning soldiers. The first Levittown sprang up in Hempstead, Long Island, in 1946, soon to be followed by others in Pennsylvania and New Jersey.

Most suburban developments were built for the "typical" American family—white, middle-class, and Christian. African Americans, Jews, and other minorities were not welcome. Although the 1948 Supreme Court decision in *Shelly v. Kraemer* made it illegal for developers and real-estate agents to restrict housing, the decision did little to integrate most suburbs. Banks rarely made home loans to minorities trying to buy in a white neighborhood.

Cozy homes were only part of the postwar dream. Veterans expected that women who had been hired while they "fought for democracy" would now relinquish their jobs. A fall 1945 *Fortune* poll discovered that 57 percent of women and 63 percent of men believed that married women should not work. Psychiatrists argued that men wanted feminine and submissive wives, not fellow workers. Fashions, like Christian Dior's "New Look," lowered skirts and accented waists and breasts to emphasize femininity.

Not all women accepted the role of contented wife and homemaker. When one ex-GI informed his wife that she could no longer handle the finances because it was not "woman's work," she indignantly reminded him that she had successfully balanced the checkbook for four years. Reflecting such tensions and too many hasty wartime marriages, the divorce rate jumped dramatically. Twenty-five percent of all marriages were ending in divorce in 1946. By 1950, over a million GI marriages had broken apart.

Despite the growing divorce rate, marriage was more popular than ever: two-thirds of the population was married by 1950 and having children. From a Depression level of under 80 per 1,000, the birth rate rose to over 115 per 1,000 within a year of the end of the war (see Figure 27.1). The so-called **baby boom** had arrived and would last for nearly twenty years.

Like women, nonwhites found that "fair employment" vanished as employers favored white males once the war was over. The skilled and industrial jobs that had opened to Latinos and African Americans during the war became scarce by 1946. In 1943, over a million African Americans were employed in the aircraft industry, but by 1950 the number had shrunk to 237,000. The decline was less marked in the automobile, rubber, and shipbuilding industries.

Mexican Americans also found themselves limited to unskilled, menial jobs, despite their rapidly growing numbers in urban areas. Discrimination, denial of educational opportunities, and language barriers combined to trap a majority of Mexican Americans as common laborers. Throughout the Southwest and West, the pattern of Mexican-American migration to urban areas continued to heighten the agricultural labor shortage. Mechanization made up for some of the loss, but more workers were necessary. In 1947, when Mexico pressed for higher wages and better working conditions for Mexicans working in the *bracero* program (see page 580), the United States allowed American farmers to contract directly for Mexican workers with virtually no restrictions on wages and working conditions. Between 1947 and 1950, nearly twice as many undocumented Mexican workers were recruited than had worked under the *bracero* program.

Nonwhite Americans at the end of World War II still lived in a distinctly segregated world. From housing to jobs, from healthcare to education, white society continued to deny nonwhites full participation in the American dream. Still, African Americans and Latinos looked eagerly toward the postwar period. Minorities had achieved social and economic gains during the war, and despite immediate postwar adjustments, it seemed that more progress was possible. One sign of such progress appeared when Jackie Robinson broke the color barrier in professional baseball and played for the Brooklyn Dodgers in 1947. Robinson was voted the National League's Rookie of the Year.

Having fought for democracy, minorities were more determined than ever before not to return to the old ways. Latino and African-American leaders

---

Shelly v. Kraemer Supreme Court ruling in 1948 that barred developers and real-estate agents from creating whites-only housing but that had little immediate impact.

baby boom Sudden increase in the birth rate that occurred in the United States after World War II and lasted from 1946 to 1964.

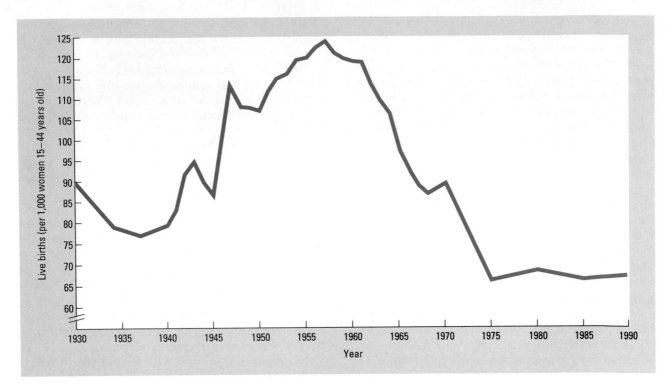

♦ **FIGURE 27.1 Birth Rate, 1930–1990** Between 1946 and 1957, families chose to have more children and the birth rate rebounded from the Depression. This increase is often called the baby boom. During the 1960s, the birth rate slowed down, and since the 1970s, it has remained fairly constant.

insisted that democracy be practiced at home. W. E. B. Du Bois stated that the real problems facing the United States came not from Stalin and Molotov but from racists like Mississippi's Senator Theodore Bilbo and Congressman John Rankin. "Internal injustice done to one's brother," Du Bois warned, "is far more dangerous than the aggression of strangers from abroad."

Truman and Liberalism

When Roosevelt died, many wondered if Truman would continue the New Deal or largely abandon it. Truman ended all speculation when on September 6, 1945, he unveiled a twenty-one-point program. One Republican critic characterized it as an effort to "out–New Deal the New Deal." The president asked Congress to continue governmental controls on the economy, especially on prices, and to renew the

Fair Employment Practices Commission (FEPC). He recommended an expansion of Social Security coverage and benefits, an increase in the minimum wage to $.65 an hour, and the development of additional housing programs and Tennessee Valley–style projects. Truman also advised Congress that he would soon ask for a national health system to ensure medical care for all Americans.

The expanded New Deal that Truman projected never fully developed. Republicans, conservative Democrats, and business leaders objected to it. They

Fair Employment Practices Commission Commission established by executive order in 1941 to curb racial discrimination in war industries; in 1946, a bill for a permanent FEPC was killed by a southern Democratic filibuster.

argued that Truman's ideas would lead to the development of a socialistic state and destroy private enterprise. Conservatives and big business embarked on a campaign to persuade the American public of the dangers of "New Deal socialism." The National Association of Manufacturers spent nearly $37 million on such propaganda in one year. Conservatives in Congress either killed or significantly modified nearly all of Truman's proposals. FEPC faded away. The full-employment act was revised to eliminate government guarantees of a job for everyone.

The numerous strikes that occurred after the war fed the conservative mood of the country. When prices rose 25 percent but wages remained unchanged during the first eighteen months after the war, nearly 4.5 million workers went on strike to demand better compensation. Congress and state governments responded with measures designed to weaken unions and end strikes. "Right to work" laws banned compulsory union membership and in some cases provided police protection for those crossing picket lines during strikes. Other laws promoted the **open shop** and company-organized workers' associations.

Even Truman squared off against the railroad and coal miners' unions. When locomotive engineers struck in late May 1946, Truman asked Congress for power to draft striking workers into the army. The railroad strike was settled without the bill. Truman responded to a coal strike involving 400,000 United Mine Workers in April 1946 by seizing the nation's coal mines. He applauded when a federal court fined the union $3.5 million and again when the miners finally returned to work on December 7.

The strikes, soaring inflation rates, and divisions within Democratic ranks fit the Republican party's prescription for a 1946 election bonanza. "Had Enough?" Republican candidates asked the voters. Voters responded affirmatively, electing Republican majorities to both houses of the 80th Congress. The new Congress ignored Truman's domestic proposals and instead passed a tax cut and anti-union legislation. The **Taft-Hartley Act,** passed in June 1947 over Truman's veto, was a clear victory for management over labor. It banned the closed shop, prevented industry-wide collective bargaining, and legalized state-sponsored "right to work" laws. The law also empowered the president to use a court injunction to force striking workers back to work for an eighty-day cooling-off period. Truman had cast his veto knowing it would be overridden.

Truman's position on civil rights was cautious but generally supportive. In December 1946, he created the Committee on Civil Rights to examine race relations in the country. In October 1947, the committee's report, *To Secure These Rights,* called on the government to correct the extensive racial imbalances that it had found in American society. The report recommended the establishment of a permanent Commission on Civil Rights, the enactment of antilynching laws, and the abolition of the poll tax. It also called for integration of the U.S. armed forces and support for integrating housing programs and education. Truman asked Congress in February 1948 to act on the committee's recommendations but provided no direction or legislation. Nor did the White House make any effort to integrate the armed forces until black labor leader A. Philip Randolph once again threatened a march on Washington. Truman then issued an executive order to integrate the military forces. The navy and air force complied, but the army resisted until it faced high casualties in the Korean War. Despite his caution, Truman had done more in the area of civil rights than any president since Abraham Lincoln.

The 1948 Election

Republicans had high expectations in 1948. Republican candidates had done well in congressional elections, and Truman's approval rating remained low. To take on Truman, the Republicans chose New York's governor, **Thomas E. Dewey,** who had run a respectable race against Roosevelt in 1944.

---

open shop Business or factory in which workers are employed without having to join a union; unlike a closed shop, which requires union membership.

Taft-Hartley Act Law passed in 1947 banning closed shops, permitting employers to sue unions for broken contracts, and requiring unions to observe a cooling-off period before striking.

Thomas E. Dewey New York governor who twice ran unsuccessfully for president as the Republican candidate, the second time against Truman in 1948.

Dewey's prospects looked very good in 1948. Not only was the Republican party strong and Truman's popularity weak, but the Democrats were mired in bitter infighting over domestic policy. Dissatisfied Democratic liberals hoped to replace Truman with General Dwight David Eisenhower or Supreme Court Justice William O. Douglas. Neither was willing to run. Grudgingly, minorities and liberals had to settle for Truman. They did secure a party platform that included a civil rights plank.

Many southerners walked out of the Democratic convention to protest the civil rights plank. Unwilling to support a Republican, they organized the **Dixiecrat party** and nominated South Carolina's governor, J. Strom Thurmond, for president. Henry Wallace's supporters also deserted Truman, forming the Progressive party.

With the Democratic party so splintered and public opinion polls showing a large Republican lead, Dewey conducted a low-key campaign. Running for his political life, Truman crossed the nation by train, making hundreds of speeches that stressed the gains made under the Democrats. He attacked the "do-nothing" 80th Congress and its business allies. He told one audience, "Wall Street expects its money to elect a Republican administration that will listen to the gluttons of privilege first and not to the people at all." Truman also emphasized his expertise in dealing with the Soviets. Comparing himself to Dewey, Truman contended that he had the guts to stand up to Stalin.

Confounding the pollsters, Truman defeated Dewey. His margin of victory was the smallest since 1916. Nevertheless, Truman's victory was a triumph for Roosevelt's New Deal coalition. Despite the Dixiecrats, most southerners did not abandon the party; Thurmond carried only four southern states. Wallace did not carry a single state. Truman's victory was made even sweeter when most of the West and Midwest voted Democrat. With Congress once again solidly in Democratic hands, Truman hoped that in 1949 he would succeed with his domestic program, which he called the **Fair Deal.** In his inaugural address, Truman called on government to ensure that all Americans received a "fair share" of the American dream. He asked for increases in Social Security, public housing, and the minimum wage. He also proposed the repeal of the Taft-Hartley Act and the institution of a national health program.

Cold War Politics

Congress responded favorably to Truman's requests for the expansion of programs already well established by the New Deal, such as Social Security. Proposals that went beyond the New Deal, however, failed to gain support. Attacks on the Fair Deal were based on the time-honored objection of too much government intrusion. In 1949, this objection found renewed meaning in the growing national fear of communism. The American Medical Association attacked the idea of a national health system by stressing its "Communistic" nature. Conservatives emphasized the "Communist" nature of government intervention in education. Civil rights legislation was held captive by the southern wing of the party, which called the FEPC part of a Communist conspiracy to undermine American unity. One of Truman's aides wrote that "the consuming fear of communism" fostered a widespread belief that change was subversive and that those who supported change were Communists.

Responding to fears of Communists within the government, Truman moved to beef up the existing loyalty program. In March 1947, the president issued Executive Order #9835, establishing the Federal Employee Loyalty Program. The order specified that, after a hearing, a federal employee could be fired if "reasonable grounds" existed for believing that he or she was disloyal. Attorney General Tom Clark provided a lengthy list of subversive organizations. Between 1947 and 1951, almost three thousand federal employees were forced to resign, and another three hundred were discharged on the basis of disloyalty. In almost every case, the accused had no right to confront the accusers or to refute evidence. Few of those forced to leave government

---

Dixiecrat party   Party organized in 1948 by southern delegates who refused to accept the civil rights plank of the Democratic platform; the party nominated Strom Thurmond of South Carolina for president.

Fair Deal   President Truman's plan for legislation on civil rights, fair employment practices, and educational appropriations.

service were Communists. Fewer still were threats to American security. Truman's loyalty program did little to calm internal fears. Instead it intensified a growing hysteria about an "enemy within."

The Second Red Scare

The Second Red Scare reflected the fears and frustrations of many Americans in the immediate aftermath of World War II. America had defeated one set of enemies in the war only to be confronted with another enemy in the form of the Soviet Union and the specter of communism generally. The Soviet domination of Eastern Europe and other Communist advances seemed inexplicable to many Americans—unless America had been betrayed from within. Ironically, the small American Communist party had already declined rapidly since the late 1930s. The end of the Depression and the Nazi-Soviet pact of 1939 had stripped communism of the attraction it had once had for some Americans.

Among those stepping forward to protect the nation from the insidious enemy within, none was more vicious than the **House Un-American Activities Committee (HUAC).** Working with FBI director J. Edgar Hoover, the HUAC announced in 1947 its intention to root out communism within the government and society. HUAC targeted State Department officials, New Dealers, labor activists, entertainers, writers, educators, and those with known liberal philosophies. Hoover proclaimed that there was one American Communist for every 1,814 loyal citizens, while Attorney General Clark warned that Communists were everywhere.

HUAC made its first Cold War splash with its investigation of Hollywood. The committee's goals were to remove leftist viewpoints from the entertainment industry and thus to ensure that the mass media promote American capitalism and traditional American values. With much fanfare, the HUAC called Hollywood notables to testify about Communist influence in the industry. Many of those called used the opportunity to strut their patriotism and denounce communism. Ronald Reagan, president of the Screen Actors Guild, testified that the Conference of Studio Unions was full of Reds. Not all witnesses were cooperative. Some who were or had been members of the Communist

party took the Fifth Amendment. Soon labeled "Fifth Amendment Communists," ten were jailed for contempt of Congress and blacklisted by the industry. The president of the Motion Picture Association, Eric Johnson, announced that no one would be hired who did not cooperate with the committee and that there would be no more films like *The Grapes of Wrath* featuring the hardships of poor Americans or "the seamy side of American life."

Anticommunism proved to be a useful weapon for a variety of causes. Manufacturers, including tobacco giant R. J. Reynolds, conducted a massive campaign to inform the nation about the Communistic nature of unions, especially the Congress of Industrial Organizations (CIO). The multimillion-dollar ad blitz successfully harnessed anti-Red hysteria to defeat the CIO's efforts to unionize southern industry. The CIO even expelled eleven unions for having Communist leaders and members. Southerners used anticommunism to fight the civil rights movement. Communities organized "watch groups" to protect themselves from the subversion of communism. These watch groups screened books, movies, and public speakers, and they questioned teachers and public officials, seeking to ban or dismiss those considered suspect. In Peekskill, New York, "loyal" Americans attacked the concert of singer, actor, and activist Paul Robeson, turning it into a riot (see Individual Choices: Paul Robeson).

HUAC's most sensational revelation came from one of the editors of *Time,* a repentant ex-Communist named Whittaker Chambers, shortly before the 1948 election. Chambers accused **Alger Hiss,** a New Deal liberal and former State Department official who had been with Roosevelt at Yalta, of being a Communist. At first Hiss denied even knowing Chambers, but under questioning by Congressman Richard M. Nixon, Hiss admitted

---

House Un-American Activities Committee Congressional committee created in 1938 that investigated suspected Communists during the McCarthy era and that Richard Nixon used to advance his career.

Alger Hiss State Department official accused in 1948 of being a Communist spy; he was convicted of perjury and sent to prison.

Speaking Out

Paul Robeson

Paul Robeson was a brilliant actor, opera singer, and civil rights activist. By choosing to support communism, whose principles he thought would advance the cause of social equality, he sacrificed his career and everything else for which he had worked. National Portrait Gallery, Smithsonian Institute/Art Resource, N.Y.

Paul Leroy Bustill Robeson was exceptional at nearly everything he did. A scholar-athlete, he earned several varsity letters and was named an All-American in football before graduating Phi Beta Kappa from Rutgers in 1919—only its third black graduate. He attended Columbia School of Law and played professional football on weekends to cover his living expenses. In 1922, Robeson took his first acting role in a play staged by the Harlem YMCA. He received his law degree the following year, but believing he could do more for African Americans as an actor than a lawyer, he returned to the theater as an actor and concert singer.

Working with playwright Eugene O'Neill, Robeson was cast as the lead in the Broadway production of O'Neill's *The Emperor Jones* and in his controversial new play about interracial marriage, *All God's Chillun Got Wings*. Critics wrote rave reviews, and Robeson was soon one of the most sought-after actors in the United States and Britain. But more than an entertainer, he was an activist—choosing to advocate equal rights, especially for blacks. "The artist must elect to fight for freedom or for slavery. I have made my choice," he explained.

In fighting for freedom, Paul Robeson walked picket lines for striking workers, demonstrated against lynchings and segregation, and refused to work on any stage that practiced

an acquaintance with Chambers in the 1930s. He denied, however, that he was or had been a Communist. When Hiss sued for libel, Chambers charged that Hiss had passed State Department secrets to him in the 1930s. Chambers even produced rolls of microfilm, hidden in a pumpkin, and showed typed copies of the stolen docu-

ments—the notorious Pumpkin Papers. In a controversial trial, Hiss was found guilty of **perjury**

perjury Deliberate giving of false testimony under oath.

segregation. In 1939, he announced that he would no longer act in movies because the film industry did not allow him to show "the life or express the . . . interests, hopes, and aspirations of the struggling people from whom I come." Also in the 1930s, he spoke out loudly against fascism, entertaining Republican troops in Spain and raising money for Jewish refugees from Nazism. In 1934, he visited the Soviet Union and was impressed with Soviet social equality. "I feel like a human being for the first time. . . . Here I am not a Negro but a human being." He told Soviet filmmaker Sergei Eisenstein, "Here . . . I walk in full human dignity."

Despite his activism and his support of the Soviet Union, Robeson's popularity continued to soar, as he performed before thousands in the United States and Europe and broke racial barriers everywhere. In 1942, he became the first African American in modern American theater to be cast as Othello. During World War II, he campaigned for war bonds and toured the European theater in the first integrated United Service Organizations (USO) show. But not everyone was tolerant. Even as he patriotically pushed war bonds, the FBI listed his name on its Detain Communist List (DetComList).

With the onset of the Cold War, Robeson's views, especially his refusal to condemn the Soviet Union and its policies, became unacceptable to most Americans and effectively ended his artistic career. Considering him a Communist, the mayor of Peoria, Illinois, canceled his concert in 1947. And in 1949, over a hundred fans were injured in Peekskill, New York, when an anti-Robeson, anti-Communist mob attacked those who came to hear him. The Peekskill riot was a direct outcome of his statement that blacks would not fight against the Soviet Union "on behalf of those who have oppressed us for generations." From over $100,000 in 1946, his income fell to under $6,000 by 1949.

Considering Robeson an undesirable representative of the country, the State Department took away his passport in 1950. For the next eight years, Robeson was a prisoner in the United States until the Supreme Court upheld his right as a citizen to travel. Free again, he left for Europe. He also published his autobiography, *Here I Stand,* proclaiming that civil rights should become a mass movement, independent of whites, and urging blacks to become aware of their African heritage.

Ill, he returned from Europe in 1963 and retired in virtual seclusion. By the seventies, however, Paul Robeson was again popular, recognized and appreciated for his great talents and—despite great personal costs—his advocacy of civil and social rights. At a Carnegie Hall celebration of his 75th birthday in 1973, Coretta King, widow of slain civil rights leader Martin Luther King, Jr., remarked that Robeson "had been buried alive because . . . he had tapped the . . . wells of latent militancy among blacks." Unable to attend the gala affair, Robeson sent a simple message from the lyrics of "Old Man River," a song he had sung in the 1936 musical *Show Boat:*

> *You can be sure that in my heart I go on singing:*
> *But I keeps laughin' instead of cryin';*
> *I must keep fightin' until I'm dyin'*
> *And Ol' Man River, he just keeps rollin' along!*

in 1949 (the statute of limitations on espionage having expired) and sentenced to five years in prison. Recent research has confirmed that Hiss was in fact a Communist and that he passed secret information to the Soviets.

As the nation followed the Hiss case, news of the Communist victory in China and the Soviet explosion of an atomic bomb heightened American fears. In many people's minds, such Communist successes could have occurred only with help from American traitors. Congressman Harold Velde of Illinois charged that a network of Communists had infiltrated the government. Congress responded by passing, over Truman's veto, the

McCarran Internal Security Act. It required all Communists to register with the attorney general and made it a crime to conspire to establish a totalitarian government in the United States.

Concern about traitors and spies seemed further justified in February 1950, when British authorities arrested nuclear scientist Klaus Fuchs for passing technical secrets to the Soviet Union. Fuchs had worked at Los Alamos, New Mexico, on the American atomic bomb project. Fuchs named an American accomplice, Harry Gold, who in turn named David Greenglass, an army sergeant at Los Alamos. Greenglass claimed that his sister Ethel and her husband, Julius Rosenberg, were part of the Soviet atomic spy ring. The prosecution alleged that the information obtained and passed on by the Rosenbergs was largely responsible for the successful Soviet atomic bomb. The Rosenbergs claimed innocence, but they were convicted of espionage in 1951 and executed in 1953. The Rosenbergs were clearly Communists, but it is doubtful that they provided significant information about the bomb to the Soviets.

Joseph McCarthy and the Politics of Loyalty

Feeding on the furor over the enemy within, Republican Senator **Joseph McCarthy** of Wisconsin emerged at the forefront of the anti-Communist movement. McCarthy entered the public arena following World War II. Running for the Senate in 1946, he invented a glorious war record for himself and even walked with a fake limp. Some regarded him as among the worst senators in Washington—available to lobbyists, without principles, and absent most of the time. In February 1950, looking for an issue on which to get re-elected, McCarthy settled on the internal Communist threat.

The senator tried his gambit first in Wheeling, West Virginia. He announced to a Republican women's group that the United States was losing the Cold War because of traitors within the government. He claimed to know of 205 Communists working in the State Department. In Denver, the senator told reporters that he had a list of "207 bad risks" in the State Department. As he crossed the country, McCarthy changed the number of people on his list but continued to hammer away at security risks. He produced no names and no list for reporters.

A Senate committee quickly refuted most of McCarthy's charges. When the chair of the committee, Democrat Millard Tydings, pronounced McCarthy a fraud, the Wisconsin senator countered by accusing Tydings of questionable loyalty. During Tydings's 1950 re-election campaign, McCarthy worked for his defeat. McCarthy even displayed a faked photograph that depicted Tydings talking to Earl Browder, head of the American Communist party. When Tydings lost by forty thousand votes, McCarthy's stature swelled. The Senate's most powerful Republican, Robert Taft, slapped McCarthy on the back saying, "Keep it up, Joe." The Korean War only increased the senator's popularity. Supported by Republican political gains in the 1950 elections, **McCarthyism** became a powerful political and social force. Politicians flocked to the anti-Communist bandwagon.

By 1952, only 24 percent of Americans polled approved of Truman's presidency. Republicans had a field day attacking "cowardly containment" and calling for victory in Korea. Compounding his problems, a congressional probe of organized crime had found scandal, corruption, and links to organized crime within the government. When Truman lost the opening presidential primary in New Hampshire to Senator Estes Kefauver of Tennessee, he withdrew from the race. As in 1948, Republicans looked to the November election with great anticipation. At last, they were sure, voters would elect a Republican president.

McCarran Internal Security Act Law passed in 1951 requiring Communists to register with the U.S. attorney general and making it a crime to conspire to establish a totalitarian government in the United States.

Joseph McCarthy Senator who began a Communist witch-hunt in 1950 that lasted until his censure by the Senate in 1954.

McCarthyism Attacks on suspected Communists in the early 1950s by Joseph McCarthy and others, which were often based on unsupported assertions and carried out without regard for basic liberties.

S U M M A R Y

E xpectations
C onstraints
C hoices
O utcomes

People hoped that the end of World War II would usher in a period of international cooperation and peace. This *expectation* vanished as the world entered a period of armed suspicion called the Cold War. To protect the country and the rest of the world from Soviet expansion, the United States *chose* to assume a primary economic, political, and military role around the globe. The *outcome* was Truman's containment policy. First applied to Western Europe, it eventually included Asia as the Cold War became a hot war in Korea. By 1952, with the "loss" of China and the stalemate in Korea, Americans turned against Truman's foreign policy. Many thought that the United States was losing the Cold War and that containment was not a strong enough policy to defeat communism and protect American interests.

At home, the Cold War acted as a *constraint* on liberalism. Moderates and conservatives alike *chose* to use the fear of communism to promote their own political, social, and economic interests. They attacked liberals, unions, and civil rights advocates as radicals, **fellow travelers,** and Communists. Economic prosperity also reduced public support for further growth of the New Deal. Politically, the *outcome* was that although Social Security, a minimum wage, and farm supports grew in scope, new initiatives like civil rights and national healthcare were rejected.

As Americans adjusted to postwar life, one of the major *outcomes* was a re-emphasis on home and family. Women experienced strong social pressure to give up their wartime jobs and take up the "domestic" life. Marriages and births rose. Although jobs and homeownership multiplied for white families, minorities found that the *constraints* of discrimination ended or limited many of the economic and social gains they had made during the war. Although pushed out of the work force or into lesser jobs, many nonwhites, joined by some white women, *chose* to resist being cast in customary roles.

> **fellow traveler**   Person who sympathizes with or supports the beliefs of the Communist party without being a member.

SUGGESTED READINGS

Bernstein, Barton. *Politics and Policies of the Truman Administration* (1970).
   An excellent collection of essays on the Truman administration from a generally critical point of view.

Gaddis, John L. *The United States and the Origins of the Cold War* (1972).
   A comprehensive and balanced view of the origins of the Cold War.

Hastings, Max. *The Korean War* (1987).
   A short and readable study of the military dimension of the Korean War.

McCullough, David. *Truman* (1992).
   A highly acclaimed, readable biography of Truman.

Reeves, Thomas. *The Life and Times of Joe McCarthy* (1982).
   A solid but critical study of Joseph McCarthy and his role in the Second Red Scare.

Theoharis, Athan. *Seeds of Repression: Harry S Truman and the Origins of McCarthyism* (1971).
   An examination of the causes of the Second Red Scare and Truman's role in contributing to it.

Tygiel, Jules. *Baseball's Great Experiment: Jackie Robinson and His Legacy* (1983).
   Reflections on the life and decisions that brought Jackie Robinson to break the color barrier in professional baseball.

Whitfield, Stephen J. *The Culture of the Cold War* (1991).
   A critical account of the impact of the Cold War on the United States.

EISENHOWER'S AMERICA During the 1950s, Americans were on the move. White Americans were moving to the suburbs, especially in the South and West. Many African Americans were leaving the rural areas of the South; others were moving against long-existing patterns of segregation. This map shows the web of interstate highways that were planned in the 1950s, the shifts of population from state to state, and the cities where the process of confronting legal segregation began.

CANADA

WASHINGTON 19%
OREGON 16%
MONTANA 14%
NORTH DAKOTA -2%
MINN. 14%
IDAHO 13%
SOUTH DAKOTA 4%
WIS. 15%
MICH. 22%
Wilkes-Barre /Hazleton, PA: 12% decrease in population, 1950–1960
VT. 3%
MAINE 6%
NEW YORK 13%
N.H. 13%
MASS. 9%
WYOMING 13%
IOWA 5%
NEBRASKA 6%
IND. 18%
OHIO 22%
PENNSYLVANIA 7%
R.I. 8%
CONN. 26%
Jersey City, N.J.: 6% decrease in population, 1950–1960
N.J. 25%
NEVADA 78%
UTAH 29%
COLORADO 32%
Topeka
KANSAS 14%
MISSOURI 9%
ILL. 15%
W. VA. -7%
KENTUCKY 3%
VIRGINIA 19%
Johnstown, PA: 4% decrease in population, 1950–1960
DEL. 40%
MD. 32%
CALIFORNIA 48%
San Jose, CA: 121% increase in population, 1950–1960
Washington, D.C. -4%
ARIZONA 73%
NEW MEXICO 39%
OKLAHOMA 4%
ARK. -6%
Little Rock
TENN. 8%
NORTH CAROLINA 12%
SOUTH CAROLINA 12%
MISS. 1%
ALABAMA 6%
Montgomery
GEORGIA 14%
TEXAS 24%
LA. 21%
Orlando, Florida: 125% increase in population, 1950–1960
Ft. Lauderdale /Hollywood, Florida: 298% increase in population, 1950–1960
FLA. 78%

PACIFIC OCEAN
ATLANTIC OCEAN
Gulf of Mexico

HAWAI'I (1959) 26%
0   100 Km.
0   100 Mi.
PACIFIC OCEAN
U.S.S.R.
ALASKA (1959) 75%
CANADA
0   250   500 Km.
0   250   500 Mi.
PACIFIC OCEAN

MEXICO
CUBA

—— Interstate highway
Topeka • Sites of civil rights activities

Population changes, 1950–1960
Gains | Loss
☐ Under 10% | ☐ Under 10%
☐ 10%–20%
☐ 20%–50%
☐ Over 50%

0   200   400 Km.
0   200   400 Mi.

Korean War begins
• Eisenhower elected
• Hydrogen bomb tested
• *Brown* case
• Army-McCarthy hearings
• Eisenhower reelected
• Castro takes power in Cuba
• Soviets shoot down U-2 plane
Korean War armistice
Montgomery bus boycott begins
Little Rock crisis

1950   1952   1953   1954   1955   1956   1957   1959   1960

1850   1900   1950   2000

Quest for Consensus, 1952–1960

The Best of Times

- What factors contributed to expectations of prosperity in the 1950s?

- What expectations led American middle-class families to embrace suburban culture? What constraints did the critics of that culture condemn?

The Politics of Consensus

- What constraints did President Eisenhower and other Republicans encounter in trying to roll back the New Deal?

- How did the outcome reflect what Eisenhower called the "middle path"?

Seeking Civil Rights

- How did African-American leaders choose to attack *de jure* segregation in American society during Eisenhower's administration?

- What role did the federal government play in the outcome of civil rights issues during the 1950s?

- What constraints strengthened the strategy of confrontation and litigation in shaping the civil rights movement?

Eisenhower and a Hostile World

- What constraints lay behind the New Look?

- What were the weaknesses of "massive retaliation," and how did Eisenhower choose to address them?

INTRODUCTION

E xpectations
C onstraints
C hoices
O utcomes

In 1952, Republicans represented change. A victory by Dwight David Eisenhower ended twenty years of Democratic control of the White House. Republicans hoped that his leadership would reverse two "dangerous" trends: creeping socialism in the form of the New Deal and appeasement of communism in the guise of containment. Most people *expected* that an Eisenhower presidency would end the Korean War, re-emphasize individual freedoms, and reduce government intervention in social and economic affairs. But most of all, Americans *expected* to enjoy their lives fully, in the strongest, most democratic, and most prosperous nation in the world.

The United States of the 1950s seemed to justify this *expectation*. The country experienced one of the longest periods of sustained economic growth in its history. This affluent America matched the image of a gentle and quiet president who presided over a prosperous nation composed of families that *chose* a stable, suburban life in which the husband worked and the wife raised their children.

For a large segment of the population, this America was real. But prosperity did not touch all Americans. Nor were all Americans, even those in the suburbs, leading happy, stable, or fulfilling lives. Many men and women were dissatisfied with their roles as husband and father, wife and mother, and *chose* other forms of social and personal expression. Many American youths *chose* to reject the values of suburban culture, turning to the driving rhythms of rock 'n' roll and displaying antisocial behavior. At the same time, intellectual and cultural critics condemned the lack of vitality of the suburban culture. The *outcome* was an American society fragmented by differing *expectations*.

For minorities in 1950, the *constraints* against achieving the American dream were formidable. Poverty, prejudice, and segregation remained the norm. But some groups nurtured *expectations* of change. By mid-decade, African Americans were tearing down barriers that blocked their access to the American dream. The *outcome* was a civil rights movement that attacked existing social and legal restrictions and forced white Americans to confront long-standing contradictions in the country's democratic image.

As president, Eisenhower recognized that a political and social consensus accepted much of the New Deal. Faced with this *constraint*, he *chose* to cut spending and reduce government regulations only where possible. In foreign policy, Eisenhower made similar *choices*. He *chose* to maintain the basic strategy of containment. *Constrained* by his desire to balance the budget, he stressed the use of atomic weapons as a cheaper alternative to conventional forces. Eisenhower shaped an *outcome* built on existing patterns of domestic and foreign policy rather than initiating new ones.

CHRONOLOGY

The Fifties

1948 Alfred Kinsey's *Sexual Behavior in the Human Male*

1950 Korean War begins
David Riesman's *Lonely Crowd*

1951 J. D. Salinger's *Catcher in the Rye*
Mattachine Society formed
Allan Freed's "Moondog's Rock 'n' Roll Party"

1952 Eisenhower elected president
Eisenhower visits Korea
Hydrogen bomb tested

1953 Korean War armistice at Panmunjom
Mohammed Mossadegh overthrown in Iran
Joseph Stalin dies
Joseph McCarthy investigates USIA and Voice of America
Alfred Kinsey's *Sexual Behavior in the Human Female*
Termination policy for American Indians implemented
Earl Warren appointed chief justice of Supreme Court
"Father Knows Best" debuts on television
Playboy established

1954 *Brown v. Board of Education*
St. Lawrence Seaway Act
Federal budget balanced
Army-McCarthy hearings
Jacobo Arbenz overthrown in Guatemala
Gamal Nasser assumes power in Egypt
Battle of Dienbienphu
Geneva Agreement (Vietnam)
SEATO founded

1955 Murder of Emmett Till
Montgomery bus boycott begins
Salk vaccine approved for use
AFL-CIO merger
Warsaw Pact

McDonald's opens in California
Geneva Summit

1956 Federal Highway Act
Gayle et al. v. Browser
Southern Christian Leadership Conference formed
Eisenhower re-elected
Suez crisis
Soviets invade Hungary
Allen Ginsberg's *Howl*
Grace Metalious's *Peyton Place*
Elvis Presley's "Heartbreak Hotel"

1957 Little Rock crisis
Civil Rights Act
Baghdad Pact
Sputnik I launched
Jack Kerouac's *On the Road*

1958 Berlin crisis
U.S. troops to Lebanon
Soviet nuclear test moratorium

1959 CENTO formed
Fidel Castro overthrows Batista in Cuba
Nikita Khrushchev visits United States
Cooper v. Aaron

1960 Soviets shoot down U-2 and capture pilot
Paris Summit

The Best of Times

According to the *Reader's Digest*, in 1954 the average American male stood 5 feet 9 inches tall and weighed 158 pounds. He liked brunettes, baseball, bowling, and steak and French fries. In seeking a wife, he could not decide if brains or beauty was more important. The average female was 5 feet 4 inches tall and weighed 132 pounds. She preferred marriage to career, but she wanted to remove the word *obey* from her marriage vows. Both were enjoying life fully, the *Digest* claimed, and buying more of nearly everything.

The nation's "easy street" was a product of big government, big business, and an expanding population. World War II and the Cold War had created military-industrial-governmental linkages that primed the economy through government spending. National security needs by 1955 accounted for half of the U.S. budget, equaling 17 percent of the gross national product. The connection between government and business went beyond spending, though. Government officials and corporate managers moved back and forth in a vast web of jobs. Few saw any real conflict of interests. Frequently, regulatory agencies were staffed by people from the businesses to be regulated. Secretary of Defense Charles E. Wilson had been the president of General Motors and voiced the common view: "What's good for General Motors' business is good for America."

Direct military spending was only one aspect of governmental involvement in the economy. Federal research funds flowed into colleges and industries, producing not only new scientific and military technology but a variety of marketable consumer goods such as polyester fabrics and Teflon. On an international level, American foreign-aid programs provided billions of dollars with which other countries bought American goods.

Technological advances also increased profits and productivity. Profits doubled between 1948 and 1958. At the same time, over four thousand mergers took place. In the steel, automobile, and aircraft industries, fewer workers used new technology to produce more goods. Union member-

♦ In the popular culture of the 1950s, one of the most memorable events in any young person's life was the high school prom. Here, on this cover of the *Saturday Evening Post* painted in 1957 by Norman Rockwell, a young man in his tuxedo and a young woman in her prom dress have an after-prom milk shake at the local diner. Is that Dad behind the counter? *Courtesy of the Norman Rockwell Family Trust and Curtis Archives.*

ship declined slightly. Agricultural and white-collar workers remained unorganized, and unions made little effort to organize the economically booming Sunbelt. Instead, they focused on getting better pensions, cost-of-living raises, and paid vacations. Another consequence of declining union rolls was the merger of the AFL and the CIO in 1955.

For most Americans, jobs and good wages were available. Except for brief **recessions** in 1953 and

recession   A decline in the economy that is less severe than a depression.

1958, unemployment remained around 5 percent throughout the 1950s. Industrial wages rose from about $55 a week in 1950 to $72 in 1960. Not everyone benefited from the growing economy. Expanding opportunities in management and sales went almost exclusively to whites. Unemployment for minorities remained at about 10 percent. But for those able to reach the fruits of prosperity, life seemed good.

Suburban and Consumer Culture

During the fifties, the suburb and prosperity formed the heart of popular images of American life. Fourteen million single-family homes were built between 1945 and 1960, most of them in the suburbs. All levels of government helped make the suburbs possible. The Veterans Administration (VA) and Federal Housing Administration (FHA) underwrote thousands of loans. **Zoning laws** were changed to ease construction of tract housing developments. States, counties, and communities spent millions of dollars on roads to connect workplaces, schools, parks, and shopping centers to suburban homes. On the national level, the **Federal Highway Act** of 1956 provided $32 billion over thirteen years to build the interstate highway system.

As Americans sought the pleasant life of suburbia, the urban core deteriorated. Shrinking tax bases made it increasingly difficult for cities to maintain services, buildings, and mass transportation. Increased automobile traffic damaged roads, left railroad stations largely deserted, and added to pollution. Programs to rebuild homes in cities rarely succeeded in meeting the needs of the poor.

The automobile industry helped shape suburbia. By 1960, 75 percent of all Americans had at least one car. Stores had to include parking lots and easy access to roads. Amusement parks like Disneyland, miniature golf courses, drive-in theaters, and fast-food restaurants took advantage of the new availability of the automobile. McDonald's, franchised in San Bernardino, California, in 1955 by entrepreneur Ray Kroc, sold a standardized hamburger for 15 cents and changed the eating habits of America.

To sell automobiles, hamburgers, and all the other products that defined the good life, Madison Avenue continued to use images of youth, glamour, sex appeal, and sophistication. Leading the advertising onslaught was the tobacco industry. When medical reports connected health risks to smoking, the tobacco giants intensified their advertising and stressed that new, longer, filtered cigarettes posed no health hazards. Cigarette advertising increased 400 percent between 1945 and 1960.

Family Culture

Many Americans were sure that the 1950s were the best of all possible times. At the center of those feelings lay the economy, the home, the family, and the church. Religion enjoyed a new popularity. Church attendance rose to 59.5 percent in 1953, a historic high. No one was more esteemed than the Reverends Billy Graham and **Norman Vincent Peale** and Catholic Bishop Fulton J. Sheen. They captivated millions with religious, patriotic, and anti-Communist pronouncements. In spirit with the times, Congress added "under God" to the Pledge of Allegiance in 1954 and "In God We Trust" to all American currency in 1955.

After the disruptions of Depression and war, family took on a renewed importance in the fifties. The divorce rate slowed, and the numbers of marriages and births climbed. The ideal place for women was in the home. Women who avoided wedded bliss were suspected of being homosexual,

zoning laws Local regulations that limit particular types of buildings, such as residences, businesses, or factories, to specified sections of a city or town.

Federal Highway Act Law passed in 1956 appropriating $32 billion for the construction of federal and interstate highways.

Norman Vincent Peale Minister who told his congregations that positive thinking could help them overcome all their troubles in life.

emotionally immature, or just irresponsible. Career women frequently were thought of as neurotic and masculine.

The home was the center of "togetherness," a term defined in 1954 by *McCall's* as the modern partnership of husbands and wives who shared housework and shopping and catered to their children's needs and desires. Popular television shows such as "Leave It to Beaver" (1957) and "Father Knows Best" (1953) reflected the ideal middle-class family. The TV families who lived in all-white neighborhoods featured hardworking fathers and attractive, savvy mothers who always knew how to solve the current week's problem. Their children provided the usually humorous dilemmas that Mom's common sense and sensitivity untangled. Reality, however, rarely matched *McCall's* or television's images.

Another View of Suburbia

Unlike the wives shown on television, more and more married women were working (see Figure 28.1). Some desired careers, but the majority worked to enhance their families' **standard of living.** The percentage of middle-class women working rose from 7 percent in 1950 to 25 percent in 1960. Most found jobs in part-time or clerical positions that paid low wages and provided few benefits. Women filled most secretary, teller, and receptionist slots in banks but held only 15 percent of upper-level positions.

Nor were all homemakers happy. Surveys discovered that more than one-fifth of suburban wives were unhappy with their marriages and lives. Many women complained of the drudgery and boredom of housework and the lack of understanding and affection from their husbands. **Alfred Kinsey's** research on women's sexuality, *Sexual Behavior in the Human Female* (1953), indicated that 25 percent of married women had affairs.

Men also showed signs of being less than satisfied with the popular role of suburban dad. In 1953, Hugh Hefner first published *Playboy,* urging men to break away from the boring middle-class, husband-father image. The growing popularity of

Playboy and other "men's magazines" signaled that many men were rejecting the ideal of togetherness. Reflecting the shadier side of middle-class life in fiction, the best-selling novel *Peyton Place* by Grace Metalious (1956) set America buzzing over the licentious escapades of the residents of a seemingly placid New England town. Hollywood kept pace with stars like **Marilyn Monroe.** Starting in 1952, movie directors repeatedly cast the "blonde bombshell" in slightly dumb but very sexy roles in which she was usually romanced by slightly older, more worldly men.

Monroe and other sex symbols represented a minor threat to the image of family, community, and nation. Homosexuality, however, appeared to threaten the moral and social fabric of society. Kinsey's 1948 study of male sexuality, *Sexual Behavior in the American Male,* shocked readers by claiming that nearly 8 percent of the population lived a gay lifestyle. According to Kinsey, homosexuality existed throughout American society. The gay bars that could be found in every major city clearly reflected Kinsey's findings.

In a society that emphasized the traditional family and feared internal subversion, homosexuals represented a double threat. The Republican national chairman warned that "sexual perverts . . . have infiltrated our Government" and were "as dangerous as . . . Communists." A Senate investigating committee worried that one homosexual could "pollute a Government office." Responding to such views, the Eisenhower administration barred homosexuals from most government jobs. State and local authorities fol-

standard of living Level of material comfort as measured by the goods, services, and luxuries currently available.

Alfred Kinsey Biologist whose studies of human sexuality attracted great attention in the 1940s and 1950s, especially for his conclusions on infidelity and homosexuality.

Marilyn Monroe American actress who became famous for her blond hair, her sex appeal, and her vulnerability; she died in 1962 at the age of 36.

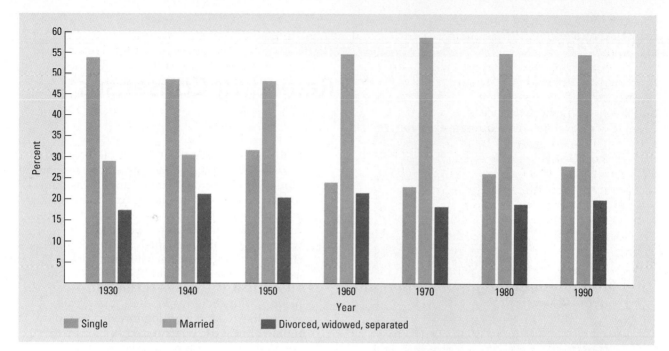

♦ **FIGURE 28.1 Marital Status of Women in the Work Force, 1930–1990** This figure shows the percentage of women in the work force from the Great Depression through 1990. While the number of women who fall into the category of divorced, widowed, and separated remained fairly constant, there was a significant shift in the number of single and married women employed. The number of single women in the workforce declined as the number of married women increased. *Source:* U.S. Department of Commerce, *Historical Statistics of the United States, Colonial Times to 1970,* Vol. I (Washington, D.C.: U.S. Government Printing Office, 1970), pp. 20–21, 131–132; and U.S. Department of Commerce, *Statistics of the United States, 1993* (Washington, D.C.: U.S. Government Printing Office, 1993), pp. 74, 399.

lowed suit. **Vice squads** began making frequent raids on gay and lesbian bars. In response to the virulent attacks, many tried to hide their homosexuality, but some confronted the attacks. In Los Angeles, Henry Hay formed the Mattachine Society in 1951 to fight for homosexual rights. In San Francisco in 1955, Del Martin and Phyllis Lyon organized a similar organization for lesbians, the Daughters of Bilitis.

Most Americans could justify the suppression of gays and lesbians because they appeared to reject the traditional values of family and community. Other critiques of American society were more difficult to reject. A number of respected writers claimed that the suburban and consumer culture stifled diversity and individuality. Mass-produced homes, meals, toys, and fashions created a gray sameness about Americans. Sociologist David Riesman in *The Lonely Crowd* (1950) argued that postwar Americans were overly concerned about fitting into a group. Peer pressure had replaced

vice squad Police unit charged with the enforcement of laws dealing with crimes such as gambling and prostitution.

Rejecting Consensus

Allen Ginsberg

Allen Ginsberg was born in Paterson, New Jersey in 1926. He graduated from Columbia University, then moved to San Francisco. Dissatisfied with his traditional job and lifestyle, he chose to stop working and start writing poetry. Eventually, he became one of the leading Beat poets and voices of his generation. Robert Kelley, LIFE Magazine, © Time Warner Inc.

In the mid-fifties, Allen Ginsberg left New York for California. "I had passed one session of my life," he remembered, "and it was time to start all over again." In the San Francisco area, he took a job with a small market-research firm and explored poetry, but he was not personally satisfied. He sought psychotherapy, and psychiatrist Philip Hicks asked him what he would like to do. "Doctor, I don't think you're going to find this very healthy," Ginsberg responded, "but I really would like to stop working forever . . . and do nothing but write poetry and have leisure to spend the day outdoors and go to museums and see friends. And I'd like to keep living with someone—maybe even a man—and explore relationships." Hicks said, "Do it."

Making his choice, Ginsberg established a long-term relationship with Peter Orlovsky, retired from work, and wrote his first long-lined poem, *Howl.*

Ginsberg's semiautobiographical cry of outrage and despair against a destructive and abusive society that worships Moloch, the god of materialism and conventionality—exploded on American society in 1956.

> *Moloch whose mind is pure machinery!*
> *Moloch whose blood is running money!*
> *Moloch whose fingers are ten armies!*
> *Moloch whose heart is a cannibal dynamo!*
> *Moloch whose love is endless oil and stone!*
> *Moloch whose soul is electricity and banks!*

At the end of the poem, Ginsberg celebrates his victory over Moloch's control of his conventional identity.

Howl not only rejected traditional American values but immediately became a target of censorship by San Francisco authorities, who claimed that the poem was obscene and pornographic. Almost as soon as it was published, San Francisco police arrested its publisher, Lawrence Ferlinghetti, and sought to confiscate existing copies of the poem. In the obscenity trial that followed, a parade of respected poets and literary critics testified that the poem had merit, forcing the judge to declare that it was not obscene. The poem and the furor over it promptly established a virtually unknown author as a leading Beat poet.

An opponent of social norms, Ginsberg believed that it was necessary to save the nation by rejecting conventionality and calling on the people to discover their true spirits. Interviewed by the *Village Voice* in 1959, Ginsberg argued that recent history was "a vast conspiracy to impose . . . a level of mechanical consciousness" on humankind and that the "suppression of contemplative individuality" was nearly complete. Fortunately, according to Ginsberg, "a few individuals, poets, have had the luck and courage . . . to glimpse something new through the crack of mass consciousness" and "have entered the world of Spirit" to battle "an America gone mad with materialism, a police-state America, a sexless and soulless America."

Ginsberg became the model for Beat writers—writing in the language of the streets about unliterary topics—and fulfilled the popular expectations of the "hipster" Beatnik. As the fifties dissolved into the sixties, Ginsberg and his Haight-Ashbury apartment became a center of the counterculture. He coined the term "flower power," while advocating spirituality and individual freedom induced by using psychedelic drugs and practicing Oriental philosophies and Buddhism. Opposed to the war in Vietnam (see Chapter 30), he asked antiwar protestors to demonstrate peacefully, arguing that flowers, bells, and chants would overcome jeers and oppression. In 1967, he organized the "Gathering of the Tribes for a Human Be-In" in San Francisco, the first of hundreds of counterculture festivals to follow.

As a poet, Ginsberg has chosen to write about his political and social concerns, attacking what he described as the evil forces in society. In 1973, his *Fall of America, 1965–1971* presented Moloch in the guise of the war in Vietnam, nuclear energy, threats to the environment, and America's rampant materialism—and won the National Book Award. From the obscenity trial to prestigious literary awards, the outcome of Allen Ginsberg's choice has been a literary Horatio Alger story, from a "dirty" Beat poet—a hipster predicted to self-destruct—to one of the country's best-known modern poets and "the biographer of his time."

individual thinking. William Whyte's *Organization Man* (1955) found the same lack of individuality and independence. Serious literature also highlighted a sense of alienation from a conformist society. Much of Sylvia Plath's poetry and her novel *The Bell Jar* (1963) depicted women torn between the demands of society and the quest for individual freedom. Contemporary novels such as Saul Bellow's *Henderson the Rain King* (1959), Sloan Wilson's *The Man in the Grey Flannel Suit* (1955), and J. D. Salinger's *Catcher in the Rye* (1951) offered similar themes.

More extreme were the **Beats,** or beatniks, a group of controversial artists, poets, and writers. Allen Ginsberg (*Howl,* 1956) and Jack Kerouac (*On the Road,* 1957) denounced American materialism and glorified a freer, natural life (see Individual Choices: Allen Ginsberg). Although some college students appreciated the beatnik critique of "square America," most Americans rejected their message and condemned their lifestyle. In an article in *Life* (1959), Paul O'Neil described the beatniks as being smelly, dirty people in beards and sandals, who were "sick little bums" and "hostile little females."

The Trouble with Kids

In the 1950s, many observers became alarmed by delinquency among many white, middle-class, suburban teens. What worried most parents was not the violent crime associated with inner-city gangs but teens running amok in cars in pursuit of amusements often involving alcohol and sex. One study of middle-class delinquency concluded that the automobile provided "a private lounge for drinking and for petting or sex episodes."

The problem with kids also seemed wedded to **rock 'n' roll,** a term coined in 1951 by Cleveland disc jockey Alan Freed. He had noticed that white teenagers were buying rhythm-and-blues (R&B) records popular among African Americans. But he also knew that few white households would listen to a radio program playing "black music." Freed decided to change the name to rock 'n' roll and play the less sexually suggestive of the R&B

records. His radio program, "Moondog's Rock 'n' Roll Party," was a smash hit.

The barriers between "black music" and "white music" quickly began to blur. White singers such as Pat Boone and Georgia Gibbs sold millions of rock-'n'-roll **cover records** and were heard on hundreds of radio stations that had refused to play the original black artists. By mid-decade, African-American artists like **Chuck Berry,** Little Richard, and Ray Charles were successfully "crossing over" and being heard on "white" radio stations. At the same time, white artists such as **Elvis Presley** were making their own contributions to rock 'n' roll. Presley blended gospel, country, and R&B into an original musical form that quickly rocked the nation. Beginning with "Heartbreak Hotel" in 1956, he recorded fourteen gold records in two years, appeared on the prestigious "Ed Sullivan Show" on television, and drove his audiences of teenage girls into frenzies with sexually suggestive movements. Although an outraged Catholic Youth Center newspaper asked readers to "smash" rock-'n'-roll records, such opponents were waging a losing battle. By the end of the decade, Dick Clark's "American Bandstand," fea-

Beats Group of American writers, poets, and artists in the 1950s, including Jack Kerouac and Allen Ginsberg, who rejected traditional middle-class values and championed nonconformity and sexual experimentation.

rock 'n' roll Style of music that developed out of rhythm-and-blues in the 1950s, with a fast beat and lyrics that appealed to teenagers.

cover record A new version of a song already recorded by an original artist.

Chuck Berry African-American rock musician and composer whose songs chronicled teenage experiences and sentiments and who helped establish rock 'n' roll in the 1950s.

Elvis Presley Rock-'n'-roll musician from a poor white family in Mississippi who gained immense popularity with songs that incorporated the driving beat and frank sexuality of rhythm-and-blues.

turing teenagers dancing to rock-'n'-roll music, had become one of the nation's most watched and accepted programs.

The Politics of Consensus

In 1952, Republicans expected to end the Democrats' twenty-year monopoly on the White House. Crying, "It is time for a change," Republicans chose war hero General Dwight David Eisenhower as their candidate. The Democrats selected Illinois governor **Adlai Stevenson,** whom the Republicans depicted as too intellectual and too liberal. Eisenhower gained many supporters by telling a war-weary public that, if elected, he would go to Korea in pursuit of peace. The Republicans also attacked the Democrats' Cold War and New Deal record. They boasted that there were "no Communists in the Republican Party" and proclaimed that a Republican administration would roll back communism. The liberal spending of the Democrats would be stopped and the New Deal dismantled.

The campaign was almost without drama. The only tense moment came when the Republicans' vice-presidential candidate, Richard M. Nixon, who had risen to prominence because of his outspoken anticommunism, was accused of accepting gifts and a secret cash fund from California business friends. Eisenhower considered dropping him from the ticket. Nixon used television to rally public opinion. In the "Checkers" speech, a teary-eyed Nixon contended that the only gift his family had ever received was a puppy, Checkers. His daughter loved the puppy, Nixon stated, and he would not make her give it back, regardless of his career. It was a sentimental speech, but it worked. Nixon stayed on the ticket.

With a smile as powerful as FDR's grin, Eisenhower buried Stevenson in popular and electoral votes. Ike's broad political coattails ensured a Republican majority in Congress. Eisenhower again swamped Stevenson in 1956, but it was his victory alone, as the Democrats maintained their 1954 majorities in both houses of Congress.

The Middle Path

Eisenhower called himself a modern Republican. He wanted to follow a "middle course" that was "conservative when it comes to money and liberal when it comes to human beings." The president's first priority was a balanced budget. Facing Truman's projected deficits for 1952 and 1953, Eisenhower knew it was necessary to end the war in Korea and to make substantial cuts in the defense budget.

Fulfilling his campaign pledge, President-elect Eisenhower flew to Korea in December 1952 for a three-day visit. Eisenhower wanted to visit the frontline to get a real sense of the war. By the time the commander in chief left Korea on December 5, he was convinced that the war could not be won. The problem was how to persuade the North Koreans and Chinese that a negotiated settlement would be in their best interests.

To prod the Communists, Eisenhower and Secretary of State **John Foster Dulles** implied that the United States would use atomic weapons unless a settlement was soon reached. By July 1953, the "atomic diplomacy" had worked. A truce signed at Panmunjom ended the fighting, brought home almost all the troops, left a divided Korea, and allowed Eisenhower to cut the military budget.

Even as Eisenhower flew home from Korea, he was contemplating other ways to reduce military spending. The answer, he decided, was to reshape the tactics of containment. Eisenhower's **New Look** policy emphasized atomic weapons

> **Adlai Stevenson**   Illinois governor who was the Democratic candidate for president in 1952 and 1956 but lost both times to Eisenhower.
>
> **John Foster Dulles**   Secretary of state under Eisenhower who called for massive retaliation with nuclear weapons to deter Soviet aggression.
>
> **New Look**   National security policy under Eisenhower that called for a reduction in the size of the army, the development of tactical nuclear weapons, and the buildup of strategic airpower employing nuclear weapons.

and airpower and thus permitted a reduction of more expensive conventional forces. The policy allowed Eisenhower to balance the federal budget in 1954. Although the New Look represented a change in tactics, it did not change the basic strategy of containment that Truman had initiated.

Eisenhower's second priority was to reverse the "creeping socialism" of the New Deal by eliminating or reducing federal programs. High on his list of government programs to reverse were those involving American Indians. A series of acts between 1953 and 1954 eliminated federal economic support to tribes and liquidated selected reservations. Critics blasted this "termination policy" as an attack on American Indian culture and society. Native Americans increasingly fell under less protective state laws, while economic pressures encouraged them to sell tribal lands. By 1960, nearly one-half of American Indians had abandoned their reservations.

Eisenhower also returned to state and private hands federally owned or controlled energy sources. Although successful in removing many federal controls over energy, Eisenhower faced bitter opposition in trying to modify agricultural policy. The strong bipartisan Farm Bloc ensured that the Agricultural Act of 1954 contained only small modifications of Roosevelt's policy (see page 545). Congress did approve lower payment rates, but because payments were based on production levels, which continued to grow, the total cost of federal subsidies rose steadily.

Eisenhower's "middle path" did not discard New Deal programs altogether or shrink the size of government. Programs such as Social Security had tremendous political support. Eisenhower believed that the Republican party could abolish Social Security only at its own peril. During his two terms, 7 million more Americans became qualified for Social Security, and 4 million more received unemployment payments. The minimum wage rose from $.75 to $1.00 an hour.

But Eisenhower's liberal nature had limits. After the **polio** vaccine developed by **Jonas Salk** was declared effective in 1955, Eisenhower strongly agreed with the American Medical Association that the government should not get directly involved in inoculating the public because it would be socialistic. Eisenhower also vetoed housing projects, public works bills, and antipollution proposals as inappropriate for the federal government.

When Eisenhower increased government spending, his rationale was generally based on national economic and security needs. He pushed the St. Lawrence Seaway project (1954), which connected the Great Lakes with the Atlantic Ocean, on the grounds that it would benefit the nation by increasing trade. He approved the Federal Highway Act (1956) to meet the needs of an automobile-driven nation and to provide the military with a workable transportation network. Following the Soviet launching of the space satellites *Sputnik I* (1957) and *Sputnik II* (1958), Eisenhower cited national security needs to support spending more federal money on education.

The successful orbiting of the Soviet satellites created a panic across the nation. Not only was the country vulnerable to missiles and bombs, but *Sputnik* appeared to underscore basic weaknesses in the American educational system. American schools, many critics argued, stressed soft subjects and social adjustment rather than hard subjects: science, languages, mathematics. *Sputnik* spurred Eisenhower and Congress to approve grants to schools for developing strong programs in those subjects. Similarly, Congress cited national defense when it established the **National Defense Student Loans** for college students.

---

polio Acute viral infection that usually struck children and often caused partial or total paralysis; it was common in the United States until the development of the Salk vaccine.

Jonas Salk American microbiologist who developed the first effective vaccine against polio in 1954.

Sputnik I Satellite launched by the Soviet Union in 1957; the first successful launch of an artificial satellite by any nation, it marked the beginning of the space race.

National Defense Student Loans Loans established by the U.S. government in 1958, designed to encourage the teaching and study of science and modern foreign languages.

The Problem with McCarthy

During the 1952 presidential campaign, Senator Joseph McCarthy had taken a prominent role in attacking Democrats as being soft on communism. With Ike in the White House, many Republicans, including Eisenhower, hoped that the Republican senator would quietly disappear. But McCarthy had no intention of fading from view. He continued his search for subversives in the State Department, the Voice of America, and the **United States Information Agency (USIA).** McCarthy's targets were discharged or pressured to resign. Although few of the individuals McCarthy attacked were guilty of any form of disloyalty, the agitation helped Republicans to rid the government of officials appointed by Democrats. McCarthy's hunt for Communists thus continued to serve partisan purposes.

McCarthy overstepped his bounds, however, when the army drafted his aide David Schine. McCarthy responded by threatening to expose army favoritism toward known Communists. Anti-McCarthy forces in Congress, quietly supported by Eisenhower, concluded that it was time to silence the senator. Charging that he was trying to blackmail the U.S. Army, the Senate investigated McCarthy. The American Broadcasting Company's telecast of the 1954 **Army-McCarthy hearings** allowed over 20 million viewers to see McCarthy's ruthless bullying firsthand. Public and congressional opposition to the senator rose. When the army's lawyer, Joseph Welch, asked McCarthy, who had accused Welch's co-counsel of belonging to a left-wing organization, "Have you no sense of decency?" the nation burst into applause. Several months later, the Senate voted 67 to 22 to censure McCarthy's "unbecoming conduct." Drinking heavily, rejected by his colleagues, and ignored by the media, McCarthy died in 1957. But McCarthyism remained for years a potent political weapon against liberal opponents.

Seeking Civil Rights

African-American leaders became determined during the 1950s to attack the racial inequalities in America. The NAACP had by 1952 won cases permitting African-American law and graduate students to attend white colleges and universities. Yet the concept of "separate but equal," established in 1896 by the Supreme Court ruling in *Plessy v. Ferguson* (see page 399), remained intact. Throughout the country, African Americans still occupied the lowest rungs of the social ladder and worked at the most menial jobs. From the delta of the Mississippi to the White House, African Americans were committed to enlarging their civil and political rights.

The *Brown* Decision

A step toward change came in 1954 when the Supreme Court considered the case of *Brown v. Board of Education, Topeka, Kansas.* The *Brown* case had started four years earlier, when Oliver Brown sued to allow his daughter to attend a nearby white school rather than the black school across town. The Kansas courts had rejected his suit, and the NAACP had appealed. In addressing the Supreme Court, NAACP lawyer **Thurgood Marshall** held that the doctrine of "separate but equal" was inherently unequal. He used statistics to show that black schools were

United States Information Agency   Agency established by Congress in 1953 to distribute information about U.S. culture and political policies and to gain support for American international goals.

Army-McCarthy hearings   The 1954 congressional investigation of allegations that McCarthy had tried to get special treatment from the U.S. Army for an aide; the televised hearings revealed McCarthy's villainous nature and ended his popularity.

Brown v. Board of Education, Topeka, Kansas   Supreme Court ruling in 1954 that separate educational facilities for different races were inherently unequal.

Thurgood Marshall   Civil rights lawyer who argued thirty-two cases before the Supreme Court and won twenty-nine of them; he became the first African American on the Court in 1967.

unequal when it came to finances, quality and number of teachers, and physical and educational resources. He also read into the record a psychological study indicating that black children educated in a segregated environment suffered from low self-esteem. He stressed that segregated educational facilities could never yield equal products.

In 1954, **Earl Warren,** appointed chief justice of the Supreme Court in 1953, announced for a unanimous court that "separate educational facilities are inherently unequal" and ruled that school segregation was illegal under the Fourteenth Amendment. In 1955, in a second *Brown* decision, the Court provided rather vague enforcement guidelines. The Court did not expect schools to desegregate overnight but wanted them to proceed with "all deliberate speed."

The Court's decision raised a loud cry of protest from white southerners. Virginia passed a law closing all integrated schools. Southern congressmen, in what was called the **Southern Manifesto,** proudly pledged to oppose the *Brown* ruling. Consequently, "all deliberate speed" amounted to a snail's pace. By 1965, only about 2 percent of all southern schools were integrated.

Southern white reactions to the *Brown* case confirmed for African Americans that efforts to undo existing social traditions would encounter strong opposition, even violence. An incident in August 1955 brought home exactly how far some were willing to go to halt threats to "tradition." **Emmett Till,** a teenager from Chicago visiting relatives in Mississippi, broke "tradition" by speaking to a white girl without being asked. For his actions, he was tortured and murdered. Roy Bryant and J. W. Milam were brought to trial and admitted to killing Till. An all-white jury acquitted both men. The verdict was not unexpected. What was a surprise was that black eyewitnesses bravely testified at the trial, despite threats against their lives.

The Montgomery Bus Boycott

In Montgomery, Alabama, African Americans decided to confront another form of white social control: segregation on the city bus line. The bus company practiced "rolling segregation," which required African-American passengers to take seats behind white riders and, if necessary, to give up seats and stand so that whites could sit. In this humiliating game of musical chairs, black Americans always lost.

On December 1, 1955, **Rosa Parks** refused to give up her seat on the bus so that a white man could sit. Mrs. Parks had not boarded the bus with the intention of disobeying the law, although she strongly opposed it. That afternoon, her fatigue and the humiliation of the demand to move were suddenly too much. She refused and was arrested. Local African-American leaders called for a boycott of the buses to begin on the day of Mrs. Parks's court appearance. They submitted proposals to the city and to bus officials calling for the hiring of black drivers and a more equitable system of seating.

On December 5, 1955, the night before the boycott was to begin, nearly four thousand people gathered at Holt Street Baptist Church to hear **Martin Luther King, Jr.,** the newly selected leader of the boycott movement. His words electrified the crowd. "We are here this evening," he announced,

---

Earl Warren   Chief justice of the Supreme Court from 1953 to 1969, under whom the Court issued decisions protecting civil rights, the rights of criminals, and First Amendment rights.

Southern Manifesto   Statement issued by one hundred southern congressmen in 1954 after the *Brown* decision, pledging to oppose desegregation.

Emmett Till   African-American teenager from Chicago who was killed in Mississippi in 1955 and whose confessed murderers were acquitted by an all-white jury.

Rosa Parks   Black seamstress who refused to give up her seat to a white man on a bus in Montgomery, Alabama, in 1955, triggering a bus boycott that stirred the civil rights movement.

Martin Luther King, Jr.   Ordained Baptist minister, brilliant orator, and civil rights leader committed to nonviolence, who led many important protests of the 1950s and 1960s; he was assassinated in Tennessee in 1968.

"to say to those who have mistreated us so long that we are tired—tired of being segregated and humiliated, tired of being kicked about by the brutal feet of oppression." He asked the crowd to boycott the buses. He urged his listeners to protest with love and, when confronted with violence, to "bless them that curse you."

On December 6, Rosa Parks was tried, found guilty, and fined $10 plus $4 in court costs. She appealed. Bus and city administrators met with boycott leaders but refused to budge. The boycott, 90 percent effective, stretched into days, weeks, and finally months. Police wrote hundreds of traffic tickets for those involved in the car pools that provided transportation for the boycotters. Insurance companies canceled automobile coverage. On January 30, 1956, a stick of dynamite destroyed King's front porch. Even in the face of personal attack, King urged supporters to avoid violence and to maintain the boycott. As the boycott approached its anniversary, the Supreme Court ruled in *Gayle et al. v. Browser* (1956) that the city's and the bus company's policy of segregation was unconstitutional. "Praise the Lord. God has spoken from Washington, D.C.," cried one boycotter.

The 381-day boycott was tremendously successful in establishing conditions for change. The traditional white view that African Americans accepted segregation had been shattered. In King, a leader had emerged determined to fight segregation throughout American society. Within weeks, he and other black leaders had formed a new civil rights organization, the **Southern Christian Leadership Conference (SCLC).** Across the South, thousands of African Americans took heart from the *Brown* and Montgomery decisions.

Ike and Civil Rights

The White House had little to say about the bus boycott. When asked, Eisenhower gave evasive replies: "I am for moderation, but I am for progress; that is exactly what I am for in this thing." Personally, Eisenhower believed that government, especially the executive branch, had little role in integration. Not all within the administration were

so unsympathetic toward civil rights. Attorney General Herbert Brownell drafted the first civil rights legislation since Reconstruction. The Civil Rights Act of 1957 provided for the formation of the U.S. Commission on Civil Rights and opened the possibility of using federal suits to ensure voter rights.

African Americans, meanwhile, made it more difficult for politicians to evade the issue of minority rights. For Eisenhower, the unavoidable finally came over the effort to integrate Central High School in **Little Rock,** Arkansas. Central High was scheduled to be integrated starting in 1957. Governor Orval Faubus, however, ordered National Guard troops to prevent desegregation.

For three weeks, the National Guard prevented nine black students from enrolling. Then, on September 20, a federal judge ordered the integration of Central High School. Faubus complied and withdrew the National Guard. But the crisis was not over. Segregationists were waiting for the black students on Monday, September 23, 1957. When they discovered that the nine had slipped into the school unnoticed, the mob rushed the police lines and battered the school doors, yelling, "Lynch the niggers!" Inside the school, Melba Pattillo Beals thought, "We are trapped. I'm going to die here, in school." School officials loaded the black students into cars and ordered the drivers not to stop: "If you hit somebody, you keep rolling, 'cause [if you stop] the kids are dead." The students escaped to safety.

The following morning, Little Rock's mayor asked for federal troops after angry white throngs began looting and burning part of the city. On September 24, Eisenhower nationalized the Arkansas

---

Southern Christian Leadership Conference Group formed by Martin Luther King, Jr., and others after the Montgomery bus boycott; it became the backbone of the civil rights movement in the 1950s and 1960s.

Little Rock Capital of Arkansas where Eisenhower sent federal troops in 1957 to protect black students entering an all-white high school and to end rioting by segregationist mobs.

♦ As Elizabeth Eckford approached Little Rock's Central High School, the crowd began to hurl curses, yelling "Lynch her! Lynch her!" and a National Guardsman blocked her entrance into the school with his rifle. Terrified, she retreated down the street away from the threatening mob. A week later, with army troops protecting her, Eckford finally attended—and integrated—Central High School. *Frances Miller, LIFE Magazine © Time Warner Inc.*

National Guard and dispatched a thousand federal troops to Little Rock. The president told the nation that he had sent the federal troops not to integrate the schools but to uphold the law and to restore order. It was a distinction lost on most white southerners.

The following school year (1957–1958), the city closed its high schools rather than integrate them. In response, the Supreme Court ruled in *Cooper v. Aaron* (1959) that such evasions of court-ordered integration were illegal. Little Rock's high schools reopened, and integration slowly spread to the lower grades. In Little Rock, as in many other communities, many white students fled the integrated public schools to attend private, segregated

schools. Federal power had been used to uphold integration in Little Rock, but meaningful integration of schools was still years away. Although Eisenhower had signed the Civil Rights Act of 1957, critics argued that he had provided little moral or political leadership.

Eisenhower and a Hostile World

Eisenhower and Secretary of State John Foster Dulles believed that the United States had a moral responsibility to protect the world from communism. During the 1952 campaign, Dulles had condemned containment as "appeasement" and promised a global "rollback" of communism. Dulles's language made good campaign rhetoric, but President Eisenhower quickly dismissed liberation and rollback as too provocative. In addition, the death of Soviet Premier Joseph Stalin shortly after Eisenhower assumed office raised the possibility of a less confrontational relationship with the Soviets. The president thus ended up seeking a modification of Truman's containment policy that would be less expensive, move the nation away from confrontation, and weaken the Soviet Union. This modification brought about the New Look policy.

The New Look

The New Look relied on cheaper nuclear deterrence, an enhanced arsenal of nuclear weapons, and the threat of **"massive retaliation"** to protect American international interests (see Map 28.1). In

> *Cooper v. Aaron*   Supreme Court ruling in 1959 that barred state authorities from interfering with desegregation either directly or through strategies of evasion.
>
> **"massive retaliation"**   Term used by John Foster Dulles in a 1954 speech implying that the United States was willing to use nuclear force in response to Communist aggression anywhere in the world.

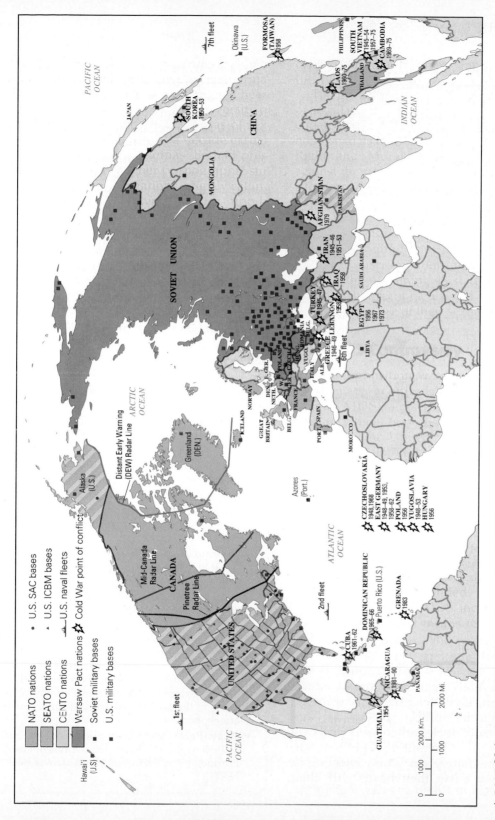

MAP 28.1 The Global Cold War During the Cold War, the United States and the Soviet Union faced each other as enemies. The United States attempted to construct a ring of containment around the Soviet Union and its allies, while the Soviets worked to expand their influence and power. This map shows the nature of this military confrontation—the bases, alliances, and flash points of the Cold War.

explaining the shift to more atomic weapons, Vice President Richard Nixon stated, "Rather than let the communists nibble us to death all over the world in little wars, we will rely . . . on massive mobile retaliation." Demonstrating its nuclear might, the United States exploded its first hydrogen bomb in November 1952. The Soviets tested theirs in August 1953.

Insiders recognized that the New Look policy was marred by several flaws. The central problem was where the United States should draw the massive retaliatory line. The Eisenhower administration's solution was to convince aggressors that the United States would rain nuclear destruction on any threat to its sphere of influence. This policy drew the label of **brinksmanship** because it required the administration to take the nation to the verge of war and trust that the opposition would back down. To convince the world of this daring boldness, Dulles and Eisenhower stressed that atomic weapons were as usable as conventional ones. Eisenhower privately was much more restrained in his willingness to "go nuclear." He recognized that a **thermonuclear** war would have no winners.

To Eisenhower's satisfaction, the nuclear threats seemed to produce immediate results. The North Koreans and Chinese signed a truce ending the Korean War. Although the death of Soviet leader Joseph Stalin now appears to have been the decisive factor, Eisenhower thought the New Look policy had paid off. To lend further credibility to atomic diplomacy, Eisenhower deployed intercontinental bombers carrying hydrogen bombs and dispatched **tactical nuclear weapons** to Europe.

The administration sought to convince the public that surviving an atomic war was possible. Underground **fallout shelters,** well stocked with food, water, and medical supplies, could, it was claimed, provide safety against an atomic attack. Across the nation, civil defense drills were established for factories, offices, businesses, and schools, including "duck-and-cover" drills in schools. Teachers would shout "Drop!" and students would immediately get into a kneeling or prone position and cover their heads with their hands.

Seeking ways to avoid a nuclear solution to international problems, Eisenhower and Dulles emphasized alliances and covert operations. Alliances would clearly mark areas protected by the American nuclear umbrella. They would also protect the United States from being drawn into limited, "brushfire" wars. When small conflicts broke out, the ground forces of regional allies, perhaps supported with American naval and air strength, would deal with them. Eisenhower concluded bilateral defense pacts with South Korea (1953) and Taiwan (1955) and a multilateral agreement, the Southeast Asia Treaty Organization (SEATO, 1954), that linked the United States, Australia, Thailand, the Philippines, Pakistan, New Zealand, France, and Britain. In the Middle East, the United States joined Britain, Iran, Pakistan, Turkey, and Iraq in the Baghdad Pact in 1957. This organization was later called the Central Treaty Organization (CENTO) after Iraq withdrew in 1959. In Europe, the United States welcomed West Germany into NATO. The Soviet bloc responded with the formation of a military alliance between Eastern European nations and the Soviet Union, the **Warsaw Pact,** in 1955.

brinksmanship Practice of seeking to win disputes in international politics by creating the impression of being willing to push a highly dangerous situation to the limit.

thermonuclear Relating to the fusion of atomic nuclei at high temperatures or to weapons based on fusion, as distinct from those based on fission.

tactical nuclear weapons Low-yield, short-range nuclear weapons designed to be used on the battlefield. By contrast, strategic nuclear weapons are used at long-range and intended to destroy large targets, such as cities.

fallout shelter Underground shelter stocked with food and supplies that was intended to provide safety in case of atomic attack; fallout refers to the nuclear particles falling through the atmosphere.

Warsaw Pact Alliance for mutual defense made in 1955 by the USSR and the nations of Eastern Europe; it was the Soviet bloc's answer to NATO.

Turmoil in the Middle East

In the Middle East, Arab nationalism, fired by anti-Israeli and anti-Western attitudes, posed a serious threat to American interests. Egypt and Iran offered the greatest challenges. Egyptian leader Colonel **Gamal Nasser** and Iranian Prime Minister Mohammed Mossadegh were attempting to expel British influence from their nations and grasp control over their valuable resources: the **Suez Canal** in Egypt and oil in Iran.

Although suspicious of Nasser, Eisenhower hoped to woo him with loans, cash, arms, and an offer to help build the **Aswan Dam** on the Nile. Nasser eventually rejected the American efforts, in large part because the United States wanted to promote an Egyptian-Israeli peace. When Nasser bought Soviet bloc weapons, Eisenhower concluded that he was an "evil influence" and canceled the Aswan Dam project in July 1956. Days later, Nasser nationalized the Anglo-French-owned Suez Canal. Israel, France, and Britain resorted to military action to regain control of the canal. On October 29, Israeli forces sliced through the Sinai toward Egypt. The French and British landed their forces in the canal zone on November 3.

Eisenhower was furious. He disliked Nasser, but he could not approve of armed aggression. Joined by the Soviets, Eisenhower sponsored a UN General Assembly resolution (November 2, 1956) calling for the removal of foreign troops from Egyptian soil. Faced with worldwide opposition, France, Britain, and Israel withdrew their forces. Nasser regained control of the canal and emerged as the uncontested leader of those opposing Western influence in Arab countries. The crisis also resulted in a growing Soviet presence in Egypt.

Elsewhere in the Middle East, Eisenhower had better luck. Nasser's actions led the Eisenhower administration to attempt to construct a Middle Eastern anti-Soviet alliance with the northern tier of Middle Eastern states. The major obstacle to such an alliance was Iran, where Prime Minister Mossadegh had nationalized British-owned oil properties and was unlikely to join an anti-Soviet alliance. Eisenhower gave the **Central Intelligence Agency (CIA)** the green light to overthrow the Iranian leader. On August 18, 1953, a mass demonstration funded and orchestrated by the CIA toppled the Mossadegh government. American money flowed into Iran to support the new government. A thankful Iranian government joined the anti-Soviet Baghdad Pact in 1956 and CENTO in 1959 and awarded the United States 40 percent of its oil production.

With Iran safely under American influence, Eisenhower redoubled his efforts to contain Nasser's **Pan-Arab movement** and an expanding Soviet presence in the region. To protect Arab friends from Communist or anti-Western rebellions, Eisenhower asked Congress for permission to commit American forces if their presence was requested. Congress agreed in March 1957 to provide $200 million in military and economic aid to the Middle East.

It did not take long for Eisenhower to use his power. When Jordan's King Hussein was threatened by an internal revolt, the White House announced that Jordan was "vital" to American interests, moved the 6th Fleet into the eastern Mediterranean, and supplied over $10 million in aid. King Hussein put down the revolt, dismissed parliament, and instituted authoritarian rule. In

Gamal Nasser   Prime minister and president of Egypt in the late 1950s; he was an Arab nationalist who sought to return valuable foreign-owned resources to Egyptian control.

Suez Canal   Canal running through Egypt from the Mediterranean to the Red Sea; it was under French and British control until 1955, when it was nationalized by Egypt.

Aswan Dam   Dam on the Nile River in Egypt intended to provide electric power and stop seasonal flooding; construction finally began in 1960.

Central Intelligence Agency   Agency established by Congress in 1947 to gather data and organize intelligence operations in foreign countries; it is responsible solely to the president.

Pan-Arab movement   Attempts to politically unify the Arab nations of the Middle East, which stressed freedom from Western control and opposition to Israel.

1958, when Lebanon's Christian president, Camile Chamoun, ignored his country's constitution and ran for a second term, nationalistic, anti-West Muslim elements rebelled. Eisenhower committed nearly fifteen thousand troops to protect the pro-American government at Chamoun's request. The American forces left in three months, after Chamoun, with American approval, had stepped down and been replaced by General Faud Chehab. Eisenhower had demonstrated his willingness to protect American interests but had done little to resolve the problems faced by Lebanon and the rest of the Middle East.

A Protective Neighbor

During the 1952 presidential campaign, Eisenhower had charged that Truman had allowed economic problems and popular uprisings to develop in Latin America and that these uprisings had been "skillfully exploited by the Communists." As president, Eisenhower intended to reverse that trend by offering anti-Communist governments economic, political, and military support. He was most concerned about Guatemala, where President Jocobo Arbenz had nationalized thousands of acres owned by the American-based United Fruit Company. These radical actions convinced the administration to use the CIA to remove Arbenz. The CIA supplied Guatemalan colonel Carlos Castillo Armas with "wads of dollar bills" and arms to overthrow the elected government. Colonel Armas launched the effort to "liberate" Guatemala on June 18, 1954, and within two weeks had established a new, pro-American government.

The other major trouble spot in Latin America was Cuba. By the mid-1950s, the corrupt and dictatorial Fulgencio Batista had become an embarrassment to the United States. Many Americans believed that **Fidel Castro,** who was leading a revolt against Batista, could be a pro-American reformer. By 1959, rebel forces had control of the island. But Castro's economic and social reforms soon seemed to endanger substantial American interests. U.S. investors controlled 40 percent of Cuba's sugar industry, 90 percent of Cuba's telephone and elec-

tric companies, 50 percent of its railroads, and 25 percent of its banking. Washington tried to push Cuba in the right direction by applying economic pressure. In February 1960, Castro reacted by signing an economic pact with the Soviet Union. Eisenhower termed Castro a "madman." In March, he approved a CIA plan to attack Castro. Actual implementation of that plan, however, would have to be approved by Eisenhower's successor.

The New Look in Asia

When Eisenhower took office, Asia was the focal point of Cold War tensions. Fighting continued in Korea, and in Indochina the Communist **Viet Minh,** led by Ho Chi Minh, were fighting a "war of national liberation" against the French.

Eisenhower continued Truman's policy of supporting French efforts to re-establish colonial rule and defeat communism. By 1954, the United States was paying nearly 78 percent of the war's cost. Articulating the **domino theory,** Eisenhower warned that if Indochina fell to communism, the loss "of Burma, of Thailand, of the [Malay] Peninsula, and Indonesia" would certainly follow, and possibly Australia and New Zealand.

The prospect of the first domino's toppling appeared imminent in 1954. By spring, Viet Minh forces had encircled the French fortress at Dienbienphu. Eisenhower transferred forty bombers to bolster the French in Vietnam. Some advisers wanted a more direct American role, but Eisenhower, believing that "no military victory is possible in that kind of theater," rejected such options. Dienbienphu fell on May 7, 1954, after a fifty-five-day siege.

Fidel Castro Cuban revolutionary leader who overthrew the corrupt regime of dictator Fulgencio Batista in 1959 and established a socialist state.

Viet Minh Vietnamese army made up of Communist and other nationalist groups, which fought the French from 1946 to 1954 to win independence from French rule.

domino theory Notion that if one nation comes under Communist control, then neighboring nations will follow.

Eisenhower was equally unhappy about the results of negotiations held at Geneva between the French and the Viet Minh. The **Geneva Agreement** "temporarily" partitioned Vietnam along the 17th parallel and created the neutral states of Cambodia and Laos. The two Vietnams were to hold elections to unify the nation within two years. American strategists called the loss of half of Vietnam a "disaster." The United States refused to sign the Geneva Agreement. To save South Vietnam, Eisenhower rushed advisers and aid to the government of Prime Minister Ngo Dinh Diem. With American blessings, Diem ignored the Geneva-mandated unification elections, repressed his political opposition, and in October 1955 staged a **plebiscite** that created the Republic of Vietnam and elected him president.

The Soviets and Cold War Politics

Although Eisenhower relied on deterrence to curb Soviet expansionism, he recognized that improved Soviet-American relations might prevent a nuclear confrontation. Negotiating with the Soviets was difficult for him. He questioned the Soviets' commitment to peace. Still, growing Soviet nuclear capabilities and the death of Stalin in 1953 provided the opportunity for reducing tensions. Soon after Stalin's death, the new Soviet leader, Georgii Malenkov, called for "peaceful coexistence." Eisenhower called on the Soviets to demonstrate their willingness to cooperate with the West. Malenkov complied. He agreed to consider some form of on-site inspection to verify any approved arms reductions. Eisenhower responded by asking the Soviets in December 1953 to work toward universal disarmament.

By then, world concern was growing not only about the threat of nuclear war but about the dangers of radiation from the testing of nuclear weapons. Worldwide pressures grew for a summit meeting to deal with the "balance of terror." In 1955, Eisenhower accepted a meeting with the new Soviet leadership of Nikolai Bulganin and **Nikita Khrushchev,** who had replaced Malenkov. Although the Geneva Summit produced no agreement, the meeting did reduce East-West tensions.

The spirit of Geneva quickly vanished when Soviet forces invaded Hungary in November 1956 to put down an anti-Soviet revolt. The Hungarians appealed to the world for help. None came from the United States. Seeing no way to help without risking all-out war, the administration could only watch as the Soviets crushed the revolt.

Eisenhower resumed discussions of a test ban with the Soviets in 1958 after Khrushchev announced a voluntary moratorium on nuclear weapons testing and called for a meeting to discuss the issue. Although the U.S. military said it needed more tests, Eisenhower agreed to hold discussions with the Soviets. Once again, however, the negotiations bogged down over the issue of **verification.** They became even more difficult when another Berlin crisis emerged. The Soviets announced in November 1958 that they intended to sign a treaty with East Germany that would terminate the West's right to occupy West Berlin. For Eisenhower, retreat from Berlin was unthinkable. American and NATO forces made plans for the defense of their zones of the city. Faced with unflinching Western determination, Khrushchev announced a permanent delay in the treaty. The crisis was over.

Khrushchev subsequently sought to smooth relations with the West. In September 1959, he made a twelve-day tour of the United States that included a stop at Camp David, the presidential retreat in Maryland. The Camp David conference produced no agreement, but Eisenhower and the

---

Geneva Agreement   Truce signed at Geneva in 1954 by French and Viet Minh representatives dividing Vietnam along the 17th parallel; the north became Communist and the south had a French-backed government.

plebiscite   Special election that allows people to either approve or reject a particular proposal.

Nikita Khrushchev   Soviet premier who denounced Stalin in 1956 and improved the USSR's image abroad; he was deposed in 1964 for his failure to improve the country's economy.

verification   In disarmament, the methods of inspection that allow each nation to ensure that the others are abiding by agreements.

Soviet premier announced that they would both attend a summit conference in Paris in May and that Eisenhower would later visit the Soviet Union.

The promising thaw in the Cold War proved short-lived once again. On May 1, 1960, an American U-2 spy plane was shot down over the Soviet Union, and its pilot, Francis Gary Powers, was captured. At first, the United States feebly denied the nature of the flight, saying the U-2 was only a weather plane. Khrushchev then showed pictures of the plane's wreckage and presented Major Powers, clearly proving the American spy mission. Eisenhower took full responsibility but refused to apologize for such flights. Khrushchev canceled from the Paris Summit, and Eisenhower canceled his trip to the Soviet Union.

Although Eisenhower was applauded for standing up to Khrushchev, the loss of the U-2, Soviet advances in missile technology and nuclear weaponry, and a Communist Cuba only 90 miles from Florida provided the Democrats with strong reasons to claim that the Republicans had been deficient in meeting Soviet threats. In 1960, turning the Republicans' own tactics of 1952 against them, the Democrats cheerfully accused their opponents of endangering the United States by being too soft on communism.

centered on affluent suburbs and a growing consumer culture. The images were partially true. Many white, middle-class Americans fulfilled their *expectations* by moving to the suburbs and living the American dream.

Economic realities, social prejudice, and dissatisfaction, however, contradicted the popular imagery. More married women *chose* to enter the work force. Many men and women behaved contrary to the supposed norms of family and suburban culture, while teens and young adults sometimes rejected or criticized established norms and values. The *outcome* was that even affluent suburbia was less stable than it appeared. African Americans *chose* to reshape the nation's social and political agendas. The *outcome* was that racial equality became an issue that neither society nor government could ignore.

Although promising change, Eisenhower *chose* foreign and domestic policies that continued the basic patterns established by Roosevelt and Truman. There were reductions in some domestic programs, but the public *expectations constrained* any large-scale dismantling of the New Deal. The New Look relied on new tactics, but Cold War foreign policies did not change significantly. Eisenhower continued containment and expanded American influence in southern Asia and the Middle East. Meanwhile, relations with the Soviet Union deteriorated with the launching of *Sputnik,* another Berlin crisis, Castro's victory in Cuba, and the U-2 incident.

SUMMARY

E xpectations
C onstraints
C hoices
O utcomes

"Had enough?" Republicans asked voters in 1952. Americans answered by electing Dwight D. Eisenhower. With Ike in the White House, the 1950s spawned popular, if flawed, images of America that reflected the *expectations* of many whose lives

SUGGESTED READINGS

Ambrose, Stephen E. *Eisenhower: The President* (1984).
A generally positive and well-balanced biography of Eisenhower as president by one of the most respected historians of the Eisenhower period.

Burk, Robert F. *The Eisenhower Administration and Black Civil Rights* (1984).
An insightful examination of federal policy and the civil rights movement.

Devine, Robert A. *Eisenhower and the Cold War* (1981).
A solid and brief account of Eisenhower's foreign policy, especially toward the Soviet Union.

Diggins, John Patrick. *The Proud Decades: America in War and Peace, 1941–1960* (1988).

A short, well-written, and well-researched examination of the postwar period.

Garrow, David J. *Bearing the Cross* (1986).

An in-depth description of the development of the civil rights movement and the role of Martin Luther King, Jr.

Halberstam, David. *The Fifties* (1993).

A positive interpretative view of the 1950s by a well-known journalist and author, especially recommended for its description of famous and not-so-famous people.

Kaledin, Eugenia. *Mothers and More: American Women in the 1950s* (1984).

A thoughtful look at the role of American women in society during the 1950s.

Miller, Douglas T., and Marion Novak. *The Fifties: The Way We Really Were* (1977).

An interesting, useful, and often-quoted description of American society during the 1950s.

THE STRUGGLE FOR CIVIL RIGHTS, 1960–1968 In the mid-1950s, African Americans chose to confront the system of prejudice and segregation that existed across the United States. This map shows the national scope of the civil rights movement from 1960 to 1968.

CANADA

WASHINGTON

Portland

OREGON

IDAHO

MONTANA

NORTH DAKOTA

SOUTH DAKOTA

WYOMING

NEBRASKA

MINN.

Minneapolis

WISCONSIN

MICH.

Flint
Pontiac
Milwaukee

Waterloo

IOWA

Chicago

South Bend

ILL.

IND.

Detroit

Cleveland

Toledo
OHIO
Youngstown
Dayton
Cincinnati

NEW YORK

Niagara
Falls

Rochester
Buffalo

White
Plains

VT.

N.H.

Boston

MASS.

R.I.
CONN.
Hartford
New York
Newark
N.J.
Philadelphia
Wilmington
DEL.
Baltimore
MD.
Cambridge

Englewood
PENN.

Pittsburgh

Washington
MAY 4

W.VA.

VIRGINIA

MAINE

NEVADA

Oakland
San Francisco
Palo Alto

CALIFORNIA

Los Angeles
(Watts)

ARIZONA

UTAH

COLORADO

Denver

KANSAS

Kansas
City

Wichita

MISSOURI

Louisville

KENTUCKY

TENN.

Nashville

Memphis

Greensboro
N.C.

SOUTH
CAROLINA

NEW MEXICO

OKLAHOMA

ARK.

Little
Rock

Pine Bluff

Itta Bena

Grenada
MISS.

Jackson
MAY 24

Birmingham
MAY 17

Anniston
MAY 14

Montgomery
MAY 20

ALA.

Atlanta MAY 13

Americus

GA.

Tucson

TEXAS

Houston

New Orleans

LA.

Tallahassee

Jacksonville
St. Augustine

FLA.

Tampa

Riviera Beach

ATLANTIC
OCEAN

PACIFIC
OCEAN

MEXICO

Gulf of Mexico

CUBA

PACIFIC
OCEAN

HAWAI'I

0 100 Km.

0 100 Mi.

U.S.S.R.

ALASKA

CANADA

0 250 500 Km.

0 250 500 Mi.

PACIFIC
OCEAN

0   200   400 Km.

0   200   400 Mi.

Major riots

● 1965
● 1966
● 1967
● 1968

■ Peaceful
demonstrations

← Route of first
Freedom Riders, 1961

● Kennedy elected

● Sit-ins begin

● Berlin
Wall
erected

● Port Huron
Statement

● King's "Letter from a Birmingham Jail"

● Kennedy
assassinated;
Johnson
becomes
president

● Johnson
elected

● Watts
riot

● Black Panthers
formed

● Martin Luther King, Jr., assassinated

● Urban riots peak

● Woodstock

| 1960 | 1961 | 1962 | 1963 | 1964 | 1965 | 1966 | 1968 | 1969 |

| 1850 | 1900 | 1950 | 2000 |

Great Promises, Bitter Disappointments, 1960–1968

Kennedy and the New Frontier

- What expectations did John Kennedy and his advisers have, and how did those expectations run into constraints?

- How did Kennedy's civil rights choices differ from Eisenhower's?

- How did civil rights activists choose to confront those resisting integration in the South?

Flexible Response

- What expectations shaped Kennedy's choices in foreign policy?

- What were some of the outcomes of Kennedy's concerns and interests in the Third World?

Beyond the New Frontier

- How did Lyndon Johnson's Great Society program expand on the expectations of the New Deal?

- How did Johnson choose to attack the constraints that African Americans and other minorities were facing?

New Agendas

- What constraints influenced the civil rights movement in the mid-1960s? What was the outcome?

- What choices did the youth movement explore? How justified were young people's criticisms of traditional American society?

INTRODUCTION

Expectations
Constraints
Choices
Outcomes

John F. Kennedy symbolized a new beginning and promised a better society for all Americans. He energized the nation, raising *expectations*, especially among the poor and minorities, that he would press for solutions to end poverty and discrimination. But Kennedy faced political *constraints* from conservatives in Congress who objected to an expansion of liberal programs and civil rights legislation. As a result, during his three years in office, Kennedy achieved only some of his goals. He *chose* to delay civil rights legislation. The *outcome* was a domestic record of legislation that expanded on existing programs but did not chart new paths of social policy.

Kennedy also vowed to intensify the global struggle against communism. To defeat communism, he *chose* to fund both an arms race and a space race with the Soviet Union. Yet the *outcome* was not a safer and less divided world. The erection of the Berlin Wall, the Cuban missile crisis, and events in Vietnam symbolized heightened tensions.

Building on Kennedy's legacy, Lyndon Johnson *chose* to create the largest expansion of New Deal–style legislation since the Depression. Johnson's Great Society waged a war on poverty and discrimination, promoted education, and created a national system of healthcare for the aged and poor. Johnson, too, faced *constraints*. Conservatives opposed the Great Society's social and political goals, and some moderates objected to its cost and the ineffectiveness of many programs. An expanding war in Vietnam also added *constraints* to Johnson's domestic program.

By 1968, growing social and political turmoil was contributing to the rejection of liberal policies. The optimistic *expectations* Kennedy had inspired were declining amid the divisions of American society. Within the civil rights movement, Black Power leaders *chose* confrontation over compromise. Urban riots and violence drove wedges between African-American leaders and some white supporters. The emergence of a youth-centered **counterculture** that *chose* to reject traditional social and moral values also worked to fragment American society. The *outcome* was that a decade that began with great optimism ended with diminished *expectations* of what the federal government could accomplish.

Kennedy and the New Frontier

Republicans had every reason to worry as the 1960 presidential campaign neared. The last years of the 1950s had not been kind to the Republican party. The Cold War seemed to be going badly as the Soviets downed an American spy plane over the Soviet Union, launched *Sputnik* into space, and supported Castro in Cuba. Domestically, there seemed little or no direction from the White House. The Democrats had gained control of Congress in 1958. The economy also had lapsed into a recession.

On the Democratic side loomed **John Fitzgerald Kennedy,** a youthful, vigorous senator from Massachusetts. Kennedy, a Harvard graduate, came from a wealthy Catholic family. Some worried

counterculture A culture with values or lifestyles in opposition to those of the established culture.
John Fitzgerald Kennedy Massachusetts senator who was elected president in 1960, established the Peace Corps, and forced Khrushchev to remove Soviet missiles from Cuba; he was assassinated in 1963.

CHRONOLOGY

New Frontiers

1960	Kennedy elected president
	Sit-ins begin
	Boynton v. Virginia
1961	Bay of Pigs invasion
	Alliance for Progress
	Peace Corps formed
	Berlin Wall erected
	Vienna Summit
	Freedom rides begin
	SNCC formed
1962	Cuban missile crisis
	James Meredith enrolls at the University of Mississippi
	SDS's Port Huron Statement
1963	Martin Luther King, Jr.'s "Letter from a Birmingham Jail"
	Limited Test Ban Treaty
	Gideon v. Wainright
	March on Washington
	Ngo Dinh Diem assassinated
	Kennedy assassinated; Johnson becomes president

1964	Civil Rights Act
	Freedom Summer in Mississippi
	War on Poverty begins
	Johnson elected president
	Escobedo v. Illinois
	Griswold v. Connecticut
	Berkeley Free Speech Movement
1965	Malcolm X assassinated
	Watts riot
	Selma march
	Voting Rights Act
	Medicaid and Medicare established
	Elementary and Secondary Education Act
1966	Stokely Carmichael announces Black Power
	Black Panther party formed
	Miranda v. Arizona
1967	More than seventy-five major urban riots
1968	Martin Luther King, Jr., assassinated
	Urban riots in more than 125 cities
	Kerner Commission report

about his young age (43) and lack of experience, and others worried about his religion—no Catholic had ever been elected president. To lessen these possible liabilities, Kennedy had added the politically savvy Senate majority leader, **Lyndon Baines Johnson** of Texas, to the ticket, called for a new generation of leadership, and emphasized that those who were making religion an issue were bigots. He challenged the nation to enter a **New Frontier,** to improve the overall quality of life for all Americans, and to reinvigorate American foreign policy against communism.

Facing Kennedy was Eisenhower's vice president, Richard M. Nixon. Trying to distance himself from the image of Eisenhower's elderly leadership, Nixon promised a forceful, energetic presidency and emphasized his executive experience and history of anticommunism. He, too, promised to improve the quality of life, support civil rights, and defeat international communism.

Politics entered a new era in 1960 when the two candidates agreed to hold televised debates. Nixon

Lyndon Baines Johnson Senate majority leader who became Kennedy's vice president in 1961 and president when Kennedy was assassinated in 1963.

New Frontier Program for social and educational reform put forward by John F. Kennedy; though charismatically presented, it was resisted by Congress.

was proud of his debating skills and thought he could score many points against Kennedy. Kennedy recognized, however, that the candidate who appeared calmer and more knowledgeable would "win" the debate. Nixon made a poor impression before the camera. He appeared tired and haggard. He looked at Kennedy and not the camera when answering questions. Worst of all, he sweated. By contrast, Kennedy appeared fresh and confident. The differences in appearance were critical. The radio audience believed that Nixon won the debates, but to the 70 million television viewers, the winner was the self-assured and sweat-free Kennedy.

The televised debates helped Kennedy, but victory rested on his ability to hold the Democratic coalition together. The Texan Johnson used his political clout to keep the South largely loyal even as Kennedy blasted the lack of Republican leadership on civil rights. Kennedy scored the narrowest of victories. Nixon carried more states, 25 to 21, but Kennedy had a narrow margin over Nixon in popular votes and won the electoral count, 303 to 219 (see Map 29.1).

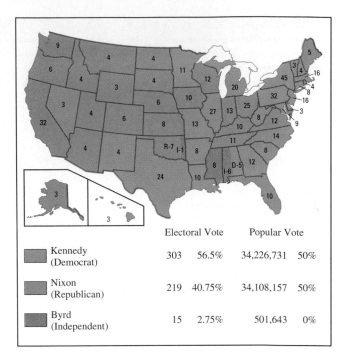

		Electoral Vote		Popular Vote	
	Kennedy (Democrat)	303	56.5%	34,226,731	50%
	Nixon (Republican)	219	40.75%	34,108,157	50%
	Byrd (Independent)	15	2.75%	501,643	0%

♦ **MAP 29.1 Election of 1960**   Although Richard Nixon won in more states than John F. Kennedy, Kennedy defeated his Republican opponent by a slim eighty-four electoral votes and fewer than nineteen thousand popular votes in the closest presidential election in the twentieth century.

The New Frontier

Kennedy's inaugural address fired the imagination of the nation. Speaking in idealistic terms, he promised to march against "the common enemies of man: tyranny, poverty, disease, and war itself." He asked all Americans to participate, exhorting them to "ask not what your country can do for you—ask what you can do for your country."

Kennedy's staff and cabinet kept up the image of change and activism. Recruiting from businesses and universities, he appointed men and women whom one reporter dubbed the "best and the brightest." Rhodes scholars and Harvard professors descended on the White House. They included historian Arthur Schlesinger, economist John Kenneth Galbraith (both personal advisers), McGeorge Bundy (national security director), and Dean Rusk (secretary of state). Ford Motor Company's president, Robert McNamara, was tapped for secretary of defense. In a controversial move, Kennedy gave the position of attorney general to his younger brother Robert. John Kennedy praised his choices as men with the "know-how" to solve

problems. Not everyone was impressed. Speaker of the House Sam Rayburn remarked that he would "feel a whole lot better . . . if just one of them had run for sheriff once."

Kennedy was politically astute enough to recognize that the new Congress was likely to be an obstacle to substantial innovation. The Democrats lost twenty-two seats in the House in the 1960 elections. Although the Democrats still controlled both houses of Congress, Kennedy could not count on many conservative, southern Democrats to support the New Frontier. Therefore, he opted to push for a limited domestic agenda that included traditional Democratic proposals such as a higher minimum wage and increased Social Security benefits. He decided to delay civil rights and social legislation and instead concentrate on shaping foreign policy and improving the economy.

To spur economic recovery, Kennedy called for more government spending and business- and income-tax cuts. The defense budget was the first beneficiary, growing by almost 20 percent. Meanwhile, the economy rebounded from the "Eisenhower recession," as unemployment fell to 5 percent.

When liberals complained about the lack of civil rights legislation and new social programs, Kennedy pointed to the coalition of Republicans and conservative Democrats. "There is no sense in raising hell and then not being successful," he observed. He promised a civil rights bill and programs to attack poverty in 1963 and 1964.

Civil Rights and the Kennedys

During the campaign, Kennedy had promised "moral leadership" in support of civil rights, but once in office, he moved cautiously. He did appoint several blacks to high office and district courts, including Thurgood Marshall to the United States Circuit Court, but civil rights advocates were far from satisfied. They noted that some judicial appointments went to recognized segregationists, including Harold Cox of Mississippi, who had once referred to African Americans as "niggers" and "chimpanzees" in court. Kennedy did not ban segregation in federal housing until November 1962.

Civil rights activists were resolved, nevertheless, to force an end to segregation. Even as Kennedy assumed office, a new wave of black activism was striking at segregation in the South. The **sit-in** movement began when four freshmen at North Carolina A&T in Greensboro, decided to integrate the public lunch counter at the local Woolworth's store. On February 1, 1960, they entered the store, sat down at the counter, and ordered a meal. A black waitress told them she could not serve them, but still they sat and waited for service. No one tried to remove or arrest them. When the store closed, they were still unserved. They returned to campus as heroes. The next day, twenty A&T students sat at the lunch counter demanding service. By the end of the week, similar sit-ins had spread throughout the South.

In April 1961, the **Student Nonviolent Coordinating Committee (SNCC,** pronounced "snick") was formed to coordinate the increasing number of sit-ins and boycotts of stores, recreational facilities, libraries, bus and train stations, and lunchrooms. Although SNCC professed **nonviolence,** it was much more militant than King's Southern Christian Leadership Conference (SCLC). SNCC spurred more than seventy thousand people to protest for integrated public facilities in more than 140 cities, including some outside the South. Many of those participating in demonstrations were young college students. In some cities, including Greensboro, demonstrators achieved equal service with a minimum of resistance, but particularly in the Deep South, whites reacted violently. Officials in Orangeburg, South Carolina, blasted protesters with high-pressure fire hoses and arrested them.

Sharing headlines with those "sitting in" were the **freedom riders.** Prior to Kennedy's taking office, the Supreme Court had ruled in *Boynton v. Virginia* (1960) that all interstate buses, trains, and terminals be desegregated. James Farmer of the Congress of Racial Equality (CORE) planned a series of "freedom rides" to force integration on southern bus lines and stations. Farmer knew that riders would meet with opposition and hoped to put pressure on the president to uphold the Court's decision. The first buses of freedom riders left Washington, D.C., in May 1961, headed toward Alabama and Mississippi. The freedom riders expected trouble. Governor John Patterson of Alabama had announced that integration would come only over his "dead body." In Anniston, Alabama, a mob of angry whites attacked the buses, setting them on fire and severely beating several freedom riders. The savagery continued at Birmingham. When asked why no police were at the station to protect the

sit-in The act of occupying the seats or an area of a segregated establishment to protest racial discrimination.

Student Nonviolent Coordinating Committee Organization formed to give young blacks a greater voice in the civil rights movement; it initiated black voter registration drives and freedom rides.

freedom riders Civil rights protesters who rode buses throughout the South in 1961 to press for integration in bus terminals.

riders, Birmingham public safety commissioner Eugene "Bull" Connor explained that it was a holiday—Mother's Day.

As Farmer had predicted, the violence forced the federal government to respond. Hoping to avoid further bloodshed, Justice Department official John Seigenthaler obtained state and local protection for the riders through Alabama. But as the buses approached Montgomery, the police and National Guard escorts mysteriously vanished, leaving the freedom riders to face a large and violent crowd alone. A brutal attack left many freedom riders injured, including Seigenthaler, who was beaten unconscious. After an hour of terror, the police finally arrived and restored order.

A livid Attorney General Robert Kennedy deputized local federal officials as marshals and ordered them to escort the freedom riders to the state line, where Mississippi forces took over. Battered and bloodied, the riders continued to the state capital, Jackson. There they were peacefully arrested for violating Mississippi's recently passed **public order laws.** The jails quickly filled as more freedom riders arrived and were arrested. The nation waited for the administration to act. Finally, in September 1961, the Interstate Commerce Commission declared that it would uphold the Court's decision prohibiting segregation. Faced with direct federal involvement, most state and local authorities grudgingly accepted the desegregation of bus and train terminals.

Hoping to steer the activism away from freedom rides and sit-ins, the Kennedy administration argued that efforts should be focused on voter registration drives. There followed the Voter Education Project, a cooperative movement among the major civil rights organizations, which with federal protection would provide the right to vote to many who had been denied since the days of Reconstruction. The results of this effort, which ended in 1964, seemed impressive: the percentage of black voters in the South increased from 29.4 percent to 43.1 percent of blacks eligible to vote. But most of the success came in urban areas, where white opposition was less pronounced than in rural areas. In addition, many of those involved in voter registration were brutally attacked and jailed. The federal government provided minimal protection on the whole.

In some instances, Robert Kennedy hoped to prevent racial violence by a show of federal force, as in the case of **James Meredith,** who integrated the University of Mississippi in 1962. Kennedy sent 500 federal marshals to guard Meredith, hoping that a show of force would prevent violence. The tactic did not work. Thousands of white students and nonstudents attacked Meredith and the marshals. Two people were killed and 166 marshals were wounded before 5,000 army troops arrived. Protected by federal forces, Meredith, who had transferred from a black college, became the University of Mississippi's first African-American graduate in May 1963.

Martin Luther King, Jr., and the SCLC focused their attention next on overturning segregation in Birmingham, Alabama. Organizers planned a series of protest marches demanding the integration of Birmingham's businesses. On Good Friday, 1963, King led the first march and along with others was arrested. From his cell, he wrote a nineteen-page "letter" aimed at those who denounced his activism in favor of patience. The "Letter from a Birmingham Jail" called for immediate and continuous, peaceful civil disobedience. Freedom was "never given voluntarily by the oppressor," King asserted, but "must be demanded by the oppressed." Smuggled out of jail and read aloud in churches and printed in newspapers across the nation, the letter rallied support for King's efforts in Birmingham.

On May 3, young and old alike filled the streets of Birmingham and confronted "Bull" Connor's police, who attacked the marchers with nightsticks, dogs, and high-pressure fire hoses. Television caught it all. Connor's brutality not only horrified much of the American public but caused many Birmingham blacks to reject the tactic of

---

public order laws Laws passed by many southern communities to discourage civil rights protests; they allowed the police to arrest anyone suspected of intending to disrupt public order.

James Meredith Black student admitted to the University of Mississippi under federal court order in 1962; in spite of rioting by racist mobs, he finished the year and graduated in 1963.

◆ On August 28, 1963, one-quarter of a million people gathered in Washington, D.C., to support racial equality. Martin Luther King, Jr., electrified the crowd by saying, "I have a dream that my four little children will one day live . . . where they will not be judged by the color of their skin but the content of their character." *Francis Miller, LIFE Magazine, © Time Warner Inc.*

nonviolence. The following day, many African Americans fought the police with stones and clubs. Fearing more violence, Birmingham's businessmen met with King on May 10, 1963, and agreed to hire black salespeople. Neither the agreement nor King's pleading, however, halted the violence. Two days later, President Kennedy ordered three thousand troops to Birmingham to maintain order.

Kennedy concluded that the time had come to fulfill his campaign promise to make civil rights a priority. In June 1963, observing that America could not be truly free "until all its citizens were free," he announced that he would send Congress civil rights legislation mandating integration in places of public accommodation.

To pressure Congress to act on the bill, King and other civil rights leaders organized the **March on Washington.** The August 28 march drew the largest crowd in American history, with over 250,000 people attending. King capped the day with an address that electrified the throng. He promised to continue the struggle until justice flowed "like a mighty stream," but he warned about a "whirlwind of revolt" if black rights were denied. "I have a dream," he offered, "that even Mississippi could become an oasis of freedom and justice" and that "all of God's children, black men and white men,

Jews and Gentiles, Protestants and Catholics, will be able to join hands and sing . . . 'Free at last! Free at last! Thank God almighty, we are free at last!'"

The march and reactions to white violence against African Americans might have been expected to work in favor of civil rights legislation. But as of November 1963, when Kennedy left for a campaign trip to Dallas, Texas, his bill was still languishing in committee in the House of Representatives.

Flexible Response

If Kennedy was slow to bring federal power to bear on civil rights, he had no reluctance to use

> **nonviolence** Doctrine of rejecting violence in favor of peaceful tactics as a means of gaining political objectives.
>
> **March on Washington** Meeting of a quarter of a million civil rights supporters in Washington in 1963, at which Martin Luther King, Jr., delivered his "I Have a Dream" speech.

◆ Soviet leader Nikita Khrushchev met with John Kennedy at the Vienna Summit in June 1961. After their first meetings, Kennedy, who had been warned that Khrushchev's style ranged from "cherubic to choleric," was convinced that the Soviet leader had bested him and that he had appeared to be a man "with no guts." Following the Vienna Summit, Kennedy was determined to be tougher with the Soviets. "If Khrushchev wants to rub my nose in the dirt, it's all over," Kennedy stated after their meeting. *Wide World Photos.*

executive power when it came to foreign policy. Kennedy increased military spending to begin a buildup of both nuclear and conventional forces. Space exploration also received a new priority. In April 1961, the Soviets had hurled the first human being, **cosmonaut** Yuri Gagarin, into space. Kennedy informed Congress that funding was needed not only to catch up with the Soviets but to beat them to the moon by the end of the decade. Congress agreed and funded the *Apollo* project.

The country's Cold War challenges were not limited to racing against Soviet arms development and space exploration. An equally important confrontation had been shaping up in the developing regions of the globe. Kennedy employed the strategy of **flexible response** to win the "hearts and minds" of developing nations for the West. This strategy involved special military units like the Green Berets who were trained to deal with Communist insurgency by living off the land and gaining the people's trust. The strategy also featured the use of American economic aid and of the **Peace Corps,** composed of idealistic young men and women who volunteered to help the people of the developing world.

Confronting the Soviets

Kennedy's biggest immediate problem in the Third World lay just to the south of the Florida Keys. The presence of a Communist regime in Cuba was simply intolerable to Kennedy. In January 1961, the newly elected president approved the operation planned by the Eisenhower administration to topple Fidel Castro (see page 636).

The invasion of Cuba began on April 17, 1961. Over fourteen hundred CIA-trained Cuban exiles landed at the **Bay of Pigs.** The predicted uprisings

cosmonaut A Soviet astronaut.

flexible response Kennedy's strategy of considering a variety of military and nonmilitary options when facing foreign policy decisions.

Peace Corps Program established by President Kennedy in 1961 to send young American volunteers to other nations as educators, health workers, and technicians.

Bay of Pigs Site of a 1961 invasion of Cuba by Cuban exiles and mercenaries sponsored by the CIA; the invasion was crushed within three days and embarrassed the United States.

in support of the invaders did not occur, however, and within three days Castro's forces had captured or killed most of the invading force. Kennedy took responsibility for the fiasco but voiced no regrets for his aggressive policy.

To blunt the growing appeal of Castroism in Latin America, Kennedy announced a sweeping foreign-aid package, the **Alliance for Progress.** He proposed over $20 billion in aid to show that "liberty and progress walk hand in hand." In return, Latin American nations were to introduce land and tax reforms. Actions fell short of promises. The United States granted far less than proposed, and Latin American governments implemented few reforms and frequently squandered the aid, much of which ended up in the pockets of government officials. Throughout the 1960s in Latin America, the gap between rich and poor widened.

To try to recapture some of the "can-do" image deflated by the Bay of Pigs disaster, Kennedy sought an opportunity to stand toe to toe with the Soviets. That opportunity came when Soviet leader Nikita Khrushchev agreed to meet Kennedy in Vienna in June 1961 to discuss Berlin, Laos, and a nuclear test ban treaty. After his first private meeting with the Soviet leader, Kennedy was shaken and angry. He thought that Khrushchev had bullied him. In following meetings, Kennedy stood his ground more firmly, stressing that the United States would remain true to its international commitments, especially in Berlin. Khrushchev was unmoved and maintained a December deadline for Allied withdrawal from Berlin.

Returning home, Kennedy asked for large increases in military spending and called fifty-one thousand reservists to active duty. Some advisers advocated the use of force if the Soviets interfered with Western control of West Berlin. To some it appeared that Kennedy and Khrushchev were moving to the brink of war over Berlin. In August 1961, the Soviets added a new point of confrontation by erecting a wall between West and East Berlin to choke off the flow of refugees fleeing East Germany. Although the Berlin Wall challenged Western ideals of freedom, it did not directly threaten the West's presence in West Berlin. The Berlin crisis finally faded when Khrushchev announced that he no longer cared about the December deadline. The wall remained as a stark re-

minder of where Soviet and American interests collided.

Far more serious than the Berlin crisis was the Cuban missile crisis of October 1962. On October 14, an American U-2 spy plane discovered that medium-range nuclear missile sites were being built in Cuba. Such missiles would drastically reduce the time the United States had to launch a counterattack on the Soviet Union. Kennedy decided on a showdown with the Soviets over the missiles.

Kennedy rejected both an invasion of Cuba and air strikes against the missiles as too dangerous. Instead, he decided on a naval blockade of Cuba until Khrushchev met the U.S. demand to remove the missiles. On Wednesday, October 24, a confrontation seemed imminent as two Soviet freighters and a Russian submarine approached the quarantine line. The Soviet vessels, however, stopped short of the line. Khrushchev had decided not to test Kennedy's will. On October 26, he sent a message that the Soviet Union was ready to remove the missiles from Cuba if the United States publicly announced it would not invade the island. The basis of a solution had been found. The United States publicly pledged not to invade Cuba, and Khrushchev ordered the removal of the missiles. In a nonpublicized, separate agreement, the United States agreed to remove its missiles from Turkey.

Kennedy basked in the victory over Khrushchev, but he also recognized how near the world had come to nuclear war. Kennedy subsequently sought to defuse Soviet-American tensions. A "hotline" telephone link was established between Moscow and Washington to allow direct talks in case of another East-West crisis. In June 1963, Kennedy suggested that the United States would halt its nuclear testing. By July, American-Soviet negotiations produced the **Limited Test Ban Treaty.**

Alliance for Progress   Program proposed by Kennedy in 1961 through which the United States provided aid for social and economic programs in Latin American countries.

Limited Test Ban Treaty   Treaty signed by the United States, the USSR, and nearly one hundred other nations in 1963, banning nuclear weapons tests in the atmosphere, in outer space, and underwater.

It prohibited nuclear tests in the atmosphere, in space, and under the seas but allowed underground testing. By October 1963, one hundred nations had signed the treaty, although the two newest atomic powers, France and China, refused to participate.

Vietnam

Vietnam represented one of the most significant challenges that Kennedy faced. South Vietnamese president **Ngo Dinh Diem** was losing control of the countryside to the South Vietnamese Communist rebels, the **Viet Cong.** Kennedy rejected arguments that American troops were needed to turn the tide, but he did send more military and civilian "advisers." By November 1963, the United States had committed sixteen thousand advisers to Vietnam—compared with only a few hundred in 1961.

The Viet Cong were only part of the problem. Diem's administration was unpopular. A Roman Catholic whose family had been French officials, Diem did not believe in democracy. He ruled through a handpicked, largely Catholic bureaucracy. Everyone else, including Vietnam's Buddhists, the religious majority, opposed his rule. With American support, Diem cracked down on his opponents. Reformers, rival officers, and protesting Buddhists were jailed, tortured, and killed. In protest, on June 10, 1963, a Buddhist monk set himself on fire. Other **self-immolations** followed. To the shock of many Americans, Diem's sister-in-law, Madame Nhu, referred to the protests as "Buddhist barbecues." To Kennedy and his advisers, Diem had become a liability. The administration secretly informed several Vietnamese generals that it would approve of a change of government. The army acted on November 1, killing Diem and creating a new military government. However, the new government brought neither political stability nor better results against the Viet Cong.

Death in Dallas

In late 1963, Kennedy decided to visit Dallas, Texas, to try to heal divisions within the Texas Democratic party. There he was assassinated on November 22. Police quickly captured the reputed assassin, Lee Harvey Oswald. The next day, a local nightclub owner, Jack Ruby, shot Oswald to death in the basement of the police station. Many wondered if Oswald had acted alone or was part of a larger conspiracy. To dispel rumors, the government formed a commission headed by Chief Justice Earl Warren to investigate the assassination. The commission announced that Oswald had acted alone. Most Americans accepted the findings at the time.

Kennedy's assassination traumatized the nation. Many people canonized the fallen president as a brilliant, innovative chief executive who combined vitality, youth, and good looks with forceful leadership and good judgment. Lyndon B. Johnson, sworn in as president as he flew back to Washington on the plane carrying Kennedy's body, was not cut from the same cloth. Kennedy had attended the best eastern schools, enjoyed the cultural and social life associated with wealth, and liked to surround himself with intellectuals. Johnson, a product of public schools and a state college education, distrusted intellectuals. Raised in the hill country of Texas, his passion was politics. By 1960, his congressional experience was unrivaled: he had served from 1937 to 1948 in the House of Representatives and from 1949 to 1961 in the Senate, where he had been Senate majority leader. Johnson knew how to wield political power and how to get things done in Washington.

Beyond the New Frontier

Five days after Kennedy's death, Johnson asked Congress for "no memorial oration or eulogy" for

---

Ngo Dinh Diem President of South Vietnam (1954–1963), who jailed and tortured opponents of his rule; he was assassinated in a coup in 1963.

Viet Cong Vietnamese Communist rebels in South Vietnam.

self-immolation Suicide by fire as an act of sacrifice to a cause.

the fallen president other than the passage of Kennedy's civil rights bill. The **Civil Rights Act of 1964** became law on July 2, 1964. The law made it illegal to discriminate for reasons of race, religion, or gender in places and businesses that served the public. Putting force behind the law, Congress established a federal Fair Employment Practices Committee (FEPC) and empowered the executive branch to withhold federal funds from institutions that violated the act.

Johnson wanted to do more, however, than pass legislation that had been initiated by Kennedy. He wanted to create his own legacy. His first step in realizing this ambition was declaring the **War on Poverty** in 1964.

Johnson's assault against the poverty that afflicted at least one-fifth of the American people was to be fought on two fronts: expanding opportunities and improving the social environment. He believed that only the federal government was capable of this task. Therefore, he projected a huge expansion of federal responsibility for social welfare. Special efforts would be made to provide education and job training for the young: "Our chief weapons will be better schools . . . better training, and better job opportunities to help more Americans, especially young Americans, to escape from squalor and misery." The Manpower and Development Training Act, the Job Corps, Head Start, and the Work Incentive Program all aimed at providing new educational and economic opportunities for the disadvantaged. In 1964, the Job Corps enrolled unemployed teenagers and young adults (ages 16 to 21) who lacked employable skills. In 1965, Head Start reached out to disadvantaged preschoolers to give them an opportunity to gain important thinking and social skills.

Conservative Response

Johnson's social programs prompted a reaction from a group of conservatives and ultraconservatives called the New Right. The New Right decried many of the political and social changes taking place in society. According to these conservatives, liberals and a national welfare state were destroying the traditional American values of localism, self-help, and individualism.

The New Right targeted the Supreme Court and Chief Justice Earl Warren as the major causes of what it regarded as the subversion of American life. The rabidly anti-Communist John Birch Society even demanded the impeachment of Warren. From the mid-1950s through the 1960s, the Supreme Court under Warren handed down one decision after another that angered conservatives. To them, the Court seemed to be forcing the liberal agenda of individual rights, social justice, and equality down society's throat. The Court, they believed, had promoted civil rights and the rights of individuals at the expense of society. In *Gideon v. Wainright* (1963) and *Escobedo v. Illinois* (1964), the Court's rulings declared that all defendants had a right to an attorney, even if the state had to provide one. In *Miranda v. Arizona* (1966), the Court held that anyone who was arrested had to be informed of his or her right to remain silent and to have an attorney present during questioning (now called the Miranda warning). The New Right argued that these decisions had tipped the scales of justice in favor of the criminal.

Conservatives believed that the Warren Court's actions also threatened traditional values by allowing the publication of sexually explicit materials and by forbidding prayers and the reading of the Bible in public schools (*Abington v. Schempp*, 1963). The Court's decision in *Griswold v. Connecticut* (1964), which overturned Connecticut's laws forbidding the sale of contraceptives, also disturbed them.

The 1964 Election

The Republican presidential candidate in 1964 offered conservatives a chance to reassert their traditional values and patriotic ideals. Senator Barry Goldwater of Arizona had voted against the Civil Rights Act of 1964 and against censuring Senator

---

Civil Rights Act of 1964 Law that barred segregation in public facilities and forbade employers to discriminate on the basis of race, religion, sex, or national origin.

War on Poverty Lyndon Johnson's program to help Americans escape poverty through education, job training, and community development.

Joseph McCarthy in 1954 (see page 629). He had opposed "Big Government" and he promised to deal with Communists more forcefully. Whereas Johnson promised not to Americanize the war in Vietnam, Goldwater was willing to commit American troops and even to use nuclear weapons.

In a war of slogans and television spots, Johnson's ads scored more points. Democrats answered one memorable Goldwater slogan, "In your heart you know he's right," by claiming, "In your guts you know he's nuts." Another Johnson ad suggested that a trigger-happy Goldwater would lead the nation into a nuclear holocaust. In a lopsided election, Americans gave Goldwater only 38.4 percent of the popular vote. Over forty new Democratic legislators swelled the Democratic majority in the House of Representatives.

Shaping the Great Society

Having beaten Goldwater, Johnson pushed forward legislation to enact his **Great Society**—his vision of an America freed of racial injustice and poverty. Between 1965 and 1968, more than sixty programs were put in place. Most sought to provide better economic and social opportunities. The Appalachian Regional Development Act (1965), Public Works and Development Act (1965), and Model Cities Act (1966) focused on developing economic growth in cities and long-depressed regional areas. The Omnibus Housing Bill (1965) provided $8 billion for constructing low- and middle-income housing and supplementing low-income rent programs.

Johnson's priorities, however, were health and education. The Elementary and Secondary Education Act (1965) was the first general educational funding act passed by the federal government. It granted more than a billion dollars to public and parochial schools for textbooks, library materials, and special-education programs. Poorer school districts were supposed to receive the highest percentage of federal support, but much of the money went to more affluent suburban school districts.

Passage of the Medical Care Act (1965) represented an even greater achievement to Johnson. This act revolutionized healthcare by providing **Medicare** to help the elderly cover their medical costs. For those on welfare, **Medicaid** provided funds to states to provide free healthcare.

Johnson also was committed to ending racial discrimination. He signed an executive order requiring government contractors to ensure nondiscrimination in jobs. He also appointed the first African-American cabinet member, Secretary of Housing and Urban Development Robert Weaver; the first African-American woman federal justice, Constance Baker Motley; and the first black on the Supreme Court, Thurgood Marshall.

Johnson followed up these appointments with proposals for a voting rights bill. Civil rights leaders had made voting rights their next major issue after passage of the Civil Rights Act of 1964. For nearly one hundred years, most southern whites had viewed voting as a privilege reserved for whites. Led by SNCC's Bob Moses, the **Freedom Summer** of 1964 called for whites and blacks to go to Mississippi to open "Freedom Schools" and to encourage African Americans to register to vote. The Freedom Schools taught basic literacy and black history and tutored African Americans so that they could pass the Mississippi voter literacy test. Prospective black voters in Mississippi had to convince a white registrar that they understood the Constitution and the duties of citizenship. White hostility made the work of registering black voters dangerous. Violence occurred almost daily in Mississippi from June through August 1964. Six Freedom Summer workers were murdered, but the crusade registered nearly sixty thousand new African-American voters. By December 1964, Johnson concurred with

---

Great Society Social program that Johnson announced in 1965; it included the War on Poverty, protection of civil rights, and funding for education.

medicare Program of health insurance for the elderly and disabled established in 1965; it provides government payment for healthcare supplied by private doctors and hospitals.

medicaid Program of health insurance for the poor established in 1965; it provides states with money to buy healthcare for people on welfare.

Freedom Summer Effort by Civil Rights groups in Mississippi to register black voters and cultivate black pride during the summer of 1964.

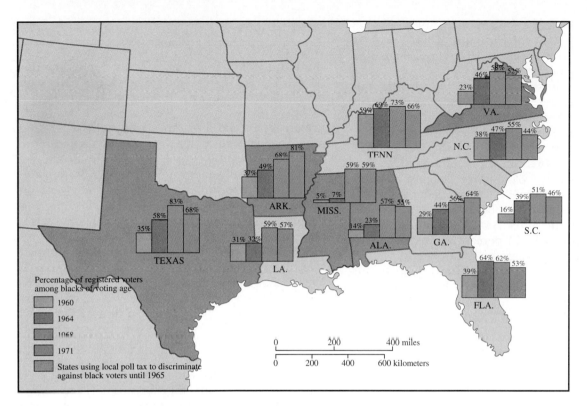

♦ **MAP 29.2 African Americans and the Southern Vote, 1960–1971**   An important part
of the civil rights movement was to reestablish the African-American vote that had been
stripped away in the South following Reconstruction. Between 1960 and 1971, with the
outlawing of the poll tax and other voter restrictions, African-American voter participation rose significantly across the South.

Martin Luther King, Jr., on the need for federal voting legislation.

Pointing to the violent response civil rights leaders had met with in Selma, Alabama, in March 1965,
Johnson urged Congress to act. King had called for a
freedom march from Selma to Montgomery because
of the former town's adamant and violent opposition to integration. On March 7, 1965, hundreds of
freedom marchers faced fifty Alabama state troopers
and Sheriff Jim Clark's mounted officers at Selma's
Pettus Bridge. After ordering the marchers to halt,
the state troopers fired tear gas and charged. As the
marchers fled back to Selma, Clark's men chased
them down, wielding rubber tubing wrapped with
barbed wire. Television coverage of the onslaught
stirred nationwide condemnation of Clarks' tactics.
Johnson told Governor George Wallace that he
would not tolerate any further interference with the

march. When twenty-five thousand people resumed
the march on March 25, the National Guard escorted
them.

In response to Johnson's pressure, Congress
passed the 1965 **Voting Rights Act.** It banned a variety of methods, such as literacy tests, that states
used to deny blacks the right to vote (see Map
29.2). In Selma, 60 percent of qualified African-
American voters registered, voted, and stopped

freedom march   Civil Rights march from Selma to
Montgomery, Alabama, in March 1965.
Voting Rights Act   Law passsed by Congress in
1965 that outlawed literacy and other voting tests
and authorized federal supervision of elections in
areas where black voting had been restricted.

Sheriff Clark's bid for reelection. By 1968, the percentage of African Americans registered to vote had risen by 30 percent; in Mississippi, it had increased from 7 percent to 67 percent.

Although Johnson's civil rights agenda met with great success, by 1966 many Great Society programs were underfunded and diminishing in popularity. An expanding American war in Vietnam, white backlash to urban riots, and partisan politics forced reductions in the budget of the War on Poverty. Still, by 1970 the Great Society had contributed to nearly a 10 percent decrease in the number of people living below the poverty line. Between 1963 and 1968, African-American unemployment fell nearly 42 percent. Johnson did not totally cure any of society's ills, but he did provide the basis for a more democratic and nondiscriminatory country. In the process, he widened the functions of the federal government more than any president since Franklin D. Roosevelt.

New Agendas

By the end of 1965, federal legislation had confirmed that *de jure* segregation—segregation established by local ordinances or state laws—was illegal in the United States. But equality depended on more than laws. Neither the 1964 Civil Rights Act nor the 1965 Voting Rights Act guaranteed justice, removed oppressive poverty, or provided jobs. *De facto* discrimination—the product of economics, social tradition, and custom—and prejudice remained.

African Americans' frustrations soon changed the nature of civil rights protest. By 1964, more than half of the nation's black population lived in northern cities, and more than a million mostly poor and unskilled blacks left the South during the 1960s. They entered an environment where unskilled jobs were declining and black unemployment was high. Poverty, false hopes, and frustrations led to increased violence and crime. African Americans saw largely white police forces as suppressors rather than protectors. By the mid-1960s, the nation's cities were primed for racial violence. Minor race riots had occurred in 1964, but it was the 1965 **Watts** riot that shook the nation.

New Voices

Watts did not look like most other ghettos. It was a community of largely single-family homes and duplexes. The fairly new buildings were usually well maintained. There was little open discrimination in Los Angeles, which was among the nation's leaders in public assistance programs, spending more than $500 million a year. But Watts had more than four times the people per block than the rest of the city. Male unemployment was 34 percent, and almost two-thirds of the residents were on public assistance. Finally, the nearly all-white Los Angeles police force had a reputation for racism and brutality.

In this climate, Officer Lee Minikus stopped Marquette Frye for drunk driving on August 11, 1965. What started as a simple arrest soon mushroomed into a major riot. A crowd of onlookers gathered as more police arrived and as Frye and Minikus began to scuffle. The police charged through the crowd of about 150 bystanders using nightsticks, and word quickly spread through Watts that the police were attacking innocent people. The Watts riot followed. Many residents pelted the police with stones and bottles and vented their anger by looting and setting fire to cars and stores. When firefighters and police arrived to restore order and to put out the flames, they had to dodge snipers' bullets and **Molotov cocktails.** It took fourteen thousand members of the California National Guard and over one thousand police and eight hundred sheriff's deputies to calm the storm. The costs were high: thirty-four dead, including twenty-eight African Americans, and over $45 million in property destroyed. Four thousand rioters were arrested.

The Watts riot shattered the complacency of many northern whites who had supported civil rights in the South while ignoring the plight of the

Watts Predominantly black neighborhood of Los Angeles where race riots in August 1965 did $45 million in damage and took the lives of twenty-eight blacks.

Molotov cocktail Makeshift bomb made of a bottle filled with gasoline.

inner cities. It also demonstrated a gap between northern blacks and many civil rights leaders. King discovered after the riot that the people of Watts had little use for his "dreams." He was shouted down and jeered. "Hell, we don't need no damn dreams," one skeptic remarked. "We want jobs."

Watts was only the beginning. More deadly urban riots followed, and a new, militant approach to racial and economic injustices erupted: the **Black Power** movement. A change in SNCC's leadership helped usher in a new era of black militancy. By the winter of 1965, Bob Moses had had too much of clubs, dogs, threats, and jails. Emotionally spent, he resigned and moved north. SNCC's new leader, **Stokely Carmichael,** exalted Black Power. "I'm not going to beg the white man for anything I deserve," he announced. "I'm going to take it." SNCC and CORE quickly changed from biracial, nonviolent organizations to Black Power movements.

Among those receptive to a more militant approach were the **Black Muslims** (the Nation of Islam), founded by Elijah Muhammad in the 1930s. The Black Muslims attracted mostly young males and demanded adherence to a strict moral code that prohibited the use of drugs and alcohol. They preached black superiority and independence from an evil white world. By the early 1960s, there were nearly a hundred thousand Black Muslims, but most whites were concerned with only one: **Malcolm X.**

By the age of 20, Malcolm Little's life of hard drugs, pimping, and burglary had put him in prison. Behind bars, his intellectual abilities blossomed. He devoured the prison library, took correspondence courses, and converted to the Nation of Islam, becoming Malcolm X. On his release in 1952, he quickly became one of the Black Muslims' most powerful leaders. A mesmerizing speaker, he rejected integration with a white society that, he said, emasculated blacks by denying them power and personal identity. "Our enemy is the white man!" he roared. But in 1964, he reconsidered the policy of rejecting cooperation with whites. Although still a black nationalist, he recognized that to achieve their goals, Black Muslims needed to cooperate with some whites. He broke with Elijah Muhammad, a defection that cost him his life. On

February 21, 1965, three Black Muslims assassinated him in Harlem. After his death, Malcolm X's *Autobiography,* chronicling his personal triumph over white oppression, became a revered guide for many blacks.

Malcolm X represented only one model for urban blacks. Others pursued direct action against white power and advocated violence. Huey P. Newton and Bobby Seale organized the **Black Panthers** in Oakland, California, in 1966. They were primarily noticeable for adopting Mao Zedong's adage that "power flows from the barrel of a gun." Their willingness to use violence frightened many, but others applauded their militance. New SNCC leader H. Rap Brown told listeners to grab their guns, burn the town down, and shoot the "honky." The summer of 1967 seemed to bring Brown's words to life. Over seventy-five major riots took place, the deadliest occurring in Detroit and Newark, resulting in a nationwide total of eighty-seven dead.

After a third summer of urban riots, President Lyndon Johnson created a special commission chaired by Governor Otto Kerner of Illinois to investigate their causes. The committee's report, issued in March 1968, put the primary blame on the racist attitudes of white America. The study

---

Black Power Movement beginning in 1966 that rejected the nonviolent, coalition-building approach of traditional civil rights groups and advocated black control of black organizations.

Stokely Carmichael Civil rights activist who led SNCC and who coined the term "Black Power" to describe the need for blacks to use militant tactics to force whites to accept political change.

Black Muslims Popular name for the Nation of Islam, an African-American religious group founded by Elijah Muhammad, which professed Islamic religious beliefs and emphasized black separatism.

Malcolm X Black activist who advocated black separatism as a member of the Nation of Islam; in 1963 he converted to orthodox Islam, and two years later he was assassinated.

Black Panthers Black revolutionary party founded in 1966 that accepted violence as a means of social change; many of its leaders were killed in confrontations with police or sent to prison.

described two Americas, one white and one black, and concluded:

> *Pervasive discrimination and segregation in employment, education, and housing have resulted in the continuing exclusion of great numbers of Negroes from the benefits of economic progress.*

The Kerner Commission believed that the solution to America's racial problem was a "compassionate, massive and sustained" commitment "backed by the resources of the most powerful and richest nation on this earth."

Just a month later, the assassination of Martin Luther King, Jr., sparked a new series of riots across the country. King had been in Memphis supporting striking black sanitation workers when, on April 4, 1968, he was gunned down by James Earl Ray, a white racist. African Americans took to the streets in over 125 cities. Sections of Washington, D.C., were engulfed in flames.

As American cities burned and cries of "Burn, Baby, Burn" and "Black Power!" emerged from the smoke, a white backlash occurred. Many Americans backed away from supporting civil rights. Republican politicians were especially vocal. California Governor Ronald Reagan argued the "riff-raff" theory of urban problems: "mad dogs" and "law-breakers" were the sole cause of the trouble. Governor Spiro Agnew of Maryland blamed activists like H. Rap Brown. Most Americans applauded as police cracked down on the Black Panthers, arresting or killing the party's membership. As the 1968 political campaign began, law and order replaced the Great Society and the War on Poverty as the main issue.

September 1967
PRICE $1

COLLEGE ISSUE

If you think the war in Vietnam is hell, you ought to see what's happening on campus, baby.

◆ "We're in a time that's divorced from the past," wrote author Norman Mailer, and from Berkeley to Harvard Yard, college campuses were becoming battlegrounds of the social, cultural, and political changes that were sweeping the nation. Whether participating in the counterculture or the Freedom Summer, or opposing the war in Vietnam or college restrictions, America's youth demanded new values and attitudes in the 1960s. *Michael Barson Collection/Past Perfect.*

The Challenge of Youth

As alarming to many Americans as the revolution that was reshaping African-American attitudes was the growing tendency of the nation's white youth to reject traditional values. Although the majority of young people remained quite traditional, an increasing number advocated alternative values. The transformation was particularly noticeable on college campuses.

Many students began to question the goal of education, particularly at huge institutions like the University of California at Berkeley and the University of Michigan. Students complained that concern for individuals was missing from education. Education seemed sterile—more like an assembly line producing a standardized product than an effort to create an independent, thinking individual. In *Growing Up Absurd*, Paul Goodman argued that schools destroyed creativity and replaced it with conformity. Reflecting Goodman's view, many students demanded freedom of expression and a new, more flexible attitude from college administrators and faculty.

Campus activists denounced course requirements and restrictions on dress, behavior, and living arrangements. By the end of the decade, many colleges and schools had relaxed or eliminated dress codes that required the wearing of coats and ties for men and dresses for women. Long hair was accepted for males, and casual clothes like faded blue jeans and shorts became common dress for both sexes on most college campuses. Colleges also lifted dorm curfews and other residence requirements. Some dorms became coed. Academic departments reduced the number of mandatory courses. By the early 1970s, many colleges had introduced programs in fields like African-American, Native American, and women's studies.

Setting their sights beyond the campus community, student activists urged that the campus should be a center for social change. **Students for a Democratic Society (SDS)**, organized at the University of Michigan in the early 1960s by Tom Hayden and Al Haber, charged that business and government ignored social inequalities. In 1962, SDS issued its Port Huron Statement, which maintained,

The search for truly democratic alternatives to the present, and a commitment to social experimentation with them, is a worthy and fulfilling human enterprise, one which moves us and, we hope, others today.

Hayden argued that the country should strive to build "an environment for people to live in with dignity and creativeness."

The earliest major confrontation between students and university authorities occurred at Berkeley in 1964. Activists led by Mario Savio protested when the administration tried to prevent students from using a plaza on campus to recruit supporters and solicit funds for various social and political causes. Fresh from the Freedom Summer, Savio demanded freedom of speech on campus. Claiming that the university was not fulfilling its moral obligation to provide an open forum for free thought, Savio asked students and faculty to disrupt the university's activities. Over six thousand students responded, seizing the administration building, boycotting classes, and yelling four-letter

words. Although Savio and two other organizers were expelled and sentenced to four months in jail, Chancellor Clark Kerr agreed to allow freedom of expression on campus.

The Berkeley Free Speech Movement encouraged other campus organizers. Student activists in growing numbers focused their attention on civil rights, the environment, and social and sexual norms. By the late sixties, though, their loudest protests opposed American foreign policy, the **military-industrial complex,** and the war in Vietnam. Opposition to the war further expanded the number of student activists.

The youth movement's discontent also found expression in what became known as the counterculture. Many young people came to spurn the traditional moral and social values of their parents. "Don't trust anyone over 30" became the motto of the young generation. The counterculture glorified freedom of the spirit and self-knowledge.

Music was one of the most prominent forms of defiance. Musicians like Bob Dylan and Joan Baez challenged society with protest and antiwar songs. Folk music and protest rock, however, were only a small part of the music challenge. For the majority, rock 'n' roll remained dominant. Performers like the **Beatles,** a British group that exploded on the American music scene in 1964, were among the most popular. The behavior and songs of other British imports such as the Rolling Stones and the Animals depicted a life of pleasure and lack of social restraints. The Grateful Dead and Jimi Hendrix turned rock 'n' roll into a new form of music, psychedelic **acid rock,**

Students for a Democratic Society Left-wing student organization founded in 1962 to criticize American materialism and call for social justice.

military-industrial complex Term first used by Eisenhower to describe the arms industry; in the 1960s, it was used by radicals to describe all those in power who benefited from U.S. militarism.

Beatles English rock group that gained international fame in 1964 and disbanded in 1970; they were known for the intelligence of their lyrics and their sophisticated instrumentation.

acid rock Rock music having a driving, repetitive beat and lyrics that suggest psychedelic drug experiences.

whose swirls of sound and lyrics acclaimed a drug culture and attacked social conventions.

The message of much music of the sixties was wrapped up in drug use—get "high" or "stoned." For many in the sixties generation, marijuana, or "pot," was the primary means to get high. Marijuana advocates claimed that, unlike the nation's traditional drug, alcohol, it reduced aggression and heightened perception. Thus, they argued, marijuana contributed to the counterculture's ideals of peace, serenity, and self-awareness. A more dangerous and unpredictable drug popular with some was LSD, lysergic acid diethylamide. "Acid" was a hallucinogenic drug that altered the user's perceptions of reality. Harvard psychology professor **Timothy Leary** argued for its widespread consumption. He believed that by "tripping" on LSD, people could free themselves from the rat race: "turn on, tune in, and drop out." Drugs offered some within the counterculture a new and liberating experience. But they also proved to be self-destructive and deadly, contributing to the deaths of musicians Jimi Hendrix, Jim Morrison, and Janis Joplin.

Another realm of traditional American values the counterculture overturned was sex. Some young people appalled their parents and society by questioning and rejecting the values that placed restrictions on sexual activities. A new openness about sexuality and a relaxation of the stigma on premarital sex turned out to be a significant legacy of the sixties. But the philosophy of **free love** also had a negative side, as increased sexual activity contributed to a rapid rise in venereal disease.

Perhaps the most colorful and best-known advocates of the counterculture were the **Hippies.** Seeking a life of peace, love, and self-awareness, Hippies tried to distance themselves from conventional society. They flocked in large numbers to northern California, especially to the Haight-Ashbury neighborhood of San Francisco. Elsewhere, some Hippie groups abandoned the "old-fashioned" nuclear family and lived together as extended families in communes. Hippies expressed their nonconformism by favoring long, unkempt hair and ratty blue jeans or long, flowered dresses. Although the number of true Hippie dropouts was small, their style of dress and grooming greatly influenced young Americans.

The influence of the counterculture peaked in the summer of 1969, when an army of teens and young adults converged on **Woodstock,** New York, for the largest free rock concert in history. For three days, through summer rains and deepening mud, more than four hundred thousand came together in a temporary open-air community while popular rock-'n'-roll bands performed day and night. Touted as three days of peace and love, sex, drugs, and rock 'n' roll, Woodstock symbolized for a few fleeting days the power of counterculture values to promote cooperation and happiness.

Timothy Leary Harvard professor and counterculture figure who advocated the expansion of consciousness through the use of drugs such as LSD.

free love Popular belief among members of the counterculture in the 1960s in having sexual activity with as many partners as they liked.

Hippies Members of the counterculture in the 1960s who rejected the competitiveness and materialism of American society and searched for peace, love, and autonomy.

Woodstock Free rock concert in Woodstock, New York, in August 1969, which attracted 400,000 people and was remembered as the classic expression of the counterculture.

SUMMARY

E xpectations
C onstraints
C hoices
O utcomes

The *outcome* of John F. Kennedy's election was a wave of renewed optimism and liberalism. Kennedy's call for a more responsible society and government was at the heart of his New Frontier. Kennedy raised *expectations*, but it was Lyndon B.

Johnson's Great Society that greatly expanded the role of government in social affairs. Heightened *expectations* were clearly visible among the African Americans who looked for legislation to end segregation and discrimination. As Kennedy took office, African-American leaders *chose* to launch a series of sit-ins and freedom marches. Kennedy responded by introducing a civil rights act in 1963 that was finally passed in 1964 after his assassination.

In foreign policy, Kennedy *chose* to expand the international struggle against communism. Confrontations over Berlin and Cuba, a heightened arms race, and an expanded commitment to Vietnam were the *outcomes*.

As president, Johnson *chose* to expand on the slain president's New Frontier. The 1964 Civil Rights Act, the 1965 Voting Rights Act, and Great Society legislation were designed to wage war on poverty and discrimination, to provide federal aid for education, and to create a national system of health insurance for the poor and elderly. But by 1968, growing societal and political divisions *constrained* liberalism. African-American activists *chose* to become more militant in their demands for social and economic equality. The nation's youth, too, seemed unwilling to accept the traditional values of society, and they demanded change. Disturbed by the turmoil, conservatives and many moderate Americans *chose* to oppose government programs that appeared to favor the poor and minorities at their expense. The *outcome* was that a decade that had begun with great promise produced disappointment and disillusionment for many.

SUGGESTED READINGS

Anderson, Terry H. *The Movement and the Sixties* (1995).

A skillful examination of the social and cultural currents of the 1960s.

Bernstein, Irving. *Promises Kept: John F. Kennedy's New Frontier* (1991).

A brief and balanced account of Kennedy's presidency that nonetheless presents a favorable report of the accomplishments and legacy of the New Frontier.

Berschloss, Michael. *The Crisis Years: Kennedy and Khrushchev, 1960–1963* (1991).

A strong narrative account of the Cold War during the Kennedy administration and the personal duel between the leaders of the two superpowers.

Carson, Clayton. *In Struggle: SNCC and the Black Awakening of the 1960s* (1981).

A useful study that uses the development of SNCC to examine the changing patterns of the civil rights movement and the emergence of black nationalism.

Kearns, Doris. *Lyndon Johnson and the American Dream* (1977).

An effective study of how Johnson's background and values shaped his career and the Great Society.

Wolfe, Tom. *The Electric Kool-Aid Acid Test* (1968).

A classic account of the dimensions of the counterculture.

Easy Rider (1969) and *The Graduate* (1967) are two period films that critique traditional social and cultural norms and provide a glimpse of the "values" of the 1960s.

● ● ● The Debate over Black Power

The Context

By 1965, the civil rights movement had made significant changes in American society. Segregation was illegal under the 1964 Civil Rights Act. Yet many African Americans still were denied equality, were mired in poverty, and felt powerless. The outcome was increasing anger among many African Americans, who replaced the philosophy of nonviolence and passive resistance with aggressive self-defense and a philosophy of "Black Power." Used initially by Paul Robeson following the Little Rock crisis (1957), the phrase burst onto the front pages on June 16, 1966, when Stokely Carmichael renewed the call for Black Power. Quickly, its advocates seemed to drown out calls for "Freedom Now." A white marcher recalled that the "thundering" demands for Black Power seemed to him "chilling . . . frightening." (For further information on the context, see pages 654–656.)

The Historical Question

The phrase "Black Power" grabbed headlines. To many white Americans, it seemed threatening. To many African Americans, it signaled the need to understand the race issue and its resolution in a different way and to make new choices. There was no standard definition of the term. What was Black Power? Was it a call for revolution and racial separation, a pronouncement of racial pride, a cry of desperation?

The Challenge

Using the sources provided, along with other information you have read, write an essay or hold a discussion on the following question. Cite evidence in the sources to support your conclusions. **What meanings did people give to the concept of Black Power? What historical and social experiences shaped these meanings?**

The Sources

1 After Stokely Carmichael called for Black Power, he wrote an essay in the *Massachusetts Review* in which he sought to explain the origins and concerns of the Black Power movement. He said:

Negroes are defined by two forces, their blackness and their powerlessness. There have been traditionally two communities in America. The White community, which controlled and defined the forms that all institutions within the society would take, and the Negro community, which has been excluded from participation in power decisions that shaped the society. . . .

In recent years the answer . . . has been . . . something called "integration." According to the advocates of integration, social justice will be ac-complished by "integrating the Negro into the . . . society from which he has been traditionally excluded.". . .

This concept . . . had to be based on the assumption that there was nothing of value in the Negro community . . . so the thing to do was to siphon off the "acceptable" Negroes into the surrounding middle-class white community. . . . Now, black people must look . . . to issues of collective power.

. . . The political and social rights of Negroes have been and always will be negotiable and expandable the moment they conflict with the interests of our "allies." If we do not learn from history, we are doomed to repeat it, and that is precisely the lesson of Reconstruction . . .

. . . To the extent that we are dependent on . . . other groups, we are vulnerable to their influence and domination.

2 Bayard Rustin, long-time civil rights advocate and a past official of CORE, opposed Carmichael's nationalism and separatism. But, as he explained in *Commentary* (1965), African Americans still faced many constraints. He wrote:

The very decade which has witnessed the decline of legal Jim Crow has also seen the rise of de facto segregation. . . . More Negroes are unemployed today than in 1954. . . . More Negroes attend de facto segregated schools today than when the Supreme Court handed down its famous decision. . . .

. . . Last summer's riots were not race riots; they were outbursts of class aggression in a society where class and color definitions are converging disastrously. . . .

We need allies. The future of the Negro struggle depends on whether the contradictions of this society can be resolved by a coalition of progressive forces which become the effective political majority.

3 In 1966, Lerone Bennett, Jr., senior editor of *Ebony*, explained the underlying problems facing black Americans and American society. He wrote:

There is no Negro problem in America. . . .

The problem of race . . . is a white problem . . . white America created, invented the race problem . . .

racism is a mask for a much deeper problem involving not the victims of racism but the perpetrators. . . .

It is fashionable . . . to think of racism as a vast impersonal system for which no one is responsible. . . . Racism did not fall from the sky; it was not secreted by insects. No: racism in America was made by man, neighborhood by neighborhood, law by law, restrictive covenent by restrictive covenant, deed by deed.

4 In 1967, President Lyndon Johnson created a commission chaired by Governor Otto Kerner to investigate the causes of racial strife that had swept across America and to recommend possible solutions. In March 1968, the final report provided a bleak image of race relations in the United States.

The events of the summer of 1967 are in large part the culmination of 300 years of racial prejudice. . . . Our nation is moving toward two societies, one black, one white—separate and unequal. . . . Discrimination and segregation have long permeated much of American life; they now threaten the future of every American. . . . This deepening racial division is not inevitable. The movement apart can be reversed. . . .

Violence and destruction must be ended—in the streets of the ghetto and in the lives of people. . . . What white Americans have never fully understood—and what the Negro can never forget—is that white society is deeply implicated in the ghetto. White institutions created it, white institutions maintain it, and white society condones it.

MOVING TO THE SUNBELT From the 1960s on, many Americans have moved to the Sunbelt — a region, shown in this map, stretching from Florida in a westward arc to the state of Washington. Pushed by harsh winters and declining economic opportunities in the North and East, thousands have sought warmer climates and jobs in states like California, Florida, and Arizona.

CANADA

WASHINGTON
44.8%
21.1%

OREGON
48.9% 25.9%

IDAHO
41.5%
32.4%

MONTANA
16.5%

NORTH
DAKOTA
3.4%

MINN.
19.4%

WIS.
19.1%

WYOMING
42.1%
41.3%

SOUTH
DAKOTA
1.4%

MICH.
18.4%

Jersey City, New Jersey:
8% decrease in
population, 1970–1980

Buffalo, New York:
8% decrease in
population, 1970–1980

Cleveland, Ohio:
8% decrease in
population, 1970–1980

VT.
31.2%
21.6% 24.8%

MAINE
16.1%

N.H.
51.8%

NEW
YORK
4.7%

MASS.
19.3%

R.I.
10.3%

CONN.
22.6%

CALIFORNIA
50.6%

NEVADA
181.1%
71.6% 63.8%

UTAH
64%
37.9%

COLORADO
64.8%
26% 30.8%

NEBRASKA
11.2%

IOWA
5.6%

ILL.
13.3%

IND.
17.7%

OHIO
11.2%

PENNSYLVANIA
4.8%

26.5% 22.9%

N.J.
21.4%

DEL.
33.2%

MD.
36%

Washington, D.C.:
–16.4%

27.1%

Las Vegas, Nevada:
70% increase in
population, 1970–1980

ARIZONA
108.7%
53.1%

36.3%

NEW MEXICO
36.9%
28.1%

KANSAS
8.5%

MISSOURI
13.8%

KENTUCKY
20.5%

W.VA.
5%

VIRGINIA
34.7%

NORTH
CAROLINA
29.1%

TENN.
28.7%

SOUTH
CAROLINA
31%

20.5%

OKLAHOMA
19.2%

ARK.
28%

GEORGIA
38.6%

*ATLANTIC
OCEAN*

*PACIFIC
OCEAN*

MISS.
15.7%

ALABAMA
19.2%

TEXAS
48.6%
27.1%

MEXICO

LA.
29.1%

FLA.
96.7%
37.1% 43.5%

Fort Lauderdale/
Hollywood, Florida:
64% increase in
population, 1970–1980

West Palm Beach, Florida:
65% increase in
population, 1970–1980

Gulf of Mexico

*PACIFIC
OCEAN*

HAWAI'I
52.4% 21.8% 25.3%

U.S.S.R.

CANADA

34.1% 32.8%

ALASKA
78.1%

0   100 Km.
0   100 Mi.

0   250   500 Km.
0   250   500 Mi.

*PACIFIC
OCEAN*

0   200   400 Km.
0   200   400 Mi.

CUBA

Increase in population,
1960–1980

Over 40%

30–40%

20–30%

10–20%

5–10%

Under 5%

State population increases
of 20% or more

1970–1980

1960–1970 20%

Kennedy assassinated;
Johnson becomes president

Gulf of Tonkin Resolution

Escalation in Vietnam begins

NOW founded

Tet offensive

Indians seize Alcatraz

EPA created

Nixon visits
China and
Soviet Union

Nixon resigns;
Ford becomes president

Fall of
South Vietnam

1963   1964   1965   1966   1968   1969   1970   1972   1974   1975

1850   1900   1950   2000

America Under Stress, 1963–1975

Johnson and the World

- What expectations led Lyndon Johnson to choose the policy of escalating America's role in Vietnam?

- What were the political, social, and military outcomes of his decision?

Expanding the American Dream

- What constraints did women, Latinos, and American Indians face in American society, and how did they organize to promote change?

Nixon and the Balance of Power

- What choices did Richard Nixon make to achieve an "honorable" peace in Vietnam?

- How did Nixon's choices in shaping Cold War policies differ from those favored by earlier administrations?

Nixon and Politics

- How did Nixon's choices in dealing with the economy and the environment reflect his pragmatic conservatism?

- Why did Nixon achieve such a huge success in the 1972 election? What expectations and constraints led to Watergate?

INTRODUCTION

E xpectations
C onstraints
C hoices
O utcomes

The Sixties began with a wave of optimism and confidence in the ability of the national government to improve society and promote American interests abroad. In 1963, those *expectations* provided the new president, Lyndon Johnson, an opportunity to create his Great Society. In foreign affairs, Johnson had less ambitious *expectations*. He seemed content to continue Kennedy's policies, especially in Vietnam. But he was determined that the United States not be beaten by the Communists of a "two-bit" nation like North Vietnam.

An array of *constraints* blocked any dramatic increase in the American military role in South Vietnam, which many regarded as necessary to defeat the Communists. Sudden escalation would be expensive, could weaken support for Johnson's domestic program, and might drive the Chinese and the Soviets to increase their support of North Vietnam. To the president, the best *choice* seemed to be a carefully controlled, gradual escalation of American force. The administration *expected* the North Vietnamese would then abandon their efforts to conquer South Vietnam.

That strategy failed miserably. North Vietnam *chose* to meet escalation with escalation, until many Americans turned against both the war and Johnson. In 1968, Johnson *chose* to start peace negotiations with North Vietnam. Unexpectedly, he also announced that he would not seek re-election.

The Republicans rallied behind Richard Nixon. He called for a restoration of national prestige and a reassertion of the values that had made the nation strong. Nixon played on the uneasy *expectations* of a society that was fragmented by the Vietnam War and by sharp demands from an array of social groups, from feminists to American Indians, seeking political, economic, and social changes.

Despite their claims of wanting to bring the nation together, Nixon and the Republicans *chose* to inflame social divisions to ensure their victories in 1968 and 1972. They *expected* to construct a solid political base around the Silent Majority: suburban, middle-class, white Americans who were tired of social reform. Promising a new, pragmatic conservatism, Nixon's first administration achieved generally successful *outcomes*. He improved relations with the Soviet Union and the People's Republic of China and gradually withdrew American forces from Vietnam. Domestically, his policy *choices* showed surprising flexibility.

Despite his successes, Nixon was not satisfied. His desire to destroy his political enemies contributed to the illegal activities surrounding the Watergate break-in. Watergate's *outcomes* included not only the unprecedented resignation of a president but a nationwide wave of disillusionment with politics and government.

Johnson and the World

Lyndon Baines Johnson saw the world in black-and-white terms: the free world on one side, the Communist world on the other. In 1964, Johnson perceived a growing Communist menace in Latin America and Vietnam.

Eyeing Castro's presence in Cuba, Johnson resolved that there would be no further erosion of American power in Latin America. Reversing Kennedy's policy, the State Department informed Latin American leaders that social and political reforms were no longer prerequisites for American aid. Johnson wanted order, stability, and pro-American governments. American military equipment and advisers were provided to regimes trying to suppress "Communist" elements. The new policy led to direct military intervention in the Dominican Republic in 1965. There, supporters of

CHRONOLOGY

From Camelot to Watergate

1962 Cesar Chavez forms National Farm Workers Association

1963 Betty Friedan's *The Feminine Mystique*
La Raza Unida formed in Texas
Kennedy assassinated; Johnson becomes president
16,000 U.S. advisers in South Vietnam

1964 Johnson elected president
Civil Rights Act
Gulf of Tonkin Resolution

1965 Voting Rights Act
U.S. air strikes against North Vietnam begin
American combat troops arrive in South Vietnam
Anti-Vietnam "teach-ins" begin
Dominican Republic intervention
National campaign for farm workers

1966 National Organization for Women founded

1967 Antiwar march on Washington

1968 Tet offensive
My Lai massacre
Peace talks begin in Paris
Johnson withdraws from presidential race
Robert Kennedy assassinated
Nixon elected president
American Indian Movement founded

1969 American Indians occupy Alcatraz
Anti-Vietnam march on Washington
First American troop withdrawals from Vietnam
Secret bombing of Cambodia
Vine Deloria's *Custer Died for Your Sins*
Alexander v. Holmes
Warren Burger appointed to Supreme Court

1970 Cambodian invasion
Kent State and Jackson State killings
Clean Air and Water acts
Earth Day observed nationally
Environmental Protection Agency created
Strike-for-Equality Parade
Harry Blackmun appointed to Supreme Court

1971 *Pentagon Papers*
Nixon enacts price and wage controls
Swann v. Charlotte-Mecklenburg
William Rehnquist and Lewis Powell appointed to Supreme Court

1972 Revenue Sharing Act
Watergate break-in
Nixon reelected
Nixon visits China and Soviet Union
SALT I treaty
Bombing of North Vietnam resumes

1973 Watergate hearings
Paris Peace Accords
War Powers Act
"Second battle of Wounded Knee"

1974 Nixon resigns
Gerald Ford becomes president
Jerry Apodaca elected governor of New Mexico
Raul Castro elected governor of Arizona

1975 South Vietnamese government falls to North Vietnamese deposed President Juan Bosch rebelled against a repressive, pro-American regime. Johnson decided that the pro-Bosch coalition was Communist dominated and sent in twenty-two thousand American troops to restore order. The troops left in mid-1966, after Joaquin Balaguer, a conservative, pro-American candidate, was elected president. Johnson claimed to have saved a free nation from communism, but many Latin Americans saw only an example of Yankee arrogance.

The Americanization of Vietnam

Latin America was not the only region where Johnson believed that American interests were threatened by communism. Although the United States had stationed sixteen thousand advisers in South Vietnam by the end of 1963, the Viet Cong, supported by North Vietnam, appeared to be winning the war. American advisers saw little hope for improvement unless American combat troops were committed to the contest. Johnson agreed, but concluded that sending troops to Vietnam in an election year was politically unwise. He decided to delay escalation at least until after the presidential election. Nevertheless, planning began immediately.

The plan that emerged relied heavily on American air power. It would be used against industrial and commercial targets in North Vietnam. Johnson's advisers believed that North Vietnamese leader Ho Chi Minh would end support for the Viet Cong rather than watch his nation's economic future go up in smoke. Without support from the North, the Viet Cong could be defeated by the South Vietnamese army (ARVN). The need for large numbers of American ground forces would consequently be limited. **General William Westmoreland,** commander of American forces in Vietnam, disagreed with that assessment. American ground forces were necessary, he argued, because the ARVN was inept. But Johnson chose not to follow this advice in an election year.

The administration did begin preparing the public for a larger American role in South Vietnam. The White House and the **Pentagon** encouraged newspapers and magazines to stress the Communist threat to South Vietnam and Southeast Asia. The White House waited for an opportunity to ask

Congress for permission to use whatever force was necessary to defend South Vietnam.

That chance came in August 1964 off the coast of North Vietnam. On August 1, North Vietnamese torpedo boats skirmished with the American destroyer *Maddox* in the Gulf of Tonkin (see Map 30.1). On August 4, experiencing rough seas and poor visibility, radar operators on the *Maddox* and another destroyer concluded that the patrol boats were making another attack. Confusion followed. Both ships fired wildly at targets shown only on radar screens. Officers on both ships soon concluded that the radar blips had not been attacking vessels. Johnson joked privately that the sailors had probably been shooting at flying fish. Still, he told the nation that the Communists were guilty of "open aggression on the high seas" against the United States. On August 7, he submitted to Congress a resolution asking approval "to take all necessary steps, including the use of armed force," to aid South Vietnam. An overwhelming majority of Congress approved the **Gulf of Tonkin Resolution;** only two senators opposed it.

The Gulf of Tonkin Resolution gave Johnson the freedom to take whatever measures he wanted in Vietnam. Before committing American forces, however, he wanted to wait until after the 1964 election and for another enemy provocation. Johnson got his provocation when the Viet Cong attacked the American base at Pleiku in February 1965, killing eight Americans. Operation Rolling Thunder, the air assault on North Vietnam, began on March 2, 1965. On March 8, the 3rd Marine Division arrived to take up positions around the American base at Da Nang. By July, American planes were flying over nine hundred missions a week and a hundred

General William Westmoreland Commander of all American troops in Vietnam from 1964 to 1968.

Pentagon The U.S. military establishment, so named because its central offices are located in a five-sided building in Arlington, Virginia, called the Pentagon.

Gulf of Tonkin Resolution Resolution passed by Congress in 1964 authorizing the president to take any measures necessary to repel attacks against U.S. forces in Vietnam.

CHINA

NORTH VIETNAM

BURMA (MYNAMAR)

Dienbienphu •

French surrender, May 7, 1954

Hanoi ⊛
Haiphong •

Red

Gulf of Tonkin

Harbor mined, 1972

LAOS

Gulf of Tonkin, 1964

Vinh •

HAINAN

Vientiane ⊛

Mekong

Udon Thani •

U.S. Seventh Fleet operations during the war

17th Parallel

KHE SAHN 1968
HUE 1968

THAILAND

Phu Bai •
A SHAU VALLEY 1969
Da Nang •

Demarcation Line, July 1954

Chu Lai •

Ubon Ratchathani •

CENTRAL HIGHLANDS
DAK TO 1967
KONTUM 1972
Pleiku •

Bangkok •

CAMBODIA

PLEI ME 1965
IA DRANG VALLEY 1965

Qui Nhon •

U.S incursion into Cambodia, 1970

SOUTH VIETNAM

South China Sea

HO CHI MINH TRAIL

LOC NINH 1967
AN LOC 1972

Phnom Penh ⊛

Gulf of Thailand

Saigon •

CAI LAY 1972

Mekong Delta

Cease-fire, Jan. 27, 1973
Last U.S. ground troops leave, March 1973
North Vietnamese victory, 1975

◆ U.S. bases
░ Area of confrontation
▓ Viet Cong base areas
→ Enemy supply routes
→ U.S. movements
✪ Major battles

0   100   200 Km.
0   100   200 Mi.

♦ **MAP 30.1 The Vietnam War, 1954–1975**   Following the French defeat at Dienbienphu in 1954, the United States became increasingly committed to defending South Vietnam. This map shows some of the major battle sites of the Vietnam War from 1954 to the fall of Saigon and the defeat of the South Vietnamese government in 1975.

thousand American ground forces had reached Vietnam. Johnson's strategy soon showed its flaws. As the United States escalated the war, so did the enemy. General William Westmoreland now insisted that victory required even more American soldiers. Reluctantly, Johnson gave the green light. Vietnam had become an American war.

Westmoreland planned to use overwhelming numbers and firepower to destroy the enemy. In the first major American offensive, a large-scale sweep of the Ia Drang Valley in November 1965, the 1st Air Cavalry forced North Vietnamese units to retreat into Cambodia. The brutal hand-to-hand fighting left three hundred Americans and an estimated three thousand enemy soldiers dead. Westmoreland and Johnson were pleased. *Time* named Westmoreland "Man of the Year" for 1965.

Throughout 1966 and 1967, both sides continued to escalate. The Viet Cong and North Vietnamese suffered heavy losses of men and supplies, but their determination to continue the struggle remained unbroken. American aircraft rained bombs on North Vietnam and supply routes south, especially the **Ho Chi Minh Trail,** but arms and provisions still moved. In the fall of 1967, Westmoreland informed Washington that half of the enemy's forces were no longer capable of combat. At the same time, he asked to increase the American presence in Vietnam to 542,000.

Unknown to Westmoreland, North Vietnamese leaders were planning an immense offensive for the Vietnamese new year holiday of Tet in January 1968. The Viet Cong struck forty-one cities throughout South Vietnam, including Saigon. In some of the bloodiest fighting of the war, American and South Vietnamese forces recaptured the lost cities and villages.

The **Tet offensive** was a military defeat for North Vietnam and the Viet Cong. It provoked no popular uprising against the South Vietnamese government, the Communists gained no cities or provincial capitals, and they suffered staggering losses. Over forty thousand Viet Cong were killed. Tet was nonetheless a "victory" for the North Vietnamese in that it seriously weakened American support for the war. Coming amid official pronouncements of "victory just around the corner," Tet destroyed the administration's credibility and intensified a growing antiwar movement.

♦ Unlike previous American wars, Vietnam was a war without fixed frontlines. At the isolated outpost of Khe Sahn, fewer than six thousand American marines fought to hold back thirty thousand to forty thousand North Vietnamese regulars for seventy-seven days, killing or wounding more than ten thousand of the enemy. Within weeks after the siege, the United States withdrew from the area. *Robert Ellison/Black Star.*

The Antiwar Movement

Throughout 1964, there was widespread support for an American role in Vietnam. Most Americans accepted the domino theory, which held that a Communist success in one country would lead to the toppling of other "free" governments. A year later, little had changed except that the largely college-based opposition to the war was more outspoken. The University of Michigan held the first Vietnam "teach-in" to mobilize opposition to the war on March 24, 1965. In April, Students for a Democratic Society (SDS) organized a protest march of about fifteen thousand in front of the White House.

> **Ho Chi Minh Trail**   Main infiltration route for North Vietnamese soldiers into South Vietnam; it ran through Laos and Cambodia.
>
> **Tet offensive**   Viet Cong and North Vietnamese offensive against South Vietnamese cities in January 1968; a military defeat for North Vietnam, it nevertheless undermined U.S. support for the war.

Those opposing the war fell into two major categories. Pacifists and radical liberals opposed the war for moral and ideological reasons. Others opposed the war for pragmatic reasons: the draft, the loss of lives and money, and the inability of the United States to defeat the enemy. In 1966, high school students hardly mentioned Vietnam or the draft as a problem facing their lives. Three years later, 75 percent of those polled listed both as major worries. By 1967, the possibility of being sent to Vietnam was becoming a concern of many college students. A University of Michigan student complained that if he were drafted and spent two years in the army, he would lose over $16,000 in income. Yet college students were not the most likely to be drafted. Far more often, those who were drafted and sent to Vietnam were poorly educated, low-income whites and minorities.

Nonetheless, it was America's middle class, especially college students, who swelled the antiwar movement and participated in the "Stop-the-Draft Week" in October 1967. That week, over 10,000 demonstrators blocked the entrance to an induction center in Oakland, California, while over 200,000 people staged a massive protest march in Washington against "Lyndon's War."

Until 1967, Johnson displayed little concern about the antiwar movement. Press and television coverage continued to emphasize American successes. Public opinion polls found that the nation stood behind Johnson's efforts to save South Vietnam. But as antiwar numbers increased and as opposition to the war spread beyond students and radicals in 1967, Johnson responded by having federal agents infiltrate, spy on, and try to discredit antiwar groups.

The Tet offensive broadened and intensified antiwar sentiments. The highly respected CBS news anchor Walter Cronkite had supported the war, but Tet changed his mind. Unable to match the administration's claims of impending victory with the fierce Communist offensive, he went on a personal fact-finding tour of Vietnam. On his return, Cronkite announced that there would be no victory in Vietnam. "If I have lost Walter Cronkite, then it's over. I have lost Mr. Average Citizen," Johnson lamented.

Johnson's own circle of advisers began opposing American policy in Vietnam. Secretary of War

Robert McNamara left the administration over its policy. Secretary of State Dean Rusk and new Secretary of Defense Clark Clifford argued that military victory was impossible. Clifford concluded that after four years of "enormous casualties" and "massive destruction from our bombing," there was no lessening of "the will of the enemy." Thus, following Tet, when Westmoreland called for more troops, most of Johnson's "wise men" urged sending fewer troops and seeking instead a diplomatic end to the war.

The 1968 Presidential Campaign

As Johnson prepared for the 1968 presidential race, rumors circulated that 200,000 more Americans were being sent to Vietnam. In the New Hampshire primary, Minnesota senator **Eugene McCarthy** challenged Johnson for the Democratic presidential nomination by opposing the Vietnam War. Hundreds of student volunteers knocked on doors and distributed flyers for McCarthy.

Expecting no real challenge to his renomination, Johnson had not entered the New Hampshire primary. But with the furor over Tet, Johnson's political advisers quickly organized a **write-in campaign** for Johnson in New Hampshire. The president beat McCarthy, but by only 6 percent of the vote. Political commentators called McCarthy the real winner of the contest. New York senator **Robert Kennedy** added to Johnson's worries when he proclaimed his candidacy for the presidency and opposition to the war.

On March 31, 1968, a haggard-looking president announced on television that the United States

---

Eugene McCarthy Senator who opposed the Vietnam War and who made an unsuccessful bid for the 1968 Democratic nomination for president.

write-in campaign An attempt to elect a candidate not registered or listed on the ballot; voters are urged to write in the candidate's name on the ballot themselves.

Robert Kennedy Attorney general during the presidency of his brother John F. Kennedy; he was elected to the Senate in 1964 and was campaigning for the presidency when he was assassinated in 1968.

would negotiate with the Viet Cong and North Vietnamese. The escalation of the ground war was over, and the South Vietnamese would assume a larger role. The bombing of North Vietnam above the 20th parallel would end. Johnson ended his speech with this bombshell: "I have concluded that I should not permit the presidency to become involved in the partisan divisions that are developing in this political year. . . . Accordingly, I shall not seek, and I will not accept, the nomination of my party for another term as president." Listeners were shocked. Lyndon B. Johnson had thrown in the towel. Nearly everyone agrees that the war ended Johnson's political career.

Negotiations with North Vietnam began in Paris in May and went nowhere. The war remained the critical issue within the Democratic political race, which now included Vice President **Hubert H. Humphrey.** McCarthy campaigned against the war and the "imperial presidency." Kennedy opposed the war and called on the government to meet the needs of the poor and minorities. Standing by Johnson's peace efforts, Humphrey relied on party regulars and White House clout to win the nomination. While Kennedy and McCarthy battled for primary victories, Humphrey concentrated on the nonprimary delegations.

By June, Kennedy was winning the primary race. In the critical California primary, he gained a narrow victory over McCarthy, 46 to 41 percent. As Kennedy left his election headquarters, he was shot in the head by Sirhan Sirhan, a Jordanian immigrant. He died the next day.

Kennedy's assassination ensured Humphrey's nomination. McCarthy continued his campaign but was unable to generate much support. By the time of the national convention in Chicago in August, Humphrey had enough pledged votes to ensure his nomination. The convention was nevertheless dramatic. Antiwar and antiestablishment groups demonstrated for McCarthy, peace in Vietnam, and social justice. In the streets of Chicago, radical factions within the SDS promised physical confrontation. The so-called **Yippies** (Youth International party), led by Abbie Hoffman and Jerry Rubin, threatened to contaminate the water supply with drugs. Chicago's mayor, Richard Daley, was determined to maintain order. Inside the convention, delegates argued and screamed support for

their positions. Outside, protesters threw eggs, bottles, rocks, and balloons filled with water, ink, and urine at the police, who responded with tear gas and nightsticks. On August 28, the police went berserk before television cameras, viciously attacking protesters and bystanders alike. The violence in Chicago's streets overshadowed Humphrey's nomination.

Many Americans were disgusted by the chaos in Chicago. **George Wallace,** the Democratic governor of Alabama, appealed to this sentiment when he left the Democratic party and ran for president as the American Independent party's candidate. The conservative Wallace, who had opposed federal civil rights legislation, took a dim view of antiwar protesters. He aimed his campaign at southern whites, blue-collar workers, and lower-income white Americans. On the campaign trail, Wallace took special glee in attacking the counterculture and the "rich-kid" war protesters, who avoided serving in Vietnam while the sons of working-class Americans died there. Wallace agreed with his vice-presidential candidate, General Curtis Lemay, that the United States should bomb North Vietnam "back to the Stone Age." Two months before the election, Wallace commanded 21 percent of the vote according to opinion polls.

The Republican candidate, Richard Nixon, also intended to tap this general dissatisfaction. He and Spiro Agnew, his vice-presidential running mate, campaigned on the need for law and order while denouncing pot, pornography, protesters, and permissiveness. He announced that he would "end the war and win the peace" but refused to specify how.

On election day, Nixon won a comfortable margin in the Electoral College, although he received

---

Hubert H. Humphrey Vice president under Lyndon Johnson who won the Democratic nomination for president in 1968 but lost the election to Richard Nixon.

Yippies Counterculture group that inflamed the protests that disrupted the Democratic National Convention in Chicago in 1968.

George Wallace Conservative Alabama governor who opposed desegregation in the 1960s and ran unsuccessfully for the presidency as an independent in 1968 and 1972.

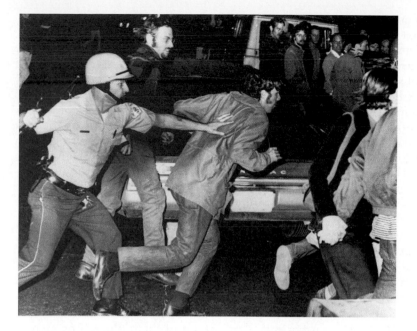

♦ Violence erupted during the 1968 Democratic National Convention in Chicago. Using nightsticks, police attacked antiwar and anti-establishment protesters who surrounded the convention hotel. The violent confrontations in Chicago did little to quell similar protests, unify the Democratic party, or help Hubert Humphrey's chances for election. *Wide World Photos.*

only 43.4 percent of the popular vote. Conservatives were pleased. Combined, Nixon and Wallace attracted almost 57 percent of the vote, which conservatives said indicated wide public support for an end to liberal social programs and a return to "traditional values." They believed that a major political realignment was taking shape.

Expanding the American Dream

The explosion of the civil rights movement during the 1960s spread African-American activism to all parts of the country. It also contributed to the growth of other groups, such as women, Mexican Americans, and Native Americans, demanding equal rights and access to the American dream.

The Women's Rights Movement

Popular social images during the 1950s showed women happiest at home raising children and running the household. Although this scenario held true for many women, a growing number were dissatisfied with their lives. As the 1960s began, more women were entering the work force, having fewer children, and getting divorced. Many women complained that they were denied access to profitable careers. A 1963 report documented that women worked for less pay (on average, 40 percent that of a man), were more likely to be fired or laid off, and had little success in reaching top career positions. Nor was it just in the workplace that women faced discrimination. Throughout the country, divorce, credit, and property laws generally favored men.

To some women, the role of housewife itself symbolized oppression. **Betty Friedan** was one who concluded that the chores of the housewife amounted to a form of servitude. As a young woman, she had dropped out of a psychology doctoral program to get married, bear children, and keep a suburban home. In her 1963 bestseller, *The Feminine Mystique,* she pondered why she was not satisfied. After reviewing the responsibilities of the housewife (making beds, grocery shopping, driving children everywhere, preparing meals and

> **Betty Friedan** Feminist who wrote *The Feminine Mystique* in 1963 and helped found the National Organization for Women in 1966.

snacks, and pleasing her husband), she asked: "Is this all?" She concluded that it was not enough. Women needed to overcome the "feminine mystique" that promised them fulfillment through the domestic arts. She called on women to set their own goals and seek careers outside the home. Her book contributed to a renewed women's movement.

Title VII of the 1964 Civil Rights Act also produced more activism. Title VII prohibited discrimination on the basis of race, religion, creed, national origin, or sex. Many women and liberals hoped that Title VII would commit the government to gender equality. But when the Equal Employment Opportunity Commission (EEOC) showed little interest in dealing with gender discrimination, proponents organized to press the government to enforce Title VII. Experienced civil rights activists like Mary King and Casey Hayden of the Student Nonviolent Coordinating Committee were anxious to push for women's rights. In "the black movement," one woman wrote, "I had been fighting for someone else's oppression and now there was a way I could fight for my own freedom and I was going to be much stronger than I ever was."

The most prominent women's organization to emerge was the **National Organization for Women (NOW),** formed in 1966 and headed by Betty Friedan. NOW launched an aggressive campaign to draw attention to sex discrimination. It sued the EEOC for not upholding the law and thirteen hundred corporations for gender discrimination. It demanded an Equal Rights Amendment to the Constitution and pushed for easier access to birth-control devices and the right to have an abortion.

NOW's membership grew rapidly, from about 300 in 1966 to 175,000 in 1968. But the movement was larger than NOW's membership. Women in droves attended **consciousness-raising** sessions and other grassroots gatherings to promote women's issues. Calls arose for new social and sexual codes for women. Some women rejected high heels, bras, and other trappings associated with a male-defined image of feminine sexuality. NOW's 1970 Strike-for-Equality Parade demonstrated the growing mass appeal of the women's movement when **fifty thousand** supporters marched down New York City's Fifth Avenue.

As within the African-American civil rights movement, divisions developed. Many women who supported equal opportunities and rights rejected the feminist label and what they believed was the movement's bias toward career and working women. At the other extreme, some called for a complete redefinition of the traditional institutions of family and marriage. Marriage was "slavery," "legalized rape," and "unpaid labor," according to radical feminist Ti-Grace Atkinson. Still, by the end of the Seventies, a general feminist critique of American society had succeeded in convincing many Americans that women should pursue goals and aspirations beyond the traditional roles of wife, mother, and homemaker.

The Emergence of Chicano Power

Mexican Americans also organized to assert their social and political rights. As the 1960s began, Mexican Americans were largely an invisible minority (see Map 30.2). Outside the Southwest, few Americans were aware of them. Prevailing stereotypes portrayed them as docile, if not lazy, and ridiculed them as poorly educated, unskilled people who spoke English badly. Statistically, Mexican Americans were near society's lowest levels of income and education.

Throughout the 1940s and 1950s, organizations like the League of Latin American Citizens and the G.I. Forum had made minor gains against legal segregation, but little had changed for most Mexican Americans. The New Frontier and the Great Society had revived hope, as organizations began to pressure American society to recognize the needs of the Latino population. In 1963, the Mexican-American majority in Crystal City, Texas,

Title VII Provision of the Civil Rights Act of 1964 that guaranteed women legal protection against discrimination.

National Organization for Women Women's rights organization founded in 1966 to improve educational, employment, and political opportunities for women and to fight for equal pay for equal work.

consciousness-raising Related to achieving greater awareness of the nature of a political or social issue through group therapy or group interaction.

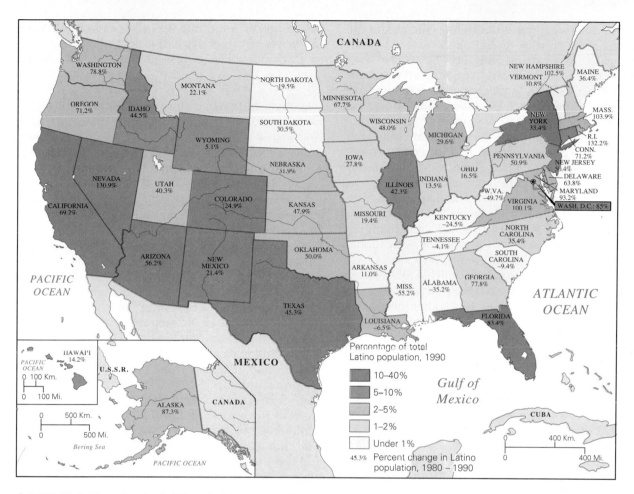

♦ **MAP 30.2 Changing Latino Population**   At one time, the great majority of Latinos
were Mexican Americans located in the Southwest. In the 1990s, Latinos resided in
nearly every major city and included Cubans, Puerto Ricans, and others from throughout the Caribbean and Central and South America. Growing rapidly, the Latino population was projected to become the largest minority in the country by the year 2000, perhaps 12 percent of the total population.

stunned the region by electing an all-Mexican-
American slate to the city council. The Crystal City
vote was, for many Mexican Americans, a revolutionary act. Across south Texas, Mexican Americans banded together to form El Partido Raza
Unida (the United People party) to spread the political "revolution" throughout Texas. The passage
of the 1965 Voting Rights Act and Johnson's War on
Poverty added more impetus. Throughout the
Southwest, the activism of Mexican Americans

frightened those supporting the status quo. Texas
governor Dolph Briscoe typified conservative sentiment when he denounced the La Raza Unida
movement as Communist inspired.

Briscoe was wrong. The Mexican-American
movement was a local one, born of poverty and
oppressive segregation. Reflecting the grassroots
character of the movement was the important role
that youths played. Many Mexican-American
teenagers and young adults adopted the term

Chicano to stress their unwillingness to accept the dictates of Anglo society. Although many Mexican Americans disapproved, the term "Chicano" was soon applied to Mexican Americans who promoted their heritage and rights. In schools, Chicanos demanded better teachers, integration, and Mexican-American (Latino) studies programs.

Under pressure from the Mexican-American community, school districts, including Los Angeles, implemented Mexican-American studies and bilingual programs, hired more Mexican-American teachers and counselors, and adopted programs to meet the special needs of migrant farm worker children. By the 1970s, calls for bilingual education had become an important educational reform focus for the Latino community.

During the 1960s, nearly one-third of all Mexican Americans worked at **stoop labor** in the fields, picking onions, carrots, grapes, and other perishable crops for less than the minimum wage. Unskilled and uneducated farm laborers were trapped at the bottom of the occupation ladder. They were not covered under minimum wage or labor laws. Established unions made no effort to organize agricultural labor. Finally, in 1962, **Cesar Chavez** created the **National Farm Workers Association (NFWA).** When Chavez called a strike against the grape growers of central California in 1965, the NFWA had reached seventeen hundred members. He demanded a wage of $1.40 an hour and asked the public to support the farm workers by buying only union-picked grapes. With varying degrees of success, the boycott and strike continued for five years until most of the major growers accepted unionization.

As Mexican Americans and other Latinos became more vocal in their demands for a fairer share of the American dream, both political parties began to reach out to moderate Mexican-American leaders. New Mexico's Manuel Lujan, a Republican, was elected to Congress, joining several Mexican-American Democrats in the House of Representatives. In 1974, Democrats Jerry Apodaca and Raul Castro were elected governors of New Mexico and Arizona.

Despite such success stories, the majority of Mexican Americans have not achieved social or economic equality. Economically, the Mexican-American population remains one of the poorest minorities in the United States. Lack of economic success has left few incentives for Latino children to stay in high school.

The Latino dropout rate was 45 percent nationwide in 1990, exceeding rates for blacks and whites.

American Indian Activism

American Indians also began to assert their rights with new vigor in the 1960s. The 1950s had been oppressive years for Indians. Although the federal government actually eliminated few reservations or tribal units, federal policies encouraged more than thirty-five thousand American Indians to leave their reservations and move to urban areas. Few urban Indians found anything but discrimination, poverty, and disease.

American Indians on and off reservations called for changes in federal and state policies. Increasingly militant Indian leaders demanded the protection and restoration of their ancient burial grounds, along with fishing and timber rights. They asked museums to return the remains of dead Indians on display. The National Indian Youth Council called for Indians to resist further loss of Indian lands, rights, and traditions. Vine Deloria's popular *Custer Died for Your Sins* (1969) informed readers that Indians asked "only to be freed of cultural oppression." "The white does not understand the Indian," he wrote, "and the Indian does not wish to understand the white." The central issue was not equality and assimilation, Deloria explained, but Indian self-determination. Indians wanted economic prosperity and opportunity,

---

Chicano   Term adopted by many Mexican Americans during the late 1960s to describe their ethnic identity; it was associated with the promotion of Mexican-American heritage and rights.

stoop labor   Field labor that involves constant bending, usually to pick fruits and vegetables.

Cesar Chavez   Labor organizer who founded the National Farm Workers Association; he believed in nonviolence and used marches, boycotts, and fasts to bring moral and economic pressure to bear on growers.

National Farm Workers Association   Migrant workers' union organized by Cesar Chavez in 1962 that used a series of boycotts to force California growers to recognize the union and improve wages and working conditions.

but on terms that would ensure their continued tribal existence.

In the 1960s, Presidents Kennedy and Johnson provided some change, ending the termination program. President Nixon continued the process by placing Indians in top-level positions within the Bureau of Indian Affairs. In 1974, Congress passed the **Indian Self-Determination and Education Assistance Act,** which gave tribes control of many federal programs on their reservations. On the issue of lost land, American Indians pressed their claims, with little prospect of success. Still, some Indian victories have occurred. In 1972, the Passamaquoddy and Penobscot tribes in Maine sued to have over 12.5 million acres, which they claimed had been illegally seized by the state, returned to them. They settled in 1980 for 300,000 acres and the establishment of a $27 million trust fund for the tribes. Also in 1980, the Supreme Court decided that the federal government owed over $106 million to the Sioux for taking the Black Hills of South Dakota in the 1870s.

Although some American Indian leaders turned to Washington and the courts to assert Indian rights, others took more direct action. In 1968, the Chippewas organized the **American Indian Movement (AIM)** to dramatize police brutality toward Indians in Minneapolis. In 1969, a group of San Francisco Indian activists seized **Alcatraz Island,** offering to buy the federally owned island for $24, the same amount that Dutch settlers had paid for Manhattan Island in 1626. They held the island until 1971, when federal authorities, without bloodshed, retook control. In 1973, AIM leaders Russell Means and Dennis Banks organized the armed occupation of Wounded Knee, South Dakota, the site of the 1890 massacre of the Sioux by the army. AIM militants controlled the town for seventy-one days before surrendering to federal authorities. Although the "second battle of Wounded Knee" failed to change federal policy, it did publicize Indian grievances and problems.

Nixon and the Balance of Power

In foreign affairs, Nixon expected to achieve an honorable peace in Vietnam and to reestablish American leadership in world affairs. To realize these goals, he turned to Harvard professor **Henry Kissinger,** his national security adviser and foreign policy expert. Nixon and Kissinger wanted to restructure Cold War policies, particularly with regard to the Soviet Union. They believed that America's military advantage over the Soviets was narrowing rapidly. Because there was little chance that Congress would support efforts to regain clear military superiority, they concluded that it was necessary to improve relations with the Soviet Union. Nixon and Kissinger recognized that the widening split between China and the Soviet Union, which had developed in the 1960s, offered promising possibilities for changing the balance of Cold War power.

Vietnamization

Nixon and Kissinger also knew that Vietnam was the most immediate problem. It dominated and shaped nearly all other issues: the budget, public and congressional opinion, foreign policy, and domestic stability. The Republicans needed a solution to Vietnam before moving ahead on other issues. The central problem was to find a means to protect South Vietnam, to encourage the North Vietnamese to negotiate, and to allow the gradual withdrawal of American forces. Nixon's solution was **Vietnamization:** reducing the American role while strengthening

Indian Self-Determination and Education Assistance Act   Law passed in 1974 giving Indian tribes control over federal programs carried out on their reservations and increasing their control of reservation schools.

American Indian Movement   Militant Indian movement organized to demand social justice for urban Indians.

Alcatraz Island   Rocky island in San Francisco Bay that was occupied from 1969 to 1971 by Native American activists who demanded that it be made available as a cultural center.

Henry Kissinger   German-born American diplomat who was national security adviser and secretary of state under President Nixon; he helped negotiate the cease-fire in Vietnam.

Vietnamization   Policy announced by Nixon in which the United States scaled back its involvement in Vietnam, returning to its earlier role of helping Vietnamese forces fight their own war.

South Vietnam's military capability. Nixon believed that large-scale opposition to the war would fade once American soldiers started coming home.

Vietnamization began in the spring of 1969. By the end of the year, American forces in Vietnam had declined by over 110,000. The withdrawal of American troops reflected a broader strategy that became known as the **Nixon Doctrine.** This doctrine stipulated that countries confronting communism would have to bear the brunt of the military burden, and that the United States would provide those countries with only economic and political support.

Vietnamization was only a part of Nixon's strategy for ending the conflict in Vietnam. The other element in the "peace plan" was to increase the economic, diplomatic, and military pressure on North Vietnam to end the war. This, Nixon hoped, would be done in two ways: by getting the Soviets and the Chinese to reduce their support for North Vietnam and by bombing enemy bases across the South Vietnamese border in Cambodia and Laos. In March 1969, Nixon ordered the heavy bombardment of Communist sanctuaries inside Cambodia. Fearful of public and political reactions, the administration tried to keep the operation a secret. When Operation MENU ended in 1973, over 383,800 tons of bombs had been dropped on Cambodia. The intense assault was also part of a "madman strategy" Nixon designed to convince the North Vietnamese to negotiate. Nixon said that he wanted Hanoi "to believe that I've reached the point where I might do anything to stop the war."

The strategy did not work. The North Vietnamese appeared unconcerned about Nixon's "madness," the increased bombing, and decreasing support from China and the Soviet Union. They still believed that victory was only a matter of waiting patiently until America was unwilling to continue the war. Consequently, talks between Kissinger and the North Vietnamese in Paris were unproductive.

Nor did American opposition to the war fade away. In November 1969, over 250,000 antiwar protesters paraded past the White House calling for an end to the conflict. News of American atrocities at **My Lai,** which came to light in 1970, added fuel to the antiwar cause. In March 1968, Lieutenant William Calley's platoon had "wasted" the small village, killing more than two hundred men, women, and children. The massacre seemed to of-

fer incontestable proof that the Vietnam War was immoral. The publication of the **Pentagon Papers,** a collection of official documents showing government officials had deceived the American public about Vietnam from the 1950s on, furthered public disillusionment with the war.

Still, Nixon refused to change course. In 1970, he ordered American troops to cross the border into Cambodia and destroy North Vietnamese and Viet Cong headquarters and supply areas. He told the public that the incursion was not to widen the war but to hasten its end. The Cambodian invasion, which involved nearly eighty thousand American and South Vietnamese troops, did destroy large amounts of supplies. But it failed to defeat the enemy or to stop the flow of supplies from North Vietnam. It also generated loud protests on college campuses. At Kent State University on May 4, 1970, the Ohio National Guard fired on protesters, killing four and wounding eleven. At Jackson State University in Mississippi, police killed two students during another demonstration. Outraged students responded by shutting down over a hundred campuses. An angry Senate repealed the Gulf of Tonkin Resolution and forbade the further use of American troops in Laos and Cambodia.

By the end of 1971, Kissinger and Nixon were frustrated. They knew that Vietnamization was not progressing well and that there seemed no sign of a settlement in Paris. The North Vietnamese refused to consider any settlement that did not replace South Vietnamese president Nguyan Van Thieu and his government with a coalition that included the Communist National Liberation Front. That condition was unacceptable to the United States. Then, in

Nixon Doctrine Nixon's policy of requiring countries threatened by communism to shoulder the bulk of the military burden, with the United States offering mainly political and economic support.

My Lai Site of a massacre of more than two hundred South Vietnamese villagers by U.S. infantrymen in 1969, an event that added to antiwar sentiment in the United States.

Pentagon Papers Classified government documents on the policy decisions that led to U.S. involvement in Vietnam, which were leaked to the *New York Times* in 1971.

◆ Together, Richard Nixon *(left)* and Secretary of State Henry Kissinger *(right)* sought to refocus American foreign policy by ending the war in Vietnam and improving relations with the Soviet Union and the People's Republic of China. *John Dominis, LIFE Magazine © Time Warner.*

March 1972, Communist forces drove toward Saigon as South Vietnamese forces tottered on the brink of collapse. Livid at the Communist offensive, Nixon ordered massive bombing raids against North Vietnam and Communist forces in South Vietnam. By mid-June 1972, American airpower had stalled the offensive and enabled ARVN forces to regroup and drive back the North Vietnamese. With their cities under almost continuous air attacks, the North Vietnamese became more flexible in negotiations. By October, a peace settlement was ready. "Peace is at hand," Kissinger announced.

Thieu, however, rejected the plan. Reluctantly, Nixon supported Thieu and ordered the Christmas bombing of North Vietnam. Nixon hoped to put additional pressure on Hanoi and to convince Thieu that the United States would protect South Vietnam. After eleven days, Nixon stopped the bombings and advised Thieu that if he did not accept the next peace settlement, the United States would leave him to fend for himself. Thieu thereupon accepted a peace settlement similar to the one offered in October. Following the signing of the Paris Peace Accords in 1973, Nixon and Kissinger proclaimed peace with honor. Kissinger shared the 1973 Nobel Peace Prize with his North Vietnamese counterpart, Le Duc Tho.

The peace accords imposed a cease-fire, required the removal of all American troops (only twenty-four thousand now remained in South Vietnam) but not North Vietnamese troops, and promised the return of American prisoners of war. The peace terms permitted the United States to complete its military and political withdrawal, but the pact did little to ensure the continued existence of South Vietnam. The cease-fire, everyone expected, would be temporary. Kissinger confided privately that the South Vietnamese government might "hold out for a year and a half."

As expected, the cease-fire soon collapsed. North Vietnam continued to funnel men and supplies to the south, but substantial American air and naval support for South Vietnam never arrived. Neither Congress nor the public was anxious to help Thieu's government. Instead, Congress cut aid to South Vietnam. In March 1975, North Vietnam began its final campaign to unify the country, and a month later, its troops entered Saigon. The few remaining Americans and some South Vietnamese were evacuated by helicopter, some from the roof of the American embassy. The Vietnam War ended as it had started, with Vietnamese fighting Vietnamese.

Congress drew one immediate conclusion in the aftermath of American involvement in Vietnam: that limits should be placed on the president's powers to commit American troops to foreign conflicts. The **War Powers Act,** passed in November 1973, required the president to inform Congress within forty-eight hours of deploying troops overseas and to withdraw those troops within sixty days if Congress failed to authorize the action.

Modifying the Cold War

Ending the Vietnam War was essential to Nixon's goal of redefining the Cold War. Nixon hoped that an "era of confrontation" would give way to an "era of negotiation." To this end, he pursued **détente,** a policy intended to reduce tensions with the two Communist superpowers. China was the key to the Nixon-Kissinger strategy. Several bloody border clashes between the Chinese and the Soviets made the Chinese receptive to better relations with the United States. Nixon hoped that American friendship with the Chinese would in turn encourage the Soviets to improve their relations with the United States. Following a secret visit by Kissinger, Nixon flew to Beijing in February 1972 to meet with Communist party chairman Mao Zedong. Suddenly, the "Red Chinese" were no longer the enemy but "hard-working, intelligent and practical" friends. The Cold War was thawing in the East.

Nixon's China policy contributed to improved relations with the Soviet Union. Kissinger followed his secret visit to China with one to Moscow, where he discussed improving relations with President **Leonid Brezhnev.** Nixon flew to Moscow in May 1972 and told Brezhnev that he believed that the two nations should "live together and work together." Needing to reduce military spending, develop the Soviet domestic economy, and increase American trade, Brezhnev agreed. The meeting was a success. Brezhnev obtained increased trade with the West, including shipments of American grain, and the superpowers announced an agreement on the **Strategic Arms Limitation Talks (SALT I),** which established a maximum number of **intercontinental ballistic missiles (ICBMs)** and submarine-launched ballistic missiles (SLBMs) for each side. It seemed as if détente had arrived.

Nixon and Politics

In his foreign policy, Nixon followed new paths in dealing with the Chinese and Soviets that did not reflect traditional Republican views. This was also true of his domestic programs. Nixon believed that Republicans needed to develop a pragmatic and socially responsible conservatism.

Pragmatic Conservatism

Nixon's brand of conservatism, the **New Federalism,** embraced federal power while proposing to make programs more responsive to state and local government. His **Revenue Sharing Act,** passed in October 1972, reflected the new approach. The government would continue to raise revenue through its broad tax base, but it would release more of the money to state and local governments and reduce federal controls on how they spent it.

War Powers Act Law passed in 1973 that set a sixty-day limit on presidential commitment of U.S. troops to hostilities abroad unless Congress authorized continued action.

détente Relaxing of tensions between the superpowers in the early 1970s, which included increased diplomatic, commercial, and cultural contact.

Leonid Brezhnev President of the Soviet Union from 1977 until his death in 1982, who worked to foster détente with the United States during the Nixon era.

Strategic Arms Limitation Talks agreement Agreement between the United States and the USSR in 1972 to limit both offensive nuclear weapons and the anti-ballistic missile systems that protected against them.

intercontinental ballistic missiles Missiles that can travel from one continent to another.

New Federalism Nixon's policy of accepting the existence of government social programs but seeking to trim waste and increase the power of state and local governments.

Revenue Sharing Act Five-year program established in 1972 to distribute large amounts of federal tax revenues to state and local governments to use as they saw fit.

Before the program ended in 1986, state and local governments had received over $83 billion in revenue sharing funds.

Nixon also wanted to redirect the flow of money and responsibility in the welfare system. Unlike many staunch conservatives, Nixon was not opposed to welfare, but he believed that the existing welfare system robbed people of their self-esteem, contributed to the breakup of nuclear families, and punished people for working. His proposal for welfare reform, the Family Assistance Plan (FAP), sought to balance work and welfare but was attacked by conservatives and liberals alike. The Senate defeated it in 1969 and 1971. After its second defeat, Nixon lost interest.

But Nixon did not abandon what he saw as the need for federal social responsibility. Under his administration, food stamps became more accessible; the elderly and the disabled received direct federal support; and Social Security, Medicare, and Medicaid payments were increased. Nixon also supported subsidized housing and expanded the Job Corps. He signed the **Twenty-sixth Amendment** giving 18-year-olds the right to vote, and his administration oversaw the formation of the Occupational Safety and Health Administration (OSHA) and the **Environmental Protection Agency (EPA).**

Nixon believed that the Republican party could not afford to ignore social needs and public concerns in the name of conservatism. The environmental issue was a case in point. When Nixon took office in 1969, the environment was not a major issue. Almost overnight, however, it became one. The ever-present Los Angeles smog, an oil slick off Santa Barbara, California, and the declaration that Lake Erie was ecologically dead provided graphic reminders of the ecological dangers facing the nation. During the second celebration of Earth Day in April 1970, nearly every community in the nation hosted some type of Earth Day activity.

Nixon was not an environmentalist, but he recognized an opportunity. Two days after Earth Day, 1970, he proposed the creation of the EPA. He also signed the Clean Air and Clean Water acts, which limited the amount of pollutants that business and industry could dump into the air and water.

Nixon proved to be flexible in economic matters as well. When he took office, the nation was experiencing a climbing rate of inflation. Nixon's initial response was to cut spending, increase interest rates, and balance the budget. He succeeded in balancing the budget in 1969, but inflation continued to rise even as economic growth slowed, a phenomenon soon dubbed **stagflation.** By 1971, the economy was in its first recession since 1958 and inflation was still climbing. Fearing that the economy would erode Republican support, Nixon radically shifted his approach. "I am now a Keynesian," he announced in April 1971. He asked for increased federal spending to boost recovery and wage and price controls to stall advancing inflation.

Nixon's battle with inflation, however, was a losing one, in part because of economic events over which he had no control. A global drought pushed up farm prices. Following the October 1973 Arab-Israeli Yom Kippur War, Arab nations instituted an oil boycott of the United States for its support of Israel. Gasoline prices nearly doubled. Many Americans were forced to wait in long gas lines. Some areas of the country even instituted fuel oil and gasoline rationing. Increases in food and oil prices pushed the 1974 inflation rate over 10 percent.

Law and Order and Southern Politics

During the 1968 campaign, Nixon had presented himself as the law-and-order candidate, who would use the power of government to combat crime. Once in office, however, Nixon seemed more interested in using the law-and-order theme for political purposes than for attacking street crime. Throughout Nixon's first term, administration officials had waged war against student, antiwar, and

---

Twenty-sixth Amendment Amendment to the Constitution in 1971 lowering the voting age from 21 to 18.

Environmental Protection Agency Agency created in 1970 to consolidate all major government programs combating pollution.

stagflation Persistent inflation combined with stagnant consumer demand and relatively high unemployment.

civil rights activists. Vice President **Spiro Agnew** denounced antiwar protesters for aiding the enemy. He called for the Silent Majority to reject "the nattering nabobs of negativism" and for authorities to take back the campuses. The White House also employed more direct tactics. The Justice Department, often acting illegally, used **wiretaps** and preventive detention against opponents and infiltrated groups viewed as the administration's enemies.

As part of Nixon's efforts to lock up the once solidly Democratic South for Republicans, the administration worked to slow integration. In response to Mississippi's request in 1969 to postpone the court-ordered integration of several school systems, Attorney General **John Mitchell** petitioned the Supreme Court for a delay. At the same time, the administration lobbied Congress to pass a weaker version of the 1965 Voting Rights Act. Neither effort was successful. Congress rejected changes to the Voting Rights Act, and in October the Supreme Court unanimously decreed in *Alexander v. Holmes* that it was "the obligation of every school district to terminate dual school systems at once." The White House suffered another loss in 1971 when the Court reaffirmed the use of busing to achieve integration in a North Carolina case, *Swann v. Charlotte-Mecklenburg.* The Nixon administration criticized the decisions but agreed to "carry out the law." By 1973, most African-American children in the South attended integrated public schools. Nixon was unable to slow integration, but he did win political support from white southerners.

A second part of Nixon's southern strategy was to alter the ideological composition of the Supreme Court. He wanted a more conservative Court that would interpret the Constitution more narrowly. His first opportunity came in 1969 when Chief Justice Earl Warren retired. Nixon nominated federal judge Warren Burger, a respected conservative who was easily confirmed by the Senate.

Liberal Justice Abe Fortas's resignation soon after gave Nixon a second chance to alter the Court. For political reasons, he wanted to appoint a southerner. Nixon selected Clement Haynesworth of South Carolina to replace Fortas. Haynesworth's record on labor and civil rights raised predictable opposition in the Senate. Democrats and several Republicans joined forces to deny his confirma-

tion. The rejection incensed Nixon, who was determined to force a southerner down the Senate's throat. His second choice was worse than the first. Not only was G. Harrold Carswell of Florida opposed to civil rights and labor, but he was a mediocre judge. A coalition of Republicans and Democrats rejected Carswell. On his third try, Nixon stopped looking for a southerner and selected Harry Blackmun, a conservative from Minnesota, who was confirmed easily. In 1971, Nixon appointed two more justices, Lewis Powell of Virginia (finally a southerner) and William Rehnquist of Arizona, creating a more conservative Supreme Court.

An Embattled President

By the end of Nixon's first term, the Republicans had every reason to gloat. Nearly 60 percent of those polled approved of Nixon's record. Nixon's southern strategy had ensured growing support in what had once been the "solid Democratic South." The law-and-order campaign had proven attractive to Middle America, while protesters and activists were losing strength. The economy, though still a worry, seemed under control. Diplomatically, Nixon had scored major successes in opening relations with China, establishing détente with the Soviets, and reducing American forces in Vietnam.

The continued disarray of the Democratic party only added to Republican confidence. The Democrats nominated **George McGovern** of South Dakota, but he was too liberal for much of the party. George Wallace again bolted the party to

---

Spiro Agnew Vice president under Richard Nixon, who resigned in 1973 amid charges of illegal financial dealings during his governorship of Maryland.

wiretap Concealed listening or recording device used to monitor communications.

John Mitchell Nixon's attorney general, who eventually served four years in prison for his part in the Watergate scandal.

George McGovern South Dakota senator who opposed the Vietnam War and was the Democratic candidate for president in 1972 defeated by Nixon.

run as a third-party candidate on the American Independent ticket. Wallace's candidacy ended on May 15, 1972, when Arthur Bremer shot and paralyzed him.

Despite almost certain victory, Nixon was plagued by a siege mentality. He was convinced that he was surrounded by enemies: Democrats, social activists, liberals, and much of the press. Repeatedly, he spoke about "screwing" his domestic enemies before they got him. He used the FBI, the Internal Revenue Service, and other government organizations to intimidate and punish his "enemies."

Throughout the campaign, Nixon was obsessed with humiliating the Democrats. To achieve this objective, Nixon's staff and the Committee to Reelect the President (CREEP), directed by John Mitchell, were willing to step outside the normal bounds of election behavior. They turned to a Special Investigations Unit, the "Plumbers," to disrupt the Democrats. The Plumbers had used illegal surveillance and even burglary to investigate sources of suspected leaks of sensitive materials, like the *Pentagon Papers.* Ex-FBI agent G. Gordon Liddy and former CIA operative E. Howard Hunt conducted "dirty tricks" against the Democrats. CREEP approved sending burglars into the Democratic National Headquarters office in the **Watergate** building to copy documents and tap phones.

There on June 17, 1972, a security guard detected the burglars and notified the police, who arrested five men carrying "bugging" equipment. Officials soon determined that they worked for Hunt and Liddy. CREEP and the White House denied any connection to the burglars. As Nixon "categorically" denied that anyone in the White House was involved, Mitchell and White House staffers destroyed incriminating documents and arranged payments to those arrested in return for their silence. The FBI was encouraged to limit its investigation. The furor passed, and the Watergate break-in had little apparent effect on the election. Nixon buried McGovern in an electoral avalanche, winning every state except Massachusetts.

Nixon began his second term by claiming a clear mandate for his policies. From the outside, it appeared that the Nixon administration had a clear field to promote its agenda. But within the White House, concern simmered over the approaching trial of the Watergate burglars. If the truth about Watergate were discovered, the Nixon administration might disintegrate. Although not directly involved in the covert actions against the Democrats, Nixon knew soon after the Watergate break-in that White House officials were implicated and approved of efforts to hide their involvement. "Cover it up," he told John Mitchell.

As the trial approached, the cover-up began to unravel. Before being sentenced, James McCord, who led the burglary team, informed Judge John J. Sirica that key Republicans had been involved in planning the operation and that the burglars had been paid to keep quiet. *Washington Post* reporters Bob Woodward and Carl Bernstein found a trail of suspicious payments that led to the White House, John Mitchell, and CREEP. Amid growing suspicions of White House involvement, the Senate convened a special committee in 1973 to investigate the break-in, chaired by a Democrat, Senator Sam Ervin, Jr., of North Carolina. White House staffer John Dean testified before Sirica and Ervin's committee that top White House officials, including Nixon, were involved in the cover-up. By May 1973, Nixon had fired Dean and watched Bob Haldeman and John Ehrlichman resign.

The cover-up further unraveled with testimony that Nixon had secretly recorded Oval Office conversations, including those with Dean. Responding to public pressure, Nixon appointed Harvard professor Archibald Cox as special Justice Department prosecutor to investigate Watergate. When Cox demanded the Oval Office tapes, Nixon had him fired in October 1973. Calls for Nixon's resignation or impeachment intensified. Adding to Nixon's troubles were accusations that he had improperly taken tax deductions. "I am not a crook," Nixon asserted. Nevertheless, the Internal

---

Watergate   Washington apartment complex that housed the Democratic party's national headquarters; it gave its name to the scandal over the Nixon administration's involvement in a break-in at those headquarters and the president's part in the cover-up that followed.

Revenue Service concluded that Nixon had made errors in his deductions and owed the government half a million dollars. Meanwhile, Vice President Agnew was convicted of income-tax evasion and influence peddling and forced to resign. Nixon named Congressman Gerald R. Ford of Michigan to replace Agnew.

In March 1974, the grand jury investigating the Watergate break-in indicted Mitchell, Haldeman, and Ehrlichman and named Nixon as an "undicted co-conspirator." Under tremendous pressure, Nixon released transcripts of selected tapes to the House Judiciary Committee. The outcome was devastating. Not only did the transcripts contradict some official testimony, but Nixon's profanity and apparent lack of moral values shocked many Americans. By August, the House Judiciary Committee had charged Nixon with three impeachable crimes: obstructing justice, abuse of power, and denying subpoenas. Once-loyal Republicans told him that he could either resign or face impeachment. Nixon resigned on August 9, 1974, making Ford president. Eventually, twenty-nine people connected to the White House were convicted of crimes related to Watergate and the 1972 campaign.

Vietnam cost Johnson his presidency and divided the nation.

It was not just the debate over the war that split the nation. By 1968, the country was aflame with riots in urban centers, and an increasing number of groups was seeking better social, economic, and political *choices*. Those advocating social reforms encountered growing *constraints* generated by a resurgence of conservatism. In 1968, Nixon *chose* to emphasize dissatisfaction with Johnson's war and the Great Society to win the presidency.

As president, Nixon *chose* to escape the quagmire of Vietnam by implementing Vietnamization. He *chose* to promote détente by working to improve relations with the Soviet Union and China. At home, Nixon *chose* an uneven course, switching between maintaining governmental activism and reducing the power of government. Politically, he sought a broader base for the Republican party by pursuing a southern strategy that diminished federal support for civil rights. Despite Nixon's domestic and foreign policy successes, however, his desire to crush opposition eventually led to the Watergate scandal. *Expecting* impeachment, the president *chose* to resign. The *outcome* of the Johnson years and Watergate was a nation with low *expectations* for politics and government, caught in a feeling of drift, disillusionment, and disunity.

S U M M A R Y

E xpectations
C onstraints
C hoices
O utcomes

President Johnson *chose* to continue President Kennedy's commitment to save South Vietnam from communism. The *outcome* was an Americanized war in Vietnam. The *expectation* that American superiority would defeat Ho Chi Minh's Communists proved disastrous for the nation.

SUGGESTED READINGS

Ambrose, Stephen. *Nixon: The Triumph of a Politician, 1962–1972* (1989).

An excellent examination of Nixon and his politics.

Caputo, Philip. *A Rumor of War* (1986).

An excellent personal account of one person's changing perspectives on the war in Vietnam. From his experiences as a young marine officer in Vietnam to an experienced journalist covering the final days in Saigon, Caputo frequently reflected the views of the American public.

Deloria, Vine, Jr. *Behind the Trail of Broken Treaties* (1974).

An examination of U.S. government policies toward Native Americans by a leading Indian activist.

Echols, Alice. *Daring to Be Bad* (1989).

An insightful and interesting account of the radical dimension of the women's movement.

Kutler, Stanley. *The Wars of Watergate* (1990).

A detailed account of the events surrounding the Watergate break-in and the hearings that led to the resignation of Nixon.

McQuaid, Kim. *The Anxious Years: America in the Vietnam-Watergate Era* (1989).

A brief and solid overview of the 1960s.

Roberts, Robert. *Where the Dominoes Fell* (1990).

A brief, well-written history of America's role in Vietnam.

Films

There are many excellent films about the American experience in Vietnam, from the PBS series on Vietnam to feature films like *Platoon, Apocalypse Now,* and *The Deer Hunter*.

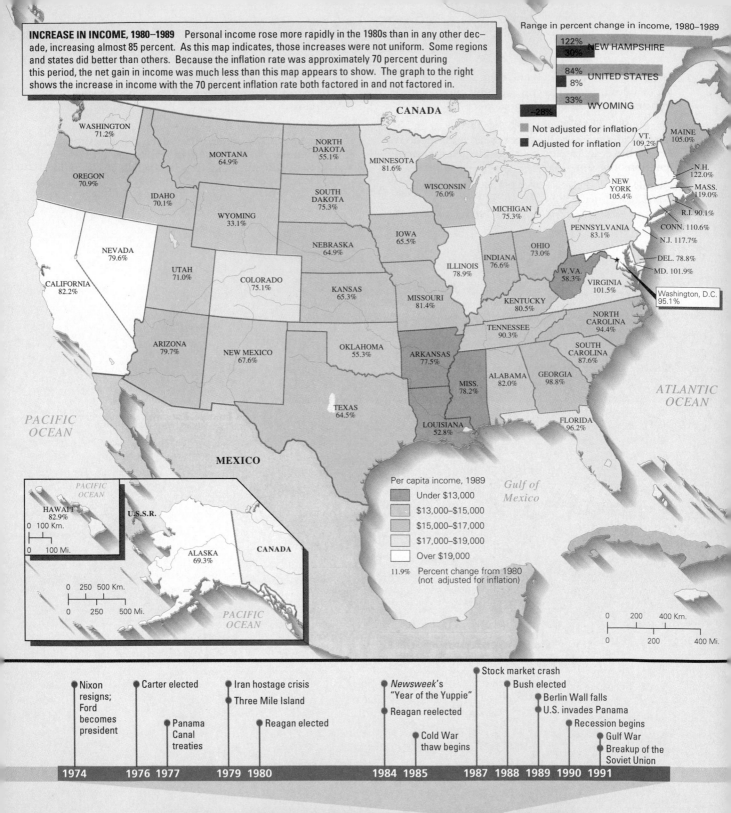

INCREASE IN INCOME, 1980–1989 Personal income rose more rapidly in the 1980s than in any other dec-ade, increasing almost 85 percent. As this map indicates, those increases were not uniform. Some regions and states did better than others. Because the inflation rate was approximately 70 percent during this period, the net gain in income was much less than this map appears to show. The graph to the right shows the increase in income with the 70 percent inflation rate both factored in and not factored in.

Range in percent change in income, 1980–1989

122% NEW HAMPSHIRE
30%

84% UNITED STATES
8%

33% WYOMING
−28%

Not adjusted for inflation
Adjusted for inflation

CANADA

WASHINGTON 71.2%

OREGON 70.9%

IDAHO 70.1%

MONTANA 64.9%

NORTH DAKOTA 55.1%

MINNESOTA 81.6%

WISCONSIN 76.0%

MICHIGAN 75.3%

VT. 109.2%

MAINE 105.0%

N.H. 122.0%

MASS. 119.0%

NEW YORK 105.4%

R.I. 90.1%

CONN. 110.6%

N.J. 117.7%

NEVADA 79.6%

UTAH 71.0%

WYOMING 33.1%

SOUTH DAKOTA 75.3%

IOWA 65.5%

NEBRASKA 64.9%

ILLINOIS 78.9%

INDIANA 76.6%

OHIO 73.0%

PENNSYLVANIA 83.1%

DEL. 78.8%

MD. 101.9%

CALIFORNIA 82.2%

COLORADO 75.1%

KANSAS 65.3%

MISSOURI 81.4%

KENTUCKY 80.5%

W.VA. 58.3%

VIRGINIA 101.5%

Washington, D.C. 95.1%

ARIZONA 79.7%

NEW MEXICO 67.6%

OKLAHOMA 55.3%

ARKANSAS 77.5%

TENNESSEE 90.3%

NORTH CAROLINA 94.4%

SOUTH CAROLINA 87.6%

TEXAS 64.5%

MISS. 78.2%

ALABAMA 82.0%

GEORGIA 98.8%

LOUISIANA 52.8%

FLORIDA 96.2%

ATLANTIC OCEAN

PACIFIC OCEAN

MEXICO

Gulf of Mexico

Per capita income, 1989
Under $13,000
$13,000–$15,000
$15,000–$17,000
$17,000–$19,000
Over $19,000

11.9% Percent change from 1980 (not adjusted for inflation)

PACIFIC OCEAN

HAWAI'I 82.9%

0 100 Km.
0 100 Mi.

U.S.S.R.

ALASKA 69.3%

CANADA

0 250 500 Km.
0 250 500 Mi.

PACIFIC OCEAN

0 200 400 Km.
0 200 400 Mi.

Stock market crash

Nixon resigns; Ford becomes president

Carter elected

Panama Canal treaties

Iran hostage crisis

Three Mile Island

Reagan elected

Newsweek's "Year of the Yuppie"

Reagan reelected

Cold War thaw begins

Bush elected

Berlin Wall falls

U.S. invades Panama

Recession begins

Gulf War

Breakup of the Soviet Union

1974   1976 1977   1979 1980   1984 1985   1987 1988 1989 1990 1991

1850   1900   1950   2000

Facing Limits, 1974–1992

Politics of Uncertainty

- What domestic problems did Gerald Ford and Jimmy Carter face? What were the political and economic outcomes of the choices they made?

- What expectations and constraints did Carter face as a Washington outsider?

Carter's Foreign Policy

- What new directions in foreign policy did Carter take? What were the outcomes of those changes?

- What constraints did Carter face in implementing a policy stressing human rights?

Enter Ronald Reagan— Stage Right

- What expectations influenced Americans who chose to vote for Reagan?

- What was "Reaganomics," and what were the outcomes of Reagan's economic policies for the economy and society?

Asserting World Power

- How did the Reagan administration's expectations about American foreign policy differ from Carter's? How did those views shape the outcomes of Reagan's policies?

In Reagan's Shadow

- What new foreign-policy choices did the United States face as a result of the collapse of the Soviet Union?

- How did the outcome of Reagan's domestic policies shape expectations and outcomes for the Bush administration?

INTRODUCTION

E xpectations
C onstraints
C hoices
O utcomes

Gerald Ford assumed the presidency after the resignation of Richard Nixon and faced an expanding set of policy *constraints* without Nixon's vision or toughness. The economy continued to flounder, and many of Nixon's foreign-policy initiatives, especially regarding détente, were being questioned by his own party. Also, the political cynicism generated by Vietnam and Watergate operated as a *constraint*. The *outcome* was a presidency with few political or foreign-policy "victories." Nevertheless, the Republican party nominated Ford for the presidency in 1976.

As the nation celebrated its two-hundredth birthday, few Americans *expected* the immediate future to match the success of the past. Limits seemed to loom everywhere. The sluggish economy responded to neither liberal nor conservative policy *expectations*. The liberalism that had attacked racism and poverty was out of vogue, challenged by more conservative *choices*. The Silent Majority seemed to set the tone of the nation, rejecting the idea that a more active government can solve problems and favoring a stronger emphasis on more traditional social values. Even James Earl Carter, the Democratic candidate for the presidency in 1976, argued that the U.S. government could not solve every problem. He urged Americans to sacrifice to overcome problems at home and abroad. As president, however, Carter failed to provide an effective domestic or foreign policy.

The 1980 Republican candidate for president, Ronald Reagan, won popular approval by promoting the *expectation* of a renewed America, powerful and prosperous. He attacked liberal economic and social policies and reemphasized a Cold War foreign policy that would "stand tall" against the Soviet "evil empire." During his administration, the economy seemed revitalized, and government was redirected away from costly social programs. Many Americans felt that business had been freed of many needless government controls, traditional social and family values had been properly reasserted, and the Cold War had been all but won.

Not everyone agreed that Reagan's *choices* produced a favorable *outcome*. Critics argued that he placed too much emphasis on wealth and too little on the needs of the poor. Others pointed to a massive national debt and a growing trade deficit as serious economic problems. Despite Reagan's personal popularity, as the Reagan administration ended, more and more Americans were uncertain about the *outcome* of Reagan's economic and social policies.

Running in the shadow of Reagan in 1988, Vice President George Bush seized the Republican presidential nomination in a nation that seemed dissatisfied but unable to pinpoint what was wrong and how to fix it. Responding to the lack of consensus in the polls, Bush offered a "kinder, gentler nation" that would show more concern for minorities, the poor, education, and the environment. Easily defeating Michael Dukakis, the Democratic candidate, Bush assumed the presidency but had little desire to implement domestic policy changes. Instead, he *chose* to focus on foreign policy. Taking office as the Soviet Union shattered, he charted foreign policy in a new international setting: the United States was the only superpower. Bush cautiously supported democratic change in the Soviet Union and Eastern Europe and *chose* to commit American military force in Panama and Kuwait. The *outcome* was that Bush's foreign policy, unlike his domestic policies, generated widespread praise.

CHRONOLOGY

New Directions, New Limits

1974   Nixon resigns; Ford becomes president
Ford pardons Nixon

1975   Fall of South Vietnam
Helsinki Summit
Jackson-Vanik Amendment

1976   Carter elected president

1977   Department of Energy created
Panama Canal treaties
SALT I treaty expires

1978   Camp David Accords
Revolution in Iran topples the shah
United States recognizes People's Republic
of China

1979   Ayatollah Khomeini assumes power in Iran
Nuclear accident at Three Mile Island,
Pennsylvania
Egyptian-Israeli peace treaty signed in
Washington, D.C.
Chrysler bailout
Hostages seized in Iran
Soviet Union invades Afghanistan

1980   Carter applies sanctions against Soviet
Union
SALT II withdrawn from Senate
Iran-Iraq War begins
Reagan elected president

1981   Iran releases American hostages
Economic Recovery Tax Act

1982   United States sends marines to Lebanon

1983   SDI funded
United States invades Grenada
Marine barracks in Beirut destroyed

1984   Reagan reelected
Withdrawal of U.S. forces from Lebanon
Boland Amendment

1985   Mikhail Gorbachev assumes power in
Soviet Union
Secret arms sales to Iran in exchange for
hostages
Gorbachev-Reagan summit in Geneva

1986   U.S. bombing raid on Libya
Gorbachev-Reagan summit in Iceland

1987   Iran-Contra hearings
Stock market crash
Intermediate Nuclear Force Treaty

1988   U.S. warship shoots down Iranian
passenger jet
Terrorists blow up a Pan American jet over
Scotland
Bush elect president

1989   Communism collapses in Eastern Europe
Berlin Wall torn down
United States invades Panama
Chinese government crushes
prodemocracy movement
Gorbachev-Bush summit at Malta

1990   Recession begins
Free elections in Nicaragua
Clean Air Act
Iraq invades Kuwait

1991   Breakup of Soviet Union
Gulf War
Gorbachev resigns

Politics of Uncertainty

When he assumed office in 1974, **Gerald Ford** offered a stark contrast to Richard Nixon. Whereas Nixon was innovative, suspicious, and arrogant, Ford was conservative, trustful, and humble. (He joked that he was a Ford and not a Lincoln.) Responding to Watergate, Ford sought to establish cordial relations with Congress and to restore the people's faith in government. That expectation faded rapidly.

An Interim Presidency

Soon after taking office in 1974, Ford pardoned Nixon for any crimes the former president might have committed. The pardon was widely unpopular. Thereafter, Democrats opposed Ford's policies to deal with the problems of inflation, recession, and the federal deficit. He wanted to cut spending, raise interest rates, and cut business taxes. Democrats instead introduced legislation to create jobs and to increase spending for social and educational programs. Ford in turn vetoed these bills. The consequence of the pardon, rising inflation and unemployment, and the battles with Congress was a political stalemate.

Ford fared only slightly better in his foreign policies. Relying heavily on Henry Kissinger, the national security adviser and secretary of state, Ford continued Nixon's policies, including Vietnamization, arms limitation, and détente (see page 678). Trying to maintain the thaw in the Cold War, Ford met with Soviet Premier Leonid Brezhnev and leaders from thirty-three other nations in Helsinki, Finland, in August 1975. Following these negotiations, the United States officially recognized the boundaries of Europe established after World War II. The Soviets in return agreed to respect an extensive list of **human rights.** The Helsinki agreements quickly came under fire as human rights violations continued in the Soviet Union. Congress responded by passing the Jackson-Vanik Amendment, which required the Soviets to allow more Jewish immigration from the Soviet Union before the United States granted trade agreements. Reading the political climate, Ford backed away from détente.

Ford's efforts to maintain Nixon's pledges of economic and military support for South Vietnam (see page 675) also met with congressional opposition. When North Vietnamese forces seized Saigon in April 1975, Ford blamed Congress for the Communist victory. Most Americans, however, were happy that the conflict was no longer an American war.

Kissinger was far more successful with his diplomacy in the Middle East (see Map 31.1). Following the Yom Kippur War of October 1973, Kissinger flew between the Israeli and Arab capitals seeking to negotiate the removal of Israeli forces from Arab territory. His so-called shuttle diplomacy continued until September 1975, when Israel agreed to withdraw from some occupied areas and Egypt resigned from the anti-Israeli Arab coalition.

The Bicentennial Election and Jimmy Carter

Against the background of the bicentennial celebration of American independence, Ford sought election in his own right. Although he faced a stiff challenge from California governor Ronald Reagan and the Republican right wing, he gained the nomination.

Ford's Democratic opponent, Jimmy Carter, had no national exposure and little political experience apart from being governor of Georgia. But people in 1976 were fed up with politics and politicians. Carter presented himself as a political outsider

> **Gerald Ford** Michigan congressman who became vice president under Nixon in 1973 after Vice President Agnew resigned; Ford became president in 1974 when Nixon resigned.
>
> **human rights** Basic rights and freedoms to which all human beings are entitled, including the rights to life, liberty, freedom of thought and expression, and equality before the law.

ROMANIA
YUGO.
MAC.
BULGARIA
GREECE
Athens
Crete
Mediterranean
Sea
Black Sea
RUSSIA
KAZAKHSTAN
UZBEKISTAN
GEORGIA
ARMENIA
AZERBAIJAN
Caspian Sea
TURKMENISTAN
Ankara
TURKEY
Cyprus
U.S. troops, 1958, 1983–1984
SYRIA
LEBANON
Damascus
Tel Aviv
ISRAEL
Amman
JORDAN
Cairo
See inset
Baghdad
IRAQ
Tehran
IRAN
AFGHANISTAN
Soviet occupation, 1979–1989
U.S. aid to rebels, 1980s
U.S. arms sales, 1955–1978:
$20.8 billion
Shah overthrown, 1979
American hostages taken,
1979–1981
PAKISTAN
U.S. and allies launch Operation
Desert Storm against Iraq, 1991
KUWAIT
Kuwait
Persian Gulf
U.S. arms sales, 1980s,
during Iran-Iraq War
Iraq invades Kuwait, 1990
BAHRAIN
Manama
QATAR
Doha
Strait of Hormuz
Dubayy
Muscat
UNITED ARAB
EMIRATES
LIBYA
EGYPT
Aswan
Dam
Red Sea
SAUDI ARABIA
Riyadh
Mecca
Oil embargo, 1973
Source of 17% of U.S. oil imports
in 1975
Largest buyers of U.S. arms, 1978
OMAN
SUDAN
YEMEN
Sana
Mukalla
Gulf of Aden
Aden
DJIBOUTI
Djibouti
SOMALIA
ETHIOPIA
Arabian Sea
INDIAN OCEAN
U.S. troops assist in relief
of famine, 1992–1993; U.S.
troops withdrawn, 1994
KENYA

Jewish state after UN partition of
Palestine, 1947
Israel after War of 1948–1949
Area controlled by Israel after
Six-Day War, 1967
Israeli-occupied area after Yom Kippur
War, 1973
By Egyptian-Israeli agreements of 1975 and
1979, Israel withdrew from the Sinai in 1982.
In 1981 Israel annexed the Golan Heights.
Through negotiations between Israel and
the PLO, Jericho and the Gaza Strip were
placed under Palestinian self-rule, and Israeli
troops were withdrawn in 1994.
In 1994 Israel and Jordan signed an agreement
opening their borders and normalizing their
relations.

LEBANON
Beirut
Damascus
SYRIA
Golan Heights
Haifa
Sea of Galilee
Mediterranean Sea
Port Said
West
Bank
Tel Aviv
Jerusalem
Gaza
Jordan
Amman
Dead Sea
ISRAEL
JORDAN
Cairo
Suez
EGYPT
Suez
Canal
Elat
SINAI
PENINSULA
Gulf of Suez
Gulf of Aqaba
SAUDI ARABIA
Sharm el-Sheikh
Red Sea
Nile
ARAB-ISRAELI
CONFLICT

Members of the Organization of
Petroleum Exporting Countries
(OPEC)
Oil fields

0   250   500 Km.
0   250   500 Mi.

◆ **MAP 31.1 The Middle East** Since 1946, the United States has tried to balance strong support for Israel with its need for oil from the Arab states. To support U.S. interests in this volatile region, the United States has funneled large amounts of financial and military aid and used overt and covert force to shape regional governments. Agreements signed in Washington in 1993 and 1994 between Israel and the Palestine Liberation Organization and between Israel and the kingdom of Jordan reduced tensions in the region.

who would heal the wounds of Watergate and Vietnam. He seemed the ideal candidate for the time. In a lackluster campaign, Ford and Carter were vague on issues but expansive on smiles and photo sessions. Carter won a close election, receiving 297 electoral votes to Ford's 240.

Brimming with enthusiasm, Carter arrived in Washington in January 1977. He emphasized that he was an outsider, untouched by the politics of Washington and the lure of special interests and political deals. He pledged an administration of honesty, simplicity, and hard work. Promoting his image as a simple farmer, Carter took the oath of office wearing a plain blue business suit. His message to the people was without frills. "We must simply do our best," he stated, to generate a "new spirit . . . of individual sacrifice for the common good." Portraying himself as the people's president, Carter delivered Roosevelt-style "fireside chats" (see page 544) on radio and television and held "phone-ins" that gave people a chance to talk with their president. The public welcomed Carter's open, informal presidency.

But not everyone was charmed. Some questioned whether Carter had the political flexibility, expertise, and muscle to handle congressional politicians. Traditional Democrats also resented Carter's appointments of Georgia friends to government posts. "I busted my butt for Carter," one Democrat complained, "and there's nobody I know who got an appointment." A rift soon developed between the Washington outsiders on Carter's staff and the insiders in Congress.

Democratic congressional leaders flew into a rage when Carter presented his first budget, which axed eighteen pet projects that would have provided jobs and revenue for home districts. Angry Democrats joined with gleeful Republicans to force Carter to restore many of the cuts. The battle over the budget established a pattern. Congress and President Carter frequently marched in different directions. By mid-1977, most of Carter's proposals were buried in Congress. Criticism increased when allegations of financial mismanagement forced the president's close friend Bert Lance to resign as director of the Office of Management and Budget in September 1977. The Lance affair further eroded public trust in Carter's judgment and raised questions about the administration's claim of honesty.

Domestic Priorities

Carter faced two major domestic problems: a sluggish economy and high energy costs due to dependence on foreign oil. He concluded that the economy could not improve until the United States stopped consuming more energy than it produced. It was then importing about 60 percent of its oil. Solving the energy imbalance was the "moral equivalent of war," Carter argued. He asked Americans to save energy by lowering thermostats, wearing sweaters, and using public transportation. Turning to Congress, he proposed regulations and taxes to encourage conservation, as well as increases in domestic production.

Lobbyists for automobile, oil, gas, and other industries immediately tried to steer Congress in another direction. They advocated increased oil production, which they said would also create jobs. The development of large oil fields in Alaska's North Slope region made it difficult for many people to believe that there really was an **energy crisis**. Congress passed only fragments of Carter's plan, creating the Department of Energy in 1977, approving some incentives for conservation, and deregulating the natural gas industry.

When oil prices rose in 1978, forced upward by a revolution in Iran, Congress reconsidered Carter's program. By 1980, Congress had approved funds for **alternative fuels** (including nuclear energy) and an excess-profits tax on the oil and gas industry. But Congress made no real effort to develop a comprehensive plan to achieve energy independence.

---

energy crisis Vulnerability to energy shortages due to dwindling fossil fuels, wasteful energy consumption, and potential embargoes by oil-producing countries.

alternative fuels Sources of energy other than coal, oil, and natural gas; alternative energy sources include solar, geothermal, hydroelectric, and nuclear energy.

The prospects of using nuclear energy as a substitute for oil dimmed considerably after a nuclear power plant at **Three Mile Island** in central Pennsylvania had a serious accident on March 28, 1979. The plant released a cloud of radioactive gas and nearly suffered a **meltdown.** Over a hundred thousand people were evacuated from the surrounding area. After the accident, more than thirty energy companies canceled nuclear building projects. Thus oil, coal, and natural gas remained the primary sources of American energy.

Carter's economic policies fared even worse than his energy policy. To stimulate the economy, Carter asked for tax reforms, the **deregulation** of transportation industries (trucking, railroads, and airlines), and passage of his energy program. He tried to use tighter credit and higher interest rates to curb inflation. Like Ford, he asked workers and producers to hold the line on wages and prices.

Carter lost the battle with inflation. By 1979, inflation was running at 13 percent, the highest rate since 1947. Unemployment, which stood at nearly 7.6 percent, was also high. Carter assumed part of the blame for the nation's economic troubles. But he also blamed the public for its unwillingness to sacrifice. Most people, however, blamed the president for the nation's difficulties.

The stagflation troubling the American economy was largely the product of a changing world economy over which presidents had little control. The booming economies of West Germany, Japan, Korea, and Taiwan cut into American markets, reducing American profits and prosperity. The new cohesion of the **Organization of Petroleum Exporting Countries (OPEC)** following the Arab-Israeli Yom Kippur War of 1973 caused the price of petroleum products to skyrocket during the rest of the decade. Drastically higher energy costs not only added to inflation and unemployment but threatened the nation's industrial base, which depended on inexpensive fuel. In the new global economy, many American industries were unable to match the production costs, retail prices, or quality of goods produced overseas. Japanese manufacturers, once the joke of international commerce, were gobbling up the electronics industry and cutting deeply into the American automobile

market. Korea and Taiwan were taking huge bites out of the American textile markets. Many of the nation's primary industries (iron and steel, rubber, automobiles and their parts, clothing, coal) were forced to cut back production, lay off workers, and even close plants.

In 1978, the giant Chrysler Corporation tottered on the brink of bankruptcy. Carter, facing soaring unemployment, agreed to help Chrysler, and in 1979 Congress underwrote a $1.5 billion private loan for the automobile maker. Critics called the Chrysler bailout welfare for the rich, but supporters argued that the loan saved jobs. With new models, effective advertising, and more efficient production, Chrysler was making more than $2.4 billion in profits by 1984, and Chrysler's chief executive officer, Lee Iacocca, was a national hero. Chrysler's success, however, was the exception. From the Great Lakes to the Northeast, the **Rust Belt** spread over the once-vibrant industrial center of the United States.

Carter's Foreign Policy

Carter's foreign policy was as controversial as his domestic policy. He said that American foreign

Three Mile Island Site of a nuclear power plant near Harrisburg, Pennsylvania; an accident at the plant in 1979 led to a partial meltdown and the release of radioactive gases.

meltdown Severe overheating of a nuclear reactor core, resulting in the melting of the core and the escape of radiation.

deregulation Removal of government regulations from an industry.

Organization of Petroleum Exporting Countries Economic alliance of oil-producing countries, mostly Arab, formed in 1960; in 1973, OPEC members placed an embargo on the sale of oil to countries allied with Israel.

Rust Belt Industrialized region containing older factories that are barely profitable or that have been closed.

policy had been preoccupied by an "inordinate fear of communism." America's recognition of the People's Republic of China in 1978 reflected Carter's beliefs. He advocated a foreign policy that would safeguard human rights, fight poverty, and promote economic and social development, especially in the **Third World.** Yet Carter also pursued traditional East-West power politics.

Carter's foreign-policy advisers reflected the split within his own mind over what American foreign policy should attempt to accomplish. **Zbigniew Brzezinski,** the national security adviser, was an uncompromising Cold Warrior who looked for chances to "stick it to the Russians." He worried that Carter's emphasis on human rights might weaken pro-American but abusive regimes in South Korea, Nicaragua, and the Philippines.

Cyrus Vance, Carter's secretary of state, was more broad-minded than Brzezinski. Vance recognized Cold War constraints but wanted to follow policies that focused on human issues and economic development. Clashes between him and Brzezinski were expected, but Carter believed he could bridge the gap between them.

A Good Neighbor and Human Rights

Latin America seemed to Carter and Vance the best place to sound a new tone in American policy. Carter wanted the United States to abandon its "paternalism" and instead fashion policies that considered each Latin American nation's internal priorities. Carter believed that Panama and the Panama Canal presented an excellent opportunity to chart a new course for U.S. policy in Latin America.

When Carter took office, negotiations to turn control of the canal over to Panama had been stalled for years. Carter assigned the canal a high priority. Within a year, two treaties were written that returned ownership and control of the canal to Panama by 1999 and guaranteed the neutrality of the canal. Carter was pleased, but the American public was not. Nearly 80 percent of those asked opposed giving up the canal. Opponents argued that the canal was built and operated by

the United States and should remain that way forever. **Ronald Reagan** labeled the agreement outright appeasement, and conservative Republican senator Jesse Helms of North Carolina promised to kill it in the Senate. He failed, but only barely.

Carter also hoped to promote human rights in Latin America. Conservatives complained that letting human rights drive policy might undermine pro-American governments in Nicaragua and El Salvador. In Nicaragua, the **Sandinista Liberation Front,** a largely Marxist-led organization, was conducting a guerrilla war to oust Anastasio Somoza, who had ruled the country since 1967. Carter considered the corrupt and dictatorial Somoza a liability and stopped all aid to Nicaragua in early 1979. With his national guard disintegrating, Somoza fled to Paraguay in July, taking much of the nation's treasury.

The Sandinistas, led by **Daniel Ortega,** assumed power and promised free elections. Hoping that Ortega would adopt moderate reform programs, Carter asked Congress for $75 million in aid for the new government. Congress agreed, but the Nicaraguan government became more radical and **autocratic.** By 1980, the Sandinistas had canceled

---

Third World   Underdeveloped or developing countries of Latin America, Africa, and Asia.

Zbigniew Brzezinski   National security adviser who favored Cold War confrontations with the Soviet Union.

Cyrus Vance   Secretary of state who wanted the United States to defend human rights and further economic development in the Third World.

Ronald Reagan   Fortieth U.S. president; succeeded Jimmy Carter.

Sandinista Liberation Front   Leftist guerrilla movement that overthrew the corrupt regime of Anastasio Somoza in Nicaragua in 1979.

Daniel Ortega   Sandinista leader who helped establish the revolutionary government that replaced the Somoza regime in 1979 and who served as president of Nicaragua from 1984 to 1990.

autocratic   Having unlimited power or authority; despotic.

elections and established close ties with the Soviet Union.

Conservatives attacked Carter's human rights policy for destroying a pro-American leader and allowing a Communist government to be established in Central America. Republican presidential candidate Ronald Reagan denounced the Communist "takeover" of Nicaragua and the Sandinistas' effort to export revolution to neighboring countries. Reagan called for support for the rebel **Contras** fighting the Sandinistas. Many Contras were former supporters of Somoza and had vowed to overthrow Ortega and restore "democracy." Carter stopped all aid to the Ortega government in early 1981.

Conservatives also called for more American support for El Salvador. There the newly created government of **José Napoleón Duarte** faced threats from both the left and the right. On the left were Farabundo Martí National Liberation Front (FMLN) guerrillas, who occupied more and more territory. On the right were elements within the military who used terrorism to eliminate opposition figures. Carter almost cut off military and economic aid when right-wing death squads murdered reform advocate Archbishop Oscar Romero. But FMLN victories prodded Carter to send millions of dollars in equipment and credit to Duarte.

As the election of 1980 neared, Carter's program for human rights in Latin America lay in ruins. He had been forced to break ties with Nicaragua and disregard murder and torture in El Salvador. His one triumph, the canal treaties, was unpopular at home.

♦ One of President Carter's greatest triumphs was the signing of the 1978 peace accords between President Anwar Sadat of Egypt (*left*) and Prime Minister Menachem Begin of Israel (*right*). The agreement followed days of personal diplomacy by Carter at the Camp David presidential retreat. Both Sadat and Begin received the Nobel Peace Prize for their efforts. *Jimmy Carter Presidential Library.*

ber 1978. Carter smoothed relations between Sadat and Begin, who did not get along well. Carter carefully negotiated agreements by which Egypt recognized Israel's right to exist and Israel returned the Israeli-occupied Sinai Peninsula to Egypt.

Carter had to rescue the **Camp David Accords** several times before they were ratified. But on March 26, 1979, he watched as Begin and Sadat

The Camp David Accords

Carter credited his success in Panama to his ability to take a new approach to an old issue. He believed that such a tactic could also be used to achieve a peace settlement between Israel and its Arab neighbors (see Map 31.1). To this end, Carter invited Egypt's president, Anwar Sadat, and Israel's prime minister, Menachem Begin, for talks at the presidential retreat at Camp David in Maryland. Surprisingly, both agreed and arrived in Septem-

Contras Nicaraguan rebels, many of them former followers of Somoza, fighting to overthrow the Sandinista government.

José Napoleón Duarte Moderate civilian named to head the government of El Salvador in 1980.

Camp David Accords Treaty signed at Camp David in 1978, in which Israel agreed to return territory captured from Egypt in the Six-Day War in 1967 and Egypt agreed to recognize Israel as a nation.

signed the first peace treaty between an Arab state and Israel. The glow of success was fleeting. Arab leaders and many Egyptians bitterly condemned both the treaty and Sadat and remained committed to the destruction of Israel.

The Collapse of Détente

The most immediate Soviet-American issue that Carter faced was the still-unfinished **SALT II** treaty. Carter decided to negotiate even deeper cuts in nuclear weapons than Ford had proposed. Despite chilly relations, the United States and the Soviet Union were able to reach an agreement on strategic arms limitations in July 1979. Many senators, however, believed that the agreement was too favorable to the Soviets.

The Senate was still debating the treaty in December when the Soviet Union invaded neighboring Afghanistan. Claiming that the Afghan government had asked for help against **Islamic fundamentalist** rebels, Soviet leader Brezhnev sent in eighty thousand troops. Carter called the invasion the "gravest threat to peace since 1945." He withdrew the SALT II agreements from the Senate, halted grain shipments to the Soviet Union, and announced an American boycott of the 1980 Moscow Olympics. The invasion ended Carter's ambiguous Soviet policy. He now called for military superiority and a renewed arms race. He also began providing support for the **mujahedeen,** the Afghan resistance fighters.

The Iranian Revolution

Islamic fundamentalism affected far more than just Afghanistan. It was also behind the 1978 revolution in Iran, which toppled the pro-American ruler, Shah Reza Pahlavi. Since Eisenhower, the United States had supported the shah as a barrier to Soviet influence in the region. The shah had received billions of dollars in American weapons and aid, but his regime had become increasingly repressive. Led by **Ayatollah Ruhollah Khomeini,** a Shiite Muslim sect that condemned the contamination of Iranian culture by Western ideas and values headed the opposition. Khomeini returned to Iran

from exile in Paris in February 1979, when the Shiites and the Iranian military forced the shah to flee. The Ayatollah Khomeini then set in motion a repressive fundamentalist Islamic revolution that attacked the United States as the main source of evil in the world.

Carter ended American aid to Iran, ordered Americans home, and reduced the embassy staff in Tehran. After the exiled shah entered a New York hospital to receive cancer treatments, an angry Iranian mob stormed the American embassy in Tehran on November 4, 1979, and took the staff hostage. These Americans were then paraded through the streets and subjected to numerous abuses as the Iranians demanded the return of the shah for trial. The press quickly dubbed the crisis "America Held Hostage."

Carter weighed the conflicting options identified by his advisers. Brzezinski wanted to use military force to free the hostages. Vance argued for negotiation, hoping that Iranian moderates would find a way to free the hostages. Carter sided with Vance and through the **Palestine Liberation Organization (PLO)** was able to negotiate freedom for thirteen hostages, mostly women and African

---

SALT II Proposal made in 1979 that the United States and the Soviet Union limit the numbers of strategic nuclear missiles in each country; Congress never approved the treaty.

Islamic fundamentalist Member of a movement calling for the replacement of Western secular values and attitudes with traditional Islamic values and an orthodox Muslim state.

mujahedeen Afghan resistance movement, supplied with arms by the United States, that fought the Soviets after the invasion of Afghanistan in 1979.

Ayatollah Ruhollah Khomeini Iranian Shiite leader who was exiled for his opposition to the shah but who returned to Iran in 1979 after the shah's downfall and established a new constitution giving himself supreme powers.

Palestine Liberation Organization Political and military organization of Palestinians originally dedicated to opposing the state of Israel through terrorism and other means.

Americans. As further discussions failed, American frustration and anger grew. In April 1980, Carter agreed with Brzezinski and ordered a military rescue mission. The operation was a disaster. A violent dust storm in the Iranian desert caused three helicopters to malfunction. Carter scratched the mission. Vance, who had opposed the operation, resigned.

Diplomatic efforts through the Canadians and the Algerians eventually resulted in an agreement in late 1980 to release the hostages. By that time, the shah had died of cancer, and Iran was at war with Iraq and needed the assets that Carter had frozen. On January 20, 1981, the last day of the Carter presidency, the hostages were freed, after 444 days of captivity.

Enter Ronald Reagan— Stage Right

According to Republicans in 1980, Carter's failure to free the hostages was typical of his administration's ineptness. Inflation remained at 12.4 percent, and unemployment was near 8 percent. Republicans claimed that Carter was incapable of maintaining either American honor abroad or prosperity at home. Ronald Reagan, a movie actor turned conservative politician, offered voters a clear alternative to Carter. The former California governor easily outran CIA director George Bush in 1980 to become the Republican candidate. Reagan named Bush his running mate. Liberal Republican John Anderson protested his party's turn to the right by running as an independent.

In his campaign for the presidency, Reagan argued that the federal government had grown too large and powerful. He promised to reduce the role of government and to lower taxes, freeing American ingenuity and competitiveness. Across the country, taxes had become a hot issue. In 1978, California had passed **Proposition 13,** which placed a limit on property taxes.

Reagan was a smooth campaigner with a sense of humor. He quipped, "A recession is when your neighbor loses his job. A depression is when you lose yours. A recovery is when Jimmy Carter loses his." Reagan presented himself as the "citizen politician, speaking out for the ideas, values, and common sense of everyday Americans." His conservative agenda called for more power for the individual and less power for the federal government. A vote for Reagan, his supporters claimed, would restore American pride, power, and traditions.

Reagan's message was welcome news not only to Republicans but also to many living in the Sunbelt (see chapter opener map for Chapter 30). By 1980, the region's population exceeded that of the industrial North and East. Politically, the Sunbelt exhibited conservative populism that opposed the power of the federal government. White southerners equated "liberal" government with altering traditional racial norms, and a **"sagebrush rebellion"** in the western Sunbelt opposed federal control and regulation of land and natural resources. Many westerners argued that federal environmental and land-use regulations blocked growth and economic development in the West. Throughout the Sunbelt, Reagan found enthusiastic voters ready to reject liberal, activist government. Further contributing to Republican totals were voters mobilized by the **New Right,** as well as younger voters attracted by the economic goals and social stability Republicans promised. Except for the size of Reagan's majority, the outcome of the election of 1980 was never in doubt.

Reagan emerged with 51 percent of the popular vote, compared to 41 percent for Carter and 7 percent for Anderson. Reagan's electoral count

Proposition 13   Measure adopted by referendum in California in 1978 cutting local property taxes by more than 50 percent.

"sagebrush rebellion"   A 1980s political movement in western states opposing federal regulations over land and natural resources.

New Right   Conservative movement opposing the political and social reforms that developed in the late 1960s and demanding less government intervention in the economy and a return to traditional values; it was a major political force by the 1980s.

was even more impressive: 489 to 49. Republicans gained a majority in the Senate and narrowed the Democratic majority in the House substantially. It appeared that a new conservative era was beginning.

The Moral Majority and the New Right

Reagan's campaign pulled vital support from the New Right. A loosely knit alliance that combined political and social conservatives, the New Right opposed the social and cultural changes spawned during the 1960s and 1970s. The New Right's social agenda promoted the movement's views of correct family and moral values, condemning abortion, pornography, and homosexuality. To mobilize support, the New Right pioneered the use of direct-mail campaigns that targeted specific segments of the population.

Highly visible among New Right groups were evangelical Christian sects, many of whose ministers were **televangelists.** With donations that exceeded a billion dollars a year, they did not hesitate to mix religion and politics. Jerry Falwell's **Moral Majority** promoted Ronald Reagan on more than five hundred television and radio stations. Falwell called on listeners to wage political war against politicians whose views on the Bible, homosexuality, prayer in schools, abortion, and communism were too liberal. Although many of the television evangelists were sincere, some were susceptible to the lure of wealth and power. In the most publicized scandal, Jim Bakker, whose "Praise the Lord" radio and television shows and enterprises earned millions of dollars, was denounced for forcing women of his church to have sex with him. He was also found guilty of fraud and conspiracy and sentenced to prison in 1987. Other scandals and abuses weakened the electronic ministry by the 1990s.

Reaganism

Reagan brought to the White House a clear and simple vision of the type of America he wanted. Called the "Great Communicator" by the press,

he and his staff used imagery and the media expertly. Reagan did not create the policies to realize his vision; instead, he delegated authority to the cabinet and executive staff while he set the grand agenda.

Once in office, Reagan hit hard at the economic crisis of inflation, high interest rates, and unemployment. The administration's economic formula to restore the economy was deceptively simple: increase military spending, reduce taxes, and end government restrictions.

This formula derived from **supply-side economics.** Supply-siders believed that lowering taxes would actually increase tax revenues by increasing the amount of money available for investments. Budget director David Stockman fashioned a tax package and budget that reduced income and corporate taxes and slashed federal spending on social programs. The **Economic Recovery Tax Act,** passed in 1981, cut income and most business taxes by an average of 25 percent. Upper-income levels received the largest tax reduction. Stockman later admitted that the tax act was really a "Trojan Horse" to help the rich. Conservative Democrats joined with Republicans to cut $25 billion from social programs, including food stamps, Aid to Families with Dependent Children, and jobs and housing programs. Reagan also ended Nixon's federal revenue-sharing programs (see page 678) and reduced the amount of federal money paid to the states for Medicare and Medicaid programs. To

televangelist Protestant evangelist minister who conducts television broadcasts; many such ministers used their broadcasts as a forum for defending conservative values.

Moral Majority Right-wing religious organization led by televangelist Jerry Falwell that had an active political lobby in the 1980s on issues such as opposition to abortion and the Equal Rights Amendment.

supply-side economics Theory that reducing taxes on the wealthy and increasing the money available for investment will stimulate the economy and eventually benefit everyone.

Economic Recovery Tax Act Law passed in 1981 that cut income taxes by 25 percent across the board and further reduced taxes on the wealthy.

halt inflation, Federal Reserve chairman Paul Volker pushed interest rates upward.

Cutting taxes and domestic spending was only part of the Reagan agenda for economic growth. Another aim of **Reaganomics** was to free businesses and corporations from restrictive regulations. This aim was most visible in environmental regulations. Interior Secretary James Watt sought to open federally controlled land, coastal waters, and wetlands to mining, lumber, oil, and gas companies. The Environmental Protection Agency under Anne Gorsuch Burford weakened enforcement of federal guidelines for reducing air and water pollution and the cleanup of toxic-waste sites.

Reagan's economic policies were not immediately effective. Although inflation fell from 12 percent in 1980 to 4 percent by 1982, economic growth failed to materialize. Unemployment climbed over 10 percent in one of the worst recessions since World War II, and small businesses and farms faced bankruptcy in increasing numbers. The **trade deficit** skyrocketed from a surplus in 1980 to a $111 billion deficit in 1984, and the federal deficit swelled alarmingly. Reagan called for patience, saying that his economic programs eventually would work.

Suddenly, in 1983, the recession ended. Unemployment dropped to 7.5 percent. Many conservative economists and Republicans praised the administration's policies for the recovery. Others said that the recovery had less to do with Reagan's policies than with increases in world trade and the lowering of oil prices. Critics also pointed out that the national "recovery" was selective. The West Coast was doing well, but the Rust Belt was still rusting. But most Americans simply sought to make the most of renewed prosperity.

The Power of Money

Reagan's support for American business and opposition to government restrictions placed an emphasis on success, profits, and individual gain. While some argued that the new business culture was based on greed, others pointed to the creativity of American capitalism. Developments such as personal computers affected almost every segment of American society. With Apple and IBM leading the way, personal computers restructured the process of handling information and offered new choices for nearly everyone. Bill Gates, who developed software and programs for personal computers, took advantage of these new opportunities to become America's youngest billionaire (see Individual Choices: Bill Gates).

Among the most successful people during the 1980s were financial wizards like Donald Trump, T. Boone Pickens, and Ivan Boesky. Trump, who proclaimed himself the king of the "megadeal," commanded national attention for both his business ventures and his social life. His ghost-written books glorified him as the master of manipulating the economic system for personal gain. Speculators took advantage of government deregulation to sell **junk bonds** to finance **leveraged buyouts.** Riding the crest of the speculative boom, they amassed vast fortunes by arranging to have huge conglomerates gobble up smaller, vulnerable companies. "Buy high, sell higher," *Fortune* proclaimed.

The culture of success filled newspapers, magazines, television, and movies, celebrating people who were making big money and living accordingly. The lifestyle of success captivated young Americans. Those about to enter the work force increasingly considered financial success as their main goal in life. In 1974, only 46 percent of college freshmen and high school seniors listed being "financially successful" as their first priority. In 1986, 73 percent of college freshmen put being "very well off financially" as their priority.

Reaganomics   Economic beliefs and policies of the Reagan administration, including the belief that tax cuts for the wealthy and deregulation of industry would benefit the economy.

trade deficit   Amount by which imports exceed exports.

junk bond   Corporate bond having a high yield and high risk.

leveraged buyout   Use of a target company's asset value to finance the debt incurred in acquiring the company.

Leading the Computer Revolution

Bill Gates

In 1974, Bill Gates made an eventful choice. Along with a friend from high school, Paul Allen, the Harvard sophomore decided to create an operating system for a new development in the computer world: the personal computer (PC). The system worked, and Gates left Harvard and formed Microsoft, creating MS-DOS and software packages for what soon became the personal computer revolution. By 1986, his operating system dominated the computer world, and he became the country's youngest billionaire. Corbis-Bettmann.

In December 1974, Bill Gates, a sophomore at Harvard, and his high school friend Paul Allen claimed that they could write a computer program for a new personal computer, the Altair 8080, which came unassembled and cost $397. Neither Gates nor Allen had seen the computer or the microchip that made the Altair run, but they were positive that the advent of personal computing was the beginning of a new era in information processing. "We realized that the revolution" had started, Gates recalled, and "there was no question of where life would focus." Gates and Allen chose to be a part of the revolution.

Having read only sketchy information about the Altair 8080, Gates and Allen invaded the Harvard computer lab and worked day and night for eight weeks. Ignoring his classes and sometimes sleeping at the keyboard, Gates modified the computer language BASIC to fit the Altair. They had no idea if the program would work—"If we had read the book wrong . . . we were hosed," Allen recalled. He then flew to New Mexico to demonstrate the program. Fortunately, it worked, and Gates and Allen were on the cutting edge of the computer revolution. Allen stayed to work for the computer company. Gates finished his academic year at Harvard. Then, over the objections of his parents, he chose to drop out of Harvard and join Allen. At 19, he and Allen formed Microsoft, a company to write software for personal computers. Microsoft made Gates, at age 31, the youngest billionaire in America.

Gates's obsession with computers began in 1968, when his high school in Seattle arranged computer time on a local company's machine.

"We were off in our own world," he remembered. "Nobody quite understood the thing but I wanted to figure out exactly what it could do." At the age of 13, he was "hired" by the company—paid with computer time—to find bugs in the system. Three years later, with Allen, Gates formed a company to analyze automobile traffic data by computer. They made about $20,000 until the government offered to analyze the traffic for no cost.

In 1980, their expectations rising, Gates and Allen agreed to design an operating system to run the software for IBM's entry into the personal computing field. IBM was already a giant in large business and institutional computers, and it was expected that IBM's personal computers would greatly expand the popularity and uses of personal computers. In 1980, each computer company wanted to capture and keep users by having a unique operating system to run software. IBM wanted Microsoft to formulate a new, exclusive system. Gates and Allen began by buying an existing system—QDOS, the "quick and dirty operating system"—and modifying it. Within a year, they had created, in great secrecy, Microsoft DOS (MS-DOS).

IBM's personal computers became the industry's leader and were soon being cloned by other companies. Gates chose to offer MS-DOS to other companies. At first, IBM was reluctant to share "its" system, but both companies benefited. By the 1990s, only two major operating systems still existed for personal computers: Apple and MS-DOS. Microsoft had become the industry giant and Gates the country's richest man.

Looking toward the twenty-first century, Gates continues to seek better and more innovative applications for personal computers, telecommunications, and information processing. His newest challenge is to integrate multimedia and communication systems with an interactive software package more effectively. Still pursuing his choice to be at the forefront of a revolution, Gates looks confidently toward a bright future. "We are going to create the software that puts a computer on every desk and in every home," he said. A billionaire, Paul Allen left Microsoft in 1983 and has since invested in and worked to develop companies in the high-technology, communications, and information delivery fields.

Although new technology and innovative ideas created some millionaires, many others were the beneficiaries of the government. Reagan's tax and economic policies favored the wealthy. The wealthiest 1 percent of Americans saw their slice of the economic pie grow from 8.1 percent to 15 percent during the Reagan years. The majority of American workers and families during the same period lost income. Still, the media spotlighted people making millions. College graduates hoping to become highly paid professionals applied to law, business, and other postgraduate schools in droves.

Not everyone was captivated by the Reagan boom. Social critic Tom Wolfe complained of a "Me Generation" that was self-indulgent and materialistic. Some economists warned that the stock market's climb rested on a weak foundation of shaky credit and fast profits. Such credit and profits, they argued, were related neither to actual economic growth nor to an increase in real buying power and wages.

On "Black Monday," October 19, 1987, their fears came true. The stock market dropped 508 points, the largest single decline in American history. Images of the 1929 Crash and the Great Depression reared up. The Reagan administration was shaken, but the Federal Reserve acted quickly to lower interest rates and to pump money into the economy. The Fed's action stopped the panic selling, and the stock market slowly turned upward again. Some warned, however, that the stock market still did not reflect real economic health and argued that more trouble lay ahead.

They soon had additional evidence when the savings and loan system began edging toward collapse. Until 1982, government regulations permitted **savings and loan associations (S&Ls)** to lend money only for single-family homes. In that year, the Reagan administration lifted nearly all restrictions on lending by S&Ls. Many S&L operators jumped into risky ventures such as office buildings, shopping malls, and junk bonds. Losses were covered by the Federal Savings and Loan Insurance Corporation (FSLIC). It was a no-lose situation for the S&L operators. If they gambled wrong, the government paid for their mistakes.

Corruption, bad loans, poor judgment, and a slowing economy soon pricked the S&L bubble. As real-estate values slumped in 1987, many S&Ls began losing vast sums of money. Some closed their doors. Charles Keating, president of Lincoln Savings and Loan in California, lost more than $2.6 billion of depositors' money. To keep his operation from being investigated, he made sizable "political" contributions to several senators. Eventually convicted of fraud, Keating was not alone in bending and breaking the law. He and scores of others left the S&L industry in ruins. The federal government had to cover more than $500 billion in losses.

By the late 1980s, the financial boom was fading along with the reputations of many who had ridden it. Donald Trump had to sell his airline and most of his real estate to pay creditors. Boesky was arrested for **insider trading** and sentenced to three years in prison.

Reputations fell in the Reagan administration as well. Secretary of the Interior James Watt and Attorney General Edwin Meese resigned following revelations that they had received money and favors for helping some businesses gain lucrative government contracts. They were not alone. Over a hundred members of the Reagan administration were found guilty of illegal behavior. Reagan was untouched by the scandals, however, and his popularity remained high. Some called him the "Teflon President" because no criticism seemed to stick to him.

Reagan's Second Term

Throughout the presidential campaign of 1984, Republicans credited Reagan's leadership and poli-

---

savings and loan associations Financial institutions originally founded to provide home mortgage loans; deregulation during the Reagan era allowed them to speculate in risky ventures and led to many S&L failures.

insider trading Trading of stocks by someone who has access to confidential information about the companies involved.

cies for renewed prosperity, restored military superiority, and "standing tall" against communism throughout the world. Using the theme "Morning in America," Reagan's re-election campaign projected a new day of economic expansion, morality, and national power. Reagan avoided specific issues while announcing that big-government liberalism was dead.

After a divisive primary season, former vice president **Walter Mondale** won the Democratic nomination. He refused to concede that liberalism was dead. He called for revitalizing social programs. He selected Geraldine Ferraro, a congresswoman from New York, to be his vice-presidential candidate. Although many people applauded Mondale for selecting a woman, others complained that Ferraro was not the best-qualified woman for the job.

Reagan won an overwhelming victory, taking 59 percent of the popular vote and carrying every state except Mondale's Minnesota. Only the poor, African Americans, and Latinos voted Democrat. A majority of organized labor, women, Catholics, white southerners, farmers, and the middle and upper classes voted for Reagan's Republican vision of "Morning in America."

A growing cloud, however, hung over Reagan's American morning: the soaring budget deficit. During his first administration, the annual deficit had gone from $73.8 billion to over $200 billion. Although reducing the deficit had bipartisan support, how to do it remained a partisan issue. Most Democrats took the view that cuts in military spending were needed. They argued that a large part of the deficit came from military spending, which had risen from $164 billion in 1980 to $228 billion in 1985. Republicans countered by blaming the debt on wasteful social programs.

In late 1985, a coalition of Republicans and Democrats passed the Gramm-Rudman-Hollings Act, which established a maximum debt level and ordered across-the-board cuts if the budget failed to match the level set. The plan never worked effectively. By 1989, federal expenditures had climbed to $1,065 billion a year, and the national debt stood at nearly $3 trillion, requiring an annual interest payment of $200 million. The United States had become the world's largest debtor nation. With the deficit seemingly out of control, many advocated a constitutional amendment to require a balanced budget.

Asserting World Power

As a candidate in 1980, Reagan had promised to re-establish the United States as the leader of the world. To accomplish that goal, he believed it was necessary to overcome what he termed the "Vietnam syndrome": the unwillingness to use military force to defend U.S. interests. As president, Reagan promised no lack of resolve to support those interests.

Cold War Renewed

At the center of Reagan's view of the world was his hostility toward the Soviet Union. He believed that the Soviet Union was an "evil empire" that would "commit any crime" to achieve world conquest. America's grand role was to defend global freedom against communism. Large increases in the military budget were necessary, Reagan argued, to close the "window of vulnerability" that Carter had created by allowing the Soviets to pull ahead in the arms race.

With almost no dissent, Congress funded Reagan's military budget. More funds were made available for nuclear weapons and new aircraft, including the B-1 bomber and Stealth fighters and bombers. The navy was enlarged; the army received more tanks and helicopters. The most controversial program called for a new defense system that would use x-ray lasers to blast incoming

Walter Mondale Minnesota senator who was vice president under Jimmy Carter and ran unsuccessfully for president on the Democratic ticket in 1984.

♦ After declaring the Soviet Union an "evil empire" responsible for nearly all the world's problems, President Reagan *(left)* reversed course in 1988 and opened productive discussions with Soviet reformer Mikhail Gorbachev *(right)*. The outcome was an intermediate-range nuclear force treaty that helped end the Cold War, as well as reduce the overall number of nuclear missiles. Here the two leaders pose in front of St. Basil Cathedral in Moscow. *Corbis-Bettmann.*

Soviet missiles. The **Strategic Defense Initiative (SDI),** or Star Wars, as it was soon dubbed, became Reagan's military priority. Between 1983 and 1989, Congress provided over $17 billion for Star Wars research despite criticism that Star Wars owed more to science fiction than to science. By 1989, Reagan had added over $100 billion a year to the military budget.

Numerous defense contractors took advantage of the money being lavished on defense. With billions of dollars available, government and industry officials padded their expense accounts and exchanged bribes and kickbacks on an unprecedented scale. They falsified test results and inflated costs artificially. Billion-dollar cost overruns became commonplace. Critics loudly opposed the military shopping spree but had little effect on Congress or the public.

The Middle East

The Middle East presented the Reagan administration with a complex series of problems that, except for Afghanistan, resisted being explained as Communist aggression. In Afghanistan, the CIA continued to supply the mujahedeen with arms to use against Soviet and Afghan forces. Elsewhere in the Middle East, problems involving Arab nationalism, Arab-Israeli disputes, and terrorism could not be so readily understood in a Cold War context.

As Reagan assumed office, Yassir Arafat's Palestine Liberation Organization had increased its raids against Israel, and shadowy militant Islamic groups had begun a campaign of terrorism against Israel and its Western supporters. Throughout the Mediterranean region, terrorists kidnapped Americans and Europeans, hijacked planes and ships, and attacked airports. Reagan linked the terrorists to Communist organizations, the PLO, and various Arab nations. With American encouragement, Israel invaded neighboring southern Lebanon in 1982 to halt terrorist attacks and to suppress the PLO. As Israeli forces approached the capital city of Beirut, all semblance of internal stability collapsed. A smoldering civil war between Christians and Muslims raged anew.

As part of an international peacekeeping effort, the United States sent nearly two thousand marines

> **Strategic Defense Initiative** Research program designed to create an effective defense against nuclear attack; President Reagan asked Congress to fund SDI in 1983.

to Beirut. They quickly became a target for Muslim terrorists. In October 1983, a suicide driver rammed a truck filled with explosives into the marine barracks at the Beirut airport, killing 241 marines. Reagan denounced the terrorist attack but quietly made plans for the marines' removal. In January 1984, the United States withdrew its forces from Lebanon, where the civil war still raged. In Lebanon, there were no victories.

Nor were there any easy solutions in the **Persian Gulf.** The **Iran-Iraq War,** which started in 1980, created two problems for American foreign policy: protecting vital shipments of oil and ensuring that neither Iran nor Iraq emerged from the war as a dominant power. The Reagan administration provided money and weapons secretly to both sides. When Iranian forces attacked several oil tankers in 1986, American warships began escorting all oil tankers in the gulf. Clashes between American and Iranian forces occurred, one of which mistakenly resulted in the shooting down of an Iranian airliner. When the Iran-Iraq War ended in 1988, it had cost over 2 million lives. American intelligence concluded that neither country could threaten the rest of the region immediately.

To counterbalance Iran and Iraq, the United States supplied Saudi Arabia with sophisticated radar detection planes, tanks, and fighter aircraft. Stores of American military supplies were also buried in the Saudi desert in case of future need.

Farther west, in North Africa, Reagan faced off against **Muammar Qaddafi,** the vehemently anti-American ruler of Libya. Reagan denounced Libya as a "rogue" nation that actively supported the PLO and terrorist groups. In April 1986, terrorists bombed a disco popular among American troops in West Berlin, wounding several and killing an American soldier. Reagan ordered a reprisal raid after American intelligence tied Qaddafi to the terrorists. American planes bombed several targets in Libya, including Qaddafi's quarters, killing a young adopted daughter. The United States had shown Qaddafi "that we could get people close to him," bragged one official.

Although Qaddafi remained in power, what seemed important to most Americans was that the United States had responded to terrorism. The White House continued to call for the economic and political isolation of Qaddafi, particularly after investigations suggested that Libya had aided the terrorists who blew up a Pan American airliner over Lockerbie, Scotland, in December 1988, murdering over 250 people.

Central America and the Caribbean

In Central America and the Caribbean, Reagan thought that any hint of Communist influence justified American action. In the southern Caribbean, Reagan focused on the tiny island of **Grenada,** where a Marxist government had ruled since independence from Britain in 1979.

In October 1983, the radical New Jewel movement took control of Grenada. The Reagan administration immediately expressed concern about the new government, the construction of a large airport runway by Cuban "advisers," and the potential threat to about five hundred Americans attending medical school on the island. (The students did not think they were in any danger.) On October 25, Reagan ordered American forces to invade Grenada. More than two thousand American soldiers quickly overcame minimal opposition, brought home the American students, and installed a pro-American government. The administration basked in the light of public approval.

Determined to uphold his campaign pledge to defeat communism in Central America, Reagan

---

Persian Gulf   Arm of the Arabian Sea that includes the ports of several major oil-producing Arab countries, including Iran, Saudi Arabia, Kuwait, and Iraq.

Iran-Iraq War   War between Iran and Iraq that broke out in 1980 over control of a disputed waterway and ended in 1988 with more than 2 million dead.

Muammar Qaddafi   Libyan political leader who seized power in a military coup in 1969 and imposed socialist policies and Islamic orthodoxy on the country.

Grenada   Country in the West Indies that achieved independence from Britain in 1979 and was invaded by U.S. forces in 1983.

provided billions of dollars in aid to the El Salvadorian government and the Contra "freedom fighters" in Nicaragua. Although the public and Congress strongly supported Reagan's invasion of Grenada, his efforts in Central America stirred considerable opposition. Some critics were disturbed by reports of human rights violations by "death squads" linked to the El Salvadorian military. Many feared that Central America would become another Vietnam. When the press uncovered large-scale American covert aid to the Contras, including the CIA's mining of Nicaraguan harbors in 1984, Congress passed legislation drafted by Representative Edward Boland that allowed only humanitarian aid to the Contras.

Reagan and CIA director William Casey soon sought ways to work around the **Boland Amendment.** In the fall of 1985, the White House believed that it had found a way to do so. National security advisers Robert McFarlane and John Poindexter arranged for the secret sale of arms to Iran. In return, Iran agreed to use its influence with terrorist groups in Lebanon who held American hostages. The cash that Iran paid for the arms was then to be routed to the Contras, allowing them to purchase supplies and weapons.

When the press broke word of the so-called arms-for-hostages deal, a special White House commission and a congressional committee began separate investigations in 1987. Both uncovered evidence that the CIA and the National Security Council had acted without congressional approval and that members of both organizations had lied to Congress to keep their operation secret. McFarlane, Poindexter, and National Security Council aide Oliver North were found guilty and sentenced to prison terms. Although neither investigation uncovered proof that Reagan knew of the operation, some of his closest aides were clearly involved. The scandal damaged his image and that of his presidency.

Reagan and Gorbachev

Reagan made no attempt to improve relations with the Soviet superpower during his first term. He suddenly changed course early in his second term. He called for the resumption of arms limitation talks, and when Soviet leader Konstantin Cher-

nenko died in March 1985, he invited Chernenko's successor, **Mikhail S. Gorbachev,** to the United States.

Gorbachev differed from previous Soviet leaders. He was determined to breathe new life into the Soviet economy, which was stagnating under the weight of military spending and government inefficiency and corruption. He also wanted to institute reforms that would provide more political and civil rights to the Soviet people.

Gorbachev declined Reagan's invitation but agreed to a summit meeting in Geneva in November 1985. The two leaders at first jousted with each other. Reagan condemned the Soviets for human rights abuses, their involvement in Afghanistan, and their aid to Communist factions fighting in Angola and Ethiopia. Gorbachev attacked the proposed development of SDI. But when Gorbachev showed an interest in Hollywood, his relationship with the former movie actor improved. The two leaders left Geneva with a growing fondness for each other.

Gorbachev shocked Reagan when they met again in October 1986 in Reykjavik, Iceland, by proposing a 50 percent reduction in strategic weapons over a five-year period and, less surprisingly, the nondeployment of SDI for ten years. Without consulting his advisers, Reagan responded that the two powers should eliminate all strategic missiles within ten years but allow the development of SDI. The summit ended without an agreement, to the relief of American advisers who considered Reagan's idea of eliminating all nuclear missiles a dangerous one.

Still, Soviet-American negotiations on arms limitations continued with new optimism. By December 1987, negotiators had reached an agreement that eliminated Soviet and American intermediate-range missiles from Europe. Reagan and Gor-

---

Boland Amendment   Motion approved by Congress in 1984 that barred the CIA from using funds to give direct or indirect aid to the Nicaraguan Contras.

Mikhail S. Gorbachev   Soviet leader who came to power in 1985; he introduced political and economic reforms and then found himself presiding over the breakup of the Soviet Union.

bachev signed the **Intermediate Nuclear Force Treaty** in Washington during their December 1987 summit. Throughout 1988, Soviet-American relations continued to improve. Gorbachev withdrew Soviet forces from Afghanistan, the Senate approved the Intermediate Nuclear Force Treaty, and Reagan visited Moscow. It seemed that the Cold War was over.

In Reagan's Shadow

As Republicans got ready for the 1988 election, the torch of Reaganism passed to Reagan's vice president, **George Bush.** Bush had devoted many years to public service and had held several important posts under Presidents Nixon and Ford: ambassador to the United Nations, chairman of the Republican National Committee, ambassador to China, and director of the CIA. After gaining the Republican nomination, Bush selected as his running mate a young, conservative, and virtually unknown Indiana senator, J. Danforth Quayle.

Bush Assumes Office

The 1988 campaign proved to be a dull affair. Both Bush and Democratic nominee Michael Dukakis, governor of Massachusetts, lacked flair and style. Dukakis ignored most issues and focused on his personal integrity and success in revitalizing the Massachusetts economy. Bush promised to fight drugs and crime, to take a special interest in education and the environment, and not to raise taxes. "Read my lips, no new taxes," he said. **Negative campaigning,** which aimed at discrediting the opponent rather than addressing issues, dominated the airwaves in 1988. Republican ads were very effective and put Dukakis on the defensive. One focused on Willie Horton, an African-American convicted of murder and imprisoned in Massachusetts, Dukakis's home state. While out of prison on a weekend pass, Horton raped a white woman. Lee Atwater, Bush's campaign manager, said that by the time he was through running the Horton ad, the public would believe that Horton was Dukakis's running mate.

Bush won election easily, gaining 79 percent of the electoral vote and 54 percent of the popular vote. The victory was not as sweet as Bush hoped it would be. His **political coattails** were very short. The Democrats remained the majority party in both houses of Congress.

Bush and a New International Order

Shortly after becoming president, Bush had to respond to unexpected and rapid changes in the Communist world, from Nicaragua to the Soviet Union. Within the Soviet Union, Mikhail Gorbachev's politics of **glasnost** and **perestroika** were producing political and religious freedom, reducing censorship and repression, and starting the development of a capitalist-style economy. Soviet armed forces were being withdrawn from Afghanistan and Eastern Europe (see Map 31.2).

The Bush administration voiced cautious support for Gorbachev's efforts. In December 1989, Bush met with Gorbachev on the island of Malta in the Mediterranean Sea. Gorbachev declared that the Cold War was over. Bush more prudently stated that they were working toward "a lasting peace." Later, Gorbachev visited Washington and signed agreements to improve trade and reduce

---

Intermediate Nuclear Force Treaty Treaty signed in 1987 by Reagan and Gorbachev that provided for the destruction of all U.S. and Soviet medium-range nuclear missiles and for verification with on-site inspections.

George Bush Politician and diplomat who was vice president under Ronald Reagan and was later elected president of the United States.

negative campaigning Presenting a political opponent as weak, dishonest, or untrustworthy instead of addressing basic political issues.

political coattails The result of voters casting their votes for all members of a political party based on voting for one particular member, generally the highest-ranking candidate on the ticket.

glastnost Policy under Gorbachev that allowed freedom of thought and candid discussion of social problems.

perestroika The restructuring of the Soviet economy and bureaucracy that began in the mid-1980s.

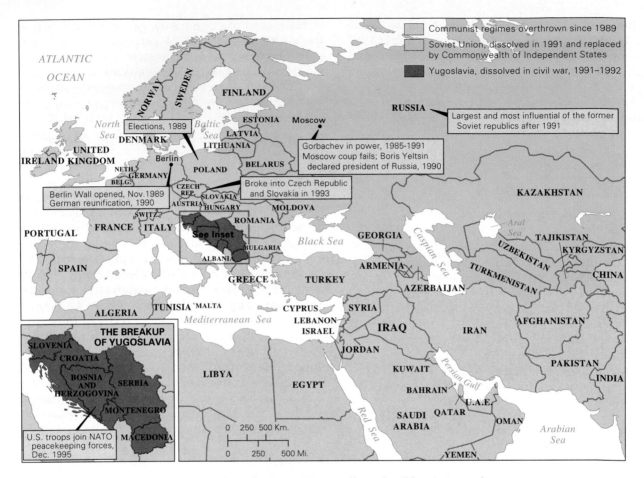

Legend:
- Communist regimes overthrown since 1989
- Soviet Union, dissolved in 1991 and replaced by Commonwealth of Independent States
- Yugoslavia, dissolved in civil war, 1991–1992

RUSSIA — Largest and most influential of the former Soviet republics after 1991

Elections, 1989

Gorbachev in power, 1985–1991 Moscow coup fails; Boris Yeltsin declared president of Russia, 1990

Berlin Wall opened, Nov.1989 German reunification, 1990

Broke into Czech Republic and Slovakia in 1993

THE BREAKUP OF YUGOSLAVIA

U.S. troops join NATO peacekeeping forces, Dec. 1995

♦ **MAP 31.2 The Fall of Communism**   As the Soviet Union collapsed and lost its control over the countries of Eastern Europe, the map of Eastern Europe and Central Asia changed. The Soviet Union disappeared into history, replaced by fifteen new national units. In Eastern Europe, West and East Germany merged, Czechoslovakia divided into two nations, and Yugoslavia broke into five feuding states.

the size of conventional and nuclear arsenals. He was cheered in the United States and around the world. At home, however, his popularity fell as the Soviet economy continued its downward spiral. Attacked by people wanting more reform and by hard-line Communists who feared any reform, Gorbachev asked the United States, Japan, and Western Europe to provide economic support to prevent "chaos and civil wars" in the Soviet Union.

Unable to slow the rush toward reform, the hard-liners on August 19, 1991, attempted a coup. They confined Gorbachev to his vacation home along the Black Sea and outlawed all political par-

ties. In Moscow, **Boris Yeltsin,** leader of the Russian Republic, declared the coup illegal and called on the Russian people to resist. Over 150,000 Muscovites surrounded the Russian parliament building to defend Yeltsin. Faced with popular opposition in Moscow and other cities, the coup collapsed

> **Boris Yeltsin**   Russian parliamentary leader who was elected president of the new Russian Republic in 1991 and promised increased democratic and economic reforms.

within seventy-two hours. Released from captivity, Gorbachev announced that he was again in control of the Soviet Union.

By 1992, there was no Soviet Union to command. All that remained was a weak federation, the **Commonwealth of Independent States.** Power rested not with Gorbachev, who soon retired from office, but with the independent republics and especially with Yeltsin.

The collapse of the Soviet Union both simplified and complicated U.S. foreign policy. The threat of war with the Soviet Union was gone, but the new relationship between the United States and the former Soviet Union had not yet been determined. Bush recognized the independent republics and Yeltsin as the spokesman for the Russian Republic and for the Commonwealth. In a June 1992 visit to Washington, Yeltsin announced that Russia was ready to eliminate nearly all of its land-based strategic missiles. Bush applauded the arms reduction proposal, promised increased economic support, and hoped that Yeltsin could bring some stability to what had once been the Soviet Union. Yeltsin, however, could barely provide stability for Russia.

Even before the Soviet Union collapsed, communism was in retreat throughout Eastern Europe. In December 1988, Gorbachev announced that the Soviet Union would no longer intervene in Eastern Europe. Within a year, Poland had a new constitution, a free market economy, and a non-Communist government. In 1989, workers tore down the **Berlin Wall.** As the wall crumbled, so too did the Communist governments of East Germany, Hungary, Bulgaria, Czechoslovakia, and Romania. By the end of 1990, a unified Germany existed, and the Baltic states of Latvia, Estonia, and Lithuania had declared their independence from the Soviet Union.

The Bush administration hoped that free market economies and stable, democratic governments would emerge in the former Soviet bloc. In some nations, there was peaceful movement toward both; in others, there was increased regional and ethnic conflict. Yugoslavia's collapse in 1991 led to a series of bloody conflicts among rival ethnic groups. By 1994, over a hundred thousand people had died, many of them in **Bosnia,** where Muslims fought better-armed Christian Serbs who were trying to dismember the Bosnian republic.

The breeze of democracy was not limited to Eastern Europe. In the People's Republic of China, Central America, and South Africa, similar movements were taking place. Chinese university students sought an end to the authoritarian policies of Deng Xiaoping. Prodemocracy protesters took to the streets in Beijing and other Chinese cities, demanding political, economic, and civil freedoms. They filled **Tiananmen Square** in Beijing, erecting a "Goddess of Liberty" statue that looked like the Statue of Liberty. Rather than relinquishing power, however, China's leaders resorted to force on June 4, 1989. Police and army forces brutally cleared the square and arrested many leaders of the democracy movement. Thousands were killed or injured as the movement for democracy across China was crushed. President Bush condemned the violent repression but resisted demands for sanctions against China. He argued that sanctions would make the Chinese leadership even more brutal.

Bush's policy toward South Africa drew praise for supporting democratic change. In South Africa, the goal was to end **apartheid.** In 1988, after South African president P. W. Botha had brutally repressed anti-apartheid demonstrations, Congress instituted **economic sanctions.** As Bush applauded the willingness of South Africa's new president,

---

Commonwealth of Independent States   Weak federation of the former Soviet republics that replaced the Soviet Union in 1992 and soon gave way to total independence of the member countries.

Berlin Wall   Wall that the Communist East German government built in 1961 to divide East and West Berlin; it was torn down in 1989 as the Cold War ended.

Bosnia   Region of the former Yugoslavia; its major city is Sarajevo.

Tiananmen Square   City square in Beijing where army forces attacked student protesters in 1989, crushing the prodemocracy movement in China.

apartheid   Official policy of racial segregation in South Africa; its outcome was political, legal, and economic discrimination against blacks and other people of color.

economic sanctions   Trade restrictions that several nations acting together impose on a country that has violated international law.

F. W. de Klerk, to work with Nelson Mandela and other black Africans to end apartheid. Bush lifted the sanctions once it became apparent that substantial progress was being made. In April 1994, South Africa held its first multiracial free elections, electing Mandela president.

In Central America, Bush broke with Reagan's policies (see pages 703–704) by reducing aid to the Contras and encouraging negotiations. His actions contributed to the acceptance of the **Contadora Plan** negotiated by a coalition of Central American nations. Under this plan, the Contras agreed to halt their military operations, and the Ortega government agreed to hold free elections. Opposition candidate Violeta de Chamorro defeated Daniel Ortega in 1990. Although friction between Sandinista and Contra supporters continued, the peaceful change in government effectively ended a bitter struggle.

In El Salvador, American-supported peace negotiations also ended a civil war. Antigovernment rebels agreed to a cease-fire and to participate in future elections. Bush proudly boasted that American efforts in both El Salvador and Nicaragua helped to produce more democratic governments.

Protecting American Interests Abroad

By mid-1991, almost everyone agreed that the Cold War was over. The Soviet Union and Soviet communism had collapsed. The United States stood as the sole superpower. Liberals and moderates called for a "peace dividend," money taken from the military budget and allocated for social programs. But Bush resisted any sizable cuts in the military budget. The world was still a dangerous place, he warned, and needed the military strength of the United States.

One place where Bush exercised that strength was in Panama. During his presidential campaign, he had promised a crackdown on the flow of drugs into the United States. In December 1989, he ordered American forces into Panama to arrest Panamanian dictator **Manuel Noriega** on drug-related charges. Implicated in the torture and murder of his political enemies, Noriega was actively involved in the transshipment of Colombian drugs to the United States.

Within seventy-two hours, American forces were in charge of the country. American casualties were light (twenty-three lost their lives). Some three thousand Panamanians died, almost all civilians. A Miami court found Noriega guilty of drug-related offenses, and he was sentenced to prison in 1992. Panama, however, remained a major route for smuggling drugs into the United States.

By the fall of 1990, President Bush faced a much more serious threat from **Saddam Hussein,** the authoritarian ruler of Iraq. Saddam claimed that the oil-rich sheikdom of Kuwait, which had long been friendly to the United States, was waging economic war against Iraq. Believing that the United States would not intervene, Saddam invaded and quickly overran Kuwait in early August 1990.

Many worried that Saddam intended to control the Persian Gulf region's oil fields, which held over 40 percent of the world's oil. Within hours of the invasion, Bush warned, "This [action] will not stand." Bush helped organize a multinational force of over 700,000, including 500,000 Americans, which was sent to Saudi Arabia in an effort to convince Iraq to withdraw from Kuwait. Many believed that the economic sanctions imposed by the United Nations would force Iraq to leave Kuwait. Bush worked within the United Nations to set a deadline of January 15, 1991, for Iraqi withdrawal from Kuwait.

Eighteen hours after the deadline expired, aircraft of the United Nations coalition began the **Gulf War** with devastating attacks on Iraqi positions in Kuwait and on Iraq itself. For nearly forty days, a

---

Contadora Plan Pact signed by the presidents of five Central American nations in 1987; it called for cease-fires in conflicts in the region and for democratic reforms.

Manual Noriega Panamanian dictator who was captured by U.S. invasion forces in 1989 and taken to the United States to be tried for drug trafficking.

Saddam Hussein Iraqi ruler who annexed Kuwait in 1990, triggering the Gulf War.

Gulf War War in the Persian Gulf region in 1991 triggered by the Iraqi invasion of Kuwait; a U.S.-led coalition defeated Iraqi forces and freed Kuwait.

high-tech air attack pounded the Iraqis. Saddam had promised, however, that the ground war would be the "mother of all battles." Concern about casualties among the coalition forces was great. Nevertheless, General Norman Schwarzkopf, coalition force commander, was confident of victory and ridiculed the Iraqi leader's military ability: Saddam is "neither a strategist, nor is he schooled in the operational arts, nor is he a tactician, nor is he a general, nor is he a soldier. Other than that he is a great military man."

The ground offensive, called Operation Desert Storm, started the night of February 23. In Kuwait, thousands of demoralized Iraqi soldiers, many of whom had gone without food and water for days, surrendered to advancing coalition forces. Within four days, coalition forces were mopping up the remaining resistance. They liberated Kuwait and humiliated the Iraqi army thoroughly. Estimates of Iraqi losses ranged from 70,000 to 115,000 killed. The United States lost fewer than 150. It was indeed the "mother of all victories," Americans quipped. Some, however, speculated that the offensive should have continued until all of the Iraqi army had been destroyed and Saddam ousted from power.

By the summer of 1991, the United States could claim victory in two wars, the Gulf War and the Cold War. It was clearly the diplomatic and military leader of the world.

A Kinder, Gentler Nation at Home?

Bush entered the White House in 1989 promising a "kinder, gentler nation." Many praised Bush for his apparent rediscovery of social issues. But others concluded from Bush's promise not to increase taxes that substantial action was unlikely.

They were correct. Bush's domestic policy reflected his belief that there was nothing fundamentally wrong with American society or the economy. He saw no reason for extensive new social programs.

Bush did support some social and environmental initiatives. By the end of his first year in office, he could point to legislation that protected disabled Americans against discrimination (the Americans with Disabilities Act) and reduced smokestack and auto emissions and acid rain (the Clean Air Act). Bush also noted that the minimum wage had risen from $3.35 to $4.25 an hour. Only two problem areas seemed to exist: the economy and his broken pledge on taxes.

In mid-1990, in part because of oil-price increases caused by Iraq's invasion of Kuwait, the nation entered into a recession. The recession, plus the growing national deficit, convinced Bush to work with Congress to raise taxes, despite his "no new taxes" pledge. Bush believed that by 1992, the recession would be over, the national debt would be reduced, and voters would happily re-elect him. The recession deepened, however, and lasted into 1992.

The recession lasted longer than Bush expected for several reasons. Fewer American goods were being sold overseas because of a slowdown in the world economy. American firms responded by downsizing to be more competitive. Between July 1990 and July 1993, over 1.9 million people lost their jobs. Sharply rising federal spending and the ever-increasing deficit also contributed to the length of the recession. Despite Bush's pledges to hold down federal spending, during his term the budget skyrocketed, reaching $1.5 trillion in 1992. At the same time, family income dropped below 1980 levels, to $37,300 from a 1980 high of $38,900. Consumers, caught between increasing unemployment, falling wages, and inflation, saw personal savings and confidence in the economy shrink.

Bush did little to halt the economic slide. He responded to Democrats' calls for tax cuts for the middle class, increased and extended unemployment benefits, and other social programs with vetoes and by asking for reductions in **capital gains** taxes. The result was political gridlock. Bush looked increasingly vulnerable as the November 1992 election approached. Unlike Reagan, Bush seemed incapable of projecting the image of a leader who knew where the nation and the world should be going.

> **capital gains** Profits made from selling assets such as securities and real estate.

SUMMARY

E xpectations
C onstraints
C hoices
O utcomes

The years between Nixon's resignation and 1992 were ones of changing *expectations*. During the presidencies of Ford and Carter, the nation seemed beset by *constraints* that limited its domestic prosperity and international status. The policy *choices* that Ford and Carter made neither recaptured people's faith in the nation nor established national goals. In his foreign policy, Carter chose to de-emphasize Cold War relationships and give more attention to human rights and Third World problems. The *outcome*, many believed, was a weakening of America's world position.

Reagan rejected Carter's notion that Americans should sacrifice to overcome the limits facing the nation. He argued that the only *constraint* on American greatness was government's excessive regulation and interference in society. He promised to reassert American power and renew the offensive in the Cold War. As president, Reagan *chose* a conservative program to restore the nation's values, honor, and international prestige. He fulfilled many conservative *expectations* by reducing support for some social programs, easing and eliminating some government regulations, and exerting American power around the world—altering the structure of Soviet-American relations. Supporters claimed that the *outcome* of Reagan's *choices* was a prosperous nation that faced few *constraints*. They applauded Reagan's assessment that his administration had *chosen* to "change a nation, and instead . . . changed a world."

Bush inherited the *expectations* that the Reagan administration had generated. But unlike Reagan, he could not project an image of strong and visionary leadership. Finding fewer *constraints* and more opportunities in the conduct of foreign policy, Bush directed most of his attention to world affairs. As the Soviet Union and communism in Eastern Europe collapsed, Bush gained public approval for his foreign policies, also demonstrating American strength and resolve in Panama and the Persian Gulf. His foreign-policy successes, however, only highlighted his weakness in domestic policy as the nation found itself mired in a nagging recession that sapped the public's confidence in Republican leadership and the economy.

SUGGESTED READINGS

Burroughs, Bryan, and John Helyar. *Barbarians at the Gate: The Fall of RJR Nabisco* (1990).

    A novel-like account (also a made-for-television movie) of hostile takeovers, leveraged buyouts, and the politics of greed that revolved around the Nabisco company.

Cannon, Lou. *President Reagan: The Role of a Lifetime* (1992).

    The most complete and detailed account of the Reagan presidency from a generally positive perspective.

Duffy, Michael, and Don Goodgame. *Marching in Place: The Status Quo Presidency of George Bush* (1992).

    An insightful but critical analysis of the Bush presidency.

Gaddis, John L. *The United States and the End of the Cold War* (1992).

    An excellent narrative of events in the Soviet Union and the United States that led to the end of the Cold War, as well as a useful analysis of the problems facing the United States in the post–Cold War world.

Kaufman, Burton. *The Presidency of James Earl Carter, Jr.* (1993).

    A well-balanced account and analysis of Carter's presidency and the changing political values of the 1970s.

Schaller, Michael. *Reckoning with Reagan* (1992).

    A brief but scholarly analysis of the Reagan administration and the society and values that supported the Reagan revolution.

Sifry, Micah L., and Christopher Cerf, eds. *The Gulf War Reader* (1991).

A collection of essays and documents that provides both insight into and an excellent overview of the Gulf War.

Wolfe, Tom. *Bonfire of the Vanities* (1987).

A best-selling novel (also a movie) about the inside world of financial deals and the quest for power and wealth.

Wall Street (1988).

A movie that provides another example of financial wheeling and dealing and Yuppies in search of wealth and power.

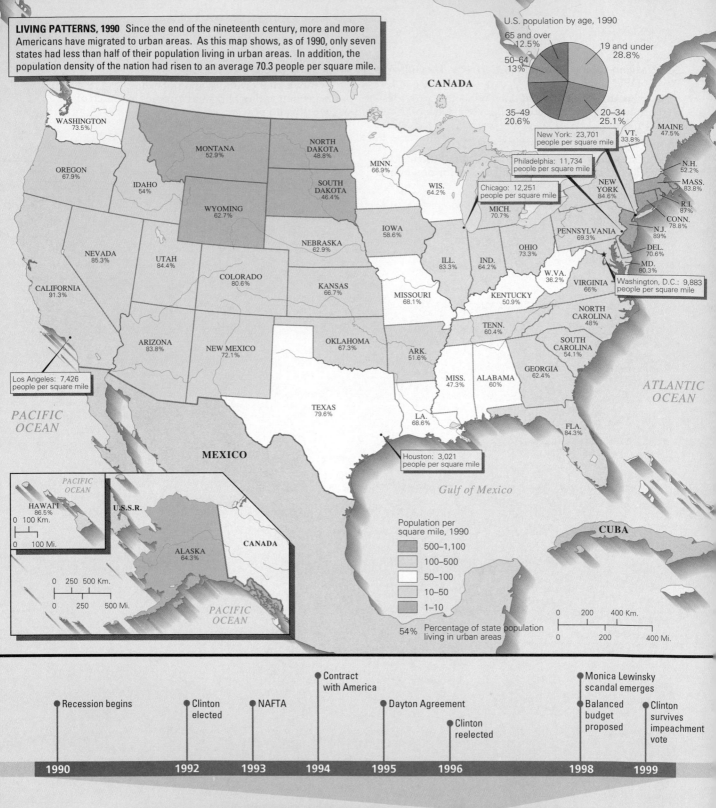

LIVING PATTERNS, 1990 Since the end of the nineteenth century, more and more Americans have migrated to urban areas. As this map shows, as of 1990, only seven states had less than half of their population living in urban areas. In addition, the population density of the nation had risen to an average 70.3 people per square mile.

U.S. population by age, 1990

- 65 and over 12.5%
- 50–64 13%
- 35–49 20.6%
- 19 and under 28.8%
- 20–34 25.1%

CANADA

New York: 23,701 people per square mile

Philadelphia: 11,734 people per square mile

Chicago: 12,251 people per square mile

Los Angeles: 7,426 people per square mile

Washington, D.C.: 9,883 people per square mile

Houston: 3,021 people per square mile

WASHINGTON 73.5%
OREGON 67.9%
MONTANA 52.9%
NORTH DAKOTA 48.8%
MINN. 66.9%
MAINE 47.5%
VT. 33.8%
N.H. 52.2%
IDAHO 54%
SOUTH DAKOTA 46.4%
WIS. 64.2%
MICH. 70.7%
NEW YORK 84.6%
MASS. 83.8%
R.I. 87%
WYOMING 62.7%
IOWA 58.6%
PENNSYLVANIA 69.3%
CONN. 78.8%
N.J. 89%
NEVADA 85.3%
UTAH 84.4%
NEBRASKA 62.9%
ILL. 83.3%
IND. 64.2%
OHIO 73.3%
DEL. 70.6%
MD. 80.3%
CALIFORNIA 91.3%
COLORADO 80.6%
KANSAS 66.7%
MISSOURI 68.1%
KENTUCKY 50.9%
W.VA. 36.2%
VIRGINIA 66%
ARIZONA 83.8%
NEW MEXICO 72.1%
OKLAHOMA 67.3%
ARK. 51.6%
TENN. 60.4%
NORTH CAROLINA 48%
SOUTH CAROLINA 54.1%
GEORGIA 62.4%
TEXAS 79.6%
MISS. 47.3%
ALABAMA 60%
LA. 68.6%
FLA. 84.3%

PACIFIC OCEAN
ATLANTIC OCEAN
MEXICO
Gulf of Mexico
CUBA

PACIFIC OCEAN
HAWAI'I 86.5%
0 100 Km.
0 100 Mi.
U.S.S.R.
CANADA
ALASKA 64.3%
PACIFIC OCEAN
0 250 500 Km.
0 250 500 Mi.

Population per square mile, 1990
- 500–1,100
- 100–500
- 50–100
- 10–50
- 1–10

54% Percentage of state population living in urban areas

0 200 400 Km.
0 200 400 Mi.

Timeline:

- 1990 Recession begins
- 1992 Clinton elected
- 1993 NAFTA
- 1994 Contract with America
- 1995 Dayton Agreement
- 1996 Clinton reelected
- 1998 Monica Lewinsky scandal emerges
- 1998 Balanced budget proposed
- 1999 Clinton survives impeachment vote

1990 1992 1993 1994 1995 1996 1998 1999

1850 1900 1950 2000

Making New Choices, 1992–1999

An Anxious Society Grows More Confident

- What changes were taking place in the American economy during the 1990s, and how did they affect people's expectations?

The Politics of Morality

- What expectations surrounded the introduction of issues of morality and values into American politics?

Calls for Change

- Given the outcomes occurring during the Clinton presidency, what policy issues seemed most important to Americans in the mid- to late 1990s?
- What was the outcome of the Clinton impeachment trial?

INTRODUCTION

E xpectations
C onstraints
C hoices
O utcomes

Before the election of 1992, many people *expected* the central issue of the campaign and perhaps of the 1990s would be the social and cultural divisions within American society. Liberals and conservatives were bitterly at odds over the values that should guide American society. Liberals believed that government should work to ensure that women, homosexuals, racial and ethnic minorities, and the disadvantaged generally have equal rights and economic opportunities. They supported the Equal Rights Amendment, affirmative action, and bans on antigay legislation. Conservatives, led by the New Right, argued that liberal policies were destroying the basic value system of the country and resulting in crime, violence, immoral behavior, and the breakdown of family life. They campaigned for a return to the traditional values of the two-parent family.

Contrary to *expectations,* the 1992 election seemed to hinge more on economic issues than on social or cultural ones. Since the 1970s, economic growth had slowed. Middle- and lower-class Americans had grown increasingly anxious as their economic circumstances either stagnated or deteriorated. Faced with a lingering recession, voters in 1992 *chose* Bill Clinton, the Democratic governor of Arkansas, over Republican incumbent George Bush and third-party candidate H. Ross Perot. Whereas Bush offered no answers to troubling economic issues, Clinton promised to support social needs while making the choices necessary to control the federal budget and reduce the national debt.

Clinton's efforts to enact major domestic legislation ran into major *constraints.* Faced with strong opposition, he had to abandon his proposed national healthcare plan and modify his goals for other social issues. In addition, the Republicans gained control of Congress in 1994. Clinton proved adept, however, at establishing himself as a centrist while making his Republican opponents appear to be too far to the right. For example, Clinton made the issue of welfare reform his own. He also was successful in foreign policy, helping to bring stability, peace, and democracy to

Bosnia and Haiti. These successes and a healthy economy translated into an easy victory for Clinton over Robert Dole and H. Ross Perot in the 1996 elections. The Republicans retained control of Congress.

As Clinton's second term began, both parties promised to cooperate with each other. *Expectations* of cooperation vanished in January 1998 when revelations that Clinton had had a sexual affair with a former White House intern, Monica Lewinsky, surfaced. By a largely partisan vote, the House approved two articles of impeachment charging that Clinton had perjured himself and obstructed justice in dealing with the Lewinsky affair. Although the Senate voted not to remove Clinton from office in February 1999, the *outcome* of the Lewinsky affair was that Clinton's presidency was permanently tainted.

C H R O N O L O G Y

New Expectations, New Directions

1969	Stonewall Riot		**1992**	Riots in South Central Los Angeles
				U.S. troops sent to Somalia
1972	Equal Rights Amendment begins ratification process			Clinton elected president
				Planned Parenthood of Southeastern Pennsylvania v. Casey
1973	*Roe v. Wade*			
			1993	North American Free Trade Agreement passed
1974	Busing confrontation in Boston			Clinton introduces national health package
1976	Hyde Amendment restricts federally funded abortions			Ruth Bader Ginsburg appointed to Supreme Court
1978	*Regents of the University of California v. Bakke*		**1994**	Withdrawal of U.S. troops from Somalia
				Nelson Mandela elected president of South Africa
1981	Beginning of AIDS epidemic in the United States			Violence Against Women Act
	Sandra Day O'Connor appointed to Supreme Court			Contract with America
			1995	Dayton Agreement
1982	Equal Rights Amendment fails to win ratification		**1996**	Welfare reform passed
				Clinton reelected
1986	William Rehnquist appointed chief justice of Supreme Court		**1997**	Madeleine Albright confirmed as secretary of state
	Antonin Scalia appointed to Supreme Court			*Reno v. ACLU*
1987	Anthony Kennedy appointed to Supreme Court		**1998**	Clinton projects balanced budget
				Monica Lewinsky scandal surfaces
1988	Bush elected president			House impeaches Clinton
1990	Recession begins		**1999**	Senate votes not to remove Clinton from office
	David Souter appointed to Supreme Court			
1991	Clarence Thomas appointed to Supreme Court			

An Anxious Society Grows More Confident

When Bill Clinton became president in 1993, Americans were worried about their economic future. The largely stagnant economy of the previous two decades made it difficult to maintain their standard of living. Those entering the work force worried that they would not be able to achieve their parents' level of affluence.

Clinton's presidency, however, coincided with the resurgence of the American economy. Sustained economic growth during the 1990s once again made the American economy the envy of the world. By the end of the decade, the unemployment rate had dropped to its lowest level in thirty years, median family income had risen significantly, and the **Dow Jones industrial average** had soared past 11,000.

The Revitalized Economy

During the 1970s, the American economy entered a prolonged period of stagnation. The economy grew at slightly more than 1 percent annually, in contrast to the robust 2.5 percent annual growth rate it enjoyed from the end of World War II through 1970. Although the causes of this slowdown were not clear at the time, what stands out in retrospect is that the basic activity of the economy was shifting from industrial production to providing information and services.

The painful effects of this transition were felt throughout the 1970s and 1980s. Regions that relied on industry saw the closing or moving of plants, the loss of jobs, and economic decline. The Rust Belt continued to decay as steel and coal companies cut back production or closed (see page 691). In addition, for the first time since the Great Depression, white-collar workers felt the effects of downsizing—companies cutting back on their work forces.

Since the early 1990s, American workers however, have been the beneficiaries of a largely successful transition to an information and service economy. American leadership in the computer software, microprocessing, and telecommunications industries, as well as the structure of the country's highly competitive retail markets, has produced a long and sustained economic boom. Between 1992 and 1998, the economy grew at an annual rate of about 3 percent, half a percentage point higher than in the decades after World War II.

During the 1990s, the American economy became the envy of the world, combining low interest, unemployment, and inflation rates. As one after another of the Asian "miracles" such as Japan went bust, the American economy surged forward. Meanwhile, many European countries experienced high unemployment.

The 1990s, like the 1980s, rewarded those at the top very handsomely. In addition, the decade saw a reversal of the long trend of falling real wages for the average American. Whereas the average real wage for men fell about 11 percent between 1979 and 1993, it rose 4 percent between 1997 and 1998. Real wages for the lowest-paid workers rose 6 percent between 1993 and 1998. By the mid-1990s, fast-food restaurants were advertising starting hourly wages that were well above the minimum wage and were offering fringe benefits in an effort to attract workers in the suddenly tight labor market.

Rising wages reflected the trend toward full employment during the decade. The unemployment rate fell from 7.5 percent in 1992 to 4.1 percent in the fall of 1999—the lowest rate since 1968. Minority unemployment rates fell in 1998 to the lowest levels ever recorded—8.9 percent for African Americans and 7.2 percent for Latinos. Even the unemployment rate for blacks ages 16 to 24 fell to a historic low in 1998, although nearly 21 percent of these workers remained unemployed.

During the 1990s, the stock market brought unprecedented returns to investors. The S&P 500, an index of the five hundred largest American companies, averaged unprecedented increases of 33 percent *per year* between 1994 and 1998, about three times the historical average. Americans who bought shares in the initial offerings of America Online, Amazon.com, or any of a number of Internet and high-technology companies saw even greater returns. The boom market of the Nineties made that of the Twenties pale by comparison.

Moreover, a broad spectrum of the American public benefited from this upsurge in the stock market. The percentage of adult Americans who owned stock rose from 10 percent in 1965 to 43 percent in 1999. This increasing stock ownership reflected the wider participation of Americans in pension and 401(k) funds that invest in securities.

The buoyant stock market indicated the fundamental confidence of investors in the American

---

Dow Jones industrial average New York Stock Exchange index representing stock prices of the thirty largest industrial corporations.

economy. With a few notable exceptions, virtually every economic indicator looked good. Inflation remained under control, averaging less than 3 percent annually. The inflation rate of 1.6 percent for 1998 was the second lowest in thirty years. Low interest rates that had not been seen since the 1960s spurred a construction and building boom. Even the federal budget, which seemed to have been careening out of control in the early 1990s, showed a surplus in 1998 and promised more surpluses in succeeding years.

Most observers were willing to overlook or minimize the few deficiencies of this generally robust economy. One of those deficiencies was that American consumers found many things to buy but had little inclination to save. As a result, the national savings rate fell to its lowest ever, less than 2 percent, and consumer debt rose to record highs. Another problem was the widening trade gap. Whereas in 1980 the United States had a modest trade surplus of $3.7 billion, by 1997 it had a trade deficit of $166 billion.

The Familiar Face of Poverty

For those at the bottom of the economic ladder, even a strong economy did little to ease existing problems. Although the poverty rate fell from 15 percent in 1992 to 13.3 percent in 1997, an estimated 36 million Americans remained mired in poverty. For minorities, the economic picture was worse. Both African Americans and Latinos experienced poverty rates of 27 percent in 1997. Households headed by women also figured prominently in the statistics on poverty. Some 30 percent of women heads of households lived in poverty.

Contributing to what some have called the "feminization of poverty" was the continuing gap between men's and women's income. Women continued to earn roughly 75 percent of the wages earned by men. Alimony was awarded less frequently in the 1990s, and child-support payments, when ordered, were likely to be too small to be of much help. Enforcement of child-support payments was frequently lax. In 1990, for example, more than one-quarter of those who owed child support paid nothing.

The Urban Crisis and Racial Tensions

During the 1980s, the problems of urban Americans seemed beyond solution. Businesses continued to leave the inner cities, taking many well-paying, full-time jobs with them. More and more urban areas came to be peopled by "the underclass," mostly nonwhite, unemployed or underemployed people with little education and even less hope. The only thriving enterprises were gangs and drug sales, especially those of **crack cocaine.**

Violence was a way of life in the inner city. Sections of many cities took on the appearance of war zones. By 1991, one-fourth of all urban school districts had installed metal detectors to prevent students from bringing weapons to school. Murder had become the leading cause of death for black males under the age of 35.

The **Rodney King** affair in Los Angeles illustrates the deeply embedded racism in many urban police departments and the seething racial tensions in many inner cities. A videotape made during the 1991 arrest of King, an African American, showed that four white policemen had clubbed, kicked, and beaten him after he had apparently been subdued. When an all-white jury acquitted three of the policemen (one was found guilty) in April 1992, South Central Los Angeles erupted in violence. For African Americans, the trial was further proof of white racism. The ensuing five-day riot resulted in 53 deaths, 2,300 injuries, 16,000 arrests, and more than $750 million in property damage.

The most famous trial during the 1990s was that of former professional football player O. J. Simpson. The issue of race pervaded the lengthy, televised trial of Simpson, who was accused of murdering his wife, Nicole Brown Simpson, and her friend, Ronald Goldman, on June 12, 1994. Although the prosecution presented the findings

crack cocaine Highly potent form of cocaine that is smoked through a glass pipe and is extremely addictive.

Rodney King African American whose beating by Los Angeles police officers was captured on videotape; the acquittal of the officers in 1992 triggered riots in which fifty-three people were killed.

◆ The April 1992 rioting in Los Angeles that followed the acquittal of three policemen for the beating of motorist Rodney King lasted five days and destroyed much of South Central Los Angeles. Fifty-three people were killed, and property damage exceeded $750 million. Many stores were looted before being set on fire, especially in what was called Koreatown. *Scott Weersing/Enterprise/Gamma Liaison.*

of DNA tests that placed Simpson's blood at the murder scene and his ex-wife's at his residence, Simpson's "Dream Team" of defense attorneys cast doubts on the integrity of police procedures. They scored many points when they showed that Detective Mark Fuhrman, who claimed to have found a bloody glove used in the murders on Simpson's property, had planted evidence in other cases and was a racist. The jury deliberated for less than four hours before proclaiming Simpson innocent in October 1995. The verdict sharply divided Americans along racial lines. Polls showed that more than two-thirds of white Americans believed that Simpson was guilty, whereas a similar proportion of African Americans believed him innocent.

Although Americans remained polarized over racial issues, urban environments improved substantially in the 1990s. Perhaps the most telling statistics concerned violent crimes such as murder, rape, and robbery. Beginning in 1992, the number of violent crimes dropped every year. The homicide rate, which doubled between the mid-1960s and 1980, also declined dramatically. In 1998, the murder rate fell to its lowest level since 1968. Drug use also fell off considerably. Cocaine use, for example, declined by about two-thirds from its peak in 1985.

Safer cities probably reflected a number of factors. First, an expanding economy provided some additional opportunities in the inner cities. Second, more police on the beat served as a deterrent to crime. Third, the enactment of tough "three strikes and you're out" legislation removed many offenders from the streets and swelled prison populations. And finally, aggressive campaigns such as that waged by New York City Mayor Rudolph Giuliani to rid the Times Square area of prostitutes and porn shops led many more urban residents to come out at night.

The Politics of Morality

While liberals continued to espouse government activism as a means to promote social equality and cultural pluralism, conservatives argued that America had become a nation of interest groups clamoring for rights and power and that a sense of national purpose was rapidly fading. They charged that liberal programs and attitudes had made victims of hardworking, thrifty middle-class Americans.

Changing Values

Many conservatives believed that there had been a moral breakdown in American society. They argued that the women's movement, the counterculture, and the **sexual revolution** had caused this breakdown. These movements, they claimed, had undermined the values of work and family by stressing personal fulfillment and advocating "fun, display, and pleasure."

The sexual revolution began with the youth movement of the 1960s (see pages 656–658). By 1970, more than half of those surveyed said that they approved of premarital sex and cohabitation outside marriage. Though still the norm, marriage had lost some of its importance.

By the 1970s, divorce rates were climbing as both men and women became less willing to stay in unsatisfactory marriages. As attitudes toward marriage and divorce changed, divorce laws also changed. **No-fault divorce** allowed spouses to dissolve their marriage because of so-called irreconcilable differences. By the 1990s, half of all those who married eventually divorced.

Divorce, the women's movement, and the sexual revolution also interacted with economic factors to affect the structure of American families. No longer was the American family the image of the typical 1950s family—white, suburban, mother as housewife. Instead, there were increasing numbers of single-parent families and families in which both spouses worked. Television reflected the changing views of American society. By the 1970s, there were few television shows showing families similar to Beaver Cleaver's (see page 622). Some nonwhite families appeared, and many of the situation comedies featured groups of single and divorced people living and working in an urban environment. A week of television in 1997 featured several programs about white and African-American "traditional" households—"Cosby," "Mad About You," "In the House," "The Simpsons"—and several

single-parent households—"The Gregory Hines Show" and "Grace Under Fire." But there were also many programs that featured divorced and never-been-married singles—"Seinfeld," "Friends" and "Ellen." The title character in "Ellen" revealed in one episode that she was a lesbian.

A new openness about sex began to pervade society after the 1960s. By the 1980s, sexual content had become standard fare in movies and on television. In 1987, an estimated sixty-five thousand sexual references were broadcast each year in prime-time television programs. During the day, sex and sex-related issues became more daring and numerous on the soaps. Violence, too, became standard. A 1997 study indicated that 44 percent of all network programming had violent content. Sexual and violent content was featured even more on cable and satellite television. One study found that on the premier cable channels, 85 percent of the programming had violent content. Sexually explicit material also could be found in magazines and books, on the Internet, and in X-rated films. Many people called for censorship and ways to limit the amount of sex and violence seen by children. By the 1990s, records, movies, and television all offered rating systems indicating the level of sex and violence in their content. In 1997, however, the Supreme Court ruled in *Reno v. ACLU* that efforts to ban sexually offensive material from the Internet were unconstitutional.

Women and Changing Values

Related to the sexual revolution's effects on American society were demands by women for more personal and economic choices. As the women's movement continued into the 1980s and 1990s, it began, like other social movements, to divide and encounter more opposition. At the center of the

---

sexual revolution Dramatic change in attitudes toward sex; it began in the 1960s as more and more Americans considered premarital sex acceptable.

no-fault divorce Divorce granted without the need to establish wrongdoing by either party.

divisions and at the heart of the opposition were differences about the meaning and importance of the sexual revolution, home, family, and children.

By the late 1960s, a growing number of women had begun to attack sexism in American society and culture. As unprecedented numbers of women began working, many became angered by the gap between their abilities and their earnings. In August 1970, over fifty thousand women marched in New York to demand better pay and equal access to jobs.

The women's movement began to call for other changes as well. These included abortion rights, the right to reject unwanted sex, and freedom from **sexual harassment.** To help achieve these goals, the National Organization for Women (NOW) and other women's groups in 1967 called for an **Equal Rights Amendment (ERA).**

Many states responded to the changing social values and to pressure from women's groups. They modified laws to reduce or eliminate gender discrimination. Some states legalized abortions. In 1972, Congress drafted the Equal Rights Amendment and sent it to the states for ratification. ERA advocates argued that it was needed to eliminate laws at the state and local levels that blocked women's equality. They pointed out that the ERA also would transfer the responsibility of ensuring equality from individuals and state governments to the federal government.

At first, ratification of the ERA appeared almost certain. Thirty-three of the thirty-eight states needed for ratification had approved it by 1974. But opposition stiffened, and only two more states voted approval before the 1978 deadline. Congress granted an extension of the deadline until 1982, but it did no good.

Conservative forces from more than 130 organizations made the ERA an effective symbol of what they said threatened the traditional family. **Phyllis Schlafly** and other STOP-ERA leaders charged that the ERA would alter the "role of the American woman as wife and mother" and destroy the American family. Their emphasis on the ERA's threat to the traditional family prevented it from being ratified.

The STOP-ERA movement also benefited from the Supreme Court's controversial 1973 decision in the case of *Roe v. Wade.* The Court invalidated a Texas law that prevented abortions. Justice Harry

Blackmun, writing for the majority, held that "the right to privacy" gave women the freedom to choose to have an abortion during the first three months of pregnancy. The controversial ruling struck down abortion laws in forty-six states that had made it nearly impossible for women to have an abortion. As the number of legal abortions rose from about 750,000 in 1973 to nearly a million and half by 1980, so too did opposition.

Although public opinion polls indicated that a majority of Americans favored giving women the right to choose an abortion, Catholics, Mormons, some Orthodox Jews, and many Protestant churches organized a "Right to Life" campaign to oppose abortion rights. The **Right to Life movement** easily merged with the conservative elements of American society. Responding to conservative and anti-abortion pressure, Congress in 1976 passed the Hyde Amendment, which prohibited the use of federal Medicaid funds to pay for abortions. As President Reagan appointed Sandra Day O'Connor and other conservative justices to the Supreme Court, many people expected the Court eventually to overturn *Roe v. Wade.* But in 1992, in *Planned Parenthood of Southeastern Pennsylvania v. Casey,* the Court confirmed a woman's right to have an abortion. The Court did assert that in some cases the state could modify that right.

---

sexual harassment Unwanted and offensive sexual advances or sexually derogatory or discriminatory remarks.

Equal Rights Amendment Proposed constitutional amendment giving women equal rights under the law; Congress approved it in 1972, but it failed to achieve ratification by the required thirty-eight states.

Phyllis Schlafly Leader of the movement to defeat the Equal Rights Amendment; Schlafly believed that the amendment threatened the domestic role of women.

Roe v. Wade Supreme Court ruling in 1973 that women have an unrestricted right to abort a fetus during the first three months of pregnancy.

Right to Life movement Anti-abortion movement that favors a constitutional amendment to prohibit abortion; it grew increasingly militant during the 1980s and 1990s.

Sexual harassment became a national issue in 1991 during Clarence Thomas's Senate confirmation hearings for the Supreme Court. Those hearings turned stormy after Anita Hill, a University of Oklahoma law professor, accused Thomas of sexual harassment. Hill testified that a decade earlier, while she was working for Thomas, he had pressured her for dates and told her pornographic stories. Thomas denied her allegations, angrily calling the hearing "a high-tech lynching for uppity blacks." The Senate hearings became a national television spectacle. The predominantly male Senate confirmed Thomas in a close vote, but the hearings focused national attention on the issue of sexual harassment. In response to growing concerns about sexual abuse, Congress passed the **Violence Against Women Act** in 1994.

Gay Rights: Progress and Resistance

Women were not the only group asking society to reconsider America's traditional views of gender. Homosexuals too were demanding equality. In the late 1960s, groups promoting gay and lesbian rights openly demanded an end to laws that discriminated against homosexuals.

The spark for the movement was a police raid in June 1969 on the Stonewall Inn, a gay bar in the Greenwich Village section of New York City. Gays and other members of the community fought back in what came to be called the Stonewall Riot. After the riot, gays and lesbians borrowed tactics from the women's and civil rights movements, formed activist groups, and demanded equality. Because visibility was a major tool and goal of the movement, gays and lesbians demonstrated in support of their lifestyles.

Throughout the 1970s, the gay liberation movement pressured government at all levels to end restrictions against homosexuals in employment, housing, and the military. Success came slowly. One victory came in 1973 when the American Psychiatric Association ended its classification of homosexuality as a mental disorder. Polls indicated that the "straight" public held confusing views. By the mid-1970s the majority of Americans considered homosexuality wrong, but a slight majority opposed job discrimination based on sexual orientation and seemed more tolerant of gay lifestyles.

The growing toleration of gays did not end legal or social discrimination. The Reagan administration equated homosexuality with a disease and denied homosexuals entry into the United States. The New Right and Moral Majority campaigned actively against the rights of homosexuals. Evangelical minister Jerry Falwell called on his followers to "stop gays dead in their perverted tracks." Although 26 states had decriminalized sexual relationships between consenting adults by 1986, only 7 states and about 110 communities had prohibited social and economic discrimination against homosexuals by 1993. In the remaining 43 states and under federal law, no legal recourse existed for those fired from their jobs because of their sexual preference.

The AIDS Controversy

Antigay opposition was strengthened by a growing fear of **acquired immune deficiency syndrome (AIDS),** a disease that was at first regarded primarily as a "gay disease." AIDS was first discovered in the United States in 1981. Within ten years, over 195,700 cases had been reported, and over 97,000 Americans had died of it. Another 1.5 million were estimated to be infected by HIV (human immunodeficiency virus), the virus that causes AIDS. Initially, because most AIDS victims were either homosexuals or intravenous drug users, official and public response to the disease was restrained. But as more and more non-drug-using heterosexuals contracted AIDS, research and educational efforts expanded.

As public fear of AIDS increased, controversy flared about the best means to prevent the spread

---

Violence Against Women Act Law passed in 1994 that provided federal funds to prevent violence against women, to aid victims, and to punish those convicted of attacks on women.

acquired immune deficiency syndrome Gradual and eventually fatal breakdown of the immune system caused by HIV; AIDS is transmitted by exchanging body fluids through means such as sex or blood transfusions.

of the disease. Claiming to be "realists," many recommended "safe sex," emphasizing the use of condoms as a means to reduce the possibility of getting the disease. Television ads used prominent movie and sports figures to advocate the use of condoms. Some advocated that high schools provide students with free condoms and information about AIDS. Others disagreed. Arguing that free condoms would encourage sexual activity, they promoted abstinence.

Contributing to the public's awareness of AIDS were revelations that Earvin "Magic" Johnson and Arthur Ashe had tested positive for the HIV virus. Ashe, the onetime U.S. Open tennis champion, contracted the disease from HIV-infected blood during a heart bypass operation. Johnson, star of the Los Angeles Lakers basketball team, caught the disease through heterosexual activity. Johnson admitted to being "naive" about AIDS and told the public, "Here I am saying it can happen to anybody." Both became spokesmen for AIDS research and prevention. Ashe died of AIDS in 1993.

By the mid-1990s, some advances had been made in research toward controlling AIDS. Combinations of drugs seemed to have a positive effect in slowing the advance of and death rate from the disease. But there remained no cure for the disease, which by 1996 had claimed more than 280,000 American lives and had infected 20 million people around the world.

Federal Intervention and the Courts

By the 1980s, many Americans who had initially supported civil rights for African Americans and other minorities were rejecting calls for continuing programs to help equalize social and economic relationships. Multiculturalism and federal intervention in support of minority rights, conservatives argued, were weakening American society and undermining traditional values. Among the most disastrous examples of federal intervention, many conservatives held, were requirements for forced busing and **affirmative action.** Both had been largely supported and influenced by the federal court system.

Busing for integration had become a national issue in the early 1970s, when state and federal courts began to order non-Southern school districts to adopt busing to achieve more equally balanced schools. Boston experienced violent protests in 1974 following a busing order, and twenty thousand white students eventually left the school system. In the 1980s, the Reagan and Bush administrations backed away from court-ordered busing. "We aren't going to compel children who don't want to have an integrated education to have one," said one Reagan official. Federal courts also began to take a less favorable view of affirmative action. In part, their rulings reflected the judicial appointments of the Reagan and Bush administrations. By 1992, Reagan and Bush had appointed nearly half of all sitting federal district and appeals court judges. In selecting candidates, they sought individuals who practiced **judicial restraint,** deferring to the views of Congress, the president, and the states on legislation and policy.

Reagan and Bush reshaped the Supreme Court in a conservative bent by appointing six justices. In 1986, five years after appointing Sandra Day O'Connor, Reagan named Justice William Rehnquist to be chief justice and appointed conservative Antonin Scalia to the Court. Anthony M. Kennedy joined the Court in 1987, adding to the conservative majority. The conservative direction of the Court was further reinforced by President Bush's two appointments, David Souter (1990) and Clarence Thomas (1991). In a case involving DeKalb County, Georgia, the Rehnquist Court declared in 1992 that busing should not be used to integrate schools segregated by *de facto* housing patterns.

Affirmative action was already under increasing attack by the time Reagan took office. As the economy slowed, a growing number of middle-class and blue-collar whites had come to believe that affirmative action programs limited their job and ed-

affirmative action Policy that seeks to redress past discrimination through active measures to ensure equal opportunity, especially in education and employment.

judicial restraint Refraining from using the judiciary as a forum for implementing social change but instead deferring to Congress, the president, and the consensus of the people.

ucational opportunities. Believing himself a victim of **reverse discrimination,** Allan Bakke sued the University of California system. Bakke claimed that the School of Medicine at the University of California at Davis had accepted black students less qualified than he and had denied him admission because he was white. In 1978, in *Regents of the University of California v. Bakke,* the Supreme Court ruled that the university should admit him to the medical school. The Court did not totally reject color and gender as considerations for hiring, but the *Bakke* decision weakened many affirmative action programs.

During the Reagan administration, racial and gender preference systems were effectively limited by the Rehnquist Court's 1989 *Croson* decision, which declared state and local government efforts to set aside jobs and contracts for minorities to be illegal. The city of Atlanta and many other municipalities subsequently abolished set-aside programs. In 1997, California voters approved a measure forbidding any consideration of racial or gender preferences in hiring, college admissions, or contracting. Governor Pete Wilson announced that it "began a new chapter in the journey toward a color-blind society."

Calls for Change

In mid-1991, Republicans believed that they had established a new alignment of conservative voters that would continue the shift away from liberalism and big government. President Bush was basking in the glow of Operation Desert Storm and the fall of communism. Most prominent Democrats expected that the president would easily win reelection, so they chose not to compete. As a result, the door was opened for less well-known Democratic candidates. Arkansas governor Bill Clinton emerged as the front-runner and easily won the party's nomination. He selected Senator Albert Gore of Tennessee as his running mate.

Bush campaigned on his presidential experience, his knowledge of world affairs, and Vice President Dan Quayle's call for family values. He blamed the Democratic Congress for the political gridlock. Calling Clinton a "tax-and-spend Demo-crat," Bush warned that the Arkansas governor's lack of experience, especially in foreign and military affairs, would ruin the country.

Clinton insisted that he was a new kind of Democrat. He called for increased taxes on the wealthy, programs to rebuild the nation's transportation and industrial base, and a strong commitment to a national healthcare program. Unlike Bush, Clinton embraced government activism. Surviving Bush's ads attacking his character, personal life, and avoidance of the draft during the Vietnam War, Clinton steadily emphasized the economy, which was languishing in a recession.

The 1992 campaign also saw the emergence of a third-party candidate. **H. Ross Perot** offered to use $100 million of his own money if supporters could get his name on the presidential ballot in all fifty states. Perot's announcement in February 1992 drew immediate support from many Americans who were disenchanted with both political parties. Perot had a simple message: the politicians had messed up the nation, and control needed to be returned to the people. "It's time to take out the trash and clean up the barn," he told listeners. The deficit was the foremost problem, he said, and he promised to shrink it. By June, one opinion poll showed the feisty Texan leading with 39 percent of the vote. Then, without warning, he withdrew from the race in July. Although Perot later reentered the race, he never regained the momentum he had had in June.

The 1992 campaign culminated in three televised debates between Bush, Perot, and Clinton in September and October. Although both Bush and Perot gained in the public opinion polls following the debates, neither could overtake Clinton, who won the election with 43 percent of the popular vote. Bush received 37.4 percent and Perot 18.9

reverse discrimination Discrimination against members of a dominant group; it results from policies established to correct discrimination against members of minority groups.

H. Ross Perot Texas billionaire who used large amounts of his own money to run as an independent candidate for president in 1992.

percent. Clinton received 370 electoral votes, 100 more than he needed to win.

Political observers wondered if Clinton's success and the success of women and minorities in elections across the nation indicated that the conservative shift in American politics that had begun with Reagan was at its end. Setting a liberal tone, Clinton stated that he wanted a "government that looks like America," and he appointed minorities and women to several posts in the judiciary, the cabinet, and other federal offices. Janet Reno became the first women attorney general, and in 1993 Ruth Bader Ginsburg became the second woman on the Supreme Court. In 1997, Madeleine K. Albright became the first women secretary of state. Clinton's most controversial appointment was his wife, Hillary Rodham Clinton, whom he named to chair the committee to draft a national healthcare plan.

Clinton, Congress, and Change

Clinton's presidency got off to a slow and shaky start. One of his first actions was to attempt to fulfill a campaign pledge to end discrimination against homosexuals in the military. Faced with substantial opposition in Congress and in the military, Clinton retreated and compromised. The compromise required the armed forces to stop asking about sexual preference as long as gays and lesbians in the service refrained from homosexual activities. The new policy pleased no one. It left even the president's supporters distressed about his willingness to sacrifice principles.

Clinton fared no better with his promise to provide national health insurance for the estimated 35 million Americans who were uninsured. Chaired by his wife, the Task Force on National Health Care Reform in 1993 proposed providing universal insurance primarily by mandating that employers offer health insurance to their employees. A barrage of criticism greeted the task force's report. Businesses objected to providing mandated health insurance. The American Medical Association complained that adopting the recommendations would mean that government would decide how much healthcare an individual could receive and deny an individual's choice of doctors. Such complaints found their mark in a public leery of big

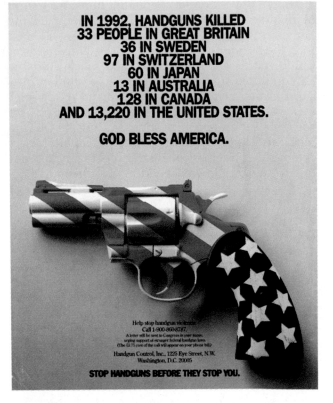

IN 1992, HANDGUNS KILLED
33 PEOPLE IN GREAT BRITAIN
36 IN SWEDEN
97 IN SWITZERLAND
60 IN JAPAN
13 IN AUSTRALIA
128 IN CANADA
AND 13,220 IN THE UNITED STATES.

GOD BLESS AMERICA.

Help stop handgun violence.
Call 1-900-860-8787.
A letter will be sent to Congress in your name, urging support of stronger federal handgun laws.
(The $1.75 cost of the call will appear on your phone bill.)
Handgun Control, Inc., 1225 Eye Street, N.W.
Washington, D.C. 20005

STOP HANDGUNS BEFORE THEY STOP YOU.

♦ Throughout the 1980s and 1990s, the issue of gun control sharply divided the nation. This ad strongly asserts the need for control. Opponents argue that the right to bear arms is guaranteed by the Constitution. Advocates for control won a small victory in 1993 when Congress passed the Brady bill, which requires a five-day waiting period and a background check before someone can buy a handgun. *Handgun Control, Inc.*

changes in medical care. By mid-1994, it was apparent that healthcare reform was a dead issue.

Success did not elude Clinton entirely during his first two years in office. Going against considerable opposition within his own party, he gained congressional approval of the **North American Free Trade Agreement (NAFTA),** which gradually re-

> **North American Free Trade Agreement** Agreement approved in 1993 that eliminated most tariffs and other trade barriers among the United States, Canada, and Mexico.

duced trade barriers between the United States, Canada, and Mexico over a fifteen-year-period. In 1993, Congress also approved the **Brady bill,** which mandated a five-day waiting period before an individual could purchase a handgun. Additionally, Clinton was able in 1993 to secure passage of a budget that he believed would reduce the budget deficit and promote economic growth. Denounced by Republicans as typical liberal "tax and spend" measures, these laws raised taxes on wealthy Americans while making major spending cuts. The failure to achieve significant social reform and Clinton's many compromises, however, more than overshadowed the president's small victories.

As Clinton sank ever lower in public opinion polls in 1994, the Republicans rallied around Newt Gingrich, a conservative member of Congress from Georgia. Some three hundred Republican aspirants to the House of Representatives pledged on September 27, 1994, to support the **Contract with America** that Gingrich promised to enact if Republicans were victorious at the polls. Reflecting Gingrich's philosophy of a minimal federal government, the contract called for various tax cuts and a balanced federal budget by 2002. Apart from specifying cuts in welfare, the contract was vague on how the budget was to be balanced.

Voters responded to Gingrich's call for a political revolution. In the 1994 elections, Republicans picked up nine Senate seats and fifty-two House seats, thereby gaining control of the Senate for the first time since 1987 and of the House for the first time in forty years. In addition, Republicans added fourteen governorships to their total. Democratic mainstays such as Governor Mario Cuomo of New York and Governor Ann Richards of Texas went down to defeat. A conservative revolution even more profound than the one that had elected Ronald Reagan president appeared to be taking shape.

True to his word, Gingrich, the new Speaker of the House, steered virtually all of the Contract with America through the House during its first hundred days in session in 1995. Republicans passed large tax cuts, strong anticrime legislation, and increases in military spending. (Ironically, the only part of the contract that was not fulfilled was the provision calling for term limits for members of Congress.) Euphoria ran high in the Republican ranks.

The contract's pledge to balance the budget by 2002 led to a confrontation between Clinton and Gingrich after the beginning of the new federal fiscal year in October 1995. Since no budget had been agreed on for fiscal year 1995–1996, a continuing resolution was needed to allow the federal government to function and to pay its bills. Gingrich attached specified reductions in Medicare, Medicaid, and welfare spending to the continuing resolution. If Clinton vetoed the resolution because he did not like these reductions, all nonessential services of the federal government would be forced to shut down.

Clinton called Gingrich's bluff and vetoed the resolution. Some 800,000 federal workers were sent home briefly in November and for more than a month beginning in mid-December. National museums, parks, passport offices, and a host of other government offices closed. As the shutdown continued into January 1996, the public increasingly pointed the finger at Gingrich and the Republicans for the budgetary impasse. "It seems like the Republicans have this my-way-or-no-way attitude, and I'm tired of it," a 37-year-old Kansan observed. Senate Majority Leader Robert Dole of Kansas, sensing the damage that the shutdown was doing to his party, finally called for a Republican retreat on the continuing resolution. Government employees went back to work in mid-January, and the leaders of the two parties sat down again to negotiate a budget.

Clinton emerged from the government shutdown with enhanced stature and a new political lease on life. The budgetary battles made him seem a moderate, whereas Gingrich and his supporters came off as extremists.

Following the government shutdowns of 1995–1996, Clinton and the Republican Congress were able to reach substantial agreement on only one major issue, welfare reform. The Republican

Brady bill   Law passed in 1993 that established a five-day waiting period for handgun purchases.
Contract with America   Pledge taken in September 1994 by some three hundred Republican candidates for the House that promised to reduce the size and scope of the federal government and to balance the federal budget by 2002.

welfare reform bill that Clinton signed late in the summer of 1996 marked a dramatic departure from the federal welfare program that had existed since the New Deal—Aid to Families with Dependent Children. Charging that AFDC payments had created a culture of poverty and dependence because the program did not require recipients to work, Republicans replaced AFDC with block grants to the states. The legislation allowed the states to experiment with a variety of approaches to handling welfare and required adults to work in order to receive welfare. Critics of the measure contended that the end of federal welfare entitlements amounted to a betrayal of the poor.

The 1996 Campaign

Perceiving Clinton as a vulnerable president, a host of Republican candidates emerged in 1995 to compete for the right to carry the party's standard. Despite sharp initial challenges from Steven Forbes, heir to a publishing fortune, and Patrick Buchanan, a conservative columnist, veteran politician Robert Dole secured the nomination easily.

Dole emerged as the Republican nominee only to find himself trailing in the polls by twenty points in June 1996. In an effort to narrow the gap, he resigned his Senate seat. Several factors operated as constraints on his ambitions. First, the economy had grown steadily though not spectacularly during Clinton's presidency. Second, Dole was a moderate Republican who failed to inspire the conservative activists who had energized Reagan's campaigns. Finally, Clinton's handling of the budgetary impasse gave him some credentials as a presidential leader.

Dole's best hopes appeared to rest on further developments in the **Whitewater scandal.** The complicated scandal got its name from the failed Whitewater real-estate development in Arkansas in which the Clintons had invested. On May 28, 1996, a jury convicted Arkansas Governor Jim Guy Tucker and two of the Clintons' other former business partners in Whitewater, James and Susan McDougal, of fraud. The three were found guilty of arranging nearly $3 million in loans from federally backed banks on the basis of falsified appraisals and of using the loans for improper purposes, including the Whitewater development, while Clinton was governor of Arkansas.

Although none of the evidence introduced in the trial implicated the president, that did not absolve him and his wife of suspected wrongdoing in many people's eyes. Hillary Clinton had been a partner in the Rose Law Firm that handled the affairs of the McDougals' failed bank. Vincent Foster, an attorney who followed the Clintons from Arkansas to the White House, committed suicide when the scandal broke in 1993, leading some to speculate that the Clintons had something to hide.

Neither Dole's attempt to question Clinton's character nor the former senator's call for a 15 percent across-the-board cut in income taxes made much of an impression on the electorate. Clinton rolled to an easy victory on November 5, becoming the first Democrat to be re-elected president since Franklin D. Roosevelt. He captured 379 electoral votes and 49 percent of the popular vote. Dole won the remainder of the electoral votes and 41 percent of the popular vote, while Reform party candidate Ross Perot captured 9 percent of the popular vote. Expecting an easy Clinton victory, less than half of all eligible voters cast their ballots. The percentage turnout was the lowest since 1924. Clinton proved to have very short coattails. The Republicans retained control of the Senate and the House.

Clinton's Foreign Policy

When Clinton assumed control of foreign policy, it still was not clear what general policy would replace that of the Cold War. Americans wanted to maintain their power and influence as a super-

> **Whitewater scandal**   A scandal involving a failed real-estate development in Arkansas in which President Clinton invested; several of the president's business partners in the Whitewater development were convicted of fraud.

power but were divided over what situations would warrant American intervention. Inexperienced in foreign affairs, Clinton proceeded cautiously and followed the general outline set by President Bush. In economic foreign policy, Clinton completed Bush's effort to pass the NAFTA and General Agreement on Tariffs and Trade (GATT) agreements, to improve trade with China, and to encourage Japan to buy more American goods. Clinton continued to support Russian leader Boris Yeltsin and to work toward agreements with former Soviet countries to destroy nuclear warheads.

Clinton inherited two highly controversial commitments from the Bush administration—in Somalia and in Bosnia. U.S. troops intervened in Somalia in 1992 as part of a United Nations effort to keep the peace between marauding factions in a civil war. But in the absence of any direct U.S. interest in the country, pressure to withdraw the troops grew. By April 1994, Clinton had done so.

Clinton inched forward on the issue of Bosnia amid considerable controversy over whether UN peacekeeping efforts would have any effect. As the carnage increased, however, the Clinton administration agreed to allow American forces to participate in a UN campaign to establish and protect "safe areas" for refugees. In the fall of 1995, the United States sponsored talks between the warring elements—the Serbs, the Muslim Bosnians, and the Croats. The resulting **Dayton Agreement** partitioned the country into a Bosnian-Croatian federation and Serbia and called for UN forces, including 20,000 Americans, to police the peace. By the summer of 1996, when most American forces were withdrawn, much had been accomplished to rebuild the shattered region. In December 1997, Clinton announced, however, that a continued American presence in that nation was necessary to oversee the task of nation building.

The Balkans continued to remain a hot spot during Clinton's second term. The conflict that erupted in 1998 again involved ancient hostilities between Orthodox Christians and Muslims, this time in the Serbian province of Kosovo. Kosovo, 90 percent of whose population consisted of ethnic Albanians, who also were Muslims, had enjoyed considerable autonomy until the breakup of

the former Yugoslavia in 1989, when Serbian president Slobodan Milosevic took control of the province. Milosevic ordered a crackdown in Kosovo in 1998 after the emergence of the Kosovo Liberation Army, which sought full independence for the province.

Milosevic's efforts to drive ethnic Albanians from their villages in Kosovo prompted NATO intervention in March 1999 after negotiations to end the conflict failed. NATO launched bombing raids against Serbian targets in Kosovo and Serbia to force a Serb withdrawal from the province. NATO's reluctance to commit troops to the conflict, however, allowed Milosevic to conduct a campaign of **ethnic cleansing** against the Albanians, who began a mass exodus from the province. Milosevic finally capitulated and agreed to sign a UN-approved peace agreement on June 9. British officials sent to investigate mass graves after the conflict ended estimated that some ten thousand ethnic Albanian civilians had been deliberately shot by Milosevic's forces between June 1998 and June 1999.

Iraq remained a problem area as well. Fearful that Saddam Hussein would replenish his chemical and biological weapons after the Gulf War, the United Nations required Iraq to allow UN inspectors access to sites suspected of storing or producing such weapons. From the beginning of these forced inspections, Saddam obstructed the UN efforts. In January 1998, he flatly refused to allow inspectors to visit some sites, including many presidential palaces.

Clinton responded by threatening military action against Iraq. Although Saddam appeared to agree to unrestricted inspections in February 1998, he soon began imposing restrictions on the UN inspections again. Tired of Saddam's delaying tactics, Clinton ordered American warplanes to bomb

---

Dayton Agreement   Agreement signed in Dayton, Ohio, in November 1995 by the three rival ethnic groups in Bosnia, which pledged to end the four-year civil war there.

ethnic cleansing   An effort to eradicate an ethnic or religious group from a country or region, often through mass killings.

♦ Following his impeachment by the House of Representatives in December 1998, a determined President Clinton announced that he would not resign his office and vowed to serve out his term to "the last hour." House Minority Leader Richard Gephart (*left*), Vice President Al Gore, and Hillary Clinton lend support.

Baghdad in December 1998. Saddam soon relented, promising once more to allow inspectors to visit all suspected sites. Few observers, however, expected Saddam's cooperation.

Bridge to the Twenty-first Century

As Clinton began his second term, most Americans were generally pleased with society and the economy and gave the president a high approval rating. The country was at peace, and the economy was growing, providing more jobs while inflation remained low. The previous years of economic growth were broad based, helping to reduce income gaps between men and women and African Americans and whites.

In his State of the Union address in 1998, Clinton focused on the economy's strength as he projected the first balanced budget in thirty years. The budget marked, he stated, "an end to decades of deficits that have shackled our economy, paralyzed our policies, and held our people back." He also suggested that any surplus should be set aside to ensure the future viability of Social Security. "Before we do anything with that surplus," he told Congress, "let's save Social Security first." Stressing "smart government," Clinton called for increased spending on education, daycare, Medicare, and Medicaid, as well as for medical and other scientific research. Republican critics argued that the budget had been balanced through the use of "smoke and mirrors" and represented the Democratic position as a continuation of "big government."

At the time Clinton gave his State of the Union Address, the emerging Monica Lewinsky scandal was rocking the White House and prompting some people to suggest that the president should resign or be impeached. Did the president have a sexual relationship with the former White House intern? Did he ask her to lie about it under oath? Although willing to believe the accusations, most Americans did not seem to care. As the investigation and stories of a cover-up and presidential sexual misconduct continued, Clinton's public approval rose to a record high of 79 percent. Polls suggested that a majority of the public was pleased with Clinton's performance as president and the overall state of the nation and thought that Clinton's private life should be his own business.

The Republican majority in the House of Representatives, however, did not agree with that assessment. On October 8, 1998, for only the third time in American history, the House launched impeachment proceedings against a president. In December, the House approved two articles of impeachment against Clinton. The first article charged that Clinton had perjured himself in his January 1998 testimony in the Paula Jones case. (Jones had filed a sexual harassment suit claiming that Clinton had asked her to perform oral sex on him in 1991 while he was governor of Arkansas. Clinton settled the case in November 1998 by paying Jones $850,000 while admitting nothing.) The second article charged that Clinton had abused the powers of his office and obstructed justice in attempting to cover up the Lewinsky affair.

Although public opinion polls clearly were against Clinton's impeachment, the Senate nevertheless agreed to proceed with the case. After a six-week trial, the Senate acquitted Clinton on both counts on February 12, 1999. Forty-five senators voted in favor of convicting the president of perjury, while fifty voted in favor of the obstruction of justice charge. Since a two-thirds majority was required to remove Clinton from office, he remained president, but with a badly stained reputation.

As Americans neared the new millennium, they appeared to have all but forgotten the high drama and low tragedy of Clinton's impeachment trial. Although some feared computer problems and stocked up on portable generators, canned goods, and extra cash, most awaited the arrival of the year 2000 with quiet confidence and assurance. The American economy was strong and showed no signs of stopping its extraordinary expansion. No great foreign threats loomed on the horizon for the world's remaining superpower. Only time would tell whether those confident expectations would be borne out. But one thing was certain: the making of America would continue.

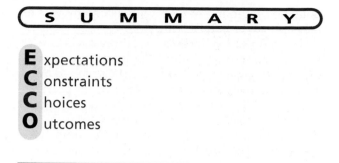

SUMMARY

E xpectations
C onstraints
C hoices
O utcomes

Americans entered and left the 1990s badly divided over many cultural and social *expectations*. Conservatives and liberals argued heatedly about the morality of the country. From both sides of the political spectrum, activists promoted their point of view. Racial and ethnic minorities, gays, and women were among those insisting that government remove *constraints* in the form of discriminatory laws and practices. Conservatives countered that government programs were already providing too many special programs for minorities and the disadvantaged. Opposed to homosexuality, abortion, and what they considered destructive values, conservatives claimed that American society was too permissive, too preoccupied with sex and violence, and too tolerant of immortality and "alternative lifestyles." They advocated less government interference in economic and social matters and argued for policy choices that stressed "traditional values."

The key issue in the 1992 presidential election proved to be not social issues but economic ones. Reminding voters of the economic recession then facing the country, Bill Clinton was able to outdistance incumbent president George Bush and third-party candidate Ross Perot. The *outcome* of Clinton's efforts to expand the welfare state by proposing national healthcare legislation failed abysmally and encouraged Republican *expectations* of a new era of conservatism. Those *expectations* appeared quite realistic in 1994, when Republicans captured both houses of Congress by proposing the conservative Contract with America.

Clinton chose to steal much of the Republican thunder by successfully proposing budgetary and welfare reforms. The *outcome* of his shift to the political center and of a growing economy was his reelection over Bob Dole in 1996.

The Monica Lewinsky scandal operated as a severe *constraint* on Clinton's political effectiveness during his second term. Although he survived a Senate trial on two impeachment charges, his presidential leadership virtually ended on the day Lewinsky became a household name in January 1998.

As America entered the new millennium, there appeared to be no clear political mandate. During the 1990s, Americans had resoundingly voted against a further expansion of "big government"—at least in the form of national healthcare. But they also had chosen to reject conservatives' calls for a thorough dismantling of the welfare state and to retain Social Security and Medicare. Radical *choices* seemed unnecessary in a country that had enjoyed nearly a decade of prosperity and that had resumed its place as the world's leading economic power.

SUGGESTED READINGS

Campbell, Colin, and Bert A. Rockman, eds. *The Clinton Presidency: First Appraisals* (1995).

An informative and speculative group of wide-ranging essays that explore many aspects of Clinton's first years in office and examine broader political issues.

Congressional Quarterly's Research Reports.

A valuable monthly resource for information and views on issues facing the United States and the world.

Garrow, David J. *Liberty and Sexuality: The Right to Privacy and the Making of Roe v. Wade* (1994).

An in-depth, scholarly account of the origins and impact of *Roe v. Wade* and the legal and political issues dealing with privacy, gender, and abortion.

Shilts, Randy. *And the Band Played On: Politics, People and the AIDS Epidemic* (1987).

A compelling book on the AIDS epidemic and the early lack of action by society; written by a victim of AIDS.

Terkel, Studs. *The Great Divide* (1988).

An interesting and informative collection of oral interviews that provide a personal glimpse of changes taking place in American society.

BIBLIOGRAPHY

Chapter 15 Reconstruction: High Hopes and Broken Dreams, 1865–1877

Herman Belz, *Emancipation and Equal Rights: Politics and Constitutionalism in the Civil War Era* (1978); Michael Les Benedict, *The Impeachment and Trial of Andrew Johnson* (1973); LaWanda C. Cox, *Freedom, Racism, and Reconstruction* (1997); Laura F. Edwards, *Gendered Strife and Confusion: The Political Culture of Reconstruction* (1997); John Hope Franklin, *Reconstruction: After the Civil War* (1961); John Hope Franklin and Alfred A. Moss, Jr., *From Slavery to Freedom: A History of Negro Americans*, 6th ed. (1988); Herbert G. Gutman, *The Black Family in Slavery and Freedom* (1976); William C. Harris, *With Charity for All: Lincoln and the Restoration of the Union* (1997); Jacqueline Jones, *Labor of Love, Labor of Sorrow: Black Women, Work and the Family, from Slavery to the Present* (1985); William S. McFeely, *Grant: A Biography* (1981); Eric L. McKitrick, *Andrew Johnson and Reconstruction* (1960; reprint, 1988); James M. McPherson, *Ordeal by Fire: Reconstruction* (1982); David Montgomery, *Beyond Equality: Labor and the Radical Republicans, 1862–1872* (1967); Michael Perman, *Emancipation and Reconstruction, 1862–1879* (1987); Roger L. Ransom and Richard Sutch, *One Kind of Freedom: The Economic Consequences of Emancipation* (1977); John David Smith, *Black Voices from Reconstruction, 1865–1877* (1996); Hans Louis Trefousse, *Andrew Johnson: A Biography* (1989); Allen W. Trelease, *White Terror: The Ku Klux Klan Conspiracy and Southern Reconstruction* (1971, reprint 1995); Vernon Lane Wharton, *The Negro in Mississippi: 1865–1890* (1965; reprint, 1974); Forrest G. Wood, *The Era of Reconstruction, 1863–1877* (1975); C. Vann Woodward, *Reunion and Reaction: The Compromise of 1877 and the End of Reconstruction*, rev. ed. (1956); C. Vann Woodward, *Origins of the New South, 1877–1913* (1951).

Chapter 16 Survival of the Fittest: Entrepreneurs and Workers in Industrial America, 1865–1900

Ralph Andreano, ed., *The Economic Impact of the Civil War*, rev. ed. (1967); Paul Avrich, *The Haymarket Tragedy* (1984); Robert V. Bruce, *1877: Year of Violence* (1959); Vincent P. Carosso, *The Morgans: Private International Bankers, 1854–1913* (1987); Alfred D. Chandler, Jr., *The Essential Alfred Chandler: Essays Toward a Historical Theory of Big Business*, ed. by Thomas K. McCraw (1988); Alfred D. Chandler, ed., *The Railroads: The Nation's First Big Business* (1965); Thomas C. Cochran and William Miller, *The Age of Enterprise: A Social History of Industrial America*, rev. ed. (1961); Carl N. Degler, *In Search of Human Nature: The Decline and Revival of Darwinism in American Social Thought* (1991); Melvyn Dubofsky, *Industrialism and the American Worker, 1865–1920*, 3rd ed. (1996); Leon Fink, *Workingmen's Democracy: The Knights of Labor and American Politics* (1983); Robert Fogel, *Railroads and American Economic Growth* (1965); John A. Garraty, *The New Commonwealth, 1877–1890* (1968); Peter George, *The Emergence of Industrial America: Strategic Factors in American Economic Growth Since 1870* (1982); Louis M. Hacker, *The World of Andrew Carnegie: 1865–1901* (1968); Robert L. Heilbroner, *The Economic Transformation of America* (1977); Matthew Josephson, *The Robber Barons: The Great American Capitalists, 1861–1901* (1934; reprint, 1962); Alice Kessler-Harris, *Out to Work: A History of Wage-Earning Women in the United States* (1982); Edward Chase Kirkland, *Industry Comes of Age: Business, Labor, and Public Policy, 1860–1897* (1961); Harold C. Livesay, *Andrew Carnegie and the Rise of Big Business* (1975); David Montgomery, *Workers' Control in America* (1979); Daniel Nelson, *Managers and Workers: Origins of the New Factory System in the United States, 1880–1920* (1975); Allan Nevins, *Study in Power: John D. Rockefeller, Industrialist and Philanthropist*, 2 vols. (1953); Nick Salvatore, *Eugene V. Debs: Citizen and Socialist* (1982); Fred A. Shannon, *The Farmer's Last Frontier: Agriculture, 1860–1897* (1945); Stephan Thernstrom, *Poverty and Progress: Social Mobility in a Nineteenth Century City* (1964).

Chapter 17 Conflict and Change in the West, 1865–1902

Albert Camarillo, *Chicanos in a Changing Society: From Mexican Pueblos to American Barrios in Santa Barbara and Southern California, 1848–1930* (1979); Sucheng Chan, *Asian Californians* (1991); Sarah Deutsch, *No Separate Refuge: Culture, Class, and Gender on an Anglo-Hispanic Frontier in the American Southwest, 1880–1940* (1987); Everett Dick, *The Sod-House Frontier, 1854–1890* (1954); Robert R. Dykstra, *The Cattle Towns* (1968); Juan Gómez-Quiñones, *Roots of Chicano Politics, 1600–1940* (1994); Wesley S. Griswold, *A Work of Giants: Building the First Transcontinental Railroad* (1962); Richard Griswold del Castillo, *The Los Angeles Barrio, 1850–1890* (1979); Frederick E. Hoxie, *A Final Promise: The Campaign to Assimilate the Indians, 1880–1920* (1984); William Issel and Robert W. Cherny, *San Francisco, 1865–1932: Politics, Power, and Urban Development* (1986); Douglas Monroy, *Thrown Among Strangers: The Making of Mexican Culture in Frontier California* (1990); Sandra L. Myres, *Westering Women and the Frontier Experience, 1800–1915* (1982); Victor G. Nee and Brett de Barry Nee, *Longtime Californ': A Documentary History of an American Chinatown* (1972, 1973; reprint, 1986); Donald Pisani, *From the Family Farm to Agribusiness: The Irrigation Crusade in California and the*

West, 1850–1934 (1984); Leonard Pitt, *The Decline of the Californios: A Social History of the Spanish-Speaking Californians, 1846–1890* (1971); Earl Pomeroy, *The Pacific Slope: A History of California, Oregon, Washington, Idaho, Utah, and Nevada* (1965); Francis Prucha, *American Indian Policy in Crisis: Christian Reformers and the Indian, 1865–1900* (1975); Glenda Riley, *The Female Frontier: A Comparative View of Women on the Prairie and the Plains* (1988); Joseph G. Rosa, *Age of the Gunfighter* (1995); Fred A. Shannon, *The Farmer's Last Frontier: Agriculture, 1860–1897* (1945); Ronald Takaki, *Strangers from the Different Shore* (1989); Robert M. Utley, *The Lance and the Shield: The Life and Times of Sitting Bull* (1993); Walter Prescott Webb, *The Great Plains* (1931); Donald Worster, *Rivers of Empire: Water, Aridity, and the Growth of the American West* (1985).

Chapter 18 The New Social Patterns of Urban and Industrial America, 1865–1917

Edward L. Ayers, *The Promise of the New South: Life After Reconstruction* (1992); John E. Bodnar, *The Transplanted: A History of Immigrants in Urban America* (1985); Ruth Bordin, *Frances Willard: A Biography* (1986); George Chauncy, *Gay New York* (1994); Lawrence Arthur Cremin, *American Education: The Metropolitan Experience, 1876–1980* (1988); Roger Daniels, *Not Like Us: Immigrants and Minorities in America, 1890–1924* (1997); Allen F. Davis, *American Heroine: The Life and Legend of Jane Addams* (1973); John D'Emilio and Estelle B. Freedman, *Intimate Matters: A History of Sexuality in America* (1988); Peter Gammond, *Scott Joplin and the Ragtime Era* (1975); William H. Gerdts, *American Impressionism* (1984); Lynn D. Gordon, *Gender and Higher Education in the Progressive Era* (1990); David F. Greenberg, *The Construction of Homosexuality* (1988); David C. Hammack, *Power and Society: Greater New York at the Turn of the Century* (1982); Louis R. Harlan, *Booker T. Washington: The Making of a Black Leader, 1856–1901* (1972); Kenneth T. Jackson, *Crabgrass Frontier: The Suburbanization of the United States*

(1985); A. T. Lane, *Solidarity of Survival? American Labor and European Immigrants: 1830–1924* (1987); Lawrence W. Levine, *Highbrow/Lowbrow: The Emergence of Cultural Hierarchy in America* (1988); Eric H. Monkkonen, *America Becomes Urban: The Development of U.S. Cities and Towns, 1780–1980* (1988); Regina Markell Morantz-Sanchez, *Sympathy and Science: Women Physicians in American Medicine* (1985); H. Wayne Morgan, ed., *Victorian Culture in America, 1865–1914* (1973); Steven Riess, *Sport in Industrial America, 1850–1920* (1995); Lewis O. Saum, *The Popular Mood of America, 1860–1890* (1990); Thomas J. Schlereth, *Victorian America: Transformations in Everyday Life, 1876–1915* (1991); Louise L. Stevenson, *The Victorian Homefront: American Thought and Culture, 1860–1880* (1991); Jon C. Teaford, *The Unheralded Triumph: City Government in America, 1870–1900* (1984); David Ward, *Cities and Immigrants: A Geography of Change in Nineteenth Century America* (1971); Ida B. Wells-Barnett, *Crusade for Justice: The Autobiography of Ida B. Wells*, edited by Alfreda M. Duster (1970); Mark Wyman, *Round-trip to America: The Immigrants Return to Europe, 1880–1930* (1993).

Chapter 19 Political Stalemate and Political Upheaval, 1868–1900

Walter Dean Burnham, *Critical Elections and the Mainsprings of American Politics* (1970); Paolo E. Coletta, *William Jennings Bryan*, 3 vols. (1964–1969); Carl N. Degler, *The Age of the Economic Revolution, 1876–1900*, 2d ed. (1977); Eleanor Flexner, *Century of Struggle: The Woman's Rights Movement in the United States*, rev. ed., 1996; Milton Friedman and Anna Jacobson Schwartz, *A Monetary History of the United States, 1867–1960* (1963); John A. Garraty, *The New Commonwealth, 1877–1890* (1968); Paul W. Glad, *McKinley, Bryan, and the People* (1964, rpt. 1991); Lewis L. Gould, *The Presidency of William McKinley* (1980); John D. Hicks, *The Populist Revolt: A History of the Farmers' Alliance and the People's Party* (1931); Ari Hoogenboom, *Rutherford B. Hayes: Warrior and President* (1995); Ari

Hoogenboom, *Outlawing the Spoils: A History of the Civil Service Reform Movement* (1961); Michael Kazin, *The Populist Persuasion: An American History* (1995); Paul Kleppner, *The Third Electoral System, 1853–1892: Parties, Voters, and Political Cultures* (1979); Suzanne M. Marilley, *Woman Suffrage and the Origins of Liberal Feminism in the United States, 1820–1920* (1996); Richard L. McCormick, *The Party Period and Public Policy: American Politics from the Age of Jackson to the Progressive Era* (1986); Robert C. McMath, Jr., *American Populism: A Social History, 1877–1898* (1993); Horace Samuel Merrill, *Bourbon Leader: Grover Cleveland and the Democratic Party* (1957); H. Wayne Morgan, *William McKinley and His America* (1963); Nell Irvin Painter, *Standing at Armageddon: The United States, 1877–1919* (1987); Norman Pollack, ed., *The Populist Mind* (1967); Carlos A. Schwantes, *Coxey's Army: An American Odyssey* (1985); Theda Skocpol, *Protecting Soldiers and Mothers: The Politics of Social Provision in the United States* (1992); Xi Wang, *The Trial of Democracy: Black Suffrage and Northern Republicans, 1860–1910* (1997); R. Hal Williams, *Years of Decision: American Politics in the 1890s* (1978).

Chapter 20 Becoming a World Power: America and World Affairs, 1865–1913

Robert L. Beisner, *Twelve Against Empire: The Anti-Imperialists, 1898–1900* (1968); Richard H. Collin, *Theodore Roosevelt: Culture, Diplomacy, and Expansion* (1985); John M. Dobson, *Reticent Expansionism: The Foreign Policy of William McKinley* (1988); Justus D. Doenecke, *The Presidencies of James A. Garfield and Chester A. Arthur* (1981); Lewis L. Gould, *The Presidency of Theodore Roosevelt* (1991); David Healy, *U.S. Expansionism: The Imperialist Urge in the 1890s* (1970); Jerry Israel, *Progressivism and the Open Door: America and China, 1905–1921* (1971); Walter LaFeber, *Inevitable Revolutions: The United States in Central America*, rev. ed. (1993); Gerald F. Linderman, *The Mirror of War: American Society and the Spanish-American War* (1974); T. J. McCormick,

China Market: America's Quest for Informal Empire (1967); Alfred Thayer Mahan, *The Influence of Seapower upon History, 1660–1783* (1890, rpt., 1957); C. Roland Marchand, *The American Peace Movement and Social Reform, 1898–1918* (1972); Ernest R. May, *American Imperialism: A Speculative Essay* (1968); Ernest R. May, *Imperial Democracy: The Emergence of America as a Great Power* (1961, rpt. 1973); H. Wayne Morgan, *America's Road to Empire: The War with Spain and Overseas Expansion* (1965); H. Wayne Morgan, *William McKinley and His America,* (1963); Thomas J. Osborne, *"Empire Can Wait": American Opposition to Hawaiian Annexation, 1893–1898* (1981); Bradford Perkins, *The Great Rapprochement: England and the United States, 1895–1914* (1968); Dexter Perkins, *A History of the Monroe Doctrine* (1963); Milton Plesur, *America's Outward Thrust: Approaches to Foreign Affairs, 1865–1900* (1971); Julius W. Pratt, *Expansionists of 1898* (1936); Emily S. Rosenberg, *Spreading the American Dream: American Economic and Cultural Expansion, 1890–1945* (1982); E. Berkeley Tompkins, *Anti-Imperialism in the United States: The Great Debate, 1890–1920* (1970); Richard E. Welch, Jr., *The Presidencies of Grover Cleveland* (1988); Richard E. Welch, Jr., *Response to Imperialism: The United States and the Philippine-American War, 1899–1902* (1979); William Appleman Williams, *The Roots of the Modern American Empire* (1969); Marilyn Blatt Young, *The Rhetoric of Empire: American China Policy, 1895–1901* (1968).

Very Different Age: Americans of the Progressive Era (1998); Louis Filler, *Appointment at Armageddon: Muckraking and Progressivism in the American Tradition,* ref. edn. (1996); Linda Gordon, *Woman's Body, Woman's Right: Birth Control in America,* rev. ed. (1990); Lewis L. Gould, *Reform and Regulation: American Politics from Roosevelt to Wilson,* 3rd ed. (1996); Louis R. Harlan, *Booker T. Washington: The Wizard of Tuskegee, 1901–1915* (1983); Samuel P. Hays, *American Political History as Social Analysis* (1980); Samuel P. Hays, *Conservation and the Gospel of Efficiency* (1959); Ari and Olive Hoogenboom, *A History of the ICC: From Panacea to Palliative* (1976); Arthur S. Link, *Woodrow Wilson,* 5 vols. (1947–1965); Richard Coke Lower, *A Bloc of One: The Political Career of Hiram W. Johnson* (1993); Richard L. McCormick, *The Party Period and Public Policy: American Politics from the Age of Jackson to the Progressive Era* (1986); Michael E. McGerr, *The Decline of Popular Politics: The American North, 1865–1928* (1986); Manning Marable, *W. E. B. Du Bois: Black Radical Democrat* (1986); Sally M. Miller, *Victor Berger and the Promise of Constructive Socialism, 1910–1920* (1973); Daniel Rodgers, "In Search of Progressivism." *Reviews in American History* 10 (Dec. 1982): 113–132; Nick Salvatore, *Eugene V. Debs: Citizen and Socialist* (1982); Melvin I. Urofsky, *Louis D. Brandeis and the Progressive Tradition* (1981); Robert H. Wiebe, *The Search for Order, 1877–1920* (1967); William H. Wilson, *The City Beautiful Movement* (1989).

Labor Board (1983); John Milton Cooper, Jr., *The Vanity of Power: American Isolationism and World War I* (1969); Patrick Devlin, *Too Proud to Fight: Woodrow Wilson's Neutrality* (1974); Robert H. Ferrell, *Woodrow Wilson and World War I, 1917–1921* (1985); Mark T. Gilderhus, *Diplomacy and Revolution: U.S.-Mexican Relations Under Wilson and Carranza* (1977); Maurine Weiner Greenwald, *War and Work: The Impact of World War I on Women Workers in the United States* (1980); Edward Haley, *Revolution and Intervention: The Diplomacy of Taft and Wilson in Mexico, 1910–1917* (1970); Ellis Hawley, *The Great War and the Search for a Modern Order,* 2nd ed. (1997); D. Clayton James and Anne Sharp Wells, *America and the Great War, 1914–1920* (1998); Robert Johnson, *The Peace Progressives and American Foreign Relations* (1995); David M. Kennedy, *Over Here: The First World War and American Society* (1980); Thomas J. Knock, *To End All Wars: Woodrow Wilson and the Creation of the League of Nations* (1992); David D. Lee, *Sergeant York: An American Hero* (1985); C. Roland Marchand, *The American Peace Movement and Social Reform, 1898–1918* (1972); Ernest R. May, *The World War and American Isolation, 1914–1917* (1959); Joseph A. McCartin, *Labor's Great War: The Struggle for Industrial Democracy and the Origins of Modern American Labor Relations, 1912–1921* (1997); Paul L. Murphy, *World War I and the Origin of Civil Liberties in the United States* (1979); Robert K. Murray, *Red Scare: A Study in National Hysteria, 1919–1920* (1955, rpt. 1964); Ruth Rosen, *The Lost Sisterhood: Prostitution in America, 1900–1918* (1982); William M. Tuttle, *Race Riot: Chicago in the Red Summer of 1919* (1970); Stephen Vaughn, *Holding Fast the Inner Lines: Democracy, Nationalism, and the Committee on Public Information* (1980); James Weinstein, *The Decline of Socialism in America; 1912–1925* (1967, rpt. 1984).

Chapter 21 The Progressive Era, 1900–1917

Paula Baker, "The Domestication of Politics: Women and American Political Society, 1780–1920." *American Historical Review* 89 (1984): 620–647; Jack S. Blocker, Jr., *Retreat from Reform: The Prohibition Movement in the United States, 1890–1913* (1976); John Morton Blum, *The Republican Roosevelt,* 2d ed. (1977); Ruth Bordin, *Women and Temperance: The Quest for Power and Liberty, 1873–1900* (1980); H. W. Brands, *T.R.: The Last Romantic* (1997); Kendrick A. Clements, *The Presidency of Woodrow Wilson* (1992); Steven J. Diner, *A*

Chapter 22 America and the World, 1913–1920

Lloyd E. Ambrosius, *Woodrow Wilson and the American Diplomatic Tradition: The Treaty Fight in Perspective* (1987); W. J. Breen, *Uncle Sam at Home: Civilian Mobilization, Wartime Federalism, and the Council of National Defense, 1917–1919* (1984), David Brody, *Labor in Crisis: The Steel Strike of 1919* (1965); Kendrick A. Clements, *William Jennings Bryan: Missionary Isolationist* (1982); Edward M. Coffman, *The War to End All Wars: The American Military Experience in World War I* (1986); Jean Conner, *The National War*

Chapter 23 The 1920s, 1920–1928

Carl Abbott, *Urban America in the Modern Age* (1987); William J. Barber, *From New Era to New Deal: Herbert Hoover, the Economists, and American Economic Policy,*

1921–1933 (1985); Daniel H. Borus, ed., *These United States: Portraits of America from the 1920s* (1992); Paul A. Carter, *The Twenties in America*, 2d ed. (1987); E. David Cronon, *Black Moses: The Story of Marcus Garvey and the Universal Negro Improvement Association*, 2d ed. (1969); Lyle W. Dorset, *Billy Sunday and the Redemption of Urban America* (1991); Martin Bauml Duberman, *Paul Robeson: A Biography* (1989); Lynn Dumenil, *The Modern Temper: American Culture and Society in the 1920s* (1995); Richard Wrightman Fox and T. J. Jackson Lears, eds., *The Culture of Consumption: Critical Essays in American History, 1880–1980* (1983); Linda Gordon, *Woman's Body, Woman's Right: Birth Control in America*, rev. ed. (1990); Edward Jablonski, *Gershwin* (1987); Kenneth T. Jackson, *The Ku Klux Klan in the City, 1915–1930* (1967); Harvey Klehr and John Earl Haynes, *The American Communist Movement: Storming Heaven Itself* (1992); Peter Iverson, *"We Are Still Here": American Indians in the Twentieth Century* (1998); David L. Lewis, *When Harlem Was in Vogue* (1981); Robert S. Lynd and Helen M. Lynd, *Middletown* (1929); Roland Marchand, *Advertising the American Dream: Making Way for Modernity, 1920–1940* (1985); Arnold Rampersad, *The Life of Langston Hughes*, 2 vols. (1986, 1988); Arthur M. Schlesinger, Jr., *The Crisis of the Old Order, 1919–1933* (1957); Arnold Shaw, *The Jazz Age: Popular Music in the 1920's* (1987); Robert Sobel, *The Great Bull Market: Wall Street in the 1920s* (1968); Ferenc Szasz, *The Divided Mind of Protestant America, 1880–1930* (1982); Bernard A. Weisberger, *The Dream Maker: William C. Durant, Founder of General Motors* (1979); Robert H. Zieger, *American Workers, American Unions, 1920–1985* (1986).

Chapter 24 From Good Times to Hard Times, 1920–1932

Francisco Balderrama and Raymond Rodriguez, *Decade of Betrayal: Mexican Repatriation in the 1930s* (1995); David Burner, *Herbert Hoover: The Public Life* (1978); Dan T. Carter, *Scottsboro* (1969); Roger Daniels, *The Bonus March* (1971);

Charles DeBenedetti, *Origins of the Modern American Peace Movement, 1915–1929* (1978); Paula Elder, *Governor Alfred E. Smith: The Politician as Reformer* (1983); Ethan Ellis, *Republican Foreign Policy, 1921–1933* (1968); Milton Friedman and Anna Schwartz, *The Great Contraction, 1929–1933* (1965); John Kenneth Galbraith, *The Great Crash, 1929* (1961); Cheryl L. Greenberg, *"Or Does It Explode?" Black Harlem in the Great Depression* (1991); David Hamilton, *From New Day to New Deal: American Farm Policy from Hoover to Roosevelt, 1928–1933* (1991); A. Iriye, *After Imperialism: The Search for New Order in the Far East, 1921–1931* (1965); Neil Macaulay, *The Sandino Affair* (1985); William Mullins, *The Depression and the Urban West Coast, 1929–1933* (1991); James S. Olson, *Herbert Hoover and the Reconstruction Finance Corporation, 1931–1933* (1977); Emily Rosenberg, *Spreading the American Dream* (1982); Louis Schraf, *To Work and to Wed: Female Employment and the Great Depression* (1980); Vicki Ruiz, *Cannery Women, Cannery Lives: Mexican Women, Unionization and the California Food Processing Industry, 1930–1950* (1987); John Shover, *Cornbelt Rebellion: The Farmers' Holiday Association* (1965); Peter Timim: *Did Monetary Forces Cause the Great Depression?* (1976); Susan Ware, *Holding Their Own: American Women in the Thirties* (1982); Joan Hoff Wilson, *American Business and Foreign Policy, 1920–1933* (1968); Donald Worster, *Dust Bowl: The Southern Plains in the 1930s* (1979).

Chapter 25 The New Deal, 1933–1940

Anthony Badger, *The New Deal: The Depression Years, 1933–1940* (1989); Ann Banks, ed., *First Person America* (1980); John Barnard, *Walter Reuther and the Rise of the Auto Workers* (1983); Edward D. Berkowitz, *America's Welfare State: From Roosevelt to Reagan* (1991); Irving Bernstein, *A Caring Society: The New Deal, The Worker, and the Great Depression* (1985); Gary D. Best, *Pride, Prejudice, and Politics: Roosevelt Versus Recovery,*

1933–1938 (1990); Roger Biles, *A New Deal for the American People* (1991); Julia Kirk Blackwelder, *No Hiring: The Feminization of Work in the United States, 1900–1995* (1997); Alan Brinkley, *Voices of the Protest: Huey Long, Father Coughlin, and the Great Depression* (1982); William U. Chandler, *The Myth of the TVA: Conservation and Development in the Tennessee Valley, 1933–1983* (1984); Kenneth S. Davis, *FDR: Into the Storm, 1937–1940: A History* (1993); Kenneth S. Davis, *FDR: The New Deal Years, 1933–1937* (1986); Sidney Fine, *Sit-Down: The General Motors Strike of 1936–1937* (1969); Colin Gordon, *New Deals: Business, Labor, and Politics in America* (1994); James Gregory, *American Exodus: The Dust Bowl Migration and the Okie Culture in California* (1989); Lawrence C. Kelley, *The Assault on Assimilation: John Collier and the Origins of Indian Policy Reform* (1983); Roy Lubove, *The Struggle for Social Security* (1968); Robert S. McElvaine, ed., *Down and Out in the Great Depression: Letters from the Forgotten Man* (1983); Patrick J. Maney, *The Roosevelt Presence: A Biography of Franklin Delano Roosevelt* (1992); George McJimsey, *Harry Hopkins* (1987); Jerre Mangione, *The Dream and the Deal: The Federal Writers' Project, 1935–1943* (1972); James T. Patterson, *Congressional Conservatism and the New Deal* (1967); Kenneth Philip, *John Collier's Crusade for Indian Reform, 1920–1945* (1977); Theodore Saloutos, *The American Farmer and the New Deal* (1982); Lois Schraf, *Eleanor Roosevelt: First Lady of American Liberalism* (1987); Harvard Sitkoff, ed., *Fifty Years Later: The New Deal Evaluated* (1985); Patricia Sullivan, *Days of Hope: Race and Democracy in the New Deal Era* (1996); Devra Weber, *Dark Sweat, White Gold: California Farm Workers, Cotton, and the New Deal* (1994); Nancy J. Weiss, *Farewell to the Party of Lincoln: Black Politics in the Age of FDR* (1983).

Chapter 26 America's Rise to World Leadership, 1933–1945

Stephen E. Ambrose, *D-Day, June 6, 1944* (1994); Dorothy Borg and Shumpei

Okamoto, eds., *Pearl Harbor as History* (1973); David Brinkley, *Washington Goes to War* (1988); Wayne Cole, *Roosevelt and the Isolationists* (1983); John Costello, *Virtue Under Fire: How World War II Changed Our Social and Sexual Attitudes* (1985); Lyn Crost, *Honor by Fire: Japanese Americans at War in Europe and the Pacific* (1994); Thomas Doherty, *Projections of War: Hollywood, American Culture, and World War II* (1993); Henry L. Feingold, *The Politics of Rescue: The Roosevelt Administration and the Holocaust, 1938–1945* (1970); Irwin F. Gellman, *The Good Neighbor Diplomacy: United States Policies in Latin America, 1933–1945* (1979); Susan Hartmann, *The Homefront and Beyond: American Women in the 1940s* (1982); Waldo H. Heinrichs, Jr., *Threshold of War* (1988); Akira Iriye, *Power and Culture: The Japanese-American War, 1941–1945* (1981); Gerald D. Nash, *The American West Transformed: The Impact of the Second World War* (1985); Judy B. Litoff, *We're in This War Too: World War II Letters of American Women in Uniform* (1994); Neil R. McMillen, ed., *Remaking Dixie: The Impact of World War II on the American South* (1997); Verne W. Newton, ed., *FDR and the Holocaust* (1995); William O'Neill, *A Democracy at War: America's Fight at Home and Abroad in World War II* (1993); Richard Polenberg, *War and Society: The United States, 1941–1945* (1972); Richard Rhodes, *The Making of the Atomic Bomb* (1987); Ronald Schaffer, *Wings of Judgment: American Bombing in World War II* (1985); Martin Sherman, *A World Destroyed* (1975); Michael Sherry, *In the Shadow of War: The United States Since the 1930s* (1995); John R. Skates, *The Invasion of Japan: Alternative to the Bomb* (1994); Gaddis Smith, *American Diplomacy During the Second World War* (1965); Mark Stoler, "A Half Century of Conflict: Interpretations of World War II Diplomacy," *Diplomatic History* 18 (Summer 1994): 375–403; Susan C. Taylor, *Jewel of the Desert: Japanese American Internment at Topaz* (1994); Studs Terkel, *The Good War: An Oral History of World War Two* (1984); Jonathan Utley, *Going to War with Japan* (1985); Allen E. Winkler, *Home Front U.S.A.: America During World War II* (1986); David S. Wyman, *The Abandonment of the Jews* (1984); Neil A. Wynn, *The Afro American and the Second World War* (1975).

Chapter 27 Truman and Cold War America, 1945–1952

William C. Berman, *The Politics of Civil Rights in the Truman Administration* (1970); Paul Boyer, *By the Bomb's Early Light: American Thought and Culture at the Dawn of the Atomic Age* (1985); Kevin Boyle, *The UAW and the Heyday of American Liberalism* (1995); Richard M. Dalfiume, *Desegregation of the U.S. Armed Forces* (1969); Robert J. Donovan, *The Tumultuous Years: the Presidency of Harry S Truman, 1949–1953* (1982); Robert Griffith, *The Politics of Fear: Joseph R. McCarthy and the Senate* (1987); John L. Gaddis, *We Now Know: Rethinking Cold War History* (1997); John L. Gaddis, *Strategies of Containment* (1982); Herbert J. Gans, *The Levittowners* (1967); William S. Graebner, *The Age of Doubt: American Thought and Culture in the 1940s* (1991); John Halliday and Bruce Cummings, *Korea: The Unknown War* (1987); Alonzo Hamby, *Man of the People: A Life of Harry S Truman* (1995); Susan Hartman, *Truman and the 80th Congress* (1971); Gregory Herken, *The Winning Weapon* (1981); Michael Hogan, *The Marshall Plan* (1987); Landon Y. Jones, *Great Expectations: America and the Baby Boom Generation* (1980); Burton Kaufman, *The Arab Middle East and the United States: Inter-Arab Rivalry and Superpower Diplomacy* (1996); Donald Katz, *Home Fires: An Intimate Portrait of One Middle-Class Family in Postwar America* (1992); Melvyn Leffler, *A Preponderance of Power* (1991); Allen J. Matusow, *Farm Policies and Politics in the Truman Years* (1967); Elaine Tyler May, *Homeward Bound: American Families in the Cold War Era* (1988); William O'Neil, *American High: The Years of Confidence 1945–1960* (1986); David M. Oshinsky, *A Conspiracy So Immense: The World of Joseph McCarthy* (1983); James T. Patterson, *Grand Expectations: The United States, 1945–1974* (1996); Arnold Rampersad, *Jackie Robinson* (1997); Gary W. Reichard, *Politics as Usual* (1988); Michael Schaller, *The American Occupation of Japan: The Origins of the Cold War in Asia* (1985); Ellen W. Schrenker, *The Age of McCarthyism* (1994); Athan Theoharis and John S. Cox, *The Boss: J. Edgar Hoover and the Great American Inquisition* (1988).

Chapter 28 Quest for Consensus, 1952–1960

Charles C. Alexander, *Holding the Line* (1985); H. W. Brands, Jr., *Cold Warriors* (1988); Wini Breines, *Young, White, and Miserable: Growing Up Female in the Fifties* (1992); Taylor Branch, *Parting the Water: America in the King Years, 1954–1963* (1988); John D'Emilio, and Estelle B. Freedman, *Intimate Matters: A History of Sexuality in America* (1988); Robert A. Devine, *The Sputnik Challenge* (1993); Robert A. Devine, *Blowing in the Wind: The Nuclear Test Ban Debate* (1978); Barbara Ehrenreich, *Hearts of Men* (1983); Robert Fishamn, *Bourgeois Utopias* (1987); Donald I. Fixico, *Termination and Relocation: Federal Indian Policy, 1945–1970* (1986); Lloyd Gardner, *Approaching Vietnam* (1988); William Graebner, *Coming of Age in Buffalo* (1990); Fred I. Greenstein, *The Hidden-Hand Presidency* (1982); Richard G. Hewlett and Jack M. Hall, *Atoms for Peace and War* (1989); Alice Kessler-Harris, *Out to Work: A History of Wage-Earning Women in the United States* (1982); Nicholas Lemann, *The Promised Land* (1991); Victory Marchetti and John D. Marks, *The CIA and the Cult of Intelligence* (1974); Karal Ann Marling, *As Seen on TV: The Visual Culture of Everyday Life in the 1950s* (1994); Waldo Martin, Jr., *Brown v. Board of Education: A Brief History with Documents* (1998); Martin E. Marty, *Modern American Religion, Vol. 3: Under God, Indivisible, 1941–1960* (1996); Joan Meyerowitz, ed., *Not June Cleaver: Women and Gender in Postwar America* (1994); William Pickett, *Dwight David Eisenhower and American Power* (1995); Stephen G. Rabe, *Eisenhower and Latin America* (1988); Mark H. Rose, *Interstate* (1979); John W. Sloan, *Eisenhower and the Management of Prosperity* (1991); Jane Smith, *Patenting the Sun: Polio and the Salk Vaccine* (1990); John C. Teaford, *The Twentieth Century City*

(1993); Mark V. Tushnet, *Making Civil Rights Law: Thurgood Marshall and the Supreme Court, 1936–1961* (1995); Alan Winkler, *Life Under A Cloud: American Anxiety About the Atom* (1993).

Chapter 29 Great Promises, Bitter Disappointments, 1960–1968

Terry Anderson, *The Movement and the Sixties* (1995); Alexander Bloom, ed., *'Takin' It to the Streets: A Sixties Reader* (1995); David Burner, *John F. Kennedy and a New Generation* (1988); Eric Burner, *And Gently He Shall Lead Them: Robert Parris Moses and Civil Rights in Mississippi* (1994); Claude Andrew Clegg III, *An Original Man: The Life and Times of Elijah Muhammad* (1997); David Farber, *The Age of Great Dreams: America in the 1960s* (1994); Alexander Fursendo and Timothy Naftali, *"One Hell of a Gamble": Khrushchev, Castro, and Kennedy, 1958–1964* (1998); David Garrow, *Protest at Selma: Martin Luther King and the Voting Rights Act of 1965* (1978); Paula Giddings and Cornel West, *Regarding Malcolm X* (1994); James Giglio, *The Presidency of John F. Kennedy* (1991); Hugh Davis Graham, *The Civil Rights Era: Origins and Development of National Policy, 1960–1972* (1990); Allen Matusow, *The Unraveling of America: A History of Liberalism in the 1960s* (1984); James Miller, *"Democracy Is in the Streets"—From Port Huron to the Siege at Chicago* (1987); Charles Murray, *Losing Ground: American Social Policy, 1950–1980* (1984); Thomas Paterson, *Confronting Castro: The United States and the Triumph of the Cuban Revolution* (1994); Thomas C. Reeves, *President Kennedy: Profile of Power* (1994); Theodore Roszak, *The Making of the Counterculture* (1969); Thomas Schoenbaum, *Waging Peace and War: Dean Rusk in the Truman, Kennedy, and Johnson Years* (1988); Bernard Schwartz, *Super Chief: Earl Warren and His Supreme Court* (1983); John E. Schwartz, *America's Hidden Success: A Reassessment of Twenty Years of Public Policy* (1983); Barbara L. Tischler, ed., *Sights on the Sixties* (1992); Irwin Unger, *The Movement: A History of the American New Left,*

1959–1972 (1974); Melvin Urofsky, *The Continuity of Change: The Supreme Court and Individual Liberties, 1953–1986* (1991); Robert Weisbrot, *Freedom Bound: A History of America's Civil Rights Movement* (1991).

Chapter 30 America Under Stress, 1960–1975

Stephen Ambrose, *Nixon: The Triumph of the Politician, 1962–1972* (1990); Larry Berman, *Lyndon Johnson's War* (1989); Robert Buzzanco, *Masters of War: Military Dissent and Politics in Vietnam* (1996); Larry Cable, *Unholy Grail* (1991); Peter Caroll, *It Seemed Like Nothing Happened* (1982); Vine Deloria, Jr., *Custer Died for Your Sins* (1969); Robert Devine, *The Johnson Years, Volumes 1–3* (1981, 1987, 1994); Juan Gomez-Quinones, *Chicano Politics: Reality and Promise, 1940–1990* (1990); Richard Griswold de Castillo and Richard A. Garcia, *Cesar Chavez: A Triumph of Spirit* (1995); H. R. Haldeman, *The Haldeman Diaries: Inside the Nixon White House* (1994); Seymour Hersh, *The Price of Power: Kissinger in the Nixon White House* (1983); Troy R. Johnson, *The Occupation of Alcatraz Island: Indian Self-Determination and the Rise of American Activism* (1996); Blanche Linden-Ward and Carol Hurd Green, *American Women in the 1960s* (1993); Kim McQuaid, *The Anxious Years: America in the Vietnam and Watergate Era* (1989); Marguerite V. Marin, *Social Protest in an Urban Barrio: A Study of the Chicano Movement, 1966–1974* (1991); George D. Moss, *Vietnam: An American Ordeal* (1994); Carlos Munoz, Jr., *Youth, Identity, Power: The Chicano Movement* (1989); Richard Nixon, *RN: The Memoirs of Richard Nixon* (1978); James S. Olson and Randy Roberts, *My Lai: A Brief History with Documents* (1998); Herbert Parmet, *The World and Richard Nixon* (1990); Kirkpatrick Sales, *The Green Revolution: The American Environmental Movement, 1962–1992* (1996); Deborah Shapely, *Promise and Power: The Life and Times of Robert McNamara* (1993); Neil Sheehan, *A Bright Shining Lie: John Paul Vann and America in Vietnam* (1988); Melvin Small, *Johnson, Nixon, and the Doves* (1988); Ronald Spector, *After Tet:*

The Bloodiest Year in Vietnam (1992); Steven J. Spiegel, *The Other Arab-Israeli Conflict: Making America's Middle East Policy from Truman to Reagan* (1985); Bob Woodward and Carl Bernstein, *All the President's Men* (1974); Daniel Yergin, *The Prize* (1991).

Chapter 31 Facing Limits, 1974–1992

William Berman, *America's Right Turn: From Nixon to Bush* (1994); John A. Booth and Thomas W. Walker, *Understanding Central America* (1989); Peter G. Bourne, *Jimmy Carter: A Comprehensive Biography from Plains to Post-Presidency* (1997); Paul Boyer, ed., *Reagan as President* (1990); Dan Carter, *From George Wallace to Newt Gingrich: Race in the Conservative Counterrevolution, 1963–1994* (1996); Paul Dukes, *The Last Great Game* (1989); John Dumbrell, *American Foreign Policy: Carter to Clinton* (1997); Carol Felsenthal, *The Sweetheart of the Silent Majority* (1981); Lawrence Freedman and Efraim Karsh, *The Gulf Conflict, 1990–1992* (1993); Raymond Gartoff, *The Great Transition: American Soviet Relations and the End of the Cold War* (1994); William E. Griffth, ed., *Central and Eastern Europe: The Opening Curtain* (1989); Samuel P. Hays, *Beauty, Health, and Permanence: Environmental Politics in the United States, 1955–1985* (1987); Haynes Johnson, *Sleepwalking Through History: America in the Reagan Years* (1991); Charles O. Jones, *The Trusteeship Presidency: Jimmy Carter and the United States Congress* (1988); Harold H. Koh, *The National Security Constitution* (1990); Walter LaFeber, *The Panama Canal* (1989); Robert S. Leiken, ed., *Central America: Anatomy of Conflict* (1984); Robert C. Liberman and Robert Wuthnow, eds., *The New Christian Right* (1983); Theodore Lowi, *The End of the Republican Era* (1995); Donald Mabry, ed., *The Latin American Narcotics Trade* (1992); David Mervin, *George Bush and the Guardianship Presidency* (1996); John Palmer and Elizabeth Sawmill, eds., *The Reagan Record* (1984); William B. Quandt, *Camp David* (1986); T. S. Reid, *The Chip* (1985); Robert Scheer, *With Enough Shovels* (1982); Peter Scott and Jonathan

Marshall, *Cocaine Politics: Drugs, Armies, and the CIA in Central America* (1991); Allan P. Sindler, *Bakke, DeFunis, and the Minority Admissions* (1978); Philip Slater, *Earthwalk* (1974); Gaddis Smith, *Morality, Reason, and Power* (1986); James B. Stewart, *Den of Thieves* (1991); Strobe Talbot, *Deadly Gambits* (1984); John Kenneth White, *The New Politics of Old Values* (1988); Clyde Wilcox, *Onward Christian Soldiers: The Religious Right in American Politics* (1996); John Woodridge, *The Evangelicals* (1975).

Chapter 32 Making New Choices, 1992–1999

Dan Balz and Ronald Brownstein, *Storming the Gates: Protest Politics and the Republican Revival* (1996); Frank Bean and Marta Tienda, *The Hispanic Population of the United States* (1988); David Bender and Bruno Leane, *Abortion. Opposing Viewpoints* (1997); Susan K. Cahn, *Coming on Strong: Gender and Sexuality in 20th-Century Sport* (1994); Donald T. Crithlow, ed., *The Politics of Abortion and Birth Control in Historical Perspective* (1996); W. Avon Drake and Robert D. Holsworth, *Affirmative Action and the Stalled Quest for Black Progress* (1996); Barbara Ehrenreich, *The Worst Years of Our Lives* (1990); Herbert Gans, *The War Against the Poor: The Underclass and Anti-Poverty Policy* (1995); Nathan Glazer, ed., *Clamor at the Gates: The New American Immigration* (1986); James D. Hunter, *Culture Wars: The Struggle to Define America* (1991); Michael Katz, *The Undeserving Poor: From the War on Poverty to the War on Welfare* (1989); Jonathan Kozol, *Rachael and Her Children: Homeless Families in America* (1988); Elliot Liebow, *Tell Them Who I Am: The Lives of Homeless Women* (1993); John Longone, *AIDS: The Facts* (1988); Manhattan Institute and Pacific Research Institute, *Strangers at Our Gate: Immigration in the 1990s* (1994); David Maraniss, *First In His Class: A Biography of Bill Clinton* (1995); Robert Morris, *Partners in Power: The Clintons and Their America* (1996); Gary Orfield and Susan Eaton, *Dismantling Desegregation: The Quiet Reversal of Brown v. Board of Education* (1996); Robert Reich, *The Work of Nations: Preparing Ourselves for Twenty-First Century Capitalism* (1991); Stanley Renshon, *High Hopes: The Clinton Presidency and the Politics of Ambitions* (1996); Hilda Scott, *Working Your Way to the Bottom: The Feminization of Poverty,* (1985); William Serrin, *Homestead: The Glory and Tragedy of an American Steel Town* (1992); Ruth Sildel, *Women and Children Last* (1986); James Simon, *The Center Holds: The Power Struggle Inside the Rehnquist Court* (1995); Christina Hoff Sommers, *Who Stole Feminism? How Women Have Betrayed Women* (1994); Lawrence Tribe, *Clash of Absolutes* (1992); Melvin Urofsky, *A Conflict of Rights: The Supreme Court and Affirmative Action* (1991); William Wei, *The Asian American Movement* (1993); William J. Wilson, *The Truly Disadvantaged* (1987).

Declaration of Independence in Congress, July 4, 1776

When, in the course of human events, it becomes necessary for one people to dissolve the political bonds which have connected them with another, and to assume, among the powers of the earth, the separate and equal station to which the laws of nature and of nature's God entitle them, a decent respect to the opinions of mankind requires that they should declare the causes which impel them to the separation.

We hold these truths to be self-evident: That all men are created equal; that they are endowed by their Creator with certain unalienable rights; that among these are life, liberty, and the pursuit of happiness; that, to secure these rights, governments are instituted among men, deriving their just powers from the consent of the governed; that whenever any form of government becomes destructive of these ends, it is the right of the people to alter or to abolish it, and to institute new government, laying its foundation on such principles, and organizing its powers in such form, as to them shall seem most likely to effect their safety and happiness. Prudence, indeed, will dictate that governments long established should not be changed for light and transient causes; and accordingly all experience hath shown that mankind are more disposed to suffer, while evils are sufferable, than to right themselves by abolishing the forms to which they are accustomed. But when a long train of abuses and usurpations, pursuing invariably the same object, evinces a design to reduce them under absolute despotism, it is their right, it is their duty, to throw off such government, and to provide new guards for their future security. Such has been the patient sufferance of these colonies; and such is now the necessity which constrains them to alter their former systems of government. The history of the present King of Great Britain is a history of repeated injuries and usurpations, all having in direct object the establishment of an absolute tyranny over these states. To prove this, let facts be submitted to a candid world.

He has refused his assent to laws, the most wholesome and necessary for the public good.

He has forbidden his governors to pass laws of immediate and pressing importance, unless suspended in their operation till his assent should be obtained; and, when so suspended, he has utterly neglected to attend to them.

He has refused to pass other laws for the accommodation of large districts of people, unless those people would relinquish the right of representation in the legislature, a right inestimable to them, and formidable to tyrants only.

He has called together legislative bodies at places unusual, uncomfortable, and distant from the depository of their public records, for the sole purpose of fatiguing them into compliance with his measures.

He has dissolved representative houses repeatedly, for opposing, with manly firmness, his invasions on the rights of the people.

He has refused for a long time, after such dissolutions, to cause others to be elected; whereby the legislative powers, incapable of annihilation, have returned to the people at large for their exercise; the state remaining, in the mean time, exposed to all the dangers of invasions from without and convulsions within.

He has endeavored to prevent the population of these states; for that purpose obstructing the laws for naturalization of foreigners; refusing to pass others to encourage their migration hither, and raising the conditions of new appropriations of lands.

He has obstructed the administration of justice, by refusing his assent to laws for establishing judiciary powers.

He has made judges dependent on his will alone, for the tenure of their offices, and the amount and payment of their salaries.

He has erected a multitude of new offices, and sent hither swarms of officers to harass our people and eat out their substance.

He has kept among us, in times of peace, standing armies, without the consent of our legislatures.

He has affected to render the military independent of, and superior to, the civil power.

He has combined with others to subject us to a jurisdiction foreign to our constitution, and unacknowledged by our laws, giving his assent to their acts of pretended legislation:

For quartering large bodies of armed troops among us;

For protecting them, by a mock trial, from punishment for any murders which they should commit on the inhabitants of these states;

For cutting off our trade with all parts of the world;

For imposing taxes on us without our consent;

For depriving us, in many cases, of the benefits of trial by jury;

For transporting us beyond seas, to be tried for pretended offenses;

For abolishing the free system of English laws in a neighboring province, establishing therein an arbitrary government, and enlarging its boundaries, so as to render it at once an example and fit instrument for introducing the same absolute rule into these colonies;

For taking away our charters, abolishing our most valuable laws, and altering fundamentally the forms of our governments;

For suspending our own legislatures, and declaring themselves invested with power to legislate for us in all cases whatsoever.

He has abdicated government here, by declaring us out of his protection and waging war against us.

He has plundered our seas, ravaged our coasts, burned our towns, and destroyed the lives of our people.

He is at this time transporting large armies of foreign mercenaries to complete the works of death, desolation, and tyranny already begun with circumstances of cruelty and perfidy scarcely paralleled in the most barbarous ages, and totally unworthy the head of a civilized nation.

He has constrained our fellow-citizens, taken captive on the high seas, to bear arms against their country, to become the executioners of their friends and brethren, or to fall themselves by their hands.

He has excited domestic insurrection among us, and has endeavored to bring on the inhabitants of our frontiers the merciless Indian savages, whose known rule of warfare is an undistinguished destruction of all ages, sexes, and conditions.

In every stage of these oppressions we have petitioned for redress in the most humble terms; our repeated petitions have been answered only by repeated injury. A prince, whose character is thus marked by every act which may define a tyrant, is unfit to be the ruler of a free people.

Nor have we been wanting in our attentions to our British brethren. We have warned them, from time to time, of attempts by their legislature to extend an unwarrantable jurisdiction over us. We have reminded them of the circumstances of our emigration and settlement here. We have appealed to their native justice and magnanimity; and we have conjured them, by the ties of our common kindred, to disavow these usurpations, which would inevitably interrupt our connections and correspondence. They, too, have been deaf to the voice of justice and of consanguinity. We must, therefore, acquiesce in the necessity which denounces our separation, and hold them, as we hold the rest of mankind, enemies in war, in peace friends.

We, therefore, the representatives of the United States of America, in General Congress assembled, appealing to the Supreme Judge of the world for the rectitude of our intentions, do, in the name and by the authority of the good people of these colonies, solemnly publish and declare, that these United Colonies are, and of right ought to be, FREE AND INDEPENDENT STATES; that they are absolved from all allegiance to the British crown, and that all political connection between them and the state of Great Britain is, and ought to be, totally dissolved; and that, as free and independent states, they have full power to levy war, conclude peace, contract alliances, establish commerce, and do all other acts and things which independent states may of right do. And for the support of this declaration, with a firm reliance on the protection of Divine Providence, we mutually pledge to each other our lives, our fortunes, and our sacred honor.

JOHN HANCOCK
and fifty-five others

Constitution of the United States of America and Amendments*

Preamble

We the people of the United States, in order to form a more perfect union, establish justice, insure domestic tranquillity, provide for the common defense, promote

---

* Passages no longer in effect are printed in italic type.

the general welfare, and secure the blessings of liberty to ourselves and our posterity, do ordain and establish this Constitution for the United States of America.

Article I

Section 1 All legislative powers herein granted shall be vested in a Congress of the United States, which shall consist of a Senate and a House of Representatives.

Section 2 The House of Representatives shall be composed of members chosen every second year by the people of the several States, and the electors in each State shall have the qualifications requisite for electors of the most numerous branch of the State Legislature.

No person shall be a Representative who shall not have attained to the age of twenty-five years, and been seven years a citizen of the United States, and who shall not, when elected, be an inhabitant of that State in which he shall be chosen.

Representatives and direct taxes shall be apportioned among the several States which may be included within this Union, according to their respective numbers, *which shall be determined by adding to the whole number of free persons, including those bound to service for a term of years and excluding Indians not taxed, three-fifths of all other persons.* The actual enumeration shall be made within three years after the first meeting of the Congress of the United States, and within every subsequent term of ten years, in such manner as they shall by law direct. The number of Representatives shall not exceed one for every thirty thousand, but each State shall have at least one Representative; *and until such enumeration shall be made, the State of New Hampshire shall be entitled to choose three, Massachusetts eight, Rhode Island and Providence Plantations one, Connecticut five, New York six, New Jersey four, Pennsylvania eight, Delaware one, Maryland six, Virginia ten, North Carolina five, South Carolina five, and Georgia three.*

When vacancies happen in the representation from any State, the Executive authority thereof shall issue writs of election to fill such vacancies.

The House of Representatives shall choose their Speaker and other officers; and shall have the sole power of impeachment.

Section 3 The Senate of the United States shall be composed of two Senators from each State, *chosen by the legislature thereof,* for six years; and each Senator shall have one vote.

Immediately after they shall be assembled in consequence of the first election, they shall be divided as equally as may be into three classes. The seats of the Senators of the first class shall be vacated at the expiration of the second year, of the second class at the expiration of the fourth year, and of the third class at the expiration of the sixth year, so that one-third may be chosen every second year; *and if vacancies happen by resignation or otherwise, during the recess of the legislature of any State, the Executive thereof may make temporary appointments until the next meeting of the legislature, which shall then fill such vacancies.*

No person shall be a Senator who shall not have attained to the age of thirty years, and been nine years a citizen of the United States, and who shall not, when elected, be an inhabitant of that State for which he shall be chosen.

The Vice-President of the United States shall be President of the Senate, but shall have no vote, unless they be equally divided.

The Senate shall choose their other officers, and also a President *pro tempore,* in the absence of the Vice-President, or when he shall exercise the office of President of the United States.

The Senate shall have the sole power to try all impeachments. When sitting for that purpose, they shall be on oath or affirmation. When the President of the United States is tried, the Chief Justice shall preside: and no person shall be convicted with-out the concurrence of two-thirds of the members present.

Judgment in cases of impeachment shall not extend further than to removal from the office, and disqualification to hold and enjoy any office of honor, trust or profit under the United States: but the party convicted shall nevertheless be liable and subject to indictment, trial, judgment and punishment, according to law.

Section 4 The times, places and manner of holding elections for Senators and Representatives shall be prescribed in each State by the legislature thereof; but the Congress may at any time by law make or alter such regulations, except as to the places of choosing Senators.

The Congress shall assemble at least once in every year, and such meeting *shall be on the first Monday in December, unless they shall by law appoint a different day.*

Section 5 Each house shall be the judge of the elections, returns and qualifications of its own members, and a majority of each shall constitute a quorum to do business; but a smaller number may adjourn from day to day, and may be authorized to compel the attendance of absent members, in such manner, and under such penalties, as each house may provide.

Each house may determine the rules of its proceedings, punish its members for disorderly behavior, and with the concurrence of two-thirds, expel a member.

Each house shall keep a journal of its proceedings, and from time to time publish the same, excepting such parts as may in their judgment require secrecy; and the yeas and nays of the members of either house on any question shall, at the desire of one-fifth of those present, be entered on the journal.

Neither house, during the session of Congress, shall, without the consent of the other, adjourn for more than three days, nor to any other place than that in which the two houses shall be sitting.

Section 6 The Senators and Representatives shall receive a compensation for their services, to be ascertained by law and paid out of the treasury of the United States. They shall in all cases except treason, felony and breach of the peace, be privileged from arrest during their attendance at the session of their respective houses, and in going to and returning from the same; and for any speech or debate in either house, they shall not be questioned in any other place.

No Senator or Representative shall, during the time for which he was elected, be appointed to any civil office under the authority of the United States, which shall have been created, or the emoluments whereof shall have been increased, during such time; and no person holding any office under the United States shall be a member of either house during his continuance in office.

Section 7 All bills for raising revenue shall originate in the House of Representatives; but the Senate may propose or concur with amendments as on other bills.

Every bill which shall have passed the House of Representatives and the Senate, shall, before it become a law, be presented to the President of the United States; if he approve he shall sign it, but if not he shall return it with objections to that house in which it originated, who shall enter the objections at large on their journal, and proceed to reconsider it. If after such reconsideration two-thirds of that house shall agree to pass the bill, it shall be sent, together with the objections, to the other house, by which it shall likewise be reconsidered, and, if approved by two-thirds of that house, it shall become a law. But in all such cases the votes of both houses shall be determined by yeas and nays, and the names of the persons voting for and against the bill shall be entered on the journal of each house respectively. If any bill shall not be returned by the President within ten days (Sundays excepted) after it shall have been presented to him, the same shall be a law, in like manner as if he had signed it, unless the Congress by their adjournment prevent its return, in which case it shall not be a law.

Every order, resolution, or vote to which the concurrence of the Senate and House of Representatives may be necessary (except on a question of adjournment) shall be presented to the President of the United States; and before the same shall take effect, shall be approved by him, or being disapproved by him, shall be repassed by two-thirds of the Senate and House of Representatives, according to the rules and limitations prescribed in the case of a bill.

Section 8 The Congress shall have power

To lay and collect taxes, duties, imposts, and excises, to pay the debts and provide for the common defense and general welfare of the United States; but all duties, imposts and excises shall be uniform throughout the United States;

To borrow money on the credit of the United States;

To regulate commerce with foreign nations, and among the several States, and with the Indian tribes;

To establish an uniform rule of naturalization, and uniform laws on the subject of bankruptcies throughout the United States;

To coin money, regulate the value thereof, and of foreign coin, and fix the standard of weights and measures;

To provide for the punishment of counterfeiting the securities and current coin of the United States;

To establish post offices and post roads;

To promote the progress of science and useful arts by securing for limited times to authors and inventors the exclusive right to their respective writings and discoveries;

To constitute tribunals inferior to the Supreme Court;

To define and punish piracies and felonies committed on the high seas and offenses against the law of nations;

To declare war, grant letters of marque and reprisal, and make rules concerning captures on land and water;

To raise and support armies, but no appropriation of money to that use shall be for a longer term than two years;

To provide and maintain a navy;

To make rules for the government and regulation of the land and naval forces;

To provide for calling forth the militia to execute the laws of the Union, suppress insurrections, and repel invasions;

To provide for organizing, arming, and disciplining the militia, and for governing such part of them as may be employed in the service of the United States, reserving to the States respectively the appointment of the officers, and the authority of training the militia according to the discipline prescribed by Congress;

To exercise exclusive legislation in all cases whatsoever, over such district (not exceeding ten miles square) as may, by cession of particular States, and the acceptance of Congress, become the seat of government of the United States, and to exercise like authority over all places purchased by the consent of the legislature of the State, in which the same shall be, for erection of forts, magazines, arsenals, dockyards, and other needful buildings; — and

To make all laws which shall be necessary and proper for carrying into execution the foregoing powers, and all other powers vested by this Constitution in the government of the United States, or in any department or officer thereof.

Section 9 *The migration or importation of such persons as any of the States now existing shall think proper to admit shall not be prohibited by the Congress prior to the year 1808; but a tax or duty may be imposed on such importation, not exceeding $10 for each person.*

The privilege of the writ of habeas corpus shall not be suspended, unless when in cases of rebellion or invasion the public safety may require it.

No bill of attainder or ex post facto law shall be passed.

No capitation, or other direct, tax shall be laid, unless in proportion to the census or enumeration herein before directed to be taken.

No tax or duty shall be laid on articles exported from any State.

No preference shall be given by any regulation of commerce or revenue to the ports of one State over those of another; nor shall vessels bound to, or from,

one State, be obliged to enter, clear, or pay duties in another.

No money shall be drawn from the treasury, but in consequence of appropriations made by law; and a regular statement and account of the receipts and expenditures of all public money shall be published from time to time.

No title of nobility shall be granted by the United States: and no person holding any office of profit or trust under them, shall, without the consent of the Congress, accept of any present, emolument, office, or title, of any kind whatever, from any king, prince, or foreign state.

Section 10 No State shall enter into any treaty, alliance, or confederation; grant letters of marque and reprisal; coin money; emit bills of credit; make anything but gold and silver coin a tender in payment of debts; pass any bill of attainder, ex post facto law, or law impairing the obligation of contracts, or grant any title of nobility.

No State shall, without the consent of Congress, lay any imposts or duties on imports or exports, except what may be absolutely necessary for executing its inspection laws: and the net produce of all duties and imposts, laid by any State on imports or exports, shall be for the use of the treasury of the United States; and all such laws shall be subject to the revision and control of the Congress.

No State shall, without the consent of Congress, lay any duty of tonnage, keep troops or ships of war in time of peace, enter into any agreement or compact with another State, or with a foreign power, or engage in war, unless actually invaded, or in such imminent danger as will not admit of delay.

Article II

Section 1 The executive power shall be vested in a President of the United States of America. He shall hold his office during the term of four years, and, together with the Vice-President, chosen for the same term, be elected as follows:

Each State shall appoint, in such manner as the legislature thereof may direct, a number of electors, equal to the whole number of Senators and Representatives to which the State may be entitled in the Congress; but no Senator or Representative, or person holding an office of trust or profit under the United States, shall be appointed an elector.

The electors shall meet in their respective States, and vote by ballot for two persons, of whom one at least shall not be an inhabitant of the same State with themselves. And they shall make a list of all the persons voted for, and of the number of votes for each; which list they shall sign and certify, and transmit sealed to the seat of government of the United States, directed to the President of the Senate. The President of the Senate shall, in the presence of the Senate and House of Representatives, open all the certificates, and the votes shall then be counted. The person having the greatest number of votes shall be the President, if such number be a majority of the whole number of electors appointed; and if there be more than one who have such majority, and have an equal number of votes, then the House of Representatives shall immediately choose by ballot one of them for President; and if no person have a majority, then from the five highest on the list said house shall in like manner choose the President. But in choosing the President the votes shall be taken by States, the representation from each State having one vote; a quorum for this purpose shall consist of a member or members from two-thirds of the States, and a majority of all the States shall be necessary to a choice. In every case, after the choice of the President, the person having the greatest number of votes of the electors shall be the Vice-President. But if there should remain two or more who have equal votes, the Senate shall choose from them by ballot the Vice-President.

The Congress may determine the time of choosing the electors and the day on which they shall give their votes; which day shall be the same throughout the United States.

No person except a natural-born citizen, *or a citizen of the United States at the time of the adoption of this Constitution,* shall be eligible to the office of President; neither shall any person be eligible to that office who shall not have attained to the age of thirty-five years, and been fourteen years a resident within the United States.

In cases of the removal of the President from office or of his death, resignation, or inability to discharge the powers and duties of the said office, the same shall devolve on the Vice-President, and the Congress may by law provide for the case of removal, death, resignation, or inability, both of the President and Vice-President, declaring what officer shall then act as President, and such officer shall act accordingly, until the disability be removed, or a President shall be elected.

The President shall, at stated times, receive for his services a compensation, which shall neither be increased nor diminished during the period for which he shall have been elected, and he shall not receive within that period any other emolument from the United States, or any of them.

Before he enter on the execution of his office, he shall take the following oath or affirmation:—"I do solemnly swear (or affirm) that I will faithfully execute the office of the President of the United States, and will to the best of my ability preserve, protect and defend the Constitution of the United States."

Section 2 The President shall be commander in chief of the army and navy of the United States, and of the militia of the several States, when called into the actual service of the United States; he may require the opinion, in writing, of the principal officer in each of the executive departments, upon any subject relating to the duties of their respective offices, and he shall have power to grant reprieves and pardons for offenses against the United States, except in cases of impeachment.

He shall have power, by and with the advice and consent of the Senate, to make treaties, provided two-thirds of the Senators present concur; and he shall nominate, and by and with the advice and consent of the Senate, shall appoint ambassadors, other public ministers and consuls, judges of the Supreme Court, and all other officers of the United States, whose appointments are not herein otherwise provided for, and which shall be established by law: but Congress may by law vest the appointment of such inferior officers, as they think proper, in the President alone, in the courts of law, or in the heads of departments.

The President shall have power to fill up all vacancies that may happen during the recess of the Senate, by granting commissions which shall expire at the end of their next session.

Section 3 He shall from time to time give to the Congress information of the state of the Union, and recommend to their consideration such measures as he shall judge necessary and expedient; he may, on extraordinary occasions, convene both houses, or either of them, and in case of disagreement between them, with respect to the time of adjournment, he may adjourn them to such time as he shall think proper; he shall receive ambassadors and other public ministers; he shall take care that the laws be faithfully executed, and shall commission all the officers of the United States.

Section 4 The President, Vice-President and all civil officers of the United States shall be removed from office on impeachment for, and on conviction of, treason, bribery, or other high crimes and misdemeanors.

Article III

Section 1 The judicial power of the United States shall be vested in one Supreme Court, and in such inferior courts as the Congress may from time to time ordain and establish. The judges, both of the Supreme and inferior courts, shall hold their offices during good behavior, and shall, at stated times, receive for their services a compensation which shall not be diminished during their continuance in office.

Section 2 The judicial power shall extend to all cases, in law and equity, arising under this Constitution, the laws of the United States, and treaties made, or which shall be made, under their authority;—to all cases affecting ambassadors, other public ministers and consuls;—to all cases of admiralty and maritime jurisdiction;—to controversies to which the United States shall be a party;—to controversies between two or more States;—*between a State and citizens of another State;*—between citizens of different States;—between citizens of the same State claiming lands under grants of different States, and between a State, or the citizens thereof, and foreign states, citizens or subjects.

In all cases affecting ambassadors, other public ministers and consuls, and those in which a State shall be party, the Supreme Court shall have original jurisdiction. In all the other cases before mentioned, the Supreme Court shall have appellate jurisdiction, both as to law and fact, with such exceptions, and under such regulations, as the Congress shall make.

The trial of all crimes, except in cases of impeachment, shall be by jury; and such trial shall be held in the State where said crimes shall have been committed; but when not committed within any State, the trial shall be at such place or places as the Congress may by law have directed.

Section 3 Treason against the United States shall consist only in levying war against them, or in adhering to their enemies, giving them aid and comfort. No person shall be convicted of treason unless on the testimony of two witnesses to the same overt act, or on confession in open court.

The Congress shall have power to declare the punishment of treason, but no attainder of treason shall work corruption of blood, or forfeiture except during the life of the person attainted.

Article IV

Section 1 Full faith and credit shall be given in each State to the public acts, records, and judicial proceedings of every other State. And the Congress may by general laws prescribe the manner in which such acts, records, and proceedings shall be proved, and the effect thereof.

Section 2 The citizens of each State shall be entitled to all privileges and immunities of citizens in the several States.

A person charged in any State with treason, felony, or other crime, who shall flee from justice, and be found in another State, shall on demand of the executive authority of the State from which he fled, be delivered up, to be removed to the State having jurisdiction of the crime.

No person held to service or labor in one State, under the laws thereof, escaping into another, shall, in consequence of any law or regulation therein, be discharged from such service or labor, but shall be delivered up on claim of the party to whom such service or labor may be due.

Section 3 New States may be admitted by the Congress into this Union; but no new State shall be formed or erected within the jurisdiction of any other State; nor any State be formed by the junction of two or more States, or parts of States, without the consent of the legislatures of the States concerned as well as of the Congress.

The Congress shall have power to dispose of and make all needful rules and regulations respecting the territory or other property belonging to the United States; and nothing in this Constitution shall be so construed as to prejudice any claims of the United States, or of any particular State.

Section 4 The United States shall guarantee to every State in this Union a republican form of government, and shall protect each of them against invasion; and on application of the legislature, or of the executive (when the legislature cannot be convened), against domestic violence.

Article V

The Congress, whenever two-thirds of both houses shall deem it necessary, shall propose amendments to this Constitution, or, on the application of the legislatures of two-thirds of the several States, shall call a convention for proposing amendments, which, in either case, shall be valid to all intents and purposes, as part of this Constitution, when ratified by the legislatures of three-fourths of the several States, or by conventions in three-fourths thereof, as the one or the other mode of ratification may be proposed by the Congress; provided *that no amendments which may be made prior to the year one thousand eight hundred and eight shall in any manner affect the first and fourth clauses in the ninth section of the first article;* and that no State, without its consent, shall be deprived of its equal suffrage in the Senate.

Article VI

All debts contracted and engagements entered into, before the adoption of this Constitution, shall be as valid against the United States under this Constitution, as under the Confederation.

This Constitution, and the laws of the United States which shall be made in pursuance thereof; and all treaties made, or which shall be made, under the authority of the United States, shall be the supreme law of the land; and the judges in every State shall be bound thereby, anything in the Constitution or laws of any State to the contrary notwithstanding.

The Senators and Representatives before mentioned, and the members of the several State legislatures, and all executive and judicial officers, both of the United States and of the several States, shall be bound by oath or affirmation to support this Constitution; but no religious test shall ever be required as a qualification to any office or public trust under the United States.

Article VII

The ratification of the conventions of nine States shall be sufficient for the establishment of this Constitution between the States so ratifying the same.

Done in Convention by the unanimous consent of the States present, the seventeenth day of September in the year of our Lord one thousand seven hundred and eighty-seven and of the Independence of the United States of America the twelfth. In witness whereof we have hereunto subscribed our names.

GEORGE WASHINGTON
and thirty-seven others

Amendments to the Constitution*

Amendment I

Congress shall make no law respecting an establishment of religion, or prohibiting the free exercise thereof; or abridging the freedom of speech, or of the press; or the right of the people peaceably to assemble, and to petition the government for a redress of grievances.

Amendment II

A well-regulated militia being necessary to the security of a free State, the right of the people to keep and bear arms shall not be infringed.

Amendment III

No soldier shall, in time of peace, be quartered in any house without the consent of the owner, nor in time of war, but in a manner to be prescribed by law.

Amendment IV

The right of the people to be secure in their persons, houses, papers, and effects, against unreasonable searches and seizures, shall not be violated, and no warrants shall issue but upon probable cause, supported by oath or affirmation, and particularly describing the place to be searched, and the persons or things to be seized.

Amendment V

No person shall be held to answer for a capital, or otherwise infamous crime, unless on a presentment or indictment of a grand jury, except in cases arising in the land or naval forces, or in the militia, when in actual service in time of war or public danger; nor shall any person be subject for the same offense to be twice put in jeopardy of life or limb; nor shall be compelled in any criminal case to be a witness against himself, nor be deprived of life, liberty, or property, without due process of law; nor shall private property be taken for public use without just compensation.

Amendment VI

In all criminal prosecutions, the accused shall enjoy the right to a speedy and public trial, by an impartial jury of the State and district wherein the crime shall have been committed, which district shall have been previously ascertained by law, and to be informed of the nature and cause of the accusation; to be confronted with the witnesses against him; to have compulsory process for obtaining witnesses in his favor, and to have the assistance of counsel for his defense.

---

* The first ten Amendments (the Bill of Rights) were adopted in 1791.

Amendment VII

In suits at common law, where the value in controversy shall exceed twenty dollars, the right of trial by jury shall be preserved, and no fact tried by a jury shall be otherwise reexamined in any court of the United States, than according to the rules of the common law.

Amendment VIII

Excessive bail shall not be required, nor excessive fines imposed, nor cruel and unusual punishments inflicted.

Amendment IX

The enumeration in the Constitution, of certain rights, shall not be construed to deny or disparage others retained by the people.

Amendment X

The powers not delegated to the United States by the Constitution, nor prohibited by it to the States, are reserved to the States respectively, or to the people.

Amendment XI

[Adopted 1798]

The judicial power of the United States shall not be construed to extend to any suit in law or equity, commenced or prosecuted against one of the United States by citizens of another State, or by citizens or subjects of any foreign state.

Amendment XII

[Adopted 1804]

The electors shall meet in their respective States, and vote by ballot for President and Vice-President, one of whom, at least, shall not be an inhabitant of the same State with themselves; they shall name in their ballots the person voted for as President, and in distinct ballots the person voted for as Vice-President, and they shall make distinct lists of all persons voted for as President, and of all persons voted for as Vice-President, and of the number of votes for each, which lists they shall sign and certify, and transmit sealed to the seat of government of the United States, directed to the President of the Senate;—the President of the Senate shall, in the presence of the Senate and House of Representatives, open all the certificates and the votes shall then be counted;—the person having the greatest number of votes for President shall be the President, if such number be a majority of the whole number of electors appointed; and if no person have such majority, then from the persons having the highest numbers not exceeding three on the list of those voted for as President, the House of Representatives shall choose immediately, by ballot, the President. But in choosing the President, the votes shall be taken by States, the representation from each State having one vote; a quorum for this purpose shall consist of a member or members from two-thirds of the States, and a majority of all the States shall be necessary to a choice. And if the House of Representatives shall not choose a President whenever the right of choice shall devolve upon them, before the fourth day of March next following, then the Vice-President shall act as President, as in the case of the death or other constitutional disability of the President.

The person having the greatest number of votes as Vice-President shall be the Vice-President, if such number be a majority of the whole number of electors appointed; and if no person have a majority, then from the two highest numbers on the list the Senate shall choose the Vice-President; a quorum for the purpose shall consist of two-thirds of the whole number of Senators, and a majority of the whole number shall be necessary to a choice. But no person constitutionally ineligible to the office of President shall be eligible to that of Vice-President of the United States.

Amendment XIII

[Adopted 1865]

Section 1 Neither slavery nor involuntary servitude, except as a punishment for crime whereof the party shall have been duly convicted, shall exist within the United States, or any place subject to their jurisdiction.

Section 2 Congress shall have power to enforce this article by appropriate legislation.

Amendment XIV

[Adopted 1868]

Section 1 All persons born or naturalized in the United States, and subject to the jurisdiction thereof, are citizens of the United States and of the State wherein they reside. No State shall make or enforce any law which shall abridge the privileges or immunities of citizens of the United States; nor shall any State deprive any person of life, liberty, or property, without due process of law; nor deny to any person within its jurisdiction the equal protection of the laws.

Section 2 Representatives shall be apportioned among the several States according to their respective numbers, counting the whole number of persons in each State, excluding Indians not taxed. But when the right to vote at any election for the choice of Electors for President and Vice-President of the United States, Representatives in Congress, the executive and judicial officers of a State, or the members of the legislature thereof, is denied to any of the male inhabitants of such State, being twenty-one years of age and citizens of the United States, or in any way abridged, except for participation in rebellion, or other crime, the basis of representation therein shall be reduced in the proportion which the number of such male citizens shall bear to the whole number of male citizens twenty-one years of age in such State.

Section 3 No person shall be a Senator or Representative in Congress, or Elector of President and Vice-President, or hold any office, civil or military, under the United States, or under any State, who, having previously taken an oath, as a member of Congress, or as an officer of the United States, or as a member of any State legislature, or as an executive or judicial officer of any State, to support the Constitution of the United States, shall have engaged in insurrection or rebellion against the same, or given aid or comfort to the enemies thereof. Congress may, by a vote of two-thirds of each house, remove such disability.

Section 4 The validity of the public debt of the United States, authorized by law, including debts incurred for payment of pensions and bounties for services in suppressing insurrection or rebellion, shall not be questioned. But neither the United States nor any State shall assume or pay any debt or obligation incurred in aid of insurrection or rebellion against the United States, or any claim for the loss or emancipation of any slave; but all such debts, obligations, and claims shall be held illegal and void.

Section 5 The Congress shall have power to enforce, by appropriate legislation, the provisions of this article.

Amendment XV

[Adopted 1870]

Section 1 The right of citizens of the United States to vote shall not be denied or abridged by the United States or by any State on account of race, color, or previous condition of servitude.

Section 2 The Congress shall have power to enforce this article by appropriate legislation.

Amendment XVI

[Adopted 1913]

The Congress shall have power to lay and collect taxes on incomes, from whatever source derived, without apportionment among the several States, and without regard to any census or enumeration.

Amendment XVII

[Adopted 1913]

Section 1 The Senate of the United States shall be composed of two Senators from each State, elected by the people thereof, for six years; and each Senator shall have one vote. The electors in each State shall have the qualifications requisite for electors of [voters for] the most numerous branch of the State legislatures.

Section 2 When vacancies happen in the representation of any State in the Senate, the executive authority of such State shall issue writs of election to fill such vacancies: Provided, that the Legislature of any State may empower the executive thereof to make temporary appointments until the people fill the vacancies by election as the Legislature may direct.

Section 3 This amendment shall not be so construed as to affect the election or term of any Senator chosen before it becomes valid as part of the Constitution.

Amendment XVIII

[Adopted 1919; Repealed 1933]

Section 1 After one year from the ratification of this article the manufacture, sale, or transportation of intoxicating liquors within, the importation thereof into, or the exportation thereof from the United States and all territory subject to the jurisdiction thereof, for beverage purposes, is hereby prohibited.

Section 2 The Congress and the several States shall have concurrent power to enforce this article by appropriate legislation.

Section 3 This article shall be inoperative unless it shall have been ratified as an amendment to the Constitution by the legislatures of the several States, as provided by the Constitution, within seven years from the date of the submission thereof to the States by the Congress.

Amendment XIX

[Adopted 1920]

Section 1   The right of citizens of the United States to vote shall not be denied or abridged by the United States or by any State on account of sex.

Section 2   The Congress shall have power to enforce this article by appropriate legislation.

Amendment XX

[Adopted 1933]

Section 1   The terms of the President and Vice-President shall end at noon on the 20th day of January, and the terms of Senators and Representatives at noon on the 3rd day of January, of the years in which such terms would have ended if this article had not been ratified; and the terms of their successors shall then begin.

Section 2   The Congress shall assemble at least once in every year, and such meeting shall begin at noon on the 3d day of January, unless they shall by law appoint a different day.

Section 3   If, at the time fixed for the beginning of the term of the President, the President-elect shall have died, the Vice-President-elect shall become President. If a President shall not have been chosen before the time fixed for the beginning of his term, or if the President-elect shall have failed to qualify, then the Vice-President-elect shall act as President until a President shall have qualified; and the Congress may by law provide for the case wherein neither a President-elect nor a Vice-President-elect shall have qualified, declaring who shall then act as President, or the manner in which one who is to act shall be selected, and such persons shall act accordingly until a President or Vice-President shall have qualified.

Section 4   The Congress may by law provide for the case of the death of any of the persons from whom the House of Representatives may choose a President whenever the right of choice shall have devolved upon them, and for the case of the death of any of the persons from whom the Senate may choose a Vice-President whenever the right of choice shall have devolved upon them.

Section 5   Sections 1 and 2 shall take effect on the 15th day of October following the ratification of this article.

Section 6   This article shall be inoperative unless it shall have been ratified as an amendment to the Constitution by the Legislatures of three-fourths of the several States within seven years from the date of its submission.

Amendment XXI

[Adopted 1933]

Section 1   The eighteenth article of amendment to the Constitution of the United States is hereby repealed.

Section 2   The transportation or importation into any State, Territory, or Possession of the United States for delivery or use therein of intoxicating liquors, in violation of the laws thereof, is hereby prohibited.

Section 3   This article shall be inoperative unless it shall have been ratified as an amendment to the Constitution by conventions in the several States, as provided in the Constitution, within seven years from the date of submission thereof to the States by the Congress.

Amendment XXII

[Adopted 1951]

Section 1   No person shall be elected to the office of President more than twice, and no person who has held the office of President, or acted as President, for more than two years of a term to which some other person was elected President shall be elected to the office of President more than once. But this article shall not apply to any person holding the office of President when this article was proposed by the Congress, and shall not prevent any person who may be holding the office of President, or acting as President, during the term within which this article becomes operative from holding the office of President or acting as President during the remainder of such term.

Section 2   This article shall be inoperative unless it shall have been ratified as an amendment to the Constitution by the legislatures of three-fourths of the several States within seven years from the date of its submission to the States by the Congress.

Amendment XXIII

[Adopted 1961]

Section 1   The District constituting the seat of Government of the United States shall appoint in such manner as the Congress may direct:

A number of electors of President and Vice-President equal to the whole number of Senators and Representatives in Congress to which the District would be entitled if it were a State, but in no event more than the least populous State; they shall be in addition to those appointed by the States, but they shall be considered for the purposes of the election of President and Vice-President, to be electors appointed by a State; and they shall meet in the District and perform such duties as provided by the twelfth article of amendment.

Section 2   The Congress shall have the power to enforce this article by appropriate legislation.

Amendment XXIV
[Adopted 1964]

Section 1   The right of citizens of the United States to vote in any primary or other election for President or Vice-President, for electors for President or Vice-President, or for Senator or Representative in Congress, shall not be denied or abridged by the United States or any State by reason of failure to pay any poll tax or other tax.

Section 2   The Congress shall have the power to enforce this article by appropriate legislation.

Amendment XXV
[Adopted 1967]

Section 1   In case of the removal of the President from office or of his death or resignation, the Vice-President shall become President.

Section 2   Whenever there is a vacancy in the office of the Vice-President, the President shall nominate a Vice-President who shall take office upon confirmation by a majority vote of both Houses of Congress.

Section 3   Whenever the President transmits to the President pro tempore of the Senate and the Speaker of the House of Representatives his written declaration that he is unable to discharge the powers and duties of his office, and until he transmits to them a written declaration to the contrary, such powers and duties shall be discharged by the Vice-President as Acting President.

Section 4   Whenever the Vice-President and a majority of either the principal officers of the executive departments or of such other body as Congress may by law provide, transmit to the President pro tempore of the Senate and the Speaker of the House of Representatives their written declaration that the President is unable to discharge the powers and duties of his office, the Vice-President shall immediately assume the powers and duties of the office as Acting President.

Thereafter, when the President transmits to the President pro tempore of the Senate and the Speaker of the House of Representatives his written declaration that no inability exists, he shall resume the powers and duties of his office unless the Vice-President and a majority of either the principal officers of the executive department[s] or of such other body as Congress may by law provide, transmit within four days to the President pro tempore of the Senate and the Speaker of the House of Representatives their written declaration that the President is unable to discharge the powers and duties of his office. Thereupon Congress shall decide the issue, assembling within forty-eight hours for that purpose if not in session. If the Congress, within twenty-one days after receipt of the latter written declaration, or, if Congress is not in session, within twenty-one days after Congress is required to assemble, determines by two-thirds vote of both Houses that the President is unable to discharge the powers and duties of his office, the Vice-President shall continue to discharge the same as Acting President; otherwise, the President shall resume the powers and duties of his office.

Amendment XXVI
[Adopted 1971]

Section 1   The right of citizens of the United States, who are eighteen years of age or older, to vote shall not be denied or abridged by the United States or by any State on account of age.

Section 2   The Congress shall have power to enforce this article by appropriate legislation.

Amendment XXVII
[Adopted 1992]

No law, varying the compensation for the services of the Senators and Representatives, shall take effect, until an election of Representatives shall have intervened.

Territorial Expansion of the United States

Territory	Date Acquired	Square Miles	How Acquired
Original states and territories	1783	888,685	Treaty with Great Britain
Louisiana Purchase	1803	827,192	Purchase from France
Florida	1819	72,003	Treaty with Spain
Texas	1845	390,143	Annexation of independent nation
Oregon	1846	285,580	Treaty with Great Britain
Mexican Cession	1848	529,017	Conquest from Mexico
Gadsden Purchase	1853	29,640	Purchase from Mexico
Alaska	1867	589,757	Purchase from Russia
Hawai`i	1898	6,450	Annexation of independent nation
The Philippines	1899	115,600	Conquest from Spain (granted independence in 1946)
Puerto Rico	1899	3,435	Conquest from Spain
Guam	1899	212	Conquest from Spain
American Samoa	1900	76	Treaty with Germany and Great Britain
Panama Canal Zone	1904	553	Treaty with Panama (returned to Panama by treaty in 1978)
Corn Islands	1914	4	Treaty with Nicaragua (returned to Nicaragua by treaty in 1971)
Virgin Islands	1917	133	Purchase from Denmark
Pacific Islands Trust (Micronesia)	1947	8,489	Trusteeship under United Nations (some granted independence)
All others (Midway, Wake, and other islands)		42	

Admission of States into the Union

State	Date of Admission	State	Date of Admission
1. Delaware	December 7, 1787	26. Michigan	January 26, 1837
2. Pennsylvania	December 12, 1787	27. Florida	March 3, 1845
3. New Jersey	December 18, 1787	28. Texas	December 29, 1845
4. Georgia	January 2, 1788	29. Iowa	December 28, 1846
5. Connecticut	January 9, 1788	30. Wisconsin	May 29, 1848
6. Massachusetts	February 6, 1788	31. California	September 9, 1850
7. Maryland	April 28, 1788	32. Minnesota	May 11, 1858
8. South Carolina	May 23, 1788	33. Oregon	February 14, 1859
9. New Hampshire	June 21, 1788	34. Kansas	January 29, 1861
10. Virginia	June 25, 1788	35. West Virginia	June 20, 1863
11. New York	July 26, 1788	36. Nevada	October 31, 1864
12. North Carolina	November 21, 1789	37. Nebraska	March 1, 1867
13. Rhode Island	May 29, 1790	38. Colorado	August 1, 1876
14. Vermont	March 4, 1791	39. North Dakota	November 2, 1889
15. Kentucky	June 1, 1792	40. South Dakota	November 2, 1889
16. Tennessee	June 1, 1796	41. Montana	November 8, 1889
17. Ohio	March 1, 1803	42. Washington	November 11, 1889
18. Louisiana	April 30, 1812	43. Idaho	July 3, 1890
19. Indiana	December 11, 1816	44. Wyoming	July 10, 1890
20. Mississippi	December 10, 1817	45. Utah	January 4, 1896
21. Illinois	December 3, 1818	46. Oklahoma	November 16, 1907
22. Alabama	December 14, 1819	47. New Mexico	January 6, 1912
23. Maine	March 15, 1820	48. Arizona	February 14, 1912
24. Missouri	August 10, 1821	49. Alaska	January 3, 1959
25. Arkansas	June 15, 1836	50. Hawai`i	August 21, 1959

Presidential Elections

Year	Number of States	Candidates	Parties	Popular Vote	% of Popular Vote	Electoral Vote	% Voter Participation[a]
1789	11	**George Washington**	No party			69	
		John Adams	designations			34	
		Other candidates				35	
1792	15	**George Washington**	No party			132	
		John Adams	designations			77	
		George Clinton				50	
		Other candidates				5	
1796	16	**John Adams**	Federalist			71	
		Thomas Jefferson	Democratic-Republican			68	
		Thomas Pinckney	Federalist			59	
		Aaron Burr	Democratic-Republican			30	
		Other candidates				48	
1800	16	**Thomas Jefferson**	Democratic-Republican			73	
		Aaron Burr	Democratic-Republican			73	
		John Adams	Federalist			65	
		Charles C. Pinckney	Federalist			64	
		John Jay	Federalist			1	
1804	17	**Thomas Jefferson**	Democratic-Republican			162	
		Charles C. Pinckney	Federalist			14	
1808	17	**James Madison**	Democratic-Republican			122	
		Charles C. Pinckney	Federalist			47	
		George Clinton	Democratic-Republican			6	
1812	18	**James Madison**	Democratic-Republican			128	
		DeWitt Clinton	Federalist			89	
1816	19	**James Monroe**	Democratic-Republican			183	
		Rufus King	Federalist			34	
1820	24	**James Monroe**	Democratic-Republican			231	
		John Quincy Adams	Independent-Republican			1	

Presidential Elections, *Continued*

Year	Number of States	Candidates	Parties	Popular Vote	% of Popular Vote	Electoral Vote	% Voter Participation[a]
1824	24	**John Quincy Adams**	Democratic-Republican	108,740	30.5	84	26.9
		Andrew Jackson	Democratic-Republican	153,544	43.1	99	
		Henry Clay	Democratic-Republican	47,136	13.2	37	
		William H. Crawford	Democratic-Republican	46,618	13.1	41	
1828	24	**Andrew Jackson**	Democratic	647,286	56.0	178	57.6
		John Quincy Adams	National Republican	508,064	44.0	83	
1832	24	**Andrew Jackson**	Democratic	688,242	54.5	219	55.4
		Henry Clay	National Republican	473,462	37.5	49	
		William Wirt	Anti-Masonic	101,051	8.0	7	
		John Floyd	Democratic			11	
1836	26	**Martin Van Buren**	Democratic	765,483	50.9	170	57.8
		William H. Harrison	Whig			73	
		Hugh L. White	Whig			26	
		Daniel Webster	Whig	739,795	49.1	14	
		W. P. Mangum	Whig			11	
1840	26	**William H. Harrison**	Whig	1,274,624	53.1	234	80.2
		Martin Van Buren	Democratic	1,127,781	46.9	60	
1844	26	**James K. Polk**	Democratic	1,338,464	49.6	170	78.9
		Henry Clay	Whig	1,300,097	48.1	105	
		James G. Birney	Liberty	62,300	2.3		
1848	30	**Zachary Taylor**	Whig	1,360,967	47.4	163	72.7
		Lewis Cass	Democratic	1,222,342	42.5	127	
		Martin Van Buren	Free Soil	291,263	10.1		
1852	31	**Franklin Pierce**	Democratic	1,601,117	50.9	254	69.6
		Winfield Scott	Whig	1,385,453	44.1	42	
		John P. Hale	Free Soil	155,825	5.0		
1856	31	**James Buchanan**	Democratic	1,832,955	45.3	174	78.9
		John C. Frémont	Republican	1,339,932	33.1	114	
		Millard Fillmore	American	871,731	21.6	8	
1860	33	**Abraham Lincoln**	Republican	1,865,593	39.8	180	81.2
		Stephen A. Douglas	Democratic	1,382,713	29.5	12	
		John C. Breckinridge	Democratic	848,356	18.1	72	
		John Bell	Constitutional Union	592,906	12.6	39	

Presidential Elections, *Continued*

Year	Number of States	Candidates	Parties	Popular Vote	% of Popular Vote	Electoral Vote	% Voter Partici- pation[a]
1864	36	**Abraham Lincoln**	Republican	2,206,938	55.0	212	73.8
		George B. McClellan	Democratic	1,803,787	45.0	21	
1868	37	**Ulysses S. Grant**	Republican	3,013,421	52.7	214	78.1
		Horatio Seymour	Democratic	2,706,829	47.3	80	
1872	37	**Ulysses S. Grant**	Republican	3,596,745	55.6	286	71.3
		Horace Greeley	Democratic	2,843,446	43.9	[b]	
1876	38	**Rutherford B. Hayes**	Republican	4,036,572	48.0	185	81.8
		Samuel J. Tilden	Democratic	4,284,020	51.0	184	
1880	38	**James A. Garfield**	Republican	4,453,295	48.5	214	79.4
		Winfield S. Hancock	Democratic	4,414,082	48.1	155	
		James B. Weaver	Greenback- Labor	308,578	3.4		
1884	38	**Grover Cleveland**	Democratic	4,879,507	48.5	219	77.5
		James G. Blaine	Republican	4,850,293	48.2	182	
		Benjamin F. Butler	Greenback- Labor	175,370	1.8		
		John P. St. John	Prohibition	150,369	1.5		
1888	38	**Benjamin Harrison**	Republican	5,477,129	47.9	233	79.3
		Grover Cleveland	Democratic	5,537,857	48.6	168	
		Clinton B. Fisk	Prohibition	249,506	2.2		
		Anson J. Streeter	Union Labor	146,935	1.3		
1892	44	**Grover Cleveland**	Democratic	5,555,426	46.1	277	74.7
		Benjamin Harrison	Republican	5,182,690	43.0	145	
		James B. Weaver	People's	1,029,846	8.5	22	
		John Bidwell	Prohibition	264,133	2.2		
1896	45	**William McKinley**	Republican	7,102,246	51.1	271	79.3
		William J. Bryan	Democratic	6,492,559	47.7	176	
1900	45	**William McKinley**	Republican	7,218,491	51.7	292	73.2
		William J. Bryan	Democratic; Populist	6,356,734	45.5	155	
		John C. Wooley	Prohibition	208,914	1.5		
1904	45	**Theodore Roosevelt**	Republican	7,628,461	57.4	336	65.2
		Alton B. Parker	Democratic	5,084,223	37.6	140	
		Eugene V. Debs	Socialist	402,283	3.0		
		Silas C. Swallow	Prohibition	258,536	1.9		
1908	46	**William H. Taft**	Republican	7,675,320	51.6	321	65.4
		William J. Bryan	Democratic	6,412,294	43.1	162	
		Eugene V. Debs	Socialist	420,793	2.8		
		Eugene W. Chafin	Prohibition	253,840	1.7		

Presidential Elections, *Continued*

Year	Number of States	Candidates	Parties	Popular Vote	% of Popular Vote	Electoral Vote	% Voter Participation[a]
1912	48	**Woodrow Wilson**	Democratic	6,296,547	41.9	435	58.8
		Theodore Roosevelt	Progressive	4,118,571	27.4	88	
		William H. Taft	Republican	3,486,720	23.2	8	
		Eugene V. Debs	Socialist	900,672	6.0		
		Eugene W. Chafin	Prohibition	206,275	1.4		
1916	48	**Woodrow Wilson**	Democratic	9,127,695	49.4	277	61.6
		Charles E. Hughes	Republican	8,533,507	46.2	254	
		A. L. Benson	Socialist	585,113	3.2		
		J. Frank Hanly	Prohibition	220,506	1.2		
1920	48	**Warren G. Harding**	Republican	16,143,407	60.4	404	49.2
		James M. Cox	Democratic	9,130,328	34.2	127	
		Eugene V. Debs	Socialist	919,799	3.4		
		P. P. Christensen	Farmer-Labor	265,411	1.0		
1924	48	**Calvin Coolidge**	Republican	15,718,211	54.0	382	48.9
		John W. Davis	Democratic	8,385,283	28.8	136	
		Robert M. La Follette	Progressive	4,831,289	16.6	13	
1928	48	**Herbert C. Hoover**	Republican	21,391,993	58.2	444	56.9
		Alfred E. Smith	Democratic	15,016,169	40.9	87	
1932	48	**Franklin D. Roosevelt**	Democratic	22,809,638	57.4	472	56.9
		Herbert C. Hoover	Republican	15,758,901	39.7	59	
		Norman Thomas	Socialist	881,951	2.2		
1936	48	**Franklin D. Roosevelt**	Democratic	27,752,869	60.8	523	61.0
		Alfred M. Landon	Republican	16,674,665	36.5	8	
		William Lemke	Union	882,479	1.9		
1940	48	**Franklin D. Roosevelt**	Democratic	27,307,819	54.8	449	62.5
		Wendell L. Wilkie	Republican	22,321,018	44.8	82	
1944	48	**Franklin D. Roosevelt**	Democratic	25,606,585	53.5	432	55.9
		Thomas E. Dewey	Republican	22,014,745	46.0	99	
1948	48	**Harry S Truman**	Democratic	24,179,345	49.6	303	53.0
		Thomas E. Dewey	Republican	21,991,291	45.1	189	
		J. Strom Thurmond	States' Rights	1,176,125	2.4	39	
		Henry A. Wallace	Progressive	1,157,326	2.4		
1952	48	**Dwight D. Eisenhower**	Republican	33,936,234	55.1	442	63.3
		Adlai E. Stevenson	Democratic	27,314,992	44.4	89	
1956	48	**Dwight D. Eisenhower**	Republican	35,590,472	57.6	457	60.6
		Adlai E. Stevenson	Democratic	26,022,752	42.1	73	
1960	50	**John F. Kennedy**	Democratic	34,226,731	49.7	303	62.8
		Richard M. Nixon	Republican	34,108,157	49.5	219	

Presidential Elections, *Continued*

Year	Number of States	Candidates	Parties	Popular Vote	% of Popular Vote	Electoral Vote	% Voter Participation[a]
1964	50	**Lyndon B. Johnson**	Democratic	43,129,566	61.1	486	61.7
		Barry M. Goldwater	Republican	27,178,188	38.5	52	
1968	50	**Richard M. Nixon**	Republican	31,785,480	43.4	301	60.6
		Hubert H. Humphrey	Democratic	31,275,166	42.7	191	
		George C. Wallace	American Independent	9,906,473	13.5	46	
1972	50	**Richard M. Nixon**	Republican	47,169,911	60.7	520	55.2
		George S. McGovern	Democratic	29,170,383	37.5	17	
		John G. Schmitz	American	1,099,482	1.4		
1976	50	**Jimmy Carter**	Democratic	40,830,763	50.1	297	53.5
		Gerald R. Ford	Republican	39,147,793	48.0	240	
1980	50	**Ronald Reagan**	Republican	43,899,248	50.8	489	52.6
		Jimmy Carter	Democratic	35,481,432	41.0	49	
		John B. Anderson	Independent	5,719,437	6.6	0	
		Ed Clark	Libertarian	920,859	1.1	0	
1984	50	**Ronald Reagan**	Republican	54,455,075	58.8	525	53.1
		Walter Mondale	Democratic	37,577,185	40.6	13	
1988	50	**George Bush**	Republican	48,901,046	53.4	426	50.2
		Michael Dukakis	Democratic	41,809,030	45.6	111[c]	
1992	50	**Bill Clinton**	Democratic	44,908,233	43.0	370	55.0
		George Bush	Republican	39,102,282	37.4	168	
		Ross Perot	Independent	19,741,048	18.9	0	
1996	50	**Bill Clinton**	Democratic	47,401,054	49.2	379	49.0
		Robert Dole	Republican	39,197,350	40.7	159	
		Ross Perot	Independent	8,085,285	8.4	0	
		Ralph Nader	Green	684,871	0.7	0	

Candidates receiving less than 1 percent of the popular vote have been omitted. Thus the percentage of popular vote given for any election year may not total 100 percent.

Before the passage of the Twelfth Amendment in 1804, the Electoral College voted for two presidential candidates; the runner-up became vice president.

Before 1824, most presidential electors were chosen by state legislatures, not by popular vote.

[a]Percent of voting-age population casting ballots.

[b]Greeley died shortly after the election; the electors supporting him then divided their votes among minor candidates.

[c]One elector from West Virginia cast her Electoral College presidential ballot for Lloyd Bentsen, the Democratic party's vice-presidential candidate.

INDEX